1743.

1811.

1825.

1846.

31st Regiment.
Uniform in bygone days.

HISTORY OF THE 1st AND 2nd BATTALIONS
THE EAST SURREY REGIMENT

HISTORY

OF THE

31st Foot
HUNTINGDONSHIRE REGT.

70th Foot
SURREY REGT.

SUBSEQUENTLY

1st & 2nd BATTALIONS
THE
EAST SURREY REGIMENT

BY

COLONEL HUGH W. PEARSE, D.S.O.

Formerly of the Regiment

AUTHOR OF 'LIFE OF GENERAL VISCOUNT LAKE'
'MEMOIR OF COLONEL ALEXANDER GARDNER' 'THE HEARSEYS' ETC.

1702-1914

The Naval & Military Press Ltd

Published by

The Naval & Military Press Ltd
Unit 10 Ridgewood Industrial Park,
Uckfield, East Sussex,
TN22 5QE England

Tel: +44 (0) 1825 749494
Fax: +44 (0) 1825 765701

www.naval-military-press.com
www.military-genealogy.com
www.militarymaproom.com

In reprinting in facsimile from the original, any imperfections are inevitably reproduced and the quality may fall short of modern type and cartographic standards.

BADGE AND BATTLE HONOURS OF THE EAST SURREY REGIMENT.

THE UNITED RED AND WHITE ROSE.

"Gibraltar 1704-5," "Dettingen," "Martinique 1794," "Talavera," "Guadaloupe 1810," "Albuhera," "Vittoria," "Pyrenees," "Nivelle," "Nive," "Orthes," "Peninsula," "Cabool 1842," "Moodkee," "Ferozeshah," "Aliwal," "Sobraon," "Sevastopol," "Taku Forts," "New Zealand," "Afghanistan 1878-79," "Suakin 1885," "Relief of Ladysmith," "South Africa 1899-1902."

DEDICATION

TO THE MEMORY OF
THE OFFICERS, NON-COMMISSIONED OFFICERS AND
PRIVATE SOLDIERS

OF THE

OLD 31ST AND 70TH REGIMENTS

AND OF THE

1ST AND 2ND BATTALIONS OF THE EAST SURREY REGIMENT

WHO FROM

MARCH 1702 TO AUGUST 1914

DIED IN THE SERVICE OF THEIR COUNTRY

PREFACE

SOME years have elapsed since the writer of the following volume was requested by the commanding officers of the Line battalions of the East Surrey Regiment to undertake the task of preparing a complete history of the two battalions, and of their predecessors, the old 31st (Huntingdonshire) and 70th (Surrey) Regiments. As the history would cover a period of over two hundred years and would be concerned with the majority of the campaigns in which the British army has taken part since the accession of Queen Anne, it was realised that the work would take some considerable time. The history was, in fact, ready for the press at the moment when the present European war broke out, but it was then decided to delay publication so that if possible a narrative of the share taken in the war by the two battalions might be included in the history. The course of events, the development of the struggle, and the consequent expansion of the East Surrey Regiment (in common with the other regiments of the army) into an organisation formed of many battalions, has rendered necessary a further change of plan.

The present volume has therefore been closed as on the third day of August 1914, the eve of the declaration of war against Germany by Great Britain.

It is the hope of the writer to supply eventually to the East Surrey Regiment a second volume, describing the war-services of all units of the regiment, of the old Line battalions, the Special-Reserve and Territorial battalions, and lastly of the new Service and Reserve battalions which sprang into existence during the expansion of the army. Their story, if competently told, will be a fine one, and it may here be mentioned that volume ii. of this history is in course of preparation and will be published as soon as possible after the termination of the war.

It may perhaps seem doubtful to some critical minds if the present is a suitable moment in which to launch a history dealing with the old wars of England, wars mostly carried through by small armies and frequently waged against badly armed and badly organised enemies. The writer hopes, however, that those of the general public who may read the pages of this volume will form a different opinion. He believes that the story he has had to tell will show that throughout its history, and whatever its name, the tasks committed to the East Surrey Regiment have not been easy ones, and that although its soldiers have not been called upon to encounter the masses of heavy artillery and the novel and inhuman methods of destruction that render the present war so terrible, its death-roll by battle has often been very heavy, while more than once each of its battalions has perished, almost to a man, through the vicissitudes of pestilence and climate that caused the greater part of the mortality in ancient wars.

Something must now be said regarding the materials from which this volume has been compiled.

Both the 31st and 70th Regiments were provided with official histories, written to order by a civil clerk of the War Office towards the end of the reign of King William IV. Little need be said of these somewhat arid productions, which, though based on official information, are full of inaccuracies and deficiencies. The records of events since the year 1836 are very bald and unsatisfactory, and owing to various accidents by fire and shipwreck both battalions possess but few documents of historical interest.

On the other hand, several books have at different times been written by officers connected with the 31st and 70th, and to them the writer is much indebted. All quotations from these books are acknowledged in the letter-press, but special reference must be made to the delightful " Recollections " of the late Colonel Robertson, which bring so vividly to the mind's eye the desperate encounters of the Sikh War of 1845. The thanks of the regiment are due to Mr. Edward Arnold for permission to make use of these extracts, each of which is formally acknowledged in the letter-press.

For the interesting letters of Captain, afterwards Lieut.-Colonel Robert Irving, relating to the American War of Independence and to the campaign in the West Indies, the regiment is indebted to the kindness of Major-General Mainguy, the great-grandson of Lieut-Colonel Irving, and the thanks of the regiment are also due to Sir Eyre Coote for permission to use various MSS. connected with Lieut.-General Sir Eyre Coote, K.C.B. To the commanding and other officers of the East Surrey Regiment who have in various ways assisted the writer, he begs to tender his best thanks, and would specially mention his debt of gratitude to the following : General Sir G. R. Greaves, G.C.B., K.C.M.G., Colonel of the Regiment; Major-General J. R. Longley, Lieut.-Colonel H. L. Smith, D.S.O., Brigadier-General H. S. Sloman, D.S.O., Lieut.-Colonel Hill-James, Colonel H. D. Lawrence, Captains H. Stacke, H. V. Bayliss and R. Streatfeild-James. He also desires to thank Mr. F. J. Batchelor and Mr. H. F. Milne of the staff of the Royal Geographical Society for the care with which they prepared many of the maps in this volume.

It may be mentioned that the maps have been made solely to assist the reader to follow the narrative, and that, as far as possible, all places mentioned in the text will be found in them, other places being omitted.

Finally, the writer desires to say that in telling, to the best of his power, the story of his former regiment, he has endeavoured to avoid all exaggeration of phrase. He has seldom ventured to award praise, and where words of eulogy appear they are mostly quotations from other writers or from official utterances. The words "glorious" and "heroic" seldom if ever appear, though many of the deeds related might well bear those descriptions. If, however, a number of fine individual actions are saved by these pages from oblivion, be sure that a very far greater number remain unrecorded, for in nearly every region of the earth, during the two centuries with which this volume has to do, the faithful soldiers of the East Surrey Regiment have laid down their lives for England. Far and wide their graves are scattered, and for the most part the plough has passed over them and no trace of them remains. This history then is their only memorial —would it were more complete and more worthy of them.

CONTENTS

PART I

HISTORY OF THE THIRTY-FIRST REGIMENT

CHAPTER I

COLONEL GEORGE VILLIERS' REGIMENT OF MARINES

Roll of the original officers—Marine uniform—The soldier's life at sea—Cadiz—Vigo—Capture of Gibraltar—The first defence of Gibraltar—Barcelona and Montjuich—The Balearic Isles—Attempted capture of Toulon—Threatened reduction of the marine regiments . . 3

CHAPTER II

THE BATTLE OF DETTINGEN

Sir Harry Goring's Regiment of Foot—Colonel William Handasyd—The war of the Austrian Succession—Ancient officers—The battle of Dettingen—King George II and "*the young Buffs*" 16

CHAPTER III

BATTLE OF FONTENOY AND ACTION OF MELLE

Losses of the regiment—The Duke of Cumberland's Despatch—The action of Melle—Raising of a second battalion, and subsequent separation from it—Service in Florida and destruction of the regiment—Trials of a commanding officer—Service in St. Vincent 30

CHAPTER IV

THE AMERICAN WAR OF INDEPENDENCE

The Thirty-first in Canada—Services of the Flank Companies with General Burgoyne—Action of Bemis Heights—The capitulation at Saratoga . 46

CONTENTS

CHAPTER V

THE FRENCH REVOLUTIONARY WAR

The Flank Companies in the West Indies—Capture of Martinique and St. Lucia—Capture of Guadeloupe—The defence of Berville—Destruction of the Flank Companies—The Thirty-first in Holland—St. Lucia again—The repulse at La Vigie—Heavy loss of the regiment—Why the attack failed—A year's casualties in the West Indies—The campaign of 1799 in Holland—Actions of Egmont-op-Zee, and of Alkmaar—An Ensign's letter—An old soldier's yarn—Action at Ferrol—Minorca—Raising a second battalion—Egypt—Action of Rosetta: heavy losses of the regiment—Services in Sicily and Italy—Action of Albaro . 56

CHAPTER VI

THE SECOND BATTALION THIRTY-FIRST IN THE PENINSULAR WAR

Battle of Talavera—Mackenzie's Brigade—Battle of Albuera—The disaster to Colborne's Brigade—Major L'Estrange's square—Lord Mulgrave's letter—Battle of Vittoria—Battles of the Pyrenees, Nivelle, and Nive—Action of St. Pierre—Sir John Byng and the Colour—Action of Garris——Battle of Orthes—Battle of Toulouse—Disbanding of the Second Battalion 98

CHAPTER VII

THE BURNING OF THE *KENT*

Gallant rescue by the *Cambria*—The camp at Rupar—Indian service . 150

CHAPTER VIII

THE FIRST AFGHAN WAR

Early history of the war—Destruction of General Elphinstone's force—The punitive campaign of 1842—The Shinwari expedition—Mountain fighting—The capture of Kabul and destruction of the Grand Bazaar—The return march to India 161

CHAPTER IX

THE SUTLEJ CAMPAIGN

The Sikhs invade the protected states—The march to the frontier—Battle of Moodkee—Lieutenant Robertson's letters—Battle of Ferozeshah—Lord Hardinge's address to the Thirty-first—" I was with you when you saved the Battle of Albuera "—Action of Budhowal—Battle of Aliwal—Battle of Sobraon—Occupation of Lahore 174

CONTENTS

CHAPTER X

THE CRIMEAN WAR

Sketch of the campaign—Siege of Sebastopol—The assault on June 18, 1855—Work in the trenches—The second assault—Evacuation of Sebastopol by the Russians. 218

CHAPTER XI

THE CHINESE WAR OF 1860

Advance on Sind-ho—The capture of Tang-koo—The Taku forts—Service in China—The Thirty-first returns home—Is linked with the Seventieth Regiment—Establishment of the Depot at Kingston-on-Thames—The Thirty-first becomes the 1st Battalion East Surrey Regiment 227

PART II

HISTORY OF THE SEVENTIETH REGIMENT

CHAPTER XII

EARLY HISTORY

"The Glasgow Greys"—Roll of the original officers—Loss of four companies—Ten years' service at Grenada—The Carib rising at St. Vincent—The remains of the regiment return to England 239

CHAPTER XIII

THE AMERICAN WAR OF INDEPENDENCE

The Seventieth detained at Halifax—The Flank Companies at New York—Captain Irving's letters—The capture of Charleston—Lord Cornwallis' operations—The Flank Companies return to New York—Services and death of Major Patrick Ferguson—The Seventieth styled the "Surrey" Regiment 248

CHAPTER XIV

THE FRENCH REVOLUTIONARY WAR

The "Standing Orders" of 1788—The West Indian Campaign of 1793—More letters of Major Irving—Capture of Martinique—The Seventieth at Morne Pied—Heavy loss of life in the regiment—Service at Gibraltar—A trip to Trinidad—Under Sir John Moore at Chatham and Shorncliffe—The West Indies again—Yellow fever—The Flank Companies at Gaudeloupe in 1810 270

CONTENTS

CHAPTER XV

YEARS OF PEACE

After the Great War—Service in Canada—Ireland in 1831—Gibraltar and Malta—The West Indies again—First tour of Indian service—Cholera at Cawnpore 305

CHAPTER XVI

THE INDIAN MUTINY

The importance of Peshawar—Colonel Chute's "Flying Column"—Military executions—The regiment supplies artillery and cavalry—An abortive rising 310

CHAPTER XVII

THE NEW ZEALAND WAR

Engagements on the Katikira, and on the Waikato rivers—Relief of Pukekohe—Action of Rangiawhia—Action of Orakau—The "Gate Pah"—Action of Okea 321

CHAPTER XVIII

INDIAN SERVICE—THE SECOND AFGHAN WAR

Home service—India again—Peshawar and Cherat in 1875—Nowshera and Multan—The second Afghan war—The Dera Bugti Desert—The advance on Kandahar—The march to the Helmand—The return to Kandahar and return march to India through Tal and Chotiali—The Seventieth becomes the Second Battalion East Surrey Regiment 335

PART III

HISTORY OF THE 1ST AND 2ND BATTALIONS THE EAST SURREY REGIMENT, JULY 1881 TO AUGUST 1914

CHAPTER XIX

RECENT HISTORY OF THE FIRST BATTALION

Home service—A trip to Gibraltar—Nine months at Aldershot—Gibraltar again—A modern voyage to India—Peaceful service—Presentation of Colours by Lord Roberts—Two years at Jersey—Ireland before the war 353

CONTENTS

CHAPTER XX

THE SECOND BATTALION AT SUAKIN

The Second Battalion in Egypt, 1884–5—At Suakin—Reconnaissance of Hashin—Engagement at Hashin and occupation of the post—Advance to Tamai 358

CHAPTER XXI

THE SECOND BATTALION IN THE SOUTH AFRICAN WAR

The Second Battalion on Home service—The South African War—The 2nd Brigade sent to Natal—The action of Willow Grange or Brynbella Hill—The action of Colenso—The Spion Kop operations—The action of Vaal Krantz—The relief of Ladysmith—Cingolo and Monte Cristo—The fight on Wynne's Hills—Battle of Pieter's Hill—Skirmish at Elandslaagte—The Volunteer Service Company—The clearing of northern Natal—Operations in the Biggarsberg—Action of Alleman's Nek—Occupation of Standerton—On the lines of communication—Minor enterprises—With Colonel Colville's column—With Colonel Rimington's column—On the line again—Record of the Mounted Infantry company—End of the war—The battalion goes to India   365

CHAPTER XXII

RECENT HISTORY OF THE SECOND BATTALION

Two years at Lucknow—Sitapur and Ranikhet—Mhow—Athletic successes—Efficiency and good health—The battalion visits Burma for the first time—A country of many detachments—Back to India—Manœuvres in Eastern Bengal—Chaubattia—The coming of war . 457

ILLUSTRATIONS

31ST REGIMENT. UNIFORM IN BYGONE DAYS	*Frontispiece*
VIGO. THE BAY AND HARBOUR	*Facing page* 3
BATTLE OF DETTINGEN. (From an old print.)	17
LIEUT.-GENERAL SIR GUY L'ESTRANGE, K.C.B. (WHO COMMANDED THE 2ND BN. 31ST REGIMENT AT ALBUERA)	122
THE BURNING OF THE "KENT"	152
GENERAL THE EARL OF MULGRAVE, G.C.B., COLONEL OF THE 31ST (HUNTINGDONSHIRE) REGIMENT, MASTER-GENERAL OF THE ORDNANCE, &C., &C.	157
THE 31ST REGIMENT AT MOODKEE	178
BIVOUAC OF THE 31ST REGIMENT, FEROZESHAH	190
THE 31ST REGIMENT AT SOBRAON. SERGEANT MCCABE PLANTING THE COLOUR ON THE SIKH ENTRENCHMENT	206
SERGEANT AND PRIVATE, 70TH REGIMENT. (PERIOD OF FRENCH WAR.)	275
LIEUT.-GENERAL THE HONBLE. SIR G. LOWRY COLE, K.C.B., COLONEL OF THE 70TH (SURREY) REGIMENT	305
70TH (SURREY) REGIMENT. OFFICERS' UNIFORM IN BYGONE DAYS	305
SERGEANT A. E. CURTIS, V.C., 2ND BN. THE EAST SURREY REGIMENT	329
GENERAL THE RIGHT HONBLE. SIR EDWARD LUGARD, G.C.B., COLONEL OF THE EAST SURREY REGIMENT	353
GALLANT CONDUCT OF FOUR SOLDIERS OF THE 31ST REGIMENT IN AFGHANISTAN	367
SPION KOP, NATAL. GENERAL VIEW OF THE BOER POSITION	383
BOER POSITION—PIETER'S HILL, NATAL. (FROM THE FOOT OF HLANGWANÉ HILL)	390
CAPTURE OF HART'S HILL, NATAL, FEBRUARY 27TH, 1900. (From a drawing by an Officer of the Devonshire Regiment)	404

PART I

HISTORY OF THE THIRTY-FIRST REGIMENT

CHAPTER I

COLONEL GEORGE VILLIERS' REGIMENT OF MARINES

Roll of the original officers—Marine uniform—The soldier's life at sea—Cadiz—Vigo—Capture of Gibraltar—The first defence of Gibraltar—Barcelona and Montjuich—The Balearic Isles—Attempted capture of Toulon—Threatened reduction of the Marine Regiments.

THE Thirty-First Regiment, the oldest of the units that to-day form the East Surrey Regiment, has been in existence over two hundred years, during which long period it has more than once been compelled to change its name, but has never lost its identity.

The augmentation of the army of England, then a very small one, which called the regiment into existence, was ordained in the last year of the reign of King William III, when it had become evident that the short-lived peace with France, dating from the treaty of Ryswick signed in 1697, must presently come to an end. When war had been decided on King William was already a dying man, and one of his last actions was the selection of the commanding and field-officers of six new regiments. On February 12, 1702, the King signed the commissions of George Villiers to be Colonel of a Regiment of Marines, of Alexander Luttrell to be Lieutenant-Colonel, and of Thomas Carew to be Major of the same regiment. Colonel George Villiers was appointed from the First Guards, in which regiment he was appointed Ensign on August 31, 1685, and Captain-Lieutenant on April 1, 1687. Eight days after making these appointments King William fell from his horse and sustained the injuries which caused his death on the morning of March 8. It therefore happened that it fell to his successor to carry out the augmentation of the army already decreed, and that one of the first acts of the warlike and glorious reign of Queen

Anne was the issue of the Royal Warrant, dated March 14, 1702, ordering the formation of six additional regiments of marines. Villiers' regiment, in accordance with the seniority of its Colonel, ranked second among the six, and is to-day the First Battalion of the East Surrey Regiment. The establishment of the new regiment consisted of twelve companies, each with a strength of two sergeants, three corporals, two drummers, and fifty-nine private soldiers, with an additional sergeant in the Grenadier company. The first six companies, three of which were commanded, as was then the custom, by Colonel Villiers, Lieut.-Colonel Luttrell, and Major Carew, were raised at Taunton and Bridgewater, and as appears from the names of the officers, a considerable proportion of them, and doubtless of the rank and file, were west-country men. With war in sight recruiting was very brisk, and within a few weeks Villiers' Marine Regiment was fully officered and had reached its prescribed strength of forty officers and 793 sergeants, rank and file.

The names of the original officers of the regiment will be found below, with such particulars as have been traced concerning their subsequent history.

COLONEL GEORGE VILLIERS' REGIMENT OF MARINES

ROLL OF ORIGINAL OFFICERS

COLONEL
George Villiers. Drowned December 6, 1703.

LIEUTENANT-COLONEL
Alexander Luttrell. Promoted Colonel December 6, 1703. Died September, 1714.

MAJOR
Thomas Carew. Promoted Lieut.-Colonel December 6, 1703. Died April 7, 1705.

CAPTAINS
Robert Hedges. Promoted Major May 8, 1705. Retired July 27, 1707.
George Blakeney. Promoted Major December 6, 1703. Lieut.-Colonel April 7, 1705. Re-commissioned in Thirty-First Foot, 1715.
Benjamin Buller. Died December 2, 1702.
Philip Docton. Retired March 10, 1706.
Francis Blinman. Retired June 6, 1709.
Edward Tynte. Promoted Major July 27, 1707. Retired June 18, 1708, on appointment as Governor of Carolina, where he died in 1710.
Thomas Adams.
Walter Pigott.
William Courtney, Grenadier Company. Drowned December 6, 1703.

CAPTAIN-LIEUTENANT
   Thomas Horner.

1ST LIEUTENANTS (11)
   Walter Elliot.
   John Salter.
   James Clarke.
   Roger Flower. Promoted Captain October 14, 1709. Re-commissioned in Thirty-First Foot, 1715.
   Mark Hildesley.
   John Taylor. Promoted Captain. Killed in action October 14, 1709.
   Solomon Balmier.
   John Carwardin.
   Robert Stawell.
   Fleetwood Watkins. Promoted Captain March 3, 1708. Re-commissioned in Thirty-First Foot, 1715.
   David Evans.

2ND LIEUTENANTS (12)
   Henry Rainsford. Died December 31, 1708.
   John Beckwith. Re-commissioned in Thirty-First Foot, 1715.
   John Thurston.
   Cutts Hassan. Re-commissioned in Thirty-First Foot, 1715.
   John Anderson. Died January 12, 1708.
   James Desbordes.
   Richard D'Oyley. Died December 15, 1705.
   William Bisset. Died December 18, 1706.
   Thomas Northcote.
   Daniel Winter.
   Samuel Bell. Died June 11, 1706.
   Thomas Sutton. Promoted Captain June 10, 1708.

CHAPLAIN
   Thomas Rose.

ADJUTANT
   Abraham Coakley.

QUARTERMASTER
   John Andrews.

SURGEON
   James Church.

It would appear that during the early days of the new regiments some uncertainty existed as to their exact status and duties when afloat and ashore, for on July 1, 1702, were issued " The rules and instructions for the better government of the Marine Regiments." These regulations directed that when on shore the Marines were to be quartered in the vicinity of the dockyards " in order to guard them from embezzlement or from any attempt that might be made on them by an enemy."

The uniform of the Marine regiments consisted of high-crowned leather caps covered with cloth of the same colour as the facings of the regiment, and ornamented with devices similar to those worn on the caps of the Grenadier company. It is believed that the badges worn were a crown with the initials A. R. beneath it, in the centre of the hat, and an anchor horizontal on the turned-up flap. The remaining uniform consisted of a scarlet frock-coat, buff waist-belt, buff gaiters, and breeches. A heavy black pouch, carried in front, was supported by a shoulder-belt, and kept steady by a bayonet belt which was attached to the pouch.

When ashore the men of the marine regiments came under the same regulations regarding clothing as prevailed in the infantry of the line, and were subject to similar deductions from their pay. When embarked on the Fleet, however, they received suitable sea-clothing and necessaries, and they also drew the same free rations as did the seamen. When serving afloat the marine regiments came under the naval officers for purposes of discipline.

No sooner was Colonel George Villiers' Regiment of Marines ready for active service than it obtained full opportunity of proving its fighting quality, for on May 4, 1702, war was declared by England against France and Spain, and the vigorous plan of campaign designed by King William was at once taken in hand by the ministers of Queen Anne. The British force already stationed in the Low Countries was considerably augmented, and the chief command in that area was bestowed on the Earl (soon to be created Duke) of Marlborough, in conjunction with Prince Eugene of Savoy. It was, however, not the good fortune of Villiers' Marines to serve under Marlborough, and so share in the glories and sufferings of the campaigns of Blenheim, Ramillies, Oudenard, and Malplaquet. Theirs was possibly an even more arduous fate, for the life of the soldier at sea, never one of comfort, was indeed one of almost incessant suffering in the days of Queen Anne, as we may learn from the picturesque language of Private George Dene of the First Regiment of Guards, written, it may be added, after a very brief experience of marine service.

"While we lay on board," writes the honest soldier, "we had continual Distruction in ye foretop; ye pox above board; ye Pleague between Decks; Hell in ye forecastle, and ye Devil att ye Helm; so that you may easely judge what course we steered."

"Ye pox" to which Dene referred was of course small-pox, as deadly an enemy to the soldiers of Queen Anne as was enteric fever to those of Queen Victoria.

The expedition against Spain, of which the headquarters and five companies of Villiers' Marines formed a part, consisted of a fleet of fifty sail of the line, partly British and partly Dutch, besides frigates and transports, the latter carrying a land force numbering 13,500 officers and men. Of this force about 9600 were British, and the remainder Dutch. The orders of the commanders of the expedition, Admiral Sir George Rooke and the Duke of Ormonde, were to capture the town of Cadiz, so often the objective of British attacks in the old wars between England and Spain.

The five companies of Villiers' Marines, with their Colonel, embarked at Plymouth in the latter part of May 1702, and joined the main body of the expeditionary force at Portsmouth, whence the fleet and transports sailed for Cadiz in July, arriving off that town on August 12. The operations at Cadiz were unfortunately unsuccessful, and after some desultory and half-hearted attempts, which only proved that the fortifications of the town were stronger, and the garrison larger, than had been reported, the commanders decided to abandon the enterprise and return to England. The troops were consequently re-embarked and sailed from Cadiz on September 30.

This seemed a disappointing end to the first active service of Villiers' Marines, but some compensation was at hand. Intelligence reached Admiral Rooke that the Spanish treasure fleet from South America had arrived at Vigo, under the additional escort of a French squadron. The position of the treasure ships was strong, but Rooke and Ormonde, who reached Vigo on October 22, 1702, at once decided to attack.

The combined French and Spanish fleet, with the treasure galleons, lay sheltered within a narrow channel, the entrance to which was defended on one side by a castle and on the other by batteries; a strong boom was thrown across the mouth of the harbour.

The British-Dutch force made a combined attack by sea and land on this formidable position, the Duke of Ormonde landing on October 23 with a portion of his troops, six miles from Vigo, and capturing by assault a battery of forty guns near the entrance of Vigo Bay. The hoisting of the British flag on this fort gave the signal for a general attack. The fleet, under full sail, ran boldly in, broke the boom at the first shock and closely engaged the enemy's ships within, while Ormonde's troops assaulted and captured one battery after another. The French and Spanish forces fought well, but were overpowered, and finding that escape was impossible, set fire to their ships. The British seamen exerted themselves nobly in extinguishing the flames, and succeeded in saving seven ships of war and six galleons. The loss of life on the enemy's side is said to have amounted to 2,000, while that of the British-Dutch force did not exceed 130 men.

The treasure captured was valued at one million sterling, and prize-money amounting to 561l. 10s. was awarded to each regiment of infantry. Villiers' Marines served in the fleet during the operations at Vigo, and on arriving in England in November 1702 were stationed at Plymouth, where they were joined by two more companies of the regiment which had been rendered efficient for service during their absence in the Spanish expedition. Great importance was attached in England to the victory at Vigo and to the heavy loss in ships, men, and treasure inflicted on the enemy; Queen Anne, attended by the Lords and Commons, going in state to St. Paul's Cathedral to return thanks for the success of British arms.

Villiers' Marines did not long remain ashore, for on January 27, 1703, Headquarters and four companies of the regiment embarked on board H.M.'s ships *Suffolk* and *Grafton*, which proceeded to join the fleet then serving under Admiral Sir George Rooke off the coast of Spain and in the Mediterranean. While serving in the fleet near Malta the regiment lost its first commanding officer, Colonel George Villiers being drowned in December 1703, less than two years after receiving his commission to raise the regiment. Captain William Courtney of the Grenadier Company was drowned with his Colonel. Colonel Villiers, whose death was considered a great loss to the service, was succeeded in the command of the regiment by Lieut.-Colonel Alexander Luttrell, whose commission as Colonel was dated December 6, 1703, the day following the death of Colonel Villiers. Colonel Luttrell, who had previously served as a captain in the present (19th) Yorkshire Regiment, became Lieutenant-Colonel of Norcott's

COLONEL GEORGE VILLIERS' REGIMENT OF MARINES

Foot in 1694. He had served in all King William's wars in Flanders. In February 1704 the regiment, now styled Luttrell's Marines, accompanied Sir George Rooke's fleet to attempt further enterprises on the coast of Spain. After a concentration at Lisbon the fleet sailed for Barcelona, where the whole body of Marines, under the command of Major-General Prince George of Hesse-Darmstadt, was landed on May 19. The force being found to be too small to attack Barcelona, was re-embarked on the following day and headed for Gibraltar, at that time neither strongly fortified nor considered of great importance. Gibraltar has, however, at all times possessed great natural defensive advantages, and its capture by the very small force at the disposal of Admiral Rooke, though of the nature of a surprise, must be considered a remarkable and memorable achievement, on its share in which the regiment may justly pride itself. On July 21, 1704, 1800 British and Dutch marines, under Prince George, effected a landing almost unopposed on the neck of land joining Gibraltar with the mainland; and three days later, after a bombardment by the fleet, aided by the vigorous attack of the Marines ashore, the Governor of Gibraltar was forced to capitulate. The Spanish garrison, though far too weak to make an effective defence, fought gallantly and inflicted a loss on the attacking force of 61 killed and 260 wounded.

After the surrender, the fleet sailed on other enterprises, leaving Prince George of Hesse-Darmstadt as Governor of Gibraltar, with a good store of provisions and a garrison of about 2000 English and Dutch soldiers. The British portion of the garrison consisted, in addition to Luttrell's Regiment, of two other Marine corps, now the First Battalion Royal Lancaster Regiment and the First Battalion Duke of Cornwall's Light Infantry. Prince George, an experienced soldier, lost no time in strengthening the fortifications, and it was well that he acted promptly, for at the end of August a Spanish force of 8000 men marched down to the isthmus which unites the Rock of Gibraltar with the mainland, while a month later 4000 French troops were landed at the head of the bay. These joint forces then began the first siege of Gibraltar. The operations were vigorously pushed forward, and the inadequate garrison was soon hard beset. At the end of October Admiral Leake, arriving from England with a squadron of seventeen English and some Dutch ships threw, with much difficulty, some stores and a small but welcome reinforcement of 200 Marines on to the Rock, together with an able engineer, Captain Bennett, whose services proved of great value.

The siege continued to throw a very heavy strain on the weak garrison, and although an attack on the eastern side made on October 17 was repulsed with heavy loss, by the end of November the garrison had no more than 1000 men fit for duty. Happily, in the middle of December detachments of the Coldstream Guards, 13th and 35th Regiments, numbering in all 2000 men, were successfully landed; and with this welcome accession of strength Prince George was able to make a series of vigorous sorties against the besiegers, who had also been largely reduced in numbers by sickness and casualties.

In the middle of January 1705 the enemy received reinforcements of 4000 men, in addition to supplies of powder and shot, both of which had previously run short. The bombardment redoubled in vigour, and a practicable breach was made in the Round Tower, which formed one of the principal defences on the western side.

On the morning of January 27, 1300 men assaulted the Round Tower, and in spite of the gallant resistance offered by the British garrison of 300 men, succeeded in carrying the town. Then pressing immediately after the survivors of the garrison the storming column attempted to gain possession of the gate which led into the main fortress. Through the good conduct and staunch fighting of the troops nearest the gateway, this attempt was frustrated and the enemy finally driven off, not only from the gate, but from their original capture, the Round Tower. This repulse, and the arrival of further British reinforcements, ended all serious attempts on the fortress, but Marshal Tessé, who was now in command of the besiegers, bombarded the town of Gibraltar, which was speedily reduced to ruins. Relief came on March 10, when Admiral Leake, with a powerful fleet, appeared on the scene, and after a severe action defeated and drove off the French squadron, with a loss of a third of its strength. By the middle of April Gibraltar was free from the presence of the last of its enemies, whose loss during the siege amounted to no less than 12,000 men.

The share taken in this gallant and successful defence by Luttrell's Regiment of Marines has been recognised by the grant of the honour

COLONEL GEORGE VILLIERS' REGIMENT OF MARINES

"Gibraltar, 1704-5," which now heads the long roll of distinctions borne on its colours by the East Surrey Regiment.

The reinforcements sent from England in the course of the siege having supplied the fortress with a sufficient garrison, the Marine corps were now relieved from duty ashore and re-distributed among the fleet under Admiral Leake, destined to continue operations against the coasts of Spain. With this fleet was an expeditionary force of about 6000 English and Dutch infantry, commanded by the celebrated Earl of Peterborough, which had arrived at Lisbon early in June. Peterborough received there a reinforcement of two regiments of Dragoons, which were already serving in Portugal, and sailing for Gibraltar, picked up a mixed battalion of Guards and three line battalions from the garrison, leaving two of his own battalions in their place. Peterborough's force now consisted of twenty battalions, including the four Marine Corps, and with this force, probably not more than 10,000 men, he sailed northward in order to attack Barcelona.

This important city had been represented to the English Government as ill-fortified and under-garrisoned, but it proved on inspection to be a formidable fortress, well stocked with supplies and garrisoned by 7000 well-commanded troops. The task before Peterborough was a formidable one, but he was a man to quail from no enterprise. On August 23, 1705, the troops of the expedition were landed and took up a position to the north-east of the town, whence a regular siege was commenced. Lord Peterborough, however, soon saw that the forces on both sides were too equal for success by such means to be probable, and after a fruitless attack, lasting eighteen days, ordered the re-embarkation of the army. This order was, however, but a feint, intended to divert attention from the design which he had secretly formed. This plan was the capture by a night-surprise of the small fort of Montjuich, distant about 1200 yards from Barcelona and situated to the south-west of that town. Montjuich crowned a hill which commanded Barcelona, and it was hoped that its capture would produce a marked effect on the defence of that city.

Peterborough kept his intention a complete secret, the troops detailed for the attack being warned to march towards Tarragona, to .the north-westward. The column, 1400 strong, marched at six in the evening of September 13, 1705, while a supporting force of 1300 men were secretly posted to guard against any attack from Barcelona during the intended assault. At 10 P.M. the attacking force was ordered to change its direction to the southward, and after a fatiguing night-march over most difficult ground arrived at an early hour before Montjuich. A body of 200 men had lost its way in the dark, but Peterborough was prepared to take all risks. Six hundred men, half the little force, were divided into two assaulting columns, which were ordered to escalade the eastern and western walls of the fort; the remaining six hundred were held in reserve. Lord Peterborough and Prince George of Hesse-Darmstadt accompanied the eastern column, which was expected to have the stiffest task to perform. A little after daybreak on September 14 the assaults were delivered, and in spite of a stout resistance both columns effected a lodgment and entrenched themselves in the bastions which they had captured. The reserve was then ordered up by Lord Peterborough, and after some confused fighting in which Prince George of Hesse-Darmstadt was killed, Montjuich was eventually taken. The siege of Barcelona was then vigorously pushed forward, and on October 9 the garrison of this important fortress surrendered. The capture of Barcelona was perhaps the most remarkable achievement of Lord Peterborough, and though the services of individual corps in the operations can hardly be distinguished, the share borne by Luttrell's Marines in the campaign may well be remembered by their representatives, the East Surrey Regiment.

Among the losses sustained by the regiment in this short but arduous campaign was Colonel Luttrell, who retired on January 31, 1706, and died at Dunster in 1714. He was succeeded in the command by Lieut.-Colonel Joshua Churchill, of the 3rd Foot (Buffs). Colonel Churchill, of Henbury, in Dorsetshire, was a member of a well-known family in that county. He was not, it is believed, related to the Duke of Marlborough.

The operations in Spain in 1706 were of no great interest. In April an attempt was made by France and her Spanish allies to re-capture Barcelona, but the English and Dutch fleet arriving with reinforcements, the siege was raised on May 11, and the French beat a precipitate retreat. The defence had, however, been of a desperate character, and

COLONEL GEORGE VILLIERS' REGIMENT OF MARINES 13

at the moment of relief the garrison had been reduced to an effective strength of but 1000 men. The British fleet then sailed for the coast of Valencia, Carthagena and Alicant being successively captured, after which successes the fleet turned its attention to the Balearic Isles. Iviça and Majorca surrendered without resistance, and detachments of the Marine corps were placed as garrisons in these islands.

The disastrous defeat of Almanza in April 1707 cast a gloom over the prospects of the allies in Spain, and the operations of the fleet then

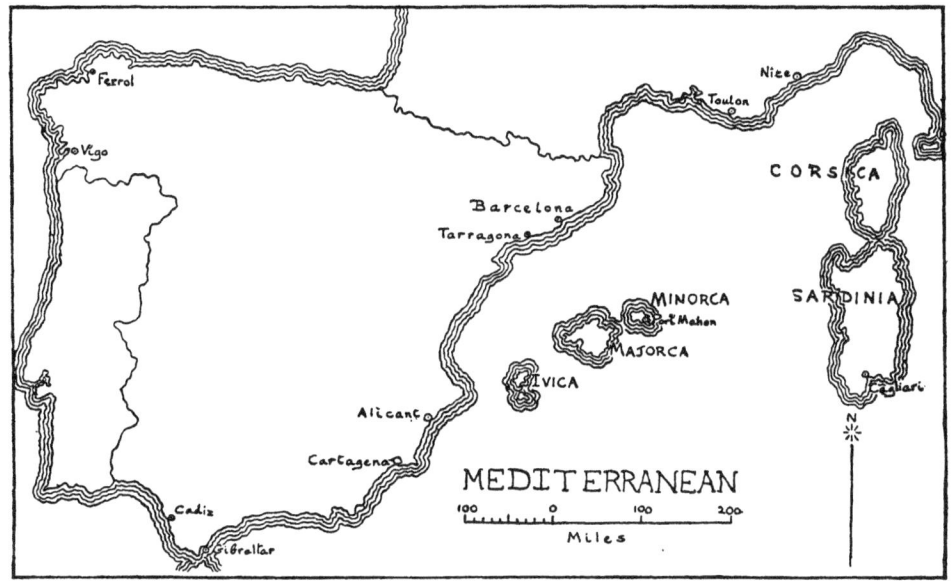

commanded by Sir Cloudisley Shovell were consequently transferred to more promising scenes. A design to attempt the capture of Toulon led to operations in conjunction with the Duke of Savoy and his more famous brother, Prince Eugene. A considerable force of English seamen and marines were landed near Nice, in order to secure a passage westward for the Italian army, but the operations were finally unsuccessful and resulted in considerable losses to the allies. Churchill's Marine Regiment formed part of the army which attacked Toulon. Soon after the abandonment of this enterprise Admiral Shovell sailed for home for the coming winter with twelve ships of the line and several small craft. The fleet got into soundings on October 22, but that night, in consequence of thick weather, several of the ships were lost on the rocks of the Scilly Islands. Between 800 and 900 lives were lost, and it is a regimental tradition that among them was a portion of Churchill's Marines. The deaths of Captain Marshall and Lieutenant Russell of the regiment occurred at this period (being reported, respectively, on November 1 and November 15, 1707), and it seems probable that those officers and their men were serving in Sir Cloudisley Shovell's fleet, though the fact has not been established.

In the following year, 1708, the fleet continued its somewhat desultory operations, a landing being effected at Cagliari, the capital of Sardinia, on August 12. The troops landed were the British Corps of Marines, in which Churchill's Regiment was included, and one Spanish regiment, and to this small force and to the guns of the fleet, Cagliari surrendered.

The next enterprise was an attack on the island of Minorca, before which place the fleet arrived on August 28, but six years of incessant warfare had done their work. The six Marine corps had been so much reduced in numbers that it was now found necessary to draft the men of two of the regiments into the remaining four regiments in order to complete the latter to a strength adequate for active service.

The garrison of Minorca made but a poor resistance, and after operations lasting about three weeks, the island surrendered, the British casualties being between forty and fifty. Minorca, it may be mentioned, was ceded to Britain at the Treaty of Utrecht, in 1713, and remained a part of our Empire until the year 1756, when it was recaptured by a Franco-Spanish force.

After the capture of Minorca in September 1708 the winter force in the Mediterranean was strengthened, Port Mahon furnishing a secure base, but no great enterprise was undertaken during 1709. In June 1710 the fleet, now commanded by Admiral Sir John Norris, defeated an attempted attack on Sardinia, but no other incident of importance in the Mediterranean is recorded from that date until the conclusion of the Peace of Utrecht. In 1711 the Seven Years' War, though still in existence, was evidently nearing its end. Colonel Churchill, consequently, being desirous of leaving the service, received Her Majesty's permission to sell his commission, and on March 1, 1711, Lieut.-Colonel Sir Harry Goring, Bart., was promoted, by purchase, to the command of the regiment. After long negotiations peace was signed in Utrecht

COLONEL GEORGE VILLIERS' REGIMENT OF MARINES

on April 11, 1713, and the employment afloat of Goring's Marine Regiment, which had lasted just eleven years, at length came to an end.

In addition to Colonel George Villiers, Captains Courtney and Marshall, and Lieutenant Russell, whose deaths have already been mentioned, the following officers of the regiment lost their lives during the Mediterranean campaigns of Queen Anne's reign: Lieutenants Anderson, Yard, Parlett, and Rainsford, who died in 1708; Captain Taylor, who was killed in action, and Lieutenant Meriam, who died in 1709; Lieutenants Sheppard and Harwood, and 2nd Lieutenant Millner, who died in 1710; Lieutenant Rogers, who died in 1711, and Lieutenant Freebody in 1712. A heavy death-roll of officers in eleven years.

As usually happens after a long war, large reductions were immediately ordered in the army, and among other regiments, all the Marine corps were threatened with disbandment. The death of Queen Anne, however, which occurred on August 1, 1714, and the consequent revival of activity on the part of the supporters of the exiled Prince James Francis Edward, son of James II, postponed the intended reductions. So active indeed were the Jacobites in many parts of the kingdom, that King George I, who had succeeded to the throne by virtue of the Act of the Protestant Succession, found it necessary to make considerable additions to the army. Six new regiments of cavalry were raised (those now numbered 9th to 14th), and in consideration of the services of the Marine corps during the wars of Queen Anne's reign, the three senior Marine regiments, those of Wills, Goring, and Borr, were restored to life and placed as infantry Regiments of the Line on the Irish establishment. Wills' Regiment was numbered the 30th Foot, Goring's the Thirty-First, and Borr's the 32nd. All three regiments, it may be observed, retain these numbers as part of their titles to the present day.

CHAPTER II

THE BATTLE OF DETTINGEN

Sir Harry Goring's Regiment of Foot—Colonel William Handasyd—The war of the Austrian Succession—Ancient officers—The battle of Dettingen—King George II and "*the young Buffs.*"

THE commissions of the officers of the Thirty-First Regiment were renewed by King George on June 1, 1715, the names of the officers being as follows:—

SIR HARRY GORING'S REGIMENT OF FOOT
(31ST FOOT)

CAPTAINS

Sir Harry Goring,[1] Colonel.
George Blakeney,[2] Lieutenant-Colonel.
Richard Prater, Major.
Roger Flower, April 25, 1714.
John Beckwith, November 19, 1714.
Cutts Hassan.
Fleetwood Watkins.
Rupert Handcock.
John Busby, Grenadier Company.

LIEUTENANTS

Alexander Wilson, Captain-Lieutenant.
William Risdall.

---

[1] Sir Henry Goring, 3rd Bart., of Highden, Sussex, Colonel of Marines (31st Foot) March 1, 1711. Half-pay 1713. Reappointed Colonel on the restoration of the above regiment in 1715. Obliged to sell his commission in September 1715 as a suspected Jacobite. Died 1732.

[2] George Blakeney was a member of an Irish family which supplied the Army with many good soldiers. He was uncle of the distinguished General William, Lord Blakeney. Colonel George Blakeney received his first commission in 1688 and became a Captain in Villiers' Marines (31st Foot) on March 10, 1702. Bt. Major March 8, 1703. He served at Cadiz in 1702 and at the taking of Vigo, at the siege of Toulon in 1707, and at the capture of Cagliari in 1708. He resigned his commission in 1718 to his nephew William, afterwards Lord Blakeney.

Battle of Dettingen.
(From an old print.)

Thomas Daracote.
Antoine Rotolph de Ladevèze.[1]
Abraham Ardesoife.
Edward Thompson.
Peter Havilland.
Edward O'Bryen, 1st Lieutenant Grenadier Company.
Lionel Seaman, 2nd Lieutenant Grenadier Company. Died March 27, 1726.

ENSIGNS
John Pierson.
Thomas Webb.
Charles Whittick.
Adam Elliot.
John Blakeney. Died February 1, 1720.
Charles Millet.
Arthur Swift.
Joseph Harding.

CHAPLAIN
John Phillips.

ADJUTANT
Ant. de Ladevèze.

SURGEON
William Scott.

It will be observed that Lieut.-Colonel Blakeney, and Captains Flower, Beckwith, Hassan, and Watkins were the survivors of the original officers of Villiers' Marines.

Partly on account of its forming part of the garrison of Ireland, and partly perhaps because its Colonel, Sir Harry Goring, was suspected by King George's Government of Jacobite sympathies, the Thirty-First Regiment took no part in the suppression of the Stuart rising of 1715. In September of this year, Colonel Sir Harry Goring was compelled, on the political grounds mentioned, to sell his commission. His successor as Colonel of the Thirty-First Regiment was Lord John Kerr, son of the 1st Marquis of Lothian, whose commission bore date September 3, 1715. Lord John Kerr held the command until his death on August 1, 1728, when he was succeeded by Colonel the Honourable Charles Cathcart, from the 9th Foot. On January 1, 1731, Colonel

---

[1] Antoine Rotolph de Ladevèze was born at the Hague in 1689, the son of the British Minister there. He was gazetted 2nd Lieutenant in Joshua Churchill's Marine Regiment in 1707, Adjutant of the Regiment 1712, Major 1732, and left the Regiment on promotion to Howard's Regiment in 1741. He died November 25, 1769.

Cathcart was removed to the 8th Dragoons, and the colonelcy of the Thirty-First was conferred on Colonel William Hargrave, of the 7th Royal Fusiliers, a veteran officer of Queen Anne's wars. Colonel Hargrave in turn was transferred on January 27, 1737, to the 9th Foot, and was succeeded in the colonelcy of the Thirty-First by Colonel William Handasyd, by whose name the regiment was long known, and under whose command it first achieved a reputation as a regiment of the line.

In the year 1739 the regiment's long period of service in Ireland, the history of which has been entirely lost, was terminated by the threatening aspect of affairs. The peace that had generally prevailed in Europe since the treaty of Utrecht was evidently nearing its end through the illness of the Emperor and the consequent impetus given to dynastic ambitions.

The Emperor Charles VI, the last male of the House of Habsburg, died on October 20, 1740, and in accordance with an agreement guaranteed by all the European Powers, his daughter Maria Theresa succeeded to the Imperial throne. The Empire, however, weakened by a long struggle against the Turks, was in no position to defend itself, and many of the Powers, particularly Prussia and France, were tempted by its weakness to increase their own territory or influence. Prussia, under Frederick the Great, asserted a claim to Silesia, and France supported the pretensions of the Elector of Bavaria to the Imperial throne. Early in 1741 Frederick of Prussia invaded Silesia at the head of 60,000 troops, and King George II, though anxious to support the Empress Maria Theresa against this aggression, was unable, through the weakness of the English army to take immediate action. Hanover was threatened by invasion from two quarters, by Prussia and France, and King George was therefore compelled for the time to stand aside, while resolved to collect his strength for future action. The small standing army of England was presently concentrated in the south-eastern counties, and among others, Handasyd's regiment was encamped at Windsor, moving afterwards to Lexden Heath, near Colchester, and joining the force employed in the camps of exercise formed at those places under General Wade. The discipline of the army had been grievously relaxed during the thirty years' peace, the veteran leaders and soldiers of Marlborough's invincible army were mostly dead or worn out, and the fighting force of England had to be reconstructed. Considerable increases to the army were sanctioned in 1741, and the British establishment for 1742 provided for a force of 62,000 men.

Prussia, having obtained her object by the cession to her of Silesia, was now at peace with Austria, but France was evidently bent on breaking up the Empire. King George II, who as Elector of Hanover was deeply concerned in the maintenance of the Empire, now found it necessary to take an active part in the struggle that appeared to be imminent; and in this decision he was upheld by the general wish of his British subjects. Englishmen at that day had no greater wish to fight in defence of the interests of Hanover than in the reign of King William III they had to fight in those of Holland; but the misconduct of Prussia and France towards the Empress Maria Theresa had deeply stirred their feelings, and the prospect of war was not unpleasing to them. Yet war was declared neither by France nor England, though both countries sent their armies into the field—a strange state of affairs.

A few words must now be said regarding the officers of Handasyd's regiment at the opening of the campaign. The year 1740 found the army, as is customary after a long peace, largely officered in the upper ranks by men past their work. A glance at the roll of the officers of Handasyd's will show that they formed no exception to the rule. The Colonel himself had at least thirty-five years' service; Lieutenant-Colonel Beckwith, a member of a well-known family of soldiers, had served forty-five years and had been one of the original officers of the regiment when it was raised as " Villiers' Marines "; and William Drummond, one of the Captains, was an even older soldier, his first commission dating from 1686. James Baird, the junior Captain, had eighteen years' service; and many of the lieutenants were of even longer standing.

The preparation for war of so elderly an army naturally resulted in wholesale retirements and promotions, and the changes in Handasyd's were of a sweeping nature. By the opening of the campaign the roll of officers were entirely reconstituted. Colonel Handasyd himself remained with the regiment until promoted to the (then permanent) rank of Brigadier-General on February 11, 1743, but long prior to that date the changes spoken of had taken place.[1]

1740

Colonel Handasyd's Regiment of Foot

	Date of Commission	Date of First Commission
Colonel		
William Handasyd.	June 27, 1737	Lieut. 1705.
Lieutenant-Colonel		
John Beckwith	July 2, 1737	Ensign 1695.
Major		
Anthony R. de Ladevèze	May 29, 1737	Lieut. April 2, 1706.
Captains		
Edward Legard	Dec. 20, 1717	Captain Dec. 20, 1717.
Robert Blakeney	April 23, 1720	Ensign Sept. 1715.
William Williamson	July 25, 1726	,, Aug. 28, 1711.
William Drummond	Mar. 1727	Lieut. 1686.
Hon. Robert Douglas	May 29, 1732	Ensign 1721.
Peter Haviland	Aug. 1727	Lieut. July 1714.
James Baird	June 20, 1735	,, Feb. 11, 1717.
Captain-Lieutenant		
John Pollock.	Feb. 21, 1736	Ensign Feb. 11, 1717.
Lieutenants		
Frederick Porter	Nov. 17, 1721	Ensign June 22, 1719.
Charles Vignoles	Oct. 22, 1723	,, Mar. 7, 1718.
Francis Mears	Aug. 11, 1730	,, Nov. 17, 1721.
Richard Abbot	Sept. 1730	,, May 26, 1704.
Robert Ryves	Nov. 30, 1730	,, Oct. 1721.
James Vignoles	Nov. 6, 1732	,, Dec. 15, 1721.
Henry Hyat	Feb. 23, 1733	,, Mar. 21, 1724.
Charles O'Hara	June 20, 1735	,, 1710.
Charles Cockburne	Feb. 21, 1736	,, 1712.
Walter Pringle	Jan. 14, 1738	,, June 20, 1735.
Ensigns		
Alexander Dalway	Dec. 5, 1729	Ensign Jan. 20, 1725.
George Dalrymple	Feb. 23, 1733	
James Hamilton	Feb. 21, 1736	
Robert Wynne	Aug. 26, 1737	
Samuel Davenport	June 14, 1738	
Pat. Clarke	June 2, 1739	
John Tatem	July 17, 1739	
Peyton Mears	Feb. 3, 1740	
Egerton Stafford	Feb. 4, 1740	

[1] Soon after Brigadier-General Handasyd's death the substantive rank of Brigadier-General was allowed to lapse, only seven officers after him receiving it; and from that period it has only been bestowed on officers on the active list as a local or temporary rank. It is now (1914) granted to certain officers on retirement.

Lieut.-Colonel Beckwith [1] died in August 1741, and was succeeded by Major Edward Montagu, of Cornwallis' (now the Devonshire Regiment). Major de Ladevèze had previously been promoted into Colonel Howard's regiment (now the 1st Battn. Yorkshire Regiment), and his majority in Handasyd's had been conferred on Edward Legard, the Senior Captain, who became Lieutenant-Colonel after Fontenoy. Only one other Captain remained, the junior, James Baird, who was promoted Major after Fontenoy. Of the remaining Captains, Drummond, Blakeney, and Haviland retired, Williams was appointed a Captain of Invalids at Hull, and the Honourable Robert Douglas was transferred to the 3rd Guards as Captain and Lieutenant-Colonel.[2] All the vacant companies were given in the regiment, so that when Fontenoy had been fought every surviving officer who had been a Lieutenant in 1740 found himself a Captain. We can understand why war was popular in the army in the brave days of old.

BRIGADIER-GENERAL WILLIAM HANDASYD'S REGIMENT OF FOOT

ROLL OF OFFICERS WHO SERVED IN THE CAMPAIGNS OF 1743-5

COLONEL (1)
  Brigadier-General Wm. Handasyd. Died April 25, 1745.
  Lord Henry Beauclerk. Promoted from 48th Foot vice Handasyd.

LIEUTENANT-COLONEL (1)
  Edward Montagu. Killed at Fontenoy.
  Edward Legard. Promoted vice Montagu.

MAJOR (1)
  Edward Legard.
  James Baird. Promoted vice Legard. Wounded and reported killed at Fontenoy. Died in 1751.

CAPTAINS (7)
  Frederick Porter.
  Charles Vignoles. Promoted Major July 1751, vice Baird, dec.
  James Baird. Promoted Major vice Legard.
  John Pollock. Killed at Fontenoy.
  James Vignoles.
  Robert Ryves.
  Francis Mears.

---

[1] Lieut.-Colonel Beckwith died in the camp near Colchester while still with the regiment. His obituary notice in the *Gentleman's Magazine* states that "King William gave him a Pair of Colours at the Siege of Namur, when he was shot through the body. He was at the taking of Gibraltar, and one of the Defenders of it above 7 months against the United Force of France and Spain."

[2] Lieut.-Colonel the Hon. R. Douglas was killed at Fontenoy. He was the second son of the 13th Earl of Morton.

CAPTAINS (continued).
    Walter Pringle.
    Charles Cockburn. Promoted vice Pollock.

ADDITIONAL COMPANIES (2). Raised June 24, 1744.
    Robert Wynne.
    James Milford.

CAPTAIN-LIEUTENANT
    James Hamilton.

LIEUTENANTS (10)
    Alexander Dalway. Killed at Fontenoy.
    George Dalrymple. Died March 30, 1742.
    Samuel Davenport. Died April 21, 1742.
    Peter Clark. Retired July 11, 1741.
    John Tatem. Died January 26, 1741.
    Peyton Mears.
    Egerton Stafford. Mortally wounded at Fontenoy.
    Frederick Porter, junr. Wounded at Fontenoy.
    William Cholmondeley. Promoted Captain in C. Howard's.
    Robert Pigot.
    Gardiner Bulstrode.
    Roger Handasyd.
    Robert Worsley. Wounded at Fontenoy.
    Robert Barker.
    John Freeman. Wounded at Fontenoy.
    Edward Bromley. Wounded at Fontenoy.
    Patrick McDowall.
    William La Chaux.
    William Marshall.

ENSIGNS (10)
    Theophilus Beaumont. Promoted in Wynyard's Marines.
    Fox Hickman. Transferred to Robinson's Marines.
    John Poole.
    Thomas Dunbar.
    Newcomen Atkinson.
    Robert Banbury.
    George Mainwaring.
    Tichborne Philip Grueber.
    Charles Cassel.
    James Grady.
    Gavin Cochran.
    Joseph Green.
    Christopher Woodward.

Note.—The two junior Ensigns were promoted from the date of the battle of Fontenoy. Joseph Green, the senior, was promoted from the rank of Corporal and Christopher Woodward from that of Sergeant. Both no doubt owed their commissions to gallant and conspicuous service, but no record of the circumstances has been traced.

ADJUTANT (1)
    John Freeman.
    William Hooker. Promoted from Sergeant-Major.

QUARTERMASTER
   Lewis Lachasselle.

SURGEON
   James Chalmers.

It is now necessary to trace very briefly the events leading to the battle of Dettingen. The force sent from England in May 1742 to support the cause of Maria Theresa, consisted of 16,000 British troops under Field-Marshal the Earl of Stair, a veteran of the wars of William III and Marlborough. The little army, which included Handasyd's regiment, was reviewed on Kew Green by King George II and his son, the Duke of Cumberland, and embarked at Deptford on May 17. Its first destination was Holland, which country, as a supporter of Austria, was now in danger of a French invasion. The British troops were therefore quartered at Bruges and Ghent, where Lord Stair hoped to be joined by the Hanoverian army, and by a contingent of 6000 Hessian troops paid by England. The concentration, however, failed from political causes too intricate to be explained here, and the British troops consequently lay inactive for nearly a year, with bad effects on their health and discipline. At last, in February 1743, the army began its march eastward, to join the Austrians, and conduct and discipline at once improved. Lord Stair desired to repeat the great exploit of the Duke of Marlborough, to march to the Danube and attack the Bavarians in their own territory, but King George, who retained all military arrangement in his own hands, ordered him to occupy the heights of Maintz and thus command the junction of the Rhine and the Main. The position finally occupied by the allied army of England, Hanover, and Austria in May 1743 ran from these heights along the north bank of the Main as far as Aschaffenburg, and opposed to them was a French army about 70,000 strong, commanded by Marshal the Duke de Noailles, and lying on the Upper Rhine near Spires.

Lord Stair was aware of the danger of his position. In the days before railways, when good roads were few and far between, and armies had but little wheeled transport, rivers were the principal lines of supply. But a river of which one bank is held by the enemy is useless for this purpose. The allied army was therefore soon on half rations and in imminent danger of starvation. Lord Stair made many representations, and despite his orders did cross the river and offer battle to Noailles. The French marshal, however declined to fight, and King George ordered Lord Stair to return to the north bank of the Main.

At last, on June 19, King George arrived from Hanover and took command of the allied army, about 40,000 strong, which was now concentrated about Aschaffenburg. The troops, though nearly starving, were in high spirits. After a delay of a week the King

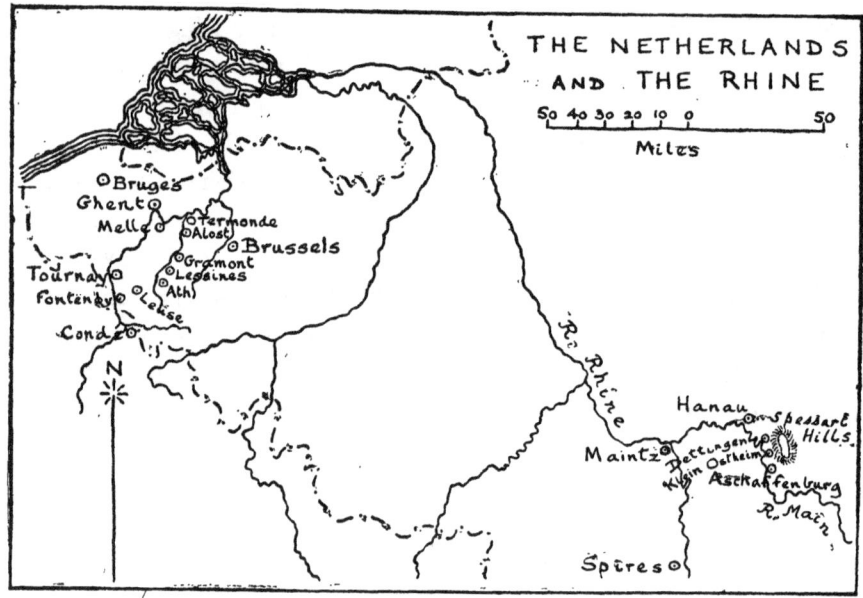

decided, on June 26, to retire to Hanau, where supplies had been collected and where a force of 12,000 men was in danger of capture.

Marshal de Noailles now had such a chance as rarely offers itself to a commander in war. The only line by which the allied army could retire was along the narrow plain between the river Main and the Spessart Hills, which was commanded throughout by five French batteries constructed on successive hills along the south bank of the river. In the rear, near Aschaffenburg, was the French main body under Noailles himself; while a force of 28,000 picked troops, under the Count de Gramont, the nephew of Noailles, had been thrown across the river and held a strong position behind the village of Dettingen, absolutely blocking the only road of escape. Never since

THE BATTLE OF DETTINGEN

Crécy had an English army with its King run such risk of capture or destruction.

The allied army marched at four in the morning of June 27, 1743, the British cavalry leading, followed by the Austrian cavalry. Then came the British, followed in turn by the Austrian infantry. A strong rear-guard was composed of the English Guards, some picked regiments of Hanoverian infantry, and the Hanoverian cavalry; for it was in the rear that the greatest danger threatened. It is stated in Cannon's Record of the Thirty-First that on the night of June 26 the regiment was on outpost duty in the direction of Dettingen, under Lieutenant-Colonel Montagu, who was in command, Colonel Handasyd having remained on duty in England.

Very early on June 27, Lieutenant-Colonel Montagu observed the movement of the Comte de Gramont's force and gave the first intimation to headquarters that the line of advance on Hanover was held.[1]

When the allied rear-guard had quitted Aschaffenburg and was making across a bend of the Main for the village of Klein Ostheim, the French main body could be seen in full march to cross the river behind them and cut off their retreat. With the Main, which they had no means of crossing, on their left, impenetrable woods blocking their right, Gramont strongly posted in their front, and Noailles closing on their rear, there seemed to be no escape for King George and his army.

Passing through Klein Ostheim at about 7 A.M. the allied army was long delayed by the narrowness of the road. The cavalry leading the way, formed up after clearing the village, and wheeled to the left, facing the river, to cover the deployment of the infantry. For an hour the cavalry stood thus, exposed to heavy artillery fire from across the river, while with much turmoil and confusion the infantry was got clear of the village and of the baggage, by which it had been

---

[1] A return enclosed in the Earl of Stair's dispatch, June 11 (N.S.), 1743, shows that of Brigadier Handasyd's regiment, there were present the Lieut.-Colonel, the Major, 8 Captains, 7 Lieutenants, 7 Ensigns, 1 Chaplain, Adjutant, Quartermaster, Surgeon and Mate, 25 Sergeants fit for duty, one sick, one left with the sick, 3 recruiting, 15 Drummers fit, 2 sick, 3 recruiting, 574 rank-and-file fit for duty, 36 sick, 2 left with the sick, 6 recruiting, 44 rank-and-file left in the hospitals. Wanting to complete, 38 rank-and-file. This return was made in the camp at Hoechst, June 7 (N.S.), 1743.

much hampered, and was formed into two lines. By now the position of Gramont beyond Dettingen had been reconnoitred and an immediate attack on his force was at once decided on. It was indeed the only thing to be done and King George, brave to a fault, was ready enough to do it.

The preparations for battle, under the difficulties described, lasted more than an hour, during which the troops, particularly the cavalry, suffered severely. At last the guns of the allies were got up from their post in rear, and presently silenced the French guns across the river. It was then possible to move the baggage forward into the shelter of a small wood on the right of the road between Klein Ostheim and Dettingen, and to complete the battle formation, which was roughly as follows.

Both infantry and cavalry were in two lines, the bulk of the latter being on the right. The first line of infantry, from left to right, consisted of the 33rd, 21st, 23rd, 12th, 11th, 8th, and 13th Foot. On the right of the 13th stood an Austrian brigade, and beyond them, in succession, the Blues, the Life Guards, 6th Dragoons, and Royal Dragoons. The second line of infantry in rear of the first line was formed by the 20th, 32nd, 37th, Thirty-First, and Buffs; and in the second line of cavalry, which also covered its first line, stood the 7th Dragoon Guards, King's Dragoon Guards, 4th and 7th Dragoons, and the Scots Greys.

Now occurred the incident which turned the fate of the day. Gramont, a young and impetuous commander, either from impatience or perhaps in the hope of striking a decisive blow while the English troops were in confusion, disobeyed his orders, and, marching forward, took up a fresh and weaker position in front of the village of Dettingen. His force was arranged in three lines, cavalry on the flanks and infantry in the centre. On the right of the French first line stood the famous "Maison du Roi," or Household cavalry. Facing them, on the extreme British left, was a gap of some 200 yards between the 33rd Foot and the river, into which the 3rd Dragoons were hurriedly thrust by General Clayton, who commanded on the left of the line. The Duke of Cumberland, the King's second son, aged twenty-two, commanded, it may be added, on the right of the first line, while the King rode close in rear of it.

The allied army now advanced, but very slowly, for the plain was

THE BATTLE OF DETTINGEN

swampy and the heavily-laden infantry had in parts to wade through morasses knee-deep. The advance though slow was not at first steady, for the troops were eager and excited, and, as has been said, discipline had suffered from the long peace. The French line was not far off and between it and the advancing allies the Maison du Roi rode somewhat aimlessly about, uncertain where to attack. Seeing them the allied infantry delivered, without orders, an irregular fire which did no harm to the enemy but caused a well-known episode of the battle by frightening King George's charger, which ran away with him towards the second line. Here it was stopped by Ensign Cyrus Trapaud, a foreign officer of the Buffs, with whom we shall meet later. The King at once dismounted and after speaking encouragingly to the regiments near him, the Buffs and the Thirty-First, turned on foot to the first line and advanced in front of it, where he remained showing a fine example of courage and giving orders to all arms throughout the battle. The first line had halted during the King's brief absence, in order to re-load and correct the alignment.

The French infantry of the right now came within the very short range of fire of the period, and opened an unsteady fire, which " the British, now thoroughly in hand, answered with a regular, swift, and continuous fire of platoons, the ranks standing firm like a wall of brass, and pouring in volley after volley—such a fire as no French officer had ever seen before." Such was the testimony of the chivalrous Noailles himself. Then by signal from Lord Stair, who rode in front of the army, the British line uttered a loud cheer, and advanced again. The French infantry, which had suffered terribly, lost heart and fell back in disorder behind their cavalry, which advanced in gallant style to attack the British left.

This imposing attack was bravely countered by General Clayton, who ordered the 3rd Dragoons, and the 33rd, 21st, and 23rd Foot, the troops on the left, to advance and meet it. Seldom have troops behaved in a finer fashion than did these brave regiments, which had already suffered heavy loss from the French artillery across the river, and it is hard to say if the conduct of the 3rd Dragoons or of the three infantry regiments is most to be admired. Still they were hard pressed, and it was not until five more British, and two Austrian cavalry regiments, reinforced the left that the French attack on that flank was beaten off. A similar attack on the allied right was much more easily repulsed, and finally after four hours of fierce fighting, the French cavalry broke and fled, losing very heavily. A great number of the Maison du Roi were drowned in endeavouring to escape across the river Main.

Thus, owing mainly to the mistake of Count de Gramont in leaving his strong position, Dettingen became a British victory instead of a defeat; but it must be admitted also that the British force, on whom the fighting mainly fell, showed fine qualities and fairly earned their triumph. The French loss is estimated at 5000 killed, wounded, and prisoners; that of the allies at about half that number, of which the British share was 265 killed and 561 wounded. The heaviest loss fell upon the cavalry, and that of the infantry fell mainly on the first line and on the troops on the left, which suffered so severely from the French artillery. Among the killed was General Clayton, whose conduct had been very distinguished, and among the wounded was the young Duke of Cumberland, whose horse, like that of his father, ran away, but carried him not to the rear but right into the French infantry.

Dettingen was the last battle in which a King of England commanded his army in person, and the regiment may therefore well be proud of having served there, and of the honour "Dettingen" borne on their colours, though through their position near the right of the second line they were but slightly engaged and only had a few men wounded.

One episode of the battle has been preserved by regimental tradition. It is said that late in the action the King went in person to lead the 20th and Thirty-First regiments forward, and was pleased by their animation and eagerness. Misled by the colour of the facings of the latter regiment, the King called out "Bravo, *Buffs*." Some of the officers are said to have replied: "Sir, we are the Thirty-First, not the *Old Buffs*." His Majesty then rejoined, "*Bravo, Young Buffs*"; and this name, highly prized for the time and manner of its being conferred, has ever since been used with pride by the regiment.

Probably in consequence of the exhaustion of the troops, King George made no attempt to follow up the victory of Dettingen, but continued his march to Hanau. The battle was the last important episode of the campaign, and in the autumn the King returned to London. Lord Stair resigned his command and retired from active service, being succeeded by General Wade, who was created a Field-Marshal. The army, as was then the custom, retired into quarters in Flanders for the winter. The results of the campaign of 1743 were considerable. France was compelled to withdraw her armies from Germany and the campaign of 1744 took place in the Austrian Netherlands, the region of many wars, known as "the cock-pit of Europe."

King Louis XV now took the wise step of giving the command of his entire field army to the famous Marshal Saxe, and the events of 1744 showed how good his choice was. As, however, the campaign was one of marches and counter-marches, rather than of fighting, its history need not be told here. Suffice it to say that from May to October the allied army was constantly on the move, with little or no result. Marshal Wade and Prince Charles of Lorraine, the principal commanders, were ready and anxious to fight, but they were constantly foiled by the inactivity of the Dutch and Austrian contingents. Marshal Saxe's game was to mark time, in order to restore the efficiency of his army, and aided by the want of harmony between the allies he played it with complete success.

CHAPTER III

BATTLE OF FONTENOY AND ACTION OF MELLE

Losses of the regiment—The Duke of Cumberland's Despatch—The action of Melle—Raising of a second battalion, and subsequent separation from it—Service in Florida and destruction of the regiment—Trials of a commanding officer—Service in St. Vincent.

ON the conclusion of the campaign of 1744 Marshal Wade resigned his command, and in March 1745 he was succeeded as Commander-in-Chief by the Duke of Cumberland, now just twenty-five years of age. This seems to-day very young for so onerous a post, but the Duke had studied war from early youth and had shown fine courage at Dettingen. It was too the custom of the period for commands in war to be held by kings or princes, and it was hoped that a royal commander-in chief would be able to control the allied contingents more effectively than Marshal Wade had been able to do. Cumberland at once showed that he meant fighting, and so did Marshal Saxe. The British contingent in Flanders had been increased to 21,000 men, and the allied army having concentrated at Brussels by May 2, began its march towards the French frontier of the following day. Its strength was about 50,000 men. Marshal Saxe was already in the field and had invested Tournay, one of the border fortresses of the Netherlands, some three days earlier. The allied army marching slowly in that direction came on May 9 in sight of Saxe's army, very strongly posted on rising ground, with its centre holding the village of Fontenoy.

On the following morning Cumberland, with the commanders of the Austrian and Dutch troops, reconnoitred the French position, which proved to be very difficult to attack. Saxe, leaving 21,000 men to

BATTLE OF FONTENOY AND ACTION OF MELLE

contain the garrison of Tournay, had selected a position of great natural strength in which to offer battle to the allies, and judging from his long experience that the French infantry was incapable of standing an attack in the open on equal terms, had with great skill strengthened his position with field fortifications. His army, with a front of two miles, lay on high ground across the two roads leading from Condé and Leuze to Tournay. The right flank, which was thrown back to the village of Anthoin and the bank of the river Scheldt, was very strong and could not be turned. The left flank was protected by the forest of Barry, at the edge of which were two strong redoubts from which the front of the position could be swept by a flanking fire of artillery. In the centre of the position the village of Fontenoy had been made into a temporary fortress of great strength, and to the right and left of it the crest of the hill was held by an ample force of infantry strongly entrenched in two lines. In front of the position the ground fell smoothly in a natural glacis, to a distance of a thousand yards, along which space of perfectly open ground Cumberland launched his attack. Seldom have troops been committed to a more desperate enterprise. It is said that Count Königseck, the veteran Austrian general, recommended an attempt to manœuvre Saxe out of his position by an attack on his communications, but was overruled by Cumberland and Prince Waldeck, the young commander of the Dutch contingent. Cumberland was a firm believer in a bold policy and was doubtless influenced by his experience at Dettingen into a belief that British valour would force its way through any difficulties. The allied generals therefore decided that the Dutch and Austrians should attack the French centre and right, the Dutch undertaking the capture of Fontenoy itself, while the British contingent was to attack the French centre and left. Saxe, anticipating this disposition, posted the flower of his army on the left to encounter the British attack, which he considered the most formidable.

To trace the full course of the battle of Fontenoy, that glorious failure, would take up too much space. A very brief narrative must suffice.

The Duke of Cumberland's orders for the attack were simple. Fifteen squadrons of British cavalry under General Sir James Campbell, a veteran of Marlborough's wars, were to lead the advance through the village of Vezon and cover the deployment of the infantry. Of the latter one brigade under Brigadier Ingoldsby, an officer of the Guards, was to attack the French left, storming the foremost redoubt (called the redoubt d'Eu) in front of the forest of Barry, and making use of the forest to gain the French flank. The remainder of the British infantry was to advance in line across the open and carry the entrenchments with the bayonet.

At two in the morning of May 11, 1745, the allied army left its camp and advanced towards Fontenoy. By five A.M. the cavalry had passed through Vezon and deployed in the plain beyond, to carry out its duty of covering the infantry while engaged in the long and cumbrous process of forming for attack. Soon afterwards General Campbell unfortunately received a mortal wound, and his orders and intentions not, apparently, being known to any of his officers, the advanced squadrons fell back in rear of the infantry (which was still in process of formation) and joined the remainder of the cavalry. Nevertheless the infantry, now fully exposed to the heavy fire of the French artillery, and in full view of the whole French army, was deliberately formed up in two lines by its commander, General Ligonier. Severe losses occurred during this process, which in the days of Fontenoy was a very long one. After a time the Duke of Cumberland ordered seven guns to the front, and these coming into action on the British right, somewhat lightened the hostile fire. At length all was in order, and Ligonier was able to send word to the Duke that he was ready to advance as soon as the Dutch would attack Fontenoy on his left, and Ingoldsby would advance against the redoubt d'Eu on his right. Thereupon the Dutch and Austrians moved forward towards Fontenoy and Anthoin, their two points of attack, but being warmly received made but a faint-hearted advance, which presently changed into a retirement. The Dutch contingent, which was largely composed of German mercenaries of inferior class, behaved particularly badly, and refused to make a second attempt to carry out their share of the programme. Brigadier Ingoldsby, on the British right, made an even worse show, for (whether with or without excuse, it is hard to say) he made no advance at all, but hung irresolutely on the fringe of the forest of Barry. The Duke of Cumberland, however, in spite of the failures on both flanks, had no idea of abandoning his attack, and with fine courage and determination he placed himself at the head of the British infantry and led them on to their desperate task—an unsupported frontal attack on a fortified position of great strength held by a largely superior force, commanded by one of the great soldiers of all time.

The British regiments which took part in the attack at Fontenoy were the following. In the first line, counting from right to left, were three battalions of Foot Guards (one of each regiment)—next to the Guards stood the following: 1st, 21st, Thirty-First, 8th, 25th, 33rd, and 19th Regiments.

On the right of the second line stood the 3rd Regiment (the Buffs), then in succession the 23rd, 32nd, 11th, 28th, 34th, and 20th Regiments, The second line was completed by some Hanoverian battalions on the extreme left.

"Then," says Fortescue,[1] in his fine narrative of the battle from which many of these details were taken, "then the word was given to advance, and the two lines moved off with the slow and measured step for which they were famous in Europe.

"Forward tramped the ranks of scarlet, silent and stately as if on parade. Full half a mile of ground was to be traversed before they could close with the invisible enemy that awaited them in the entrenchments over the crest of the slope, and the way was marked clearly by the red flashes and white smoke that leaped from Fontenoy and the Redoubt d'Eu on either flank. The shot plunged fiercely and more fiercely into the serried lines as they advanced into that murderous cross-fire, but the gaping ranks were quietly closed, the perfect order was never lost, the stately step was never hurried."

At last the crest of the ridge was gained, and despite their heavy losses and the sight of the picked troops of France awaiting them in their trenches, the British infantry pressed steadily on till they arrived within fifty yards of the French. Then occurred the famous incident of the officers of the English and French Guards each inviting the other side to fire first, not from misplaced politeness, but because it was a point of discipline in both armies to reserve their fire as long as possible, and on discipline, in great measure, depended victory.

Not until the two lines were within thirty yards did the fire com-

---

[1] *History of the British Army*, vol. ii. p. 114.

mence, by battalion volleys from right to left of the line. The British fire, as usual in those days, was terribly effective and the French losses were very heavy, but Marshal Saxe was prepared and brought up reinforcements. Still the deadly fire of the British prevailed, and their glorious infantry pressed steadily on, driving the French before them, over the entrenchments, three hundred yards beyond the flanking batteries, and into the very centre of the French camp. Victory seemed very near, the French gun ammunition had run low, and the Duke of Cumberland actually sent two battalions to make a flank attack on Fontenoy, and so, perhaps, induce the Dutch to come forward. To Saxe the triumph of the British seemed almost inevitable, and he advised the King of France and the Dauphin, who were watching the battle from a windmill in rear, to retire for safety across the Scheldt. Under Saxe's orders the French cavalry made three charges on the British infantry, attacking them from both flanks and in front, but were repulsed by fire alone. At last came the limit of endurance. The British halted in the midst of the French camp, waiting for the little help from their allies that alone was wanted to secure the victory. None came, and the exhausted troops at length fell back below the crest of the French position, where they readily rallied and were re-formed for a second advance. In response to Cumberland's appeal, Prince Waldeck agreed to make another attempt on Fontenoy, and Cumberland, once more heading his diminished lines, again moved doggedly forward.

Now, however, the task before them was heavier than before, while their losses had been terribly heavy. All the French troops of the first line had been rallied, while strong reinforcements had been hurried up by Saxe from the rear, the most formidable being the Irish Brigade. This brigade, of six battalions, was composed of Irish, English, and Scottish exiles, compelled by their religion or by loyalty to the House of Stuart to enter the French army. With this great body of infantry, largely outnumbering the British, Saxe pressed Cumberland's weary men irresistibly, bearing so hard on both flanks of his two lines that they were compelled to fall back until the British troops took nearly the form of a square. The attack, it was evident, had finally failed, for no help came from the Dutch, and thus heavily attacked in the rear and on both flanks the British infantry slowly fell

BATTLE OF FONTENOY AND ACTION OF MELLE

back over the long space of open ground over which they had so proudly advanced. Not less majestic was their retirement. Steadily and in perfect order they fell back, halting by word of command, where required, to fire battalion volleys on the enemies; while the cavalry, in spite of heavy losses, came to their assistance, repeatedly charging the French infantry.

Fontenoy was indeed, as far as the British troops were concerned, a failure, and a glorious failure, rather than a defeat. Seldom, if ever, has our infantry shown finer fighting qualities. By sheer grit it won its way into the heart of a position of immense strength, and when by the default of its allies it was compelled to retire, it drew off in such good order and showed itself still so full of fight that the brilliant Saxe himself thought it wise to attempt no pursuit of so dangerous a foe. Fontenoy does not figure as a battle honour in our army, but that bloody field may be remembered with pride by the representatives of the heroic soldiers who there fought and fell.

The British losses at Fontenoy were of course very severe, and Handasyd's regiment,[1] from its position in the centre of the first line, was among the heaviest sufferers, with 133 of all ranks killed and 141 wounded. In these casualties the officers bore their full share. Lieut.-Colonel Montagu,[2] who had distinguished himself at Dettingen, fell at the head of his regiment, as did Captain Pollock and Lieutenant Dalway. The officers wounded were Captain Baird, Lieutenants Stafford (mortally) and Porter, Ensigns Worsley, Bromley, and Freeman. Four sergeants were killed and six wounded. Captain Baird's wounds were such that he was reported killed, but he eventually recovered, was promoted Major in the Fontenoy death vacancy, and lived till June 1751, The Grenadier company of the regiment, which went into action seventy-five strong, brought only eleven men out of the field of Fontenoy, its officers being all killed or mortally wounded.

---

[1] Brigadier-General Handasyd died in April 1745, and had been succeeded in his colonelcy by Lord Henry Beauclerk, from the 48th Foot, then stationed at Ostend. The Thirty-First was however called "Handasyd's"—or "late Handasyd's"—in all accounts of Fontenoy.

[2] Lieut.-Colonel Edward Montagu was the second son of Brigadier-General Edward Montagu, and younger brother of George Montagu, of Roel, in Gloucestershire, the friend and correspondent of Horace Walpole. George and Edward Montagu were grand-nephews of the first Earl of Halifax of the Montagu family, the statesman and poet.

In the official statement of the Duke of Cumberland regarding the battle, published in the *London Gazette*, Handasyd's regiment, together with the Guards, the Royal Highlanders, and Duroure's (Suffolk Regiment) were selected for mention as having specially distinguished themselves. To be thus chosen for notice, when the conduct of all the British troops had been so admirable, may be regarded as one of the most honourable distinctions ever earned by the regiment.

Action of Melle

After Fontenoy the allied army fell back a few miles to Ath, and thence retired on May 16 to Lessines. Here the right wing was joined by three British battalions which had not been hitherto engaged, and by reinforcements of Austrian and Hessian troops. The Dutch having sustained very slight losses at Fontenoy, the strength of the allied army was thus restored to 70,000 men. This large force was, however, much hampered by divided counsels and want of harmony, for the selfish policy of the Dutch Government and the general ill-feeling towards their troops made a spirited line of action impossible. Soon indeed a great part of the Dutch contingent was withdrawn into frontier garrisons, the Duke of Cumberland's available force being thus reduced to little over 40,000 men, while the pusillanimous surrender of Tournay by the Dutch governor on June 19 enabled Marshal Saxe to make use of his whole strength of 70,000 men.

Saxe at once assumed the offensive and advanced towards Ghent, in which place was a great mass of stores for the British army. Cumberland took up a position at Gramont and invited attack. He was even anxious to attack Saxe once more, and promised his allies that in spite of the odds the battle should make amends for Fontenoy. The Dutch however would not fight, and Cumberland found himself compelled to fall back for the defence of Brussels. Unwilling, however, to lose his valuable stores at Ghent he attempted to throw a force of 4000 men, under Lieutenant-General Count von Moltke, into that city. In von Moltke's force were three British infantry regiments, the Royal (1st Foot), Bligh's (20th), and Lord Henry Beauclerk's (Thirty-First Foot), all very weak from their losses at Fontenoy. Von Moltke marched to Alost on July 8, and on the same day Marshal Saxe despatched a force of 15,000 men towards Ghent, the outposts of which were only eight miles from the British column. On July 9 von Moltke continued his march towards Ghent, the Royal Regiment leading and the rearguard being formed of five squadrons of Dutch cavalry. When the head of the column reached Melle Priory (three miles from Ghent) a French brigade was found drawn up across the road, on both sides of which houses and hedges were lined with infantry; there was moreover a battery of twelve guns about forty yards from the road on the left.

The Royal Regiment gallantly charged and drove off the French infantry in front, and turning to the left captured the French battery, but two other French brigades now advanced to the attack and von Moltke found that his task of reaching Ghent with his whole force was impossible. With his right wing, however, composed of the Royal (1st Foot) Rich's Dragoons (now 4th Hussars) and some Hanoverian cavalry, he pushed gallantly through the enemy and forced his way into Ghent after losing a third of his numbers, leaving the left wing under Brigadier-General Bligh (the Colonel of the 20th Foot) to shift for itself. Bligh made two determined attacks on the French, first with his own regiment, and then with Handasyd's, but finding that it was impossible to force his way directly to Ghent through the largely superior hostile force, posted as it was in an advantageous position open only to frontal attacks, decided to retreat to Alost. Thence he proposed to march to Termonde, and if possible find his way eventually to Ghent.

Bligh carried out the first part of his programme in the most determined manner. With his small force (20th and Thirty-First Foot and five squadrons of Dutch cavalry) he fought a rear-guard action through woods and narrow lanes, losing his tents and baggage, but escaping capture by sheer determination, good marching, and hard fighting. The two weak British infantry regiments sustained no less than 294 casualties in killed, wounded and prisoners in this honourable, if unsuccessful action, the losses in Handasyd's being three officers killed and two wounded, and 160 sergeants, rank-and-file killed, wounded, and prisoners.

The two following letters, written by Brigadier Bligh to H.R.H. the Duke of Cumberland on the day following the action, give an interesting and fairly clear description of this almost unknown affair. Although unfortunate in its results, it is undeniable that Bligh's and Handasyd's regiments may look back with satisfaction to the fight at Melle.

STATE PAPERS, FOREIGN

Military Expeditions, Vol. 17

Alost July ye 9th (should be 10th), 1745.
Saturday, 4 o'clock in the morning.

I am sorry that I am obliged to acquaint your highness that upon attempting to throw ourselves into Ghent we were cut by the enemy who were coming down in full march about three mile from Ghent where they attacked us on each side from houses and a battery of canon from the right, our losses are very great having fought a long time against a great part of their army, having only the remains of my regiment and Handisides not knowing anything of the Royal which General Mulk took along with him at the head of the Cavalry, I am affraid the General is either killed or taken prisoner I cant give your highness a very particular account and can only tell you, that I had but five squadrons of the Dutch (Ligne's and Styrum's Dragoons) that stayed to make the retreat with me to Alost. I am affraid I shall not be able to maintain this post and propose marching to Dendermond where I shall wait your highness' order and am with great respect,

Your highness most obedient servant
to command THO. BLIGH.

Dendermond, July ye 10th, 1745.

I had the honour of your highness' letter this day, and as you desire some particular account, I must inform your Highness first of the disposition the General made that day for the march, the Hussars marched first then the Royal which he had, next the three Squadrons of Sir Robert Rich's with the Hanoverian Squadrons that joined in that day, then I marched at the head of my own Regiment, with five or six Squadrons of the Dutch, next Handyside's with Styrum's and Ligne's Dragoons and in this manner we attacked them on the march by single Regiments at a time for the horse coud do nothing but get out of the way into a field of one side; they fell first on the General as he passed along the road, and what is become of the Hussars, the Royal and the six Squadrons of Dragoons, I have not been able to hear anything since ; then I marched up at the head of my own Regiment and attacked them in the road, till my Regiment suffered so much by the continued fire in front and both sides, that they were obliged to get out of the road and draw up in the field, by this time the squadrons in my rear got out of the way into the field and then Handysydes came up which I drew up in the field and marched them to attack them in Flank but was then exposed to their battery of Canon which fronted us, and when I found it was to little purpose I retired back in the same field wher my Regiment was and thought it best to think of retreating before they were quite broke which I did with the squadrons that remained in the field thro the woods and narrow roads keeping of the causeway till I came near Alost. I have missing of my Regiment 120 men, and nine officers, Handysides 160, three officers killed and two wounded, we have lost all our tents and baggage horses by a thousand Hussars and Grassans that were posted near the road and when we were engaged came in the rear and carryed of every thing we had, both our Surgeons and one Chaplain ; I have in obedience to your Highness' commands given you as particular account of what has happened as I can, and shall tomorrow endeavour to get to Ghent with the troops I have left, that are allmost jaded with marching day and night these six days, and am with great respect

Your most humble and
most obedient servant,
THO. BLIGH.

Fortunately for Handasyd's, Brigadier-General Bligh was unable to make his way to Ghent, and the regiment thereby escaped sharing in the subsequent capture of the garrison of that fortress.

Two months after the affair of Melle the Highland rising under Prince Charles Edward assumed a formidable aspect. The victory of the Prince at Prestonpans opened the way to an invasion of north-western England, whose Jacobite sympathies were strong. A rising in the eastern counties was also imminent, and the extreme weakness of the army at home rendered the triumph of the Stuart cause by no means improbable. Early in December Prince Charles arrived at Derby, and London was in a state of panic ; but the King and his Ministers kept their heads and relied with justice on the general adherence of the country to the Protestant succession, and on the measures that they had adopted to meet the danger. The greater part of the army in the Low Countries had been brought to England in the month of October, and among other regiments that now left Flanders was the Thirty-First. On arrival in England, the regiment was placed under the command of Brigadier Douglas, and moved northwards as part of the Duke of Cumberland's army. Before, however, the Duke entered Scotland more regiments became available, and Douglas' brigade, being much reduced in numbers from casualties at Fontenoy and Melle, returned to the south of England and was retained near London as part of the defence force of the capital. Handasyd's regiment was thus spared the trial of taking part in the Culloden campaign.

The defeat of Culloden having dealt a death-blow to the hopes of the House of Stuart, several regiments were sent back to Flanders, but the Thirty-First remained in Great Britain until the Peace of Aix-la-Chapelle, signed on October 7, 1748, put an end to the War of the Austrian succession. The share in this war borne by the Thirty-First is commemorated by the honour "Dettingen" on the colours. It may perhaps be regretted that the distinguished part played by the regiment at the glorious defeat of Fontenoy cannot be similarly rewarded, but the Thirty-First should as long as it endures, and whatever name it may bear, look back with pride to the high distinction won by its predecessors on that eventful day, when among a whole army that covered itself with honour, it was among the small number of regiments singled out for special praise.

On May 8, 1749, Lord Henry Beauclerk, who had been colonel of the regiment since the death of Brigadier-General Handasyd, retired from the service, and was succeeded in the colonelcy by Colonel Henry Holmes. Colonel Holmes, who was promoted to the rank of Major-General in 1756 and to that of Lieutenant-General in 1759, retained the colonelcy until his death in 1762.

It may here conveniently be mentioned that in the Royal Warrant dated July 1, 1751, for ensuring uniformity in the clothing, standards and colours of the army, and regulating the numbers and ranks of regiments, the facings of the Thirty-First regiment were ordered to be buff. The first, or King's colour, was the Great Union; the second, or

Regimental colour, was of buff silk, with the Union in the upper canton, in the centre of the colours the number of the rank of the regiment, in gold Roman characters, within a wreath of roses and thistles on the same stalk.

In the year 1749 the Thirty-First was ordered on foreign service and embarked for Minorca, which island had been retained in the possession of England since the regiment had taken part in its capture in 1708. In 1752, the regiment returned to England from Minorca, which, it may be mentioned, was re-captured by an overwhelming French force four years later.

The Thirty-First remained in England until the year 1754, when it proceeded to Scotland, in which country it was stationed for seven years, for the most part of the time at Glasgow.

Mention has already been made of the attack on Minorca made by France in June 1756, but the preparations for the attack on that island were not the first indications of the coming outbreak of war. Hostilities indeed had begun in America as far back as the spring of 1753, when the French Governor of Canada sent a strong expedition to establish itself and to build a line of forts in the western fringe of British territory in what is now the north-eastern portion of the United States. After some minor operations with the scanty local forces, war, though still not formally declared, began in 1755 with the disastrous expedition under General Braddock. At last, after three years of hostilities, the threatened attack on Minorca drove the long-suffering British Government to declare war against France, and the Seven Years' War began on May 18, 1756. The garrison of Minorca, after an exceptionally fine defence, was compelled to surrender on June 29 of the same year, and the necessity of an immediate increase of the army and navy being at last recognised, fifteen regiments of infantry serving in Great Britain were authorised to raise second battalions, the order bearing date August 25, 1756. Among these regiments was the Thirty-First, then stationed at Glasgow, which was assisted by a draft from the 29th Regiment and enlisted a large number of local recruits. The establishment of officers was nearly doubled, the consequent promotions, for the most part, going fairly in the regiment. After completing its second battalion the Thirty-First remained at Glasgow under command of Lieutenant-

Colonel Lambert, Major Charles Vignoles, the senior Major, commanding the 2nd Battalion. Two years later, on a further increase in the army, the fifteen second battalions raised in 1756 were constituted regiments, and the 2nd Battalion Thirty-First became the Seventieth Regiment, carrying with it its complete establishment of officers from the parent stock. To mark, however, its entire independence the new regiment was given grey facings in place of the buff of the Thirty-First, and it was officially styled the " Glasgow Lowland Regiment ; " the 71st (raised at the same time) being styled the " Glasgow Highland Regiment." The independent history of the Seventieth Regiment from the year 1758 until it rejoined the Thirty-First in 1881, will be found in chapters XII to XVIII.

OFFICERS OF THE THIRTY-FIRST REGIMENT, 1757

COLONEL :—Henry Holmes (Major-General).

LIEUT.-COLONEL :—(1) Hamilton Lambert.

MAJORS :—(2) Charles Vignoles.
        (1) James Vignoles.

CAPTAINS (16)

- (2) Robert Pigot.
- (1) Peyton Meares.
- (1) Thomas Troughear.
- (1) Edward Bromley.
- (1) Robert Barker.
- (1) Henry Yelverton.
- (1) Patrick M'Donall.
- (2) William Piers.
- (1) Francis Laye.
- (1) Thomas Dunbar.
- (2) Daniel Hamilton.
- (2) Tichborne Grueber.
- (2) Hector Munro.
- (2) George Grant.
- (2) William Nesbitt.
- (1) Thomas Northey.

CAPT.-LIEUTENANT :—(1) Caleb Woods.

LIEUTENANTS (21)

- (2) John Fowle.
- (1) Thomas Varloe.
- (2) John Crofton.
- (2) William Hooker.
- (1) James Campbell.
- (1) Thomas Hodgson.
- (1) Thomas Malile.
- (1) John Bolton.
- (1) John Warren.
- (1) James Bruce.
- (1) Francis Vignoles.
- (1) James Moore.
- (1) Wager Russell.
- (1) Gregory Drummond.
- (1) Thomas Pembroke.
- (2) John Stevens.
- (2) William Smith.
- (2) Robert Clements.
- (1) —— Dunn.
- (1) Edward Crofton.
- (1) Joseph Farmer.

ENSIGNS (18)

(1) Alexander Nesbitt.	(1) Robert Grant.
(1) Henry Sampson.	(2) Charles Sutherland.
(2) Mussenden Johnson.	(2) Anthony Morgan.
(1) Lewis La Chapelle.	(2) Henry Norman.
(2) John Dumaresque.	(1) William Talbot.
(2) Arthur Lysaght.	(2) Uniacke Prendergast.
(2) George Whichcot.	(1) Thomas Hale Adderley.
(2) Arthur Thompson.	(1) John Keatinge.
(2) Roger Bristow.	(1) Henry Vignoles.

CHAPLAIN :—(1) George Lillington.

ADJUTANTS :—(1) William Hooker.
           (2) Williamson Legard Hooker.

QUARTERMASTERS :—(1) Lewis La Chapelle.
                    (2) George Williamson.

In June 1762 the Thirty-First Regiment moved from Scotland to England and remained on home service during 1763 and 1764.

Lieutenant-General Henry Holmes, who had been Colonel of the regiment for nearly thirteen years, died on August 19, 1762, and was succeeded by Major-General James Adolphus Oughton, transferred from the colonelcy of the 55th Regiment. Early in the year 1765 the Thirty-First was ordered to proceed to Pensacola, the capital of West Florida, which country had been ceded to Great Britain by Spain at the peace of Fontainebleau in return for the retrocession of Havannah de Cuba. The westward journey of the regiment was a disastrous one, for on the passage to Florida the transports put into Bluefield Bay, Jamaica, in which island a violent epidemic of yellow fever was then raging. The Thirty-First was at once attacked by the disease, which accompanied the regiment to Pensacola, where the soldiers sustained a terrible loss of life. It is related that so great was the mortality and so general the sickness in the regiment that at times men could not be furnished to carry their comrades to the grave. In many instances men who attended funeral parades in the morning were themselves buried in the evening. It is stated in Cannon's " Historical Record " that on one occasion the regiment had only one corporal and six private soldiers fit for duty.

If Pensacola was a fatal station to the rank-and-file of the Thirty-First, it came near being disastrous in another way to Lieutenant-Colonel Ralph Walsh, their commanding officer.

Florida, when taken over from the Spanish authorities in 1763, had been divided into two provinces, called respectively East and West Florida, the civil governors of which were captains in the Royal Navy. Captain George Johnstone, the governor of West Florida, was a notoriety of his day, and was generally known as " Governor Johnstone." He at once came to loggerheads with the military commanding officers stationed in his province, carrying on a series of disputes; and in particular one with the colonel of the 35th Regiment. When the Thirty-First relieved the 35th at Pensacola, Lieutenant-Colonel Walsh found himself the inheritor of the quarrel of his predecessor, and as time went on the dispute became more and more violent. In January 1766 matters reached a climax on Governor Johnstone ordering Lieutenant-Colonel Maxwell, 21st Regiment, commanding at Mobile, to proceed with a strong body of his regiment to Pensacola, and there to take over command, by force of arms if necessary, from Lieutenant-Colonel Walsh. On the arrival of the troops under Lieutenant-Colonel Maxwell in the harbour of Pensacola, Colonel Walsh ordered the Thirty-First under arms, had the fort gates closed, and the guns loaded. Moderation happily prevailed on both sides, and Lieutenant-Colonel Walsh submitted to be placed under arrest. The Council of West Florida supported their Governor, and resolved that Lieutenant-Colonel Walsh should be tried by the Chief Justice for mutiny. On being brought to trial Lieutenant-Colonel Walsh pleaded in his defence that Governor Johnstone had no authority to give him orders to hand over his command, and that in that regard he, Lieutenant-Colonel Walsh, was under the sole authority of Major-General Gage, the Commander-in-Chief in North America. The chief Justice apparently concurred in this view, and considered that all that had happened was only a part of long-existing disputes. He therefore ordered the discharge from arrest of Lieutenant-Colonel Walsh. Soon after these unusual occurrences the Thirty-First was moved to St Augustine, the capital of East Florida, and Governor Johnstone to another sphere of activity. Peace once more reigned between the civil and military authorities of West Florida and the regiment remained, garrisoning Pensacola and St. Augustine alternately until the autumn of 1772, when it was ordered to the island of St. Vincent, to take part in quelling a rising of the Caribs.

St. Vincent had been captured from the French in 1762 and had been ceded to Great Britain at the peace of 1763. Its aboriginal inhabitants, the Caribs, were devoted to the French interest and proved to be turbulent and dangerous neighbours to the English planters. It was consequently found necessary to enforce certain restrictive measures, which soon resulted in a rising of a formidable nature. The Caribs were brave and hardy and possessed great advantages in the tropical climate of St Vincent and in the natural difficulties of the interior of the island, to which they retired. In these thickly-wooded and mountainous fastnesses they for a time defied all the efforts of the regular troops who had been sent to suppress the rebellion, and it is stated in the island records that the engagements between the troops and the rebels were "extremely desperate and bloody." On January 14, 1773, a small party of the Thirty-First, forming the escort of Lieutenant-Colonel Ralph Walsh, commanding the Regiment, fell into an ambuscade while marching through thick bush, Lieutenant-Colonel Ralph Walsh and three private soldiers being killed. Major Mackenzie was promoted to the lieutenant-colonelcy, and all the steps were given in the regiment.

After arduous operations lasting over a year, the troops, under Brigadier-General Dalrymple, succeeded in February 1774 in bringing the Caribs to terms, twenty-eight of the chiefs signing the treaty of peace. The chiefs agreed to acknowledge the sovereignty of Great Britain, but were permitted to preserve their own laws and customs. The losses of the British troops, which included a wing of the Seventieth, as well as the Thirty-First, 68th and other regiments, amounted to 150 killed and wounded; 110 of all ranks had died of disease; and 428 had been invalided: figures which show the severity of the twelve months' campaign.

Peace having been restored, the Thirty-First proceeded to England, moving in the autumn of 1774 to its old quarters at Glasgow, where its skeleton ranks were quickly refilled. The regiment remained at Glasgow about a year and a half, at the end of which period it was once again ordered on active service.

CHAPTER IV

THE AMERICAN WAR OF INDEPENDENCE

The Thirty-First in Canada—Services of the flank companies with General Burgoyne—Action of Bemis Heights—The capitulation at Saratoga.

THE American War of Independence had broken out in April 1775, in the winter of which year the insurgent States sent an expeditionary force, some 7000 strong, under Generals Montgomery and Benedict Arnold, to invade Canada and attempt the capture of Quebec. Lieutenant-General Carleton, who commanded the troops in Canada, relying on the loyalty of the Canadians, had sent nearly all his regular troops to Boston, the head-quarters of the English army in the field. For the defence of Quebec he had about 1200 Canadian troops, mostly of no very regular nature, and only sixty British soldiers. The American detachment which attacked Quebec, led by the two able officers named, was of equal strength with the garrison, and under their orders made a bold and skilful attack on Quebec on the last day of the year. The simultaneous assaults of two columns were met with like courage and better fortune by General Carleton and the garrison, with the result that the Americans were completely defeated, General Montgomery killed, and General Arnold severely wounded. Among the reinforcements ordered to North America at this moment was the Thirty-First Regiment, which, early in 1776, moved to Cork, whence it embarked for Canada in the month of April. The transports conveying the regiment arrived at Quebec on May 28, very shortly after General Carleton had attacked and dispersed the Americans under Arnold, who had been lying before Quebec, on the plains of Abraham. By the end of June the last remaining American soldier had been driven from Canada, and from sickness, war casualties, and desertion the 7000 invaders had been reduced to a strength of 2000.

During the autumn of 1776 General Carleton continued his operations against Arnold's diminishing forces, crossing Lake Champlain in pursuit and arriving on November 3 within fifteen miles of Fort Ticonderoga. Here he halted and went into winter quarters, the Thirty-First furnishing posts along the frontier at Sorel, St. Charles, St. Denis, St. Antoine, and St. Ours.

Early in 1777 General Carleton received orders from Lord George Germaine, the Secretary for War, to hand over a force of above 7000 men, nearly the whole of his command,[1] to Lieutenant-General Burgoyne, who was ordered to march southward to Albany and there to place himself under the orders of Sir William Howe, the Commander-in-Chief in North America. General Howe, however, instead of being ordered to move northward to meet Burgoyne, was allowed to march southward and operate against General Washington's army about Philadelphia. Gereral Burgoyne's expedition was therefore foredoomed to failure, and it was happily for itself, though doubtless much to its regret at the time, that the Thirty-First was ordered to remain in its posts along the Canadian frontier. The flank companies, however, 200 picked men under picked officers, served in the expedition with the Grenadier and Light battalions, which showed signal gallantry and suffered heavy losses throughout Burgoyne's arduous campaign. Captain William Cotton commanded the Grenadiers and Captain Noah Simpson the Light Infantry of the Thirty-First. Captain Charles Green, an officer of the regiment who had distinguished himself as a subaltern at St. Vincent, also served in the expedition as A.D.C. to Major-General Phillips. Captain Green, it may be here mentioned, who did excellent service in this campaign and was severely wounded, eventually rose to the rank of General and was created a Baronet. Lieutenant-General Burgoyne's little army, amounting to nearly 8000 of all ranks, composed mainly of British and German with a few Colonial troops, assembled on June 20, 1777, at Cumberland Point on Lake Champlain.

---

[1] The troops left under General Carleton for the defence of Canada consisted of the 29th, Thirty-First, and 34th Regiments, part of the 11th Regiment, and some German troops.

Having descended the lake in boats, Burgoyne marched from Crown Point and arrived before Ticonderoga on July 1. The American garrison numbered 3000 men, who occupied a very strongly defended position, but one commanding point had been neglected. This point at once caught the eye of Major-General Phillips, an artillery officer who had originally distinguished himself at the battle of Minden. A battery was immediately constructed at this spot, which commanded the whole American position, and Ticonderoga was in consequence hurriedly abandoned. The American garrison then retired on July 6 by way of Castleton on Skenesborough, hotly pursued by the Grenadier and Light Infantry battalions under Major-General Fraser. The remainder of the army, under General Burgoyne, made for the same place by boat along the south river. Major-General Fraser's small force marched with all speed from four in the morning until one in the afternoon, when a short halt was made to enable General Riedesel to bring up the German brigade in support. Determined, however, to bring the American troops to a halt, General Fraser again pushed on until nightfall and found his little column of 850 men within three miles of the enemy. At three in the morning of July 7 Fraser renewed his march, and at five came, at Huberton, on the American picquets, who fired and fell back.

The Americans were about double Fraser's strength, and the ground in their front being thickly wooded was not suited to the British troops of that period, trained to shoulder-to-shoulder tactics. The flank battalions, however, pressed gallantly on, adapting themselves quickly to bush-fighting, and meeting without flinching the fire of the very superior force opposed to them, who also fought bravely under a most gallant and skilful leader, Colonel Francis. After two hours' close fighting the German brigade came up and decided the action in Fraser's favour. Colonel Francis and 200 of his men lay dead on the field and about the same number were captured. The British loss was 140 killed and wounded, several of the casualties among the Grenadiers being caused by the treacherous conduct of sixty American soldiers, who fired on them at close quarters after having surrendered.

On July 10 General Burgoyne's entire force was assembled at Skenesborough, and on the 30th of the same month had arrived at Fort Edward. This was a march of twenty miles which took twenty days, owing to the extraordinary difficulty of the road, which the

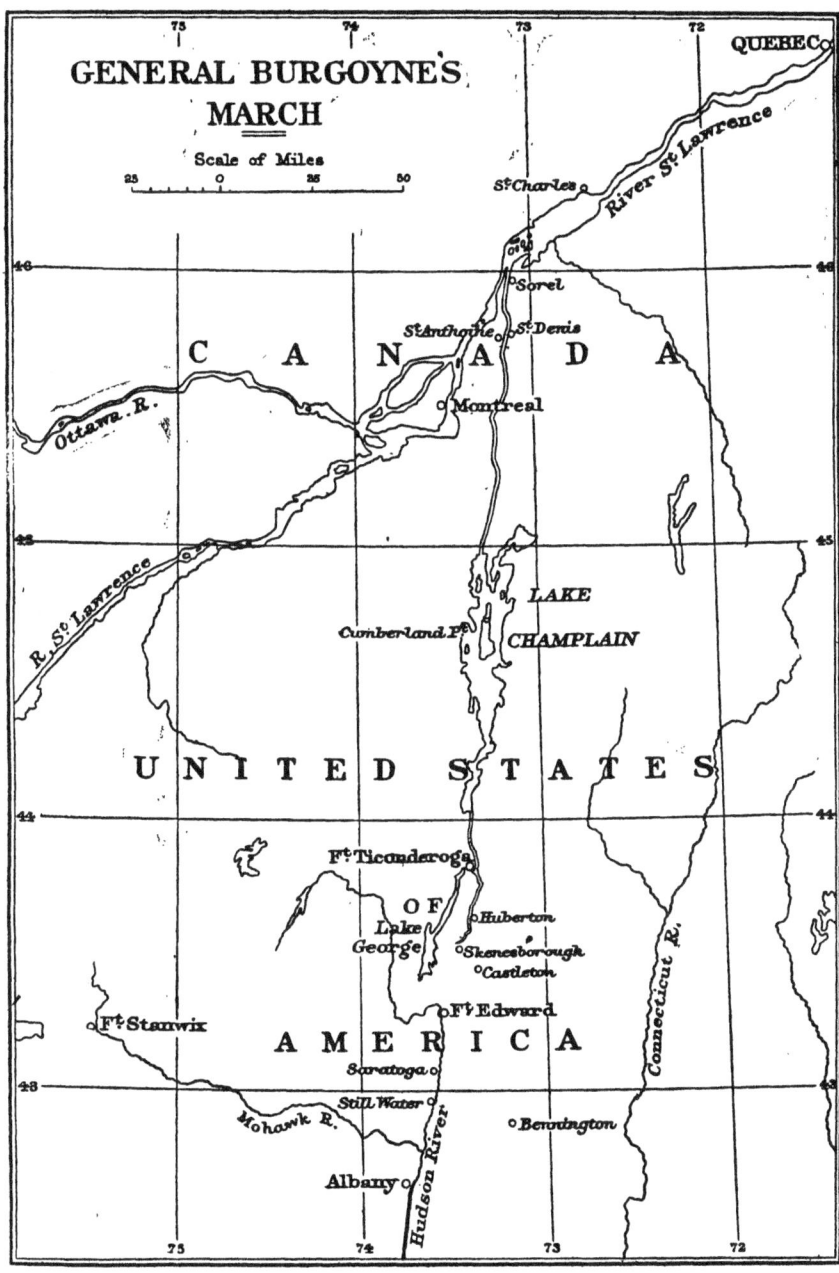

American army in its retirement had blocked in the most skilful manner. In the twenty miles traversed it had been necessary to build

no less than forty bridges, some of great length. Meanwhile General Schuyler, who commanded the American army opposing Burgoyne, had fallen back yet further to Stillwater, only thirty miles from Albany, Burgoyne's objective.

General Burgoyne now, in spite of the complete success of his march to this point, began to experience great difficulties of supply and transport, yet his orders were so definite, giving him absolutely no latitude, that he was compelled to advance at all costs. As a preliminary he endeavoured, on August 13, to capture the horses, ammunition, and provisions that had been stored by the Americans at Bennington, about thirty miles to the south-east of Fort Edward. A force of 500 German troops under Colonel Baum was despatched on this enterprise, supported at some distance by another German column of similar strength. Meanwhile General Burgoyne's main body moved down the eastern bank of the Hudson towards Saratoga.

Through no fault of Colonel Baum and his Germans, the attempt to seize Bennington met with disaster, resulting in a loss to General Burgoyne of about 500 men and four guns; moreover, about the same time a detached force, mainly composed of irregular troops, operating under Colonel St. Leger against Fort Stanwix, was compelled to suspend its operations. Burgoyne was now in a very critical position. His force had been reduced by casualties, and by the detachment of a garrison for Ticonderoga, to little over 5000 men, and the Americans before him were daily increasing in strength. Still his orders were explicit and he endeavoured to carry them out, first using every exertion to collect thirty days' supplies with which to make a forced march to Albany. On September 13, the necessary supplies had been collected, and on that and the following day Burgoyne crossed to the western bank of the Hudson by a bridge of rafts and encamped on the heights and plain of Saratoga. He was then delayed by rain till September 19, when he marched to attack the Americans, now 14,000 strong, and strongly posted and entrenched on Bemis Heights, near Stillwater. General Burgoyne attacked this formidable position in three columns, that of General Fraser (Grenadier, Light Infantry, and 24th Regiment) having to make a wide detour before reaching the American left. The march of the three columns through thickly-wooded country was admirably timed and General Burgoyne's well-laid plan was gallantly put into execution by his troops, but the American position was too strongly held to be carried by a force so inferior in numbers, however ably handled. After a very severe fight, in which the British force lost nearly a third of the numbers engaged, Burgoyne's column bivouacked on the ground which they had won, and on the following day they entrenched themselves just out of cannon shot of the American position. Among the severely wounded in the action of Bemis Heights was Captain Green, of the Thirty-First, A.D.C. to Major-General Phillips. Captain Green, after the fashion of the day, had provided himself on joining the Staff with richly-laced saddlery and appointments. He was in consequence singled out by an American marksman, who, when Green fell from his horse, exclaimed exultantly that he had shot General Burgoyne. The end of the sad story of Burgoyne's force is well known. General Burgoyne had heard that a force under General Clinton was advancing from New York against the rear of the American army, and hoped that this co-operation might enable him to complete his task. General Clinton's little column made a gallant and successful advance to Fort Montgomery, arriving there much diminished in strength on October 8. On the previous day, Burgoyne, whose situation had become desperate, had made a last attempt to attack the American left, their vulnerable point. For this forlorn hope Burgoyne could employ no more than 1500 men with ten guns, placing his German troops in the centre with the British on both flanks. The British attack was bravely delivered, but a sudden counter-stroke made by 4000 Americans under General Morgan proved effective. The British Grenadiers on Burgoyne's left held their ground with great firmness, but a battalion of Brunswickers in the centre gave way. The brave General Fraser, whose services throughout the campaign had been conspicuous, was mortally wounded, and Burgoyne with great difficulty effected a retreat to his entrenched camp. Here he was immediately attacked by the Americans, and after a fine fight, in which the Light Infantry behaved very gallantly, was compelled to fall back by night to some commanding ground in rear of his camp. Among the severely wounded officers was Major Acland, the gallant commander of the Grenadier Battalion, who had but recently recovered from a previous wound. As General Burgoyne's little column fell back, fighting desperately, towards camp,

Major Acland appealed for help to his friend Captain Simpson, of the Thirty-First. Captain Simpson, a very powerful man, carried Major Acland on his back for a considerable distance, but was then compelled to return to his company. Major Acland was then carried by a Grenadier of the Thirty-First, but the soldier being unable to keep up with the retreating troops, both fell into the hands of the enemy. On the following morning, October 8, Burgoyne found that the Americans were marching round to cut off his retreat, and was consequently compelled to fall back on Saratoga, leaving 500 sick and wounded men to the enemy. By October 14 the little British army was entirely surrounded and was starving, and three days later General Burgoyne capitulated. It was agreed that his troops should march out with the honours of war, pile their arms, and be conducted at once to Boston for conveyance to England. The army marched out accordingly, 3500 men fit for duty, just half the strength who had started from Canada four months before in all the confidence of perfect discipline and an established reputation. The American General Gates and his army, it may be mentioned, treated the vanquished troops with all courtesy and consideration, but the American Congress, the civil government of the insurgent states, shamelessly violated the terms of the capitulation. Not only did they keep the British and German troops imprisoned for three years, but they used every possible pressure to induce them to desert their colours and join the American army. All pressure and temptations alike were nobly resisted by the British soldiers during a long and arduous captivity, in which a large number of the officers and men died or permanently lost their health.

Although the issue of General Burgoyne's expedition was so unfortunate to himself and his troops, the Thirty-First Regiment had no cause for shame in that the capitulation of Saratoga included its flank companies. The services of the Grenadier and Light Battalions, in which these companies served, were conspicuous in every action during the expedition, and most people who study its vicissitudes, will agree with the words of the historian of the British Army, who writes as follows :

" As to Burgoyne's campaign . . . . it seems to me that no more honourable attempt of British officers and men to achieve the impossible is on record. . . . It is surely a marvellous instance of gallantry and discipline that fifteen hundred men should have moved out cheerfully and confidently as they did on the 7th of October in spite of much hardship and heavy losses, to attack an enemy of five times their number ; that when forced back they should have retired with perfect order and coherence ; and that though fighting all day and marching or entrenching all night, they should never have lost heart. . . . In fact what men could do, Burgoyne and his army did." [1]

The East Surrey Regiment may remember with pride, that these gallant 1500 soldiers included the survivors of the flank companies of the Thirty-First.

The capitulation of Saratoga proved to be the turning-point of the American War of Independence. It was speedily followed by a declaration of war by France against Great Britain, and the despatch of a powerful French fleet and a large body of troops in aid of the insurgent states. In 1779 Spain and Holland also declared war against England, but it was the temporary loss of sea power that in the end turned the scale against us, caused the fall of Yorktown, and won for the United States their independence.

During the remainder of the war, which dragged on its slow course until the surrender of Yorktown in October 1781, the Thirty-First remained in Canada. Here about the end of the previous year they had been rejoined by the flank companies on their release from captivity. Life on the Canadian frontier at this time must have been irksome and dull in the extreme, all the vigilance of war being demanded, with little or none of its pleasant excitement for reward.

In the spring of 1781 the Light Company, now commanded by Captain Andrew Ross, was detached, together with a party of Canadian militia and a few Indians, to reconnoitre the southern shores of Lake Champlain, and to destroy the military stores left at Fort Ticonderoga by General Burgoyne. These duties were performed at a season when the ice was just breaking up, and entailed great privations and very hard work. So great was the fatigue entailed that by degrees the provincials and Indians dropped off, and the party was reduced on its return to the Light Company only. Captain Ross was highly commended for his conduct of these operations.

Fortescue's *History of the British Army*, vol. iii. p. 242.

During its service in Canada, which continued to the autumn of 1787, the Thirty-First lost its Colonel, Lieutenant-General Sir James Adolphus Oughton, K.B., who died on May 3, 1780, and was succeeded in the colonelcy by Major-General Thomas Clarke, from the Coldstream Guards, an officer who had received his first commission in the regiment. Sir Adolphus Oughton, who was a favourite officer of King George III, was an accomplished man. Of him Dr. Johnson is recorded to have said : " Sir, you will find few men of any profession who know more. Sir Adolphus is a very extraordinary man ; a man of boundless curiosity, and unwearied diligence." There is a tablet to his memory in Westminster Abbey. It must also be recorded that in the year 1782, on the introduction of county titles for the regiments of infantry, the Thirty-First severed its recruiting connection with Glasgow, and was directed to assume the name of " the Huntingdonshire Regiment," which it bore until 1881, very nearly a century.

After completing eleven years' service in North America the Thirty-First embarked on October 4, 1787, at Quebec and landed at Portsmouth on November 7. Its service at home was apparently, however, destined to be short, for less than two years later (in July 1790) on a threat of war with Spain, the regiment embarked at Spithead in order to serve in the fleet in its original capacity of Marines. After long negotiations the quarrel with Spain was adjusted and the regiment was released from service afloat.

In July 1791 the Thirty-First was again called upon to perform exceptional service, and in this instance the duty was of an unpleasant nature. Revolutionary riots had broken out at Birmingham on the occasion of the celebration of the first anniversary of the destruction of the Bastille and the commencement of the French Revolution. Serious disturbances had taken place, and the opponents of the revolutionary party at Birmingham had burned a number of the houses of those with French sympathies. The Thirty-First were despatched hurriedly to Birmingham, and, together with the other troops employed, showed much discretion and forbearance in dealing with the situation. When order had been restored the regiment was despatched to Whitehaven, and was there employed in assisting the civil power to suppress an outbreak of the miners.

On February 8, 1792, a change occurred in the colonelcy of the regiment, Lieutenant-General Thomas Clarke being transferred to the 30th Regiment. He was succeeded in the colonelcy of the Thirty-First by Major-General James Stuart, promoted from the half-pay of the 9th Regiment. Major-General Stuart, however, only lived exactly one year from the date of his appointment, dying on February 8, 1793, and being succeeded by Colonel Henry, Lord Mulgrave, from the Grenadier Guards. Lord Mulgrave, a highly distinguished officer, who saw much active service, retained the colonelcy of the regiment for no less than thirty-eight years.

CHAPTER V

THE FRENCH REVOLUTIONARY WAR

The flank companies in the West Indies—Capture of Martinique and St. Lucia—Capture of Guadeloupe—The defence of Berville—Destruction of the flank companies—The Thirty-First in Holland—St. Lucia—The repulse at La Vigie—Heavy loss of the regiment—Why the attack failed—A year's casualties in the West Indies—The campaign of 1799 in Holland—Actions of Egmont-op-Zee and of Alkmaar—An Ensign's letter—An old soldier's yarn—Action at Ferrol—Minorca—Raising a second battalion—Egypt—Action of Rosetta : heavy losses of the regiment—Services in Sicily and Italy—Action of Albaro.

In April 1792 the Thirty-First had been transferred to Ireland and was stationed at Waterford, when the outbreak of war with France, consequent on the execution of Louis XVI, again caused the despatch of the flank companies on active service. The initiative was taken by the French National Convention, which declared war against Great Britain and Holland on February 1, 1793. France was in a state of extreme military weakness, but, owing to the neglect of the British army customary in times of peace, England was at the moment unable either to protect her ally from invasion or to deal a blow at France, which might well have averted the immense expenditure of lives and treasure entailed on England by the twenty-two years of warfare that ensued.

After considerable delay a small British contingent under Frederick, Duke of York, was sent to Holland, where it formed part of a mixed army of 60,000 British, Dutch, Austrian, and Prussian troops, and served in the unfortunate campaign of 1793–4. The Thirty-First was included in the British contingent, but the share taken in this campaign by the regiment was a small one, and will be mentioned later.

The flank companies, however, were destined to serve actively

THE FRENCH REVOLUTIONARY WAR 57

in a different quarter of the globe, for in September 1793 they formed part of the force despatched from Cork to Barbados, thence to operate against the French West India Islands.

By the end of January 1794 the force, commanded by General Sir Charles Grey, was ready to begin operations. It consisted of nearly 7000 men, escorted by a fleet of nineteen ships of war under Admiral Sir John Jervis. The force included three battalions of Grenadiers and three of Light Infantry, the Grenadier company of the Thirty-First serving in the first Grenadier battalion, and the Light company in the 2nd Light Infantry battalion. It may here be mentioned that the force also included the Seventieth Regiment, but the flank companies of that regiment served in other battalions than those to which the flank companies of the Thirty-First belonged.

The first enterprise of the expeditionary force was directed against the large and rich island of Martinique. The French garrison was dispersed among the fortified bays and harbours of the island, and to take advantage of this dispersion and prevent a concentration, General Grey attacked in three divisions. Landings were effected on February 5, 6, and 7, and vigorous operations against the various French fortified posts followed. General Grey was proverbial for his love of the bayonet, and on several occasions adopted his favourite method of insuring that there should be no firing. This method was the simple one of removing the flints from the muskets. The capture of Martinique was completed after severe fighting by March 23.[1] The French garrison had made a gallant resistance, but were completely overwhelmed by the skill and vigour displayed by Sir Charles Grey and his Brigadiers, and by the good conduct in action and the remarkable marching power of his troops. The hearty co-operation and gallant services of the fleet under Sir John Jervis contributed in no small degree to the rapid success of the operations. The casualties of the troops did not exceed 350 in killed and wounded, but the work had been very severe, and the hardships, which the officers shared in every respect with their men, had been very great.

During the fighting in Martinique Prince Edward (afterwards

[1] The operations at Martinique will be found more fully described in the history of the Seventieth Regiment. See chapter xiv.

Duke of Kent and father of Queen Victoria) joined the army, and was placed in command of the brigade of Grenadiers.

Leaving six regiments, including the Seventieth, at Martinique,

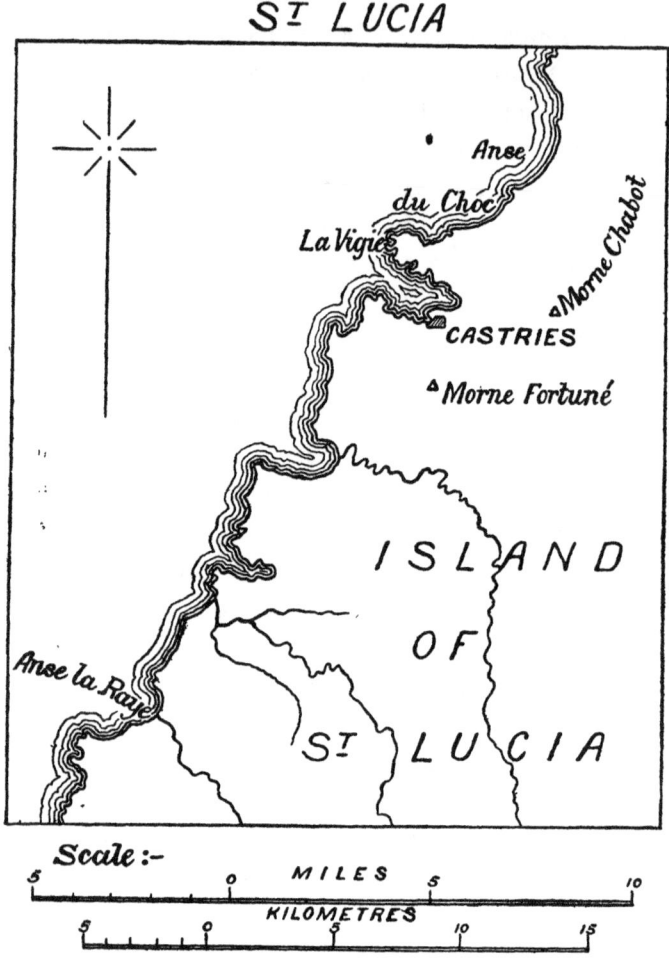

Sir Charles Grey sailed on March 30 for St. Lucia. His force was now reduced to three regiments, with the Grenadier and Light Infantry brigades, each of which had also been reduced to two battalions, as after the capture of Martinique the flank companies of the corps placed in garrison there rejoined their regiments. St. Lucia was reached on April 1, and, having been attacked in like manner as Martinique, and being very weakly held, was captured after three days' active operations. The only serious fighting occurred in the storming of a redoubt and two batteries near the fortress of Morne Fortuné. The assault was led by Colonel Coote of the Seventieth, who had accompanied the expedition in command of the 1st Light Infantry. Colonel Coote's party achieved a complete success, killing thirty of the enemy without losing a man. St. Lucia was now left in charge of two regiments, and Sir Charles Grey returned on April 4 to Martinique for supplies and stores, sailing thence on the 8th for Guadeloupe, and arriving two days later off the entrance to Pointe-à-Pitre in that island.

Without waiting for the arrival of his whole force General Grey landed under a heavy fire from the French forts at the head of 1000 men, and by the evening of April 11 the remainder of the transport had arrived, and six battalions of Grenadiers and Light Infantry, besides 500 seamen, had disembarked. The most formidable in appearance of the defences was Fort Fleur d'Epée, which was strongly held. It was situated on the summit of a hill, with a half-moon battery cut out of the slope below it, and from the front it was difficult of approach. It was, however, commanded at close quarters from the rear by another fort on a hill, named Morne Mascotte. General Grey divided his forces into three columns, one of which was to assault Morne Mascotte, while the two others were to assault Fort Fleur d'Epée in rear from different directions. The time of assault was five in the morning of April 12, and strict orders were given that there was to be no firing, but that the whole of the work must be done with the bayonet. The assaults were delivered with punctuality and despatch, and after a stout resistance in which they lost sixty killed, fifty-five wounded, and one hundred prisoners, the French fled in every direction. The British loss was fifteen killed and sixty wounded, thirteen of the wounded being sailors. In his despatch Sir Charles Grey stated—" Brevet-Major Ross of the Thirty-First Regiment, who was with the Light Infantry, behaved with great gallantry and good conduct on this occasion, as he has done on every other." Major Ross was promoted to the brevet rank of lieutenant-colonel from March 1, 1794.

Leaving garrisons at Fleur d'Epée and Mascotte, General Grey sailed on April 14 across Grand Bay, landed at Petit Bourg, and marched along the coast on Basseterre, the principal town of

Guadeloupe. Here he carried out a series of attacks on the French forts, on the same principle that he had practised so successfully at Martinique. That is, he either captured the forts by an attack in rear, or if they proved too strong for this process they were assaulted at night with the bayonet. By April 21, the last French fort round Basseterre had been captured, and the commandant, General Collot, capitulated.

Thus, with total casualties of no more than eighty-six killed and wounded, General Grey captured the large and important island of Guadeloupe, defended by many strong forts and held by a garrison of 4000 men. The short campaign shows clearly the impotence of a numerous but immobile force against a small but efficient army, boldly handled by a competent commander and supported by an equally efficient and well-handled fleet. General Grey, after the surrender of Guadeloupe, left Brigadier-General Thomas Dundas in charge of the island, and went on a tour of inspection of his previous captures and the British islands of Antigua and St. Kitts. His campaign of conquest had so far been completely successful, and feeling quite secure from any effort of re-capture by France, Grey left the newly-acquired islands with very small garrisons and collected the bulk of his force in Jamaica for further operations in St. Domingo. The arrangements were made with the full concurrence of the Home Government, who thought also that by no possibility could France send any considerable force westward.

Nevertheless on April 23 a French squadron with a convoy of transports slipped out of Rochefort and on June 4 arrived at Guadeloupe. Yellow fever had raged among the weak British garrison, General Dundas being among the first victims, and on the arrival of the French squadron at Pointe-à-Pitre the regular garrison of Fleur d'Epée numbered no more than 120 men fit for duty. The commandant, Colonel Drummond of the 43rd, and his men made a determined resistance, but owing to the repeated misconduct of a body of 200 brave but undisciplined French royalists who had volunteered to share in the defence, the fort was eventually captured with the loss of two-thirds of its garrison.

The French troops numbered no more than 1500 men, but Victor Hugues, the French Commissioner in charge of the expedition, had

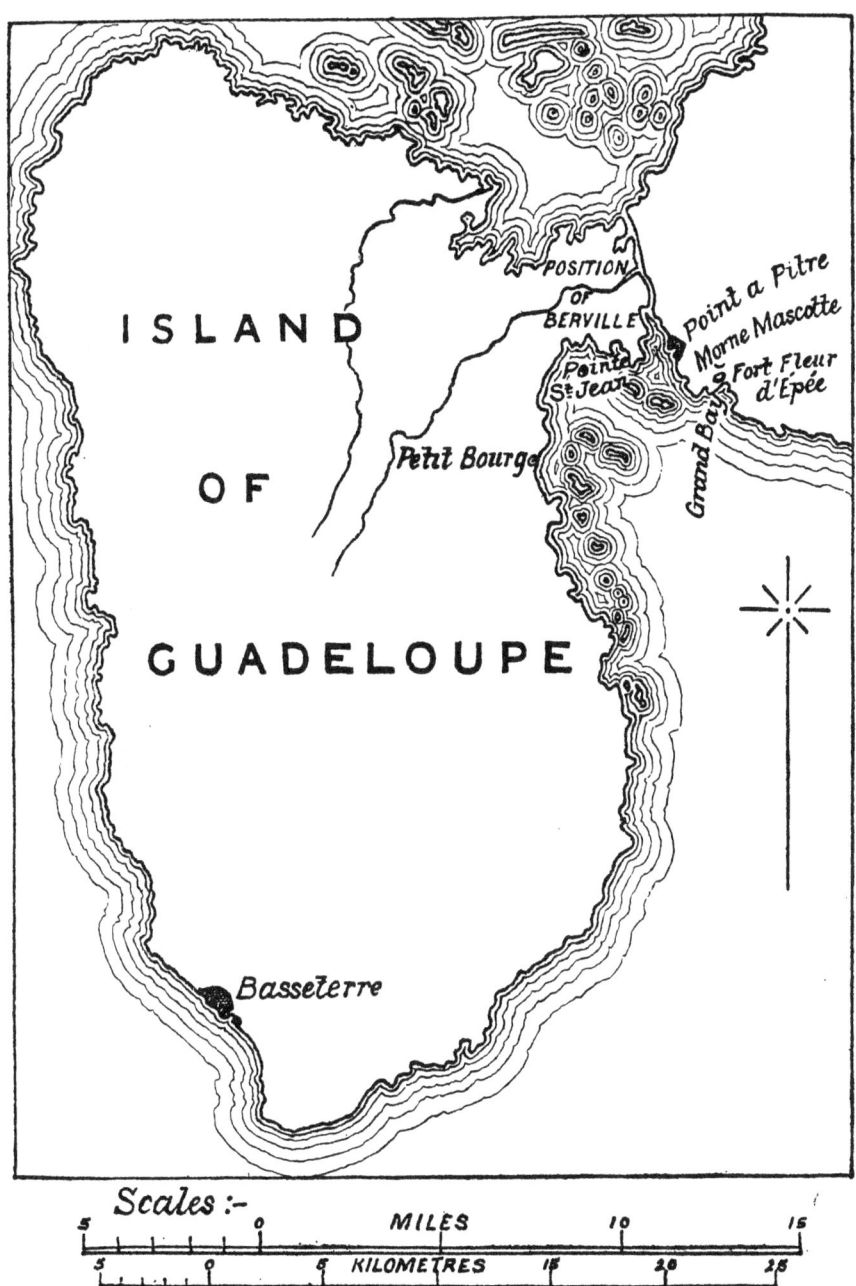

issued proclamations inciting the whole black and coloured population to take arms against the enemies of the Republic, and the French force thus at once assumed formidable proportions.

Sir Charles Grey, ordering up what scanty reinforcements could be spared from the other Windward Islands, proceeded at once to Guadeloupe, bent on vigorous action. He made Basseterre his headquarters.

Hugues, a bold and enterprising man, having the whip hand, made the first move, sending a force on June 11 to establish itself at Pointe St Jean. Two days later this force was attacked by night with the bayonet by the British troops from Petit Bourg, the fortified post overlooking Pointe-à-Pitre. The attack, well led by Colonel Francis Dundas, was a complete success, nearly 200 French being killed on the spot, with under twenty British casualties.

Sir Charles Grey's reinforcements arrived soon after this, and on June 19 the General began to throw up batteries against Fort Fleur d'Epée, and after two successful attacks on detached parties of the enemy, Grey's main body, under Brigadier-General Symes, on June 27 attacked the French position on all sides, drove the enemy in confusion to Morne Mascotte and from thence into Fort Fleur d'Epée. The loss of Morne Mascotte infuriated the French commanders, who with every available man of all colours, made two desperate attempts on June 27 and 29 to re-capture the Fort. Both attacks were repulsed by the Grenadiers and Light Infantry engaged, who displayed the finest courage and discipline. The Light Company of the Thirty-First served in these operations, and Brevet-Lieutenant-Colonel Ross commanded the 2nd battalion of Light Infantry.

Now, however, the incessant fighting began to tell heavily on the sickly and debilitated British soldiers. Since they had left England no stores had been sent to them; their clothes and boots were completely worn out. The rainy season had set in with the usual steamy heat, alternating with the fierce glare of a vertical sun. The hurricane season too was approaching, when the fleet could no longer remain at sea. Clearly it was necessary to finish off the campaign—if possible —at a stroke. Sir Charles Grey therefore decided to make—with the greater part of his force under Brigadier-General Symes—an attack on the French main position at Pointe-à-Pitre, while he, with the remainder of the force, waited in readiness to storm Fort Fleur d'Epée as soon as he saw that Symes' attack had succeeded. Brigadier-General Symes made his attack on the night of July 1, but owing to the weakness of his force and to the many mischances to which night operations are liable, the attack was unfortunately a failure, the British loss being very heavy. From June 10 to July 2 thirteen officers and 107 of other ranks had been killed; thirteen officers and 347 wounded; and seventy-two were missing. Of these casualties, heavy in so weak a force, it is estimated that five-sixths occurred in the attack of July 1.[1] Brigadier-General Symes, in his report on this action, makes special mention of Brevet-Lieut.-Colonel Ross, of the Thirty-First, who though wounded remained with the troops and rendered essential service.

Feeling that further enterprise was for the time impossible, Sir Charles Grey now decided to leave a portion of his force in a central position, so as to maintain his hold on Guadeloupe, and to withdraw the remainder until the time should come for renewed operations. He therefore left about 1800 men, together with local corps of emigrants and loyalists, under Brigadier-General Graham, at Berville; he himself returned to Martinique, and the survivors of the reinforcements brought by him to Guadeloupe were returned to their stations.

The position at Berville was strategically sound, being difficult to attack and separating the two portions of the island of Guadaloupe; but it was low-lying and marshy, and proved very unhealthy. The French forces, which had also suffered severely in the fighting prior to Sir Charles Grey's departure, made no active attack until September 26, but by the 1st of that month no less than 330 English soldiers had died at Berville, 1500 were sick, and but 500 were fit for duty.

On September 26 a large body of the enemy, under Hugues, attacked and captured Petit Bourg, where the British hospital lay under a weak guard of convalescents and royalists. The guard was driven off and many of the sick in hospital were cruelly massacred by the French; it is to be hoped by the black troops. The only survivors were those

---

[1] An episode of interest to the East Surrey Regiment occurred in Brigadier-General Symes' attack. Four companies of grenadiers, commanded by Bt.-Major Irving of the Seventieth Regiment, advanced to support the main body (which included the Light Company of the Thirty-First), and covered its retreat.

rescued by the boats of the fleet. The French, having captured also another small post, were enabled to invest Berville on the land side and to construct a battery on commanding ground. The weak British force, composed of men hardly able from sickness to use their arms, made one of the most gallant defences on record. Brigadier Graham was severely, and his second in command mortally, wounded in the first day's fighting. The command was then, as it appears, exercised by successive officers who fell, killed or disabled, at their post. Berville held out for a week under incessant assaults in which the French who also fought courageously, lost 900 out of a force of 3000 men. Of the British, two officers and twenty-five men had been killed, and five officers and fifty-one wounded, when on October 6, the wounded Graham with but two days' supply of food remaining, and his surviving men scarcely able to stand, surrendered on condition that the British troops should march out with the honours of war and be shipped by the first opportunity to Great Britain. To the shame of the French republic the terms of surrender were violated as basely by its representatives as by the Americans on the occasion of the capitulation of Saratoga.

In the words of Fortescue,[1] in describing the surrender of Berville : " One hundred and twenty-five ghastly figures staggered out of the lines, fitter for hospital than to be under arms—all that remained of what had once been three battalions and twenty-three companies of infantry and two companies of artillery." For a whole year, despite the capitulation, these poor fellows were detained as prisoners ; and they died so rapidly in the weeks that followed the surrender that probably few of them ever saw England again. Yet though the tale of their noble service must remain for ever but half told, the records of the British army contain no grander example of heroism than this of the dying garrison of the camp of Berville. In the " General State " of the troops in the Windward and Leeward Islands, dated October 1, 1794, it is stated that the flank companies of the Thirty-First were included in the surrender at Berville, and regarding the surrendered troops the sad note is added over Sir Charles Grey's signature : " All reduced by sickness to the greatest distress."

[1] *History of the British Army*, vol. iv., Part i., p. 381.

THE FRENCH REVOLUTIONARY WAR

Perhaps the only survivor of Berville belonging to the Thirty-First who reached England was Brevet-Lieutenant-Colonel Ross. Among those who died at Guadeloupe, and presumably at Berville, were Lieutenants J. M. Davies, Mackenzie, and J. T. Williams of the regiment.

While the flank companies were thus sharing in the honours and misfortunes of Guadeloupe, the Headquarters and battalion companies of the Thirty-First remained in Ireland until July 12, 1794, on which date the regiment embarked at Wexford for England, disembarking at Bristol and marching thence to Southampton. On the 25th of the same month the regiment was augmented to ten battalion and two flank companies, and on August 17 embarked for Holland, where it was stationed at Middelburg and Flushing in the island of Walcheren; places whose names a few years later became sadly familiar to English ears. The stay of the Thirty-First at Walcheren was uneventful, and early in 1795 the regiment, with others then stationed in Holland, returned to England, landing at Plymouth on February 27.

The regiment was, however, not destined long to enjoy the pleasures of the south of England, for in September of the same year it was ordered to proceed to a camp at Nursling, near Southampton, there to join a large force preparing for service in the West Indies. At Nursling the regiment received a large accession of strength, as far as numbers were concerned, drafts from the 43rd, 88th, 92nd, and 94th Regiments raising the Thirty-First to its new establishment of 1000 rank-and-file. The regiment also received a second lieutenant-colonel, a second major, and an additional lieutenant to each company.

The strength of the expedition and the duties which it was intended to perform suffered several changes, which need not be detailed here. Eventually it was decided that Lieutenant-General Sir Ralph Abercromby at the head of about 18,000 men was to undertake the recapture of St. Lucia and Guadeloupe from France, after which he was to attack the Dutch possessions of Surinam, Berbice, and Demerara. At the same time Sir Ralph was to devote a considerable part of his force to assisting in the operations against the French in St. Domingo.

The portion of the expeditionary force that could be got ready in time sailed from Portsmouth on November 16. General Abercromby accompanied it, and the large convoy was escorted by a squadron under Admiral Christian. The infantry of the force was divided among six brigades, the Thirty-First, together with the 3rd, 19th, and 33rd Regiments, forming the second brigade. This organisation was, however, short-lived, as most of the operations of the campaign were perforce carried out by small columns.

After being driven back by a disastrous gale near Weymouth, which caused the loss of many ships and of a large number of men, the fleet and convoys made a second start on December 3, to meet with even worse fortune than at the first attempt. Of the 12,000 troops only about 1000 arrived at Barbados, the remainder being driven after great suffering into various and distant ports.

At last, after difficulties which we in the days of steam can hardly realise, Sir Ralph Abercromby arrived at Barbados on March 17, 1796, where he found about 5000 troops at his disposal; and by a month later further detachments had dribbled in, bringing the available force up to nearly 8000 men. With this number Abercromby decided to attack St. Lucia.

Sailing from Barbados on April 21, the expedition touched at Martinique on the 23rd and arrived early on the 26th at Anse-du-Cap, a bay at the north-western extremity of St. Lucia. Here, nearly unopposed, a landing was effected by the 14th Regiment and 42nd Highlanders under Brigadier (afterwards the famous Sir) John Moore. Two more battalions landed later in the day, and on April 27 Moore advanced southward along the coast towards the French main position about the town of Castries. The first position of any strength encountered by Moore was at Anse-du-Choc, and here he met with an easy success, taking all the batteries, which faced the sea, from the rear. The enemy therefore abandoned this position without fighting. More troops, under Abercromby himself, now landed at Anse-du-Choc, and on April 28 an attack was made on Morne Chabot, a strong position on high ground. Owing to the rawness and consequent unsteadiness of the troops under General Moore, the two days' fighting which ensued cost some seventy casualties, but thanks to the fine leading of Moore and his staff, Morne Chabot was taken and the outposts of the force were pushed on towards Morne Fortuné, a large and strong post to the south-west of Castries. On May 1 further outpost fighting cost the British about fifty casualties; the troops engaged being a division which had landed three days earlier at Anse-la-Raye, south of Castries, and had moved northward in order to complete the investment of the French position.

When therefore the Thirty-First Regiment arrived on this day from Barbados, they found Sir Ralph Abercromby's force scattered along a wide circle of thickly-wooded hills, fighting with no marked advantage against the French revolutionary forces, which of course occupied a central, and therefore concentrated, position, well supplied, and in most of its front strongly entrenched. The regiment, which, like a great part of the army, was largely composed of very young soldiers little more than recruits drafted from four other regiments, had suffered greatly from the hardships of the long and tedious life at sea, broken by brief and uneasy periods ashore, which had lasted no less than six months. A great number of the officers, too, were as young and inexperienced as the men, and others had been recently transferred to, or promoted into, the regiment, and were almost strangers to the men they had now to command in a campaign to be carried on in difficult country and in a bad climate.

OFFICERS OF THE THIRTY-FIRST REGIMENT, 1796

COLONEL
Lord Mulgrave. In England.

LIEUTENANT-COLONELS
Adam Hay.[1] Mortally wounded at La Vigie.
Robert Arbuthnot. Mortally wounded at La Vigie.

MAJORS
William Hepburne. Promoted Lieut.-Colonel vice Hay.
George Fearon. Retired April 1, 1797.

CAPTAINS
Richard Johnston. Killed at La Vigie.
Richard Murray. Mortally wounded at La Vigie.
Clements George Massey.
Randolph Marriott. Promoted Major vice Hepburne.
David Erskine.
William Southwell.
James Smith.
William Walker. Killed at La Vigie.
John M'Cumming.
Alexander Irvine. Retired 1797.
Alexander Leith.

CAPTAIN-LIEUTENANT AND CAPTAIN
  William Sorell. Wounded at La Vigie. Promoted Captain vice Johnston.

LIEUTENANTS
  Lewis Davies.
  William Sullivan. Wounded at La Vigie.
  John Stewart Hawkshaw. Wounded at La Vigie.
  Thomas George Waggot.
  Thomas Clarke.
  R. Wigg.
  James Walker.
  John Hill.
  Charles Hay.
  Robert Brice Fearon.
  Joseph Curtis. Transferred to 80th Foot.
  Henry Rochfort.
  John Ball.
  Henry Heatley.
  James George Waddel. Transferred to Ward's Regiment
  Edward William Webb.
  George Wilkins. Transferred to McDonald's Regiment.
  Richard Mullens.
  Thomas Sharp.
  D. H. Spark.
  William M'Kenna.
  William Gordon.
  Thomas Edwards. Promoted in 68th Foot.
  Samuel Wright.

ENSIGNS
  Robert Bateman, Quartermaster. Died 1797.
    Gillespie. Retired 1797.
  Henry Annesley. Retired 1797.
  Francis M'Guire. Exchanged to 111th Foot.
  Joseph Orme. Retired in 1797.
  James Turner.
  Hugh Buchanan. Promoted in 57th Foot.

CHAPLAIN
  William Clay.

ADJUTANT
  William Sorell.

QUARTERMASTER
  Robert Bateman. Died 1797.

SURGEON
  Benjamin Worship.

The Thirty-First, under Lieutenant-Colonel Adam Hay, an officer who had joined the regiment as junior ensign on May 1, 1772, disembarked on May 1 at Anse-du-Choc, with a strength of 776 of all ranks, and went into camp near its landing place, there to prepare as quickly as possible for a share in the forthcoming fighting. Of the doings of the regiment during the first fortnight after its disembarkation we have no record, but on May 16 Sir Ralph Abercromby's batteries, of no more than eighteen guns, opened an ineffective fire on Morne Fortuné. On the following day the Thirty-First were ordered to make a night attack on a strong detached post called La Vigie, on the north side of Castries harbour, distant about two miles from its encampment. Sir Ralph considered the immediate capture of the post necessary, as the fire of its batteries hampered his operations. He also considered a night attack essential, as three batteries of the enemy flanked the neck of land which connected La Vigie with the mainland. The attack was to be supported by a Grenadier battalion. The post at La Vigie was extremely strong, both from the natural advantages of its position and from the manner in which it had been strengthened. The post had been constructed on a lofty peninsula, accessible only by a narrow isthmus, and was defended by two batteries, the inner of which, at the summit of the ascent, commanded the lower, which was itself half-way up the hill which led from the isthmus. The approach from the isthmus to the two batteries was by a circuitous path, and by a mischance the only guide supplied to the regiment was killed by the first fire from the French picquet posted on the isthmus. Lieut.-Colonel Hay, therefore, was confronted by a difficult task, for the ground before him was both steep and thickly-wooded; it was pitch dark, and he had no exact knowledge of the enemy's position or strength. He, however, ordered an advance, and coming presently on the lower battery, the regiment gallantly carried it by storm; spiked the three eighteen-pounders with which it was armed, and tumbled them over the precipice.

It was then necessary to advance against the upper battery, into which the defenders of the lower one had retreated, and now it was that the youth and inexperience of a large proportion of the regiment contributed to the failure of the attack. Instead of advancing rapidly without firing, a method which in all the fighting in the West Indies invariably achieved success, the young soldiers opened fire as they climbed the steep ascent, and after severe losses in killed and wounded, mainly caused by grape-shot from the two guns in the battery, Lieut.-Colonel Hay ordered the regiment to retire.

The losses of the Thirty-First in this unfortunate affair were very heavy. Captains Richard Johnston and William Walker, four sergeants and eighty rank-and-file were killed on the spot. Lieut.-Colonels Adam Hay and Robert Arbuthnot, Captains Richard Murray and William Sorell, Lieutenants William Sullivan and John Stewart Hawkshaw, four sergeants and one hundred and twenty rank-and-file were wounded. Lieutenant-Colonels Hay and Arbuthnot and Captain Murray died of their wounds. A great number of the casualties were caused by grape-shot, a fact which proves that the regiment arrived close up to the French position before the repulse of the attack, and the fact that both the field-officers and four of the company commanders were killed or wounded speaks well for the leading of the officers. All the officers of the Light Company were wounded, Captain Murray mortally, and Lieutenants Sullivan and Hawkshaw severely.

The failure of the attack on La Vigie is commented on in severe terms by Sir John Moore in his diary, but in reference to the remarks of that gallant soldier and high authority a few considerations may be advanced. In the first place La Vigie was a position of great natural strength. In 1778 it had been held by 1300 English soldiers against 9000 French veterans, who made repeated attacks with the utmost determination and were defeated with 1500 casualties, more than the whole strength of the defenders.

Secondly, Sir John was not present at the attack, and his remarks are based on the account of the repulse given to him by Sir Ralph Abercromby, who had planned and was in command of the operation. Thirdly, Sir John Moore, while blaming the regiment for its failure, adds that in his opinion General Abercromby was himself to blame, in that the attack was planned in a hurry, and that the General failed to make successive attacks with, if necessary, regiment after regiment, until La Vigie had been taken. Had this been done, the operation, instead of being a failure, would have been a success, and no more would have been heard of the repulse of the first assault. The officer commanding the Grenadier Battalion is stated in Sir R. Abercromby's report to have " advanced handsomely " in support with a portion of his battalion, and to have secured the retirement of the Thirty-First. The Grenadiers, however, only sustained three casualties, so can hardly have advanced to close quarters. Sir John Moore's remark as to the proper method of carrying out the attack shows that gallant soldier well in advance of the military ideas of his day, and foreshadows the successive waves of a much later period.

During the week following the affair of La Vigie the operations against Morne Fortuné were pushed forward with vigour, and on May 24 Brigadier-General Moore stormed an outwork in a decisive position on the east of the French position. On the following day the garrison of Morne Fortuné, 2000 strong, capitulated, and the island of St. Lucia consequently again fell into the possession of Great Britain.

The total number of killed and wounded in Sir Ralph Abercromby's force during the month's operations included thirty-nine officers and 520 non-commissioned officers and men, a proportion falling, as we have seen, on the Thirty-First Regiment largely exceeding that of the remainder of the force. Sir Ralph Abercromby, anxious to continue his task, lost no time in leaving St. Lucia for St. Vincent and Granada. Much to the disappointment of Brigadier-General Moore, he was left by Sir Ralph in command of St. Lucia, where further trouble was expected at the hands of the insurgent population. The garrison allotted to the island numbered about 4000 men, composed of four British regiments, including the Thirty-First, a foreign corps styled the York Rangers, and some black troops.

The duties which now devolved on the garrison of St. Lucia were harassing in the extreme, and unfortunately the hard work imposed on the ill-nourished and already sickly troops resulted in an appalling loss of life. Small bodies of the French troops who had deserted from the different fortresses at their capitulation withdrew into the interior of the island and joined the runaway slaves and the Caribs ; the mixed rebellious forces thus produced, being, appropriately enough, designated " Brigands." Taking full advantage of the impenetrable nature of the country, and of the assistance given by the climate against the unsuitably dressed and badly-fed British troops, the Brigands formed themselves into bands of a convenient strength for the purpose of molesting the British columns and plundering the planters and other white residents of the island. Brigadier-General Moore, with all his remarkable energy and zeal, penetrated in pursuit of these predatory bands into the wildest quarters of the mountains of St. Lucia; with the result that by November his 4000 effectives had been reduced to 1000 fit for duty. Of the remainder half were dead and the remainder in hospital. Among other sufferers none fared worse than the Thirty-First, the deaths among the men, for a time, numbering sixteen a day. At last, on December 22, in hope of saving some few lives, the regiment was sent to Barbados, hardly a soldier remaining fit for duty. On disembarkation at Barbados on December 26 it was found necessary to send the entire regiment into hospital, as had previously happened in Florida in the year 1765.

During the year 1796 the Thirty-First regiment is stated in Cannon's Record to have lost seventeen officers and 870 men, including those who fell in the attack at La Vigie. These figures speak for themselves, and show the appalling realities of service in the West Indies in the eighteenth century.

In Fortescue's "History of the British Army"[1] it is stated as the result of a careful study of official returns, that the campaigns of 1793 to 1796 cost the army no less than eighty thousand men, of whom half were killed or had died and the other half had been invalided, or double the total losses from all causes of the Duke of Wellington's army in the Peninsular War. A great part of this terrible loss of life was mainly attributable to mismanagement, a fact by no means peculiar to our own army; yet, whatever the cause, and however little the result, for which they suffered, the forty thousand dead British soldiers of the West Indies and of Holland died for England just as truly as if they had fallen on the field of honour, and their successors should recall their memory with the same respect as is paid to the brave dead of some famous battlefield.

[1] Vol. iv. p. 496.

THE FRENCH REVOLUTIONARY WAR

In June 1797 the survivors of the Thirty-First embarked for home, and landed at Gravesend early in the following month. The regiment numbered only eighty-five men, including sergeants, drummers, and rank-and-file. Shortly after disembarkation the regiment marched to Doncaster, where it remained for the next two years, finding detachments at Hull and York. In October of this year a treaty of peace was signed at Campo Formio between Austria and the French republic, so that Great Britain was left for a time to continue the struggle single-handed against the rapidly-growing strength of the French republic.

The year 1798 was one of great difficulty and danger for England. The Irish rebellion and the attempted French invasion of that country, together with the capture of Egypt by a French army under Napoleon Bonaparte, and the threatened attack by France on the British possessions in India, kept Great Britain strictly on the defensive. By the end of the year, however, circumstances had entirely changed. The Irish rebellion had been suppressed, the French expeditionary force in Ireland had been captured, and Nelson's victory of the Nile had not only removed any fear of an attack on India, but had isolated the French army in Egypt. Austria had concluded peace with the French republic, but in December 1798 Russia decided to unite with England in war against France, and the British Government decided again to attempt operations in Europe, and to attempt in conjunction with a Russian contingent, to expel the republican forces from Holland and replace the House of Orange in power in that country.

Owing to the terrible loss of life in the West Indies the army was reduced to a mere skeleton, but during the period of stress above alluded to, the militia had been largely increased. Early in 1799, in order to provide the men necessary for the intended expedition to Holland, the militia was invited to volunteer into the line for service in Europe only, and recruits coming forward freely the Thirty-First and thirteen other regiments detailed for active service were thus quickly raised to war strength. The Thirty-First, still very weak from its losses at St. Lucia, received 853 recruits from the militia, other regiments receiving even larger numbers. These men were of fine physique and of mature age, and with a short time and opportunity for equipment and training would have become excellent soldiers. Unfortunately this necessary time was not granted, but the newly-constituted regiments, full of young and inexperienced officers and of undrilled men, were hurried into the field. In many cases there was not even time to change the militia uniform for that of the regiments, and many regiments actually took the field for a winter campaign without greatcoats.

There was great uncertainty in the minds of the Government as to the most suitable plan for the commencement of operations. Finally it was decided that, without waiting for the arrival of the Russian contingent, a force of 10,000 men under General Sir Ralph Abercromby should be thrown into the extreme north of Holland and there establishing itself, wait for the arrival of the whole intended force of 30,000 men.

Sir Ralph Abercromby sailed from England on August 13, 1799, and after a very rough passage arrived off the coast of the Texel on August 21. The gale continued, and no appliances for disembarkation had been provided, but early on August 27 a landing under the guns of the fleet was successfully accomplished without much loss. The French force in Northern Holland, commanded by General Daendels, was of about the same strength as that of Abercromby, but offered no very effective opposition. A confused fight continued all through the day, at the conclusion of which Abercromby's whole force had been landed, and the French and Dutch, giving up the struggle, retired four miles southward. By August 30 the whole of the Helder and the Dutch fleet of thirty-two men-of-war had passed into the hands of the British fleet and army—a brilliant and unexpectedly rapid success. General Abercromby also had received a reinforcement of 5,000 men on August 28, and he therefore decided to make a cautious advance southward so as to take up an advantageous position pending the arrival of the whole force from England. Further enterprise seemed inadvisable in view of the very raw state of his troops, which the operations of August 27, in spite of their success, had clearly shown.

General Abercromby's halt enabled General Brune, who commanded the French army in Holland, also to concentrate his troops and prepare for a stout defence of Amsterdam, and by September 8 he had joined

THIRTY-FIRST REGIMENT, 1799

COLONEL
Lord Mulgrave

LIEUTENANT-COLONELS
Charles McMurdo.
William Hepburne.

MAJORS
John Smith.
Randolph Marriott.

CAPTAINS
David Erskine.
William Southwell.
James Smith. (Wounded at Egmont-op-Zee.)
John McCumming.
William Sorrell.
Alexander Leith. (Wounded at Alkmaar.)
Lewis Davies.
Paul Anderson.
John Grosser.
Thomas Pickering. (Wounded at Alkmaar.)

CAPTAIN-LIEUTENANT AND CAPTAIN
William Sullivan.

LIEUTENANTS
John Stewart Hawkshaw.
Thomas George Waggott.
Thomas Clarke.
John Bateman.
R. Wigg.
James Walker. (Wounded at Alkmaar.)
John Hill.
Robert Brice Fearon.
John Ball. (Wounded at Alkmaar.)
Henry Heatley.
Richard Mullens. (Wounded at Alkmaar.)
Thomas Sharp.
D. H. Spark.
William McKenna.
Samuel Wright.
Johnstone.
William Stewart.
James Burke.
William Roach.
Michael Coast.
Thomas Turner.
Francis Forster. (Killed at Alkmaar.)
John Stafford.
George W. Whyte.

ENSIGNS
James Turner.
Henry Heatley.
Henry Gazotte.
Benjamin Impey.
William Mason. (Wounded at Alkmaar.)
Thos. Augustus Douce.
Edward Hawkshaw.
George Sutton.
P King. (Wounded at Egmont-op-Zee.)
William Williams. (Wounded at Alkmaar.)
William Murphey.

General Daendels and had taken command of a force of 21,000 men, two-thirds Dutch and one-third French. Being thus considerably stronger than Abercromby, he decided to attack him at once. A severe action followed on September 10, in which both sides fought well, but which ended in a repulse of the Franco-Dutch army with a loss of over 2000 men, the British losing only about 200. This brilliant affair inspired Abercromby's force with great confidence in themselves and their leader, from whose competent hands the chief command was, however, now to pass. Between September 12 and 15 large reinforcements arrived in Holland, 21,000 British and 12,000 Russians joining the army. With the troops from England came the Duke of York, second son of the King, whose appointment had been considered necessary on account of the presence of the Russian contingent. The Duke, though brave and not without experience and knowledge of war, was not a skilful commander in the field. Among the recently-arrived troops was the Thirty-First Regiment, which with the three battalions of the 4th Foot, formed the 7th Brigade, commanded by Major-General the Earl of Chatham.

Encouraged by the recent repulse of the Franco-Dutch army, and having a large though badly-equipped force of 48,000 men at his disposal, the Duke of York decided on an immediate attack on the position taken up by General Brune after his defeat on September 10. This position ran from Bergen to Oudkarspel, a distance of about six miles, and had been selected in order to defend Alkmaar.

The country being intersected by innumerable canals, and the roads being broken and every defensive point skilfully strengthened, it was found necessary to attack the French position in four columns. Of these the right column was mainly composed of Russians and was ordered to attack Bergen, on the French left. The second column was ordered to attack Warmenhuizen and to co-operate with the first column. The third column was to attack Oudkarspel, while the fourth, a strong body under Sir Ralph Abercromby, was to make a wide turning movement round the French right, which had been left open, on Hoorn, and thence on Purmerend. Lord Chatham's brigade formed part of the fourth column.

The attack was to begin at dawn on September 19, and Sir Ralph Abercromby's column of 10,000 men, having far to go, marched on the evening of the 18th towards Hoorn. After a fatiguing night march of twenty miles on bad roads, Hoorn was surprised at two in

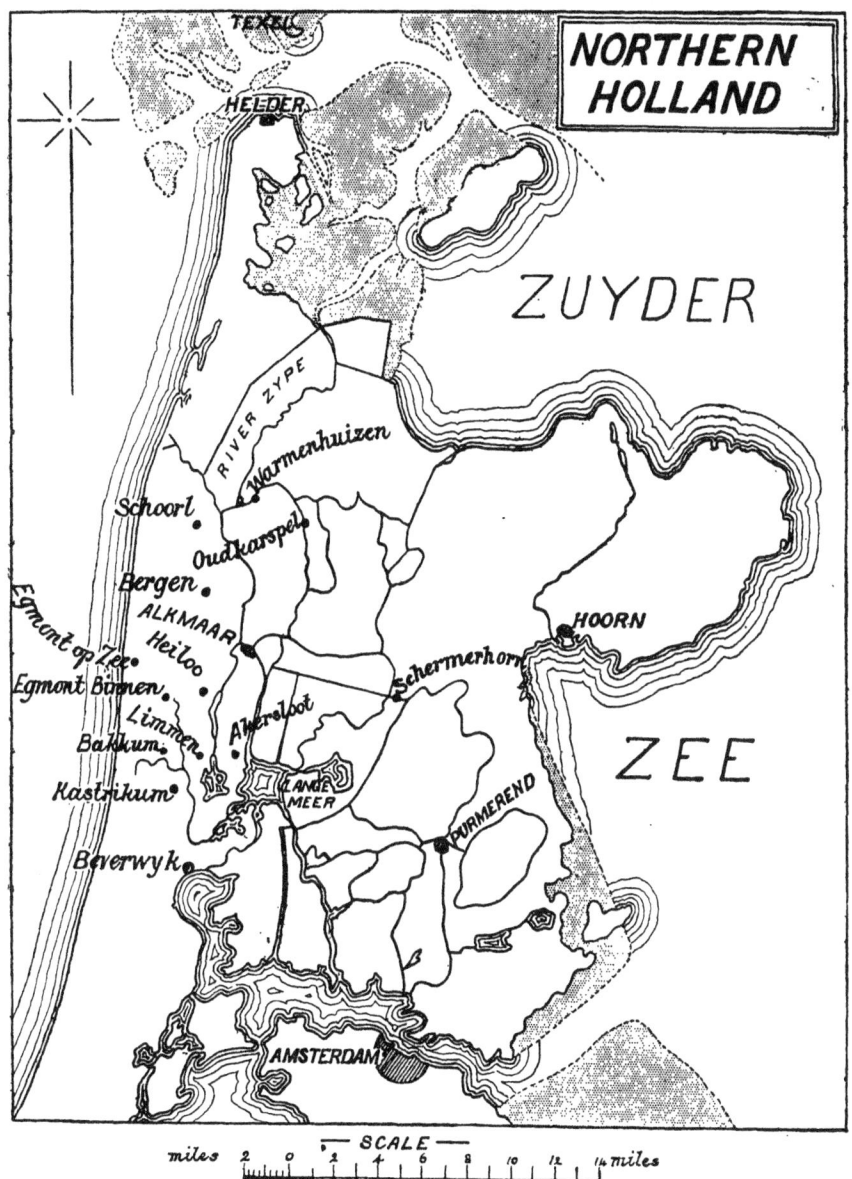

the morning and the weak Dutch garrison captured. Finding his troops much fatigued General Abercromby decided not to advance further south until he heard how matters went with the other columns.

The decision was a wise one, for owing to the weak discipline of the Russian troops, and the incompetence of their general, the attack on Bergen, though at first successful, resulted in a complete defeat of the first column. The Duke of York loyally sacrificed his own troops in the effort to save the Russians, but after suffering heavy losses decided, in spite of the successes of his two centre columns, to withdraw his entire army to the line of the Zype. Sir Ralph Abercromby's column, which had not fired a shot all day, therefore fell back to its original position.

In this unfortunate action the Russian contingent lost about 3000 men, a quarter of its strength. The British troops of the 1st, 2nd, and 3rd columns lost fifty officers and 524 soldiers killed and wounded, with a large number of prisoners. The Franco-Dutch force lost 3000 prisoners, with other casualties that about equalled those of the Duke of York's army; but although three out of the four British columns were successful in carrying out the tasks allotted to them, the main result of the day's fighting was undoubtedly a moral victory for the French, and a corresponding loss of confidence in the Anglo-Russian army.

From September 20 until October 1, both armies remained inactive, strengthening their lines of defence, and both during this period received reinforcements. On September 24 a new corps of between 3000 and 4000 Russians arrived from Kronstadt and on the 29th the French army was joined by French and Dutch troops, which brought up its numbers to about 25,000 men. An attack on lines similar to those of the action of September 19 had been planned for the 29th, to anticipate the arrival of the French reinforcements, but was postponed in consequence of a south-west gale which made marching over the sand-hills near the coast an impossibility.

At last, early on the morning of October 2, the Duke of York's army, about 29,000 men, advanced in four columns, the orders for the day being again similar to those of September 19. The first, or right column under Sir Ralph Abercromby was to attack Egmont-op-Zee[1] and endeavour to turn the French left. The second column, composed of Russian troops, was to march on Bergen. The third

---

[1] The correct name is Egmont-aan-Zee, but the more familiar form is used here.

column, under Sir David Dundas, which included Lord Chatham's brigade, numbered only 4500 men and was intended to support the operations of the first and second columns, Lord Chatham's brigade being specially detailed to support the Russian attack on Bergen. The fourth column was to march wide on the east, threaten the French right, and take advantage of any opportunity that might offer.

The Duke of York's advance began at six in the morning, and Sir Ralph Abercromby's column was almost immediately engaged, and forced its way forward fighting hard all day. At last the exhausted troops halted for the night near the village of Wimmenum, within two miles of Egmont-op-Zee. The Russian troops of the second column, with both flanks protected by British brigades, had advanced as far as Schoorl, but beyond this point the Russian commander declined to budge. This was shortly before mid-day, when General Dundas decided to advance with the brigades of Major-General Coote [1] and Lord Chatham only and attempt to capture Bergen. General Dundas handled his small force skilfully, advancing Lord Chatham's brigade so as to turn the left of the French force opposing him. A counter-attack made by the French was repulsed by the 85th Regiment. General Dundas next moved three battalions of Coote's brigade to the right of Lord Chatham, and Major-General Macdonald's brigade opportunely came up at the moment and prolonged the line further to the right. With these three brigades Sir David Dundas made a general advance in line, thus severing the garrison of Bergen from the French to the westward of that town. This closed the action in the west. On the east the fourth column had successfully advanced to Oudkarspel, threatening the French right.

It is stated in Cannon's Record that the Thirty-First Regiment specially distinguished itself in the attack on Bergen, taking two guns from the enemy. The casualties of the regiment were one sergeant and twenty-seven rank-and-file killed; Captain James Smith, Ensign P. King, and fifty-five rank-and-file wounded.

The action of October 2, 1799, was a British victory, and is commemorated by the honour " Egmont-op-Zee," granted to some of the regiments which took part in it. The Thirty-First, in spite of the

---

[1] Major-General Eyre Coote, formerly Lieut.-Colonel of the Seventieth, who had earned a high reputation in the West Indian campaign of 1794.

honourable part which it bore in the engagement, and of its considerable casualties, does not bear the honour Egmont-op-Zee on its colours.

During the night after the engagement the Russo-British army bivouacked on the ground which it had won, and on the following day, finding that the French army had retired, the Duke of York made a short advance, occupying Egmont-op-Zee, Egmont Binnen, Alkmaar, Heiloo, and Schermerhorn; Lord Chatham's brigade being posted at Alkmaar. General Brune meanwhile had taken up a strong and more concentrated position. He had received six more French battalions from Belgium and his force now lay in three lines of strongly-fortified posts, his front running from South Bakkum, through Limmen to Akersloot and the Lange Meer.

Anxious to make a further advance, and, if possible, to seize Beverwyk, an important step towards the capture of Amsterdam, the Duke of York on October 6 directed General Abercromby's division to continue its march along the beach, while the Russians under General Essen were to attack South Bakkum, Major-General Coote's brigade to attack Limmen, and Major-General Burrard's brigade to attack Akersloot. All three villages were easily captured, the French falling back on their second line of defence, but General Essen, without orders, made a further advance to Kastrikum. Here he was checked by three French battalions, but the Russians first being reinforced, and then the French, a stiff fight of three hours' duration ensued, in which first one side and then the other gained the advantage. Eventually General Brune, gaining the upper hand, drove the Russians through Kastrikum part of the way to South Bakkum and Limmen. Here the Russians were only saved from destruction by a timely charge of a small body of the 7th Light Dragoons under that famous cavalry leader, Lord Paget, and by the arrival of Sir Ralph Abercromby with one of his own brigades from the west, and two of General Dundas's battalions from the east. The details of the action of October 6 are so obscure that it is very difficult to say what share in it was taken by individual battalions. The total British casualties were, however, something like 800 in killed and wounded, of which the 4th Regiment had 150 killed and wounded and over 500 taken prisoners. The Thirty-First had a total of 130 killed and wounded, including seven officers. It seems therefore sufficiently clear that the two battalions named as coming to the help of the Russians from the east were a battalion of the 4th and the Thirty-First Regiment.

The casualties of the Thirty-First in detail were as follows :—Killed: Lieutenant Francis Forster, one sergeant, and thirty-five rank-and-file; wounded: Captains Alexander Leith and Thomas Pickering; Lieutenants James Walker, John Ball, and Richard Mullens; Ensigns William Williams and William Mason; three sergeants, and eighty-four rank-and-file.

The action of October 6 was the last event of the campaign in Holland of 1799. While not to be described as a defeat, it had convinced the Duke of York's advisers, the four lieutenant-generals with the army, that the enterprise of the campaign must be abandoned. Not only did they realise that no further advance was possible, but they plainly saw that it was necessary to retreat. The army since landing had fought five actions, costing between 9000 and 10,000 casualties, and had made but little progress. It was moreover impossible with their inadequate transport to continue military operations in Holland after the end of October. The French had been reinforced, and if the Anglo-Russian army could defeat them, which was very doubtful, they certainly could not follow them up.

Accordingly, on October 7, the Duke retreated to the lines of the Zype, leaving his wounded behind him for want of transport. The French followed the retiring army, but made no great attempt to molest it. It was next decided to evacuate Northern Holland and to take back the army to England, but it was evident that the embarkation would be no easy matter and heavy loss of guns and of horses, if not of men, was fully expected. The proposal of a convention by the French Commander-in-Chief was therefore received with satisfaction, and after four days' negotiations, terms were arranged on October 18. These were that hostilities should cease and the British should evacuate Holland by the end of November. Eight thousand French and Dutch prisoners in England were to be released, and the prisoners on both sides taken during the operations were to be exchanged.

In accordance with these terms the Russo-British army embarked as best it might and crossed the North Sea in very stormy weather, several hundred lives being lost by shipwreck. The Russian contingent, it is recorded, after surprising the people of Yarmouth by drinking the oil from the street lamps, were quartered for a time in the Channel Islands.

An interesting sketch of the operations in Holland is given in the following letter, written by Ensign Edward Hawkshaw of the Thirty-First, who with his brother served in the flank battalions formed of the Grenadier and Light companies of the army:—

Holland October 30th 1799.

Believe me, my Dearest Mother, it has given me very great pain to have been so long in your debt for your most affectionate letter, particularly as I am afraid my last letter was not allowed to go on account of a slight repulse we met with (the action of Alkmaar), which it was feared we might write of in such a manner as to alarm the people and give them ideas of our not succeeding. But as hostilities are now at an end here, and the French by this time withdrawn from the country, I seize the first opportunity of relieving my Dearest Mother from the anxiety she is good enough to say she will experience for our safety, and letting her know that, thank God, both John [1] and I are as well as possible and have enjoyed our health during this campaign, which though it has proved a short one, is allowed by the oldest officers to be the most severe one they ever served. From our first landing until the action of the 2nd of this month, we had nothing to do but a little lagging in long marches which we made to surprise some towns and succeeded in doing so, but owing to some unexpected failure on the right, where the Russians made an attack, we were reluctantly obliged to give up all we had gained, and retire to our old position.

On the night of our retreat (the 11th of last month), we made a forced march of 26 miles, which in this sandy country where every step you take you sink to the ankles, is a very tiresome thing. We gained our old quarters, with the loss of a few men, who, not being able to get on, were taken by the French.

John and I kept up famously. You may judge of the fatigue we underwent by a stout grenadier dropping down dead on the march. On the morning of the 2nd of this month I thought myself amply rewarded for all my toils, by the sight of our whole army drawn up for the attack. The morning was a most lovely one, and I never saw so fine a sight—40,000 men were drawn out

---

[1] Lieut. John Stewart Hawkshaw, also of the Thirty-First, who served in the Light Battalion commanded by Lieut.-Colonel Gideon Shairpe. Lieut. J. S. Hawkshaw was slightly wounded at Alkmaar.

along the Beach and on a kind of Bowling-green, while the sun just rising out of the sea made their arms glitter. At seven o'clock the engagement commenced, and continued with the greatest obstinacy, every inch of ground being disputed until the same hour at night, when the French were beat back to a strong fortified place they had entrenched themselves in, from whence they amused us with a few shot and shells which did no great execution. All night we continued under arms on the sand-hills, and a dreadful one it was, the wind was driving the sand so as almost to cover us. The rain came in torrents, and we were without any refreshment or even a fire. Next morn the French retreated in good order, and our Battalion (the Light Infantry) advanced to join Sir Ralf Abercrombie. We marched all the night to surprise a town which we thought was in possession of the enemy, and I do not think I will ever forget our march. It was so dark as to prevent us seeing the men before us, except by the flashes of lightning, which added to the silence of the army every minute expecting to come into action, and the roaring of the sea, while we were completely drenched with rain, made it the most awful night I ever passed.

I forgot to mention that our rout lay over sandhills almost impassable. Yet our troops were in the greatest spirits and never complained. Early in the morn: we arrived at the town and found the French had left it, so we took possession of a snug home, got some potatoes, salt, and a little hay, and slept soundly.

On the 6th, we marched out of this town (Egmont op Zee) with only the Lt. Infantry Battalion and some Cavalry to reconnoitre, and having met a large party of the enemy, both horse and foot, our lads charged them and the horse men cut them up severely and took some prisoners. Their column was four times our number, and they had reinforcements coming up every minute. Once more we took to the sand hills, and were engaged until 4 o'clock, when fresh troops coming up on either side the engagement became general, and we soon regained the ground we had been forced to lose in the morning to prevent our being flanked and cut off.

A most dreadful fire was kept up until the darkness put a stop to the business, and the French retired, leaving us masters of the field of battle.

John and I continued the greatest part of both days fighting together, and when chance separated us, I leave you to guess the pleasure of our meeting in the plain where hundreds were falling and where we could not be sure of each other's lives one moment, for the French fought very gallantly, and as no doubt you have seen by the returns of killed and wounded, we had not an easy victory. I need not tell you of our retreat or the reason of it, as the papers have left nothing for me to say, except that our usual bad fortune as to the weather attended us, and during the whole march of 30 miles by night along the sea shore, it literally never ceased raining a moment. We are now in almost daily expectation of sailing for the " Sweet little island." The terms are not, I fear, very favourable for us. All damages done the country are paid for by us, and all our works, batteries, etc., etc., are to be left standing.—The cannon we got at the Hildar to be left, and in short, we are to take nothing out of the country. None of us regret leaving this confounded place, where everything is getting more and more dear and scarce, and I am sure the inhabitants have no reason to be sorry for our departure, as we have nearly consumed all their provision.

Meat is here very cheap. You can buy a very good sheep for a dollar and a large fat cow for 6½Ds. But there is now no such thing as bread or potatoes. There are great numbers of swans here, and I am ashamed to say I have spent several days in hunting them for the sake of their skins, and we have now got half a doz. very nice ones, which we hope soon to have the pleasure of either giving or sending to our family, and it is the only thing we have got like plunder since we came. We regretted much our being obliged so soon to leave Alkmaar and Horne, both of which towns are as beautiful ones as I have seen with a great number of good houses and respectable people.

The French army is drawn off supposed to Switzerland against the Arch Duke, and another expedition is talked of to keep our present army employed. If that is the case, I am afraid neither John nor I will be able to get leave to go to Ireland, but we must be content, and I hope that some future time will make us, if possible, more sensible of the happiness of meeting our affectionate parents and restore us to your kind wishes when we will enjoy ourselves the more for our long absence. . . .

I am sorry to put you to the expense of postage for this, but I really cannot beg, borrow or steal half a sheet of paper to enclose it in. This I got, with the greatest difficulty, from our Captain. . .

John writes by this packet, so I will say nothing of him, except that every day makes me love him better. We have constantly lived together, slept together, and shared every comfort and danger since we landed in Holland, and are not yet tired of it.

Be good enough to give my most affectionate love and duty

to my Father, and thank him for his letter, which shall be answered immediately. And now, my dearest Mother, I must conclude, so I beg you will believe me what I shall ever remain, your most sincerely affectionate and dutiful son,

E. HAWKSHAW.

October 30th, 1799.

The writer, afterwards Lieutenant-Colonel Edward Hawkshaw, saw much service. He commanded one of the battalions of the Lusitanian Legion in the Peninsular War, and was severely wounded at its head when leading the final and decisive charge at the battle of Albuera.

The following letter written by an old Thirty-First soldier sixty years after the event is also interesting from its reference to the tradition that the British and French Thirty-First regiments met in a charge at Egmont-op-Zee. The story of the two men who buried one another is not devoid of a quaint military humour :—

Knutsford, July 4th 1866.

DEAR SERGEANT MAJOR,—I take the pleasure of writing these few lines to you, for I wish the Regiment well being (*i.e.* having served) under Major Eagar, the Colonel's Father, who gained some of the honours in the Peninsula, and this is the reason why I wrote these few lines.

A RESURRECTION IN 1799

The 31st Regiment was serving in Holland and at Egmont op Zee crossed bayonets with the French Regiment bearing the same number, a ball fired during the retreat of the latter regiment passed through the jaws of a soldier of the 31st named Robert Hullock. In the course of the afternoon he was buried in the sand hill where he had fallen by a soldier of his regiment named Cames. During the night Hullock recovered and having been lightly covered with sand, crept out and crawled to a picquet of his regiment posted near. He was sent to the Hospital recovered and was serving with his regiment in Malta in 1806. His face having been much discoloured and his voice scarcely intelligible (a part of his tongue and palate having been carried away) he had for some years served as a pioneer to his company. A soldier of it died and Hullock as part of his duty dug the grave in which he was found on the arrival of the body for interment still at work though nearly ten feet deep; on being drawn out and asked his reason for making it is so unusually deep he replied " Why Sir it is for poor John Cames who buried me and I think Sir if if I get him that deep it will puzzle him to creep out as I did." On the burial service being read he proceeded to fill up the grave and actually buried the man who ten years previously buried him. Hullock was discharged and pensioned in 1814. And I served with the same two men in the year 1806, so I conclude by wishing you, the Colonel, all the Officers and the Regiment well.

(Signed) JOHN LOWE.

Market Place,
Knutsford, Cheshire.

The Thirty-First Regiment embarked at the Texel on November 16, and landing at Deal three days later, marched immediately to Canterbury, where the effects of the Dutch campaign made themselves felt. Before the army left Holland dysentery had broken out, owing to cold, damp, bad food and insufficient clothing, and the Thirty-First lost a large number of men from this cause in the course of the winter of 1799.

On May 15, 1800, the Thirty-First Regiment embarked at Dover for Ireland, under orders to join an expedition proceeding on secret service. Arriving at Cove on June 6, the regiment marched immediately to Cork, where the expeditionary force was assembling under Brigadier-General the Honble. Thomas Maitland, who had met the Thirty-First on service in St. Lucia. On June 27 the force embarked, and on July 8 the expedition reached its destination, which proved to be Quiberon Bay, on the coast of Brittany. The intended object of the expedition, which consisted of 6000 troops, was an attack on Belle Isle; but after the receipt of various contradictory orders from England, this enterprise was abandoned and the troops were ordered to join the force under Lieutenant-General Sir James Pulteney, then a part of the army in the Mediterranean, commanded by General Sir Ralph Abercromby. Both these officers had served in Holland with the Thirty-First. Sir James Pulteney's force numbered about 13,000 men, and his instructions were to disembark, first at Ferrol and subsequently at Vigo, in order to destroy arsenals, dockyards, and fortifications.

Pulteney's expedition, escorted by a squadron under Admiral Sir John Warren, arrived off Ferrol on August 25, and landed very early on the following morning. After a brisk skirmish, in which the Thirty-First was engaged, the enemy's troops were driven off the heights commanding the town, and the general and his brigadiers proceeded to reconnoitre the position. On inspection it was found impossible to attack Ferrol, which was strongly fortified and amply garrisoned. It could not be carried by assault, and a long siege was out of the question. General Pulteney therefore decided to proceed to Vigo. The British losses in the skirmish mentioned above were eighty-four killed and wounded, the Spanish losses being somewhat heavier.

After re-embarking his troops Pulteney proceeded to Vigo, but deciding that it was undesirable to attack that place, he passed on to Gibraltar, where he arrived on September 19. At Gibraltar Sir Ralph Abercromby took over the command of the expedition, which with his own troops formed a force over 20,000 strong, and sailed early in October to attack Cadiz. Partly owing to the presence at Cadiz of the plague, and partly from the great difficulty of landing troops at that tempestuous time of the year, this enterprise was also abandoned; and eventually Sir Ralph Abercromby, with 16,000 men, sailed for Egypt, there to win the battle of Alexandria and to end his honourable career. The greater part of the men of the Thirty-First were not liable to service outside Europe, and consequently the regiment was not included in the Egyptian expedition; and together with six other battalions similarly constituted was ordered to Lisbon, where it arrived on November 27, having suffered much from five months' confinement on board ship and the prolonged use of salt provisions.

On January 27, 1801, the Thirty-First was again at sea, and on February 14 disembarked at Minorca, which island had surrendered to Great Britain in 1798.

The successes of British arms in Egypt, resulting in the expulsion from that country of the French Republican army, brought about the Peace of Amiens, signed on March 27, 1802, between Great Britain, Spain, Holland, and the French Republic. One of the clauses of the treaty provided for the restoration of Minorca to Spain, and in consequence the Thirty-First sailed for home in May 1802, arriving at Portsmouth early in June. On the 19th of that month it was reduced to a peace establishment.

The Peace of Amiens proved very short-lived. Early in May 1803 war again broke out and the Thirty-First was consequently moved to Jersey, where it remained for about eighteen months. While stationed at Jersey a private soldier of the Thirty-First performed an act of courage and devotion, which saved a great part of the town of St. Helier from destruction. After firing the salute on the King's birthday (June 4, 1804) the bombardier in charge neglected to see that the slow-match used for firing the guns had been properly extinguished. The match was placed still alight in the magazine, which it presently set on fire. In the magazine were 325 barrels of gunpowder. The following narrative of what then occurred is given in Cannon's Record."

" Private William Pentenny of the Thirty-first Regiment, assisted by two inhabitants of Jersey, broke open the magazine, when another moment's delay would probably have been too late, the fire having nearly reached the spot where the powder was deposited, when he entered. With infinite coolness and decision, he carried the nearest barrels away in his arms, and continued so to act until the whole stock was removed out of danger. This important service was highly appreciated. The Patriotic Fund at Lloyd's awarded Private William Pentenny a pension of £20 a year, while the States of Jersey conferred an additional £12 on this deserving soldier, and presented to him a gold medal, struck on purpose to commemorate the achievement, which he was permitted to wear. The Governor, Major-General the Honble. William Stewart, ordered a ring of silver lace to be worn round his arm as a further distinction."

It may be added that the brave action of this good soldier is still gratefully remembered in Jersey.

In consequence of the threat of the Emperor Napoleon to invade England, large increases of the defence forces of Great Britain were effected in the years 1803 and 1804. In the former year " the Army of Reserve Act " was passed, authorising the raising of men for home service by ballot, and in addition to the consequent large increase of the militia, numerous yeomanry and volunteer corps were raised all over the kingdom. The arrangements having proved inadequate to the requirements of the situation, Pitt, who became Prime Minister in May 1804, decided on an increase of the regular army. Fifty line regiments on the Home establishment were ordered to raise second battalions, and among them was the Thirty-First. The men for the second battalion of the regiment were ordered to be raised in the county of Chester, and to be enlisted for " limited service."

LIST OF OFFICERS
FIRST BATTALION THIRTY-FIRST (HUNTINGDONSHIRE) REGIMENT
WHO SERVED IN THE FRENCH REVOLUTIONARY WAR

COLONEL
   Henry, Lord Mulgrave (Lieut.-General).

LIEUT.-COLONELS
   Hon. Robert Meade. Brigadier-General. Severely wounded at Rosetta.
   Henry Bruce.
   Alexander Leith. Also served with 2nd Battalion in Peninsular War.

MAJORS
   George Augustus Tonyn.
   John Stewart Hawkshaw } Also served with 2nd Battalion in Peninsular
   Robert Brice Fearon   }   War.
   Michael Coast.

CAPTAINS
   Charles Ashe A'Court. Promoted Major in a Greek Corps.
   John Robertson. Killed at Rosetta.
   Henry Cumming.
   Patrick Cruice. Wounded at Albaro.
   Alexander Stewart. Wounded at Albaro.
   Robert Elder.
   William Gildart. Retired in 1810.
   Edward Stafford.
   Patrick Dowdall. Wounded at Rosetta. Also served with 2nd Battalion
      in Peninsular War.
   Edward Knox. Wounded at Rosetta. Also served with 2nd Battalion
      in Peninsular War.
   Richard Cust.
   Peter Fearon. Wounded at Rosetta. Also served with 2nd Battalion in
      Peninsular War.
   James Maxwell.
   J. W. Nunn.
   John Taylor Mackenzie.

LIEUTENANTS
   George Isitt. Died June 1, 1809.
   Richard Birch.
   George Blomer.
   John Thornton. Wounded at Rosetta.
   Joseph Burton.
   William Pitt Gilland. Died in 1811.
   Francis John Ryan. Wounded at Rosetta.

Duncan Rankin.
John Hutton.
William Shaw (Adjutant).
Richard Lodge.
William Sladden. Mortally wounded at Rosetta.
Peter Gapper. To 64th Regiment.
Cuthbert Ward. To 60th Regiment.
Thomas Willingham.
Matthew Kearney.
Richard Kirby. Wounded at Rosetta.
George M'Cullock.
Samuel Shaw.
Henry Harman Young.
John Collins. Died in 1810.

ENSIGNS
Ralph Blaney. To 96th Regiment.
Henry Harcourt Wynne. To Royal Horse Guards.
James Cashell.
Charles C. Bailey. Also served with 2nd Battalion in Peninsular War.
Howard Paterson.
Thomas Podmore. Retired in 1813.
Alexander Haswell.
William Ryan.
Charles Shaw.
Walter Forster Kerr.

PAYMASTER
Thomas Sunderland.

ADJUTANT
William Shaw (Lieutenant).

QUARTERMASTER
James Spence.

SURGEON
John Ives.

ASSISTANT-SURGEONS
S. F. Hayes.
Thomas Soden. Resigned in 1811.

Recruits for the Second Battalion Thirty-First came in briskly, but to assist in its formation the regiment was brought over from Jersey, arriving at Portsmouth on November 27, and marching thence to Winchester, where it received a number of recruits from the militia, which had been reduced in establishment and consequently had surplus men. In July 1805, the Second Battalion Thirty-First was fully formed, and in October marched to Winchester, where the First Battalion was still stationed.

THE FRENCH REVOLUTIONARY WAR

Leaving for the next chapter the history of the Second Battalion, we will now briefly trace that of the First Battalion during the war against Napoleon, which continued with but one brief interval from 1803 till the battle of Waterloo.

Spain having been drawn into an alliance with France declared war against England on December 12, 1805, and nine days later the combined fleets of France and Spain were defeated at Trafalgar. On January 9, 1806, the Thirty-First assisted to line the streets at the public funeral of Lord Nelson.

Italy having fallen under the sway of France and Ferdinand IV, King of Naples, having been driven from his dominions in Italy to the Kingdom of Sicily, the British Government determined to preserve this island from the sway of Napoleon. A force of about 6000 men, which had for a short time been employed in Southern Italy in the vain attempt to support the Bourbon cause, was concentrated in Sicily in February 1806. A reinforcement of four battalions, one of which was the First Battalion Thirty-First, was despatched from England in April of that year under Brigadier-General the Honble. Robert Meade, the senior Lieut.-Colonel of the Thirty-First. Embarking at Tilbury on April 26, the brigade arrived at Messina exactly three months later. During this voyage important events had occurred in the South Italian scene of action. The French had assembled a considerable force in Calabria, with which they proposed to attack Sicily; but they had been anticipated by Major-General Stuart, who then commanded the British garrison. General Stuart, crossing the Straits of Messina, had on July 4 suddenly attacked a French army of superior strength under General Regnier, and had won the victory of Maida, the first decisive triumph of the war with France. Three weeks later the First Battalion Thirty-First arrived at Messina. The disappointment naturally felt by the battalion at missing this signal victory was temporary only, for it was evident that further fighting was in store. Further British reinforcements continued to arrive during the year 1806 and by December the force in Sicily amounted to 19,000 men.

Early in 1807, in consequence of the conduct of Turkey, which country still favoured the cause of France, a British naval demonstration was made at Constantinople. The fleet under Sir John

Duckworth forced the Dardanelles and destroyed some Turkish vessels. Having no landing force, the demonstration was a failure, and the British Government decided to seize Alexandria, in order to prevent any attempt at a second French landing in Egypt. For this task General Fox, then commanding in Sicily, sent a force of 6000 men to Alexandria, under command of Major-General Mackenzie-Fraser, with Major-General Wauchope as second-in-command. Three British infantry regiments were included in the expedition, the senior being the First Battalion Thirty-First, which embarked on February 21, with a strength of forty-two officers and 970 non-commissioned officers and men. The first detachment of the expedition arrived at Alexandria after a very rough voyage on March 16, and the town surrendered four days later.

On March 23, General Mackenzie-Fraser was informed by Major Missett, the British Consul, that there was a scarcity of provisions in Alexandria, and that it would be necessary to occupy Rosetta, a town forty miles distant, where supplies abounded. General Fraser consequently ordered a weak brigade under Brigadier-General the Honble. Robert Meade of the Thirty-First to march on Rosetta. The brigade was composed of the First Battalion Thirty-First—less its light company; the Chasseurs Britanniques, a foreign corps, originally composed of French royalists, also less its light company; two six-pounder guns and two small howitzers. The total strength was about 1600 of all ranks, and Major-General Wauchope accompanied the brigade.

The column marched on March 29, and arrived at Rosetta on the 31st. The town appeared to be deserted, and it appears that Major-General Wauchope incautiously marched the troops into the narrow streets without any military precautions. Rosetta, like most oriental towns, is peculiarly adapted to defensive fighting. The houses are high, the lower half of each being a dead wall, with a small door leading into a narrow passage, well secured with bolts and bars of iron. The chambers are above, with trellised windows projecting over the streets. The garrison of Rosetta, mainly Albanian troops, remained completely hidden until the British column was involved in the narrow streets, and then without the slightest warning opened a murderous fire from the windows of every house and from specially prepared loopholes. A great number of the officers were immediately shot down, Major-General Wauchope being killed and Brigadier-General Meade dangerously wounded in the head, and over a quarter of the force were soon lying dead or wounded on the ground. In these trying circumstances the troops remained steady and amenable to orders. Lieut.-Colonel Bruce of the Thirty-First, the senior officer unwounded, ordered an immediate retirement from the town, which was carried out in good order, the troops carrying their very numerous wounded with them, and taking up a strong position on high ground near the town. This was an achievement of no ordinary merit, and reflects the highest credit on those engaged in this unfortunate affair. The Albanian troops followed up the retiring British for a while, killing any stragglers who fell into their hands, but soon abandoned the pursuit, permitting the survivors of the column to effect their retreat to Alexandria.

It is estimated that the Thirty-First on this occasion took about 770 men into action, of which number seventy-six were killed and 145 wounded; or 221 casualties in all. The detail was as follows:

Killed. Captain John Robertson, three sergeants, three drummers, and sixty-nine rank-and-file.

Wounded. Brigadier-General the Honble. R. Meade, Captain Patrick Dowdall, Lieutenants Edward Knox, Peter Fearon, John Thornton, William Sladden (mortally) and Francis John Ryan, Ensign Richard Kirby, seven sergeants, one drummer, and 129 rank-and-file. The total losses of the column were 108 killed and 282 wounded, including a heavy proportion of officers.

A second attempt to capture Rosetta with a larger force was made during the month of April, but the Thirty-First was not engaged in this expedition. It is therefore enough to say that the enterprise resulted in a disastrous failure, part of the force being defeated with heavy loss in the action of El Hamed. Reinforcements were sent to Alexandria from Sicily towards the end of May, but it had become apparent to the authorities in England that the force at their disposal was insufficient to hold both Sicily and Alexandria. Negotiations were therefore opened which resulted in the withdrawal of the British force on condition of the release of the prisoners taken at El Hamed. Consequently in September 1807 the British force in Egypt evacuated its position at and near Alexandria and returned to Sicily, arriving there on October 16.

The First Battalion Thirty-First remained at Sicily nearly a year after this incident, being removed to Malta in September 1808, and remaining there until August 1810, when it returned to Sicily and was quartered in the citadel of Messina until April 1811. In April 1810 the battalion was ordered to proceed to Portugal, to join the army under Sir Arthur Wellesley, with which the Second Battalion Thirty-First was already serving. The order was, however, subsequently cancelled. In April 1811 it was ordered that the battalion should return to Malta, to be replaced in Sicily by a stronger corps, the Thirty-First having been reduced in numbers by war casualties and sickness. This move, however, proved to be temporary only and four companies first, and subsequently the whole battalion, was recalled to Sicily by the end of August 1811.

With the exception of the grenadier company, which shared in an abortive expedition to Alicant, in Eastern Spain, in November 1812, the battalion remained in the citadel at Messina until near the end of the year 1813, when in consequence of disturbances at Palermo, the capital of Sicily, the Thirty-First took the field for a time, but was not engaged. In January 1814 the battalion returned to Messina.

On March 28, 1814, the First Battalion Thirty-First under Colonel Bruce embarked at Melazzo as part of an expedition ordered to operate in Italy under command of Lieutenant-General Lord William Bentinck. The greater part of the force landed in two divisions, one near Genoa and the other at Leghorn, and, after a rapid march, united and attacked the French under General Rouger St. Victor at Sestri on April 8, gaining some advantage. The third division of the British force, which included the Thirty-First, attempted to land at Recco during the action, but was repulsed. Further fighting on the part of the troops ashore continued until April 13, on which date the third British division landed at Nervi and immediately attacked the French on the heights of Albaro. The infantry of this division consisted of the First Battalion Thirty-First Regiment and the 8th battalion of the King's German Legion, and both battalions executed their attack with great spirit in spite of the very broken and difficult ground over which they had to advance. The right of the French position was guarded by a battery of four guns, which was stormed with conspicuous courage by the light company of the Thirty-First, led by Captain Nunn, in spite of a galling flank fire of musketry and artillery from another battery close by.

In this gallant affair the losses of the Thirty-First were one sergeant and thirteen rank-and-file killed; Captains Stewart and Cruice, three sergeants, one drummer, and thirty-six rank-and-file wounded. In

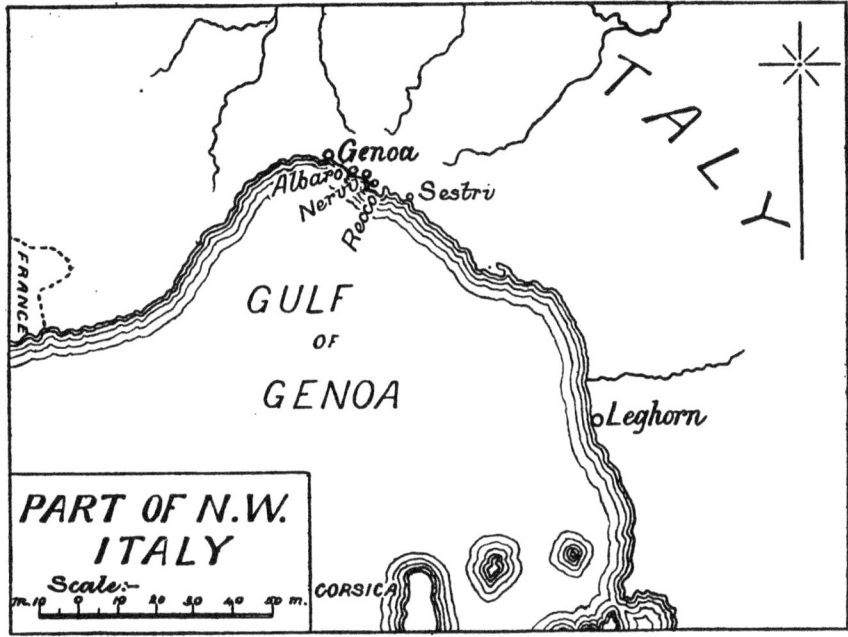

the divisional orders of the following day, by Major-General Montressor, special mention is made of "the very gallant manner in which the Thirty-first Regiment, and the 8th King's German Legion, dashed in amongst the enemy after their debarkation, and the conspicuous bravery of the light company of the Thirty-first Regiment in carrying the battery on the left."

Fighting continued daily, and by April 18 disaffection against the French rule had taken great hold on the population of Genoa. On April 19 the advance on that city continued and the Thirty-First drove the French from a strong battery of ten brass guns and two $13\frac{1}{2}$-inch brass mortars, without sustaining any loss. During the night a convention was signed, and on the following morning the French garrison marched out of the city of Genoa and evacuated all the defences.

In Lord William Bentinck's orders, dated Genoa, April 24, 1814, special mention is made of the services of Colonel Bruce, commanding First Battalion Thirty-First Regiment, and of the conduct of Captain Nunn and the light company of that regiment.

On April 27, the first battalion sailed as part of a force ordered to capture the island of Corsica, but on arrival at Ajaccio, the capital, it surrendered. The battalion then sailed for Bastia, the birthplace of Napoleon, where it landed on May 11 and remained until June 24, when it embarked for Sicily, and again went into garrison at Messina on July 18, 1814. Meanwhile great events had come about in France and Spain, culminating in the abdication of the Emperor Napoleon on April 4, 1814, and the restoration of the French monarchy. On October 14, 1814, the Second Battalion of the Thirty-First, whose share in the glories of the Peninsular War will be related in the next chapter, was disbanded at Portsmouth, and the officers and men fit for service were transferred to the first battalion, which they joined at Messina on May 6, 1815.

By this date it had become evident that the peace of Europe was not yet assured. The Emperor Napoleon had escaped from Elba at the end of February, had landed in France on March 1, had been joined by the army and re-established on the throne. The King of Naples, the Emperor's brother-in-law, at once repudiated his alliance with England and her allies, and issued a proclamation declaring the independence of Italy. The King then commenced hostilities with the Austrian army in that country. In consequence of these events Naples was invested by the Austrians in co-operation with the British fleet under Admiral Lord Exmouth, to whom the city presently surrendered.

The Thirty-First Regiment was consequently ordered from Sicily to Naples, where it arrived on May 25, 1815, and remained there until the restoration to his capital of the exiled Bourbon king, Ferdinand IV, which occurred on June 17, the day before the battle of Waterloo.

Being no longer required at Naples, the Thirty-First, early in July, was moved to Genoa, where it remained while the Sardinian dominions were being restored to their original ruler. In February 1816 the regiment embarked at Genoa for Malta, where it remained stationed until June 1818, when it returned home, landing at Deal on July 22, after a tour of foreign service of rather more than twelve eventful years. Although it had not been the good fortune of the First Battalion Thirty-First to share in the more famous actions of the Napoleonic war, it had served long and not ingloriously, often in bad climates, and once at least in very arduous conditions. Through these twelve years it had maintained a high character for courage and strict discipline in the field and for good conduct in quarters.

CHAPTER VI

THE SECOND BATTALION THIRTY-FIRST IN THE PENINSULAR WAR

Battle of Talavera—Mackenzie's Brigade—Battle of Albuera—The disaster to Coborne's Brigade—Major L'Estrange's square—Lord Mulgrave's letter—Battle of Vittoria—Battles of the Pyrenees, Nivelle, and Nive—Action of St. Pierre—Sir John Byng and the Colour—Action of Garris—Battle of Orthes—Battle of Toulouse—Disbanding of the Second Battalion.

LIST OF OFFICERS
SECOND BATTALION THIRTY-FIRST (HUNTINGDONSHIRE) REGIMENT WHO SERVED IN THE PENINSULAR WAR.

LIEUT.-COLONELS
    William Howe Campbell. Brigadier in Portuguese Army. Died in Portugal January 2, 1811.
    Alexander Leith. Commanded Battalion at Nivelle, and all subsequent actions in Peninsular War. Wounded at St. Pierre. Appointed K.C.B.

MAJORS
    John Williams Watson. Commanded Battalion at Talavera. Promoted Lieut.-Colonel Regiment of Dillon.
    Guy G. C. L'Estrange. Commanded Battalion at Albuera. Promoted Lieut.-Colonel 26th Regiment. Appointed C.B.
    John Stewart Hawkshaw.
    Robert Brice Fearon.

CAPTAINS
    William Lodge. Killed at Talavera.
    Edward Hawkshaw. Wounded at Albuera when serving with Portuguese Army.
    Thomas Samuel Nicols. Wounded at Talavera. Promoted Brevet-Major. Afterwards took name of Trafford by Royal Warrant.
    Francis Eagar.
    Charles Blomer.
    Edward Fleming. Wounded at Albuera. To 2nd West India Regiment in 1813.
    William Fagell. Retired on half-pay in 1810.

Edward Knox. Wounded at Albuera and at Garris. Previously wounded when in 1st Battalion.
George Coleman. Wounded at Talavera.
Thomas R. Hemsworth.
Hon. Thomas Henry Stewart. Died in Portugal, August 19, 1810.
Peter Fearon. Promoted Brevet-Major for Nivelle. Mortally wounded at Garris. Previously wounded at Rosetta with 1st Battalion.
Richard Cust.
William Beresford.
James Girdlestone. Wounded (1) Talavera; (2) Vittoria; (3) Pamplona; (4) Maya.
Patrick Dowdall. Wounded at Rosetta with 1st Battalion.

LIEUTENANTS

James Maxwell.
Samuel Hawkins.
Henry Simmonds. Adjutant vice Bayley.
Charles Bayley. Adjutant. Promoted in 36th Regiment.
William Gibson.
Hugh Lumley.
George Beamish. Wounded at Talavera.
Adderley Beamish. Wounded at Talavera. Afterwards took name of Bernard.
James Nangle.
William Butler. Wounded at Albuera.
Charles Kirby.
Richard Gethin. Wounded at Albuera.
Samuel Bolton. Wounded at Albuera.
James Cashell.
Andrew William Gamble. Wounded at Talavera.
Charles C. Bailey.
David McPherson.
Francis Knox.
Edward C. Thompson.
John W. Owens. Also served at Coruña attached to 50th Regiment.
Charles McCarthy.
Charles Kirby.
Loftus Nunn.
J. Maynard Goodliff. Wounded at Badajos.
James Elwyn.
Cornelius O'Connor.
George L'Estrange.

ENSIGNS

William Raymond.
R. Conyngham Soden. Mortally wounded at Talavera.
James Spence.
S. Boyle. Drowned November 28, 1809.
Samuel Wilson. Wounded at Albuera.
Thomas Clark.
George Miller.
James Eagar.
Ralph Nicholson. Wounded at Albuera.

Thomas Kirkblank.
James Thompson.
William Smyth.   Wounded at Pamplona.
G. H. Marsack.
James Hardy.
William Augustus Hardcastle.   Wounded at Aire.
Cornelius O'Connor.
Walter F. Kerr.
H. Astier.

ADJUTANTS
Charles Bayley.   Lieutenant.
Henry Simmonds.   Lieutenant.

PAYMASTER
R. Nangle.

QUARTERMASTER
William Wilcocks.
Andrew McIntosh.   Wounded at Pamplona.

SURGEONS
Fletcher Wells.
J. G. Van Millingen.

ASSISTANT SURGEONS
Henry Edwards.   Mortally wounded at Talavera.
Maurice Quill.
Edward Graham.

ON the departure, in April 1806, of the First Battalion Thirty-First from Winchester for service in Sicily, the Second Battalion, which had been raised some nine months before, remained for a time in that pleasant station. In June, however, the battalion was ordered to Gosport, and in January 1807 it embarked for Guernsey, arriving at St. Peter Port on the 15th of the month. Constant change of air seems to have been thought good for the young battalion, for in May of the same year it was moved to Ireland and was quartered at Limerick, whence it again moved in March 1808 to Dublin. Finally in August 1808 the battalion marched to Fermoy.

In this year England embarked on the great enterprise of the Peninsular War; the triumphant issue of which was the expulsion of the armies of Napoleon from Portugal and Spain and the turning of the tide of victory of that great conqueror. The campaign of 1808 in the Peninsular may be summarised in a few words. Sir Arthur Wellesley, afterwards the great Duke of Wellington, who commanded the force of about 14,000 British troops first thrown into the field, defeated a portion of the French army in the actions of

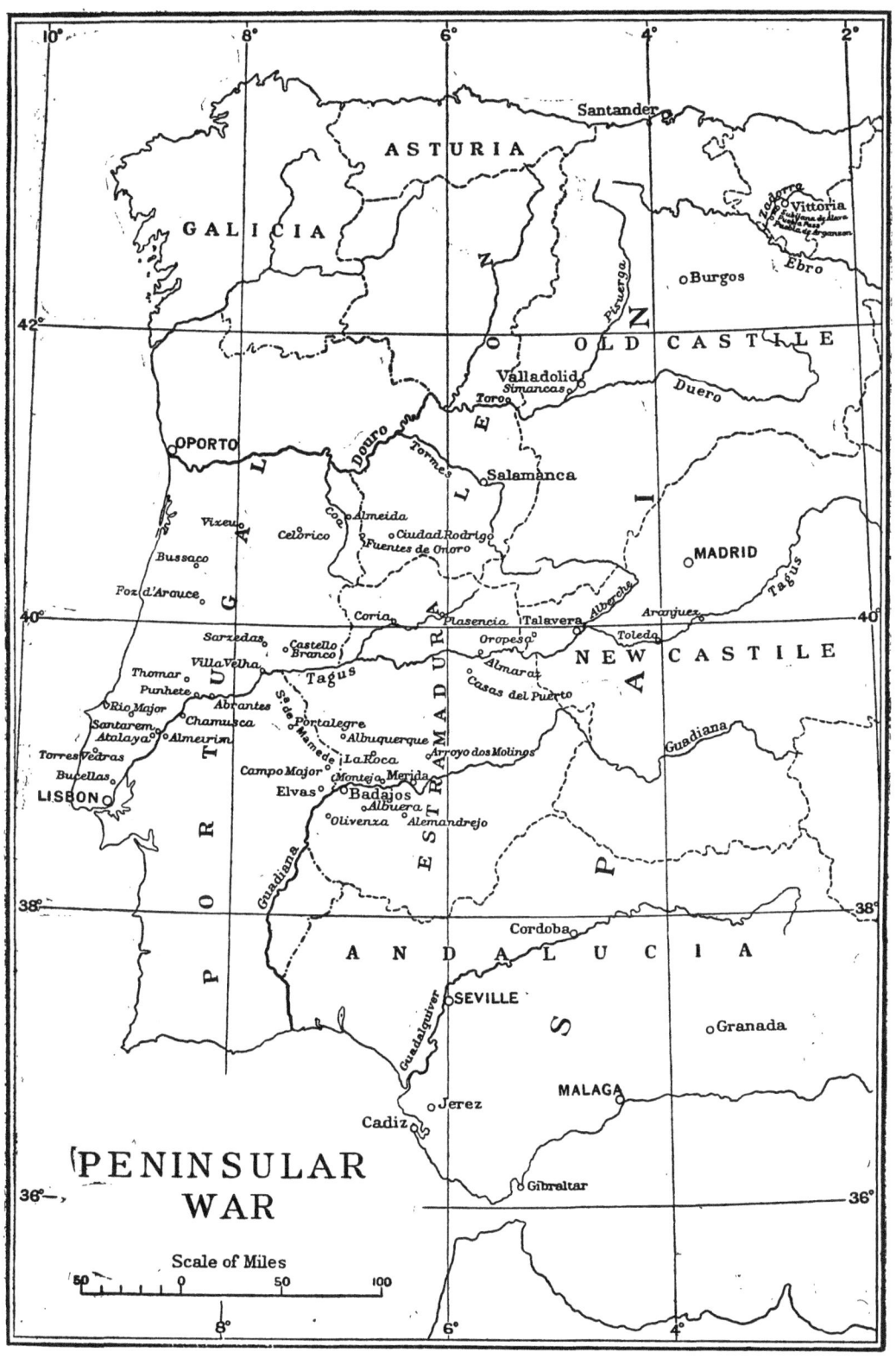

Roliça (fought on August 17) and of Vimeiro (fought on August 21). The command then passed out of Sir A. Wellesley's hands, and he, with the two general officers senior to him who had arrived in Portugal, concluded the convention of Cintra with Marshal Junot, the French Commander-in-Chief, by the terms of which the French army in Portugal was permitted to withdraw from the country and was to be conveyed back to France in British ships. On September 9 the British troops marched into Lisbon, and the campaign of 1808 in Portugal came to an end.

It was now decided by the British Government to make a vigorous advance into Spain, Lieutenant-General Sir John Moore being selected for the command of this enterprise; and large reinforcements for the army in the field were despatched from the United Kingdom. Among the corps selected for service was the Second Battalion Thirty-First, which after a stay of less than a month at Fermoy, marched under Lieut.-Colonel William Howe Campbell on September 8 to Monkstown for embarkation, and sailed a few days later to Falmouth, where a fleet was assembling to convoy the contingent for service in Spain under Lieutenant-General Sir David Baird. After some delay, General Baird's force, about 16,000 strong, sailed from Falmouth on October 9, and arrived at Coruña after a good passage on the 13th. Here the Second Battalion Thirty-First, together with the 3rd Battalion 27th Regiment, left Sir David Baird's army, being sent down to Lisbon to be changed for the Buffs and the 50th, old and seasoned regiments. Very soon after the arrival of the Thirty-First in Portugal, Lieut.-Colonel Campbell accepted employment in the Portuguese army under Marshal Beresford, who thus wrote of him to Sir Arthur Wellesley: "Campbell is really a most precious officer for this service: he has the principles necessary, he makes himself both feared and loved, and he is a very excellent disciplinarian." Major Guy L'Estrange of the Thirty-First also joined the Portuguese army at this period. The battalion arrived at Lisbon on November 5, and after a stay of some six weeks marched, under Major Watson, north-eastward towards the Spanish frontier as part of a force under Brigadier-General Richard Stewart ordered to reinforce the army of Sir John Moore. General Stewart's force, 2700 strong, arrived on December 28 at Castello Branco, on the frontier of Spain and Portugal, and, communications with Sir John Moore having been interrupted, was first ordered to halt, and subsequently, on January 1, 1809, to fall back on Lisbon.

When Brigadier-General Stewart had retired as far as Santarem, the news reached Sir John Cradock, who was in command of the army in Portugal, that Sir John Moore was advancing on Sahagun; and no attack on Portugal consequently being probable, General Cradock ordered Brigadier Stewart to halt at and about Santarem. The Second Battalion Thirty-First occupied cantonments at Bucellas, and after a month's marching in incessant rain the young battalion found much benefit in a rest in this pleasant quarter, where it was possible to repair the very inferior shoes in which the men had had their first experience of campaigning conditions.

The embarkation of Sir John Moore's army at Coruña, and its return to England at this period, did not affect the position of the troops under Sir John Cradock in Portugal. They were not molested by the French, and additional troops having arrived from England during March 1809, Lieutenant-General Cradock, on the 24th of that month, began once more to move towards the Spanish frontier. The total force in Portugal was then about 17,000 men, of whom, after providing the necessary garrisons and depôts, not more than 12,000 were available for service.

Up to this date it had been the intention of the British Government to do no more with the troops in Portugal than to defend that country from being again invaded by the French, while the task of freeing Spain was to be attempted from another direction, probably from the south. In March 1809, however, it was suddenly decided to raise the army in Portugal to as great a strength as means permitted, and to confer the command on Sir Arthur Wellesley, now considered the most capable commander in the British army. Never was there a more fortunate and timely appointment.

Sir Arthur Wellesley arrived at Lisbon on April 22, bringing with him 9200 troops, so that the total British force in Portugal numbered about 26,000 men. Sir Arthur determined to organise every available man of this force to take the field as quickly as possible, in order to attack the French army under Marshal Soult, which, after the embarkation of Moore's army at Coruña had been ordered by Napoleon to invade Portugal and had defeated the Portuguese troops and stormed the city of Oporto a month previously.

The " Division " as an unit, though not unknown in our army at this period, was only occasionally formed, and for his advance on Oporto Sir Arthur Wellesley contented himself by organising his infantry into eight British and one Hanoverian brigades, a Portuguese battalion being added to each brigade of the line.

The Second Battalion Thirty-First, with an effective strength of 784 rank-and-file; together with the 2nd Battalion 24th, 3rd Battalion 27th, and the 1st Battalion 45th, formed the Second Brigade, commanded by Major-General J. R. Mackenzie; and when in the first days of May 1809 Sir Arthur moved northward to attack Soult, this brigade, together with 7000 Portuguese troops, was left to guard southern Portugal against a possible attack from Estramadura by the First French Corps under Marshal Victor. The quarters allotted to the Second Battalion Thirty-First by Major General-Mackenzie were at Thomar, where the battalion remained until the army under Sir Arthur Wellesley had forced the passage of the Douro and captured Oporto from Marshal Soult, who was compelled to retire northward into Spain with the loss of all his guns, stores, and treasure. No sooner had Sir Arthur Wellesley thus disposed of Soult's army than he turned southward in order to attack that of Marshal Victor, in order to free the whole frontier of Portugal from any threat of attack. This operation was to be undertaken in conjunction with a Spanish army under Marshal Cuesta, and in the distribution of troops required for the new campaign the mixed force to the east of Lisbon under Major-General Mackenzie was broken up; the Portuguese troops going northward to join the army under Marshal Beresford, whose task it was to guard northern Portugal against the corps of Soult and Ney; while the Second Brigade joined the main army under Sir Arthur Wellesley.

Sir Arthur now formed his infantry in Divisions, and the Second Brigade, now consisting of the 2nd Battalion 24th, Second Battalion Thirty-First, and 1st Battalion 45th, together with the Third Brigade, formed the Third Division. The Division in the absence of a Lieutenant-General was placed under the command of Major-General J. R. Mackenzie, who also generally commanded his own brigade.

Having completed his preparations and arranged his plan of

campaign with Marshal Cuesta, Sir Arthur Wellesley marched from Abrantes on June 27, 1809, at the head of 23,000 British and German troops, with thirty guns, the Spanish army of 30,000 men under Marshal Cuesta being somewhat in advance and on his left. The British army crossed the frontier of Portugal at the end of June and arrived at Plasencia on July 9 and 10. On the latter day the Spanish army was at Casas del Puerto, not far from Almaraz, where was the right of Marshal Victor's position in rear of the river Tagus. The French left rested on Talavera and the main strength of Victor's Corps (about 23,000 men) lay on the river Alberche, a little east of that town.

After a long consultation on July 11 and a halt caused by almost insuperable difficulties regarding transport and supplies, the allied armies moved forward on Talavera on July 17, the British force being reduced by detachments to 21,000 men. The British marched on the right, the Spanish on the left. At this time the direction of Sir Arthur Wellesley's advance had been discovered by the French King, who hurried from Madrid with 5000 troops to reinforce Victor, while Marshal Soult at the head of three Corps was ordered southward on Plasencia, in order to fall on the left and rear of the allied British and Spanish armies.

Such was the position when on July 22 the allies bivouacked for the night, Mackenzie's (Third) Division, with Anson's Cavalry Brigade, being in advance, and close to Marshal Victor's position. Wellesley was anxious to attack on the next morning, but the Spanish General, who was old and worn out, though at first assenting, could not make up his mind to the enterprise and failed to advance. Marshal Victor was therefore permitted to retire unmolested in the night of July 23, and on the 24th was joined by the 4th Corps, his numbers then being raised to 43,000 men; and on finding before him Cuesta's army, which with rashness as great as its former timidity had advanced unsupported to within fifteen miles of Toledo, Victor at once came forward to the attack. The Spanish army beat a hurried and disorderly retreat, and it was thanks only to the sluggishness of the French pursuit that Cuesta arrived without serious loss at the Alberche on the evening of July 25. Here he found the north bank of the river held by Sherbrooke's and Mackenzie's Divisions, with Anson's cavalry brigade; and it was with the greatest difficulty that Sir Arthur Wellesley persuaded the Spanish Marshal to cross the river to the strong position near Talavera that Sir Arthur had selected during Cuesta's absence.

Battle of Talavera

Still unmolested, the Spanish army crossed the Alberche early on the morning of July 27, followed about 9 A.M. by Sherbrooke's Division; Mackenzie's Division and Anson's cavalry brigade remaining on the north side of the river to gain time for the allied army to take up its position. Soon the leading French troops came in sight, and about noon Mackenzie's regiments, forming the rear-guard of the Spanish army which was streaming across the plain to its post on the English right, fell back slowly, forded the stream, and presently made a stand in wooded ground about a mile distant from the south bank, near a ruined house called the Casa de Salinas. The ground being covered with dense underwood, it was considered that Anson's cavalry could not help and his brigade therefore was withdrawn to the rear of the infantry, which was ordered to protect its front by a chain of picquets. The Peninsular army, staff and regiments alike, it must be remembered, had still but little experience of war, and it appears that in some part of the Division out-post duty was on this occasion negligently performed.

Donkin's brigade, which was nearest to the river, was suddenly attacked early in the afternoon by the leading Division of Marshal Victor's corps, and two of Donkin's battalions fell back in confusion. In their retreat they came upon the Second Battalion Thirty-First, the left battalion of Mackenzie's own brigade, which with the 45th on the right and a half battalion of the 60th on the extreme left, made a stout resistance, thanks to which the two battalions above mentioned were presently rallied. "The Thirty-first," writes Mr. Fortescue,[1] "though only a second battalion, behaved remarkably well, bearing apparently the brunt of the fight, for it lost over one hundred killed and wounded. The Forty-fifth, a tough old regiment, was never shaken for a moment."

Mackenzie's Division now fell back slowly and steadily until it

[1] *History of the British Army*, vol. vii., page 227.

had cleared the wooded ground, when Anson's cavalry was able to come up and secure its flanks. In the course of the afternoon the retirement of the Division continued very steadily, though it was still hotly followed by the French, until in the dusk of evening the weary troops took up their allotted places in the Talavera position.

The losses of the Third Division in the action of Casa de Salinas amounted to 447 killed, wounded, and missing; those of the Second Battalion Thirty-First being Captain William Lodge and twenty-three sergeants, rank-and-file killed; five officers and eighty-eight sergeants, rank-and-file wounded, and two missing. Total 119. Mackenzie's Division, on joining the rest of the army, took up the ground that remained vacant; Mackenzie's own brigade in rear of the Guards' Brigade, and Donkin's on the left of the front line. In consequence of the confused state of the Spanish army, far away on the extreme right, Sir Arthur Wellesley had found it necessary to go and take charge of that flank. The dispositions of the British brigades on the left were consequently left, in some cases, to the judgment of their commanders, who acted as seemed to them best in the circumstances; with the unfortunate result that the high ground on the left of the British portion of the position, a point of vital importance, was very weakly held.

Meanwhile the whole of Marshal Victor's corps had crossed the Alberche, and the Marshal determined to follow up his surprise of the rear-guard by an equally-unexpected attack on the position taken up by the allied army. Observing that the Cerro de Medellin, the high ground mentioned above, was weakly held, Marshal Victor ordered General Ruffin's Division (nine battalions) to attack this point as soon as it was quite dark, while another portion of the French army boldly approaching the Spanish position on the right at about 7 P.M. drew from the Spaniards a heavy but ineffective fire, which disclosed their position. Alarmed as it appears by their own fire, the four left Spanish battalions threw down their arms and fled, leaving a great gap in the line, which Sir Arthur Wellesley filled with a British brigade from the second line.

The attack of Ruffin's Division on the British left was delivered soon after 9 P.M., and after a partial success was repulsed with considerable loss. In consequence of this dangerous attack and of a second panic outburst of fire in the Spanish position at midnight, the whole allied army spent a very disturbed night. Marshal Victor, too, finding that this night attack had failed, prevailed on King Joseph to make an attack in full strength in the early morning, and the noise caused by the preparatory movement of his guns by torchlight effectually prevented rest. The moon rose between one and two o'clock, and by its light the dark masses of Victor's troops could be seen marching into position for the coming battle.

At last dawn came and was eagerly hailed by both armies. The British troops, described by an observer as looking pale but determined, were ready for the encounter, while the French veterans came on in their usual gallant and imposing style.

Deducting the losses incurred on the 27th, and in the night attack, the French had over 45,000 troops in the field, with eighty guns. The Spanish army, which had been but very slightly engaged, numbered 32,000, and the British something over 22,000 of all ranks, with thirty guns; but the numbers who actually were engaged and did the fighting in the battle of Talavera, were 30,000 French infantry, who were opposed by 16,000 to 17,000 British infantry and some 2000 Spaniards.

The details of the battle, though deeply interesting to all students of the achievements of our army, can but be very briefly sketched in these pages, which have only to follow the fortunes of one of Sir Arthur Wellesley's battalions. Suffice it to say that at 5 A.M. on July 28, a signal gun set Marshal Victor's three Divisions in motion; and that after a very heavy artillery fire on the British left, to which but a weak reply could be made, the French columns came quickly forward, covered by a dense cloud of skirmishers. Protected by the steepness of the ground the French suffered little loss until they reached the summit of the Cerro de Medellin. Here they were immediately charged with the bayonet by the British regiments of the left, and after a furious fight were completely repulsed and pursued by the victorious English down the hill and across the Portina brook which ran at its foot. In this struggle, which lasted some forty minutes, Lieutenant-General Hill's troops lost between 700 and 800 men, while Marshal Victor's casualties were certainly heavier. Victor's attack had been made against King Joseph's judgment, the King wishing to wait for the arrival of Marshal Soult and his army from the north, but just after the repulse of the attack news came that Soult could not arrive for a week or more. It was then decided to make another attempt, Victor again attacking the Cerro de Medellin, while King Joseph, holding the Spanish army in check with a large force of cavalry, was to fall with the remainder of his infantry upon the British centre and right. The troops entrusted with this latter task were General Sebastiani's Division, 8000 strong, and the German Division of General Leval. In all the French infantry numbered about 30,000, while the British infantry had been reduced to little over 17,000 men. Sir Arthur Wellesley's position was, however, strengthened in one particular, General Cuesta sending at his request a considerable force of cavalry and infantry, of which Sir Arthur posted the cavalry in his left rear to guard against a turning movement, while the infantry was sent with the same object to some high ground clear of the British left.

At about half-past eleven the battle began on the British right, when General Leval's Germans attacked prematurely and were easily repulsed. Immediately after this a very strong attack was delivered by the French Divisions of Lapisse and Sebastiani against Lieutenant-General Sherbrooke's First Division, which had already suffered heavily from the French artillery. The French came on in two lines, with twelve battalions in each. Sherbrooke's Division (of three brigades) received this imposing attack with perfect steadiness, and having shattered the first French line with a single volley, charged and drove back the French in great confusion across the Portina brook. A little beyond the brook the centre British brigade was halted, but the brigade of Guards on the left and the Hanoverian brigade on the right unfortunately carried on the pursuit too impetuously, and came disconnectedly into contact with the French second line. These veteran troops at once saw their advantage, charged the Guards and Hanoverians and drove them back in confusion, and also drove back the centre British brigade from the advanced position that it had taken up. Had there been the slightest unsteadiness in Sir Arthur Wellesley's second line the day would have been lost.

Now was the time of trial for Mackenzie and his brigade, and nobly did they answer the call of duty. No order reached the Brigadier, for Sir Arthur was busily engaged in directing troops to support the broken Hanoverians, but no order was needed. Mackenzie without hesitation brought his brigade forward to meet the rush of the oncoming enemy, and they with the 48th Regiment (sent up on their left by Sir Arthur) stood firmly in line to hold the broken line of defence. Wheeling back to allow the Guardsmen to pass through their intervals, as did the 48th for the Hanoverians, Mackenzie's brigade quickly reformed line, opened a hot fire and engaged Sebastiani's vastly superior numbers in a savage infantry duel at close quarters. The strain on their endurance was great, but not of long duration. The Guards' brigade with fine discipline rallied instantly in their rear, and together with the Hanoverians quickly came forward and reinforced the first line, which, thus strengthened, soon established a superiority of fire over the French. Lapisse's veterans stood bravely for a time, but the General himself was killed and his Division soon afterwards fell back. Sebastiani's troops gave way next, and were charged in flank by Sir Stapleton Cotton's cavalry brigade which had been ordered forward by Sir Arthur Wellesley at the same time as the 48th Regiment. "Thus," says Mr. Fortescue, "the contest in the centre came to an end, both sides having suffered appalling losses in one of the stubbornest fights that occurred during the whole course of the war."

The repulse in the centre did not end the battle of Talavera. Leval's Germans came forward once more against the British right, where they were easily repulsed. As the Germans fell back they were charged by a Spanish cavalry regiment, which showed both courage and skill and inflicted heavy loss. About the same time Marshal Victor made an attempt to turn the British left, but this movement was easily checked and the French lost heavily from the Hanoverian heavy guns on the Cerro de Medellin. A courageous premature attempt by Anson's cavalry brigade to charge the French infantry resulted in failure. The battle, however, was now won, the French gradually drawing off out of range, and retiring altogether from contact with the British during the night.

The losses at Talavera were very severe on both sides. Those of the French are stated by Professor Oman to be 7268 killed, wounded and missing. On the side of the allies, the Spanish can have lost but little, but Sir Arthur Wellesley's losses on July 27 and 28 are thus detailed by the same authority : *Killed*, thirty-four officers, 767 men ; *wounded*, 196 officers, 3719 men ; *missing*, three officers, 639 men (chiefly Hanoverians). Grand total, 5363 : over a quarter of the number engaged.

Among the heaviest sufferers were Mackenzie's brigade, whose gallant commander was himself killed in the fine fight that saved the day at Talavera. Of his three battalions, the 2nd Battalion 24th sustained 352 casualties, all but nine of which occurred on July 28. The 1st Battalion 45th had twenty-five casualties on the 27th and 158 on the 28th, a total of 183. The Second Battalion Thirty-First which went into action on the 27th with a strength of 733 suffered 119 casualties on the 27th and 131 on the 28th, a total of 250. The losses of the Thirty-First in detail were : *Killed*, one officer, and forty-four of other ranks ; *wounded*, eight officers and 190 other ranks, and seven missing. The officer killed was Captain William Lodge, who fell on July 27, and those wounded were Captains T. S. Nicols and G. Coleman, Lieutenants George Beamish, Adderley Beamish and J. Girdlestone ; Ensigns A. W. Gamble and R. C. Soden ; and Assistant-Surgeon H. Edwards. When the wounded shortly afterwards fell into the hands of the French, by whom it may be added they were most kindly treated, Assistant-Surgeon H. Edwards remained in charge of the wounded and died at Talavera.[1]

It is unfortunate that, owing to the death of Major-General Mackenzie, no immediate report of the conduct of his Division on July 27, nor of his brigade on the 28th, was made to Sir Arthur Wellesley. Sir Arthur (who was created Lord Wellington for the victory of Talavera), consequently made no reference, in his original order concerning the

---

[1] Another casualty at Talavera was Peter, whose owner, Captain Edward Hawkshaw of the Thirty-First, writes of him : " Mr. Peter, my dog, fell most gloriously at Talavera. He had been found, after straying from me, by a soldier of the Regiment, who had kept him for almost two months, and at his feet he was shot. The poor fellow told me the story almost with tears. He himself had his arm shot so badly as to be unfit for any purpose. I happened to say, speaking of Peter : ' Poor fellow, I wish to God his master had been there too.' He replied immediately, ' Ah, Sir, I wish you had, I assure you we all pitied your Honour very much.' It was a most soldier-like reply of a poor fellow, pitying anyone who had not seen him (*i.e.* Peter) fall in such a glorious action."

Captain Hawkshaw was employed with the Portuguese army, and was not at Talavera. His subsequent distinguished services at Albuera will be mentioned later.

battle, to the fine conduct of Mackenzie's troops in the two days' fighting, and a supplementary order issued by him two days later has been generally overlooked. Sir William Napier, who for many years was the only historian of the Peninsular War recognised as an authority, was not present at Talavera, nor, as it appears, thoroughly aware of what took place. Consequently it was not until the publication of the second volume of Professor Oman's " History of the Peninsular War," in 1903, that Mackenzie and his regiments received the honour that was their due. It is primarily then to Professor Oman that the East Surrey Regiment owes a deep debt of gratitude for telling the full story of Talavera, and for the tribute that he pays to the conduct of Mackenzie's brigade in that battle. Mr. Fortescue, the historian of the British Army, it may be added, fully concurs in Professor Oman's opinion that Mackenzie's brigade saved the fortunes of the day on July 28, 1809.

The general order referring to the services of the Second Battalion Thirty-First ran as follows :—

Talavera de la Regna, 31st July, 1809.

"The Commander of the Forces omitted in his orders of the 29th instant to draw the attention of the army to the conduct of the . . . 2nd Battalion 31st Regiment, as intended to have been reported by the late Major General M'Kenzie . . . not having received these reports when the orders were issued. He begs that . . . and Major Watson will accept his acknowledgements for the behaviour of the gallant corps under their command respectively, and he will not fail to report their good conduct."

It is understood that the promised report was written by Lord Wellington, but was lost through shipwreck on its way to England.

Major John Williams Watson, who commanded the battalion in the battle, was awarded a gold medal, and was very soon after rewarded by promotion to the rank of Lieutenant-Colonel in the Regiment of Dillon.

The death of Major-General Mackenzie and the heavy losses of the Third Division at Talavera caused radical changes to be made in its composition. Major-General Robert Crawfurd's light brigade, which reached the army, after its famous forced march, on the morning after the battle, joined the Division, and Crawfurd himself succeeded to its command. Donkin's and Mackenzie's brigades were amalgamated, and became Donkin's brigade. This arrangement, however, did not long affect the Second Battalion Thirty-First, for on September 15, 1809, it was transferred to Major-General Tilson's (Third) Brigade, forming part of the Second Division (Hill's). The other battalions of the Third Brigade were the 1st Battalion Buffs, the 2nd Battalion 48th, and the 2nd Battalion 66th.

We must now briefly trace the movements of the army after the battle of Talavera.

On July 29, and perhaps for a day or two afterwards, Lord Wellington was unable to march. His troops were exhausted by two days' hard fighting, with but little to eat; but it soon became evident that a move must be made westward, where Marshals Soult and Ney were threatening the lines of communication. After some disputes between Wellington and Cuesta, it was decided that the British should undertake this task, while the Spaniards were to hold Talavera; and on August 3 Wellesley set out for Oropesa. No sooner had the British marched off than Marshal Cuesta abandoned Talavera, in which town the British wounded had been left. All of them who were disabled from marching, to the number of 1500, consequently became prisoners-of-war when that town was occupied by Marshal Victor on August 5. Among those who became prisoners-of-war at Talavera were five wounded officers of the Thirty-First, who remained in captivity until the peace of 1814. The history of the wounded non-commissioned officers and men has not been traced, but in all probability a small proportion of them escaped during the march to France and the remainder, with the officers, remained prisoners until 1814.

There followed a period of marches and counter-marches, in which the British and Spanish armies repeatedly changed their positions, in the endeavour to check the operations of the French commanders. All Lord Wellington's movements were carried out in the face of incessant obstruction and contradiction on the part of Marshal Cuesta, and in spite of deficiencies of supplies which reduced the British army almost to a state of starvation. These privations, coupled with hard work and the great heat of the weather, at length compelled Wellington to fall back. A letter written by him on August 19 to Marshal Beresford, the Commander-in-Chief of the Portuguese army, gives an idea of the sufferings of the British :—

" Our men are falling sick, and we have nothing to give them in the way of comforts; and our horses are dying by hundreds in the week. We have not had a full ration of provisions ever since the 22nd of last month; and I am convinced that in that time the men have not received ten days' bread, and the horses not three regular deliveries of barley. We have no means of transport, and I shall be obliged to leave my ammunition on the ground on quitting this place."

Fortunately the French were little, if at all, better off, and so with both combatants brought to a standstill by starvation, the campaign of Talavera flickered out. On September 3, Wellington moved his headquarters to Badajos near the Portuguese frontier, and cantoned his army from Campo Mayor and Olivenza in the west to Merida and Alemandrejo on the east. The Second Battalion Thirty-First was cantoned at Montejo, where the sickness caused by the privations of the campaign, no longer kept at bay by its excitement, caused a considerable number of deaths. On November 1, the strength of the battalion was: Officers twenty-five, sergeants forty-three, drummers twenty, rank-and-file 674, of whom no less than 405 were sick.

The Campaign of 1810

In the Talavera campaign Lord Wellington, as we have seen, adopted a bold, aggressive line of action. Taking advantage of the dispersion of the French armies in Spain and of the jealousies of Napoleon's Marshals, he had struck out, first to the north and then to the east, sweeping the French invaders clean out of Portugal, and by a hazardous advance he had at Talavera arrived within no great distance of Madrid. Had the Spanish commander and his army been as efficient as the individuals of the latter were brave and patriotic, Madrid might well have been occupied and the French cause rendered desperate in one campaign. As it was, the campaign, thanks to the skill of the English general and the determination of his troops, ended in a great victory, but the victory had narrowly missed being a defeat, and the Spanish army was conclusively proved to be an untrustworthy ally, ready to fight but unable to manœuvre. It had been found too that Spanish promises of food and money, the sinews of war, could not be trusted, and Wellington, after Talavera, saw plainly that for some time to come he must satisfy himself by defending Portugal and leave the liberation of Spain to be undertaken later.

Napoleon, on the other hand, blamed his brother King Joseph and his Marshals for the failures of 1809. He declared that they must be retrieved in 1810, and with this object in view he poured reinforcements across the Pyrenees, raising the strength of King Joseph's army to 297,000 men. With this force, the Emperor wrote, Spain and Portugal must be subdued and the English driven into the sea. The campaign of 1810 should have shown Napoleon how completely he underrated his opponent.

Put as briefly as possible, the plan of Napoleon for the subjugation of Portugal was as follows. That country was to be invaded at two points. The northern and main attack was to be made in the neighbourhood of Ciudad Rodrigo by *the army of Portugal*, 80,000 strong, under Marshal Masséna. In the south Marshal Soult, who could dispose of 60,000 men, was to pierce the frontier near Badajos. In support of these attacks was a third army, numbering 24,000 men, under King Joseph.

Lord Wellington, to meet this formidable movement, divided his forces into two parts. He himself, with 25,000 men, mainly British but partly Portuguese, established his headquarters at Celorico. To Lieutenant-General Hill, who had gained his complete confidence in the campaign of Oporto and Talavera, he entrusted 10,000 men, of whom about half were British and half Portuguese. With this force Hill was to act as a right flank guard to Lord Wellington and too protect the south-eastern frontier against Soult's *army of the south*. General Hill's own Division was included in his little army, and the Second Battalion Thirty-First therefore served the campaigns of 1810 under that able and kindly soldier, who was trusted and beloved by every man of the Peninsular army, from Lord Wellington downwards.

Unlike his opponents Lord Wellington was compelled to put all his available troops fit for active service in his front line, but in support he had 30,000 men of the Portuguese army, rapidly ripening for war under the firm hand of Marshal Beresford; and a like number of militia, who were fairly qualified for garrison duty and the defence of fortified posts.

As it happened by the fortune of war that the corps of Lieutenant-General Hill (promoted to this rank for his services at Oporto and Talavera) saw much marching and countermarching, but next to no fighting in 1810, the story of its operations must be briefly told. When the year opened, the headquarters of the Second Division were at Abrantés, and there General Hill's force gradually collected. Lord Wellington had gone north a little before, and on January 12 had established his own headquarters at Vizeu. Hill remained quietly at Abrantés, his depôt for supplies, till February, being aware that Marshal Soult could not advance suddenly or swiftly. On February 12 news was received that a corps commanded by Marshal Mortier had marched on Badajos, and General Hill at once issued orders to his various brigades and units to prepare for an advance to the frontier, which began on the following day. General Hill's headquarters arrived at Portalegre on February 18, where a strong position was taken up. General Hill was instructed to hold Portalegre as long as possible. On April 21 a portion of the Spanish army under General Romana was attacked and destroyed at La Roca, near Badajos, by General Reynier. Hill at once moved forward to meet this threatening movement, marching through the Serra de Mamede towards Albuquerque. Reynier then fell back on Merida and Hill returned to Portalegre on April 26. On May 15 Hill again advanced, on this occasion in the direction of Badajos, but in a few days returned to his old position.

Lord Wellington's headquarters at this time were at Celorico, with a corps of observation under Brigadier-General R. Craufurd pushed far to his front along the frontier. On July 23 Craufurd, who had acted contrary to his orders, was attacked beyond the Coa by a largely superior force under Marshal Ney, and narrowly escaped losing his whole brigade.

Hill at the beginning of the month had been at Campo Major, with the intention of again operating in Spain in conjunction with General Romana, but it was now apparent that his services would be essential further to the north, General Reynier having marched from Merida towards Almaraz, crossing the Tagus on July 16. Hill consequently made a parallel movement and crossing the river at Villa Velha arrived at Castello Branco¹ on the 20th, and on the 23rd at Atalaya, where he was within two marches of Lord Wellington's right. Here Hill halted by Wellington's order, for Reynier had continued his northward march, and on July 27 headed for Ciudad Rodrigo. His mission was in fact to occupy, and puzzle Hill. Lord Wellington believing that Masséna was about to concentrate his army for a sudden attack, now prepared to fall back. On July 31 General Reynier turned westward again and marched into Portugal, threatening Hill and keeping his force continually on the alert, and effectually preventing him from joining Lord Wellington.

Soon after this the orders of Napoleon to Masséna fell into the hands of Lord Wellington, who being consequently aware of the destination of Reynier's Corps ordered Hill on August 3 to Sarzedas; Hill's cavalry under Major-General Anson meanwhile keeping touch with Reynier.

In August Masséna's army besieged the fortress of Almeida, which was held by a Portuguese garrison. In consequence of a disastrous explosion Almeida was compelled to surrender on August 28, and early in September Lord Wellington was obliged to draw back slightly from the frontier. Marshal Masséna, however, advanced with great difficulty through want of supplies, and from sickness and other losses was now compelled to call Reynier's Corps to join him.

His strength thus raised to 65,000 men Masséna on September 15 began a steady advance, which continued until eleven days later he found Lord Wellington's army drawn up ready to receive his attack at Bussaco. Hill's corps had joined the main body by nine o'clock in the morning of that day, and had then been posted by Wellington on the extreme right of the Serra de Bussaco, where he had decided to block Masséna's further advance towards Lisbon.

The battle of Bussaco took place on the following day, September 27, resulting in one of Wellington's most famous victories, but as Masséna's attack was delivered against a distant portion of the long position, General Hill's troops were not engaged and sustained no casualties. It must, therefore, be sufficient to say that in his two main attacks

---

¹ While at Castello Branco Captain the Honourable Thomas Henry Stewart, Thirty-First Regiment, was seized with fever and died at that place on August 19, 1810. Captain Stewart was a younger brother of Lord Castlereagh and of Major-General the Honourable Charles Stewart, afterwards Third Marquess of Londonderry.

Marshal Masséna actually employed 26,000 men, who were decisively repulsed by about 15,000. The defending force was, it is fair to add, aided by a strong position, and the French attacked gallantly, their officers especially showing great courage and self-devotion.

After Bussaco Masséna drew off for a time, endeavouring to find some means of slipping past Wellington's position, and owing to the superior strength of the French Lord Wellington considered it necessary to fall back towards the great defensive position of Torres Vedras, which he had prepared in anticipation of an invasion of Portugal. Lieutenant-General Hill's corps still acted as a right flank guard during this retirement, which was most difficult of execution, as the whole Portuguese population with its entire moveable property was also to retire in rear of the lines.

In such circumstances it was practically impossible to fight another rear-guard action, so Wellington's retirement continued, much to the surprise of Masséna, who was unaware of the existence of the lines of Torres Vedras, and could not imagine why the army which had beaten him at Bussaco was now fleeing before him. However he pushed on, and the British-Portuguese army, hampered by the flying population of central Portugal, marched away from him until, on October 10, they entered and passed through the great defensive lines, so secretly prepared by the wisdom of Wellington. On the following day the leading brigade of French cavalry found stretching before it a long line of earthworks, and by October 15 Marshal Masséna was gazing at the task before him and wondering what he should do. By November 10 the French army, having exhausted the scanty resources of the country that there had not been time to remove, saw starvation staring it in the face, and Masséna, who had found no means of attacking Torres Vedras, ordered a general retreat on Santarem. As soon as it was clear that the French were retiring, Wellington issued from his lines and followed the invaders up. He did not, however, find it expedient to make a serious attack on his powerful enemy, and the campaign of 1810 ended somewhat tamely, with the main French army, very short of food, settled between Thomar and Santarem, with a detachment at Punhete; while Wellington's field army was established by December 1 along the line Rio Major—Valle de Santarem, with Hill's Division, still on the right, stationed along the south bank of the Tagus between Almeirim and Chamusca.

As will be seen from the above very condensed narrative of the campaign of 1810, the Second Division and Hill's corps generally, though taking a full and important part in the year's work, had by the fortune of war a record of hard marching and constant vigilance rather than of fighting. Hill himself, who had gained a reputation second only to that of Lord Wellington in the Peninsular Army, was compelled to go home on sick leave when he had settled his troops in their winter quarters. As for his regiments, the year's campaign had hardened them into magnificent and experienced troops, equal to any trial of war. The Second Battalion Thirty-First had started the year with a strength of no more than twenty-seven officers and 400 men, and when it entered the lines of Torres Vedras, this strength was practically unaltered. The battalion found itself, however, under different commanders, for during General Hill's absence his Division and corps were commanded by Major-General the Honourable William Stewart, and the command of Stewart's brigade (formerly Tilson's) was taken over by Lieutenant-Colonel Colborne of the 2nd Battalion 66th Regiment, afterwards Field-Marshal Lord Seaton. Colonel Colborne remained in command of the brigade until its destruction at the battle of Albuera.

Campaign of 1811

The Anglo-Portuguese and French armies remained face to face until March 1811. Marshal Masséna for some time hoped for substantial assistance from Marshal Soult, who had been ordered by the Emperor Napoleon to advance into Portugal by way of Badajos. Soult duly advanced and took possession of Badajos from a cowardly or traitorous Spanish commandant on March 10, but in consequence of the defeat of his southern army by General Graham at Barossa on March 5, found himself unable to assist Masséna. The latter on the same day decided to withdraw his starving army from Portugal, which difficult operation he carried out with great skill. Masséna's rear-guard was commanded by Marshal Ney, who displayed the same tactical skill and tenacity that subsequently were so conspicuous in the French retreat from Moscow.

Marshal Masséna's army in its retirement from Portugal was closely pressed by Lord Wellington and endured great suffering. It is estimated that his army while in that country lost no less than 30,000 men, of whom a great number died of starvation or disease; about 6000 perishing in the retreat from before Torres Vedras alone. This loss might perhaps have been made greater, but for the detemination of Lord Wellington to husband his troops for the offensive campaign on which he had decided.

We are not concerned with the pursuit of Marshal Masséna from Portugal, as on reaching Foz d'Aronce, Lord Wellington had despatched Marshal Beresford at the head of about 20,000 British and Portuguese troops to attempt the re-capture of Badajos. The British troops in this force numbered about 7000 men, and included the Second and Fourth Divisions of infantry, a cavalry brigade, and other troops. Before coming into contact with Soult's army, Marshal Beresford was joined by 14,000 Spanish troops, so that his total force was about 35,000 men. Beresford arrived before Badajos on April 20, after some delay caused by his having to bridge the Guadiana, and by the movements of the corps commanded by Marshal Mortier. Lord Wellington, whose troops had invested Almeida on April 9, rode down to consult with Beresford, and reaching his headquarters on April 22, reconnoitred Badajos with him. Immediately after this Lord Wellington returned to his own army, in anticipation of an attack by Marshal Masséna; and he arrived in fact in good time to command at the battle of Fuentes de Oñoro fought on May 3 and 5.

Meanwhile Beresford, who had begun his siege of Badajos on May 6, found that Soult was coming forward in strength to attack him, and on May 13 was obliged to raise the siege and march towards a fairly strong postition which he had selected behind the river Albuera, where he was attacked on May 16. There followed one of the most bloody battles of the Peninsular war, in which the Second Battalion Thirty-First bore a fortunate and distinguished part.

The force with which Marshal Beresford determined to face the attack of Soult in round numbers was as follows; British, 10,400; Portuguese, 10,200; Spanish, 14,600: Total, 35,200. Marshal Soult's army numbered slightly over 24,000 men. Marshal Beresford's position consisted of a long rolling line of low hills, extending for several miles along the Albuera brook. The stream was fordable in many parts and offered no obstacle to the attack, but owing to the gentle slope up to the British position there was no dead ground, a circumstance which strongly favoured the defence. Marshal Beresford considered that the weakest part of his position was his centre, posted in Albuera village, and drew up his army in anticipation of an attack in that quarter. His right stood on higher ground, and was entrusted to 12,000 Spanish troops under General Blake, disposed in two lines, each of three brigades. In the centre of the position were the Second Division, under Major-General the Honourable William Stewart, and in advance of them Albuera village was held by two Hanoverian battalions. On the left was a Portuguese Division, with a British brigade in support, guarded on the flank by a weak cavalry brigade of 800 sabres. In rear of the centre, as a general reserve, were two brigades of the Fourth Division, one British and one Portuguese, and a weak Spanish brigade. The bulk of the cavalry was divided between the extreme right and the reserve. All Marshal Beresford's troops were hidden from view except the two German battalions in Albuera, the Portuguese cavalry away on the left flank, and the Spanish cavalry on the extreme right.

Marshal Soult, who was under the impression that the Spanish army had not arrived, determined to occupy his enemy's attention by a feint attack on his centre, while making a circling movement in order to make his real attack on the allied right. Believing as he did that he had only to deal with the British and Portuguese contingents, he naturally thought that so extended a position must be weakly held, and that the long line could be rolled up from a flank. He therefore despatched one brigade (3500 men) to attack Albuera, and two complete Divisions and an additional brigade to attack the allied right. Marshal Soult began operations at 8 A.M., and about an hour later his main body, supported by a magnificent cavalry force of 3500 men under General Latour Mauburg, came on very rapidly against the right flank and caught the unfortunate Spaniards in the act of changing front to meet the French attack. One Spanish brigade alone faced 8400 French infantry, while six other Spanish battalions hurriedly sent to the rescue, though they came on bravely, could not reinforce until the French attack had begun. The Spaniards, however, all fought gallantly, Marshal Beresford himself posting the reinforcements as they came up, and for a time it seemed as if the right might hold its own until the Second Division, who had been summoned from the centre, could come to the rescue.

On they came, straining every nerve to be in time, with Colborne's brigade leading. In front were the Buffs, followed in succession by the 48th, 66th, and Thirty-First. With them came not only their Brigadier, one of the coolest and bravest soldiers in the army, but Stewart the Divisional General also, equally brave, but impetuous to a fault.

Marshal Beresford had intended that the Second Division should be formed in line and so attack the great French column, but Major-General Stewart, who had only received general orders to support the Spaniards, decided to move up on the Spanish right and take the French in flank. This movement might well have succeeded, and as time to Stewart seemed everything, he ordered the battalions of Colborne's brigade to hurry to the front and deploy in succession. This resulted in an echelon movement, with the Buffs clear of the Spanish right, the 48th and 66th passing through it, and the Thirty-First, still in column, coming up in the left rear. Now a dreadful catastrophe befell Colborne's unfortunate brigade, strung out as they were in this weak formation. General Latour Mauburg, a brilliant cavalry leader, was waiting for an opportunity to charge, which was suddenly given him by a blinding shower of rain and hail. Under its cover the French cavalry charged the Buffs in flank and rear, rolled them up in an instant, and then swept down on the two next battalions. The word annihilation is rarely justifiable in military history, but it is stated that in five minutes these three of Colborne's four battalions lost fifty-eight officers out of eighty, and 1160 men out of 1568: a very large proportion were killed, Latour Mauburg's Polish Lancers showing no mercy and slaughtering the wounded. The Second Battalion Thirty-First being, as we have said, slightly in rear and still in column, happily escaped the fate of their brothers-in-arms. The French cavalry immediately attacked them, but the little battalion, which only numbered 418 of all ranks, was ably handled by Major L'Estrange, whose men displayed the finest qualities of coolness and discipline. L'Estrange,[1] quick as thought, formed square by an original manœuvre of his own devising,

[1] Major L'Estrange was in the prime of life, having entered the army in 1798. His "Albuera square" formation continued to be practised in the Thirty-First until the year 1856.

Lieut.-General Sir Guy L'Estrange, K.C.B.
(who commanded the 2nd Bn. 31st Regiment at Albuera).

and had no difficulty in withstanding the attack of the French Lancers and Dragoons; and then having cleared his front, moved up to the summit of the hill, where he bore for a considerable time the entire brunt of the French infantry attack. In his report on this unfortunate episode of the battle, Major-General Stewart reported that the conduct of the First Brigade was very gallant; well-deserved praise, for the three battalions whose formation was broken fought doggedly to the last, forming groups or rallying squares round their officers, neither asking nor receiving quarter; while the conduct of the weak battalion of the Thirty-First, in beating off the sudden attack of an imposing force of cavalry flushed with success, and commanded by one of Napoleon's finest leaders, received universal praise.

Marshal Beresford's next action was to bring up two brigades to relieve the exhausted Spaniards, and the second stage of the battle consisted in the famous resistance offered by the right brigade (Hoghton's), aided by the Second Battalion Thirty-First, against the attack of the entire Fifth Corps; a line of 1900 men two deep opposed to a mass of 8000, twelve deep on an equal front. "This," says Professor Oman, "was the hardest and most splendid fighting done that day."[1] It was in this struggle that the 57th Regiment earned the proud title of "the Die-hards," and it was not the only regiment that might have received it. Lord Londonderry in his "History of the Peninsular War," names the 57th and Thirty-First as equal in bravery in this action.

Marshal Soult had now discovered the large numbers opposed to him and decided to act with caution, but still the attack on Beresford's right continued and seemed likely to succeed by sheer weight of numbers. Eventually the day was saved by an advance of Cole's Fourth Division, so long held in reserve. Major-General Cole had a long distance to cover and the move was a dangerous one in the presence of Latour Mauburg's cavalry. He, however, boldly moved forward in line, his flanks carefully guarded by battalions in column; on the right a battalion of nine Light Infantry companies, and on the left a battalion of the Loyal Lusitanian Legion, commanded by Major Edward Hawkshaw of the Thirty-First, who had served in Holland with the regiment.

---

[1] Oman's *History of the Peninsular War*, vol. iv. p. 386.

Cole's [1] attack, thus ably planned and executed, won the victory. The French cavalry charged again, but were stopped by the steady firing of a Portuguese brigade ; and after a desperate struggle, in which the British Fusilier brigade lost half its strength, the French infantry broke and was driven down the hill in confusion. The final and victorious charge of the brigade was led by Major Hawkshaw, who at the last moment received a wound at close quarters, from which he suffered to the end of his life. The Brigadier and all the other commanding officers in the brigade had been killed or disabled previously. Drenching rain came on, and so ended this terrible day's fighting, the most bloody in all the long Peninsular War.

The number of British troops in the field at Albuera (including the Hanoverian battalions) was 10,449 men. Their total loss was 206 officers and 3953 men. Five-sixths of this loss, moreover, fell on the three brigades of Colborne, Hoghton, and Myers, which actually sustained 3502 casualties out of 5732 men; a proportion seldom exceeded in a victorious army. The Portuguese casualties numbered 389, of which 171 were in Major Hawkshaw's Battalion of the Lusitanian Legion. The Spanish casualties numbered 1368. The French lost about 7000 out of 24,000 in the field, and were unable to attack Beresford again before Lord Wellington with two Divisions came to his assistance. The Second Battalion Thirty-First went into action at Albuera with twenty officers and 398 of other ranks. Its casualties were three sergeants and forty-five rank-and-file killed or mortally wounded ; seven officers and one hundred sergeants, rank and file wounded ; or 155 casualties out of 418 present. The names of the sergeants and rank-and-file who were killed or who died of their wounds were as follows :

SERGEANTS
　Hugh Blair.
　William Elliot.
　John Marshall.

CORPORALS
　John Mullon.
　William Swan.
　James Synnet.
　James Scanlan.

PRIVATES
　James Brown.
　Pat Carney.
　Daniel Cronin.
　John Dowde.
　James Evans.
　Thomas Fisher.
　John Flannagan.
　John Frost.
　Thomas Fryer.

[1] Major-General the Hon. G. L. Cole gained his first experience of war as a young captain in the Seventieth Regiment in the West Indies, 1793–94.

John Harwood.
James Hulton.
Owen Kenony.
John Nelson.
John Orrell.
Thomas Peale.
John Quinn.
George Rafferty.
John Robertson.
Thomas Snipe.
John Stanley.
James Woods.
John Edwards.
William Hagerty.
Joseph Hamilton.
James Kennedy.

John Major.
James Parkinson.
Thomas Connor.
James Harper.
John Hill.
James Sheehy.
John Gosling.
Dennis Dougherty.
Peter Bradley.
John Sheridan.
Edward Taylor.
George Shaw.
Owen Murphy.
Anthony Collins.
Edward Marshall.
John Murphy.

The officers wounded were Captains E. Fleming and E. Knox; Lieutenants W. Butler, R. Gethin, and S. Bolton; Ensigns J. Wilson and R. Nicholson. Lord Wellington in a letter to the Military Secretary to the Commander-in-Chief thus wrote of the Second Battalion Thirty-First and its commanding officer at Albuera: "There is one officer, Major L'Estrange of the Thirty-First, whom I must recommend in the strongest manner for promotion in some way or other. After the other parts of the same brigade were swept off by the cavalry this little battalion alone held its ground against all the *colonnes en masse*." Lord Wellington thus confirms the statement that after the disaster to the remainder of Colborne's brigade, the Thirty-First, single handed, held the crest of the hill and defended the Spanish infantry against the assault of Soult's massed columns. It appears from the following letter written to Major L'Estrange by Lord Mulgrave, the Colonel of the Thirty-First, that the services of the Second Battalion were fully recognised in England:

Harley Street. June 6th, 1811.

My Dear Sir,—When I received your very interesting and intelligent, and (as it turned out) most modest letter of the 18th of May I was not aware from its contents, that you had at the Head of the 31st Regiment arrested the successful progress of the enemy, and turned the tide of battle.

The publication of the "Gazette," determined me to discharge as soon as possible, the duty incumbent upon me as Colonel of the Regiment of stating your claims to the Commander-in-Chief, but before I could carry that intention into effect, the vigilant justice of his Royal Highness the Commander-in-Chief had rendered it unnecessary, by your promotion, on which I most cordially congratulate you.

Never was rank more nobly achieved or more honourably borne. My praises can add nothing to the general applause which the conduct of the 31st and its leader on the glorious 16th of May has excited, but I beg of you not to let them think me insensible of their merit or of the Impression which it has made on their countrymen.

The interesting anecdote which you told me of Marshal Beresford has not been generally known and I have felt much obliged to you for enabling me to give others, who like myself feel a personal interest in everything which relates to him, an opportunity of enjoying with me that Trait of his energy, gallantry and presence of mind.

I cannot conclude without again congratulating you on the mode of acquiring that most important step in the scale of professional rank.

Believe me with great regard,
Yrs very sincerely and faithfully,
MULGRAVE.

Lt.-Col. L'Estrange.

On the morning after the battle Marshal Beresford and his generals found themselves employed in a strange task. From shattered brigades they had to form battalions, while the survivors of many battalions had to be grouped together to form fighting units. For a time the remains of the two brigades, those of Colborne and Hoghton, were formed into as many battalions; one formed of the two battalions of the 48th Regiment, and the other of the survivors of the Buffs, 29th, Thirty-First, 57th, and 66th Regiments.[1] In time, however, slightly-wounded men rejoined the ranks, and on a subsequent redistribution of units the Second Battalion Thirty-First and 2nd Battalion 66th were united and styled the First Provisional Battalion. Major Alexander Leith having arrived in Spain on being posted to the Second Battalion from the First Battalion Thirty-First, was appointed to the command of the battalion thus formed, and retained it until the end of the war. As the title "Provisional" shows, it had not been Lord Wellington's intention to maintain this arrangement. In other

[1] Strength of Lieut.-Colonel Colborne's Provisional Battalion, June 24, 1811. Buffs 79, 29th Regiment 135, 2nd Thirty-First 202, 57th Regiment 242, 66th Regiment 155. Total, 813.

cases, regiments that had suffered very heavy losses were sent home to England to recruit, or were brought up to fighting strength by drafts. The First Battalions of the Thirty-First and 66th being, however, also on active service, there was no possibility of recruiting up their Second Battalions, and so, as has been stated, they remained a composite corps until the end of the Peninsular War. The services of Major L'Estrange at Albuera were promptly rewarded by his promotion to a Brevet-Lieut.-Colonelcy, and soon afterwards to that substantive rank in the 26th Regiment.

After the battle of Fuentes de Oñoro Lord Wellington considered himself strong enough to attempt the capture of Badajos. Leaving, therefore, nearly 30,000 men to guard the Portuguese frontier and repair Almeida (which had been evacuated by its French garrison), he marched rapidly with two divisions to join the army under Marshal Beresford. Outstripping his troops, Lord Wellington arrived at Elvas on May 19 and there received Beresford's despatch describing Albuera. Soult and his army were now in retreat, followed by the allied cavalry, and Lord Wellington calculated that he had a month in which to take Badajos before the French armies could again advance to attack him. A few days later Lieutenant-General Rowland Hill rejoined the army from England, and, Marshal Beresford returning to his special duty of training the Portuguese army, Lord Wellington placed General Hill in command of Beresford's Albuera army and ordered him to take up a position to cover Badajos against a French attack. The Second Battalion Thirty-First thus found themselves under their old commander, for they remained in the Second Division. The old First Brigade of that division was, however, reconstituted, and the Thirty-First were posted to the Second Brigade under Brigadier-General John Byng, who commanded it for the remainder of the war. The Brigade consisted of the 1st Battalion Buffs; 1st Battalion 57th; First Provisional Battalion (Thirty-First and 66th); and one company of the 5th Battalion 60th Regiment.

The second siege of Badajos lasted from May 29 till June 10, during which time two assaults had been repulsed with considerable loss, and it had become evident that the town could not be taken in the time at Lord Wellington's disposal. Marshal Marmont marching southward from Salamanca had joined Soult, and Lord Wellington was compelled to retire towards Elvas, where he also concentrated his army by calling General Spencer down from the north.

It now devolved on the French Marshals to invade Portugal once more, or to disperse, for they could not long keep their large army supplied. Not caring to venture an attack on Lord Wellington they adopted the second alternative, Marshal Marmont returning to Salamanca and thence to the valley of the Tagus, and Marshal Soult marching to Seville. Lord Wellington then turned northward once again and commenced a blockade of Ciudad Rodrigo, while General Hill resumed his post of the year before, guarding the south-eastern frontier of Portugal with a corps of 14,000 men. This was towards the end of August 1811.

About six weeks later General Hill performed a brilliant feat of arms, marching suddenly into Estramadura and taking completely by surprise the corps of General Girard at Arroyo dos Molinos. This exploit, which cost the French over 2000 casualties, chiefly prisoners, need not be described, as Byng's brigade was not employed, having been left to guard the frontier. General Hill after his exploit returned to his headquarters at Portalegre, arriving there on November 3 and remaining quiet until December 27. On that date he was ordered by Lord Wellington to advance against the Fifth Corps, in order to draw Marshal Soult's troops southward while Wellington delivered his long-prepared blow against Ciudad Rodrigo.

Campaign of 1812

General Hill, in accordance with his instructions, marched on Merida, arriving there on January 6, 1812; and Marshal Soult, as had been anticipated, immediately called his scattered forces together for the defence of Badajos. Two days later Lord Wellington commenced the siege of Ciudad Rodrigo, which strong fortress was, through the determined fighting of the British infantry, carried in twelve days: a marvellous achievement. The capture of Ciudad Rodrigo was, however, only the first portion of Lord Wellington's plan of campaign for 1812. The next step was to be the third attempt on Badajos. For this enterprise also the preparations were conducted with great secrecy, and as a first measure of deception General Hill was again ordered to fall back on Portalegre and the adjoining frontier.

All preparations having been completed, Lord Wellington marched southward in the first week in March, crossing the Tagus at Villa Velha on March 9 and 10. One week later, on March 17, Badajos had been fully invested by 22,000 men under Wellington, while Sir Rowland Hill (who had been made a Knight of the Bath for Arroyo dos Molinos) and Sir Thomas Graham, at the head of 30,000 British and Portuguese troops, moved forward to cover the siege. Sir R. Hill was posted about Medellin and Almendralejo; and Sir T. Graham about Zafra and Llerena.

The siege of Badajos which, as stated, began on March 17, was pressed on with astonishing vigour and brought to a successful issue on April 7, through the gallantry and devotion of the army under Lord Wellington. Every soldier should study the story of the assault of Badajos, so that he may realise that to brave men ready to die nothing is impossible. That story must not be told here, for the Second Battalion Thirty-First, being in the covering army, took no part in the siege. They were, however, not altogether unrepresented. Lieutenant James M. Goodliff of the regiment, one of the line officers acting as engineers, conducted the forlorn hope of the Third Division (Picton's), which, with the Fifth Division, performed the apparently impossible feat of escalading the castle of Badajos. Lieutenant Goodliff was mainly instrumental in dragging the leading ladders up the castle height, and in planting them against the walls. "One of the first up the ladders, he received a bayonet thrust in the head and was precipitated down." The words quoted are from a letter written by the officer commanding the storming party to General Picton's Aide-de-Camp. General Picton, immediately after the assault, ordered a letter to be written to the officer commanding the Thirty-First expressing his approbation of the gallantry displayed by Lieutenant Goodliff in the assault.[1]

After the fall of Badajos the British army, much exhausted by its winter campaign and heavily reduced by casualties, was given complete rest for one month, during which breathing space Lord Wellington completed his preparations for the advance into Spain. The recently captured fortresses of Ciudad Rodrigo and Badajos were

---

[1] From information kindly supplied by Major N. H. C. Dickinson, late 100th (Royal Canadian) Regiment.

strengthened, victualled, and garrisoned by the Portuguese and Spanish Goverments, Sir Rowland Hill's force protecting Badajos during the process.

Lord Wellington decided that before advancing he would make communications difficult between Marshals Marmont and Soult. All permanent bridges over the Tagus had been destroyed in the course of the war, but the French had constructed a bridge of boats, defended by strong enclosed works, at Almaraz. Sir Rowland Hill, whose action at Arroyo dos Molinos had shown his fitness for such an enterprise, was ordered to surprise Almaraz, and setting out on May 11, 1812, from his position near Badajos arrived after a rapid march near Almaraz on May 17. General Hill, undeterred by an initial failure, waited his opportunity and two days later, with slight loss, captured one of the French bridge-head forts and destroyed the bridge, works, boats and stores. Byng's Brigade remained in position on the Guadiana during this enterprise, and the Second Battalion Thirty-First was therefore not engaged at Almaraz.

On June 13 Lord Wellington again entered Spain, heading for Salamanca, and on the 17th he crossed the River Tormes by ford above and below that city. Sir Rowland Hill's corps was meanwhile employed on its old duty of guarding Lord Wellington's right and holding Marshal Soult's armies in check. For this purpose Hill's corps, which still included his own British Division, was raised to a strength of 20,000 men. Other operations were also planned in the south and east of Spain, with the object of further occupying Marshal Soult's attention. Sir Rowland Hill, during the Salamanca operations, remained on guard near the fortress of Badajos, and here we may leave him while very briefly sketching Lord Wellington's triumphant advance.

After Lord Wellington reached the river Tormes, his first task was the capture of the forts of Salamanca, into which Marshal Marmont had thrown an adequate garrison, while falling back himself to collect his scattered forces. Lord Wellington immediately attacked the forts, which were all taken by June 27. Marshal Marmont by July 8 had posted his army of 42,000 men with 100 guns, along the north bank of the flooded Douro, between Toro and Simancas; and the allied army, about 46,000 strong, faced him along the south bank.

There followed a period of highly interesting manœuvres in which Marmont showed a military talent only excelled by that of his opponent, the leader of each army seeking to take his adversary at a disadvantage. On July 17, by means of a brilliant feint, Marmont threw his army unopposed across the Douro, and then pursued his movements, which were intended to turn Lord Wellington's position and cut him off from his line of communications with Portugal. At last, on July 22, Marshal Marmont, in pursuing this object, made a hurried and unguarded movement which enabled Lord Wellington to cut his army in two. The leading French corps, that of Thomières, was suddenly attacked on the front and flank in overwhelming force, and General Clausel's Division, coming gallantly up to the assistance of Thomières, was surprised by the British cavalry. In forty minutes the whole French left wing was completely defeated. Marshal Marmont had been severely wounded, and General Clausel, who succeeded to the command, could do no more than draw off the remainder of his army from the field, which he effected with great courage and skill. The battle of July 22, 1812, known as the battle of Salamanca, is generally considered Wellington's most brilliant feat of generalship. It has been well said of it that " there was no mistake ; everything went as it ought ; and there never was an army so beaten in so short a time."

After the battle Lord Wellington continued his advance, and made a triumphant entry into Madrid on August 12. Marshal Soult now marched northward to join King Joseph and Clausel, and Sir Rowland Hill having no longer to guard Badajos consequently marched eastward and took up a position covering Madrid on the south.

On September 1 Lord Wellington was compelled to leave Madrid and march towards Valladolid against the French army of the north. Clausel retired before him and on September 18 Wellington commenced the siege of the Castle of Burgos. This siege proved a failure on account of Wellington's deficiency in heavy guns, and on October 21 the retreat from Burgos began, an operation in which the allied army suffered such severe privations that portions of it lost for a time much of their discipline.

Sir Rowland Hill's Corps was stationed at Aranjuez during the siege of Burgos, and the Second Battalion Thirty-First was consequently engaged neither in the siege nor in the early part of the retreat. Having repulsed an attack on the bridge of Aranjuez on October 30, Sir R. Hill retired unmolested, and it was not until the whole army had crossed the Tormes that his corps really felt the hardships of the retreat. In consequence of this good fortune Hill's Corps was almost exempt from the heavy loss of life that occurred in the remainder of the army during the winter of 1812.

The army passed this season in cantonments about Ciudad Rodrigo, Sir Rowland Hill's Corps still guarding the right flank and occupying Coria and Plasencia. The Second Battalion Thirty-First with a strength of 359 rank-and-file was cantoned in the latter place, and with the remainder of the army soon attained an excellent state of health. Writing on April 26, 1813, Lord Wellington stated: "I have never seen the British army so healthy or so strong. We have gained in strength 25,000 men since we went into cantonments in the beginning of December, and infinitely more in efficiency."

During this period of much-needed rest for the army the exertions of its commander continued unabated. Lord Wellington, who had been raised to an Earldom after the capture of Ciudad Rodrigo, and to a Marquisate after the battle of Salamanca, left the army to recover its health and went to Cadiz in order to concert measures with the Spanish Government. At this time his financial difficulties were very great, the war with the United States adding greatly to the burden of the Peninsular War; yet largely as the result of his personal efforts, Lord Wellington was enabled to take the field in May 1813 at the head of a well-equipped army of 43,000 British and 27,000 Portuguese troops, which was to be supported in the north by 20,000 Spaniards; while in the east 50,000 Anglo-Spanish troops were to occupy the attention of Marshal Suchet. During the period of rest and recuperation the Second Battalion Thirty-First received a welcome reinforcement in the shape of the strongest draft of recruits that reached it during the war. This draft, which numbered over one hundred, were volunteers from the King's County Militia, an Irish regiment commanded by the brother of Major Guy L'Estrange. With the draft came Ensign George L'Estrange, a lad of sixteen, son of the Militia Colonel, who was to prove himself the worthy nephew of his gallant uncle. In consideration of his name and of the valuable reinforcement that he had brought to the regiment, young L'Estrange was immediately posted to the Light Infantry company, a high compliment. George L'Estrange, who entered the Guards after the Peninsular War, and was eventually knighted, published a book of recollections from which many personal details of the Second Battalion Thirty-First have been taken.[1]

While the British army had improved so materially, the French had been reduced both in numbers and in efficiency, by the withdrawal from every regiment of drafts of old soldiers who were required by Napoleon to train the raw levies with which he was endeavouring to replace the army lost in Russia. The Peninsular struggle between Wellington, with small means in his own hands, and Napoleon, with great resources handled by others, was now in fact turning in favour of the man on the spot, and the allied armies were almost or quite equal in numbers to the French. Fighting as they were in aid of the inhabitants and against invaders, the odds were at last in their favour. On May 22, 1813, Lord Wellington said his last farewell to Portugal and entered on his new campaign. Dividing his army into three corps he despatched the left, 40,000 strong, under General Graham to advance over most difficult mountain country in order turn the French right on the Douro. Lord Wellington, commanding the centre corps in person, with General Hill's Corps, as usual on the right, advanced on Salamanca. Graham's advance, which was not expected by the French, compelled them to fall back from the Douro, and on June 3 the whole allied army was united at Toro, on the right bank of that river. On the same day King Joseph had collected 45,000 men on the Pisuerga, but finding himself outmatched was compelled to fall back to the line of the Ebro, and being still pressed, retired further behind the Zadorra near the town of Vittoria. Here *the army of the south* under General Gazan faced west, with *the army of the centre* behind it, while General Reille, with two divisions, barred the roads from the north.

BATTLE OF VITTORIA

On June 21 Lord Wellington, with 50,000 men, attacked Gazan, while Graham, with 20,000, attacked Reille and seized the Bayonne

[1] *Recollections of Sir George B. L'Estrange, late of the 31st Regiment.* London: Sampson Low, Marston, Low, and Searle. N.D.

Road, the main line of communication with France. The French army fought well, but encumbered as they were with a huge train, were speedily forced to retreat on Pamplona by a bad road and in great confusion.

This, in a sentence, is the story of the battle of Vittoria, the share in it taken by Sir Rowland Hill's Corps being as follows. The French left, commanded as has been said by General Gazan, rested on the heights of Puebla, which overlook the village of Puebla de Arganzon; in front was the river Zadorra, of variable depth, crossed by several stone bridges which had not been destroyed. Lord Wellington's army was formed for the attack into four columns, of which the right under General Hill and the left under General Graham were timed to attack as nearly as possible simultaneously. This difficult operation was carried out with great precision, a fact which proves the effect on Wellington's staff of long experience of war. General Hill's column, about 20,000 strong, crossed the Zadorra by Puebla de Arganzon, and its first task was to gain the heights of Puebla and force the Puebla Pass. General Hill opened his attack on the heights by sending forward General Morillo's Spanish division. The Spaniards met with a partial success, but had to be reinforced before the heights were taken. General Hill then pushed through the Puebla Pass and carried the village of Subijana de Alava, on the French side of it. General Gazan then attacked the village in force, but Hill, though his losses were considerable, held his ground. Meanwhile the remaining allied columns pressed forward all along the line and gradually forced the French army from their positions into the plain of Vittoria, when they were hopelessly encumbered by their inordinate mass of baggage and cut off by General Graham's Corps from their line of retreat towards Bayonne. The battle had begun at ten in the morning and by dusk the French, in spite of a gallant resistance, had been driven from their last position a mile west of Vittoria. The pursuit was continued for six miles beyond the town, when darkness put an end to it.

The allied troops, British, Portuguese and Spanish, all behaved well at Vittoria and bore a fair share of the work and of the casualties, which rose to above 5000. The French loss in men was about a thousand more, and in addition 151 guns and an immense plunder fell into the hands of the victors. The Second Battalion Thirty-First was employed at Vittoria as escort to General Hill's artillery, and its casualties were slight. Privates Bernard Milligan and Michael Taylor were killed, and Captain J. Girdlestone of the Light Company and twelve men were wounded. This was Captain Girdlestone's second wound.

The battle of Vittoria decided the fate of the French invasion of Spain and Portugal, the remainder of the fighting taking place on or beyond the French frontier.

After the battle King Joseph with the main body of the French army reached Pamplona in great confusion on June 24. Leaving a garrison there the King continued his retirement, closely followed by Lord Wellington, and, crossing the Pyrenees, joined other French forces on the river Bidassoa. The allies then occupied all the principal passes in the Pyrenees opposite the French position, while Lord Wellington set about reducing the fortresses of St. Sebastian and Pamplona; the siege of the former commencing on July 19, while Pamplona was blockaded by a force under Sir Rowland Hill, of which the Second Battalion Thirty-First formed part.

As soon as the Emperor Napoleon heard of the successes of the allies, he sent Marshal Soult from Dresden to take command in the south. Soult arrived at Bayonne on July 12 and quickly reorganised the troops near the frontier as *the army of Spain*. It consisted of three corps, Reille's, D'Erlon's, and Clausel's; and a reserve, and had a strength of 70,000 men. Wellington had 82,000, but a third were Spanish, still of uncertain fighting value; moreover he was blockading two fortresses and had fifty miles of the Pyrenees to guard.

Soult decided to relieve Pamplona and on July 25 D'Erlon's corps forced the pass of Maya, and those of Reille and Clausel the pass of Roncesvalles. Roncesvalles was held by Brigadier-General Byng's brigade, which had moved up from before Pamplona on July 7, and the brigade, which included the Second Battalion Thirty-First, held its ground for several hours against an overwhelming force. At length, finding that his position had been turned, Byng was compelled to fall back. The loss of the Thirty-First in this action was Privates Thomas Keegan and Charles Stubbs killed and three privates wounded. On July 28, 29, and 30, the allied army returned to the attack, and after severe fighting re-occupied the heights in front of Pamplona. Byng's brigade was again hotly engaged and the Thirty-First had Privates

Michael Quinnan and George Turbitt killed, and three officers and thirty-three rank-and-file wounded, a heavy loss when the numerical weakness of the battalion is remembered. The wounded officers were Captain J. Girdlestone (for the third time), Ensign W. Smith, and Quartermaster McIntosh.

On July 30 Marshal Soult moved to his right intending to turn the allied left and relieve St. Sebastian, but Wellington fell upon the French left and drove it in disorder over the mountains. In the nine days' fighting, known as the battle of the Pyrenees, the loss of the allies had been over 7000 men, and that of the French double as much. The siege of St. Sebastian was then renewed and the town was stormed on August 31. The castle surrendered on September 9; Pamplona also surrendered on October 31; and Lord Wellington was then able to invade France at the head of 90,000 men. As a preparatory step towards this enterprise Wellington, by ably-planned operations, effected the crossing of the Bidassoa on October 6 and 7. The operations entailed severe fighting and a loss of about 1600 killed and wounded, that of the French being somewhat less. Byng's brigade was not engaged.

The surrender of Pamplona having set free the allied army for the invasion of France, Lord Wellington ordered a general advance through the Pyrenees against the position on the river Nivelle which Soult had strongly fortified. The position ran from the sea in front of St.-Jean-de-Luz, through the heights about Sarre to those of Mondarin, which formed the French left. Beyond the left was a detached division at Bidaray, near the Nive. Marshal Soult held this very strong position with 80,000 troops, disposed in three lines of fortified posts, while Lord Wellington for the attack had about 10,000 more, a very small preponderance when it is remembered that the Spanish portion of the army could never be relied on with any confidence.

The allied army was divided by Wellington into three corps, of which Sir Rowland Hill's was on the right, Sir John Hope's [1] on the left and Marshal Beresford's in the centre. General Hill's first task was to capture the heights of Mondarin, after which his corps and that of Marshal Beresford were to converge and pierce the French centre,

---

[1] Lieut.-General Sir John Hope had recently joined the army in place of Sir Thomas Graham, who had been invalided home.

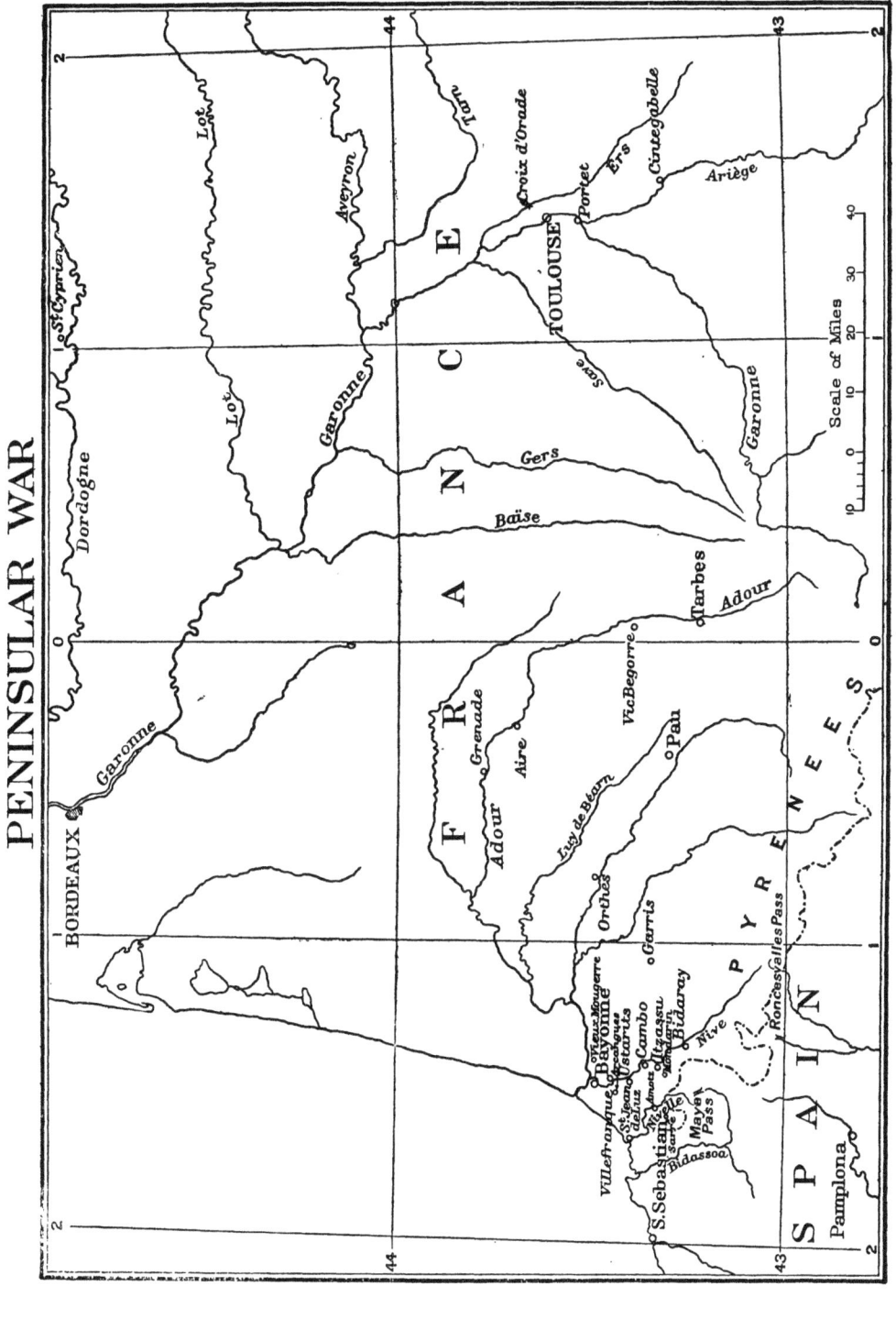

near the bridge of Amotz. This programme was carried out with complete success, fighting continuing from dawn to dusk on November 10, and the advance recommencing early on November 11. The French, however, had abandoned St.-Jean-de-Luz during the night and had retreated northward to Bayonne. During the battle of the Nivelle, in which one of the ablest soldiers of the day was driven as if by an irresistible force from a position of great strength, the fighting in many places was of a severe nature. The loss of the allies was about 2700 men, while Soult lost, including prisoners, over 4000, with fifty-one guns and all his field magazines. The Second Battalion Thirty-First, which went into action only 260 strong, had Private James Southworth killed, while Captain J. Girdlestone and eleven rank-and-file were wounded. This was the fourth occasion on which the gallant Captain of the Light Company was wounded at the head of his men. In his report on the Nivelle to Lieut.-General Stewart, Major-General Byng mentioned that the light companies of the provisional battalion conducted themselves admirably, and that Captain Girdlestone of the Thirty-First received a severe wound "while leading on his company in a most handsome style." "Lieut.-Colonel Leith," he adds, "led on the provisional battalion in the most gallant manner, and was the first who entered the redoubt I ordered him to attack." Captain Nicols, Thirty-First, acting as major, was "very forward, and contributed towards the success and good conduct of his battalion." Sir William Stewart made a special report to Sir Rowland Hill of the gallant conduct of Lieut.-Colonel Leith.

Captain Thomas Samuel Nicols, who afterwards assumed the name of Trafford, was promoted to the rank of Major in the army for his services at the Nivelle. He had been wounded at Talavera.[1]

After his repulse from the line of the Nivelle, Marshal Soult, seeing that his men were much discouraged, fell back on the entrenched camp at Bayonne and so posted his army in and near the camp as to command the high roads to Bayonne on both sides of the river Nive. Heavy rain fell from November 11 to 19, so that no serious attack was possible to the allies. General Hill, however, advanced on the 16th on Cambo,

---

[1] Captain and Brevet-Major Thomas Samuel Nicols, of Swithamley, assumed the name and arms of Trafford by Royal Warrant on succession to the property of that family. Major Trafford rose to the rank of Major-General and died in 1857.

and on November 23 the heights near Arcangues were also occupied. In addition to the weather the attitude of the Spanish Government caused a serious difficulty, and it was for a time doubtful if Great Britain would be able to maintain an army in Southern France. Eventually the firmness of Lord Wellington triumphed and early in December he was enabled to resume his advance. At this time Sir Rowland Hill's Corps, with which we are chiefly concerned, formed the right of the allies' line, running from Marshal Beresford's right at Ustaritz, by Cambo to Itzassu. The French right being extremely strong, Lord Wellington decided to hold the troops in that quarter by a demonstration on his own left, and to strengthen his right in order to force the river near Ustaritz and Cambo, moving afterwards down the right bank towards Bayonne.

This programme was exactly carried out on December 9. Sir Rowland Hill, with the Second Division and his Portuguese Division, two brigades of cavalry and a troop of horse artillery, forded the Nivelle above and below Cambo, though the fords were so deep that several men were drowned. Morillo's Spanish Division made a similar crossing further to the right, and the day's work ended with the capture of Villefranque. The passage of the Nive was thus accomplished with a loss of about 800 men, that of the Second Battalion Thirty-First being only one sergeant wounded.

There was, however, much more severe fighting to come before Bayonne could be approached, and from the dangerous position which Lord Wellington had been compelled to take up, with the broad and flooded Nive dividing his army, Soult was able to concentrate in turn superior numbers against both of Wellington's wings. The first attack was made on December 10, when Soult with 60,000 men and forty guns fell suddenly upon Sir John Hope's corps of about half that strength. The action was long and severe, but the British and Portuguese troops gallantly held their ground, but in the afternoon Wellington threatened an attack with fresh troops on Soult's left and compelled him to retire. Further fighting followed on December 11, and on the 12th, Soult prepared for a great effort against Hill's corps on the British right.

Lord Wellington saw the attack coming and ordered the Sixth Division to reinforce Hill, but unfortunately the floating bridge across the Nive near Villefranque was carried away during the night by the river, which was in flood, and consequently in the battle of December 13, termed by English writers the action of St. Pierre, Hill was seriously outnumbered. To his own fine generalship and to the determined courage of his troops was due the success of the day, the story of which was as follows. The Nive runs into the Adour through the town of Bayonne, and Sir Rowland Hill's corps was posted on hills running across the angle formed by these two rivers. A mile in rear of Hill's centre was a commanding hill called Horlopo, from which he had the advantage of seeing all his line of battle, the rivers which protected his flanks, the line of approach from Bayonne by which he must be attacked, and the country to his left rear, from which he had to rely on Wellington's support.

Late on the evening of December 12, Hill had himself seen that Soult's troops were moving out of Bayonne with the obvious intention of attacking him, and during the night Lieutenant L'Estrange of the Thirty-First, who was in command of an advanced picket close up to the walls of Bayonne, sent in information of the coming trial. L'Estrange, a lad of seventeen, who had already seen nearly a year of eventful service with the Light Company of the Thirty-First, writes in his recollections :

" I was very much on the alert, as I felt I was in a responsible position, and I took no rest that night, for I heard a rumbling noise going on during the whole period, from the movement, as it appeared to me, of guns and wagons through the strongly fortified town. So convinced was I that there was something in the wind that I sent my Corporal to say what I had observed and heard, and to communicate the intelligence at the proper quarter in the rear.

" Shortly after daylight," L'Estrange continues, " our pickets were called in, and very shortly afterwards a tremendous attack was made on our portion of the army."

Sir Rowland Hill's three brigades were posted along a ridge stretching some three miles from river to river, Major General Byng's (Buffs, Thirty-First, 57th and 66th) being on the right ; Pringle's on the left, and the 50th, 71st and 92nd, together with Ashworth's Portuguese, in the centre. In reserve was Le Cor's Portuguese Division behind the ridge of Lostenia. The battle began by a furious attack on the British centre, which was, save in one place, sustained and eventually repulsed by the gallant fighting of Ashworth's Portuguese, the 50th and 92nd. That hard fighter, Lieutenant-General Sir William Stewart, was in command in this part of the field, and was, as ever, in the post of danger.

While the desperate fighting in the centre was in progress, an equally violent attack was made under General Darmagnac on the British right, and, much outnumbered, the Buffs retired from their position on the Partouhiria ridge on General Byng's right front. Darmagnac's strong column was presently seen advancing through the village of Vieux Mouguerre. This movement, if unchecked, meant disaster, for Byng's brigade was in imminent danger of being taken in flank and rear, and rolled up. The centre too had been pierced in one place. Happily Sir Rowland Hill and Byng were both men for an emergency.

Hill immediately galloped to the front, and sending one of his Portuguese reserve brigades under Brigadier-General Buchan to rally and reinforce the Buffs, he personally led the remaining brigade to assist the 71st, which had been withdrawn from the centre. It is enough to say that the 71st willingly responded to the call, and the French attack on the centre was soon completely repulsed, the Portuguese battalions here employed showing the most distinguished courage.

While this hard fighting was in progress, a somewhat similar process was going on on the British right.

Buchan's Portuguese brigade had crossed the valley to the right under a galling flank fire of artillery, joined hands with the retiring Buffs, who readily rallied, and with the Portuguese tackled Darmagnac with such determined courage that they not only stopped his advance but drove him back, through Mouguerre and clean off the Partouhiria ridge. Byng's right was now secure, but close in his front was a hill on which the French were very strongly posted and supported by artillery. Byng was therefore ordered to form up his brigade and advance to the attack. Byng, a man of personal courage conspicuous even in the Peninsular Army, carried out the order with alacrity, and presumably to give a directing point to the line of his brigade took the King's colour of the Thirty-First from the officer who was carrying it, and led the charge in person. The result of the charge was the capture of the hill, and of two guns abandoned by the French, which fell into the hands of Captain Hemsworth's company of the Thirty-First. The day was now won, and at about 12.30 P.M., soon after General Byng's charge, Lord Wellington, who had quickly had the bridge over the Nive re-made, arrived at the head of strong reinforcements. Sir Rowland Hill had, however, already repulsed with 14,000 men the determined attack of 35,000 French, and Lord Wellington justly exclaimed: "Hill, the day is your own." The action of St. Pierre is not borne as an honour on the colours of the regiment engaged, the several actions before Bayonne being all included in the honour "Nive," but the action was one of the most honourable and severe of the Peninsular battles.

The British losses were very heavy, and those of the French terribly so. The Second Battalion Thirty-First, which went into action only 230 strong, sustained the following casualties. *Killed*: seven rank-and-file.[1] *Wounded*: Lieutenant-Colonel Alexander Leith (slightly), Ensign James Hardy (mortally), three sergeants, two drummers, and twenty-seven rank-and-file: forty-one casualties in all. Captains Patrick Dowdall and Peter Fearon were promoted Brevet-Majors for service at the Nive.

Lieut.-General Sir William Stewart reported to Sir Rowland Hill that the Major-General (Byng) reports warmly in praise of Lieut.-Colonel Leith and of the provisional battalion on this occasion.

The following extract from Lieutenant L'Estrange's recollections throws an interesting light on the episode relating to Major-General Byng and the Colour.

After stating that Byng's brigade bore the brunt of the French left attack and highly distinguished himself, Lieutenant L'Estrange adds:

"He (General Byng) took the King's Colour out of the hands of Elwyn who carried it, and headed the charge, for which he has now the colour of the Thirty-First in his armorial bearings and the words 'Vieux Mouguerre,' and as supporters two soldiers of the grenadier company of the Thirty-First. Poor Elwyn, who was a very sensitive man, felt this very much, and, as I heard, shed tears. . . . Elwyn

---

[1] Only the names of Privates John Burchell and William Nuttall are recorded as killed on December 13. The other five men were presumably mortally wounded.

who as I have already said, was a very high-minded and accomplished officer, as brave and bold as a lion, felt it was a sort of slur on his courage ; but no other officer or soldier in the brigade had any other opinion of him than that he was everything that a soldier ought to be."

General Byng, it may be added, stated in his report that Lieutenant-Colonel Leith led his men most gallantly, and showed emphatically his high opinion of the Thirty-First Regiment by his choice of supporters. After the battle of December 13, which like the other actions round Bayonne, had been fought in very severe weather, both armies rested for a time in winter quarters, and the campaign of 1813 came to a peaceful conclusion. Soult took up an extended position behind the Adour, with his right resting on Bayonne. Lord Wellington faced him ; Hope's corps before Bayonne forming the left, Beresford's the centre, and Hill's the right. The Second Battalion Thirty-First, being again very weak in numbers, was comfortably accommodated in the village of Vieux Mouguerre, where all ranks enjoyed the remainder of the winter in spite of somewhat scanty resources of amusement, and were soon in the best of health and ready for another campaign.

So severe had been the losses of the First Provisional Battalion that on January 16, 1814, it only numbered 549 effectives, of which number the 2nd Battalion Thirty-First found 271 and the Second Battalion 66th the remaining 278. H.R.H. the Duke of York, the Commander-in-Chief, tried for the second or third time to persuade Lord Wellington to send these and other weak battalions to England, to be recruited up to strength. Lord Wellington, however, had had ample proof that battalions filled up with recruits immediately broke down under the hardships of active service, and declined to part with these veteran and case-hardened troops. In a letter of this period to Lord Liverpool Lord Wellington mentioned the Second Battalion Thirty-First as one of the second battalions that were formed of the best and most experienced soldiers in the Army, and were much more efficient than first battalions that had served at Walcheren.

Action of Garris

Early in February 1814 Lord Wellington continued his advance into France, with the corps of Marshal Beresford and Sir Rowland Hill, about 35,000 strong, Sir John Hope, with about the same number, being left to deal with Bayonne. Marshal Soult's field army was also about 35,000 strong.

Lord Wellington moved to his right, towards Pau, in order to draw the French away from the point at which he intended to throw a bridge over the Adour, a formidable undertaking. In this movement Hill's corps fought a severe action on February 15 at Garris, against General Harispe's corps, which occupied a strong position on commanding ground and fought very bravely. In this action the Light Company of the Thirty-First distinguished itself, and Captain Edward Knox, who now commanded it and was severely wounded, was promoted to the rank of Major in the army. Captain Knox had also been wounded at Albuera. The other casualties in the Second Battalion were: *killed*, Private John Ward; *wounded*, six rank-and-file. Captain and Brevet-Major Peter Fearon, a distinguished officer of the Thirty-First, was also killed at Garris, in command of the Fifth Portuguese Caçadores.

After the French position had been captured in the dusk, the troops lay on the hills for the night—("Uncomfortably enough"—as Lieutenant L'Estrange tells us)—and marched off about noon next day to take part in the coming battle of Orthes.

"When," writes L'Estrange, "our corps (Sir Rowland Hill's) came in sight of the field at Orthes the battle had been virtually gained. We saw the greater part of the French army scattered over the plain like a flock of sheep in full retreat, or rather running away, throwing down their knapsacks, their muskets, and everything that could impede their flight, for such it must be called, and all moving in an oblique direction from the left towards our right, in the hope of gaining a certain bridge."

L'Estrange adds that this was a great opportunity for our cavalry, but that it was not available where it was wanted. He also adds, in justice to a brave enemy, that the spectators of the strange flight described above fully thought that the French would not fight again, but Marshal Soult was able, before many days, again to show a front.

Battle of Orthes

The story of the battle of Orthes, told as briefly as possible, is as follows. The troops engaged were about equal on both sides and Lord

Wellington attacked Marshal Soult in a very strong position. Marshal Beresford attacked the French right, Picton the centre, and Sir Rowland Hill attempted to turn the left, and so block the only line of retreat of the French army. The attacks on the French right and centre both failed and Generals Reille and D'Erlon made a counter-attack on Beresford's corps. In so doing their corps became for a time separated, and Wellington, always swift to take advantage of a tactical error, immediately delivered a strong counter-stroke and changed a threatened reverse into victory. Soult was completely defeated and it was only by a very hurried movement that his army secured a retirement by way of the bridge over the Luy de Béarn mentioned by Lieutenant L'Estrange. The retreat began in good order, but ended in broken flight, the French, however, fighting hard and losing very heavily. Lord Wellington was himself among the British wounded, and his injury was sufficiently severe to interfere with his management of the latter stages of the battle. After crossing the Luy de Béarn the French destroyed the bridge and were safe from further pursuit.

The Second Battalion Thirty-First had only two private soldiers wounded at the battle of Orthes, but the valuable services of the Second Division in the battle were rewarded by a grant of the honour to the units composing it.

After the battle of Orthes Marshal Soult took up a position near Aire across the road to Toulouse. Lord Wellington had thus succeeded in his intention of drawing Soult away from Bayonne, which town was besieged by 28,000 men under Lieutenant-General Sir John Hope. The Adour was bridged, an operation of extraordinary difficulty, on the day before the battle of Orthes, and Hope was consequently able completely to invest the town.

Returning to the operations of Lord Wellington against Soult, whose army we left at Aire, Sir Rowland Hill with the right corps of the allied army reached Aire on March 2, and after a sharp fight turned the French right, and compelled them to continue their retreat towards Tarbes. In this action the Second Battalion Thirty-First had one sergeant and two rank-and-file wounded. Ensign William Hardcastle (Captain in the Third Portuguese Caçadores) was also wounded. At this moment the French royalist party at Bordeaux offered to declare for the Bourbons if Wellington would send troops to that town. Lord Wellington consequently detached Marshal Beresford with 12,000 men to Bordeaux, which on March 12 abandoned the cause of Napoleon. At the same time, too, the armies of the Emperor were being driven through north-eastern France by those of Austria, Prussia and Russia, and it was evident that the star of the Empire was fast setting. Soult, however, fought hard for his master till the last, and had manœuvred skilfully in an endeavour to prevent the dispatch of Beresford to Bordeaux. In this attempt he was foiled by Wellington, who on March 17 fought an action at Vic Bigorre, and on the following another, short but severe, at Tarbes. After the latter action Soult retired on Toulouse, which he entered on March 24, hoping to be reinforced there by Marshal Suchet. The allied army arrived before Toulouse two days later, but before engaging Soult again it was necessary for them to cross the river Garonne.

Battle of Toulouse

Lord Wellington desired to attack Toulouse on the south side, as being the most open and also in the direction of Suchet's advance, and therefore on March 27 he endeavoured to cross the Garonne at Portet, but found the river too wide and rapid at that point. On March 31, Sir Rowland Hill effected a passage of the Garonne at a point higher up the river, and also crossed the Ariége at Cintegabelle, but, the country proving impracticable for the manœuvres of an army, he was recalled.

On April 3, while Hill's corps was left facing St. Cyprien, the fortified suburb west of the Garonne, a pontoon bridge was thrown over that river at Grenade, fifteen miles below Toulouse. Over this bridge Marshal Beresford advanced with three divisions of infantry and three brigades of cavalry, taking up a strong position near the bridge, which was injured by a flood after the crossing. Beresford was thus isolated, but was protected here from any attack by Soult by a large number of Lord Wellington's guns, which from the opposite bank of the Garonne swept the ground over which Soult must have advanced. On April 8 the Garonne fell, Beresford's bridge was repaired, and the British cavalry secured that at Croix d'Orade over the Ers near Toulouse on the north. The Garonne was also bridged at Seilh, to open communications with Hill's corps. Lord Wellington then marched up the left bank of the Ers and on April 10 attacked Toulouse, the following being the plan of action. Sir Rowland Hill's corps was to threaten St. Cyprien. General Freyre, with the Spanish corps, was to attack from the north-east, from the direction of Croix d'Orade, in conjunction with an attack by Marshal Beresford from the east and a threatened attack by General Picton from the north.

The advance began at 6 A.M. and Sir Rowland Hill made a successful opening by carrying the outer defences of St. Cyprien. The Spanish corps, however, attacked gallantly but prematurely, before Marshal Beresford's corps, which had much further to go, could reach its point of attack. The Spaniards suffered very heavily, and, to save them, General Picton converted his feint into a real attack, which was also repulsed with loss. All now depended on Marshal Beresford and his troops, who rose nobly to the occasion. After a flank march of more than two miles over very heavy ground, exposed to artillery and in parts to infantry fire, Beresford's veterans repulsed in turn the French infantry and cavalry who assailed them, and after suffering heavy loss, captured the St. Sypière redoubt, which formed the right of the French position on the ridge of Mont Rave. At half-past two Beresford resumed his attack with those of his troops which had suffered least in the morning, and stormed two more redoubts along the ridge, three-quarters of which was in his hands by 4 P.M. The Spaniards gallantly attacked the north end of the ridge and were again repulsed, but at five o'clock Soult abandoned the whole ridge and fell back behind the canal. On the night of April 11 the French evacuated Toulouse, retiring to Villefranque, and on April 12 Lord Wellington entered Toulouse to find all the population wearing the Bourbon colours.

The loss of the allied armies at Toulouse amounted to nearly 5000 men, but, as we have seen, Sir Rowland Hill's corps was but slightly engaged. The Second Battalion Thirty-First in this, their last engagement, had only one private soldier wounded, and not only had the battalion fought its last fight, but it was very near the end of its existence.

Immediately after his triumphal entry into Toulouse, Lord Wellington received the news of the abdication of Napoleon, which had occurred before both the battle of Toulouse and the bloody sortie from Bayonne on April 14, which latter operation cost the French and allied armies a large number of further unnecessary casualties.

The war being now ended, the Second Battalion Thirty-First was presently ordered to return to England. The battalion marched from Toulouse to Bordeaux on June 3, embarked on H.M.S. *Rodney* on July 12 and landed at the Cove of Cork on July 23, marching thence to Middleton. On September 23 the battalion was conveyed to Portsmouth, where it was disbanded on October 24, 1814, the majority of the officers being placed on half-pay, and men who were fit for service being transferred from that date to the First Battalion, then stationed in Sicily. The colours of the battalion were presented to Major-General Sir John Byng, the gallant and kindly soldier who had so long had the battalion under his command. Sir John Byng, who gained further distinction at Waterloo, was eventually raised to the peerage, and the Peninsular Colours of the Second Battalion Thirty-First are preserved at Wrotham Park, the residence of his grandson, the present Earl of Strafford.

The existence and war services of the battalion are commemorated by the honours, " Talavera, Albuhera, Vittoria, Pyrenees, Nivelle, Nive, Orthes, Peninsula," borne on the colours of the East Surrey Regiment.

Lieutenant-Colonel Alexander Leith, who commanded the battalion during the greater part of the Peninsular War, was appointed a Knight Commander of the Bath for his services, and Lieutenant-Colonel Guy L'Estrange, who had so highly distinguished himself at Albuera, was appointed a Companion of the Bath.

Twenty-five officers and one hundred and fifty-four non-commissioned officers and privates, the survivors of the Second Battalion, received the War Medal with a varying number of clasps on its distribution in 1848, but although the majority of the Peninsular veterans of the Thirty-First dropped, unknown to fame and unrewarded, into their graves, we, their inheritors, can turn with pride to the fields of Talavera and Albuera, where they showed themselves as brave and staunch as the best of Wellington's glorious army.

OFFICERS OF THE SECOND BATTALION THIRTY-FIRST REGIMENT WHO RECEIVED THE WAR MEDAL

Name and Rank when Medal was earned.	Name and Rank when Medal was claimed.
Astier, Ensign Henry.	Major, late 41st Regt.
Bailey, Lieutenant Charles C.	Lieutenant 5th Royal Veteran Battalion.
Bayley, Lieutenant and Adjutant C.	Lieut.-Colonel.
Beamish, Lieutenant George.	Captain.
Beamish, Lieutenant Adderley.	Bernard, Adderley Beamish.
Butler, Lieutenant William.	Late Lieutenant.
Fleming, Captain Edward.	Major-General.
Gamble, Ensign Andrew William.	Captain, late 20th Regt.
Girdlestone, Captain James.	Captain, Half-pay unattached.
Goodliff, Ensign J.	Late Lieutenant.
Graham, Assist. Surgn. Edward.	Surgeon, late 4th Dragoon Guards.
Hawkshaw, Major J. S.	Lieutenant-Colonel.
Knox, Captain Edward.	Lieut.-Colonel, late 31st Regt.
Knox, Lieutenant Francis.	Lieutenant H.P.
L'Estrange, Lieutenant George.	Ensign and Lieut. 3rd Guards H.P.
McIntosh, Quartermaster Andrew.	Lieutenant, late 4th Royal Veteran Battalion.
Millingen, Surgeon I. G. van.	First-Class Surgeon to the Forces, H.P.
Nicholson, Ensign Ralph.	Lieutenant H.P., 101st Regt.
Nicols, Captain T. S.	Trafford, Lieut.-Col. H.P., 24th Regt.
Owens, Lieutenant J. W.	Lieutenant H.P.
Simmonds, Lieut. and Adjt. Henry.	Lieut.-Col. Ceylon Rifles.
Smyth, Ensign William.	Lieut. 3rd Guards, H.P.
Thompson, Lieutenant E. C.	Late Captain.

The Medal was also granted to 154 Sergeants, rank-and-file; and to Lieutenant Benjamin Thompson (Retired on full pay) for services as a Sergeant, and to Captain John Longworth, 2nd Huron Militia, for services as a private soldier.

CHAPTER VII

THE BURNING OF THE *KENT*

Gallant rescue by the *Cambria*—The camp at Rupar—Indian service.

THE fall of Napoleon restored peace to Europe, and for many years after the battle of Waterloo the history of the Thirty-First was comparatively uneventful.

Lieut.-Colonel Guy L'Estrange, C.B., who had earned high distinction in command of the Second Battalion at Albuera, had exchanged back into the regiment from the 26th Regiment in 1815.

The regiment on its return from Malta in 1818 was stationed at Dover, with detachments at Colchester, Chatham, and Sheerness. In August 1819, in consequence of disturbances in the manufacturing districts, three companies of the Thirty-First proceeded to Manchester, three to Macclesfield, and three to Stockport; and Manchester proving to be the chief centre of disturbance, the regiment was concentrated there on August 10. On August 16 an assemblage of people, estimated at from 40,000 to 60,000, gathered in an open space in Manchester called St. Peter's field, with the avowed intention of petitioning Parliament. Such meetings having previously been forbidden by proclamation, the civil authorities took the steps that appeared to them necessary to disperse the gathering. The regular troops on the spot, consisting of the 15th Hussars, the Thirty-First, and the 88th Regiments, under command of Lieutenant-Colonel Guy L'Estrange, C.B., were for the most part held in reserve, the actual work of dispersing the rioters being performed by the local yeomanry. About ten of the crowd were killed and a considerable number wounded or injured during this operation.

Lieutenant-Colonel L'Estrange performed his difficult duties with much coolness and judgment, and the troops generally showed great self-restraint in trying circumstances; which facts were fully recognised by the local authorities, and by the Government. In the Home Secretary's letter on the occasion, dated August 21, 1819, Lord Sidmouth conveyed to "Lieutenant-Colonel L'Estrange and to the officers, non-commissioned officers, and privates, that served under his command at Manchester on the 16th of August, the high approbation of His Royal Highness (the Prince Regent) of the exemplary manner in which they assisted and supported the civil authorities of the County Palatine of Lancaster on that day." The Magistrates of Lancashire and Cheshire also wrote on August 17, requesting that Lieutenant-Colonel L'Estrange would "accept for himself and convey to the officers, non-commissioned officers and privates under his command, their best and sincerest thanks for the energy, tempered by the greatest humanity, displayed in their conduct yesterday, a conduct peculiarly characteristic of the British soldier"—a striking and well deserved tribute.

The neighbourhood of Manchester remaining in a disturbed state, it was not until June 2, 1820, that the Thirty-First was released from its highly unpleasant duties. Throughout the winter the troops at Manchester had been much harassed, and had given their services with a readiness which earned from the municipal authorities of that town and of Salford letters expressing their esteem of the Thirty-First regiment and their regret at its departure.

The regiment arrived from Manchester at Sunderland on June 10, 1820, and was stationed there till March 1821, when it marched to Port Patrick, there to embark for Ireland. Landing on March 8, at Donaghadee, the Thirty-First marched on the following day to Belfast. While quartered in that town the establishment of the regiment was reduced from ten to eight companies, and detachments were stationed at Coleraine, Downpatrick, and Carrickfergus. These detachments were employed on the revenue and other civil duties, which at that time were performed by the army in Ireland.

In April 1822 the regiment left Belfast and was stationed at Armagh, Newry, and Dundalk; in October 1823 it was moved to Naas; and in January 1824 to Dublin, in anticipation of proceeding shortly on foreign service. In July and August the regiment moved by wings to Gosport, where it remained for the rest of the year.

On January 12, 1825, the Thirty-First marched from Gosport to Chatham, arriving there on January 20, and on February 7 the regiment embarked for Calcutta at Gravesend, the right wing and headquarters under Lieutenant-Colonel Fearon, on the Honourable East India Company's ship *Kent* of 1400 tons; the left wing under Major Tovey, on board the *Scaleby Castle*. The two ships parted company off Portsmouth at the end of February; the *Scaleby Castle*, after a good passage, arrived in the Hooghly on June 7. During this long confinement on board ship only two men of the wing had died, and on arrival in India only eight were in the sick list.

The voyage of the right wing was destined to be of a very different nature, and to subject Lieutenant-Colonel Fearon and his men to the sternest trial of courage and discipline which soldiers are likely to experience. The *Kent* sailed from Gravesend, as had been said, on February 7, 1825. On March 1, when in the Bay of Biscay, towards the end of a violent gale, the ship was found to be on fire. The discovery was made about ten in the morning, and was reported to Lieutenant-Colonel Fearon shortly before noon, when the sea was still high and the ship rolling heavily. The fire, which occurred through an unavoidable accident and was actually caused by one of the ship's officers, very speedily obtained such complete hold on the *Kent* that it was evident that the only thing to be done was to endeavour to save the lives of those on board. Perfect discipline had been maintained from the first, and all ranks of the Thirty-First had shown the same ready obedience to the orders of their officers, and the same manly resignation in face of an imminent and dreadful death, that many of them had already exhibited on the field of battle. Lieutenant-Colonel Fearon, an officer who had been wounded at Rosetta with the First Battalion and who had served with the Second Battalion through a great part of the Peninsular War, gave in the following letter a plain, straightforward account of the burning of the *Kent*, which can hardly be improved on.

Falmouth,
4th March 1825.

Sir,—It is with feelings of the deepest regret I have to report, for the information of H.R.H. the Commander-in-Chief, the

The burning of the "Kent."

melancholy calamity which has befallen that portion of the Thirty-first regiment under my command, embarked on board the Honourable Company's ship *Kent* for conveyance to Bengal, owing to her loss, she having taken fire towards the close of a heavy gale of wind on the 1st instant, about noon, in the Bay of Biscay.

The moment it was discovered bursting from the afterhold of the vessel every possible effort was made to get it under, and by the immediate application of wet blankets, soldiers' great-coats, and other woollen articles that could be obtained on the emergency, we had for a short period every hope these efforts would prove successful; but unhappily, having communicated to the spirits, the hope of extinguishing it was soon dispelled, and all further exertion to save the vessel appeared evidently vain; the conflagration, owing to the state of the weather, gaining ground so rapidly. Under these circumstances it became the imperative duty of Captain Cobb and myself to endeavour to save the lives of as many of the people as possible, for which purpose the boats were hoisted out, and some rafts hastily constructed, and as many of the women and children put into the former as we could at the moment assemble. At this instant, by the Divine interposition of Providence, a sail hove in sight, which discerning our perilous situation, came promptly down to our relief; and owing to the persevering heroism of the commander, at the evident risk of losing his own vessel, and by the cool and intrepid conduct of Captain Cobb, whose attentions were unremitting, a larger portion of the troops than could ever have been anticipated under so unforeseen a calamity were preserved, though, I lament to add, sixty-eight men, one woman, and twenty-one children appear to have perished, exclusive of five seamen.

It is some alleviation to our afflictions to be enabled to state, that the origin of the fire was in no way attributable to the troops; a pleasing part of my duty to bear testimony to the cool and subordinate conduct of both officers and men under my command, —the former affording me every aid which so critical and trying an occasion demanded, and none more so than Major McGregor, to whose collected counsel and manly example, throughout this agonizing scene of distress, I feel greatly indebted.

I have, etc.,

(Signed) R. B. Fearon,
Lieut.-Colonel Com^{dg} 31st Foot.

To the Adjutant-General,
   Horse-Guards,
      London.

The vessel mentioned by Lieutenant-Colonel Fearon as so promptly coming to the assistance of the *Kent* proved to be the brig *Cambria*, of only 200 tons burden, outward bound from Falmouth to Mexico. The *Cambria*, whose crew numbered only eleven men, carried thirty-six passengers, mostly Cornish miners, and some gentlemen, their employers. This little body of Englishmen, under Captain W. Cook, the master of the *Cambria*, who proved himself a British seaman of the very best stamp, behaved nobly, and it was, thanks to the courage and determination with which Captain Cook lay close to the *Kent* until she was in imminent danger of blowing up, that so many lives were saved. The only woman lost, with her three children, was unable to escape from the orlop deck, and was unfortunately suffocated there. Four of the other children lost their lives through a sad accident. While the women and children were being lowered into the boats, Mrs. Jack, the wife of Sergeant Jack, fell overboard. The sergeant, a good old soldier who had seen much service in the Peninsular War, leaped into the sea to save his wife, and both were drowned. Their four children were unfortunately lost sight of. It was supposed that, missing their parents, they sought refuge in Colonel Fearon's cabin, and no one knew until it was too late that they were still on board. Every effort indeed was made to save all the children, many men tying them on their backs and swimming with them to the boats.

The loss of life that did occur was mainly caused by the impossibility of reaching all parts of the *Kent*, and the refusal of some men, at the end, to jump into the sea. These men doubtless could not swim. Several men were drowned while swimming from the *Kent* to the *Cambria*, and others were crushed between the boats and the ships.

Captain Cook and Lieutenant-Colonel Fearon were the last men to leave the *Kent*, which blew up at 2 A.M. on March 2. The loss of life was fortunately further reduced by the fact that fourteen survivors of the men who remained on the *Kent* were picked up on the following day by the *Caroline*, a vessel bound from the Mediterranean to Liverpool, and carried by her to that port.

The Head-quarter wing of the Thirty-First numbered twenty officers and 344 of other ranks, with forty-seven women and seventy-three children. Total 484. Of this number there were lost fifty-four men, one woman, and twenty-one children.

The *Cambria*, though dangerously over-crowded, arrived safely at Falmouth on March 4, and the surviving passengers and crew of the *Kent* were speedily landed. All had lost everything that they possessed, except the clothes they stood in, and these in many cases were extremely scanty. Their sufferings and good conduct had caused them, however, universal sympathy, and the soldiers, women and children received generous help from the people of Falmouth. On March 16, the wing of the Thirty-First embarked in the *Diadem* transport, and ten days later arrived at Chatham, where the officers of the wing received a brotherly welcome from those of the Division of Royal Marines at that station, the origin of the Thirty-First Regiment as a Marine Corps being well remembered.

In due course Lieutenant-Colonel Fearon received from the Military Secretary the following commendation by H.R.H. the Duke of York, of his conduct and that of the wing of the Thirty-First Regiment:

> Horse-Guards,
> March 9, 1825.

> SIR,—The Court of Directors of the East India Company having transmitted to the Commander-in-Chief the report made to them by Captain Cobb of the circumstances attending the destruction of the ship *Kent* by fire on the 1st instant, I have received His Royal Highness's commands to assure you of the high sense His Royal Highness entertains of the admirable conduct of the detachment of the Thirty-first regiment embarked in that ship under your command, and more particularly of the steadiness and coolness which you evinced under circumstances so critical and trying. His Royal Highness is well aware that no occasion could offer in which the effects of a well-established system of discipline and subordination would be more apparent, or in which they would in a more important degree tend to assist the efforts of those who so nobly afforded their aid towards preserving the lives of all concerned; and he desires that you will convey his thanks to the officers and soldiers forming the detachment embarked, under your orders, in the ship *Kent*, and assure them that he gives them due credit for their orderly and meritorious conduct. He considers his thanks due more especially to yourself for the example which you set them, and for the persevering and gallant

exertions which contributed so essentially to lessen the sad result of the catastrophe.

His Royal Highness orders me to add that he shall deem it his duty to report to His Majesty a conduct, on your part and that of the officers and men committed to your charge, which so well deserves His Majesty's approbation.

I have, etc.,
(Signed) H. TAYLOR.

King George IV was pleased to confer upon Lieutenant-Colonel Fearon the distinction of a Companionship of the Bath for his conduct at the burning of the *Kent*. Major Duncan McGregor was subsequently promoted to the command of the 93rd Highlanders.

Having been equipped and clothed, the Head-quarters and part of the wing of the Thirty-First embarked on April 10 on the H.E.I.C. ship *Charles Grant*, and after a good passage reached Calcutta on August 16. On September 12 the detachment arrived at Berhampore, where it found the left wing. Almost immediately afterwards the regiment was ordered to return to Calcutta, and was assembled in Fort William by November 17. Towards the end of the month the regiment was attacked by cholera, and moved into camp on the south glacis of the fort, remaining there under canvas until the epidemic ceased.

On January 18, 1826, the Grenadier Company and part of No. 1 Company arrived from England and completed the regiment to a strength of thirty-nine officers, fifty sergeants, seventeen drummers, forty-eight corporals, and 812 privates. On February 13 the regiment moved by water to Dinapore, unfortunately losing a large number of men from cholera during the move. The disease was of so virulent a type that the men at first died before they could reach the hospital boat, which was in rear. Subsequently the officers were supplied with medicine, so that those attacked could be treated at once; but the loss of the regiment on this occasion shows the danger and inconvenience of the old methods of travelling in India. It was not until May 2 that the Thirty-First reached Dinapore, a journey that now occupies a few hours. During the journey the regiment lost Lieutenant-Colonel Fearon, C.B., who exchanged to the 64th Regiment; his successor being Lieutenant-Colonel James Cassidy.

General the Earl of Mulgrave, G.C.B.,
Colonel of the 31st (Huntingdonshire) Regiment, Master-General of the Ordnance,
&c., &c.

After passing the hot weather at Dinapore the regiment was ordered to Meerut, and set out on November 8 on its first march in India. The route was by Buxar, Ghazipore, Secrole, Allahabad, Etawah, Shekohabad, Aligarh, and so on to Meerut; sixty-seven marches in all, Meerut being reached on January 13, 1827.

The colours of the Thirty-First had been destroyed in the burning of the *Kent*, and advantage was taken of the arrival of the Governor-General, Lord Amherst, to have new colours formally presented to the regiment. The ceremony was performed by Lady Amherst on March 7, 1827, and in his speech to the regiment the Governor-General made use of the following words: " I am persuaded that Lady Amherst will consider herself fortunate in having been selected to bear so distinguished a part in the ceremony of this day. It will be her earnest prayer that so dire a calamity as that which befel your former colours may never occur to those which she has had the honour to present to you. *From the ordinary perils of war they are safe in your hands*, and she confidently trusts that His Majesty's Thirty-first will ever march to victory under the colours now consigned to your charge."

The Thirty-First remained at Meerut during the years 1827–1831. In 1829 the regiment had an effective strength of 1086 and was in excellent health and a high state of efficency. The establishment in this year was reduced to 736 rank-and-file, and consequently no recruits were required for a considerable time.

Early in January 1831 the regiment was ordered to Kurnal, a new station then being formed on the frontier of the Sikh kingdom of the Punjab. Marching on January 27 the regiment reached Kurnal in five days and encamped on bare ground facing to the west of the native city, the barracks not having yet been built.

General the Earl of Mulgrave, G.C.B., who had been Colonel of the Thirty-First since the year 1793, died on April 12, 1831, and was succeeded in the colonelcy by General Sir Henry Warde, G.C.B., an officer who had seen much and distinguished service.

It was not until the month of June that the new barracks of Kurnal were ready for occupation, and therefore until the hottest part of the year was nearly over the regiment remained under canvas on the bare plain, a trial which only those who know the heat of northern India can appreciate. It is stated in Cannon's Record that there was not a single tree to give shade to the camp, but no serious sickness appears to have been caused by this exposure.

In October 1831 the Thirty-First marched from Kurnal as part of the escort of Lord William Bentinck, the Governor-General, who was about to meet Maharaja Ranjit Singh, the celebrated ruler of the Punjab. The meeting took place at Rupar, a place on the British side of the river Sutlej, and the escort, in addition to the Thirty-First, consisted of two squadrons of the 16th Lancers, two battalions of native infantry, two squadrons of Skinner's Horse (now the 1st Duke of York's Own Lancers, Indian Army) and eight guns. Ranjit Singh's escort was much larger, consisting of 10,000 of his best cavalry, and 6000 regular infantry, which had been trained by European officers. Maharaja Ranjit Singh at this time was fifty-one years old and near the summit of his extraordinary career. By birth no more than chief of one of the smaller confederacies of the Sikhs, he had during the first twenty years of the century formed that turbulent and divided people into a loyal and united nation under his own absolute rule. He had, moreover, by the judicious employment of European officers made from an undisciplined rabble host of no remarkable fighting value, a formidable army 80,000 strong, of which a large proportion were highly efficient regular infantry and artillery. Such a ruler, whose people formed an efficient barrier between the Company's territory and the Muhammadan Kingdoms and States situated in and beyond the Himalaya mountains, might be a dangerous enemy or a valuable ally; and it was to establish friendly relations with Ranjit Singh that Lord William Bentinck had taken the unusual step of travelling to the very boundary of the Company's territories.

A bridge of boats having been thrown across the Sutlej, the Maharaja, attended by a mounted escort 3800 strong, crossed the river on October 26 to visit the Governor-General. Great preparations had been made to give a fitting reception to Ranjit Singh, and as an honour which he, it was felt, would most appreciate, a street was formed from the river to the durbar tent by the 16th Lancers and the Thirty-First regiment. The Maharaja, one of the most remarkable soldiers that the Eastern world produced prior to the birth of the modern Japanese army, was greatly struck by the British cavalry and infantry, enquiring into every detail of their dress and equipment and inspecting them most narrowly. On a second visit the troops of the Governor-General's escort went through a field day for the Maharaja's benefit, and he not only observed the movements with the greatest interest, but drew the attention of his attendant officers to the details of the evolutions. The interview being over, the Thirty-First returned to Kurnal, arriving there on November 16, and remaining at that station during the next three and a half years.

General Sir Henry Warde, G.C.B., Colonel of the Regiment, died on October 9, 1834, and was succeeded by Lieutenant-General Sir Edward Barnes, G.C.B., a very gallant officer of the Peninsular War, who had been Adjutant-General at the battle of Waterloo.

In December of the same year Major Bolton, one of the surviving Peninsular officers of the Thirty-First, rejoined from England, and, in November 1835, he was promoted Lieutenant-Colonel of the regiment, by purchase, vice Colonel Cassidy, appointed to the charge of a recruiting district.

The Thirty-First, which had been extremely healthy during its long stay at Kurnal, left that place in January 1836 and marched back to its old quarters at Dinapore. Owing to the heat of the weather the distance from Cawnpore (thirty-one marches) was performed without a halt, yet there were only fifteen men sick on arrival at Dinapore, There, however, the health of the regiment quickly changed for the worse. During the hot weather of 1837, in particular, it is recorded that for several days the thermometer in the barracks remained at 115°, and that many deaths occurred from apoplexy.

On March 19, 1838, the regiment lost its Colonel, General Sir Edward Barnes, G.C.B., who was succeeded by another distinguished officer of the Peninsula and Waterloo, Lieutenant-General Sir Colin Halkett, K.C.B., G.C.H. In November of the same year the Thirty-First left Dinapore for Ghazipore, a station distant forty-six miles from Benares, in the direction of the frontier of Nepal. This move was in consequence of the threatening attitude of the Gurkha kingdom, but hostilities did not break out in this quarter.

It is recorded by Cannon that early in the year 1839 the strength of the regiment was reduced to 632 rank-and-file; it had then been fourteen years in India, during which time the casualties by death had amounted to fourteen officers and 677 men. On April 3 of this year, however, the regiment was augmented to an establishment of ten companies, with fifty officers and 1052 sergeants, rank-and-file.

The Thirty-First remained at Ghazipore until October 1840, the men suffering much from fever and dysentery. The regiment then marched to Agra, arriving there on November 30 with an effective strength of 740. Agra proved to be a much healthier station than Ghazipore, and the strength of the regiment was largely increased by the arrival in March 1841 of strong drafts of recruits from England. In the capable hands of Lieutenant-Colonel Bolton the regiment was soon restored to a state of high efficiency, with a strength of 992 bayonets. Its war value was ere long to be tested.

CHAPTER VIII

THE FIRST AFGHAN WAR

Early history of the war—Destruction of General Elphinstone's force—The punitive campaign of 1842—The Shinwari expedition—Mountain fighting—
—The capture of Kabul and destruction of the Grand Bazaar—The return march to India.

TOWARDS the end of 1841 serious disasters befell the British army occupying the principal towns of Afghanistan. We are not here immediately concerned with the early history of the Afghan War, a very brief sketch of which will sufficiently explain the situation which had arisen.

In the year 1838, Lord Auckland, who had become Governor-General of India in 1836, resolved to dethrone Dost Muhammad Khan, an Afghan chief who had seized the government of that country; and to replace Shah Sujah, the deposed king, who then resided in India as a pensioner of the British Government. With this object Lord Auckland concluded a treaty whereby Ranjit Singh, the ruler of the Punjab, agreed to give free passage through his country to troops and supplies going to and from Afghanistan. In December 1838 Afghanistan was invaded by a British army from the south, and on April 25, 1839, Kandahar, the capital of the southern province of that country, was occupied with slight loss. A strong garrison under Major-General Nott having been left at Kandahar, the main army under General Sir John Keane marched northward, and on July 23 captured the strong fortress of Ghazni in a very gallant manner. Pursuing its march, the army reached Kabul, the Afghan capital, on August 6, Dost Muhammad, who had narrowly escaped capture, having withdrawn to the mountainous region of the Hindu Kush, to the northward. Shah Sujah was then replaced on the throne, and for two years governed the country as far as his authority was supported by the British contingents, each about 5,000 strong, which were stationed at Kabul and Kandahar. Most of the people and their chiefs, however, remained loyal to Dost Muhammad, even after his personal surrender, and early in November 1841 a violent insurrection broke out at Kabul. Sir William Macnaghten and Sir Alexander Burnes, the two principal political officers, were murdered by the insurgents, the former by the hand of Akbar Khan, a son of Dost Muhammad.

Major-General Elphinstone, who commanded at Kabul, who was in bad health and had repeatedly asked leave to resign his command, proved unequal to cope with the emergency, and after severe fighting entered into a convention with the Afghan leaders, whereby he consented to evacuate Afghanistan. The Afghans, a race proverbially considered treacherous throughout the East, violated the terms of the convention, and in the retirement from Kabul towards Jalalabad the whole of General Elphinstone's force was massacred or died of exposure, with the exception of a few prisoners whose lives were spared, and of one officer who reached Jalalabad. Major-General Nott, however, who commanded at Kandahar, refused to acknowledge the convention, as did Major-General Sale, who, with a small garrison, held the walled town of Jalalabad. An even smaller force of 250 Sepoys under Captain Craigie also held their own in the fort of Kilat-i-Ghilzai.

OFFICERS OF THE THIRTY-FIRST (THE HUNTINGDONSHIRE) REGIMENT AT THE TIME OF THE FIRST AFGHAN WAR.

COLONEL
    Lieutenant-General Sir Colin Halkett, K.C.B., G.C.H. (in England).

LIEUTENANT-COLONELS
    Chatham Horace Churchill. Quartermaster-General in India. Killed at Maharajpore, 1845.
    Samuel Bolton. Appointed C.B. and A.D.C., Brevet-Colonel.

MAJORS
    Thomas Skinner. Appointed C.B. Brevet-Lieutenant-Colonel. Died May 5, 1843.
    H. C. Van Cortlandt.

CAPTAINS
  John Byrne.
  James Spence.
  Charles Shaw. Died at Kati, near Pesh Bolak.
  L. B. Urmston.
  G. C. Marshall. Died at Fatehabad, August, 1842.
  G. Baldwin. A Waterloo officer. Promoted Brevet-Major.
  W. G. Willes.
  Thomas Bulkeley.

LIEUTENANTS
  G. D. Young. ⎫
  G. F. White. ⎬ Promoted Captains.
  J. C. Stock. ⎪
  R. Norman.   ⎭
  T. Pender. Mortally wounded. Died November 18, 1842.
  J. C. Kelly.
  E. Lugard (Adjutant).
  Frederick Spence.
  R. J. Eagar.
  J. C. Brooke. Wounded September 9, 1842.
  J. S. Scott.
  H. K. Sayers. Died of small-pox.
  Dalway McIlveen. Killed in action, July 26, 1842.
  T. J. Bourke.
  J. Æ. Duncan.
  Joseph Greenwood.
  G. B. Shaw. Wounded September 8, 1842.
  T. H. Plasket.
  E. C. Mullen.

ENSIGNS
  E. W. Bray.
  D. Brown.
  J. L. Wilton.
  G. F. Moore.
  W. F. W. Atty.
  J. L. R. Pollard. Severely contused, September 13, 1842.
  H. W. Hart.
  R. Law.
  R. B. Tritton. Died of dysentery.
  R. Sparrow.

Directly the news of the outbreak at Kabul reached India, Mr. Robertson and Mr. Clerk, the principal Indian civilians on the north-west frontier, made a most spirited attempt to restore the situation by despatching four native battalions from Ferozepore, the frontier station, through the Punjab. Maharaja Ranjit Singh was dead, but his son Shere Singh, then on the throne, loyally adhered to his treaty, and the Ferozepore Brigade safely arrived at Peshawar. Further native troops followed, and early in February 1842 British troops began to arrive. A fortnight earlier (on January 19), on an urgent request for help from Jalalabad, Brigadier-General Wild, the commander of the Ferozepore Brigade, made a brave attempt to advance with native troops only into the Khaibar Pass; but this enterprise failed, with considerable loss.

Major-General George Pollock, commanding at Agra, a veteran officer of the Bengal Artillery, who had learned the art of war under Lord Lake, was placed in command of the army intended to re-capture Kabul, and among other regiments ordered to join the force assembling at Peshawar was the Thirty-First regiment, which marched from Agra on January 15, 1842, mustering 996 bayonets, and in the highest state of disciplined efficiency. The Punjab was entered on March 10, and on April 21 after a long and hot march the regiment arrived at Peshawar, where it was hospitably entertained by General Avitabile, the celebrated Italian governor of that unruly province.

Before this date, however, Major-General Pollock had effected a complete change in the aspect of affairs. Having arrived at Peshawar on February 5, he had at once taken steps to restore the *moral* of the Sepoy brigade which had been repulsed on January 19, and to prepare to force the Khaibar Pass and relieve Jalalabad. Such were the difficulties that Pollock had to overcome that it was not until March 31 that he arrived at Fort Jamrud at the mouth of the Khaibar, at the head of a force of some 9000 men. Baggage had been reduced to a minimum never before approached in Indian warfare, but even so Pollock's little army was hampered by an immense train of camels and elephants. Disregarding or brushing aside all difficulties, Pollock fearlessly entered the dreaded Khaibar Bass, and by a series of movements so skilfully planned as to have remained to the present day the model of mountain welfare, he forced a passage through the Pass at the trifling cost of 135 casualties. Marching on without a pause General Pollock arrived at Jalalabad on April 16, to find that the garrison had, nine days earlier, sallied forth and completely defeated the investing army of Akbar Khan, a son of Dost Muhammad.

The first duty imposed on General Pollock had now been performed, and owing to the defective transport arrangements of the Indian Government, he found a further advance impossible for a con-

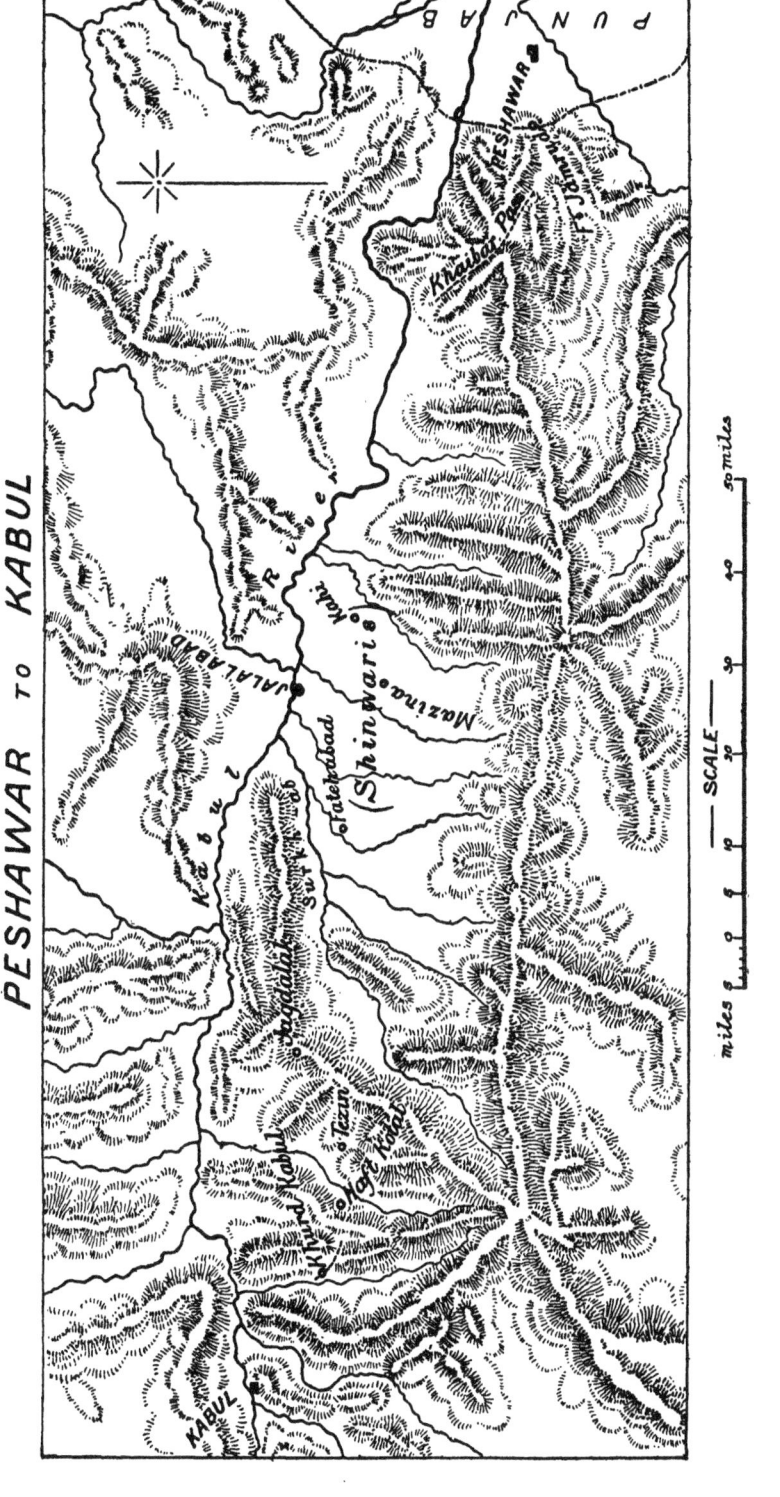

siderable time. On May 5 his army, still too small for an advance on Kabul, even had transport been available, received a welcome reinforcement by the arrival of the Thirty-First regiment, and other troops, which under the command of Lieutenant-Colonel Bolton, had pressed to the front by forced marches from Peshawar.

While delayed at Jalalabad, General Pollock maintained a long correspondence with Lord Ellenborough, who had succeeded Lord Auckland as Governor-General, and at length enforced his view that for the British army to evacuate Afghanistan without first entering Kabul would entail disaster on British rule in India. In this opinion Pollock was firmly supported by Major-General Nott, who after long correspondence was at last authorised by Lord Ellenborough to retire from Kandahar by way of Kabul.[1] General Pollock at once decided to meet Nott at the capital.

On arrival at Jalalabad, the Thirty-First was posted to the 4th Brigade, commanded by Brigadier-General Monteath, C.B., a distinguished officer of the Indian army. The regiment hoped for an immediate advance, and great disappointment was felt when days of delay lengthened into weeks, and the weather grew hotter and hotter. Crowded as they were into their tents, in one of the hottest places on earth, and living in insanitary conditions, the troops soon became unhealthy and the death-roll heavy. Partly to reduce the overcrowding and to occupy the minds of his soldiers, General Pollock decided to detach the 4th Brigade, under Brigadier-General Monteath, against the Shinwaris, a neighbouring tribe which had shown itself persistently hostile to the British, and had taken a conspicuous part in the treacherous massacre of Elphinstone's force.

Monteath's column, numbering 2300 men, left Jalalabad in the middle of June and moved through the entire country of the Shinwaris for a period of seven weeks, returning to Jalalabad on August 3. During these operations all the offending fortified villages of the Shinwaris were successively stormed and destroyed, and the fruit-trees cut and left to perish; the last punishment, harsh as it may sound, being the only manner of inflicting a lasting penalty on these lawless mountaineers.

[1] This may be compared to a retirement from Bristol to London by way of Edinburgh.

The Thirty-First regiment had its first experience of hill-fighting in the Shinwaris operations, and benefited greatly in health from the constant movement and change of scene. The transport animals also (which had been nearly starved at Jalalabad and on the march to that place) rapidly recovered their efficiency. The operations, however, were not accomplished without loss of life, Captain Charles Shaw of the regiment dying of exhaustion from the great heat at Kati, soon after leaving Jalalabad. The only severe fighting of the expedition occurred at Mazina, a stronghold in one of the most difficult portions of the Shinwari territory, situated at the head of a long and narrow valley. This position was reconnoitred on July 25 by a small column under Captain Willes, Thirty-First regiment, and attacked in force by Brigadier-General Monteath on the following day. The whole column carried out the attack with much spirit, the finest possible example being set by the Thirty-First regiment, which led the attack.

The regiment lost a gallant young officer, Lieutenant Dalway McIlveen, who was mortally wounded while storming a breast-work at the head of only five soldiers. The Lieutenant and one private fell wounded at the same moment, and fifty Shinwaris immediately charged down on the small party. Lieutenant McIlveen, with noble self-abnegation, told the remaining men to leave him, but the four soldiers (whose names have unfortunately not been preserved), gallantly held their ground and eventually carried off their wounded comrade and the dead body of their officer. Those who know Indian frontier warfare will realise how fine an achievement this was. The action of Mazina resulted in heavy loss to the Shinwaris, who after being driven successively from all their posts and defences, were scattered in flight through the neighbouring mountains. Their loss was very great and included most of their leaders.

The Thirty-First, in addition to Lieutenant McIlveen, lost several men who died from exhaustion and thirst, and seven rank-and-file were wounded. In his report on the operations, dated Mazina, July 27, 1842, Brigadier-General Monteath stated that the enemy " were driven in gallant style from their positions by the advanced troops, consisting of the light and two battalion companies of Her Majesty's Thirty-First regiment, the light companies of the 33rd and 53rd regiments of native infantry, and the corps of Jezailchees, under Major

Skinner of the Thirty-First." The Brigadier also records " the cheerful and praiseworthy manner in which the soldiers of the Thirty-First laboured to drag the guns up such places as the horses could not surmount."

Among the officers mentioned for good service this day were Lieutenant-Colonel Bolton, Major Skinner, and Lieutenant Lugard of the Thirty-First. The last-named officer, who was adjutant of the regiment, acted on this occasion as Major of Brigade, or, in modern phraseology, Brigade-Major.

Monteath's Brigade, which returned to Jalalabad on August 3, marched from thence on the 22nd of the same month, forming part of the force detailed by Major-General Pollock for the advance on Kabul. No opposition was experienced during the first portion of the advance, but the troops suffered great fatigue in dragging the artillery and stores along the very rough roads. Among other deaths in the regiment at this period was that of Captain G. C. Marshall, an excellent officer, who died at Futehabad. On leaving Surk-ab for Jagdalak on September 8, the Afghans showed themselves in force and the rear-guard of the army, under Lieutenant-Colonel Bolton, was hard pressed and suffered considerable loss. Lieutenant-Colonel Bolton had his horse shot under him, and Lieutenant G. B. Shaw of the regiment was wounded.

A spirited account of this rear-guard action is given by Lieutenant Greenwood of the regiment, in his " Narrative of the late Victorious Campaign in Afghanistan." [1] Greenwood first describes how he himself was posted by Brigadier Monteath in a breast-work on high ground guarding the entrance to the Jagdalak Pass, and then writes :

" From the *sungah* (breast-work) of which I had taken possession, I could see our gallant little rear-guard coming leisurely along the road in rear of the long line of camels, literally enveloped in fire and smoke. Clouds of Ghilzees were following it up, and the rattling of their *jezails* was incessant. Ever and anon a party of the soldiers would be sent out, and I could see them driving the enemy before them like sheep. They again, however, returned to the attack as soon as the pursuit was discontinued, and although numbers of them were continually dropping under the well-directed fire of our men, still they came on like so many devils. . . . In about two hours the whole of the baggage was got through (the entrance to the pass) while we kept the enemy

[1] Published by Henry Colburn. London. 1844.

off by constant fire on them from our position. The rear-guard, having effectually routed the Afghans with whom they had so long sustained the arduous and bloody contest which I have endeavoured to describe, effected its junction with us. They had suffered severely, and their gallant leader had his horse wounded in two places under him, but the enemy had received a severe lesson."

On the following day similar fighting, though on a smaller scale, took place, and Lieutenant Brooke and several men of the Thirty-First were wounded.

On September 10, it having been ascertained that Akbar Khan had assembled 20,000 men about the Khoord Kabul Pass, General McCaskill's division was ordered to make a forced march and join the main body at Tezin. This was performed on the 11th, after a running fight which lasted all day. The camp was attacked on the night of September 12, but the enemy made no impression, and soon after daybreak on the 13th the army moved off to attack the Tezin Pass: two companies of the Thirty-First under Captain Baldwin and Lieutenant Greenwood forming part of the advanced guard. The position of the enemy having been disclosed by fire on the advanced guard, it was found necessary to carry the heights on both flanks. This was performed in fine style by three companies of the 13th Light Infantry on the right, and by three companies of the 9th Regiment and two of the Thirty-First on the left. In this advance Lieutenant Pollard of the Thirty-First was severely contused by a large block of stone while gallantly attempting to capture a standard. The enemy's first position having thus been seized, General Pollock quickly pushed forward large reinforcements and ordered a general advance. The Afghans offered a short resistance, but disciplined and well-directed valour prevailed, and the enemy were driven back to their second position on the Haft Kotal, a group of seven hills of great height. Here the Afghans made a brave resistance, but Pollock's army, personally led by their veteran commander, pressed firmly on and at length forced the enemy from their very strong positions. A detached force of a strength of seven companies (including one from the Thirty-First), commanded by Major Skinner, performed valuable service as a right flank guard, and by turning movements materially assisted the advance of the main body.

The British casualties at the action of Tezin numbered 185. The Afghans lost between 700 and 800 men.

In his despatch to the Commander-in-Chief, General Pollock made special mention of Lieutenant-Colonel Bolton and Major Skinner, Thirty-First regiment, and Captain Baldwin received the brevet rank of Major for his services in command of the left attack of the advanced guard.

The Afghan army was completely defeated in the fighting at Tezin and Haft Kotal, and the British army advanced without further opposition, arriving at Kabul on September 15, and encamping on the old race-course of the massacred garrison. On the following day Nott's force arrived from Kandahar, and the British standard was hoisted on the Bala Hissar, the citadel of Kabul, the flank companies of the Thirty-First forming part of the garrison of that fortress.

The English prisoners, who, in addition to a few officers and a large number of women and children, included three sergeants and thirty-three rank-and-file of the 44th Regiment, had been released from captivity on September 16, and the united forces of Generals Pollock and Nott were now free to return to India. As a punishment for the treacherous conduct of the Afghan people in the massacre of General Elphinstone's brigade after it had been assured of a safe conduct to British territory, it was decided to destroy the Grand Bazaar of Kabul. This was carried out on October 9, four companies of the Thirty-First being on duty on the occasion; and three days later the army set out on the return march to India, which took exactly one month.

This march was a most difficult operation, for the army, now of considerable strength, was encumbered not only by its own baggage train, but by a number of political refugees, Afghans who had befriended the British during the four years' occupation of Afghanistan, and by some 2000 survivors of the camp followers of Elphinstone's brigade. All, or nearly all, of the last-named unfortunates were cripples, having lost hands or feet from frost-bite. The duty of guarding all the helpless refugees from Kabul to Peshawar was imposed on General Pollock's troops, and in consequence much hard work fell upon them. Owing to this fact, and to the insanitary state of the ground throughout the retirement, dysentery raged among the troops, and many men of the regiment died during the march. The hostile tribes, moreover, constantly attacked stragglers, detached bodies, and rear-guards, and numerous casualties occurred. The Thirty-First were so unlucky as to lose three officers during the march. Lieutenant Thomas Pender, senior subaltern of the regiment, was mortally wounded while on flank-guard, soon after passing the Tezin Pass. Lieutenant Pender, who is described by Lieutenant Greenwood as " as noble a fellow and as brave an officer as ever held Her Majesty's commission," though terribly wounded, survived the sufferings of the long march to Indian territory, but unfortunately died at Nowshera in the Punjab through the neglect of his Indian servants. Lieutenant H. K. Sayers also died of smallpox, and Ensign R. B. Tritton of dysentery, during the march.

Having marched through the Punjab without misadventure, the Thirty-First regiment reached Ferozepore on December 19, 1842, having been in the field for eleven months. The regiment had been so unfortunate as to lose six officers and a large number of men in this short campaign. It has not been found possible to ascertain the names of the sergeants and rank-and-file who lost their lives.

In recognition of the services of the regiment during the campaign Her Majesty Queen Victoria was pleased to authorise that the honour " Cabool, 1842 " should be borne on the regimental colour and appointments. For his services in command of the regiment, Lieutenant-Colonel Bolton was made a Companion of the Bath and appointed Aide-de-Camp to the Queen, with the rank of Colonel in the army. Major Thomas Skinner was also appointed a C.B. and granted the brevet rank of Lieutenant-Colonel. Lieutenant-Colonel Skinner, an officer of high merit, died on May 5, 1843, from disease caused by the hardships of the Afghan campaign.

On the breaking up of the army at Ferozepore, the Thirty-First was ordered to Umballa, a place about 170 miles to the south, where it had been decided to form a cantonment. The regiment arrived at Umballa on January 27, 1843, and the lines having been marked out, barracks were commenced for the men and ground allotted for the erection of bungalows for the officers. The expense of building bungalows fell upon the officers themselves, who were permitted to build on a small or large scale, as suited their fancy and pocket.

In May 1843, at the hottest season of the year, the regiment was ordered to join a force under Major-General Fast, which had been detached to reduce the neighbouring rebellious state of Khytul to subjection. The object of the expedition having been attained without fighting, the regiment returned to Umballa, but it was not until July that the men could be housed and a few of the officers' bungalows were completed. Meanwhile the intense heat caused such suffering as can only be realised by those who have lived under canvas in the hot weather in the Punjab.

In October an event occurred at Lahore which pointed to danger in the near future, Maharaja Shere Singh being shot dead at a review of the army by a Sikh chief named Ajit Singh. Dhulip Singh, a boy aged ten, who had been recognised as the last-born son of Maharaja Ranjit Singh, was now placed on the throne; but the overgrown Sikh army rapidly became more and more difficult to restrain, and it seemed probable that at any moment it might throw off all discipline, and declare war against the British government. So threatening was the aspect of affairs that in November 1843 the Thirty-First was ordered to reinforce the border station of Ferozepore, and arrived there under Colonel Bolton, C.B., on December 1. Shortly after this date a draft of ninety-three recruits arrived from England, and active training for war was carried out. The regiment was inspected in January 1844 and again in the following month, and was highly commended for its soldier-like bearing and high state of discipline.

The weather becoming very hot, the regiment left Ferozepore on April 19 and arrived at its barracks at Umballa on May 2, 1844. No event of interest occurred during the year, though war with the Sikhs was generally expected throughout British India. The Punjab, after the murder of Maharaja Shere Singh, remained in a state of anarchy, and the assassinations of prominent chiefs and statesmen frequently occurred.

In December 1844 the Thirty-First was inspected by General Sir Hugh Gough, the Commander-in-Chief in India, and was again highly commended for its soldier-like appearance. The regiment at the time was weak in numbers, but in March 1845 a large draft of recruits from England, and of volunteers from regiments proceeding homewards, joined head-quarters. This draft consisted of eight officers and 471 rank-and-file, under the command of Major James Spence. Umballa proved a healthy station, but men continued to die from the effects of the Afghan campaign, and in July the regiment was visited by a severe outbreak of cholera. From July 26 to August 5 the regiment was in cholera-camp, about two miles from the barracks, and during the epidemic the deaths from cholera included eighty-nine men, women, and children—a heavy roll in so short a period.

CHAPTER IX

THE SUTLEJ CAMPAIGN

The Sikhs invade the protected states—The march to the frontier—Battle of Moodkee—Lieutenant Robertson's letters—Battle of Ferozeshah—Lord Hardinge's address to the Thirty-First—" I was with you when you saved the Battle of Albuera." Action of Budhowal—Battle of Aliwal—Battle of Sobraon—Occupation of Lahore.

SOON after this misfortune the storm which has so long threatened burst on the Indian frontier, and on December 11 the main body of the Sikh army, numbering about 40,000 men, crossed the Sutlej, and thus invaded the territory of the Sikh States that had been under British protection since 1809.

In his anxiety to avoid giving any pretext for war, Sir Henry Hardinge, the Governor-General, who was an able and experienced soldier, had taken considerable risks. Close up to the river Sutlej which formed the Sikh frontier, were two British garrisons in the territory of the Sikh protected States. These stations were Ferozepore, held by a force of about 7000 troops, mainly native, under Major-General Sir John Littler; and Ludhiana, eighty miles east of Ferozepore, where there were about 5000 men under Major-General Hugh Wheeler, who afterwards fell at Cawnpore. The nearest support to Ferozepore and Ludhiana was Umballa, where the Thirty-First formed part of a Division, about 10,000 strong, commanded by Major-General Walter Raleigh Gilbert, a gallant and active soldier. Umballa was eighty miles from Ludhiana and double that distance from Ferozepore, and no other troops could be quickly collected to meet an attack on the frontier, the next station in support of Umballa being Meerut, which was 130 miles away.

The Sikh plan on taking the offensive was to fall upon the weak and isolated force at Ferozepore, and destroy it before the Umballa division could come to the rescue. The Sikh army having a great preponderance of strength, particularly in artillery, should undoubtedly have been able to carry this plan into execution, but as it turned out, the army, though well trained and brave to the highest degree, was unprovided with competent leaders : it could fight admirably on the defensive, but could not make a really effective attack. This fact was, however, as yet unknown when, on December 12, 1845,

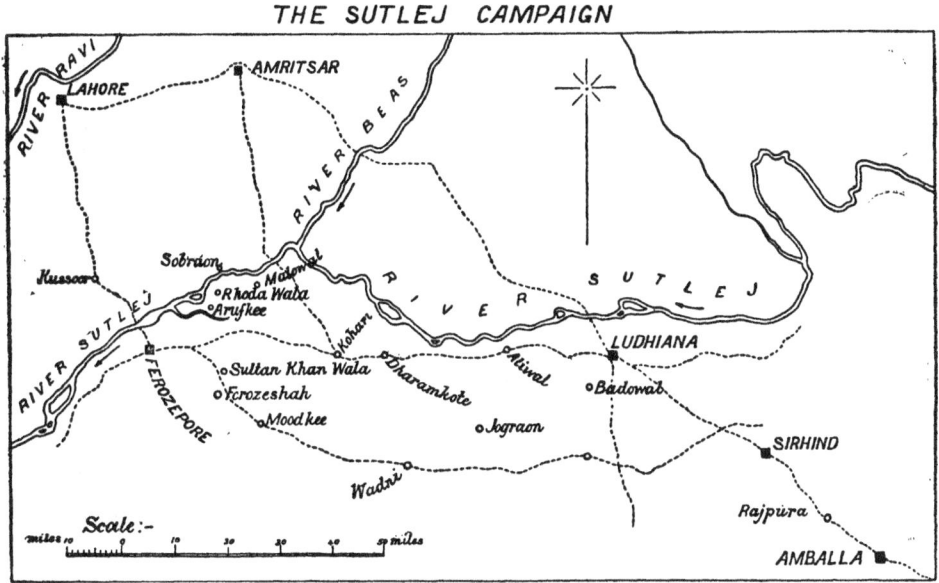

Sir Henry Hardinge heard that the Sikh army had crossed the Sutlej, and so complete were the British preparations that on the same day the Umballa Division made its first march of sixteen miles towards Ferozepore. Pressing on with the utmost speed, though marching over most fatiguing ground, heavy sand or almost equally heavy ploughed land, or through thorny jungle, day after day the Umballa troops pressed on to the rescue of their comrades at Ferozepore. The first march of sixteen miles took them to Rajpura; the second, eighteen miles to Sirhind; the third, twenty miles to Isru; the fourth, thirty miles to Lattala; the fifth, also thirty miles, to Wadni, where they joined hands with the Ludhiana force. The Umballa troops were now much exhausted, and the following days'

march, that of December 17, was comparatively short (about fourteen miles). On December 18 the army marched early and covered twenty-one miles, arriving at Moodkee, then an unknown place, early in the afternoon. Thus the Umballa Division had covered " about 150 miles in seven days over tracks heavy with sand, under clouds of dust which almost smothered the men in column, with little or no water or regular food, and under a sun which was hot and oppressive in the day."[1] A fine performance, possible only to veteran troops such as were the infantry of the Umballa Division, for there were few young soldiers in the ranks of the British regiments and none in those of the native corps. While, however, the British infantry reached the battle-field weary of body but undaunted in spirit, their Indian brothers-in-arms were more seriously affected by their exertions. Partly through the reverses of the Afghan War, and partly through various causes of dissatisfaction, the Indian sepoys of 1845 met the Sikh army in no confident spirit, and in many instances played a sorry part in the actions of the brief campaign now begun.

Battle of Moodkee

When the little British-Indian army approached Moodkee, a patrol of the 9th Irregular Cavalry reported that the village was held by the enemy, and the force immediately formed up for battle under the orders of Sir Hugh Gough. In spite of their fatigue the prospect of action gave new life to the troops, and they quickly formed up in two lines, cavalry and artillery in front, and the infantry in second line. The infantry was formed in two complete divisions, that of Major-General Sir Harry Smith (The Umballa Division) being on the right, and that of Sir John McCaskill on the left; and in the centre was a brigade of native infantry, all that had arrived of Major-General Gilbert's Division.

The Thirty-First regiment, with the 24th and 47th Native Infantry, formed the 1st Brigade, which was commanded by Colonel Bolton, C.B. The Thirty-First was consequently commanded by Lieutenant-Colonel Byrne, the next senior officer, and, after Lieutenant-Colonel

[1] *The Sikhs and the Sikh Wars.* By General Sir Charles Gough, V.C., G.C.B., and Arthur Innes. A. D. Innes & Co., London, 1897.

THIRTY-FIRST REGIMENT

Officers who Served in the Sutlej Campaign

Names	Remarks
Lieutenant-Colonel and Brevet-Colonel Samuel Bolton, C.B. (Commanding the 1st Brigade)	Mortally wounded at Moodkee.
Lieut.-Colonel John Byrne	Severely wounded at Moodkee. Appointed C.B.
,, James Spence	Promoted from Major vice Bolton. Appointed C.B.
Major George Baldwin	Mortally wounded at Ferozeshah.
Captain William Gibson Willes	Mortally wounded at Moodkee.
,, T. Bulkeley	Dangerously wounded at Moodkee.
,, G. D. Young	Dangerously wounded at Moodkee.
,, G. F. White	Acting Paymaster, but commanded his company until after Aliwal.
,, J. Garvock	Severely wounded at Sobraon. Promoted Brevet-Major.
,, D. F. Longworth	Promoted Brevet-Major.
,, E. Lugard	Wounded at Moodkee. Promoted Brevet-Major.
Lieutenant T. H. Plasket	Severely wounded at Ferozeshah.
,, W. F. Atty	Wounded at Aliwal.
,, John Lucas Romulus Pollard	Wounded at Moodkee. Killed at Ferozeshah.
,, Henry William Hart	Killed at Moodkee.
,, Robert Law	Severely wounded at Sobraon.
,, J. P. Robertson	
,, A. S. Bolton	Severely wounded at Sobraon.
,, Graham Elmslie	Severely wounded at Sobraon.
,, Poole Gabbett	Severely wounded at Sobraon.
,, S. J. Timbrell	Dangerously wounded at Sobraon.
,, John Brenchley	Mortally wounded at Moodkee.
,, A. Pilkington	Severely wounded at Ferozeshah.
,, Edward Andrew Noel	
Ensign James Paul	Wounded at Ferozeshah.
,, H. P. Hutton	Wounded at Ferozeshah.
,, Charles Hill Grant Tritton	Mortally wounded at Sobraon.
,, William Jones	Killed at Sobraon.
Lieutenant and Adjutant William Bernard	Killed at Ferozeshah.
Assistant-Surgeon Robert Beresford Gahan (attached)	Killed at Moodkee.

Byrne was wounded, by Major Spence. The regiment had been detached from the remainder of the force during the day's march, and was hurried up from the rear at high speed by Colonel Bolton, who was aware that an action was impending.

It is stated in Cannon's record that the distance actually covered by the regiment during the day's march was not less than twenty-five miles, and that it had been hurried up at such speed that at the last halt, about two miles from Moodkee, scarcely fifty men were left with the colours, and for miles to the rear the rest of the regiment might be seen staggering forward through the soft sand in an exhausted state from want of water and rest. This was at about 2 P.M., and two hours later the action commenced, by which time the stragglers had come up, the camp was being pitched, but as yet the men had eaten nothing.

On the alarm being given the regiment at once rushed to their arms, and falling in without a moment's delay, moved forward under Brigadier Bolton's orders to their place in the line. The Thirty-First was formed up in quarter-distance column, on the right of their brigade; but owing to the regiment having been in rear during the day, the extreme right of the line was taken on this occasion by Major-General Wheeler's brigade; Bolton's brigade coming next.

While the infantry was getting ready for its advance, the cavalry, under Sir Hugh Gough's orders, advanced in brilliant style, and attacked both flanks of the Sikh line, which extended far beyond those of the small British force, and threatened to envelop it. Thus boldly engaged, the Sikh horse at once fled, and the British and native cavalry swept down along the rear of the Sikh infantry, disconcerting them for the time. Their front thus cleared the British infantry after a march to the front of about two miles, halted, deployed into line, and advanced to attack the Sikh infantry and artillery, whose exact position was masked by the dense jungle. The British advance was made in an echelon of brigades from the right, and Sir Harry Smith's division, therefore, came first into action, and as events turned out, bore the brunt of the fight. The main incidents of the battle of Moodkee, as far as the Thirty-First was concerned, can be told in a few words.

As soon as Bolton's brigade received the order to advance, the regiment moved steadily and rapidly on, almost immediately forging ahead of the sepoy battalions on either flank. The old Brigadier,

The 31st Regiment at Moodkee.

mounted on his grey Arab, with his orderly bugler by his side, rode in front of the colours of the regiment under which he had been wounded at Albuera more than forty years before. Hardly had the advance begun than a terrific fire from fourteen or fifteen guns broke from the jungle in the very teeth of the regiment, and among the first to fall was Brigadier Bolton, brought down by a mortal wound. Immediately afterwards Lieutenant-Colonel Byrne, who was in command of the regiment, also fell severely wounded, thereupon Major Spence assumed the command. Lieutenants Hart and Brenchley, the officers carrying the colours, both fell mortally wounded, and with them the remainder of the colour party. The colours were immediately raised from the ground by Quartermaster-Sergeant Jones, who carried them during the remainder of the action and was given a commission as Ensign in the regiment in recognition of his gallant service on this occasion. (Colonel Robertson, a survivor of Moodkee, described Quartermaster-Sergeant Jones to the writer as "a splendid man.") By now, however, it had become clear to the officers that the immediate capture of the enemy's position could alone save the regiment from destruction, and, each company led by its officers, the Thirty-First dashed with a wild shout into the thick jungle before it, shooting or bayonetting every Sikh who stood before them. The Sikh artillerymen stood to their guns nobly, firing to the last moment, and almost all fell at their post. Their infantry, too, offered a stout resistance, but the bayonet in the hands of the veteran British infantry was a terrible weapon, and after an hour and a half's continuous fighting the Sikhs had been driven clear off the field, leaving all their advanced guns in the hands of our troops.

The regiment, which had been much scattered during the pursuit, was now assembled and reformed in quarter-distance column, and then, marching back under Major Spence to within a mile or so of Moodkee, bivouacked on the sand for the night until daylight, when it returned to its camp.

In this short but severely-contested action the losses of the Thirty-First were very heavy. The regiment had gone into action with a strength of thirty officers and 844 sergeants, rank-and-file. Of this number nine officers (in addition to Brigadier-General Bolton) and 155 sergeants, rank-and-file were killed or wounded, the details of the casualties being as follows:

OFFICERS KILLED OR MORTALLY WOUNDED

    Brigadier-General S. Bolton, C.B., A.D.C.
    Captain W. G. Willes.
    Lieutenant H. W. Hart.
    ,,   T. Brenchley.
    Assistant-Surgeon R. B. Gahan. Attached for duty.

OFFICERS WOUNDED

    Lieutenant-Colonel J. Byrne (severely).
    Captain T. Bulkeley (dangerously).
    ,,   G. D. Young (dangerously).
    ,,   E. Lugard (slightly).
    Lieutenant J. L. R. Pollard (slightly).

SERGEANTS, RANK-AND-FILE

Killed	34
Wounded	121
Total	155

NAMES OF THE SERGEANTS, RANK-AND-FILE KILLED OR MORTALLY WOUNDED

Sergeant-Major Hugh Mulligan.
Sergeant Michael McRedmond.
Corporal William Quelch.
Private William Whelan.
  ,, Charles McCarthy.
  ,, Robert Biggs.
  ,, Thomas Cowley.
  ,, Keiron Towers.
  ,, John McCaffry.
  ,, Thomas Kennedy.
  ,, John Barrett.
  ,, Thomas Bassett.
  ,, George Deane.
  ,, Peter Murphy.
  ,, Joseph Yates.
  ,, Henry Wilson.
  ,, Richard Roberts.

Private Henry McManus.
  ,, John Marmoy.
  ,, Thomas Marow.
  ,, Alexander Matley.
  ,, Philip Ollarton.
  ,, Henry Sullivan.
  ,, John Humphrey.
  ,, William Bentley.
  ,, Edward Connors.
  ,, John Dongan.
  ,, William Leyfield.
  ,, William Larkin.
  ,, James Wheeler.
  ,, John Grady.
  ,, John Doyle.
  ,, Patrick Hartin.
  ,, Thomas Purdue.

Among the subalterns of the Thirty-First who did good service at Moodkee was Lieutenant J. P. Robertson, afterwards Colonel J. P. Robertson, C.B., a distinguished soldier of the Indian Mutiny campaign, who died in February 1916.

By the kind permission of Mr. Edward Arnold and of the late Colonel Robertson, extracts from his letters describing the actions on the Sutlej follow the account of each battle, and give vivid impressions of war as it appeared to a young and high-spirited combatant officer who was in the thick of every fight. The letters were written soon after the campaign to a brother subaltern, and are, therefore, a little unconventional in parts. After describing the march from Umballa, Lieutenant Robertson mentions that he had nothing to eat on December 17, not having arrived in camp till after dark, when what little food there was in the officers' mess had been eaten.

"On the 18th," he continues, "about twelve o'clock I got some chapatties and milk out of a village which we looted to a small extent but only for grub; the sepoys took all they could get, and forced open doors and windows wherever they went—the *Soors*[1]! We were regularly done up when we got into camp at Moodkee, and lay down on the ground to sleep as the tents were not up. I was just dozing off when I heard a running of men and the order to fall in sharp. We formed at quarter-distance column and went forward immediately, some of the officers with their swords drawn, without their belts, and the men with their jackets off. Old Quigley of the Grenadiers was dressed this way. You may remember him as one of the oldest 31st men. Forward we went, no one knew where to, but all the other regiments were doing the same. Presently the artillery began to blaze away ahead of us, and we saw the shells bursting in the air. We all forgot sore feet then and went on at a kind of run for about three miles, the men calling out, 'Come on boys, or they will be away before we get at them.' Old Willes was riding his white charger, as he was quite done up and couldn't walk. Tritton and I were his subs. We deployed into line, a short distance from a low, thick jungle, on the other side of which there were lots of dust, smoke, and what the men called 'A ——— row going on.' Just as No. 1 was formed something hit the dust in front of us and went whiz over my head. One of the men called out, 'Holy Jesus! that was a bullet!' It was the first I had heard, and sounded very nasty.

"We moved forward with lots of sepoy regiments behind us and the 80th on our left. Presently I saw them form square and some cavalry came out of the dust. This proved to be some stragglers from (our cavalry). Two or three of them halted close behind me, and one called out, 'Go on, boys, there are lots of them before you. We were through them from right to left.' The man was plastered with dirt, and his sword blood-stained. On we went into the jungle, with a tremendous fire of musketry and guns in front of us. Of course we were much broken by the bushes, which would have done well for Light Infantry, but for nothing else, and the men were beginning to get hit. The first person I saw on the ground was Bulkeley, who looked quite dead, and just then there was a sort of rush to the rear of a chief and

[1] This was in friendly territory and the sepoys were looting from their own countrymen, so we may pardon Lieutenant Robertson's warmth.

his followers on horseback, who had been with us all the morning to show us the shortest way. How he got into the fight I know not, but he made the best of his way out again. A beast with two tom-toms, who had been tormenting us all the day with his thumping, nearly rode over us. He was followed by the Hooka Burda, standard-bearer, and the "Bhai-log"[1] in a terrible hurry. The sepoys were doing the same, and one was shot by our men for running away. I saw a batch of them behind a big tree, firing straight up in the air, and shouting to us ' Barrow, Broders, Barrow.'[2] But no ' Barrow ' in them !

"The last words I heard Bolton say were ' Steady, 31st, steady, and fire low for your lives ! ' Cockins, the bugler, was trying to hold the grey horse, when they were all three hit and went down together. This was from the first volley by the enemy. Shortly after Willes was hit, and I took command of No. 1 (which I had all through the campaign). The ball entered his right arm, below the shoulder, and went into his chest, making only one wound. He said he was hit from behind by the sepoys. Young was hit in the back of the neck, and the buckle of his stock saved him, as the ball ran round and came out in front. Hart and Brenchley were both hit in the body, and did not live long.

"We soon got into a regular mob, blazing away at everything in front of us, and nearly as many shots coming from behind us as in front. I saw Napier,[3] the Umballa ' Wattle and dab ' man, in a blue pea-coat and black sailor's hat, laying about him, and Sir H. Hardinge in a black coat and ' tile,' with his ' star on.' Sir Hugh Gough rode up to us and called out, ' We must take those guns.' Law was standing near us with his legs wide, shouting out, ' Charge ! Charge ! and hitting the ground with his sword, and sometimes the men's toes (just as he used to set Growler on Shaw's dog). I called out to Sir Hugh Gough : ' Where are the guns, and we will soon take them ? ' and Somerset[4] put his hat on his sword, and called out, ' Thirty-first, follow me ! ' We rushed after him through the smoke, and had the guns in a moment. On we went and came upon two light guns which the enemy were trying to take off the field ; but some of our shots hit the horses and brought them to a stand. They then took a shot at us, not twenty yards off ; down we went on our noses at the flash, and the grape went over our heads in a

---

[1] Bhai-log = brethren. [2] Go on, brothers, go on.

[3] Captain Napier, the Engineer officer who had helped the Thirty-First to build their barracks. He became Field-Marshal Lord Napier of Magdala.

[4] Captain (Brevet-Major) A. W. F. Somerset, Grenadier Guards, eldest son of Lord Raglan. Major Somerset, who had distinguished himself and had been severely wounded at Maharajpoor, was mortally wounded at Ferozeshah. He was Military Secretary to Sir Henry Hardinge.

shower. I felt it warm ; then a rush, and the guns were ours, the gunners not attempting to run away, but cutting at us with their tulwars. I think those two guns were taken away by the Sikhs later on that night, as I never saw them afterwards. Pollard was shot in the leg at Moodkee, and the sergeant-major, old Mulligan, was cut all to pieces. After it was quite dark the firing was kept up, the men blazing away at nothing, or at each other, and the bugles sounding ' cease firing ' in all directions. At last they left off firing, and we got something like a regiment formed at quarter distance, but no colours or bugler to sound the Regimental Call, so we got a nigger bugler to try it, and just as he got out a squeak someone nearly knocked the bugle down his throat ; this was Sir Harry Smith, who asked what on earth we were making such a row for. We were a long time collecting the men, and then marched back towards camp, but were halted some way in front of it, and had to sleep on the sand till morning. So much for my first battle." [1]

Such is Lieutenant Robertson's narrative of the battle of Moodkee, a victory won, as his plain tale shows, by the individual gallantry of the officers and men of the British regiments engaged.

Lieutenant Noel stated in a letter to his father that the Thirty-First captured fourteen guns at Moodkee, and that Lieutenant Bolton, adjutant of the regiment and son of Colonel Bolton, greatly distinguished himself in personal combats at the guns.

In another letter Lieutenant Robertson tells us that on the day after the battle volunteers were called for to bring in the dead and wounded, but scarcely had they arrived on the field than they were ordered back, an immediate attack by the Sikhs being expected. The attack was not made, but the troops were kept standing under arms all day in the sun. In the evening Lieutenants Hart and Brenchley were buried in one grave, below a large tree on the west side of the village of Moodkee. Brigadier-General Bolton survived until January 4, 1846, on which day he died in his tent outside Ferozepore fort.

On the day following the battle, December 20, the troops had a rest, and reinforcements joined the army. The losses at Moodkee had amounted to 215 of all ranks killed and 657 wounded, a total of 872 ; but these casualties were more than replaced by the arrival of two fine British regiments, the 29th and the 1st European Light

[1] From *Personal Adventures*, by Col. J. P. Robertson. (London, Edward Arnold.) By permission.

Infantry, with a division of heavy guns. There were no means of sending the wounded back to British India, and they were consequently lodged in a small native fort at Moodkee, where they were left under the protection of two native infantry battalions.

During the rest day, December 20, the troops were reorganised for a renewed attack on the main Sikh army under Sardar Lal Singh, and on that night Sir John Littler received orders to march out of Ferozepore, leaving two battalions to guard that town and fort, and to join hands with Sir Hugh Gough.

Owing to the death at Moodkee of Major-Generals Sir Robert Sale and Sir John McCaskill, and the disablement by wounds of three brigade commanders, several changes had to be made in the distribution of the army. The Governor-General, Sir Henry Hardinge, though senior to Sir Hugh Gough, offered his services as Second-in-Command, and the offer was thankfully accepted. The newly-arrived troops were also allotted to brigades. An immediate attack on the Sikh army being intended, an issue of sixty rounds of ammunition and two days' cooked rations was made to every soldier; and at four in the morning of December 21 the whole force at Moodkee was formed up in line of columns, ready to advance against the Sikh position or towards the column from Ferozepore, as might be ordered. The Sikh army under Lal Singh was known to lie about two miles north of the road to Ferozepore, and to be entrenched about the village of Ferozeshah.

Sir Hugh Gough, who knew that Sir John Littler's Division would soon be on the march to join him, desired to attack Ferozeshah early in the morning, with the troops under his own command, leaving Sir John Littler the duty of supporting him. This plan was, however, overruled by the Governor-General, who considered that the Sikhs had fought so well at Moodkee that a junction of the British army was imperatively necessary before Ferozeshah could be attacked; and to this decision Sir Hugh Gough was, of course, compelled to give way. This he did in the most loyal manner.

Battle of Ferozeshah

The order to advance to the attack on Ferozeshah was consequently postponed until at about one o'clock, Sir John Littler, who had skilfully withdrawn from Ferozepore without being attacked by the Sikh army of observation under Sardar Tej Singh, arrived at a point about two miles distant from the Ferozeshah position.

In one respect the delay was unfortunate, for December 21 is the shortest day of the year, and it was nearly four in the afternoon before the now united army could be formed up for attack. The Moodkee troops had then been nearly fourteen hours under arms, and the Ferozepore Division about eight hours. The latter now occupied the left of the infantry line, while Major-General Gilbert's Division was on the right and Brigadier-General Wallace's in the centre. Sir Harry Smith's Division was in reserve, with the 1st Brigade in its proper place on the right, and with the Thirty-First on the right of the brigade.

The battle of Ferozeshah began at 4 P.M., the British artillery advancing and pouring an effective fire on the Sikh position, which could plainly be seen. The infantry meanwhile were ordered to lie down and rest prior to their attack.

From some unexplained cause the Ferozepore Division appears to have advanced prematurely to the attack, and as its left brigade, which was composed of three native battalions, sustained no casualties, its share in the attack must have been slight. The right brigade, however, advanced gallantly and marched steadily towards the entrenchment under a storm of grape which caused heavy losses. The European regiment in the brigade, the 62nd Regiment, lost 104 killed and 195 wounded, and the two native battalions also lost heavily. Finally the attack came to a standstill at 150 yards from the position, and seeing that success was for the moment impossible the Brigadier ordered a retirement.

The news of this repulse soon reached the troops on the right, and the two divisions on that flank were at once ordered to attack. The advance was made in echelon of brigades from the right, the Commander-in-Chief personally leading the right brigade of Gilbert's Division, while Sir Henry Hardinge took command of Wallace's Division. Gilbert's attack was gallantly delivered, the 29th and 80th Regiments advancing in eager rivalry, while McLaren's brigade coming up on their left and holding its fire, marched steadily on the entrenchment. Presently the whole of Gilbert's Division successfully assaulted and carried the portion of the entrenchment before them, their success being crowned by a glorious charge of the 3rd Light Dragoons, one of the finest feats ever performed by British cavalry.

Wallace's Division now came up on the left of Gilbert, and through blinding dust and smoke, and with much consequent confusion, also succeeded in penetrating the Sikh entrenchment and in capturing some of the guns which had repulsed Littler's troops. Then in increasing darkness part of the 9th Regiment, with other detached parties of troops, advanced on the village of Ferozeshah, which they found before them, but discovered that it had already been captured by Sir Harry Smith's Division. This division, on the right of which stood the Thirty-First, had at the beginning of the attack been held in reserve, and stood inactive for about twenty minutes during the advance of the right and centre divisions. During this time several men of the regiment were killed and wounded by round shots which passed over the first line of troops. In consequence of the heavy losses sustained by Gilbert's and Wallace's Divisions, that of Sir Harry Smith was now ordered to advance and reinforce them, and moved forward in excellent order. The first line troops were at this time slowly advancing through the Sikh position, losing heavily as they did so, and the Thirty-First found the ground strewn with dead and wounded men, particularly of the 29th, 80th, and 1st Europeans; and the wounded men warned the regiment not to fire, as they still had friends before them. Presently, however, the Thirty-First found itself with the first line, with a clear front, and opened as hot a fire as possible, though much over-matched by that of the Sikh guns still in action.

At this time many casualties occurred in the regiment, and the horses of all the mounted officers were shot. Major Baldwin and Lieutenant Pollard (who were both mounted) were mortally wounded, and Lieutenant Bernard, the Adjutant, was killed. Lieutenant Pollard, who had distinguished himself by his forward gallantry in the Afghan campaign, had been wounded in the leg at Moodkee. He was, however, able to ride, and was employed at Ferozeshah in giving orders for Major Spence, who had nearly lost his voice. While performing this duty Lieutenant Pollard was mortally wounded by a shot through the body, dying of his wound three days later. So fell a gallant young soldier.

It was now becoming dark, but Sir Harry Smith gave orders to his division to charge the entrenchment, and himself cheered them on to the attack. Once through the entrenchment Sir Harry turned his left brigade towards the village of Ferozeshah, and captured it; but in the darkness and confusion his right brigade, with which was the Thirty-First, became detached and remained with the remnants of Gilbert's division, which soon afterwards were ordered by the Commander-in-Chief to draw off about 300 yards from the Sikh position, reform battalions, and bivouac for the night. Similar orders had been given by Sir John Littler on the left, and the position, therefore, when night fell was as follows.

In the centre Sir Harry Smith, with one of his own brigades (Ryan's) and portions of Gilbert's left brigade (McLaren's) held the village of Ferozeshah. In his right rear, at no great distance, but entirely separated by the darkness, were Sir Harry Smith's right brigade (Hicks') and the remainder of Gilbert's and Wallace's Divisions; on his left rear, but farther away, were the remains of Sir John Littler's Division.

Thus scattered, the British troops, with the Commander-in-Chief and the Governor-General in their midst, passed the night of December 21. It was impossible to ascertain the position of the various bodies of troops, and it was certain that the losses had been very heavy. To many, indeed, in the various detached bodies it seemed that only those troops around them had held their ground, or might even possibly be the only survivors. The men and officers on the right and centre were all worn out with fatigue, having been at work since 2 A.M.; hungry and parched with thirst, for no water could be found; bitterly cold, without great-coats or shelter, and unable to light fires without bringing down the enemy's fire upon them; the night seemed interminable, while the Sikhs made the darkness hideous by their shouts and clamour.

Lieutenant Robertson, in his letter describing the battle, gives a vivid picture of the scene when Sir Hugh Gough ordered the troops on the right to retire from the half-captured Sikh entrenchment. Having described the long, wandering march from Moodkee and the advance through the killed and wounded of Gilbert's Division, Lieutenant Robertson writes:

"It was now getting dark and we got the order to move forward, and a little way on we formed a complete line of men and muskets on the ground, with here and there a man or officer standing, or on one knee, keeping up a fire as well as they could, our men calling out, ' Give them it now, there is nothing but the Sikhs in front of us.' Just then a shell burst in my company and knocked a lot of us down. I thought it was all over with me, but got up and found I was not hurt. About twenty men were smashed, and some appeared to have been blown two or three yards off their feet. Baldwin was a little to my left, behind No. 2, and I heard him call out, just as if on parade, ' Captain White, keep your men together, sir, and fill up that gap!' And immediately after, he said, ' I am hit, men, take me off!' One of the men caught him as he fell, and he was taken to the rear. Poor Bernard was shot about the same time, quite dead. His sword was brought to me by Sergeant Kelly of No. 1, and I told him to keep it. The next day Noel took it, as he had broken his own in the final charge. We stood our ground and kept up a sharp fire for a long time, every now and then advancing a little till we were close up to the entrenchment. Many of their tents were on fire, and by that light I saw a large gun, just in front of us, and not a man left with it. The Sikhs had retired, and we had possession of this part of their camp; but instead of holding what we had got with so much loss, we were ordered to retire for the night. We then went back in a sort of mob, men of all regiments being mixed together, and every officer shouting for his company or regiment. One man would say, ' Where is the 80th?' ' Here it is,' would say another. ' No, this is the 31st,' would say a third, and so on. The colours of two or three regiments were all together, and everyone would have it that he was right. I ran up against Law,[1] who was crying out, ' Where is Paul and the colours?' and at last seeing him, he held on, and called out, ' Here is the 31st; this way 31st,' etc., till we got into some sort of order. But there was no firing in front of us then, and we thought the battle was over. We formed at quarter-distance column, and lay down on the cold sand. It was then we began to feel the most frightful thirst, and not a drop of anything was to be had. I had a little gin in a flask, and took a pull at it, giving the rest to the men with me. But this only made us the worse, and the cold was so intense that we were quite frozen.

" I shall never forget the miseries of that night. There was no end of a row in the Sikh camp and a constant dropping fire, but we thought this was our own people, and by the light of the tents I could see there were lots of men moving about, but presently one or two guns opened on us with grape and round shot. We just lay where we

---

[1] Of Lieutenant Law his brother officer Lieutenant Noel wrote at a later date: " My old friend Law... a very fine gallant officer, who cut a man's head clean off during that war, at Ferozeshah; a very fine swordsman and a very good comrade."

were and let them pepper away. There was a horrid bugler sounding some nigger regimental call, and every time he sounded, bang! bang! came the grape amongst us. At length Sir Hugh, who was just behind us with those of his staff who were left, ordered the 80th to form line and retake the guns. It was just as well he did this, for they had not gone far before they met an immense number of Sikh infantry crawling down upon us, to find out where we were. After a sharp fire, and losing a section of grenadiers by one discharge of grape, they took the guns. . . . The cold was very severe and we had nothing to cover ourselves with, so I took little Tritton in my arms and put Sergeant Murphy at my back, with two or three fat men for blankets and pillow, and there we lay all night, one above the other, to try and keep ourselves warm. I was soon fast asleep, for even the shot could not keep me awake."[1]

FEROZESHAH—(Second day, December 22)

We have seen how the main body of the British army, with which were the Commander-in-Chief and Governor-General, passed the night of December 21. The small force under Sir Harry Smith, in its advanced position by Ferozeshah village, was, of course, even more exposed. Sir Harry only knew that he was isolated, and that there was apparently no hope of support from the rear, and feeling therefore that he could not hope to withstand a strong attack by daylight, he decided to fall back in the direction of Sir John Littler's Division. Accordingly at 3 A.M. on December 22, he evacuated Ferozeshah, and guided by the light of Littler's bivouac, he quickly effected a junction with Sir John's troops, near the village of Misreewallah.

At early dawn the troops under Sir Hugh Gough were ordered to form line and renew the attack on the Sikh position. Fatigue and thirst were for the moment forgotten, and line was quickly formed. In front of the right rode the Commander-in-Chief, while Sir Henry Hardinge placed himself in front of the left. Generals Gilbert and Wallace headed their respective divisions. On the extreme right of the line were the Thirty-First, with the remains of the two native infantry regiments of Hicks' brigade; the horse artillery were posted on the flanks of the line, and the heavy guns and a rocket battery were in

---

[1] From *Personal Adventures*, by Col. J. P. Robertson. (London, Edward Arnold.) By permission.

the centre. The guns opened as effective a fire as was possible upon the Sikhs, under cover of which the infantry advanced in fine style, unchecked by the enemy's fire, until the charge was sounded. Thereupon the whole line rushed upon the Sikhs, when a wild fight ensued, the bayonet opposed by the Sikh sword. One soldier of the Thirty-First had his four fingers cut clean off against the barrel of his musket as he drove the bayonet home. The position was quickly carried, and then, changing front to the left, our infantry swept the whole camp clear of their brave enemy, who had fought with the utmost courage and determination. The British line then halted and drew up victorious on the hard-fought field; and presently received Sir Hugh Gough and Sir Henry Hardinge with loud cheers as they rode together down the line. Soon afterwards Sir John Littler's Division and Sir Harry Smith's 2nd brigade came up, and the whole army was concentrated in the Sikh position.

Lieutenant Robertson's letters again give some interesting details concerning the doings of the Thirty-First. He mentions that when line was formed in the early morning some of the guns were placed ready for action immediately in front of the regiment. Major Spence, with good judgment, moved the regiment to the right and got clear of the guns. There was at the time a thick mist and they could only see a few yards ahead. Presently a Sikh battery opened on our guns on the right, which answered the fire. Had not Major Spence moved the regiment many casualties would have occurred. Lieutenant Robertson continues:

"We advanced very quietly upon a strong battery on the left of the Sikh camp and just at the angle; they did not see us till we were right upon them, and they had only time to fire one or two rounds when we gave them a volley and charged right into them. Spence was on foot in front[1] and was one of the first over the ditch. We bayonetted a great many artillerymen and infantry who stood to the last; we also took a standard,[2] and then charged on through the camp, polishing off all we could get at."[3]

[1] His horse had been shot on the previous day.
[2] This standard was captured by Lieutenant Noel. It is now in the possession of his son, Colonel W. F. N. Noel. In a home letter Lieutenant Noel mentions that he took prisoner at Ferozeshah "one Porter," an Englishman, who held a high command in the Sikh artillery. Porter, he adds, was a Maidstone man.
[3] From *Personal Adventures*, by Col. J. P. Robertson. (London, Edward Arnold.) By permission.

Bivouac of the 31st Regiment, Feroseshah.

The troops which had won this hard-fought struggle now felt greatly exhausted, and suffered particularly from thirst. The Thirty-First found a well. Lieutenant Robertson says:

"I got a bucket and made a long line for it by cutting off a lot of ropes from the tents and tying them together. There was such a rush to the well that I was nearly pushed in and had to get a party of men to stand behind and protect me. I drew the water as fast as possible, while the mob standing round almost fought for it, and during the time I was at work, Sir Hugh Gough came up with one or two of his staff, and it was some time before he got any water, as there was nothing to drink out of but my bucket; the men were too mad with thirst to pass it even to the Commander-in-Chief." [1]

A little food was found in the Sikh camp: some oranges, a supply of grain and parched peas, and coarse sugar. This was better than nothing to the exhausted soldiers, but before even the oranges could be eaten the alarm was given that the enemy's cavalry was advancing, and the infantry were ordered to fall in and form battalion squares.

The newly-arrived enemy was the large Sikh army under Sardar Tej Singh, which before the battle had been threatening Ferozepore. Tej Singh, finding at length that Sir John Littler had evaded him, had marched very early in the morning of December 22, and now approached the entrenchment occupied on the day before by Lal Singh's army. This he soon discovered to be in the possession of the British, and having no confidence in his own generalship, he drew up at no great distance from the entrenchment, hesitating whether or not to attack. The little British army was now in most imminent danger. The losses on December 21 had been heavy; the men were much exhausted from want of rest and food; and the ammunition was expended. Tej Singh drew up his army as if preparing for an attack, and sending his artillery to the front opened a heavy fire on the British squadrons, and he also made successive attacks on the left and right British flanks, both of which were repulsed. A general assault must almost inevitably have resulted in the complete destruction of the British force, and at this most critical moment a large part of Sir Hugh Gough's cavalry and horse-artillery left the field. This was in consequence of an order given by an officer of the staff, who was afterwards found to have been

---

[1] From *Personal Adventures*, by Col. J. P. Robertson. (London, Edward Arnold). By permission.

suffering from sunstroke. There was, however, no sign of wavering on the part of the little British army in the entrenchment. The Governor-General sent some non-combatants, and a Prussian Prince who was present, off the field under the charge of his own escort; but he himself determined to share the fate of the army. Riding into the square of the Thirty-First, says Lieutenant Robertson, "the Governor-General thus addressed us in a firm voice: 'Thirty-first, I was with you when you saved the Battle of Albuera; behave like men now.'"

Tej Singh and his army remained looking at the task before them for more than three hours—(Lieutenant Robertson writes that the artillery fire went on for hours and that he fell fast asleep)—and in the end no decisive attack was made. It is believed by some that the strange retirement of part of the British cavalry and horse artillery alarmed Tej Singh, who could not understand the movement and imagined that a turning movement was in progress against him. Others hold that, hearing of the heavy losses incurred by Lal Singh's army, though holding a strong position, Tej Singh thought an attack on the British, now holding the same position, was impossible. Whatever the cause, Tej Singh, after a three hours' heavy and effective bombardment of the exhausted British infantry, suddenly limbered up his guns and marched away northward towards the Sutlej; his cavalry, which covered his retirement, being most gallantly and effectively charged as it moved off by a squadron of the 3rd Light Dragoons. So ended the memorable battle of Ferozeshah, one of the most critical ever fought in British India.

The losses of our army were very heavy. The killed numbered 694, of whom 499 were British. The wounded were 1721, of whom 1142 were British. It therefore seems clear that the native troops did not take a fair share of the fighting.

The Thirty-First (which had had ten officers killed and wounded at Moodkee) went into action with a strength of 721, and lost three officers killed or mortally wounded, and four wounded at Ferozeshah. Of the sergeants and rank-and-file, seventy-three were killed or mortally wounded, and eighty-two wounded. The total casualties were therefore 162, which added to the 165 Moodkee casualties, reduced the strength of the regiment by 327.

THE SUTLEJ CAMPAIGN

The officers killed or mortally wounded at Ferozeshah were:

Major George Baldwin.
Lieutenant J. L. R. Pollard,
Lieutenant and Adjutant W. Bernard.

The wounded officers were:

Lieutenant T. Plasket, severely.
,, A. Pilkington, ,,
Ensign J. Paul, slightly.
,, H. P. Hutton, ,,

The names of the sergeants, rank-and-file, killed or mortally wounded were:

Sergeant John Kinnaly.
,, Samuel Tivelly.
Corporal Martin Collier.
,, John Tritton.
Drummer William Dougherty.
Private John Barrett.
,, Abraham Bottles.
,, John Brankin.
,, James Bridgeman.
,, Patrick Burns.
,, John Cahill.
,, John Callaghan.
,, John Candler.
,, Michael Clarke.
,, James Cleary.
,, James Coapes.
,, Maurice Coffey.
,, Joseph Cornelius.
,, James Crossley.
,, Patrick Dalton.
,, John Daniel.
,, Michael Donohoe.
,, Matthew Doolan.
,, Patrick Dowlan.
,, William Emerson.
,, Andrew Finnegan.
,, Richard Fishwick.
,, John Garner.
,, Charles Gilbert.
,, John Grady.
,, Andrew Handridge.
,, Patrick Healy.
,, John Hiscox.
,, William Hitchcock.
,, Charles Hopgood.
,, John Hughes.
,, Arthur Hunt.

Private George Jones.
,, James Kehoe.
,, John Kelly.
,, Robert Kennaway.
,, Anthony Kennedy.
,, Michael Kenney.
,, Michael Lawler.
,, Timothy McDermot.
,, Charles McQuillan.
,, Hugh Macready.
,, Samuel Marlow.
,, John Moran.
,, Patrick Muldoon.
,, William Mullins.
,, Peter Murphy.
,, James Neagle.
,, Michael Nunan.
,, James O'Brien.
,, John O'Neill.
,, Samuel Petch.
,, Edward Poulton.
,, Stephen Prout.
,, John Regan.
,, John Ryan.
,, Henry Saunders.
,, Charles Scales.
,, Patrick Sheridan.
,, Charles Sheppard.
,, James Stapleton.
,, John Stephens.
,, John Stewart.
,, John Tatton.
,, William Tudor.
,, Andrew Tully.
,, William Wildridge.
,, Nevin Williamson.

As has already been stated, Brigadier-General Bolton, C.B., A.D.C., died of his wound received at Moodkee, as did Captain Willes; and Major Baldwin, a veteran officer who had served at Waterloo, died of the wounds received by him at Ferozeshah. Major Spence, who had highly distinguished himself in both actions, was promoted to the vacant Lieutenant-Colonelcy by Sir Hugh Gough, the promotion being subsequently confirmed by the Commander-in-Chief at the Horse Guards. Captains Bulkeley and Young, who had both been dangerously wounded at Moodkee, were promoted to the vacant Majorities. It need only be added that in the Governor-General's General Order, congratulating the army on the victories of Moodkee and Ferozeshah, Sir Henry Hardinge stated that "Her Majesty's infantry regiments . . . distinguished themselves by the most devoted courage in braving the destructive fire of the enemy's batteries, and valiantly capturing their guns." In Sir Harry Smith's "Autobiography" that distinguished soldier writes of Ferozeshah: "The 1st Brigade of my Division especially Her Majesty's Thirty-first Regiment, greatly distinguished itself and suffered severely."

Action of Badowal

After Ferozeshah the Sikh army, much shaken by a loss of some 5000 men and nearly 100 guns, recrossed the Sutlej, while Sir Hugh Gough encamped at Sultan Khan Wala and awaited the arrival of reinforcements. On December 27, Sir Hugh moved closer to the Sikhs, halting at Arufkee, while Sir Harry Smith's Division was placed on the right at Malowal, from which two points the fords on the Sutlej that were within reach of the Sikh position at Sobraon, could be closely watched.

On January 6, 1846, reinforcements amounting to about 10,000 men, under Sir John Grey, reached the army; and about 2000 men also reinforced the weak garrison of Ludhiana. The Sikh army had also been largely reinforced and equipped with new guns from Lahore, and about the same date began to cross the Sutlej and threaten Ludhiana. Sir Hugh Gough, therefore, on January 17, despatched a force under Sir Harry Smith with orders in the first instance to reduce a fort called Dharamkot, midway between Ferozeshah and Ludhiana, in which the Sikhs had a garrison. Sir Harry Smith reduced Dharamkot without

THE SUTLEJ CAMPAIGN

fighting on January 17, and two days later marched further eastward to Kohari. On the following day (January 20) he marched to Jograon, where he was joined by the 53rd Regiment, which had marched up from Delhi. Sir Harry's force then consisted of three regiments of cavalry, eighteen guns and four regiments of infantry, including the Thirty-First and 53rd. Of these the Thirty-First and the two native regiments were weak in numbers. The total strength of the force was about 5000 men.

On January 21 Sir Harry marched towards Ludhiana, but while on the march, at about 11 A.M., he unexpectedly found the Sikh army under Sardar Ranjur Singh posted at the village of Badowal, directly in his path. Sir Harry had ordered the Ludhiana troops to meet him, but they had not moved, and in view of their isolation he decided that it was necessary for him to force his way past the Sikh army, in order to join hands with the Ludhiana troops. The action which resulted, known as the action of Badowal, proved to be very critical to the small British force, which was most ably handled by Sir Harry Smith.

Ranjur Singh's army, estimated by Sir Harry himself at 30,000 men with fifty guns, was posted in the direct line of advance on Ludhiana, which Sir Harry had intended to follow. Had he carried out this intention, the fortified town of Badowal would have been on his right and the Sikh army on his left; and the small British force would probably have been crushed by numbers, though a large proportion of the Sikh army were irregulars. Sir Harry, however, on discovering that the town of Badowal was strongly held and the Sikh army was close by, instead of thirty miles away as he had been informed, at once decided to strike off to the right, and if possible to march round the Sikhs and evade a general action. His troops had already marched between sixteen and eighteen miles, and in order to carry out his plan Sir Harry was compelled to advance in battle array over heavy ploughed land, while from the walls of Badowal and a string of villages which afforded shelter to the Sikh army, Ranjur Singh's artillery poured a heavy flank fire on the British column, causing considerable losses. In order to ward off a close attack on his left flank, and to prevent his advance being blocked, Sir Harry Smith placed his cavalry and artillery in front; his infantry marched in column at wheeling distance, so that at any moment line could be formed towards the enemy; his baggage, with the sick and wounded, marched on the right flank and were ordered to keep well up towards the front.

As the column moved on in this formation, Ranjur Singh, with a tactical skill unusual among the Sikh leaders, planned a formidable attack on the British rear. Pouring in a heavy artillery fire on Sir Harry Smith's left, and thus delaying his advance, the Sikhs moving (as Sir Henry states in his "Autobiography") "with a dexterity and quickness not to be exceeded," formed a line of seven battalions directly across his rear, with guns in the intervals between battalions. This able movement threatened an attack in line against the fatigued British infantry marching in column. Sir Harry accepted the challenge, and under a fierce cannonade, ordered the Thirty-First to carry out a difficult parade movement, *a counter-march on the centre by wings*, thus forming line facing the Sikhs. The other regiments conformed to the movement, and, thus coolly handled in the face of danger, the infantry, British and native alike, showed perfect steadiness. Sir Harry Smith, however, found his men so exhausted that he decided not to attack the Sikhs, but to continue his march towards Ludhiana. The Sikhs, overawed by this bold front, and reluctant to lose the protection of the walls of Badowal, made no further advance, and Sir Harry marched on unmolested, reaching Ludhiana early in the evening.

The losses of the small British force in the action of Badowal were considerable, the proportion of killed to wounded being unusually high. The Thirty-First had fourteen men killed, seven wounded, and nineteen taken prisoners.

The names of the killed were as follow:

Corporal Thomas Woodcock.	Private James McDermott.
Private Charles Brown.	,, John O'Hara.
,, John Carroll.	,, William Pickford.
,, John Charters.	,, Thomas Rylance.
,, James Eagan.	,, Edward Smithson.
,, Samuel Hocker.	,, John Taylor.
,, Patrick McCarthy.	,, Daniel Smith.

The prisoners, men who had fallen exhausted during the fighting, fell into the hands of the Sikh regular regiments, and were kindly treated by them until the end of the campaign, when they were released. Unhappily this treatment was not extended to the sick and wounded, who were all murdered without mercy, perhaps by the camp followers and villagers, as they lay in their *doolies*. Lieutenant Robertson writes:

"After two or three days we returned to Badowal, as the Sikhs had retired to the banks of the Sutlej, and we found our poor sick men lying killed in the jungle, most of them in the *doolies*, as they had been shot as they lay in bed by the muzzle of a musket being put against their side. You can imagine how savage the men were after such a sight."

The bodies of these unfortunates were buried by their comrades on January 24, and two days later Sir Harry Smith's force was joined by his 2nd Brigade from Headquarters of the army. This reinforcement, added to the Ludhiana troops, brought his force up to a strength of about 10,000 fighting men. That of the 1st Brigade was as follows:—Thirty-First Regiment, 544; 24th Native Infantry, 481; 36th Native Infantry, 571. Total, 1596.

Sardar Ranjur Singh's army was also reinforced by 4000 regular infantry of the best quality, and twelve guns; and thus strengthened he took up a position at Aliwal, about sixteen miles distant from Badowal, and awaited an attack. Finding that Wheeler's Brigade were in want of rest after their rapid march to join him, Sir Harry Smith halted his force on January 27, and marched at daybreak on the 28th to attack the Sikh army.

Battle of Aliwal

Sir Harry Smith advanced in the following order. In his front were two brigades of cavalry in contiguous columns of squadrons, with two troops of horse-artillery. The cavalry scouted the country while advancing, as it had been reported that the Sikh army was in motion and intended to take the initiative. In rear of the cavalry, the infantry marched in contiguous columns of brigades at deploying intervals, so that whenever it might be desired to form line each brigade could deploy immediately on its leading company; the field-guns being placed in the intervals between brigades. Godby's brigade, composed of regiments from Ludhiana, was placed on the right, and next came Hicks's brigade (Thirty-First, 24th and 47th Native Infantry). In the left centre was Wheeler's brigade (50th Regiment, 48th N. I. and the Sirmur Gurkha Battalion) and Wilson's brigade (53rd Regiment, 30th N. I. and Shekawatti Battalion) marched on the left.

In this order Sir Harry Smith's force advanced six miles, when a distant view of the enemy was obtained. The Sikhs, as had been reported, were in motion, and held a long ridge directly facing the British line of advance. The village of Aliwal was in the left centre of the position, and the Sikh left, beyond it, was entrenched. On nearing this position Sir Harry ordered his cavalry to clear off to the flanks, thus displaying the heads of his infantry columns, which, on reaching some hard level ground, deployed into line. The flank brigades were at first slightly drawn back.

Presently, on a further inspection of the Sikh position, Sir Harry saw that its left outflanked his right, and he, therefore, ordered his infantry to break into open column and take ground to that flank. In his own narrative of the fight he writes :

" When I had gained sufficient ground, the troops wheeled into line. There was no dust, the sun shone brightly. These manœuvres were performed with the celerity and precision of the most correct field day. The glistening of the bayonets and swords of this order of battle was most imposing ; and the line advanced."

It speaks well for the courage and discipline of the Sikh army that it remained steady in its position while these formidable preparations for attack went on under its eyes. Scarcely had the British line advanced 150 yards, when, at ten o'clock, the enemy opened a fierce cannonade from his whole line.

Sir Harry, having now advanced close up to the Sikh position, was able to select his point of attack, which was the Sikh left. He, therefore, brought Godby's Brigade forward into line with the 1st Brigade under Brigadier-General Hicks, and ordering a charge led the two brigades in what he styles " A rapid and noble charge " into the village of Aliwal. Sir Harry then ordered the two brigades to swing round to their left and then again advancing, they swept up the whole Sikh left and drove it in confusion on to its centre. Sir Harry, in his narrative adds :—" Her Majesty's Thirty-first Foot and the native regiments contended for the front, and the fight became general."

Meanwhile the troops under Brigadier-Generals Wheeler and

Wilson advanced with equal spirit against the Sikh right, and as they approached the Sikh regular infantry and guns on that flank, their task was aided by a magnificent charge by the 16th Lancers and 3rd Bengal Light Cavalry, the 16th in particular breaking more than one well-formed infantry square.

The whole Sikh force was now driven from its guns, which were all captured at the point of the bayonet, the Sikh gunners dying bravely at their posts. Being hotly pursued by the British of all arms the Sikh infantry rushed in confusion to the ford in rear of their position, and struggled across the Sutlej, suffering very heavy losses.

Sir Harry Smith's losses were not severe, thanks in great measure to his brilliant leadership. In his 10,000 men there were 151 killed, 413 wounded, and twenty-five missing; a total of 589. The Thirty-First escaped with astonishingly few casualties: one officer, Lieutenant Atty, being wounded, Private John Chapman killed, and fourteen men wounded. Lieutenant Atty, a first-rate soldier, died at Meerut on May 8, 1846, in his twenty-fourth year, and no less than eleven of the wounded men also died in hospital.

In his despatch Sir Harry Smith speaks in terms of high praise of the regiment, referring to the " glorious services " of the Thirty-First and 50th. He also offered his warmest thanks to Lieutenant-Colonel Spence, commanding the Thirty-First, and to Captains Lugard and Garvock of the regiment for services on the staff. " To Captain Lugard," he writes, "I am deeply indebted, and the service still more so; a more cool, intrepid, and trustworthy officer cannot be brought forward." [1]

In his General Orders of February 2, the Governor-General made the following reference to the regiment : " Great praise is due to Brigadier Hicks, who, with Her Majesty's Thirty-first regiment, the 24th and 47th Native Infantry, stormed the village of Aliwal, drove the enemy from it, and seized the guns by which it was defended."

After Aliwal, the left bank of the Sutlej was cleared of the Sikhs, with the exception of the force entrenched at Sobraon, which was being

---

[1] Captain Lugard attained to high rank and distinction, and died as General The Right Hon. Sir Edward Lugard, Colonel of the East Surrey Regiment on the 31st October, 1898.

watched by the Commander-in-Chief. There was no more danger of a Sikh advance, nor of any attack on the British lines of communication. The siege train from Delhi, moreover, was approaching the army, and, the Sobraon force once disposed of, all was ready for an advance to Lahore. Sir Hugh Gough, however, was not strong enough to attack Sobraon in the absence of Sir Harry Smith's force, and the latter was, therefore, ordered to rejoin Headquarters immediately after his victory at Aliwal had cleared up the situation to the eastward.

While awaiting the return of Sir Harry Smith, the Commander-in-Chief once more changed the composition of his army, so that when the 1st Division arrived at Headquarters, on February 8, the 1st Brigade found itself reduced to two battalions, the Thirty-First and the 47th Native Infantry. The Thirty-First had been reduced by its losses to about 450 bayonets and was left almost without senior officers. Lieutenant-Colonel Spence was removed from the regiment, as owing to the absence of Brigadier-General Hicks he had assumed command of the 1st Brigade. Captains Lugard and Garvock being employed on the staff, and Captain White being in hospital at Ludhiana suffering from the effects of the sun, the regiment was now commanded by Captain Longworth, the only captain remaining on regimental duty. Lieutenant Atty, though so recently wounded, was present with his company, but as from his wound he was unable to ride, Lieutenant Law acted as second in command. The remaining officers were Lieutenants Robertson, Bolton (Adjutant), Elmslie, Gabbett, Timbrell, Noel, Paul, Hutton and Tritton, Ensign Jones, and Quartermaster Benison. Ensign Jones, who held the appointment of Quartermaster-Sergeant at the beginning of the campaign, had been promoted to a commission after the battle of Ferozeshah, but his career as an officer was destined to be very short.

Sir Henry Hardinge, who had been at Ferozepore, rejoined the army on the same day as Sir Harry Smith (February 8th), and on the following afternoon Sir Hugh Gough summoned the Generals of Division and the Brigadiers of his army, and explained to them very clearly his plan of attack for the next day.

The Sikh position on the left bank of the Sutlej opposite Sobraon had originally consisted of a circular entrenchment covering a bridge of boats. During Sir Hugh Gough's pause after the battle of Ferozeshah, however, the Sikh army at Sobraon had gradually grown in strength until there were in the position at least 20,000 men, and according to some authorities a number nearer 30,000. To give cover to this great assemblage the Sikhs had constructed a second line of entrenchments in advance of the original one, and eventually a third line about two miles in length, yet further in advance. This outer line was in a semicircular form, and in the centre and left portions was strongly constructed. The breastworks had a command of six feet and were provided with deep ditches. They were also loopholed for musketry and had well-constructed gun-epaulements. The left of the semicircle rested apparently on the river bank, and it had been intended to carry the right also to the river. Sir Hugh Gough had, however, ascertained from a native spy that the works on this flank were not continuous, were of slight strength, and did not reach the river. The guns in the works on the right were only light swivel guns, but on the other hand they were effectually supported by a battery of heavy guns on commanding ground on the right bank of the Sutlej.

Sir Hugh decided to make his main attack on the Sikh right, and entrusted it to Sir Robert Dick, a gallant veteran of the Peninsula and Waterloo, who had succeeded Sir John McCaskill in the command of the 3rd Division. Sir Robert Dick's Division had been made especially strong in British troops, and, for the attack, he was given a third brigade as a reserve. Sir Robert, therefore, had at his disposal nine battalions, five of which were British; he was to be supported by the fire of thirteen field-guns, and his flank to be guarded by a cavalry brigade.

General Gilbert's Division (the 2nd) was detailed to make a feint attack on the Sikh centre, and that of Sir Harry Smith was to make a similar feint against the enemy's left, the strongest part of the position. Of the cavalry, commanded by Major-General Thackwell, two brigades were to be posted in rear of the flanks, to act as required, while the third, under Colonel Cureton, an able soldier, was to distract the attention of the Sikh commanders by threatening a crossing higher up the river.

Sir Hugh Gough's total force was about 15,000 men, and with them he felt confident of his ability to carry the Sikh position, whatever its strength might be, and to destroy their army.

Sir Hugh proposed to launch his attack early in the day, and therefore, taking advantage of the carelessness of the Sikh army, the British army moved towards their position soon after 3 A.M. on February 10. No sound or sign of the coming attack reached the Sikhs and before daylight the British army was in position, waiting in perfect silence for the dawn of day. When it came, a dense fog so covered the ground that nothing could be seen, and a further delay was necessary. At length, as an eye-witness writes :

"The rising sun rapidly dispelled the fog, when a magnificent picture presented itself. The batteries of artillery were seen in position ready to open fire, and the plain covered with our troops, the fortified village of Rhoda Walla on our left rear being strongly held by our infantry. The enemy appearing suddenly to realise their danger, their drums beat the alarm, their bugles sounded to arms, and in a few minutes their batteries were manned, and pouring shot and shell upon our troops."

The artillery duel thus begun lasted for two hours, at the end of which period of time it was evident that the superiority of fire still rested with the Sikhs. The British fire was slackening and it was reported to General Gough that ammunition was running short. Sir Hugh's decision was instantaneous, and he immediately sent orders to Sir Robert Dick to commence the attack.

Sir Robert received the order at 9 A.M., and his leading brigade at once moved forward in line. Marching very steadily, it advanced, covered till within 300 yards of the Sikh entrenchment by a brigade of horse artillery, which took up successive positions in front of the infantry. On arriving within charging distance, Dick's leading brigade rushed forward with a cheer and carried the first line of entrenchment. A further advance was checked until Sir Robert Dick, in person, brought up his second brigade, in which act he fell mortally wounded. His troops, however, pressed forward, driving the enemy towards the centre of the great space enclosed by the entrenchment. The Sikhs now, seeing their right pierced, made a general rush towards the 3rd Division and in spite of the stout fighting of the two leading brigades, and the assistance of the third brigade, which was also thrown into the fight, drove them back nearly to the outer line of defences.

Sir Hugh Gough, seeing the repulse of his main attack, now sent orders to Generals Gilbert and Harry Smith to convert their demon-

THE SUTLEJ CAMPAIGN

strations into serious attacks, and at the same time he ordered the cavalry under General Thackwell to support the left and centre attacks.

To deal briefly with General Gilbert's attack, it must suffice to say that the 2nd Division, gallantly led, made two unsuccessful attempts to assault the entrenchment in their front, the earthworks being so high and strong that it proved impossible to carry them without scaling ladders. A third attempt, further to their left, and therefore nearer to the 3rd Division, proved successful, and with heavy loss Gilbert's brave fellows forced their way into the Sikh entrenchment. This success, and the fact that the 3rd Division was able to hold its ground, was however due in no small measure to the remarkable feat of arms performed by the cavalry under Major-General Thackwell.

On receiving the Commander-in-Chief's order to assist the infantry, Thackwell, a veteran who had distinguished himself in the Peninsular War and had lost an arm at Waterloo, at once rode forward at the head of two squadrons of the 3rd Light Dragoons, followed by the same strength of the 4th and 5th Bengal Light Cavalry regiments. When General Thackwell arrived within 120 yards of the Sikh entrenchments, he rode forward alone and discovered a place where it was possible to get through them in file at a walk. Disregarding the ill-aimed fire of a flanking battery, Thackwell led the leading squadron through the entrenchment, and then ordering it to form to the front, at once led it in a charge against the dense mass of Sikhs in its front. The first charge was repulsed, as was the charge of the second squadron, but the cavalry continued to press into the entrenchment, each squadron charging in succession, and finally succeeded in driving the great mass of Sikhs back towards their bridge and ford, killing great numbers of them. This feat of Thackwell and his six squadrons must ever rank as one of the most surprising achievements of cavalry.

We must now turn to Sir Harry Smith and the 1st Division, which had been encamped at some little distance from the rest of the army, clear of the British right.

Leaving its camp at about 4 A.M., the Division marched in strict silence through the jungle to its allotted post, close to the bank of the Sutlej. On reaching its position the 1st Brigade, under Lieutenant-Colonel Spence, deployed into line on the Grenadier company of the

Thirty-First, the right resting on the river. The 2nd Brigade, close in rear, also deployed into line, the 50th Regiment covering the Thirty-First, and the two native regiments prolonging the line of the 50th to the left. Pickets were then thrown out in front by the 1st Brigade, arms were piled, and the men ordered to lie down and rest until they were wanted. When the day dawned the 1st Brigade found itself about three-quarters of a mile distant from the enemy's works.

During the two hours' cannonade with which the battle of Sobraon opened, occasional shots only were aimed at the 1st Brigade, and these did no damage.

At about half-past nine o'clock the Commander-in-Chief's order for Sir Harry Smith's Division to advance and attack, was brought by an Aide-de-Camp, and the 1st Brigade (Thirty-First and 47th Native Infantry) immediately sprang to their arms, formed line, and moved forward. Seeing very soon that the entrenchment in front of the brigade was very high, Sir Harry ordered the brigade to take ground to the left in column of sections, until it arrived opposite a more favourable point which he had selected. This done, the sections wheeled again into line, and the brigade advanced to storm the works. The 2nd Brigade at first followed closely in rear of the 1st, but when the latter arrived within 300 yards of the entrenchment, the enemy's fire became very heavy. The 2nd Brigade therefore moved again to its left until clear of the left of the 47th Native Infantry, when it again advanced in line, following the 1st Brigade in echelon of brigades.

Meanwhile the 1st Brigade moved on steadily over very rough ground, entailing a slow advance, under a galling fire of shell, grape, and musketry. Many fell killed and wounded, among the latter, being Captain Garvock (Major of Brigade), and Lieutenant and Adjutant Bolton, whose father had so recently been mortally wounded at the head of the regiment. Lieutenants Law and Gabbett were also seriously wounded before the works were reached, and Lieutenant-Colonel Spence's horse was killed under him, and his sword bent nearly double by a grape shot. Still the line pressed bravely on, and presently reaching the foot of the lofty Sikh entrenchment, endeavoured to rush up it and attack its defenders with the bayonet. The Sikhs, however, as brave as the attacking force, fought at a great advantage. Standing on the superior slope of their parapet they fired down on the English soldiers and sepoys as they struggled up the sandy work, which gave no secure foot-hold to the stormers. The Sikh sword proved a deadly weapon in defence, inflicting terrible wounds on the heads and arms of the assailants. Worst of all, the formation of the brigade in line gave no weight to the attack. The first rush once checked, there were no successive waves of stormers to carry the leaders over the earth works; so the first attack failed, and the soldiers of the 1st Brigade, still facing the enemy, recoiled from a task beyond even their powers.

Sir Harry Smith, seeing the repulse of his first line, at once brought up his 2nd Brigade, which was considerably stronger than the first, and advanced to the attack with equal steadiness and determination. Its losses were very heavy, particularly in the 50th Regiment, which had shared so many fights with the Thirty-First. In the very short interval between the repulse of the first line and the assault of the second, an incident occurred which filled the British troops with fury. The Sikhs, rushing down from their entrenchment, barbarously hacked and mangled every wounded soldier who lay on the ground at their mercy. Infuriated at this sight, the Thirty-First instantly rallied, and returned to the attack, together with the 2nd Brigade. The Sikhs offered the same desperate and successful resistance to the second attack as to the first, but the soldiers, burning to avenge their murdered comrades would not be denied, and a third assault was carried to a successful issue.

While the regiment was reforming for the second attack, Captain Longworth, who alone remained mounted, ordered line to be formed on the colours. This was done, but Lieutenant Tritton, who carried the Queen's colour, was shot through the head, dying in the evening, while Ensign Jones, who carried the regimental colour, was killed almost at the same moment. The Queen's colour was seized by Lieutenant Noel; the regimental colour fell for a moment to the ground, but a brave soldier, Sergeant Bernard McCabe,[1] rushed

[1] In recognition of his gallant conduct, Sergeant McCabe was gazetted to an Ensigncy in the 18th (Royal Irish) Regiment. He eventually rose to the rank of Captain in the 32nd Regiment, and showing throughout his career the same distinguished courage which had first brought him to the front, he was mortally wounded while leading a sortie from the Residency of Lucknow during the Indian Mutiny.

Captain McCabe's memorial tablet in Christ Church, Lucknow, is thus inscribed: "To the glory of God and in memory of Captain Bernard McCabe, H.M.'s 32nd Regiment, who served with conspicuous gallantry in the defence of the Residency of

forward, seized the colour, crossed the ditch and planted it on the ramparts. The men, cheering, scrambled into the entrenchment as best they could, and aided by the entry into the works of some men who found a way by the river bank, drove the Sikhs before them, Lieutenant Noel gallantly carrying in front of the regiment the Queen's colour, the staff of which was shivered in his hand.

The attack, being now everywhere successful, and all three Divisions within the entrenchment, the slaughter of the Sikhs was very great. There was on their part no panic flight; but, unable longer to hold their ground, they retired at a walk to the bridge and ford, fighting staunchly as they fell back. Their ferocious cruelty to the British wounded deprived them of the mercy that might have been granted to their courage, and the artillery, coming into action within the entrenchment, inflicted a terrible loss on the great mass of men struggling across the wide river. Sir Harry Smith, who had seen much of war, wrote of Sobraon:

"By Jupiter! the enemy were within a hair's breadth of driving me back. Their numbers exceeded mine. And such a hand-to-hand conflict ensued, for twenty-five minutes I could barely hold my own. Mixed together, swords and targets against bayonets, and a fire on both sides. I never was in such a personal fight for half the time, but my bull-dogs of the Thirty-first and old 50th stood up like men, were well supported by the native regiments, and my position closed the fight which staggered everywhere. Then such a scene of shooting men fording a deep river, as no one I believe ever saw before. The bodies *made a bridge*, but the fire of our musquetry and cannon killed every one who rushed."

In another letter Sir Harry wrote:

"My gallant Thirty-first and 50th literally staggered under the war of cannon and musquetry. . . . For twenty-five minutes we were at it against four times my numbers, sometimes receding (never turning round, though) sometimes advancing. The old Thirty-first and 50th laid on like devils."

The task allotted to the 1st Division was indeed a tough one, and

Lucknow. He was mortally wounded when leading his fourth sortie, and died on the 1st October, 1857. He obtained his commission when serving with H.M.'s 31st Regiment at the battle of Sobraon for distinguished bravery in planting the Regimental Colour on the enemies' works under a heavy fire."

The 31st Regiment at Sobraon. Sergeant McCabe planting the Colour on the Sikh entrenchment.

THE SUTLEJ CAMPAIGN

the fine services of Sir Harry Smith and his men were thus recognised by the Commander-in-Chief in his despatch to the Governor-General:

" In his attack on the enemy's left Major-General Sir Harry Smith displayed the same valour and judgment which gave him the victory of Aliwal. A more arduous task has seldom, if ever, been assigned to a division. Never has an attempt been more gloriously carried through."

The report of Captain Longworth, who commanded the Thirty-First at Sobraon, gives an interesting though too brief narrative of the doings of the regiment, and makes it clear that the failure of the original attempt to surmount the Sikh earthworks showed that an unaided frontal attack was impossible, and that eventually a way in was discovered at the extremity of the entrenchment, on the very bank of the river. This fact is also mentioned (though not very clearly) by Sir Harry Smith in his "Autobiography," and he adds that, if left to himself, he would have originally attacked at this point.

Captain Longworth's Report

Camp, Attia, 11th February, 1846.

Sir,—I have the honour to state for the information of the Brigadier, that Her Majesty's Thirty-first regiment, under my command, marched from Camp Tulwondee yesterday morning at 4 A.M., in quarter distance column, right in front, being the leading regiment of the first brigade, first division. We advanced in this order till within about two miles of the enemy's position, and then halted, formed line, and waited till daybreak, when we advanced some distance and halted till sunrise, and again advancing, halted with our right resting on the Sutlej within range of the enemy's guns; here we remained about two hours, when we were ordered to advance. This was no sooner discovered by the enemy than they opened upon us a most tremendous fire of round shot from the whole of the guns upon the left flank of their entrenched camp; shell, grape, canister, and a very heavy fire of musketry were showered upon us as we neared the fortifications—but in spite of this, I am proud to say, the regiment advanced steadily and in the best order till within thirty paces of the entrenched camp, when a most destructive fire from overpowering numbers forced us to retire for a short distance, for the purpose of re-forming, as we left a full third of the regiment upon the ground; and I feel convinced that had the regiment remained for five minutes longer in its exposed situation it must have been annihilated, as our fire was totally ineffectual against the enemy's strongly fortified position, which completely protected them, until by a desperate charge, in conjunction with Her Majesty's Fiftieth Regiment, we succeeded in penetrating the extremity of their works extending to the river, and thereby were enabled to bring our fire to bear upon their gunners, who with the most desperate courage turned their guns upon the portion of their camp in our possession, and fought till bayoneted where they stood. Their infantry in masses now retiring, we followed them up, and, in concert with the other branches of the army, shot and bayoneted them into the river, where immense numbers were brought down by our fire. Shortly after the battle was over the regiment was ordered into camp.

I beg to bring to your notice the gallant conduct of Sergeant McCabe of the Light Company, who planted the regimental colour on the highest point of the enemy's fortifications, and maintained his position under a most tremendous fire, the colour being completely riddled by the enemy's shot;—he did this after the officer carrying the colour was shot. I beg further to bring to your notice Private Williams of No. 7 Company, and Private Biffen of the Light Company, who each took a colour from the enemy, one of which is supposed to have belonged to their artillery. I have much pleasure in expressing my high approbation of both officers and men under my command for their gallant conduct throughout the day. I regret to add that Lieutenant Law, my second in command, and Lieutenant and Adjutant Bolton, were both severely wounded.

Regarding Lieutenant-Colonel Spence, Sir Hugh Gough wrote in his despatch: "Brigadier Penny and Lieutenant-Colonel Spence commanded the two brigades of Major-General Sir H. Smith's Division, and overcame at their head the most formidable opposition. I beg to bring both in the most earnest manner to your notice." Captain Garvock (Major of Brigade) and Captain Lugard (Deputy Assistant-Adjutant-General) were also specially mentioned in the despatch. Both officers rose to high rank in the army. Captain Garvock served in the Boer War of 1848, the Kaffir War of 1850–1852, and in the Umbeyla campaign of 1863, holding the chief command in the concluding phase of that campaign. He died a General and a Knight Grand Cross of the Bath in 1878, while commanding at Portsmouth.

The Thirty-First, which went into action at Sobraon with fourteen officers (including the Quartermaster), and 490 sergeants, rank-and-file —in addition to three officers serving on the staff—sustained no less than 145 casualties. Two officers and thirty-six rank-and-file were killed, and six officers and 101 rank-and-file were wounded. The wounds of all the officers and of most of the men were very severe, being for the most part inflicted by artillery fire or the sword, and a large number of the wounded died in hospital. Two Sikh colours were captured by the regiment in this battle; one had been taken at Ferozeshah and one at Aliwal.

The names of the officers who fell under the colours of the Thirty-First at Sobraon have already been mentioned. Those wounded were:

Captain John Garvock, Major of Brigade (severely).

Lieutenant R. Law (severely).
,, and Adjutant A. S. Bolton (severely).
,, G. Elmslie (severely).
,, P. Gabbett (severely).
,, S. J. Timbrell (dangerously).

Both Lieutenant Timbrell's legs were shattered by a grape shot, but after long sufferings he recovered, with the loss, it is recorded, of four inches of his height.

The names of the non-commissioned officers and rank-and-file killed at Sobraon were as follows:

Corporal John Marsh.
,, Frederick Irvin.
Drummer John Cunningham.
Private George Arthurs.
,, John Barker.
,, John Chamberlain.
,, Charles H. Corbett.
,, Michael Davy.
,, William Downie.
,, George Hewston.
,, John Hogan.
,, William Holt.
,, Thomas Kenna.
,, James Kenna.
,, Edward Lilley.
,, Augustus McCormick.
,, Michael McDermott.
,, William McDonnell.

Private John McIntire.
,, John McQuillan.
,, George Morris.
,, Thomas Newbury.
,, John Owers.
,, Francis Pickett.
,, George Pitts.
,, William Pheaton.
,, Frederick Pope.
,, Michael Rafferty.
,, William Ross.
,, George Sherrin.
,, John Sholders.
,, William Stalliard.
,, Edward Street.
,, Daniel Sullivan.
,, Patrick Thorpe.
,, John Ticker.

The services of the Thirty-First at Sobraon were rewarded by the award of the following individual honours:

Lieutenant-Colonel James Spence, who had highly distinguished himself in every engagement of the campaign, was made a Companion of the Bath; and Captains Garvock, Longworth, and Lugard received Brevet Majorities. The commission conferred on Sergeant Bernard McCabe has already been mentioned.

The battle of Sobraon proved to be the last of the campaign, in which both sides had fought so hard and suffered so severely, and a few words may be said here of the fine quality shown by the officers and men of the regiment during the eventful two months, December 12, 1845, to February 10, 1846.

Of the thirty officers who marched from Umballa on the former date, ten (including Assistant-Surgeon Gahan, attached) lay in their graves in the cemetery at Ferozepore, and of the remainder but four came unwounded through the battles of the campaign. These figures speak for themselves.

As for the rank-and-file, they were fully worthy of the officers who led them. Weary but undaunted, they showed at Moodkee the true spirit of the British soldier; at Ferozeshah they proved themselves ready to die at their post; at Badowal and Aliwal the trial was less severe, but still the tale of losses mounted up; finally at Sobraon, reduced to little over half the strength with which they had gone into action at Moodkee, the Thirty-First showed themselves game to the last, and in the words of Sir Harry Smith, a man who knew war as few have known it, the "bull-dogs of the Thirty-first stood up like men."

A monument, bearing the names of the officers of the regiment who were killed or mortally wounded in the Sutlej campaign, was erected in their memory by their surviving brother officers. It stands, close to their graves, in the civil cemetery at Ferozepore. In Canterbury Cathedral there is also a handsome monument in memory of the nine officers and 203 non-commissioned officers and men of the Thirty-First who fell in the Sutlej campaign. Over the monument hang the colours carried in the campaign, and inscribed on silver bands on the colour-poles are the names of the officers who were killed when carrying them.

THE SUTLEJ CAMPAIGN

The numbers of non-commissioned officers and men who were killed in the various actions of the campaign have been stated in the narrative as follows:

At Moodkee	34
,, Ferozeshah	73
,, Badowal	14
,, Aliwal	1
,, Sobraon	36
Total	158

In addition to this heavy total, the fifty-one men whose names follow died of their wounds, bringing the total number of deaths caused by wounds to 209, or six more than the number given on the Canterbury monument.

The names of those who died of wounds were as follows:

Corporal Peter Fitzgibbons.
,,   Frederick Spring.
Private John Birmingham.
,,   Robert Brewer.
,,   Darby Burns.
,,   John Cahill.
,,   Alexander Cameron.
,,   Patrick Campbell.
,,   John Cantwell.
,,   James Carey.
,,   Samuel Chadwick.
,,   Patrick Coleman.
,,   James Colley.
,,   James Crossley.
,,   William Denton.
,,   Thomas Flannigan.
,,   Joseph Fuller.
,,   Patrick Garaughty (1).
,,   Patrick Garraughty (2).
,,   James Garvey.
,,   Jacob Gibton (1).
,,   Jacob Gibton (2).
,,   John Grady.
,,   John Hennessy.
,,   Thomas Higgins.
,,   Edwin Hockenhall.

Private Charles Hopgood (1).
,,   Charles Hopgood (2).
,,   John Maxwell.
,,   Bernard McCabe (2).
,,   Daniel McGhee.
,,   Robert McGinn.
,,   John Merlin.
,,   Daniel Monaghan.
,,   John Moran.
,,   George Murphy.
,,   James Parrion.
,,   Henry Pearce.
,,   Lawrence Renihan.
,,   William Rice.
,,   Richard Roberts.
,,   John Rock.
,,   Patrick Sheridan.
,,   James Stapleton.
,,   Henry Sullivan.
,,   Isaac Tanner.
,,   James Taylor.
,,   William Tudor.
,,   John Turley.
,,   Daniel White.
,,   Dennis Wholonghan.

Altogether then, ten officers and 209 sergeants, rank-and-file, lost their lives in the short Sutlej campaign, and doubtless many others died of their wounds after the preparation of the medal roll, from which the list of casualties has been compiled.

As the first shot was fired at Moodkee on December 18, 1845, and the last at Sobraon on February 10, 1846, it must be remembered that this very bloody campaign only lasted six weeks, into which short period most severe losses and sufferings were crowded without any consequent deterioration of the fighting value of the regiment, a fact which speaks volumes for the quality of the old long-service soldier.

Lieutenant Tritton died of his wounds on the evening of the battle of Sobraon, and early on the following morning the Thirty-First marched towards the pontoon bridge which had been thrown across the Sutlej, on the direct road to Lahore. The distance to the capital was less than fifty miles, and Sir Hugh Gough had decided to clench his victory by an immediate occupation of the Sikh capital. Between its camp and the bridge the regiment was joined by a detachment of sixty men, under Lieutenant McKenzie, from the depôt at Umballa. This detachment formed part of the escort of some heavy guns and a great supply of ammunition, and all of them were much disappointed to find themselves a day late for the battle. By nightfall on February 12, the bridge over the Sutlej was ready for use, and Sir Harry Smith's Division, parading at 10 P.M., marched all night and crossed the Sutlej at sunrise on February 13, the men of the Thirty-First in high spirits at the prospect of invading the Punjab.

The forced march of Sir Harry Smith's Division prevented any attempt on the part of the Sikhs to oppose the crossing, and a halt of some days was made at Kussoor, while the army closed up from the rear. The advance on Lahore then began, the army marching in battle array straight across country, each regiment keeping its own place in line, through fields and jungle, and forcing its way through every obstacle. " It was," writes an eye-witness, " indeed a grand sight to see this splendid army on the morning of the 20th of February approaching the city of Lahore over a boundless and perfectly open plain, on which it encamped about two miles from the city."

On February 22 the British standard was hoisted on the citadel of Lahore.

Immediately after the termination of the Sutlej campaign orders were issued for the Thirty-First regiment to return to England, but as seasoned soldiers were much wanted in India, tempting terms were offered to the men to volunteer for regiments remaining in the Bengal

Presidency. The old soldiers of 1846 belonged to a class who, when once they had found their way to India, generally made that country their home, and of the 420 rank-and-file who remained fit for duty after the campaign, no less than 329 volunteered to remain in India. In addition, several of the officers exchanged into regiments with whom they had been associated in camp or quarters, Lieutenant-Colonel Byrne [1] joining the 53rd, Major Young [2] the 10th, and Brevet-Major Lugard the 29th Regiment.

The following farewell Divisional Order by Major-General Sir Harry Smith is of interest, as a testimony coming from that most gallant and distinguished soldier:

Camp, Lahore, 3rd March, 1846.

"Comrades—Officers and Soldiers of the gallant Thirty-first regiment,—you and I have been so associated in the recent conflicts, where your services have been distinguished, that I cannot lose you from under my command without an expression of the deepest regret; that regret is, however, mitigated when I know that you are about to return to your native country from which the regiment has been absent twenty-one years,—much diminished in numbers—caused by your valiant conduct and recent glorious victories; but the former renown of your distinguished corps has acquired additional fame by the valour of Lieut.-Colonel Spence, the officers and soldiers; and the long list of triumphant victories now recorded on your colours has been much increased by your services in India. Farewell, my gallant comrades, for the present; may every success, happiness, honour, and prosperity attend you, the gallant Thirty-first regiment, in peace, as it has gloriously done in war! and believe me, one of the most happy and proud recollections of my life will be that I have witnessed the indomitable valour of the corps."

---

[1] Lieutenant-Colonel John Bryne (born 1786), exchanged as Captain into the Thirty-First regiment in 1825. Promoted Major in 1843, and Lieutenant-Colonel in 1844. Severely wounded at Moodkee when in command of the regiment. Appointed C.B. On the Thirty-First going home in 1846, Lieutenant-Colonel Byrne exchanged into the 53rd Regiment. He retired by sale in May 1851, and died at Simla on July 21 of the same year.

[2] Major George Dobson Young (born 1801), exchanged into the Thirty-First regiment as Lieutenant in 1823. Promoted Captain in 1841. Served in the Afghan War. Dangerously wounded at Moodkee. Promoted Major, January 5, 1846. On the regiment going home he exchanged into the 10th Regiment. Served in the Sikh campaign of 1848-49 as Lieutenant-Colonel of that regiment. Appointed C.B. Died at Wazirabad, February 20, 1850.

This was indeed a spirit-stirring address, such as soldiers seldom receive in these colder days; and the Thirty-First also had the pleasure of receiving a farewell Brigade Order, couched in similar terms of approbation, from Brigadier-General Monteath, under whom the regiment had served in Afghanistan.

The occupation of Lahore and the arrangement of terms of peace with the Sikh Government having removed all fear of further hostilities, it was decided that as many of the severely wounded as could bear the journey should be sent to England before the coming of the hot weather, and the command of this detachment was conferred by Sir Hugh Gough on Lieutenant Robertson of the Thirty-First, one of the four officers who had come unwounded through every engagement of the campaign. The party of invalids consisted of 158 men, of whom thirty-four belonged to the Thirty-First, and an escort of sixty-three duty men was also provided by the regiment.

The detachment sailed from Ferozepore on March 14, 1846, arrived at Bombay on April 27, and sailing thence on May 14, reached Gravesend on September 29.

The regiment having handed over its volunteers to their new units, quitted the army of the Punjab on March 4 and arrived at Umballa on March 20, where a halt was made to enable the officers to dispose of their bungalows and other properties, and to settle th affairs of the regiment.

The Thirty-First left Umballa on March 28, and, having marched through Meerut to the Ganges, embarked for Calcutta, arriving there, after a long and tedious voyage, on July 6. On July 30 the arms of the regiment, which had done such long and good service in camp and quarters, were withdrawn and handed over to the ordnance department, and the stay at Calcutta of the Thirty-First and 16th Lancers (also about to embark for home) was made an occasion for the open-hearted hospitality for which India in olden days was celebrated.

Prior to the embarkation of the two regiments, the following complimentary Order was issued by the Commander-in-Chief, now created Lord Gough:

Head-Quarters, Simla, May 23rd, 1846.

Those distinguished regiments, the 16th Lancers and the Thirty-First Foot, are about to return to their native country after a service in India, the former of 24, the latter of 21 years; and although the Commander-in-Chief has recently, and so frequently, had occasion to laud the gallant conduct of these corps before an intrepid enemy, he cannot permit them to embark without again expressing his admiration of their continued and conspicuous bravery in all the battles they have been engaged in during the long and eventful period of their Indian service, whether in Afghanistan or at the more sanguinary conflicts of 1845 and 1846. . . . The Thirty-first Regiment will have recorded on their already highly decorated colours—Cabool, Moodkee. Ferozeshah, Aliwal, and Sobraon. Again must Lord Gough express the gratification it affords him thus to be able to record his opinion of their merits; and both these corps are assured that their correct conduct in quarters, and almost total absence of crime for many years, have mainly conduced to the gallant achievements in the field to which their good fortune has afforded them the opportunity to contribute."

By Order of H.E. the Commander-in-Chief.
(Signed)   H. G. Smith, Major-General,
Adjutant-General in India.

The regiment embarked for England on August 2 and 3, 1846, Head-Quarters, consisting of ten officers and 220 of other ranks with twenty-one women and thirty-two children, on the *Madagascar*, and the left wing, five officers, 118 of other ranks, ten women and ten children on the *Plantagenet*. Lieutenant R. Sparrow and five men on the *Madagascar*, and seven on the *Plantagenet*, died on the homeward voyage, and it is recorded that of the 215 men who landed with the Head-Quarters of the regiment, only eighty were unwounded.

The Thirty-First landed at Gravesend on December 4, 1846, where the regiment received an enthusiastic reception, the officers being entertained in high style by the officers of the Royal Marines, who have never lost an opportunity of recalling their ancient alliance with the Thirty-first regiment. In consideration of its long service abroad, and of its distinguished services, the regiment received immediate furlough, without any restriction as to numbers, in order that the soldiers might visit their friends without delay. All officers who could be spared were also granted leave of absence. Another highly-valued compliment was also received by the regiment in the shape of a letter from its distinguished Colonel, General Sir Colin Halkett, G.C.B., in which the General, after reviewing the course of the Sutlej campaign, justly remarked : " Never will your country's banner suffer a stain so long as its soldiers shall equal those who stormed the Sikh camp of Ferozeshah. Greater fortitude and gallantry than those of which you had given proof in these actions, could not possibly be displayed."

After transferring to the invalid depôt the men selected for discharge on account of wounds or other disabilities for further service, the regiment was moved from Chatham to Walmer, where it arrived on December 20, having been greeted while on the march with similar honours to those accorded to it by the people of Chatham.

On June 30, 1847, sanction was published in Army Orders that the honours Moodkee, Ferozeshah, Aliwal, and Sobraon should be borne on the colours and appointments of the regiment. On July 12 Lieutenant-General the Honourable Henry Otway Trevor (afterwards Lord Dacre) was appointed to the Colonelcy, in succession to General Sir Colin Halkett, G.C.B., removed to the 45th Regiment. On September 6 Lieutenant-General Sir Harry Smith, who had been appointed Governor and Commander-in-Chief of the Cape of Good Hope, came to pay a visit to the regiment, which he reviewed on the following day. Sir Harry expressed his satisfaction at seeing the regiment, which had so recently returned home a mere skeleton, in a perfect state of discipline. The regiment was inspected by other general officers on May 4 and October 1 ; and on November 10 by His Grace the Duke of Wellington, who expressed his approbation in the highest terms. The strength on parade was thirty-nine officers and 846 of other ranks. In the same month the Thirty-First was moved to Manchester by railway, probably the first occasion of its being so conveyed, and on April 7, 1848, the regiment was transferred to Dublin. On May 19, new colours were presented to the regiment by Major-General His Royal Highness Prince George of Cambridge, K.G., afterwards so well known as Commander-in-Chief of the Army. The Prince, in making the presentation, made special reference to the gallant conduct of Sergeant McCabe, in seizing and rushing forward with the colour when Ensign Jones had fallen mortally wounded at the battle of Sobraon.

In February 1849 the establishment was reduced to 750 rank-and-

THE SUTLEJ CAMPAIGN

file, and on July 20 of the same year Lieutenant-Colonel Spence, C.B., who had so highly distinguished himself in the Sutlej campaign, retired after forty-one years' service. His successor in the command was Major Staunton, who had exchanged into the regiment on its leaving India.

The Thirty-First remained in Ireland until the end of 1852, being stationed successively at Athlone, Dublin, Enniskillen, Limerick, and Fermoy. On December 31, 1852, the regiment was formed into six service and four depôt companies, and on January 22, 1852, the service companies embarked at Cork in H.M.S. *Simoon* for Corfu, one of the Ionian Islands, at that time under British protection.

CHAPTER X

THE CRIMEAN WAR

Sketch of the campaign—Siege of Sebastopol—The assault on June 18, 1855—Work in the trenches—The second assault—Evacuation of Sebastopol by the Russians.

THE Thirty-First arrived at Corfu on February 11, and furnished detachments at Cerigo, Ithaca, Zante, Santa Maura, and Cephalonia. Service in the Ionian Islands was very popular, and it may be doubted if the regiment ever found itself in pleasanter quarters.

General Lord Dacre, Colonel of the Thirty-First, died in June 1853, and was succeeded by General Sir Alexander Leith, K.C.B., an old and highly distinguished officer of the Thirty-First. Sir Alexander had been wounded, losing an eye, at Alkmaar and commanded the 2nd Battalion Thirty-First during the greater part of the Peninsular War.

About this time the relations of the Powers of Western Europe with Russia became seriously strained, and war appeared probable. The original cause of quarrel was a dispute between the priests of the Greek and Latin churches in the Holy Land, the former being supported by Russia and the latter by France. This dispute, after long negotiations, was settled by liberal concessions on the part of Turkey, but it subsequently became evident that Russia was not to be appeased, but had serious designs on Constantinople. The possession of this great port and trade centre had for centuries been the dream of the Russian rulers, and the Czar Nicholas, being persuaded that England and France were both determined to live at peace, and that his influence over the young Emperor of Austria was secure, thought that his opportunity had arrived.

In July 1853, therefore, the Czar invaded the Danubian Principalities, then a part of Turkey. The maintenance of Turkey being a part of the policy of the Western Powers at this time, and an attempt to arrange terms between Turkey and Russia, at a conference at Vienna, having failed, war broke out between those countries in October of the same year. In the following month great indignation was caused in England and France by the merciless destruction by the Russian Fleet of a small Turkish squadron at Sinope, and in February 1854 these countries demanded the evacuation of the Danubian Principalities.

Russia took no notice of the demand, and England and France declared war against her on April 30. This, it may be observed, was one of the very few occasions in modern times on which a declaration of war preceded hostilities.

At first it seemed that the region of the Danube would be the theatre of war, and English and French armies were despatched to Varna with a view to checking the expected Russian advance on Constantinople. Austria, however, was then induced to take part in the movement, and, by massing her army on her southern frontier, so menaced the Russian rear as to make her position south of the Danube untenable; and, early in August 1854, the Russian army recrossed that river and the invasion of Turkey was at an end. England and France, however, having put their armies into the field, determined not to withdraw them until they had dealt a blow which, they hoped, would check Russian enterprise in the south for a considerable period. With this object they determined to attack and destroy the great fortress of Sebastopol, in the Black Sea, which had obviously been constructed as a standing menace to Constantinople. The operations which followed are called by us the Crimean War.

The course of the war in its early stages must be described in the shortest possible space.

The Crimea, it must be mentioned, is an extensive peninsula in the Black Sea, its size about double that of Yorkshire. The distance from Varna to its coast is about 300 miles, and the allied expedition being escorted by the British Fleet, was too powerful to be attacked at sea by the Russians. The expedition sailed from Varna on September 7, 1854, and landed unopposed on the coast of the Crimea, at a point some twenty-five miles from Sebastopol, between September 14 and 18. The British contingent numbered about 27,000 men, including 1000 cavalry; the French were slightly stronger, and the Turks numbered 7000, but neither had any cavalry. When therefore the advance on Sebastopol began on September 19, it was decided that the British army should take the left, or exposed flank, while the French and Turks marched close to the sea, protected by the guns of the fleet.

On September 20 the Russian field army, about 37,000 strong, with thirty-six guns, were defeated on the river Alma, the heavier part of the fighting falling on the British contingent, which behaved very gallantly and sustained over 2000 casualties. The loss of the French and Turks was trifling. The way to Sebastopol being then clear, the allied armies moved forward unopposed, and, on September 26, took up a position on high ground facing the southern front of Sebastopol. The choice of ground being offered to Lord Raglan, the British General, he chose the right, with the port of Balaklava as a base. This choice, though recommended by the British Admiral, proved to be a bad one and caused infinite suffering and great loss of life during the winter of 1854. On October 17 the first bombardment of Sebastopol took place, the civil population of the town having been removed a fortnight earlier. The bombardment was a failure owing to mischances to the French artillery, but the Russians suffered severely and an assault might possibly have succeeded. None, however, was made, and soon afterwards the Russian field army, which had been reinforced, took the offensive.

On October 25 Prince Menschikoff, the Russian commander, advanced against the British naval base at Balaklava, which was weakly garrisoned and inadequately fortified. The local garrison, which included some Turkish troops, made a stout defence, and two British Divisions were sent in good time from the position before Sebastopol to take part in the action. Before they, however, could come into action the fate of the day had been decided by the British cavalry, which by now had been raised to the strength of two brigades. These brigades both acted with great gallantry, and one of them, the Heavy Brigade, with great efficiency. The celebrated charge of the Light Brigade, though justly admired on account of the devotion and discipline shown by the individual regiments, had no material result, and resulted in the annihilation of the brigade as a fighting force. The action of Balaklava ended in the partial retirement of the Russians, who, however, maintained possession of some high ground, formerly used by our cavalry for outpost purposes.

After this action Balaklava was securely fortified, but on November 5 occurred the great Russian attack which we call the battle of Inkerman, which, but for the undaunted fighting of the British regimental officers and rank-and-file, would have destroyed the invading armies. In this very severe action the British fought with every disadvantage. Largely outnumbered, taken by surprise, and fighting as best they could in small groups, the British infantry showed its finest qualities, and Inkerman may well be called " the soldiers' battle." After some six hours' desperate fighting, the Russians, who also had shown great gallantry and devotion, were completely driven off the field, but the losses to the small British army were terribly severe : 597, including thirty-nine officers, being killed, and 1760, of whom ninety-one were officers, were wounded.

Until after the battle of Inkerman the British army had suffered no great hardships except from over-work in the trenches, but in the middle of November a great storm destroyed a large number of store-ships at Balaklava and wrecked the British camp before Sebastopol. Very severe weather then set in, and the sufferings of the British army became almost intolerable. Men died in hundreds of sheer starvation and over-work, and by the end of February nearly 14,000 men were sick in the hospitals. Towards the end of February the aspect of affairs began to mend. Immense exertions had been made to supply the army with warm clothing and other necessary stores, and troops from all quarters were drawn in to the seat of war. Among other regiments despatched to the Crimea was the Thirty-First, which received from England a draft of seven officers and 306 of other ranks. The establishment of the regiment was at the same time raised to 1000 rank-and-file.

On May 15, 1855, the regiment, under Lieut.-Colonel Staunton, embarked at Corfu with a strength of twenty-five officers and 692 of other ranks, and arrived ten days later at Balaklava, where it took possession of the huts vacated by the 79th Cameron Highlanders. The regiment remained at Balaklava for about a month, busily employed in preparation for the hard fighting that was shortly expected. The assault on Sebastopol, so long anticipated, was fixed for June 18, the anniversary of the battle of Waterloo, and it was hoped that a victory earned by the allied armies of England and France would obliterate all memories of their ancient wars.

The Thirty-First, having been replaced at Balaklava by another regiment, marched on June 15 to the heights before Sebastopol, where it was brigaded with the Buffs and the 72nd Highlanders. On June 17 the brigade took up its allotted position in the right rear of the Twenty-one gun battery, and on the following day it lay in reserve during the attack on the Redan, formed in three lines, the Buffs being in front. As is well known, the assault of June 18 resulted in failure, and entailed heavy losses on the allied armies; but as the reserves were not brought into action the Thirty-First bore but a passive part, and the assault need not be described. The regiment hardly came under fire, and had only three private soldiers wounded.

One sad consequence of the repulse of June 18 was the death of Lord Raglan, who, worn out by hard work, anxiety, and disappointment, succumbed to an attack of cholera on June 28. It may be added that Marshal St. Arnaud, the French Commander-in-Chief, had already died, as had the Emperor Nicholas of Russia, so that the war had quickly proved fatal to the heads of the three armies engaged.

The siege continued to be pressed with vigour, and the Thirty-First was continuously employed in the trenches between the assaults of June 18 and September 8, at first serving in the 2nd Brigade, 2nd Division, and being transferred in September to the 2nd Brigade, 1st Division. The strength of the regiment was well maintained by the arrival from England of drafts amounting to two officers and 245 of other ranks. The working parties in the trenches were frequently attacked by the Sebastopol garrison, and on September 4 a detachment of the Thirty-First, under Lieutenant R. E. Leeson, performed distinguished service by capturing, under heavy fire, a line of rifle-pits, the occupants of which had inflicted much loss on the French troops in the neighbouring entrenchments. Lieutenant Leeson and his men rushed the intervening space without firing a shot, and carried the rifle-pits at the point of the bayonet. For this service Lieutenant Leeson and Privates Ruth, Lackey and Ryan received the French decoration of the Legion of Honour. Private John Spelman, who was severely wounded on the same occasion, was subsequently granted the French military medal.

The second assault on Sebastopol was delivered on September 8, and was only partially successful. The losses of the allies approached 10,000 officers and men, but those of the Russians were much heavier, and the southern defences of Sebastopol were practically ruined. A renewed assault was ordered for the following day, but during the night the Russian garrison, which had earned undying honour by its stubborn defence, was withdrawn to the north of the harbour, and the magazines were blown up. The remainder of the Russian Fleet was also set on fire and destroyed.

The siege of Sebastopol thus ended in a victory to the allies, but the losses in the opposing armies had been very heavy, and it was not clear how the war was to be brought to an end. Eventually, after long diplomatic efforts, peace was concluded in April 1856.

During the previous winter the Thirty-First, in common with the remainder of the British army, had entirely regained health and efficiency. The men were employed in the destruction of the great docks and defences of Sebastopol, and in road-making, hut-building, and other works of utility. By the coming of spring all was in readiness for an active campaign, should one have been necessary, and the British army was in greater strength than at any time since the end of the Peninsular War. No less than 22,000 men had succumbed to battle or disease, but when peace was concluded the British troops in the Crimea numbered 55,000 efficients, in addition to a Turkish contingent of 20,000 men and 10,000 Germans : all in British pay. There were also 18,000 troops still available in England.

Early in 1856 the Thirty-First received a final draft of one officer and 100 rank-and-file, which kept up its strength to the end of the war. Its losses in the Crimea, principally caused by disease, included Captain F. S. Attree, Captain C. Anderson (both killed in action), and 112 non-commissioned officers and men, in whose memory a monument was erected by the regiment in St. Mary's Church, Huntingdon.

THIRTY-FIRST REGIMENT—CASUALTIES IN THE CRIMEAN WAR

Killed

Captain Charles Anderson.
,, F. S. Attree.
Colour-Sergeant Thomas Behan.
Sergeant John Thompson.
Private Thomas Gilman.
,, Michael Glennon.
,, James Goom.
,, John Hickey.
,, John James.
Private Thomas Jones.
,, Benjamin Lang.
,, Philip Larkin.
,, Michael McElroy.
,, Edward Neill (1).
,, Edward Neill (2).
,, Henry Oaten.
,, William Potter.
,, Henry Richards.

Total, 18 killed.

Wounded

Colour-Sergeant Thomas Behan (afterwards killed in action).
Colour-Sergeant James Foley.
Sergeant James Forrest.
,, Samuel Lee.
,, Dennis McCarthy.
,, William Molony.
Corporal James McMarry.
,, E. Prevost.
,, William Roberts.
,, Patrick White.
Drummer M. Cunningham.
,, James Holder.
,, S. Martin.
Private James Bliss.
,, J. Brien.
,, Thomas Cardell.
,, Thomas Cardell (previously wounded).
,, John Cardle.
,, George Coleman.
,, William Critchley.
,, Thomas Cuthbert.
,, Cornelius Dalury.
,, John Daly.
,, John Devoy.
,, Solomon Dockett.
,, Patrick Dunn.
,, James Fee.
,, John Flannagan.
,, Edward Gleeson.
,, W. Haynes.
,, Martin Heagney.
,, Martin Hogan.
,, Patrick Holmes.
,, H. Houghton.
,, Charles Hutton.
,, John Jenner.
Private Malachi Keogh.
,, Terence Kernan.
,, Charles Laxton.
,, Edward Leeson.
,, Jesse Lockhurst.
,, John Madden.
,, J. McCabe.
,, Peter McGrath.
,, John McGuire.
,, Patrick McNabe.
,, John McQuade.
,, John Miller.
,, John Mooney.
,, Patrick Murphy.
,, Patrick Neagle.
,, Edward Neill (afterwards killed in action).
,, Matthew Perrin.
,, Lewis Prince.
,, James Procter.
,, Thomas Purcell.
,, Joseph Rennox.
,, J. Roberts.
,, Denis Rosney.
,, Michael Ryan.
,, George Shaw.
,, James Shaw.
,, Michael Sheridan.
,, Charles Smith.
,, John Spellman.
,, John Talbot.
,, George Thomas.
,, John Tracey.
,, Thomas Wade.
,, Henry Walton.
,, John Weekly.
,, James Weir.
,, William Woods.

Total, 73 wounded.

SUMMARY

   Killed, 2 officers and 16 other ranks 18
   Wounded, sergeants, rank-and-file 73

                Total 91

In addition to the Legion of Honour awarded to Lieutenant Leeson, Colonel Staunton and Major F. Spence received the same decoration. Captain R. J. Eagar was promoted to the brevet rank of Major and also received the Legion of Honour for services on the Staff.

On the withdrawal of the army from the Crimea, the Thirty-First was ordered to proceed to Gozo, an island which forms part of the Malta group. The strength of the regiment on arrival at Gozo was thirty-seven officers and 942 of other ranks. The Thirty-First remained at Gozo until February 1857, when it was moved to Gibraltar; and, in May 1858, it was again moved to the Cape of Good Hope, where it was stationed at King William's Town, with detachments at Fort Peddie, Leni Drift, and Tamacha. The stay of the Thirty-First in South Africa was, however, very short, for in December 1858 it was again on the high seas, landing at Bombay early in 1859, and moving by rail to Poona, there to be stationed. While at Poona Lieut.-Colonel Staunton, who had commanded the regiment with great efficiency for ten years, handed over command and returned to England. On February 19, 1859, the Thirty-First lost its Colonel, General Sir Alexander Leith, K.C.B., who was succeeded by Major-General Peter Edmondstone Craigie, C.B. During this year (1859) the regiment was supplied with khaki (dust-coloured) clothing, and wicker helmets, which were worn on all parades and duties during the hot weather. The helmets had a *pagri* of dark slate-coloured linen. This uniform had been generally adopted by the army in India in the course of the Mutiny campaign of 1858–9. For use in the cold weather, red serge tunics were issued in place of the cloth shell jackets then worn on home and colonial service.

Towards the end of 1859 the Thirty-First was brought up to a strength of 1000 by the arrival from England of a draft of 115 men, and by volunteering from other regiments; and on December 29 the regiment was ordered to hold itself in readiness for active service in China.

OFFICERS OF THE THIRTY-FIRST (HUNTINGDONSHIRE REGIMENT) WHO RECEIVED THE WAR MEDAL WITH CLASP FOR SEBASTOPOL

Lieut.-Col. and Brevet-Col. George Staunton.
Lieut.-Col. Thomas C. Kelly.
Major Fredrick D. Lumley.
,, Frederick Spence.
Captain Frederick S. Attree (killed in action, Sept. 8, 1855.
,, Charles Anderson (killed in action, Sept. 5, 1855).
,, George W. Baldwin.
,, Alexander F. Ball.
,, Amyatt E. Brown.
,, Robert J. Eagar.
,, William Frederick McBean.
,, Charles Prevost.
,, James P. Robertson.
,, Arthur J. Schreiber.
,, Charles J. O. Swaffield.
,, Edward Temple.
Lieutenant George Bayley.
,, Annesly Cary.
,, Frederick Y. Cassidy.
Lieutenant William G. H. T. Fairfax.
,, George R. R. Fitzmaurice.
,, John W. T. Fyler.
,, George J. Hamilton.
,, George F. Herbert.
,, Charles E. Jeffcock.
,, Ralph Leeson.
,, Richard W. Litton.
,, Alexander Mitchell.
,, George N. Pepper.
,, George Spaight.
,, Thomas E. Swettenham.
Lieut. and Adjt. Charles K. Pearson.
,, Thomas C. Rycroft.
Paymaster Julius B. Travers.
Quarter-Master Patrick Hopkins.
Surgeon W. F. T. Ivey.
Asst. Surgeon Thomas J. Atkinson.
,, William Grantt.
,, John Meane.
Actg. Surgeon R. H. Beal.

The Medal with clasp for Sebastopol was also issued to nine hundred and ninety-one non-commissioned officers and men of the Regiment.

CHAPTER XI

THE CHINESE WAR OF 1860

Advance on Sind-ho—The capture of Tang-koo—The Taku forts—Service in China—The Thirty-First returns home—Is linked with the Seventieth Regiment—Establishment of the Depot at Kingston-on-Thames—The Thirty-First becomes the 1st Battalion East Surrey Regiment.

ENGLAND and France entered into an alliance for the purpose of enforcing, if necessary, by arms the stipulation of their respective treaties made at Tientsin in 1858 with the Imperial Government of China; and it was agreed that the British contingent should number 10,000 men, and that of France about 7000. The command of the British force was entrusted to Major-General Sir Hope Grant, a cavalry officer who had served in the Sikh campaign of 1848–49, and had earned a high reputation during the suppression of the Indian Mutiny.

Sir Hope Grant's force, which numbered about 11,000 of all ranks, included eight British infantry regiments, the strongest of which in point of numbers was the Thirty-First, which arrived at the seat of war with a strength of thirty officers and 970 men. The regiment, which was in good health and in a highly efficient state, was commanded by Lieut.-Colonel F. Spence,[1] the next senior officer being Major Eagar, both members of families long connected with the Thirty-First.

The voyage to China was not without incident, as one of the transports conveying the regiment ran short of water when off the coast of Cochin China, and a fatigue party sent ashore to obtain water was attacked by hostile natives. The captain of the transport, and

---

[1] Colonel W. Sutton, the senior Lieut.-Colonel of the regiment, commanded a brigade until his death during the war.

Captain Baldwin, the commanding officer of the detachment of the Thirty-First, went ashore with a flag of truce, but were seized by the natives and dragged inland. After two days' captivity they were released by the local mandarins, with suitable apologies. The whole regiment had arrived at Hong Kong by April 23, when it was encamped on the Kowloon Peninsula, a tract of land which had been acquired on lease by Sir Hope Grant for the accommodation of the force.

The ground allotted to the Thirty-First proved to be damp and malarious, and caused the outbreak of a considerable amount of fever and ague in the regiment.

The whole British expeditionary force had not arrived in China until the month of June, and on the 29th of that month the Thirty-First (which had left Hong Kong on the arrival of the bulk of the force) disembarked at Talienwan Bay, which had been selected as the base of the operations in North China. The British contingent, which was admirably provided with transport, supplies, and all the requisites of an army in the field, was ready for immediate action, but the much weaker French contingent was still in a backward state, and required nearly another month before it could take the field. The situation of the two little armies was, in fact, the exact reverse to that at the beginning of the Crimean War.

While at Talienwan Bay the British force was brigaded, and the Thirty-First, with the 1st Royal Regiment (now the Royal Scots), formed the 1st Brigade of the 1st Division, the 2nd Brigade of which was commanded by Colonel Sutton. The commander of the 1st Brigade was Brigadier-General Charles Staveley, C.B., the commander of the Division being Major-General Sir John Michel.

On July 24, the allied expedition, being ready for active service, embarked at Talienwan Bay, and on August 2 arrived at the Peiho River, landing near the town of Pehtang, out of reach of the guns of the Taku Forts. A British naval attack on these forts had sustained a disastrous defeat in 1859, and Sir Hope Grant desired that their capture should be undertaken as soon as possible. Owing to the very swampy nature of the ground, it was no easy matter to select the best way of approach to the forts, and on this subject a strong difference of opinion arose between Sir Hope Grant and General de Montauban, the commander of the French expeditionary force. Sir Hope, however, whose choice of ground was proved by the event to be perfectly right, maintained his point of view firmly, though in a friendly manner, expressing his intention of attacking the forts single-handed if necessary. Finding that his English colleague was not to be moved, General de Montauban gave way and loyally co-operated in the attack to which he had objected. Both commanders, in fact, deserved high credit.

All arrangements for the attack having been completed, the allied force advanced from Pehtang at daybreak on Sunday, August 12, 1860, the 2nd Division and cavalry leading. Much rain had fallen and the country was deep in slush and water; but after advancing some three miles along a raised road, line was formed with much difficulty to both flanks of the road, the 2nd Division and cavalry forming on the right and some distance in advance, while the 1st Division formed line to the left of the road. The point of attack was an entrenched position, at a place called Sind-ho, some eight miles distant from Pehtang. Had the Chinese, who were numerically strong, attacked the force while advancing along the causeway, much loss would have been caused; but happily, rendered confident by their success of the previous year, the Chinese allowed the small allied force to deploy unopposed for attack. The intention of the Chinese commander was to envelop the whole force with his numerous Tartar cavalry, and this, he thought, could be better done in the marshy plain.

The deployment of the allied force, some 3000 strong, having been completed, and the advance on Sind-ho having commenced, the Tartar cavalry made a brave attack on the right, but were easily driven off by the two regiments of Indian cavalry, Fane's and Probyn's Horse, supported by two squadrons of the King's Dragoon Guards. Demoralised by the fire of the British and French artillery, which both made admirable practice, the brave but undisciplined Tartars were swept off the field with heavy loss after a very short resistance. The infantry then advanced and captured the Sind-ho position almost unopposed.

The action over, the force bivouacked for the night and the light baggage came up on the following morning. Before advancing to the attack of the Taku Forts Sir Hope Grant found that it would be necessary to capture an entrenched position at Tang-koo, distant about two and a half miles to the south-east of Sind-ho. As a preliminary measure the Thirty-First, with 250 men of the 60th Rifles and a party of Madras Sappers and Miners, marched at nightfall on August 13 to ground within close fire of the fort of Tang-koo, where a long shelter trench was dug by the regiment during the night. The work was carried out without loss, and the detachment marched back just before dawn on August 14 and rejoined the remainder of the brigade. After an hour's rest the 1st Brigade advanced to the attack, the Thirty-First marching in line when the ground permitted, and when necessary advancing in fours from the left of companies. On approaching the position, a Chinese rocket battery firing from the high reeds on the opposite bank of the Peiko caused considerable annoyance, but was soon silenced by the sharp-shooters of the Thirty-First, under Major Eagar. The fort and entrenched position were then carried, the Royal, Thirty-First, and 60th Rifles racing for the lead, and the enemy being pursued through and beyond the works, which were very extensive, though of no great strength. The attack had been much aided by the efficient fire of the French and British artillery, which had been brought up to within 450 yards of the walls.

After the capture of Tang-koo the allied force was compelled to halt for a few days while the heavy guns and ammunition were being brought to the front for the intended attack on the Taku Forts. The captured position at Tang-koo was occupied by Sir Robert Napier's Division, as that experienced Engineer officer was destined to carry out the difficult operations of bridging the Peiho and attacking the forts on its northern bank. It thus fell to the lot of part of Sir John Michel's Division to hold the lines of communication, and the Thirty-First was ordered to return to Sind-ho, where it occupied an old Tartar entrenchment, arriving there on August 19.

On August 21, the Taku Forts were captured, after a gallant resistance on the part of the Chinese.

On August 30, the Thirty-First, with the remainder of Major-General Sir John Michel's force, advanced on Tientsin, distant about thirty miles, reaching that city after slight resistance on September 2. The force remained at Tientsin until September 22, when orders were received for an immediate advance on Pekin, Sir Hope Grant and General de Montauban having found that nothing short of a

MEDAL ROLL OF THE THIRTY-FIRST (HUNTINGDONSHIRE) REGIMENT

Rank.	Name.	Taku Forts 1860.	Pekin 1860.	Remarks.
Lieut.-Col. & Bt.-Col.	William Sutton, C.B.			
Lieut.-Col.	F. Spence, C.B.	1		
Major	R. J. Eagar	1		
,,	C. J. O. Swaffield	1		
Captain	G. W. Baldwin	1		
,,	W. F. McBean	1		
,,	S. Christian	1		
,,	T. E. Swettenham	1		
,,	J. S. C. Harcourt	1		
,,	A. Mitchell	1		
,,	A. Gammell	1	1	Attached to the Royal Artillery.
,,	F. Y. Cassidy	1		
,,	G. J. Hamilton	1		
Lieutenant	R. J. Gould	1		
,,	H. P. Deane	1		
,,	A. Jebb	1		
,,	C. C. McIntyre	1		
,,	J. T. A. Gardiner	1		
,,	A. J. Danyell	1		
,,	A. G. S. Maynard	1		
,,	J. M. B. Wood	1		
,,	W. E. Tibbetts	1		
,,	A. C. Gow	1		
Ensign	R. E. Huxam	1		
,,	F. W. H. D. Butler	1	1	Attached to the Chinese Coolie Corps.
,,	R. T. Masefield	1		
Adjutant	W. Hill James	1		
Asst.-Surg.	W. Grantt	1		
,,	B. T. Giraud	1		
,,	C. H. Giraud	1		
Qr. Master	C. Kettyles	1		
Paymaster	W. E. Adams	1		

The Medal and Clasp "Taku Forts, 1860" was also issued to nine hundred and seventy-six non-commissioned officers and men of the regiment.

threat to the capital would decide the Chinese Government to offer satisfactory terms of peace.

The Thirty-First, however, was again fated to serve on the communications, two companies being left after the second day's march at the town of Tong-tsin, and on the fourth day the headquarters of the regiment, with other troops, under Lieut.-Colonel Spence, occupied the town of Ho-see-woo, an important port in which the hospital and store-depôt had been located. Here the regiment remained until the termination of hostilities on October 24, on which date the treaty of peace with England was ratified by the Chinese Government. The treaty with France was ratified a week later.

Under the terms of the treaty England was entitled to maintain garrisons at Tientsin, the Taku Forts, and Canton until the war indemnity of £8,000,000 promised by China had been paid, and the Thirty-First, having been selected as part of the garrison of Tientsin, marched to that city on November 18, 1860, where it was stationed, under command of Brigadier-General Staveley, until April 1862.

Colonel William Sutton and Colonel Frederick Spence were created Companions of the Bath for their services during the campaign, and the regiment was granted the honour " Taku Forts " on the regimental colour. The period of time spent by the Thirty-First at Tientsin afforded the regiment a novel and not unpleasant experience. Brigadier-General Staveley quickly established friendly relations with the Chinese civil authorities, who delivered all supplies required by the troops at local market rates. For this purpose they employed the same contractors as had previously supplied the Chinese garrison of Tientsin, the only apparent difference to the contractors being that they were regularly paid by the British, whereas their previous experience had been widely different. The climate in the winter months was very severe, but the troops were sensibly dressed, each regiment being allowed to buy fur, with which their coats and caps were lined on a regimental pattern. Lieutenant, now Lieut.-Colonel, Hill-James, Adjutant of the Thirty-First in China, mentions, in some notes on the campaign in China, that on New Year's Day 1861 he

" saw the porter issued by the commissariat to the regiment carried to the men's quarters by fatigue parties in *sacks*. It was solid ice, and had to be broken up with crowbars and picks, and then melted in pots and cauldrons before it could be measured out to the several messes, a warm and frothy beverage. The men, for the nonce, rather liked the novelty. The bread was sometimes frozen so hard that it had to be sawn, instead of cut, into slices."

In the summer months, on the other hand, the heat was extreme, and a large number of men of the Thirty-First suffered from sunstroke, and it was thought necessary to forbid the men from going into the sun during the heat of the day, except when absolutely necessary.

Advantage was taken by the Chinese Government of the residence among them of British troops, two battalions of regular infantry being raised at Tientsin during the occupation, one of which was commanded by Lieutenant Jebb of the Thirty-First. A battery of field artillery was also raised, horsed with English horses. These troops, however, were not allowed to join General Charles Gordon's " Ever victorious army," to which they would have formed so valuable an addition, but the Thirty-First was permitted to lend a number of non-commissioned officers and men to Gordon, to act as drill instructors, when his army was in process of formation.

The Chinese Government having paid the war indemnity early in 1862, the regiment left Tientsin in April, and embarked at the mouth of the Peiho on H.M.S. *Vulcan* for conveyance to Shanghai, where they arrived on April 22. Here the regiment joined a field force, under Brigadier-General Staveley, C.B., operating against the Taiping rebels, and was present at the capture of the cities of Khadin, Sing-poo, and Tso-lin, and of the stockades of Nart-siang and Najow. At the attack on Khadin, on December 24, 1862, Captain Alexander Mitchell was severely wounded.

On the last day of May 1862 the Thirty-First lost its Colonel, Major-General P. E. Craigie, C.B., the appointment of his successor, General Sir Edward Lugard, G.C.B., dating from June 1. Sir Edward was an old Thirty-First officer of great distinction who had been severely wounded in the Sutlej campaigns and had held important commands in the Persian and Indian Mutiny campaigns.

The regiment remained at Shanghai till June 27, 1863, when it embarked for England, arriving at Plymouth in November with a strength of twenty-six officers and 622 of other ranks.

It was not the fortune of the Thirty-First to see active service for fifty-one years after its return from China, and as this history deals chiefly with the campaigns of the regiment, the remaining eighteen years of its existence as a separate unit will be but briefly described.

On landing from China in November 1863 the Thirty-First took over quarters in the Raglan Barracks, Devonport, where the regiment remained nearly a year. In October 1864 Headquarters moved to Aldershot, where the Thirty-First was stationed until March 1866, when it moved to Portsmouth, being quartered in the Cambridge Barracks until July, when Headquarters and five companies embarked in the *Avoca* for Dublin. The remaining five companies quickly followed, and the regiment took up quarters at the Curragh by August 7. On the departure of the Thirty-First from Portsmouth a complimentary farewell Order testified that "the appearance of the Regiment on parade, the steadiness and quickness of its drill, its good discipline in quarters and its general efficiency upon all occasions leave nothing to be desired." The commanding officer at the time was Colonel R. J. Eagar.

In December 1866 the Thirty-First moved to Kilkenny, and in the following month detachments were sent to Tipperary and Templemore. These moves were in consequence of the disturbed state of Ireland, and during March 1867 the detachments were employed in the suppression of Fenian riots at both places, but particularly at Tipperary. For their conduct in the performance of this duty the officers, non-commissioned officers and soldiers employed received an expression of the high approval of General Lord Strathnairn, commanding the forces in Ireland, and of H.R.H. the Duke of Cambridge, the Field-Marshal Commanding-in-Chief.

The Thirty-First again proceeded on foreign service in 1867, after a home tour of less than four years. The regiment, raised to a strength of forty-five officers and 884 of other ranks, embarked at Queenstown on June 1 and arrived at Malta on June 22, where it was quartered in hut barracks at Pembroke Camp. Before leaving Ireland the colours presented to the regiment in 1848 by Prince George of Cambridge, together with the four Sikh standards captured during the Sutlej campaign, were sent to the county town of Huntingdon, there to be placed over the regimental monument erected in St. Mary's Church in memory of the officers and soldiers who fell in the Crimea.

While at Malta the regiment made the usual move from barrack to barrack, being stationed in turn at Pembroke Camp, Isola Gate Barracks, Fort Manoel, Pembroke Camp again, Saint Elmo, and Verdala Barracks.

In 1871 "The most satisfactory state" of the regiment met with the approval of His Royal Highness the Commander-in-Chief, and in May of that year Lieut.-Colonel R. J. Eagar, commanding the regiment, was appointed a Companion of the Bath.

On the last day of February 1872 the Thirty-First, under Colonel Eagar, C.B., embarked in H.M. troopship *Jumna* for conveyance to Gibraltar, taking up quarters in Buena Vista Barracks.

In April 1873 a tentative re-organisation of the army took place, single battalion infantry regiments being linked together in pairs and formed into sub-district brigades. This organisation was generally looked upon in the army as a step towards the universal adoption of a double battalion system, and, though unpopular in the army and entailing many disadvantages, was eventually loyally accepted by the officers and men.

The Thirty-First (Huntingdonshire) Regiment was linked with the 70th (Surrey) Regiment, which had been originally raised in 1756 as its Second Battalion.

The establishment approved for the new organisation was as follows :

31st Regiment	33 officers	658 other ranks.
70th ,,	32 ,,	886 ,,
Depôt .	9 ,,	216 ,,
Total	74 ,,	1760 ,,

The "Brigade Depôt," a title changed subsequently to "Regimental District," was localised at Kingston-on-Thames.

In March 1874 Colonel R. J. Eagar, C.B., retired on full pay after nearly forty-four years' service in the regiment, in which he had been born. He was succeeded in the command by Brevet-Lieut.-Colonel Scrase-Dickins.

The Thirty-First returned to England from Gibraltar in April 1876 and was stationed at Portland. During its stay of four years at Gibraltar it had maintained its high character. In 1877 the regiment moved to Aldershot, and in the following April the then existing reserves were for the first time mobilised. The result, as regards the regiment, was that 294 of the Militia Reserve (soldiers belonging to the First and Third Royal Surrey Militia Regiment), and eleven men of the 1st class Army Reserve joined the colours. In July 1878, the mobilisation being complete, the regiment moved to Fleetwood with a strength of 907, exclusive of officers. The reserves were demobilised at the end of the month, leaving the regiment with 620 rank-and-file only. In the month of October a draft of three officers and 147 of other ranks was despatched to the linked battalion (the 70th Regiment) in India, leaving the Thirty-First with only 448 rank-and-file. The Depôt at the same time could furnish only seventy recruits to the home battalion. The linked battalion system, in fact, was as yet far from perfection.

In March 1879 Lieut.-Colonel and Brevet-Colonel Scrase-Dickins handed over command to Lieut.-Colonel Swettenham, and at the end of the month the regiment moved to Chatham, where it remained until October 1880, when it again moved to Dover.

While stationed at Dover the existence of the Thirty-First Regiment came to an end, for on July 1, 1881, the long-contemplated re-organisation of the infantry took effect and from that date the regiment lost its separate existence and became the 1st Battalion of the East Surrey Regiment, the Seventieth Regiment becoming the 2nd Battalion, and thus rejoining its parent corps after a separation of 123 years.

The Thirty-First at the same time lost its old territorial designation of "the Huntingdonshire Regiment," and its buff facings, which had been worn from a date prior to the battle of Dettingen.

It cannot be denied that the wholesale destruction of old regimental distinctions, which marked the introduction of the Territorial system, made the change highly unpopular. For many years regiments resented the abolition of their time-honoured numbers and distinctive marks, and it is in comparatively recent days that certain advantages of the double battalion system have been recognised, and that the Territorial associations of regiments have proved their value.

PART II
HISTORY OF THE SEVENTIETH REGIMENT

CHAPTER XII

Early History

"The Glasgow Greys"—Roll of the original officers—Loss of four companies—Ten years' service at Grenada—The Carib rising at St. Vincent—The remains of the regiment return to England.

THE peace of Aix-la-Chapelle, signed in 1748, did not long preserve harmony between England and France, but its immediate result was the reduction of the English army to a dangerous weakness. The British establishment of the year was fixed at 30,000 men, two-thirds of whom were at home and one-third in the Colonies. The rest of the army was stationed in Ireland and paid by that country, and consisted of thirty-seven very weak regiments mustering perhaps 10,000 men. When therefore the hostilities initiated in America by the French culminated in July 1755 in the disaster to General Braddock's expedition, and war was seen to be again inevitable, steps had to be taken to increase the English army. This, however, was at first done on a meagre scale. In the winter and in the following spring fifteen infantry regiments stationed in Great Britain were ordered to raise second battalions. Among the regiments thus augmented was the Thirty-First, then stationed at Glasgow; the actual date of the Order authorising the new battalion being August 25, 1756. The Thirty-First Regiment was well known in Scotland, and service in the army being very popular in that country at the time, no difficulty was experienced in bringing both battalions quickly to their full strength. The Second Battalion Thirty-First was entirely supplied with senior officers from the First Battalion, the subaltern ranks being filled by gentlemen, who were authorised to supply the prescribed number of recruits. Nearly all the officers and men of the regiment were Scots by birth, and this long continued to be the case. Two years later, on May 9, 1758, a further augmentation of the army having been decided on, the Second Battalion Thirty-First Regiment was constituted a separate regiment and was numbered the Seventieth of the Line. It remained stationed at Glasgow, and its facings being light grey, while it was mainly composed of Scotsmen, the regiment was commonly known as "The Glasgow Greys."

The Colonelcy of the Seventieth Regiment was bestowed on Lieutenant-Colonel John Parslow, a Captain and Lieutenant-Colonel in the First Foot Guards, and an officer of long service. Colonel Parslow's connection with the Seventieth was of short duration and it does not appear that, beyond attending occasional musters, he took personal command of the regiment, though this was the usual practice of colonels at the time. Major Charles Vignoles of the Thirty-First Regiment, who had commanded the new regiment during its existence as a 2nd battalion was promoted to the Lieutenant-Colonelcy; and Captain Robert Pigot, the senior of his rank in the Thirty-First, to the Majority. The names of the original officers of the Seventieth are given below. All those senior to Lieutenant William Tulloch had previously served in the Thirty-First.

ORIGINAL OFFICERS OF THE SEVENTIETH REGIMENT
(1758)

COLONEL
    John Parslow.

LIEUT.-COLONEL
    Charles Vignoles. — Retired February 1760.

MAJOR
    Robert Pigot. — Promoted Lieut.-Colonel February 4, 1760.

CAPTAINS
    William Piers. — Promoted Major and transferred to 96th Regiment.

    Daniel Hamilton.
    Tichborne Grueber. — Transferred to 96th Regiment.
    Hector Munro. — Promoted Major in 89th Regiment. Afterwards Lieut.-General Sir Hector Munro, K.B.

    George Grant.
    William Nesbit. — Promoted Major February 4, 1760.
    Hon. Spencer Compton. — Afterwards 8th Earl of Northampton.

CAPTAIN-LIEUTENANT
    John Fowle. — Promoted Captain, February 4, 1760.

LIEUTENANTS
    John Crofton. — Promoted Captain. Transferred to 96th Regiment.

John Stevens.
William Smith.
Robert Clements.
Mussenden Johnstone.   Promoted Captain. Transferred to 96th Regiment.
Edward Hicks.
John Dumaresq.
Arthur Lysaght.   Promoted Captain in 96th Regiment.
George Whichcot.
Arthur Thompson.
Roger Bristow.
Charles Sutherland.
Anthony Morgan.   Transferred to 96th Regiment.
Henry Norman.   ditto.
Uniack Prendergast.   ditto.
William Tulloch.
James Cusack.
Williamson Legard Hooker.   Adjutant. Transferred to 96th Regiment.

ENSIGNS

George Williamson (Quartermaster).
George Kinloch. Promoted Lieutenant and transferred to 96th Regiment.
Robert Jephson.
Charles Gordon.
Robert Orrock.
William Talbot.
Robert Wilson.
J. Rosenhagen.

CHAPLAIN
Thomas Parslow.

ADJUTANT
Williamson Legard Hooker.

SURGEON
Samuel Bright.

QUARTERMASTER
George Williamson.

NOTES

1. It will be observed that the Adjutant was gazetted as junior Lieutenant, and that the Quartermaster held rank as senior Ensign. Ensign Williamson was succeeded in 1760 by another George Williamson (perhaps his son) as Quartermaster, and subsequently George Williamson, junior, also became a combatant officer, afterwards serving as Lieutenant of the Grenadier Company in North America.

2. Captain Hector Munro remained in the regiment until 1760, although he had been appointed Major in the newly-raised 89th Regiment (afterwards disbanded) in October 1759. He was at a later date known to fame as Lieutenant-General Sir Hector Munro, K.B., Commander-in-Chief of the Madras Army. Sir Hector's victory of Buxar in the year 1764 is regarded as one of the decisive battles of Indian history. He died in 1805, aged seventy-nine.

In 1759 the regiment, being raised to full strength, was moved to Canterbury, and shortly afterwards to Dover, at which station it remained during the remainder of the Seven Years' War. Early in 1760 the Seventieth, then stationed at Dover, consisted of a Grenadier company and eight battalion companies, with a strength of 802 in addition to officers. The regiment had recently furnished a small draft to the army in Germany, but was strong and efficient, and might well have been selected for active service on the continent or in India, in which region the war with France was being actively waged. Unfortunately for the regiment, its fate was otherwise decided; and in the month of April 1760 the four strongest companies were ordered to proceed " on command " to the East Indies, there to form the nucleus of a new regiment, afterwards numbered the 96th. What steps, if any, Colonel Parslow took to protest against the wrecking of his regiment is not recorded, but the four companies duly embarked for India in two ships of the Honourable East India Company's fleet, one of the companies being Colonel Parslow's own, with a strength of four officers, six sergeants and ninety-nine rank-and-file. The Grenadier company, 100 strong, also went to India, and after the departure of the wing the unfortunate Seventieth found itself with a strength of no more than 372 of all ranks. There are no means of ascertaining the feelings of Colonel Parslow on this sad occasion, but very shortly afterwards he was compensated, if not consoled, for the wreck of the Seventieth by transfer to the Colonelcy of the 54th Regiment.

The following officers of the Seventieth accompanied the wing to India and were subsequently transferred to the 96th Regiment:

Major: William Piers.
Captains: Tichborne Grueber, Mussenden Johnstone, John Crofton, and Arthur Lysaght.
Lieutenants: Anthony Morgan, Henry Norman, Uniack Prendergast, Williamson Legard Hooker, George Kinloch, and Francis Baillie.
Ensigns: George McCormick, Andrew Grant, George Phillips, and Bernard Ward.

The wing of the Seventieth, it may be added, arrived in due course at Bombay, its voyage to India (according to the log of the *Neptune*, one of the ships in which it was conveyed eastward) being attended by " pleasant gales." From Bombay the wing sailed round the peninsula towards Madras, but it was found advisable to land it at Tellicherry, to avoid the risk of capture by the French fleet, then in alarming strength in eastern waters. Early in 1761 the wing was transferred to the 96th Regiment, which was at the same time completed to full strength by the arrival from England of five independent companies, which had been transferred to it. The history of the 96th, this child of the Seventieth, was very short, for it was disbanded at the peace of 1763, the officers being placed on half-pay and the rank-and-file discharged or drafted to other units. The disbanding of the 96th Regiment brought the career of the officers of the Seventieth who were transferred to it to an untimely end. Major Piers remained for many years on the half-pay list, and most of the other officers remained also on half-pay until they died or retired. Of the Captains, two eventually effected exchanges to the active list, Captain Johnstone joining the 8th (The King's) Regiment in 1766 and retiring in 1770 ; while Captain Arthur Lysaght joined the 63rd Regiment, also in 1766, and retired in 1770. Lieutenant Morgan became a Captain in the 96th before it was disbanded, and exchanged from half-pay into the 7th (Royal Fusiliers) in 1775. He retired about 1778.

The transfer of Colonel John Parslow to the 54th Regiment has been mentioned. His successor in the Colonelcy of the Seventieth was Lieut.-Colonel Cyrus Trapaud of the 3rd Regiment or "Buffs." Colonel Trapaud, a member of a distinguished French family and nearly related to the celebrated Marshal Turenne, had been driven from France by religious persecution, for he was a Protestant. Entering the English army at an early age, Trapaud, as mentioned in Chapter II. of this history, distinguished himself at Dettingen, when an Ensign in the Buffs, by saving the life of King George II. Colonel, afterwards General, Trapaud saw much active service, both before and after joining the Seventieth, which regiment he commanded for eighteen years, save when employed in higher commands.

On December 31, 1760, the strength of the regiment was 396 sergeants, rank-and-file, and the establishment being 900, there was a deficiency of no less than 504. The new Grenadier company alone was 100 strong, the average strength of the eight battalion companies being thirty-seven. Efforts were evidently being made to replace the lost wing whose history has been related, as no less than nineteen officers are shown in the " state " as " on recruiting duty," but the regiment, having no chance of seeing active service, remained considerably below strength during 1761 and 1762. The Seven Years' War having been brought to a conclusion in the year 1763, the Seventieth, together with the rest of the army, was placed on a reduced establishment; but being shortly afterwards warned to proceed on foreign service, its establishment was fixed at 890 sergeants, rank-and-file. The regiment, then stationed at Hilsea Barracks, had on January 1, 1763, a strength of 639, leaving a deficiency of 261, and shortly afterwards it was moved to Ireland, where it remained about a year. In 1764, the regiment, still much under strength, embarked for its first tour of foreign service, its station for no less than ten years being the little island of Grenada. To be ordered on service in the West Indies at this period, and long afterwards, was with good reason looked upon in the army generally as a sentence of death. Barrack construction and the science of sanitation were then in their infancy, and yellow fever raged yearly in the unhealthy harbours round which, for defensive purposes, the British garrisons of the islands were stationed. It was no uncommon event for regiments to be swept off, almost to a man, within a few months of their arrival. This being so, the despatch of a regiment to the West Indies was followed, except in a time of actual active service, by the exodus of a large proportion of the officers, all who possessed sufficient influence securing transfers to some more desirable station, while the richer officers paid large sums for exchanges. The Army List of the years 1764, '65, and '66 shows that this procedure was followed in the Seventieth, the field officers and one or two of the seniors of each rank alone remaining in the regiment. Those who determined, for various reasons, to stand fast, naturally were rewarded by rapid promotion. Thus by exchange, transfer, and the survival of the fittest, after a couple of years or so the Seventieth, like other regiments in similar quarters, was furnished with a number of hardy and seasoned officers who triumphantly lived through the ten years of West Indian service that lay before the regiment, and many of whose names remained for long years afterwards on its rolls.

So distant, in 1764, did the West Indian Islands appear, and so little known were they to the home-staying headquarter staff of the army, that the very name of the island in which the regiment was stationed was too much for the compiler of the Army List of that year. He wrote it down as "Grenadoes," thinking no doubt that the name was something akin to that of another island that he spelt "Barbadoes." By 1765 some enlightened person appears to have pointed out that the spelling "Grenadoes" was unusual, so for the rest of the regiment's tour of service its station was described by the general term "Charibbee Islands," which evaded comment and no doubt satisfied everybody.

On December 19, 1768, presumably by desire of the Colonel, who at that period had almost uncontrolled authority in all matters relating to uniform, the facings of the Seventieth Regiment were changed by Royal Warrant from grey to black. Black facings were worn from 1768 to 1881, those of the officers being of velvet, and those of warrant officers, sergeants, and rank-and-file of cloth.

Among the officers of the Seventieth during its West Indian service was a young Ensign who long served in the regiment and subsequently rose to high rank in the army. This was George Hewett, born in 1750, the son of Major Shuckburgh Hewett, of the Buffs. George Hewett was given an Ensigncy in the Seventieth at the age of twelve by General Cyrus Trapaud, who was a friend of his father, and before his fifteenth birthday young Hewett had purchased a Lieutenancy and had joined his regiment in the West Indies, where he remained nearly ten years. Lieutenant Hewett had been left an orphan and almost alone in the world since the age of seven, but he was fortunate in being cared for by Captain Collins of the Seventieth, a man of exemplary character, who had served under General Wolfe at the taking of Quebec.

Responsibility soon fell on the young Lieutenant, for soon after he arrived at Grenada he was sent in command of a small detachment of the Seventieth, with two howitzers, charged with the duty of guarding properties in the centre of the island from insurgent slaves and other natives. Lieutenant Hewett was sent in 1771 to New York in charge of a number of invalids from Grenada, and while there was employed on recruiting duty. He obtained a large number of recruits, but no one born in the country would enlist. During the operations in St. Vincent Lieutenant Hewett was employed as Major of Brigade, and in 1774 he purchased the command of a company, returning with the regiment to England. Captain Hewett, it may be here added, subsequently served with distinction, in command of the Grenadier company, in the American War, and in 1781 was promoted by purchase to a Majority in the 43rd Regiment. He afterwards rose to high rank in the army, and after being Commander-in-Chief in India, and subsequently in Ireland, was created a Baronet, and died in 1840, at the age of ninety, a General and a Knight Grand Cross of the Bath.

In the year 1772, when the Seventieth had spent eight long years in Grenada, a formidable rebellion broke out in St. Vincent, another of the group of the West India Islands under the same government as Grenada. As has already been explained in the history of the Thirty-First, the Caribs, the original inhabitants of St. Vincent, had resented the transfer of the island to Great Britain at the peace of 1763, and after many warnings broke into open rebellion nine years later. Owing to the densely wooded and mountainous nature of the island, the repression of the rebellion proved a difficult task, and no less than six whole regiments, and parts of two more, were employed at various periods before the end of the operations. Among the complete regiments employed against the St. Vincent Caribs was the Thirty-First, and one of the detachments borrowed from neighbouring garrisons was furnished by the Seventieth Regiment, this being the first, but not the last, occasion on which the Seventieth met its parent corps in the field.

No detailed narrative of the suppression of the rebellion in St. Vincent exists, either in the Home Record Office or in the archives of the Island, but a few details of this forgotten campaign may be of interest.

The detachment of the Seventieth arrived at St. Vincent from Grenada on June 23, 1772, and completed the force (a very small one) required by Major-General Dalrymple for an encircling movement which he had planned. Owing to the weakness of the staff, Captain George Chamberlayne of the Seventieth was taken from duty with the detachment and employed as Quartermaster-General to the troops. Lieutenant George Hewett was also employed as Major of Brigade. A special corps, called the Rangers, was also formed, under a captain of the 14th Regiment, into which Lieutenant Nicholas Darrah and an unascertained number of men of the Seventieth were permitted to volunteer. In November 1772, all preparations having been completed, a detachment under Major Mackenzie of the Thirty-First was despatched by sea to effect a landing at Grande Sable, in rear of the rebel position. The landing at Grande Sable was stoutly opposed, and while it was being effected under a heavy fire, one boat was capsized. Lieutenant Nicholas Darrah of the Seventieth, with one sergeant, two corporals, and fifteen privates (all probably also of the regiment), were unfortunately drowned, but the landing was made. Encouraged by the disaster to the boat, the Caribs boldly rushed down to the shore, and in the hand-to-hand fight that followed two more privates were killed and nine wounded. On January 18, 1773, Lieutenant-Colonel Walsh of the Thirty-First, who had visited the Grande Sable detachment, escorted by a small party of his regiment, was attacked in a thick wood by Caribs. The Colonel and three of his men were killed, and their bodies mutilated in a shocking manner. The landing at Grande Sable had, however, the desired effect. The Carib army, being completely surrounded, was soon afterwards reduced to a state of starvation, and nine of their leading chiefs surrendered on February 12, 1773. For a time, however, it was not thought expedient to reduce the garrison to its normal strength, and in May 1773 an additional company of the Seventieth is mentioned as having been brought to the Island. The Caribs showing no inclination to resume hostilities, later in the year the detachment of the Seventieth rejoined its Headquarters at Grenada, and early in 1774 the regiment, reduced to a mere skeleton, returned to England to recruit its numbers; the companies at the same time numbering from ten to twenty men only. Having been quickly raised to an effective strength, the Seventieth, early in 1776, marched to Scotland, and was stationed at Edinburgh Castle until the spring of 1778.

In May 1778 Lieut.-General Cyrus Trapaud was removed to the 52nd Regiment, and was succeeded in the Colonelcy of the Seventieth by Major-General William Tryon, Major of the First Regiment of Foot Guards (now the Grenadier Guards). Major-General Tryon, who had been Governor of North Carolina, and subsequently of New York, had done good service during the War of Independence and the Colonelcy was bestowed on him in consequence.

CHAPTER XIII

THE AMERICAN WAR OF INDEPENDENCE

The Seventieth detained at Halifax—The flank companies at New York—Captain Irving's letters—The capture of Charleston—Lord Cornwallis' operations—The flank companies return to New York—Services and death of Major Patrick Ferguson—The Seventieth styled the "Surrey" Regiment.

ABOUT the date of General Tryon's appointment to the Seventieth, the regiment was ordered to North America, where at the time a great part of the army was employed in the defence of Canada and the attempted subjection of the rebel States.

The Seventieth itself was stationed at Halifax, Nova Scotia, during the greater part of its service in North America, and the battalion companies in consequence saw no fighting. The flank companies, however, were sent almost immediately after the arrival of the regiment at Halifax to join the Grenadier and Light Infantry battalions serving with the field army at New York, then commanded by Lieut.-General Sir Henry Clinton; and under that officer, Lord Cornwallis, and other general officers saw much active service.

The Grenadier company of the Seventieth, the officers of which were Captain George Hewett and Lieutenants George Williamson and C. F. Phillips, was posted to the 2nd battalion of Grenadiers, commanded by Lieut.-Colonel Yorke; and the Light company, under Captain Robert Irving, with Lieutenants Mackenzie, Zachary Hall, and T. H. Swymmer, formed part of the 1st battalion of Light Infantry, commanded by Colonel Abercromby. Later in the war Captain Irving, an experienced and highly-trusted officer, who had joined the Seventieth in 1762 and was now senior captain of the regiment, acted as major to his Light Infantry battalion (which for a time he commanded), and Captain Thomas Dunbar, who had purchased a company in the Seventieth from the 43rd Regiment, was appointed to command the Light Infantry company.

Lieutenant Phillips acted throughout the war as Adjutant of the 2nd battalion of Grenadiers, or of the " Flank battalion " into which owing to their heavy casualties the remains of the Grenadier and Light battalions were eventually merged.

The identity of the various companies of which the Grenadier and Light Infantry battalions were composed in the wars of the eighteenth century, were so merged in that of the battalions, that it is a most difficult matter to trace their history. In the case of the Seventieth companies, however, the broad facts can be stated positively, though details are lacking. It happens that, as Captain George Hewett of the Grenadier company subsequently rose to high rank, particulars of his early service have been preserved, and in a privately-printed memoir of his career the movements of his company in the American War are recorded. Captain Irving also, in an interesting series of letters to his wife, enables us to trace the movements of the Light company.

It appears from Captain Irving's first letter that the flank companies joined the army at New York on or about May 20, 1779, and went almost immediately into the field. On May 30 they were present at the capture of Fort Lafayette, at Stony Point on the Hudson. This fort, it may be mentioned, was recaptured on July 15 by General Washington, but during the great heat then prevailing neither army was prepared to undertake serious operations. As Captain Irving's letters show, the Light Company of the Seventieth shared in all that was done, but it was not until the end of the year that Sir Henry Clinton had sufficient strength to enter into any serious enterprise. It was necessary for him to maintain a strong garrison in Canada and also to guard the extensive positions at New York and Long Island; and when therefore on December 26 Clinton sailed from New York for the capture of Charleston he could take with him no more than 6700 men. In this force were one battalion of Light Infantry and two of Grenadiers, which included both the Seventieth flank companies. Major Ferguson, late of the Seventieth, now in command of a corps of American loyalists, was also with the army, and did brilliant service.[1]

[1] See Fortescue's *History of the British Army*, vol. iii. p. 309.

Charleston fell on May 9, 1780, the British casualties amounting to 265 killed and wounded, and shortly afterwards the flank battalions returned to New York and remained with the force there during the rest of the year.

In December 1780 a small force was sent from New York to form a base at Portsmouth on the James River. This force, chiefly composed of American loyalists and other irregulars, was commanded by Brigadier-General Benedict Arnold, who had recently deserted from the American army and had returned to his British allegiance. In March 1781 Arnold's force was threatened with destruction by the French fleet and army, and Sir Henry Clinton hurriedly despatched a force under Major-General Phillips to rescue Arnold, and in this force the flank companies of the Seventieth were included. Some of the adventures of the Light Company can be traced in Captain Irving's letters of May 11 and June 29. It appears from the States of the flank companies at the Record Office that at this time Captain Irving was acting as Major of the 1st battalion of Light Infantry, and the Seventieth Light Infantry company was commanded by Captain Thomas Dunbar.

In the action of July 6, described in Captain Irving's letter of August 16, the Seventieth company had one man killed and several others (probably wounded) became prisoners of war. Little other positive information concerning the flank companies can be gleaned from the few extant documents concerning them, but the Grenadier company and all or part of the Light Company were sent back to New York before Lord Cornwallis took up his fatal position at Yorktown. Among the troops which sailed from New York in the attempt to reinforce Lord Cornwallis at Yorktown, was the Grenadier company of the Seventieth under Captain Hewett, which was conveyed in Admiral Digby's flagship, in which Prince William, afterwards King William IV, was serving as a midshipman. Unhappily the reinforcements were so long delayed that Lord Cornwallis had been compelled to surrender four days before their arrival at Yorktown.

Captain Irving, and perhaps a portion of the Light company, served through the siege, and Captain Irving is known to have done good service there, acting as Major of the Light battalion. He was

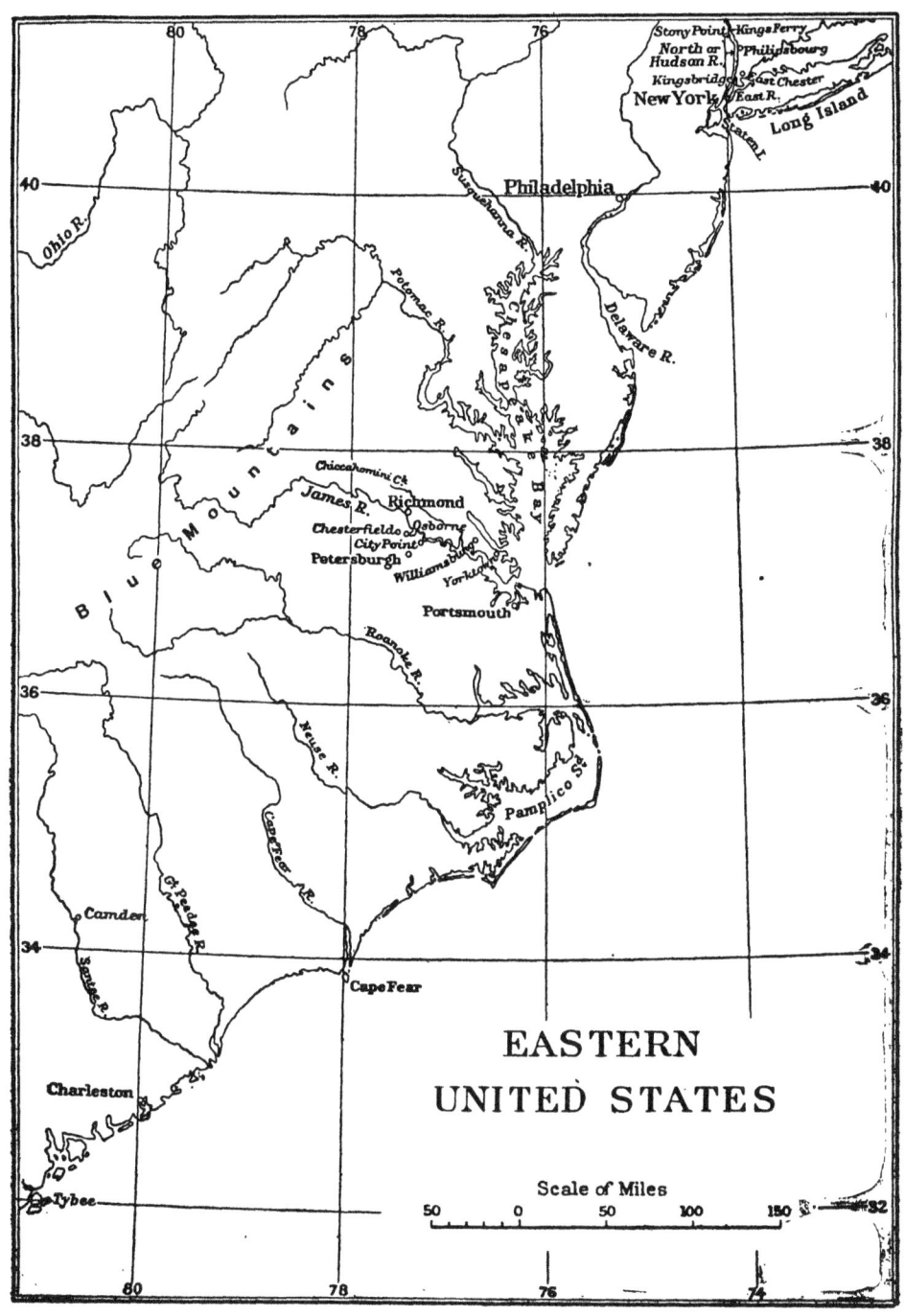

EASTERN UNITED STATES

included in the surrender, and, having been released on parole, was permitted to return to England.

Captain Irving, like many of the officers of the Seventieth in 1779, hailed from Scotland, being the son of John Irving of Bonshaw, co. Dumfries. There is a monument to him in the churchyard of St. Michael's Church, Dumfries. This and the following letters were written by Captain Irving to his wife, and from them we can glean some particulars of the little known operations of the War of Independence, and learn the impressions of the rebellion formed by the mind of a thoughtful and intelligent observer. For permission to make use of the letters of Captain Irving the East Surrey Regiment is indebted to the kindness of his great-grandson, Major-General F. B. Mainguy, late Royal Engineers. A few instances of irregular or old-fashioned spelling in the letters are left unaltered.

Camp near Fort Lafayette,
10th June, 1779.

My Company with the other light Troops from Halifax joined the Light Infantry of the Army at Hell Gate, near New York, about the 20th of last month where we remained four or five days, during which time the Army were preparing to take the field. About the 25th the whole were put in motion and took post five miles from Kingsbridge, forming one line with the right to the East River and left to the North River, extending about seven miles from right to left. When the Troops had been encamped for two or three days, it was generally believed that they would remain in that situation till the month of August, as the intense heat of the weather makes it impossible to go through any active service before that month, and even then marches are generally made in the night—but on the 29th just after dinner we received orders to march, and to be ready to quit our ground in ten minutes, which we did; and that evening the whole army with Sir H. Clinton embarked at Philipsbourgh on the North River; we landed next day about 10 o'clock, eight miles below this place; and marched immediately with about 3,000 men to attack the Fort: we could not possibly make the attack till next day, so much time was spent in halting, reconnoitring &c. Next morning we advanced within a mile of it, and from the fire which the Rebel Artillery kept up on our shipping, gun boats, and a battery our men erected in the night on the opposite side at Stony Point taken the preceding day by three regiments from the Rebels, and from every other appearance, there was reason to expect a desperate resistance. A disposition was made for the attack by General Vaughan, who was to command it, but when Jonathan understood that the Artillery were within three hundred yards of him, that the Light Inf^{try} and Grena^{drs} of the Guards were at the same distance with Ferguson's Corps,[1] that the Light Inf^{try} and Grena^{drs} of the Army were within a mile of Fort Lafayette, and that no quarter would be given if the Garrison thought proper to risk a storm, he very prudently surrendered. Two of the Rebels were killed, and one wounded by a shell—none of ours hurt. The work is very small but strong; and if they had been resolute, we could not have carried it without losing at least two hundred fine fellows; it contained about 80 Rebels. This post is of no other consequence than that of commanding King's ferry, where the Rebel Army have always crossed the North river; and they cannot now cross it without going 40 miles further up, over mountains and bad roads scarcely passable for Artillery. The River here is about three q^{rs} of a mile broad; and we are so strongly posted on both sides that no enemy can give us much trouble, without fighting on very unequal terms, which is an error the continental army are by no means liable to fall into: the day after the surrender of this impertinent little Fort, the Army on this side of the river marched to Peak's Hill six miles up the river, where we expected to find a few hundreds of the Enemy; but they had gone off the night before, and we saw only a few of their Light horse, some of whom were shot by our advanced guard. The Light Infantry then made a detour of fourteen miles further, with two other corps, and we returned to our quarters at 2 o'clock in the morning, with a quantity of cattle, after having been twenty hours on our legs. This was the first Exhibition of my Company, and they all stood the fatigue extremely well. My Trumpeter picked me up a little horse, and I assure you I will take as little fatigue as possible, whilst I can get one to carry me. I have got quite the better of that folly of despising a horse because I am a Lt Infantry man. Since that time we have not had anything to do, nor do we expect any further employment till the arrival of the reinforcement, which is expected very soon. It is confidently reported that the Rebels have in their turn sent Commissioners to France to negotiate a peace, convinced that the losses of their new Allies will soon make them desert from the engagements they are under to them. I hope in God Great Britain

---

[1] A corps of picked marksmen commanded by Captain Ferguson of the Seventieth; who was subsequently promoted Major in the 71st Regiment.

will keep her dignity on the occasion, and confirm all her rights, even though she never intends to exercise them—it was a wanton and unprovoked Rebellion ; I, therefore, think we should have no peace whilst there is a particle of that poison remaining in their blood, which has cost us so many valuable lives. I am clear for peace with America, but their submission ought to be ample, as their crime has been great ; and if their penitence is sincere they have still much happiness to expect from the protection of the most indulgent parent and most powerful State in the world, who has a heart to forgive, as well as a spirit to chastise.

15th. The Comm^r in Chief has been at New York and is returned,—it is said, to see the Fortifications here completed ; and then to withdraw part of the Troops to their former post near Kingsbridge, when everything is likely to remain quiet till the Reinforcement arrives, and I shall be within reach of the Post Office when a Packet arrives. I fear you will be very angry at my paper being filled with matters of so little consequence, to both you and me, as the taking of a little dirty Fort ; but as you will probably see some Newspaper accounts of this Expedition I thought I would give you one which you know you can depend on.

. . . . .

Our Colonel, General Tryon, is Govr of New York.

(S^d). R. IRVING.

Maraneck Camp,
July 15th 1779.

Since the last little letter I wrote you nothing has happened of any consequence—the Reinforcement is not arrived and the Army is loitering in a state of Inactivity and indolence in Camp—some trifling motions which we have made perplex Mr. Washington a good deal, as he acknowledges himself at a loss how to judge of our real intention, and I believe this entirely answers the Comd^r-in-Chief's present purpose, for little more can be done with the small numbers now under his command than to tease and vex the Enemy. Genl Tryon's expedition which I mentioned in my last, went up the East river some days after. He landed in two or three different parts in New England and burnt some Stores and small towns inhabited by people notorious for their violence in the Rebel interest, and for their cruelty to, and depredations on the friends of Government on the opposite shore in Long Island About the time of their first landing, we marched from our encampment at East Chester with the British and Hessian Grenadiers, the 17th

Dragoons, Queen's Rangers and Legion towards Connecticut to favour their operations by alarming the Country near them, and I am convinced they received some advantage by this movement. Our little Army advanced by Byam's Bridge, which is the Entry into New England, lay there one night, and returned five miles on the way to East Chester next day, where we now are and expect to remain till the Dragoons eat up the Forrage. We heard some cannonading when Gen. Tryon landed, but were not near enough to see anything that happened,—he lost two Officers besides some wounded; and a few men were killed and wounded.—We have no accounts of the loss of the Rebels—I am very anxious about the arrival of the packet. . . .

. . . .

25th. East Chester. The day after I wrote the other side, we marched from our Encampment at Marraneck, and returned to this ground; the cause of which was, that an attack had been made the preceding night upon Stony Point opposite to Verplank's Point by the Rebels who carried it by storm in half an hour tho' it was strongly fortified, and garrisoned with about 500 of our best Troops, vizt the 17th Reg^t, the two Grenadier Companys of the 71st, and the rest were a Detach^t from a very good provincial Corps. . . . An Officer was killed and several wounded. . . . As soon as they had possession of the place, they turned the guns upon the Shipping and the opposite Fort—the shipping were obliged to cut their cables and run—but Colonel Webster (the Minister's son) with the 33rd Reg^t, Ferguson's Corps and Robinson's provincials defended it in the most gallant manner for three days till part of the Army went up the river to their relief—our Battal^n was among the number. When we got so near that the Rebels thought we might push on shore in boats in the night, they set fire to all the works, having first carried off the Cannon &ca. and then evacuated them. The Light Infantry landed next day to re-take the place, not knowing that they were gone, but there was not a Rebel to be seen, nor a shot fired at us,—we left it in the night and returned next day to E. Chester, where the Army will remain for some weeks.—I am in great distress to hear that the packet sailed with two mails on board long before the "Greyhound" Friggate which arrived with Lord Cornwallis the 22nd. I begin to fear that fortune is determined I shall not hear any more from you.[1] . . . By the Edinburgh Reg^t I expect many letters . .

(S^d) R. IRVING.

[1] He received four letters from his wife a few days later.

New York,
28 Augt 1779.

I wrote you a few days ago by the Cork fleet. . . . Since that the Fleet is arrived from England with the Troops. They have been very sickly, some of them on board for above twenty-two weeks. . . . The June Packet was taken, and all the letters thrown overboard—the date of the last I had from you was the 15 April—. . . The army is all Encamped at present in the neighbourhood of New York, that is, on York Island, Staten Island, and the West end of Long Island. I am told that some grand Expedition was intended on the arrival of the reinforcement, but the general opinion now seems to be, that the Governm^t has not sent a sufficient one to enable the Com^{dr} in Chief to put such a plan in execution—in short, many experienced Officers think we shall have no Campaign, from the weakness of the Army—that some troops will be sent to Georgia, and the rest endeavour to preserve what we have here—unless the Ministry can support us better, I fear the Country will not be easily subdued—Treasure will be wasted, and nothing done. I should not have wrote you by this packet if I had not come to Town by accident, for she sails to-morrow, and I knew nothing of it. . . .

(S^d)   R. IRVING.

THE EXPEDITION TO CHARLESTON

Jamaica, Long Island,
Decr 1779.

6th Decr Our Battalion has just rec^d orders to hold themselves in readiness to embark with all the British and Hessian Grenadiers and other Corps to the amount of about 8,000 men—our destination, as usual in such cases, is a secret, but let it be where it will, the Enemy have no strength to oppose such a force with the smallest chance of success. We certainly must go to the southward from the season of the year—I hope to Virginia, where a few Tobacco Hogsheads may fall into our hands, and assist to defray the expenses of the Expedition. Don't be uneasy about the fighting that we are to have—the Rebels made no resistance agst that Expedition which did not consist of half our number. We expect to return here before April.

10*th.* Our Battⁿ is divided into two. I am in the first, commanded by Col. Abercromby—Col. Dundas has got the second. Our ships are allotted to us—Mine is called the Neptune, a very good ship which was one of our Transports on the passage from Greenock to Halifax—I imagine we shall soon return, as we leave our heavy baggage. . . . Again I intreat you not to be uneasy. . . .

Ever &c.
(S^d) R. Irving.

P.S. *New York. 16th Dec'*. I am come to Town to put my letters in the bag. No acc^{ts} of our embarking yet. The Genl is not certain that the French Fleet has left the coast yet—and we won't sail till they do. The weather is so cold, I can hardly hold the pen. God bless you all.

New York,
22nd Decr 1779.

I have written you a long letter by a Man of War, and a very long one by Captn McMurdo, who is sailed in another ship of the same fleet. The packet is just ordered to be made up, and to sail directly. This is merely intended as a Bill of health, and I suppose will arrive before either of the others—8,000 Troops are embarked on an Expedition supposed against Charlestown—the name of my Transport is the Neptune. We expect no fighting and a great deal of prize money.—I will write you by the first oport^y from thence if I know of it.—I am just going on board.

. . . .

&c. &c.
(Signed) R. Irving.

James's Island,
8th March 1780.

I wrote you two or three letters just before we left New York. I am just informed that a ship is going back there, and a packet to sail from thence immediately for England. . . .

Our voyage was tedious by contrary winds and bad weather—all are at last safely arrived except one ship which lost her masts and went to the West Indies. The Fleet rendezvoused at Tybee in Georgia, came from thence to John's Island and landed the 11th of last month. Our aproaches are greatly retarded by the Inland navigation through which we are obliged to bring our cannon, provisions &c., but we expect that a few days more will bring us before Charlestown, when a regular siege will commence, and it will probably be agreeable news to you to be informed that in such an attack every thing is done by Artillery so that the rest of the Army will not be near so much exposed as in the field—I am in perfect health. . . .

Your &c. &c,
(Signed) R. IRVING.

P.S. We have hitherto met no opposition—Our Fleet consisting of 40 Guns Ships and Frigates, are to attack by sea whilst we invest the Town by land ; and it is expected a very few days well employed will oblige them to capitulate.

I imagine this scrawl is very incorrect but I had not time to make it better. We have the greatest plenty of good fresh provisions, and there never was so healthy an army.—Some Regiments have not a sick man. The Lt Infantry return to New York after the siege. All my company are in perfect health.

Camp before Charlestown,
18th April 1780.

I have had the happiness of receiving three letters from you since the Army came to the Southward, the last dated the 26th November, and I sincerely thank God for the health which you and my children enjoy, and pray to Him for the continuance of that and the attainment of every other blessing this world affords to you and them. . . .

. . . . . .

25th. The siege goes on with great expedition it is expected that a fortnight more will put us in possession of the Town, Troops, Magazine etc. . . General Tryon is relieved from all his Employments in America, another Governor being arrived at New York ; and he goes home soon. . . .

Charlestown 12th May. My dearest wife will rejoice to hear that the Town has this day surrendered to His Majesty's Arms, and that your husband has not received even a scratch in the midst of constant danger during a siege of six weeks. I thank God for my safety

Considering the constant firing of Cannon, Mortars and Small Arms which has been kept up since the 2nd of April by the Enemy, you will be surprised to see so small a list of killed and wounded as the Gazette will produce, which can only be accounted for by the ability of those who directed our operations— our approaches were regular, carried on with great caution, and at the same time with the utmost expedition. The whole proceeding does much honor to Sir Henry Clinton, whose humanity on the occasion appears in a very conspicuous light. I believe the conduct of the Rebels would have provoked any other man to have stormed their Works and put every man to the Sword. I must refer you to the Gazette for particulars, you will there receive a much better account of the Siege than any I could give—indeed, were I inclined I have not time, for the Light Infantry march this night or to-morrow morning into the Country, to take possession of some rich Stores the Rebels have on the Santi River. . .

May Almighty God bless you and my dear Children.

. . . .

Your ever aff^{te} and most faithful
Husband,
(Sd.) R. I.

P.S. Major Ferguson desires me to mention that he is well, lest any accident happen to his letters.

New York,
30th November 1780.

. . . . . .

Before this reaches you, you will have heard of Lord Cornwallis's Victory[1] to the Southward. Never did any General or Army acquire more honor than they did on this occasion. But tho' the Rebel Army was entirely cut to pieces they have since collected a sufficient number of troops to enable them to give some trouble to his Lordship's Army. Genl Leslie sailed with an expedition to Virginia in Oct^r, which landed without oposition took Tobacco & Stores to a great amount. Lord Cornwallis having sent for them, they have re-embarked & sailed for Carolina, we are now under orders to embark in a few days, and the general opinion is that we are going to take up Genl Leslie's post and finish the business he went about, namely, to take all the shipping & stores we can lay our hand on, & destroy what we cannot bring away. The last Fleet was only five days on their passage, and I hope we won't be longer. . . . It will perhaps please you to hear that they had no fighting there, and that it is most probable we shall finish our work without broken bones, if there should be a few scratches we will most likely get enough to pay the Doctor, tho' if judgment is to be formed out of our success at Charlestown, we shall lie long out of our money. That matter is never yet settled, but is before the King and Council whose determination we expect soon. . . .

---

[1] Battle of Camden, August 16, 1780.

It gives me great concern to inform you of the death of one whom you know I had a most affectionate regard for—Poor Major Ferguson is no more—he was left in Carolina by Sir Henry Clinton (who had a very just opinion of his abilities and worth) to execute a Plan for raising Militia in that province—he had succeeded beyond the General's expectations, for no person could be better qualified to gain the hearts of the people, or convert them from their erroneous principles, than he was—but he unfortunately fell in an attack which the Rebels made with very superior numbers on the Post where he commanded, he has not left a man of superior abilities or possessed of a better heart behind him in this Army. His superior talents in a professional as well as in a general view, had deservedly gained him a degree of confidence and esteem from the Com^{dr} in Chief above what his rank entitled him to.

Our Expedition is stopped & only three Reg^{ts} go, under the Com^d of Genl Arnold. We are in Winter Quarters about three miles from New York, and shall remain quiet for some months—most probably till the end of the war, for little more can be done here unless the French fleet gets a hearty drubbing.

(S^d). R. IRVING.

Staten Island,
18 Jan^y, 1781.

About a fortnight ago we were ordered here with other Troops of the Army in all about 6,000 men to be in readiness to favor a Revolt in part of the Rebel Army to the amount, as report says, of two Thousand. The cause of it by our information is their want of clothing, proper and regular supplies of provisions, and a determination they have made not to serve any longer unless paid in hard money, their paper Currency being by no greater Value in their markets than as one is to a hundred, and of real value, worth nothing. All the other Corps but the Gren^{drs} & Lt. Infantry are returned to their winter quarters, and we expect to go in a day or two, as the last advices from the Rebel Country mention that their requests are agreed to by Congress—if this should be true they have only put off the evil day a little longer, for there is not a possibility of their being able to fullfill their obligations, particularly that part where they promise to pay them in hard money—other accounts say that Congress have proposed meeting the Revolters at a place to treat with them, where they intend to surround them with the Militia and reduce them to their own terms—some Revolution will undoubtedly soon take place among them—they begin to lose confidence in their leaders, and the inhabitants as well as their military show themselves exceedingly discontented with the Hardships they suffer by the continuance of the War. Our quarters here are not very good, mine is one of the best. We are cantooned at the Farm-houses, which are not so good as in Long Island, the officers sleep in the houses, & the men sleep in the barns.

We are just informed that the Packet sails immediately, and tho' it may not go before we return to our quarters I think it best to inform you of my health without risking a delay till then, to prevent any chance of your not hearing from me which might make you more than commonly uneasy at a time, so interesting an event has occasioned a general movement of the Army—a report prevails to-day that the Packet which sailed about three weeks ago is taken by the rebels, so that I fear you will be very impatient before you receive this—in these cases the letters are always thrown overboard & sunk.

. . . .

Winter Quarters on Long Island,
22 Jan^y.

The Army for the present are all returned to their winter quarters, and the Disputes in the Rebel Army are abated for a time, but I am convinced the Reconciliation cannot be permanent, what has now happened is only a prelude to something of great importance, and I am firmly convinced that we shall see America return to her Allegiance again in a short time, but it will be from inability to carry on the War, not from friendship to Brittain.

. . . .

Your most aff^{te}
R. IRVING.

Captain Irving was quite right as to his facts, but not right in his anticipations. Washington's difficulties at the beginning of 1781 appeared to be insurmountable, but his fine perseverance overcame them in the end, and almost single-handed he held the rebel armies together until France came to their assistance and turned the scale against England.

Long Island,
3rd March, 1781.

. . . .

I have written you a long letter by the Packet, to which I must refer you. She is not sailed yet, but will in a few days.

We are ordered to embark again, and are supposed to be going to Virginia to join Arnold, whose situation at present is a little irksome, being blocked up by two or three French ships, but the appearance of Adm^l Arbuthnot's Fleet will soon set that matter right & then I hope we shall visit some of their Tobacco Stores —be not apprehensive about the fighting business of this Expedition, I believe that will fall to the share of the Navy— they have no land forces that can oppose the number of our Army which will be there. Two months will probably bring us back here, and if I dare hazard a conjecture about our operations in this part of America for the rem^r of the Summer, I think they will be defensive

The War must be carried on somewhere else, nothing can be done here. You see I always inform you without delay when we are ordered on any Service, it is certainly the best way to prevent your being more alarmed than is necessary from other people's accounts. . . .

Your most faithfull &c.

R. IRVING.

Petersburgh,
Virginia,
11th May, 1781.

After I last wrote you from New York we lay for some time on board Transports at Sandy Hook, then sailed, and after a good passage of five days arrived at Portsmouth in this Province, from whence I wrote you soon after, and sent my letter to Willie Armstrong at New York to forward to you; on the 18th April about 1900 men embarked at Portsmouth and sailed immediately up James's River to complete the destruction of such Stores as Gen. Arnold had left on his former expedition—the Infantry were in boats that hold about 85 men each; the Queen's Rangers and Jägers in Bateaux; the 76th & 80th Reg^{ts} in Transports— about 50 miles up the River part of the Army landed and marched to Williamsburgh and York Town, but no Public Stores being found there, they left these places immediately and re-embarked the Lt Infantry whom they had landed, went near twenty miles further up the River, and having taken and destroyed the Shipping Dockyard and Stores on Chiccahomini Creek, and returned to our Boats on the 23rd, landed at City Point on the 24th distance from this place twelve miles—Genl Phillips having got good intelligence with respect to the Enemy's position and strength, the whole Army marched the next morning to attack them, having halted and refreshed about a mile from their advanced posts the Army moved on about 2 o'clock. The Enemy was posted on a Hill within a mile of Petersburgh with a Rivulet in their front. The Action began about 3 o'clock, & before 5 we beat them from three different positions equally advantageous, to which they retreated successively, and got possession of the Towns and Hills on both sides of the river it stands on, which entirely command it, and likewise the villages of Blandford & Pocahunta, the former joining the Petersburgh, the latter on the opposite bank of the Apamattoc, on which they stand—a branch of James River— The Rebels in the action lost in killed & wounded between 60 & 70. One cannon ball killed & wounded 15 of them. Our loss was one Jägar, killed in a skirmish before the Action began, and ten Light Infan^{try} wounded. Major Armstrong, who commands the 1st Battalion being detached, I had the honor of commanding it that day. The Rebels had the advantage of us in numbers by a hundred or two—they were all militia and we have never heard of them since. Next day was employed in destroying all the Tobacco and other Public Stores, which were great & very valuable. On the 27th Genl Arnold, with the rest of the Army, went to Osborne, whilst the Lt Infantry made a detour by Chesterfield Court House, burnt Barracks for 2,000 men, 300 barrels of flour, & all public buildings, & joined line in the evening. He had taken, on his arrival there, 2 Ships, 2 Brigs, & some small Vessels with some Tobacco in them, which with what they found in store houses amounted to about 800 hogs-heads, and was brought off in these Ships. The Enemy defended their Ships for some time against a six pounder of ours. On the 30th the Army marched to Manchester, opposite to Richmond, on the other branch of the River, & destroyed all the Public Stores, in the face of the Enemy, who were strongly posted there. Not a shot was fired, tho' in the reach of musquetry. The whole time that evening the Army marched on its return to the Shipping. The whole embarked the 3rd May, sailed the 4th, and when we had got as far down the River on the way back to Portsmouth, as where we first landed, near Williamsburgh, Genl Phillips received an Express from Lord Cornwallis, informing him that he would march from Cape Fear for Petersburg immediately, and desiring that by such proceedings as he might think best calculated for that purpose our little Army would favor his passing the Roanoque River, which divides North Carolina & Virginia. We returned immediately, and are now strongly posted, to watch the motions of La

Fayette's Army, or act otherwise, according to the intelligence we have of the Southern Army under Lord Cornwallis.

I am sorry to find I have filled up my paper with a long Story, which will, I fear, afford very little amusement.

. . . .

Don't imagine, from what has happened, that we are likely to have much fighting here. I believe they will not look at us again. When our two armies meet, every thing here will fly before us, and that will probably happen in three or four days.

. . . .

Most affectionate,
R. IRVING.

Williamsburg,
29th June 1781.

Since writing you last, the Army has been employed in endeavouring to bring the Rebel Army, under the Marquis De la Fayette, to an Engagement, but finding that impossible we are returned to Williamsburg, only 80 miles from the sea, where, or at York Town on York River (5 miles distant) it is imagined Lord Cornwallis will keep his quarters during the two hot summer months, July and August.

We pursued the Marquis till within 50 miles of the Blue Mountains which we had a very fine view of, and at that distance appear as high as any I have seen in Scotland. I looked at them with pleasure from their resemblance to the Moffat Hills, when they are seen on the road from Penrith to Carlisle. . . . We gave up the pursuit at Elk Hill, remained there some days, and on our return called at Richmond, where I met with your Cousin Dr. Currie. . . . The damage we have done the Enemy in this part of America is immense, not only in the destruction of their Tobacco and Military Stores, but in feeding 4,000 men so long on the Country. If Great Britain can only keep her other enemys at bay, the American contest will soon be over. I have had an opportunity of knowing the sentiments of all classes—they are, to a man, tired of the War, and the lower degree often declare to us that they have discovered the Selfish and Ambitious designs of their leaders, and are most unhappy under their Yoke; but acknowledge they have not resolution to embrace the most ready and effectual method to shake it off, which would be to take Arms and join the British Troops, and their reason is not only just, but mortifying to Brittain, 'tis this—" After the loyal Inhabitants of different parts of America have openly professed their friendship for, and taken part with Great Brittain, the King's Troops have often, from necessity, or some important object in view, left them to the barbarous Ravages and persecutions of their merciless neighbours and countrymen." The Resources of the Rebels are nearly exhausted, and without French re-inforcements they must very soon submit.

Probably it will not displease you to hear that the Lt. Infantry are ordered back to New York, as you are always more anxious for my being out of the way of broken heads, than in the way of preferment. Lord Cornwallis hesitates about obeying the order, and I am told will make an effort to keep us, but I do not think the Com^r-in-Chief will consent to it. I enjoy the most perfect health; the summer weather in America is very hot, but does not effect me as the W. Indies did. I never have even so much as a cold that lasts above one day. . . .

Yours etc.,
R. IRVING.

York Town,
Virginia,
16th August, 1781.

. . . .

The Feb^{ry} Packet brought me a letter, the March Packet was taken, the April and May Packets are arrived and I have none by either. . . .

Since I wrote you last the Army has marched through a good deal more of the country and destroyed all the Tobacco and Public Stores of every kind upon or near James River; the beginning of July Lord Cornwallis left Williamsburg and marched to Jamestown on the north side of the river; distance six miles where the Army took post till the Baggage etc., crossed the River, after which they were to follow. The Marquis de la Fayette having intelligence on the 5th that the troops were all crossed over but the rear guard consisting of six hundred men marched next day with an intention to destroy these poor fellows, but to his astonishment and sorrow instead of the handfull he expected, he found Lord C., with his whole Army, ready to receive him. The Rebels did not appear till 4 o'clock in the afternoon (of July 6) and perceiving their mistake endeavoured to waste the time in the edge of a wood that was in our front, by making every appearance of a resolution to come to a general engagement whilst his real design was to avoid it if possible, and retreat through the Woods as soon as night favoured him.

For some time Lord C. was in hopes that they intended to fight, but at length he perceived what they were about and the afternoon being far spent he attacked them and gave them a most hearty drubbing.[1] They stood a little firing but fled when the British Army attempted to close with them, and night coming on, the pursuit was very short—the Edinburgh Reg^t and Lord McDonald's who were in the hottest of the Action, behaved remarkably well—Lord Cornwallis pays them a very handsome compliment in next day's Orders. The Enemy's loss was above 100, our's about 70. The Army crossed the river next day, and nothing worth notice has happened since that time, except the evacuation of the garrison at Portsmouth in Elizabeth River, in the room of which one is established here, the situation being thought a better one.

When the Works are finished, the Lt. Infantry [2] and some more troops expect to return to New York.

· · · · · · ·

The War must soon be over, and then we will meet.

· · · · · · ·

Yours for ever,
R. IRVING.

York Town,
Virginia,
19th October, 1781.

· · · · · · ·

When you receive this, if not before, you will hear of the Surrender of the Garrison I date it from, to an Army of French and Americans of near 20,000 men, after the hottest siege that ever happened in any part of America, and I believe, for the time it lasted, equal to any that ever was known in any Country. The killed, wounded and sick amount to near half of our Army.

---

[1] In this action, in which Lord Cornwallis showed great skill, Private J. McGuire, of the Light Company, Seventieth Regiment, was killed, and in the "state" in which McGuire is shown as "killed in action" ten privates of the Light Company are shown as "prisoners of war." These were probably wounded men who had fallen into the hands of the Americans, for the action of July 6 was a decided victory to Lord Cornwallis' army.

[2] As the following letters show, Captain Irving remained at Yorktown and was included in Lord Cornwallis' surrender. He was released on parole and returned to England. As second in command of the 1st Battalion of Light Infantry, Captain Irving took part in the sortie from Yorktown on October 16, 1781, when the battalion distinguished itself by the capture of a French battery at the point of the bayonet. This was the last British success in the American War. The Seventieth Light Company was not at Yorktown, and had apparently been sent back to New York before the siege began.

In the midst of perpetual danger your husband has been preserved not only from the accidents of War but in the most perfect health. . . .

I do not yet know the terms of the capitulation, but hope, from report, that they are very favourable. . . .

I will write you by every opportunity till I can inform you what we are to do, and when I shall see you. If we go to the back country very few opportunities will offer but whatever are the terms I have some hopes of getting home very soon.

I am, for ever, etc., etc.,

R. IRVING.

York Town,
Virginia,
22nd October, 1781.

. . . .

This Post under the Com^d of Lord Cornwallis has been besieged since the 27th September by a very powerfull Army of French and Americans, and reduced to the necessity of capitulating on the 19th instant. Our worthy general has obtained the most favourable terms for us. A proportion of Officers stay in the Country with the Men, this was determined by Draft, and I was fortunate for the second time in my life. Paroles are given to all the other officers and they are allowed to go to New York or Europe. I need not tell you that I made choice of the latter and I must add that I hope to be with my beloved wife by the beginning of the year. We all go to New York first, which is very convenient, for there are few of us but what have some business there. . . .

The siege has been the hottest ever known in this, and I believe equal to what has been known in any, country. There was not one spot of safety large enough to hold a man, within the garrison. The fire was astonishing from the 9th when they opened their Batterys, till the 17th when hostilities ceased. The number of killed and wounded are great—most of those that are safe have had narrow escapes. I had three or four hair-breadth ones. A bomb-shell fell under the table where seven of us were sitting at dinner one day but did not burst till we had time to crawl on our Bellys to a little distance, by which means we saved ourselves. . . . This goes with the Dispatches to France and I must conclude as the letter is sent for.

God preserve you and my children.

Yours for ever,

R. IRVING.

In addition to the eight officers who served with the flank companies, and to Major-General Tryon, whose services after he became Colonel of the Seventieth were mainly of a civil nature, one other officer of the Seventieth performed conspicuously good work in North America, and earned for himself a reputation quite exceptional for one of his modest military rank. This was Captain Patrick Ferguson, a member of the family of Ferguson of Pitfour, who was born in 1744, and, after serving in the Seven Years' War as a young subaltern in the Scots Greys, purchased in 1768 a company in the Seventieth. Captain Pat Ferguson, as he was always called, served several years with the regiment in Grenada and St. Vincent and did good service in the Carib insurrection, but he was best known in the army for his inventive genius and for his extraordinary skill as a marksman. Ferguson invented a breech-loading rifle, called after him, which was patented in 1776, and with it could fire with extraordinary speed and accuracy. In the following year Captain Ferguson was allowed to go to New York as a volunteer, taking with him a small corps of selected riflemen drawn from regiments serving at home, armed with his rifle, and trained by him. With this corps Ferguson did admirable service, showing great skill and enterprise, until he was very severely wounded in the battle of Brandywine, September 11, 1777. Immediately before he was wounded Captain Ferguson had an opportunity of shooting General Washington, but held his hand; a chivalrous action, which materially affected the course of history. While Ferguson was in hospital from his wound, Sir William Howe unfortunately broke up the corps of riflemen and sent the men back to duty with their regiments. In the autumn of 1778 Captain Ferguson was entrusted by Sir Henry Clinton, who had succeeded Sir William in the command in North America, with a detached command, in the execution of which duty he showed remarkable enterprise and skill.

In 1780 Ferguson, then in command of a corps of loyal American Militia, styled "Ferguson's Rangers," was again severely wounded in a night attack, and about the same time he became a Major in the 71st Regiment (Fraser's Highlanders), but apparently never joined that regiment. With his corps of Rangers, Ferguson did valuable service under Lord Cornwallis in the Southern States, and at last, after a career of extraordinary activity, he was killed in action at King's Mountain in North Carolina on October 6, 1780. Major Ferguson's death was as honourable as his life, for he died fighting against overwhelming odds and keeping up to his last moment the courage and steadiness of his irregulars. The death of Major Ferguson has been declared by more than one American writer to have been the real turning-point of the War of Independence, and it undoubtedly resulted in the total loss of his corps of 1100 men, and in the consequent abandonment of Lord Cornwallis' active plan of campaign in North Carolina. Major Ferguson, who is described by Mr. Fortescue[1] as "the most expert rifleman in the British Army, and an admirable partisan leader," was an officer of whom the Seventieth Regiment has every right to be proud, and by it his memory should be preserved.

To return to the history of the regiment itself, and of its flank companies, it only remains to say that the Seventieth led an uneventful life at Halifax throughout the war, completing the flank companies from time to time, as vacancies occurred in them. All fighting, as has been mentioned, ceased in America after the surrender of Lord Cornwallis at Yorktown in October 1781, but it was not until the year 1783 that the Seventieth returned to England.

During its stay at Halifax (in the year 1782) the regiment received an English county title, being ordered to style itself the Seventieth (Surrey) Regiment. At the same time an additional (or depôt) company was formed, which was stationed at Kingston-on-Thames for recruiting purposes. This company enlisted men of the county of Surrey for the regiment, and passed them on in small parties to the general depôt for English regiments at Chatham, whence they were sent in annual drafts to the regiments in North America. In consequence of complaints made by certain regiments, an enquiry into the quality of the drafts for America was made, and the Surrey recruits of the Seventieth were reported by a board of officers to be of good quality.

[1] *History of the British Army*, vol. iii. p. 324.

CHAPTER XIV

THE FRENCH REVOLUTIONARY WAR

The " Standing Orders " of 1788—The French revolutionary war—The West Indian campaign of 1793—More letters of Major Irving—Capture of Martinique—The Seventieth at Morne Pied—Heavy loss of life in the regiment—Service at Gibraltar—A trip to Trinidad—Under Sir John Moore at Chatham and Shorncliffe—The West Indies again—Yellow fever—The flank companies at Guadeloupe in 1810.

ON its return from North America, the Seventieth was stationed at Exeter. On August 16 of this year Lieutenant-General William Tryon, Colonel of the regiment, was removed to the Colonelcy of the 29th Foot, and was succeeded in the Seventieth by Colonel the Earl of Suffolk, an officer of the First Foot Guards. Lord Suffolk joined the regiment at Exeter and took over command from Lieut.-Colonel St. George, who was granted long leave of absence. Nearly all the rank-and-file of the regiment had been discharged as unfit for further service, a fact which testifies to the severe strain imposed on the army by the American War, and the regiment was consequently very weak in numbers. In the following year the Seventieth, under Lieut.-Colonel Richard St. George, remained at Exeter, being still low in strength, and in 1785 it moved to Plymouth Dock. Whether or not change of air was considered likely to increase the strength of the regiment we cannot say, but early in 1786 we find it stationed at Guernsey, the eight companies having a total strength of 310 and the establishment being only 360. It appears from the " Standing Orders " of the regiment, printed in 1786 by order of Lieut.-Colonel St. George, that an annual change of station was the normal arrangement, it being expressly stated that clothing was to be issued annually " on arrival at the new station."

In December of the same year, Headquarters had moved to Jersey, and the regiment numbered 306. In 1787 the Seventieth proceeded to Ireland, in which country it remained for six years, with constant changes of station. It is recorded that in 1787 the nationality of the officers of the regiment was as follows: English, thirteen; Scottish, eleven; Irish, four; Foreign, one.

In the following year, Major Eyre Coote, nephew of the celebrated General Sir Eyre Coote, was promoted from the 47th Regiment to the Lieutenant-Colonelcy of the regiment, vice Lieutenant-Colonel R. St. George, transferred to the 8th Light Dragoons. Lieutenant-Colonel, afterwards Major-General, Sir Eyre Coote was the second son of the Rev. Charles Coote, Dean of Kilfenora, and brother of Charles Henry Coote who succeeded as second Lord Castlecoote. Dean Coote was an elder brother of General Sir Eyre Coote, Commander-in-Chief in India, a famous soldier. Members of the Coote family were formerly Earls of Mountrath and of Bellamont and Barons Castlecoote, but all three peerages are now extinct.

Lieutenant-Colonel Coote was born in 1762 and was therefore only twenty-six years of age on attaining to the command of the Seventieth, but he had had considerable experience of war from the time when as an Ensign of fourteen he had carried the colours of the 37th Regiment at the battle of Brooklyn, and he was now considered an officer of great promise.

Sir Eyre Coote of West Park, Damerham, possesses a copy of the "Regimental Standing Orders of the Seventieth (or Surrey) Regiment of Foot," issued by the field officers at Kilkenny soon after Lieut.-Colonel Coote assumed the command. The orders follow generally those issued two years previously at Jersey by Lieut.-Colonel Richard St. George, but are much more detailed, and contain excellent regulations for the conduct of the officers of the regiment in relation to the men. The officers are enjoined to set an example by the utmost regularity in their own conduct and invariably to wear uniform when in quarters, except when going out riding or shooting. They are called upon to make themselves thoroughly acquainted with the character of every man in their company: no difficult matter, as the companies were weak and the men as a rule were never changed. The details of interior economy as laid down for the Seventieth in 1786 and 1788 are in principle those of to-day, although with improved education and the great increase of sobriety shared by the soldier with the general public, much less restraint is now considered necessary than was the case 130 years ago.

A few of the orders to the non-commissioned officers and men may be quoted for their quaint wording, as well as for their excellence, *e.g.* :

"*The Non-Commissioned officers* are expected to shew an example of Obedience, Alertness, and Regularity to the Men of the Regiment. When their Companies assemble either with or without Arms, they are to go through the Ranks before the Officers, inspect the Men, to see the Hats well put on, their Hair well Tied and Powdered; the whole Dress perfectly Neat and Clean; that their arms, Pouches, Gaytors, and Scabbards have a perfect Polish; examine what Repairs are wanting, and to give strict Orders (which they must be very particular to have obeyed) that those discovered be immediately mended.

. . . .

"They are never to connive at the irregular behaviour of the Soldiers in any point whatever. They are to keep up a proper command, and closely attend to their Improvement in Writing and Cyphering; to make themselves Master of all forms of Duty and Returns. To be careful and honest in all Money Matters; to make themselves thoroughly acquainted with the Exercise in every respect, and to be fully able to Instruct and take Charge of any Squad that may be put under their Direction.

"They are to treat the men as civilly as possible; and to endeavour to keep up Harmony, good Order, and Obedience, and to assist all Recruits in the different Branches they are to Learn.

. . . .

"If a Corporal should ever be found to have sent the Soldier to his Post, without going himself regularly to plant him, or shall have allowed the Centinels to relieve each other, he must never expect to be pardoned.

. . . .

"The non-commissioned Officers are not to suffer the Women to iron the Men's Linen on the Barrack Blankets.

. . . .

"The non-commissioned Officers of each Room to be answerable that the Barrack Maids keep themselves as well as the Room, at all times clean, and have the Beds properly turned up by ten o'clock every morning.

. . . .

"Every time a tailor gets drunk, he is to lose payment of a Waistcoat, and be sent to the Black-hole; and whatever Money may arise from those Fines, such Sums shall be appropriated to the use of Sick in Hospital."

. . . .

Under the heading "Dress" the following regulations regarding the distinctions between Grenadier, Light Infantry and Battalion Companies are of archæological interest:

"Article 3. The Officers to wear their hair Queu'd, the Sergeants also, their Queus to be eighteen inches; the men to appear at all times with their hair Clubb'd, the Grenadiers and Light Infantry excepted. The former when with Caps to wear their hair Boxed, with their Hats to wear Queus. The latter to wear their hair in a loose plait."

In the year 1793 the course of the French Revolution, and particularly the execution of Louis XVI, caused the British Government to declare war against the revolutionary Government. An active campaign against the French colonies, the source of a great part of supplies of that country, having been decided on, an expeditionary force was collected in the south of Ireland for service in the West Indies under Lieutenant-General Sir Charles Grey. The Seventieth Regiment, having been selected for service in the expedition, sailed from Queenstown under Lieutenant-Colonel Coote, in company with eight other regiments, in September 1793. The expedition, which was conveyed in a large number of transports and was escorted by the fleet under Vice-Admiral Sir John Jervis, met with very rough weather, and it was not until January 10, 1794, that it was collected at Barbados. Here the nine infantry regiments of the expedition were brigaded, the Seventieth with the 6th and 58th Regiments forming the Third Brigade, under Brigadier-General John Whyte, an officer with long experience of West Indian service. In addition to his three infantry brigades, Sir Charles Grey had with him three Grenadier battalions, formed of the Grenadier companies of his own regiments, and of fourteen regiments stationed in Ireland; and three similarly constituted battalions of Light Infantry. These flank battalions were composed of picked officers and men, and the Light Infantry battalions had the further advantage of being trained while at Barbados to perform their duties on a uniform system, their instructor, Major-General Thomas Dundas, having gained his experience in light infantry duties during the American War.

On arrival at Barbados Lieutenant-Colonel Eyre Coote was selected by Sir Charles Grey to command the First Battalion of Light Infantry, in which the Light Company of the Seventieth was included. Brevet-Major Evatt of the regiment was appointed Major of the battalion, and Brevet-Major Robert Irving, whose services in the American War are familiar to us, also served at Martinique in an extra regimental capacity, being appointed Major of the First Battalion of Grenadiers. In consequence of the employment of Lieutenant-Colonel Coote the command of the Seventieth devolved on Brevet-Lieutenant-Colonel Boulter Johnstone, an officer who had been with the regiment throughout his service. The Grenadier Company of the Seventieth was posted to the Third Grenadier Battalion, with which it did good service in the capture of Martinique, after which, together with the Light Company, it rejoined the regiment and shared in its almost complete destruction by yellow fever, as will be related presently.

Two letters, written from Barbados by Major Irving to his wife, give an idea of the expectations of Sir Charles Grey's army with regard to the coming campaign:

>	Carlisle Bay,
>		Barbadoes,
>			11th January, 1794.

I take the first leisure moment after arriving here to acquaint my beloved wife and children of my safe arrival here on the 6th instant in perfect health. . . . We thought for some time we were going to Toulon, but after trying for two or three days to beat up to Gibraltar, the 12th Reg^t Dragoons left us, and we proceeded to the W. Indies. Our fleet was soon after dispersed in a gale of wind, and we lost sight of the 74 gun-ship that was our convoy—soon after I spoke to the Agent of Transports, on whom the command devolved—I represented to him the impropriety of keeping 19 transports together, who could be no protection to each other if attacked by two or three Ships of War belonging to the enemy, and if that should happen, half of the Army would be lost. I

Sergeant and Private, 70th Regiment. (Period of French War.)

told him my opinion was, the fleet should disperse, and proceed by two or three together, that were equal sailers, and make the best of their way—by this means they would be secure against privateers and if they met with a strong force it was better to lose two or three ships than the whole. He did not agree with me, but after consulting the Officers on board on the subject, he made the signal to disperse about two hours after. I proceeded with two other ships, all copper bottomed, and consequently fast sailers, and arrived on Monday last, after a passage of 6 weeks and a day. My ship was the first of the whole Fleet at anchor; we found Sir John Jervis, the Admiral, and Sir Charles Grey had only arrived two or three hours before us. Sir Ch. Grey sent a boat directly for the Commanding Officer to come to him; I was ready and went on board. I found Genl Dundas on the quarter deck who introduced me to the General and Admiral. They were very happy to see any part of the Cork Fleet, for they had doubts that it might have been stopped, one express having been sent from London for that purpose.

I dined with the Admiral and General. Gen. Dundas told me that I had been mentioned very particularly to Sir Chas. Grey and he certainly would do something for me, but I shall probably hear of it no more for a week or two, till the arrangements are made, and perhaps when I do it will be of no great value. . . .

I suppose in less than three weeks we will attack Martinico, which is only twenty-four hours' sailing from this place. We expect it will be an easy conquest, as there are few white troops, and the slaves they have armed will not stand above one fire, much less allow the bayonet to come near them. I understand Prince Edward is coming here from Quebec, and I suppose his regiment will come with him. . . . I understand there is a packet every fortnight to this Island, from whence letters will be forwarded to us wherever we are; therefore I will expect always to hear from you. Direct to M.I. 70th Reg^t, with Sir Chas. Grey's Army, W. Indies, by Barbadoes. The sickness in this part of the world is abated and almost gone. I live close on board-ship for health —the contagion never reached Martinico. Almost all the Fleet is arrived.

13th. The General has made part of his arrangements and I am appointed Major to the 1st Battalion of Grenad^{rs}. I would have preferred the Lt Infantry but could not obtain it. You will perhaps be better pleased as the Grenadier Service is less hazardous. . . .

Report says the people at Martinico will receive us with open arms—perhaps the troops in the Fort may make some efforts to a defence, but we hold it in great contempt.

The Lt Infantry were seen by Sir Ch. Grey to-day, and to-morrow he is to see the Grend^{rs}. I will add a few lines after. There is not one Ship of War at Martinico and few disciplined troops. *14th.* 9 *o'clock.* I am just come from the Review of the 3 battalions of Grenadiers and such a body of men was hardly ever seen before. We were on the ground before daylight, and back to our Ships by 8 o'clock. . . .

God bless you all.

Yrs. etc.,
R. IRVING.

Barbadoes,
21st Jan^y, 1794.

I wrote a long letter since I arrived here by a ship bound to Liverpool, and I hope she will have a short passage that not only your mind, but that of many others who have the same cause of anxiety, may be relieved. I am so hurried by duty, and likewise in preparing to move to one of the Ships of the Grenadiers that I am appointed to, that I have not time to say much for the packet which arrived yesterday sails to-morrow. . . . As I am appointed Major to the 1st Batt^n of Grenadiers, I hope I shall go wherever they do during the War and that we will not remain long in the W. Indies.

Preparations for our Enterprize are going on rapidly and it is expected that we are to proceed in a few days. Success we have no doubts of. . . . I have been so busy since I came here that I have not yet had time to examine the list of the Army particularly, but I believe I am the eldest (*i.e.* senior) Captain now here, (Lt. Col. Hallows of 56th Regt. being sent from this Army, with the Reg^t, to some of the other English Islands). I have no doubt but Sir Chas. Grey will do me and every Officer justice. My appointment to the Grenad^{rs} does nothing for me in the pecuniary way, but it is a distinguished and honourable situation, and will strengthen the claim to promotion which I derive from seniority. I shall endeavour to write to you a long letter before we sail, if there is any opport^y to send it. May God bless and preserve you and my dear children is the earnest prayer of

etc.,
R. IRVING.

. . . .

Officers of the Seventieth (Surrey Regiment) who Served at Martinique, 1794

LIEUT.-COLONEL
  Eyre Coote. Promoted Brevet-Colonel.

MAJORS
  Boulter Johnstone. Brevet Lieut.-Colonel, October 12, 1793. Promoted Lieut.-Colonel 65th Regiment, July 15, 1794.
  Mungo Paumier. Promoted from Captain and Brevet-Major 15th Foot vice Johnstone.

CAPTAINS
  Robert Irving. Brevet-Major. Killed in action, September 29, 1794.
  John Evatt.[4] Brevet-Major. Transferred to a Veteran Battalion.
  Thomas Nicoll. Brevet-Major. Sent to England on recruiting duty.
  Thomas Dunbar. Brevet-Major.
  George Strange Nares. Died April 21, 1794.
  Charles Irvine. Exchanged to an independent company, 1794.
  Hon. George Lowry Cole.[2] Promoted Major in 102nd Regiment, October 31, 1793.
  Charles Atkinson. Promoted from 15th Regiment. Died April 1794.
  Richard Newton Ogle. A.D.C. to Sir Charles Grey. Died June 29, 1794.
  James Rose. Promoted from 9th Regiment vice Nares.
  Hon James Stopford. Exchanged from 65th Regiment, December 6, 1794.

CAPTAIN-LIEUTENANT
  James Bruce. Died May 23, 1794.

LIEUTENANTS
  Courtland Skinner. Promoted Captain vice Irving.
  George Spry. Promoted Captain, February 11, 1794—vice Cole. Sent home on recruiting duty.
  James Eiston.[3] Promoted Captain, May 5; died May 12, 1794.
  Jasper Grant. Promoted Captain in 41st Regiment, December 1793.
  Henry Elliot. Promoted Captain-Lieutenant vice Bruce.
  John Grueber. Resigned commission, 1794.
  Charles Morley Balders. Promoted Captain independent company, May 14, 1793.
  Henry Gifford. Died April 1794.
  William Cox. Died May 10, 1794.
  William Coplen Langford. Promoted Captain in 15th Regiment.
  Henry Leader. Retired January 1795.

ENSIGNS
  John Floyer. Promoted Lieutenant. Died April 21, 1794.
  William B. Johnston. Promoted Lieutenant vice Spry.
  George Otway. Promoted Lieutenant in 41st Regiment.
  John Scott. Promoted Lieutenant and retired in 1794.
  John Crawford. Promoted Lieutenant vice Floyer, dec.
  Patrick Crawford. Promoted Lieutenant vice Scott.
  Henry Roberts. Promoted Lieutenant vice Elliot.
  Usher Boate. Promoted Lieutenant vice Eiston.
  Henry Thornhill. From Volunteer. December 6, 1794. Promoted Lieutenant vice Langford in same Gazette.

Edward Grove. Promoted Lieutenant vice Visscher.

William Hutchinson. From Quartermaster. Promoted Lieutenant vice Cox, dec.

James Bathurst. From Volunteer. December 6, 1794. Promoted Lieutenant vice Skinner.

CHAPLAIN.
John Jones.

ADJUTANT
Benjamin Lawrence. Appointed Ensign vice Oliver promoted, and promoted Lieutenant vice Leader, ret.

QUARTERMASTER
William Hutchinson. Appointed Ensign and promoted Lieutenant vice Cox, dec.

SURGEON
James Kay. Died August 15, 1794.

John White. Promoted from " Hospital Mate " (corresponding to Assistant Surgeon) " without Purchase " vice Kay, dec.

NOTES.

1. The deaths and retirements from ill-health among the officers had occurred so rapidly during 1794 that the London Gazette failed to keep up with them.

On December 6 of that year no less than thirteen promotions in the regiment were gazetted, with the result that Volunteer Thornhill, gazetted in one place as junior Ensign, was promoted at the end of the Gazette as Lieutenant by seniority ; an unusual circumstance.

2. Captain the Hon. Galbraith Lowry Cole accompanied the regiment to Barbados, but was there informed that he had been promoted to a Majority in the 86th Regiment. Major Cole embarked for England, but his ship being becalmed was overtaken by the fleet conveying the expedition to Martinique. Major Cole volunteered to rejoin for service, and was appointed Aide-de-Camp to Sir Charles Grey, in which capacity he served during the operations at Martinique. Major Cole subsequently rose to the rank of General, and earned high distinction in the Peninsular War in command of the 4th Division. In 1814 he was appointed Colonel of the Seventieth Regiment, with which he had first seen active service.

(See Appendix).

3. Captain Eiston's company was purchased by Lieutenant Visscher, 65th Regiment, but he did not join, having exchanged with Captain Hon. James Stopford, also of the 65th.

4. Brevet-Major Evatt, one of three brothers who held commissions in the army during the French war, was the son of Humphry Evatt of Mount Louise, co. Monaghan. The family had been located in Ireland since the year 1613, and has given many of its members to the army. Major Evatt died in 1815. His nephew, Captain George Evatt of the Seventieth, died at Peshawar during the Indian Mutiny.

Sir George Grey and Sir John Jervis, who had arranged their plans during the voyage from England, and worked in complete harmony with one another, lost not a moment in getting to work. The expeditionary force was prepared for service with great rapidity, and on February 3 sailed from Barbados for Martinique with a strength of nearly 7000 men, escorted by Admiral Jervis' fleet of nineteen vessels of varying strength. Martinique was the strongest of the French West India Islands, and was garrisoned with 6000 troops, but Sir Charles Grey knew that the garrison had been dangerously dispersed and saw his way to attack the island with success. It seemed also advisable to him to attack the strongest island first with his entire force, as it would be necessary to garrison each of the islands in succession after its capture.

In order to prevent the concentration of the scattered French garrison, the General and Admiral had decided to throw ashore detached columns, each strong enough to deal with the garrisons which it would find before it; and this policy was executed with complete success. The landing places selected were (1) the Bay of Galion, on the east coast of the island; (2) Case de Navire, near Fort Royal Bay, on the west coast; and (3) Baie de Marin, at the eastern angle of the south coast, at which the main landing under the Commander-in-Chief was to be made. This force included the three infantry brigades, while the first and second landing forces were composed of the brigades of flank battalions under Major-General Dundas and Brigadier-General Sir Charles Gordon.

After landing his own troops on February 5 and destroying a battery on Point de Borgnesse, General Grey re-embarked and made a second landing on February 6 at Trois Rivières, a little to the west of Sainte Luce. From this point Sir Charles advanced with his division by a very difficult and mountainous road to Rivière Salée, at the same time detaching a Light Infantry battalion under Brigadier-General Whyte to capture batteries in his rear at Cape Solomon and Point Bourgos. General Whyte carried out his task on February 7, attacking the batteries in rear and capturing their garrisons. General Rochambeau, however, the French Commander-in-Chief, now sent a force across from Port Royal to cut off General Whyte from the main body, and this apparently threatening movement gave Sir Charles Grey an opportunity for one of his favourite movements, the execution of which he entrusted to the Seventieth Regiment.

Sir Charles had been known in the American War of Independence as "the no flint General," from his habit of making surprise attacks

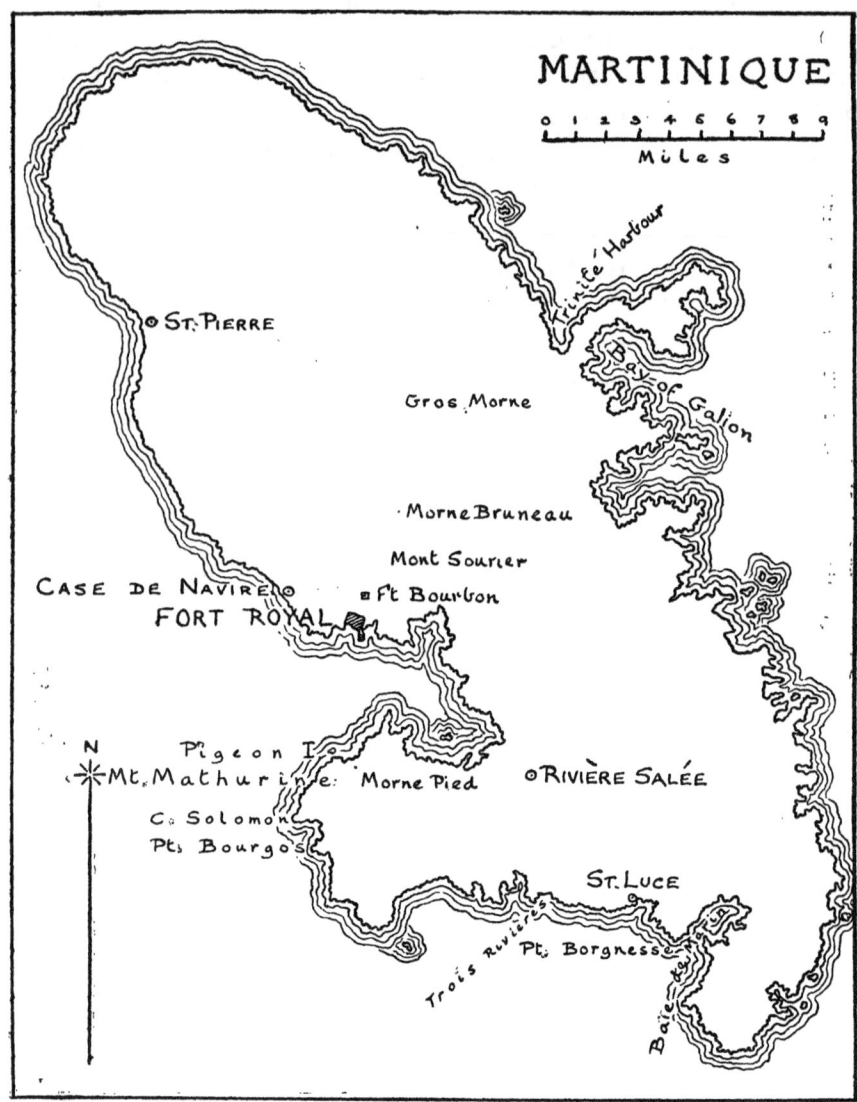

with the bayonet after removing the flints from the soldiers' muskets as an effectual safeguard against unauthorised firing. In accordance with this practice Sir Charles Grey now ordered the Seventieth, under Brevet-Lieut.-Colonel Johnstone, to march on the following night (February 8) and attack the French detached force. In his despatch written a week later, Sir Charles Grey thus describes the incident:

"In the meantime I had received intelligence of the enemy's landing troops and taking post on Morne Pied, to cut off the communications between Brigadier-General Whyte and the headquarters at Sallée, and ordered the Seventieth Regiment, with two Howitzers to march the same night and dislodge them, which was executed with great spirit, and the post taken possession of early in the morning of the 9th, under the good conduct of the Adjutant-General, Colonel Dundas, the Seventieth Regiment being commanded by Lieutenant Colonel Johnstone and the enemy completely defeated at the first charge."

While the Seventieth was thus engaged, an engagement on a larger scale and conducted with equal spirit took place under Major-General Dundas on the east coast of the island, where a force of coloured troops under General Bellegarde, a mulatto, were quickly dispersed with the bayonet. This success occurred near Trinité Harbour, and pushing inland from that point General Dundas quickly seized Gros Morne, a high point which secured the only road from the north to the south of Martinique. Leaving a garrison at Gros Morne, Dundas pushed on southward, and on February 9 came in view of Fort Bourbon, the strongly-fortified centre of the French defences.

In Sir Charles Grey's orders of February 9, these two successes are thus recorded:

"The Commander-in-Chief has again the pleasure to announce to the troops the further success of his Majesty's arms towards the conquest of the island of Martinico, by the able conduct of Major-General Dundas, and the gallantry and spirit of the troops under his command, in attacking the enemy's troops under the command of Mons. Bellegarde at Trinité with bayonets, and putting them totally to the rout with great slaughter, he narrowly escaping with a few followers into Fort Royal. The Major General with great spirit followed up the blow, and took possession of the very strong fort of the Gros Morne, where the English colours are now flying. He has also the pleasure to add the gallantry of the Seventieth Regiment, commanded by Lieutenant Colonel Johnstone, and led by Colonel Dundas, who with so much spirit and promptitude attacked the enemy posted upon Morne Charlotte Pied, and put them totally to flight, taking possession of that important commanding ground looking down upon Pigeon Island, which, when attacked (in conjunction with Brigadier General Whyte) and taken, will enable the English fleet to come up into Fort Royal Harbour, in full view of the enemy's forts of Bourbon and Royal. The Commander-in-Chief is happy in the opportunity of making honourable mention of Captain Nares of the Seventieth Regiment, who led the advanced guard with so much true courage and judgment in the above attack, as reported to him in the strongest manner by Colonel Dundas."

The casualties of the Seventieth in this highly-successful attack were limited to a few private soldiers wounded, only two being disabled. Slight wounds were not officially returned at this period.

As foreshadowed by Sir Charles Grey's order, quoted above, the expeditionary force proceeded without any delay to its next task, the capture of Pigeon Island. This was a strongly-fortified, rocky islet which guarded the entrance to Fort Royal Harbour.

On this occasion the Seventieth Regiment again earned the commendation of the General for good service in dragging by hand two $5\frac{1}{2}$-inch howitzers to Mount Mathurine, a high point which effectually commanded the defences of Pigeon Island. The bombardment from this point was so effectual that after two hours the French garrison of 200 men was compelled to surrender, with a loss of forty killed and wounded. This important success took place on February 11, and on the following day the fleet entered Fort Royal Bay, keeping close to the southern shore and anchoring near the military base at Rivière Salée. On February 13 Sir Charles Grey sent part of his force (including the Seventieth) forward to join hands with Dundas at Bruneau, and moved the remainder of the force to that point on February 14. Dundas then returned with two battalions and two light companies to Trinité Bay, and thence made a most remarkable march across the rugged and hilly island to the town of St. Pierre, which he captured on February 17. All that then remained to be achieved was the capture of Forts Bourbon and St. Louis, the two permanent defences of Fort Royal, the capital town of Martinique.

Fort Bourbon was a large and formidable work, and the task of attacking it was complicated by the position taken up by General Bellegarde, with a considerable force on high ground to the north of it. General Grey intended to attack Bellegarde with the bayonet on

February 19, but the latter made a rash attack on the British left on the previous afternoon. Bellegarde had left a garrison to hold his own position on Mount Sourier, but Sir Charles Grey immediately ordered the Third Battalion of Grenadiers (which included the Seventieth Company) and two battalions of Light Infantry to attack it, Colonel Coote of the Seventieth commanding the Light Infantry. The Sourier position was quickly captured at the cost of about sixty casualties, and ten days later General Bellegarde with the remainder of his force, which now had no base, was compelled to surrender.

General Grey without loss of time at once occupied the Sourier position, and thence disposed his force round Fort Bourbon and Fort St. Louis. The sailors of the fleet were landed and worked indefatigably in conjunction with the soldiers in making roads and dragging their heavy guns to the hill tops selected as the positions for batteries. All the reward that the gallant sailors asked was permission to have a battery of their own, a favour gladly granted by the General. With this spirit in the combined force, work was quickly done in spite of unusually heavy rain, and on March 7 a heavy fire was opened on both forts. One of the principal batteries on the north side of Fort Bourbon was constructed and guarded by the Seventieth Regiment, and was called by its name.

The French garrisons of the two forts made a stout defence, but on March 20 Fort Louis was attacked by the boats of the fleet and carried by escalade by the sailors, headed by the gallant Captain Faulkner, R.N. At the same time the town of Fort Royal was captured by two flank battalions (one of which was the Third Grenadier Battalion), while Colonel Coote with his light battalion, in which the light company of the Seventieth was included, prevented the escape of the garrison which was endeavouring to take refuge in Fort Bourbon.

Seeing the loss of the town, with all his stores and supplies, and finding his garrison reduced from 1200 to 900 men, without the slightest hope of relief, General de Rochambeau hung out the white flag. In consideration of its brave defence the garrison of Fort Bourbon was allowed to march out on March 23 with the honours of war, and was sent to France on condition of not serving again during the war.

Some letters of Major Irving give interesting details of the campaign.

Camp La Coste,
Martinico,
12th March, 1794.

. . . .

I told you in my last that our Batterys had opened on the morning of the day I wrote. They have since that time kept up a regular fire (but not half so heavy as the French kept upon us at Yorktown) and with good effect as we believe. I was in a situation two days ago where I could see the French carrying the killed and wounded out of the fort by a back road and many were seen by different people of my party in the course of twenty-four hours. A Flag of Truce is gone into the Fort [1] this morning, it is supposed by people like myself, not in the secret, with an offer of terms; whether they will be accepted or not I don't know, but if they are rejected it will be unfortunate for the enemy for I am certain the place must fall, and if they don't accept of the present offer I am convinced they will get no terms at all, but it will be highly necessary for our fleet at home to take care that no reinforcement is sent from France. After this place is taken, which must happen very soon, whether they listen to the proposals of this day or not, we expect to proceed to Guadaloupe and St. Lucia where there is little resistance to be looked for. I hope to be in that part of the Army which goes to the former. After our operations are over there, perhaps the remainder of the troops, after leaving proper garrisons, may go to St. Domingo, to complete the conquest of that part of the Island belonging to the French, for we are already in possession of part of it, and then the Flank Corps, if they can be spared, will return to Europe. The hope of returning with them will induce me to remain close with the Grenadiers, if Sir Chas. Grey will permit me, which I hope he will: for besides this private motive, that of continuing to serve with the first Corps in the world, you may believe is a very strong one.

We shall certainly get some prize money, but nobody can guess at the amount. The chief town, St. Pierre, has been in our hands since the 16th of last month, where a considerable number of Shipping and public stores were taken. Fort Royal, where our sentries are within speaking of the French, we are told has much more riches in it, and must, with Fort St. Louis, which we are erecting Batterys against, be in our hands in a few days and little loss is to be feared in obtaining this advantage. I imagine we shall after that take a position very near the great Fort,[2] in which we shall be entirely secure against every effort of the enemy to

---

[1] Fort St. Louis.   [2] Fort Bourbon.

injure us. In the situation of this army, every man must be exposed to some degree of danger, but be assured it is not half so great as you and our other anxious friends at home apprehend. The French have fled before us everywhere. They have more than once insulted us, but we cannot persuade them to fight us. In this however they are in some degree justified by our superiority in numbers, and in every other sense of the word. . . .

Our army is wonderfully healthy, I am convinced they would would not be more so in England; this we in some measure attribute to the whole wearing flannel shirts and drawers and no linen. The Officers in general do the same. I have only had a linen shirt once on since we landed and never was so comfortable in this climate before. I likewise think the air here cooler and better than in any of the other Islands I am acquainted with. . . .

. . . .

I hear Prince Edward is to have the three Batallions of Grend^{rs} under his immediate command.

Yours for ever,
(Sd.) R. IRVING.

Martinico,
14th March.

P.S. The ans^r from the Fort is that they cannot think of surrendering till they have deserved the esteem of a generous enemy by a good defence.

Martinico,
24th March, 1794.

MY DEAREST WIFE,—I wrote you not many days ago and predicted the news you would hear in a fortnight or three weeks after, and I suspect that you will receive this letter a week or two sooner than you expect it.

. . . .

On the 20th Fort Royal was stormed by a body of seamen, supported by four flank corps (of which the first Grend^{rs} was one) Our batterys kept up a tremendous fire for an hour before the attack was made and the place was taken without almost any loss. Yesterday two Bat^{ns} of Grend^{rs} and two of Light Inf^{try} took possession of the gates, the Lt. Col. of our Bat^n remained at the gate which was open, with two Comp^{ys}, all night. I was at the distance of a hundred yards on the side of the hill with the other seven Comp^{ys} to support him, and we had a very quiet night. We are now relieved from that situation, and returned to camp to prepare for marching into Fort Bourbon tomorrow morning when the French will give it up and embark for France, except the Negroes, who I understand are to be at the disposal of Sir Chas. Grey. There was about 26 ships taken in the harbour of Fort Royal and many public stores in the town so that our hopes of a considerable Dividend of prize money is greater than when I wrote you last, for besides the captures, I have heard there are several valuable plantations forfeited. . . .

I had a present from Dunbar[1] yesterday of a horse worth 40 or 50 guineas, which he took out of Rochambeau's Stables the day Fort Royal was stormed. This horse comes very a propos, for I ought always to be on horseback.

. . . .

Dunbar says the General opinion in the Army is, that I am to get one of the vacant majoritys. I have strong hopes, but am ignorant. In a few days we expect to sail for Guadaloupe or St. Lucia, at neither of which Islands any kind of serious resistance is expected. I did not expect the accounts of our success would be sent home in less than a week after the surrender, but I am just informed the Frigate that carries them sails tomorrow, when I shall have no time to write for I am informed that Prince Edward,[2] who takes possession at the head of our Batallion, enters the Fort early.

This day's Orders announce that His Royal Highness is to command the three Batallions of Gren^{drs} from this time, which I am very happy to hear. I had the honour to dine with him the other day. I think him clever, he is active to a great degree, you may be sure he is zealous, and from all I have seen (as far as my opinion goes) I think he will make an excellent Off^r; he is extremely pleasant in Company. His Royal Highness is very like the King, but I think handsomer.

. . . .

Your most affect^{te} husband,
(S^d) R. IVRING.

24th March.

Thus Martinique was captured at a cost of no more than 350 killed and wounded, but the labours of the troops and fleet had been very severe, and were soon to cost them dear; no regiment suffering more terribly than the Seventieth, which together with the 15th, 39th,

---

[1] Captain Dunbar of the Seventieth, who had served in North America with the Light Company.

[2] H.R.H. Prince Edward, afterwards Duke of Kent, father of Queen Victoria.

56th and 64th Regiments was left to garrison Martinique; while the remainder of the expeditionary force sailed on March 30 to capture St. Lucia and Guadeloupe. With the expedition sailed Lieutenant-Colonel Coote, Brevet-Majors Irving and Evatt, and Captain Ogle, all of the Seventieth. Colonel Coote earned further high distinction in command of the Light Infantry, and showed his devotion to duty in a critical period by returning to Guadeloupe while still dangerously ill from an attack of yellow fever for which he had been invalided home. No officer in Sir Charles Grey's force earned a higher reputation than did Colonel Coote.

Of the other Seventieth officers two perished during the campaign. Brevet-Major Irving serving on the Staff as D.A.Q.M.G., after rendering exceptional service throughout, earned special notice in the disastrous action of July 1, 1794, at Point-à-Pitre in Guadeloupe, when four companies of Grenadiers under his command secured the retirement of Brigadier-General Symes' defeated force. Major Irving was lying sick in the hospital at Petit Bourg when most of the inmates were massacred by the French republican troops on September 29, 1794. He was one of the fortunate few rescued from this horrible fate by the boats of the fleet, but his hour had come, for on the same day he was killed in the cabin of H.M.S. *Assurance* by a round shot from a French gun-boat. So ended the career of a good soldier. Owing to the numerous casualties among officers at this period, the death of Major Irving was long unreported. Nearly six months afterwards he was gazetted to the brevet rank of Lieut.-Colonel, but about the same time the fact of his death was ascertained and his vacant company in the Seventieth filled up.

Captain Newton Ogle, who had not served long in the regiment, died of yellow fever at Guadeloupe on June 29, 1794. In Willyams' "Account of the Campaign in the West Indies," a work of considerable interest, the following observation is recorded: "On the 29th the Commander-in-Chief sustained a heavy loss in the death of Captain Newton Ogle of the Seventieth Regiment, one of his excellency's aid-de-camps. He was a young man of an excellent understanding, and had distinguished himself on all occasions where his exertions had been called forth."

The remaining officer of the Seventieth was Brevet-Major John

Evatt, who served in Colonel Coote's battalion of Light Infantry at St. Lucia, and was among the few officers mentioned by Sir Charles Grey as having done good service there.

Some further letters by Major Irving to his wife give certain details of the campaign, and afford interesting glimpses of the army more than a century ago.

Guadaloupe,
April 23rd, 1794.

I wrote you yesterday since which time the Commander in Chief has sent for me, and offered me an Office of £600 a year if I would sell my commission and reside here. As this would both have cut me off from the promotion which I have a right to expect, and from my family, (for I never would think of bringing any of you to this country) I declined it. The General then said that he would appoint another person to the Office, with half the emoluments and that I should have the other half, and might attend my duty as an Officer of the 70th., and have nothing more to do but receive the money. This I readily accepted with proper acknowledgments, and I go to the Reg^t at Martinico from whence I will write you directly.

Yours etc.,
R Irving.

Fort Royal,
(Martinique),
16th May, 1794.

I came from my quarters at Marin Bay two days ago upon some business, and have only time to say that I still enjoy perfect health. I brought with me seven bad subjects[1] that I took up by the Gen$^{l's}$ orders after a very long night march. (I was on horseback) and received his thanks, with further orders on the same subject, which will occasion the arrest of a great many more of infamous character. I return to-morrow. It is necessary to sweep these conquered islands of all republicans, both for the sake of our present tranquility, and to prevent their being ready to join the Enemy, if any should dare to attack us.

I was yesterday informed by one of the French Council, that many Estates will be forfeited for the benefit of the Army. We expect a dividend of prize money soon.

Sir Charles Grey told me this day he will apply for the rank of Lieut. Colonel for me, agreeable to Prince Edward's request.

[1] French republicans.

The General says I must remain a while and command the Grenadiers. All the Comp^ys in my Battalion belong to Regiments in Ireland, and I have reason to believe they will soon be ordered to join them. . . The 70th Reg^t, which is quarterd here, have been very unhealthy. About 70 men and several Officers have died since the 1st of this month, they are now removed to a place at three miles distance, and I hope will be better. I return to my healthy quarters tomorrow, where we have not yet lost a man, and have hardly any sick.

Yours etc.,
R. IRVING.

Marin,
Martinico,
6th May, 1794.

I wrote you from Guadeloupe after the surrender of that Island, that the Gren^drs were under orders to return here, and we sailed accordingly the day following, and arrived here on the 1st inst.

This quarter of the Island is reckoned the most healthy part of the West Indies; people I am informed come from every other district of Martinico here, for the recovery of their health and I can readily credit this account for there are several very old people here, even some of 80 years of age, and I do not hear of any person being sick, either in this little town or in the neighbourhood. The country is beautiful and well cultivated; it encircles a bay 10 miles deep, on one side of the bay there is a ridge of high mountains with sugar plantations at the bottom, and coffee, Cotton and Cocoa to the summit. On the other side of the bay is the parish of St. Ann. The Estates are all in sugar, and the face of the country is superior in beauty to anything I have seen in the West Indies. Most of the Inhabitants who had emigrated to the British Islands are returned and are the happiest people on earth. They treat us with more than hospitality, and drink the health of their deliverers with tears of joy. They give a shocking account of the cruelty and bad usage they met with from the republicans, of whom there is still a nest in this neighbourhood, that I hope to harry in a few days. A very genteel man, who has a fine sugar plantation within a mile of us, tells me he was obliged to catch fish at St. Vincent's and sell it for the support of his family; and they tell me many stories of their distresses that were still much greater than that. A number of the principal inhabitants dined with us yesterday. A very large fleet passed in sight, but too far off for us to distinguish their colours. The Republicans flattered themselves it was a French fleet coming to take all the Islands. The worthy royalists were a little apprehensive but they assured me if they were French Troops, they would join me in a few hours with Fifteen hundred men, for they would much rather be shot than leave the country again; however two ships anchored in our bay—a 40-gun ship with our baggage ship under her convoy. The Captain of the man-of-war came on shore in the evening, and told us the Fleet was English. The arrival of the baggage ship will afford us some comforts. I shall get to naked bed tonight, which will be pleasant enough after sleeping three months on the ground with my clothes on. . . .

Tho' this is a pleasant quarter in many respects, there are some disagreeable things attending it. We have not the same opport^y of either hearing from our friends, or writing to them, that Officers have at St. Pierre's or Fort Royal. You must recollect this and not be surprised if you hear from me seldom for the future, or get two or three letters by one ship. The nearest Troops and the nearest Town is Fort Royal—distance 36 miles and there is not an article of any kind to be got here. . . .

The Prince has applied to the Comm^r in Chief to obtain me the rank of Lieut. Colonel.

I hear from Port Royal that some of the Seventieth Officers are dead. (S^d) R. IRVING.

. . . .

Grandeterre,
Guadeloupe,
4th July, 1794.

You will be surprised to hear from me from this Island. The Comm^r in Chief's dispatches in the newspapers will give you the reasons for it. I arrived here with my little Batt^n of Grenadiers on Friday last. Next day we marched to the Army. The day following we were in action, and gained some credit, but since then, we received a check.[1] We now embark for Guadeloupe to wait, I suppose, for reinforcement. You will hear from me by next oport^y a full account of everything. In the meantime be satisf^{ed} to hear that God Almighty has preserved me unhurt in the midst of danger, for your sake, and my dear children's.
God bless and preserve you all.
Yours etc.,
R. IRVING.

I am much hurried and have not time to write more just now. . . .

[1] The reverse at Point à Pitre, when Major Irving distinguished himself.

THE FRENCH REVOLUTIONARY WAR

Guadeloupe,
10th July, 1794.

I wrote you a few lines after our unfortunate miscarriage at Point-à-Pitre. We lost many brave fellows that day and the Officers killed, wounded and taken prisoners, amount to about sixteen. My Grenad^{rs} with the 65th Regt., and a body of sailors were on a hill close to Fleur D'Épée Fort, which we were to have stormed if the others had succeeded. We retreated to the Guadaloupe side of the Rivière Salée three or four days after and are now throwing up strong works. I imagine to wait for a reinforcement from home. Pray what is the English Fleet about that this French Army was suffered to go out ? . . .

Sir Charles Grey sent the Adj^t General to me, offering to appoint me Dep^y Quarter Mr Genl for the West Indies. Sir Charles afterwards wrote a very handsome answer to my letter and appointed me D. Q^r Mr Genl . . . It is now probable I shall remain in the West Indies till next Spring, when I hope we shall have entire possession of the Island again. . . .

This is a charming country and of great extent.

. . . .

Bless you all.
Yours most affectionately,
R. IRVING.

Guadaloupe,
18th July, 1794;

I mentioned in my last letter that Sir Chas. Grey had appointed me Dep^y Q^r Mr Genl and Genl Symes being gone home to England, I am head of that Department. . . .

Sir Chas. Grey has at last discovered that I am not unworthy of his attention. He has besides the above Office recommended me for the Majority of the 70th[1] and requested that notwithstanding the business I shall have to transact as Q^r Mr Genl, I will continue to command the whole Grenadiers of the Army; who are formed into one Battalion.

This is the first command in the Army and you may suppose I did not refuse it. His Excell^y has likewise assured me he will move Heaven and earth to serve me. He is sensible of the bad usage I have met with, in being refused both the Lieut. Colonelcy of Genl Fox's and Col. Hewett's regiment, because I was absent (on the service of an ungratefull country). I believe he is likewise

---

[1] Vacant through the promotion of Major Boulter Johnstone to the Lieut.-Colonelcy of the 65th Regiment.

very well pleased with my conduct, and that of three Comp^{ys} I brought from Martinico, in an action we had the second day after we arrived here. I mentioned to you that we received a little check—we are now fortifying, and will remain inactive till reinforcements arrive.

Remember me most affectly to all friends and to my dearest girls and boy, say everything that can express the most tender affection.

Your's for ever most aff^{tely},
R. IRVING.

This is the last of Major Irving's letters that has been preserved. He was unfortunately killed two months later before his long and gallant services had been rewarded.

On the departure of the army and fleet for St. Lucia and Guadeloupe the six regiments left to form the garrison of Martinique were distributed by Lieut.-General Prescott between the most important fortresses, the Seventieth and 58th Regiments forming the garrison of Fort Bourbon, which had been re-named Fort George. Soon after the departure of the expedition, the health of the garrison of Martinique, already in an unsatisfactory state, became rapidly worse, and during the months of April, May and June an epidemic of yellow fever raged throughout the West India Islands, causing an appalling loss of life. It is the opinion of Mr. Fortescue, who has made an exhaustive study of the subject, that no less than 5000 men, out of the 7000 with whom Sir Charles Grey began his campaign, perished during 1794, and that, including the Royal Navy and the fleet of transports, 12,000 Englishmen were buried in the West Indies that year. No regiment of Sir Charles Grey's expedition suffered more heavily than the Seventieth, as will be seen by the following figures taken from the monthly returns of "the troops in the Windward and Leeward Islands," preserved in the Record Office.

On arrival at Barbados early in February the regiment had twenty-four officers and 503 men "fit for duty," with 110 sick. The sickness is stated by Sir Charles Grey to have occurred during the voyage, doubtless from over-crowding and bad food. It may be mentioned that another regiment is stated to have had double that number of sick on arrival, and yet another regiment had an equal number.

On April 1, the day on which the Seventieth went into garrison at

Fort George, the short but arduous campaign of Martinique had done its work. War casualties had been very light, and only six men had died, but the effective strength was already reduced to twenty-three officers and 400 men, with 234 sick. The deaths among the rank-and-file in April, May and June numbered no less than 265, and on June 1, at the height of the yellow fever epidemic, the strength was as follows: Nineteen officers (including surgeon and surgeon's mate) and 128 men, fit for duty. Sick in hospital, 167. Sick in quarters, 143. Total sick, 310, the sick in quarters being simply men for whom there was no room in hospital. By August 1 the epidemic had spent its strength, but with sad results. On the first day of that month the Seventieth was the strongest regiment at Martinique, with nineteen officers and 209 men fit for duty. Nine officers and 299 men had died since the arrival at Barbados, six months earlier.

It will be observed that in spite of their heavy death-roll, the strength of the regiment in officers was well maintained. This resulted from all vacancies being promptly filled by promotions from other regiments in the expedition, or in a few cases from home. The only existing vacant commissions were those of six Ensigns, required to complete establishment.

In consequence of the very weak state of the garrison of Martinique, the regiments were ordered to send home officers on recruiting duty, those of the Seventieth being posted at London, Birmingham, Killarney, and Newry respectively. Sir Charles Grey, moreover, recommended soon afterwards that the six weakest regiments should return to England, their effective men being induced by bounties to consent to be drafted into regiments remaining. One of the regiments selected for drafting was the Seventieth, which in October 1794 gave 188 effective soldiers to other regiments at Martinique. In the same month the regiment lost thirteen men by death, and was reduced to a skeleton. All that remained were seventeen officers, six sergeants, five drummers, and thirty rank-and-file, of whom only nine rank-and-file were fit for duty. Of this small number six died during November, and it may be doubted if any British regiment was ever more completely worked out than was the Seventieth at Martinique in the year 1794.

On leaving the army in the West Indies, Colonel Coote was desired by Sir Charles Grey to name some old and deserving officers and non-commissioned officers serving under his command who appeared to Colonel Coote deserving of Sir Charles Grey's "countenance and protection."

Colonel Coote accordingly made his recommendations, confining himself principally to his own regiment, in the following terms:

> (1) Acting-Major Evatt—70th Regiment—who has been in the army near thirty-three years.
> (2) — ——
> (3) Sergeant-Major John McKay of 70th Light Infantry, who has served twenty-five years.
> (4) — ——
> (5) Sergeant John Russell, 70th Light Infantry, "who has been my orderly sergeant during this campaign and has been of essential service to me—and who has been in the Army twenty years.
> (6) Sergeant John McDonald of the 70th Lt Infantry Company, "who has been in the Army twenty years—and who has a large family, and whom any little assistance that could be given him at Martinique, where his Regt is, would essentially serve."

Colonel Coote added to his recommendations the following words:

"Were I to enumerate all the deserving people with whom I am acquainted, I should recommend more than perhaps your Excellency could provide for—I therefore beg leave to recommend to you those above stated—who I am certain will do all in their power to prove themselves deserving any mark of your Excellency's goodness."

Colonel Coote was evidently permitted to make some further recommendations, and wrote a second letter, as follows:

> SIR,—I beg to recommend to your Excellency's consideration Ensign Scott of the 70th Regt, who served most of the Campaign with the 3rd Batt^n Grenadiers, and who has been an Ensign in the 70th Regiment since the beginning of the year 1791. Could your Excellency give him a Lieutenancy he would feel himself under many obligations to you.
> Allow me to name to you all the Volunteers serving with the 1st Batt^n Lt Inf^y.

The second of the five volunteers recommended was Volunteer

Thornhill, who in due course received an Ensigncy in the Seventieth. He had served in the campaign attached to the Light Company of that regiment.

For no discoverable reason the honour "Martinique" was not at the time bestowed on the Seventieth Regiment, although its services had earned the unqualified approval of Sir Charles Grey. Formal application for the award was made on at least one occasion. In the year 1909 the honours granted for the campaigns in the West Indies received special consideration by a War Office Committee, and various awards in connection with those campaigns were made to regiments whose claims had not previously been recognised. The honour "Martinique 1794" was accorded to the East Surrey Regiment by Army Order 295 of 1909, in recognition of the distinguished services of the late Seventieth Regiment in the campaign of 1793–94.

The surviving officers and a handful of sergeants, drummers, and rank and-file of the Seventieth arrived in England from Martinique in July 1795, and on August 1 had the following strength present and fit for duty. Officers, seven; sergeants, fifteen; drummers, fifteen; rank-and-file, nineteen. In addition there were two rank-and-file present sick, and three men had died during July. Recruiting proceeded briskly for 'some months and by the end of the year the regiment was fairly on its legs again and was considered fit to return to foreign service. Lieutenant-Colonel Coote, who had recovered from yellow fever, was employed on the staff in Ireland, and Major Nicoll, now senior Major of the regiment, consequently held the command for about three years.

In December 1795 the Seventieth, with a strength of twenty-two officers and 488 of other ranks, embarked for Gibraltar, where it remained for a little over five years. During this period the strength of the regiment varied from about 500 to 600, in addition to the officers; the strength at the end of the five years on the Rock being, by a coincidence, precisely the same as on arrival there—488 sergeants, drummers, rank-and-file. The strength of officers present had increased to twenty-nine.

In February 1800 the Seventieth was ordered to return to the West Indies, and Headquarters and six companies under the command of Colonel the Hon. Arthur Wolfe,[1] arrived in due course at Trinidad, where it was intended that the regiment should be stationed. The remaining four companies, however, under Lieutenant-Colonel Thomas Nicoll,[2] had an abrupt end put to their voyage. The ship in which the companies were being conveyed to Trinidad sprung a leak at sea and put into Lisbon harbour, whence she was ordered to proceed to Jersey, presumably being unfit for a longer voyage. It was then decided that the six companies from Trinidad should return home, and in May 1801 the regiment was assembled in Jersey, whence it proceeded seventeen months later to Chatham, arriving at Deal towards the end of October 1802. The Seventieth was conveyed on this occasion in ships of war, and having landed at Deal marched to Dover Castle, and thence, after a halt of three weeks, to Chatham. The garrison of Chatham, which was commanded by Sir John Moore, consisted of the Staff Corps, the first and second battalion of the 52nd, and the Seventieth.

Among the officers who joined the regiment at Jersey was Ensign Jonathan Leach, afterwards Colonel Leach, C.B., of the Rifle Brigade. Colonel Leach in 1831 published his military recollections, under the title of "Rough Sketches of the Life of an Old Soldier," and in this very interesting book gives a good idea of life in the West Indies at the beginning of the nineteenth century. Colonel Leach informs us that soldiering at Chatham in 1802, even under Sir John Moore, was anything but interesting. "To the winter which we passed at Chatham," he writes, "with little to vary the scene except dock-yard guards main guards, and sundry other guards, on which I constantly found myself posted, I do not look back with any particularly pleasurable recollections." In the early spring of 1803, however, Sir John Moore was permitted to pick out the finest and most effective men of the two battalions of the 52nd, and the 1st battalion thus formed was made a regiment of Light Infantry under Lieutenant-Colonel Kenneth McKenzie. This regiment was the model (writes Colonel Leach) on which the other Light Infantry regiments of the army were afterwards formed. Very soon afterwards the 52nd and Seventieth marched to Shorn-

---

[1] Lieut.-Colonel and Brevet-Colonel the Honourable Arthur Wolfe exchanged into the Seventieth with Lieut.-Colonel M. Paumier, from half-pay of 108th Regiment, April 19, 1799.

[2] Major T. Nicoll was promoted second Lieut.-Colonel vice Colonel Coote, transferred to 17th Foot, August 9, 1799.

cliffe, where they were encamped, and with the 4th and 59th Regiments and five companies of the 95th formed Sir John Moore's original Light Brigade, intended to bear the brunt of Napoleon's expected invasion of England. "Everyone knows, or ought to know," writes Colonel Leach, "that at this time Bonaparte threatened our shores with a visit from his numerous army and flotilla, which were in and about Boulogne. We had no difficulty in seeing the immense mass of white tents on the French coast, when the day happened to be clear." Colonel Leach adds that every precaution against surprise was taken at night, the beach being constantly patrolled until daylight, and all guards being kept standing under arms from one hour before day-break until it could be clearly seen that no flotilla was approaching. Sir John Moore at this time was in the prime of his strength and energy, and it is now known, through the publication of his diary, that he was ready at the head of the Shorncliffe Brigade to encounter the flower of Napoleon's grand army. The volunteers of England, with a strength of 320,000 men, stood in support, and so fine was the fighting spirit of the people in 1803 that it was the belief of Sir John Moore that Napoleon's veterans could be met successfully. He at any rate was fully prepared to take the risk. As we all know the threatened attack was never made. The "Army of England" broke up its camp at Boulogne and marched away to conquer the greater part of Europe, and the unfortunate Seventieth found itself doomed to yet another tour of service in the West Indies.

"Towards the end of October," writes Colonel Leach, "a sudden and on our part unexpected order arrived for our Regiment to march immediately to Portsmouth, to embark for the West Indies. This intelligence caused some long faces among a few of our old hands who had previously served in that part of the world; but the greater part of us being young and thoughtless, the order for moving, being a novelty, was received with pleasure rather than dislike."

Poor lads, little did they guess what lay before them.

On the march to Portsmouth an unfortunate affair occurred. At Battle an affray took place at night between some men of the regiment and a party of artillerymen, in which two of the latter were shot and a third man bayonetted in the body. A corporal and two privates soldiers were left behind in custody, and were subsequently tried and acquitted by the civil power; it having been proved that they had acted in self-defence and had no other means of saving their lives. Early in November the regiment embarked in the *Pandour*, an old forty-four gun war-ship fitted up for troops, and during the voyage westward met a vessel which was pronounced to be a hostile frigate. The *Pandour* was at once cleared for action, the Grenadier Company was posted on the forecastle, and the Light Company on the poop; the remaining companies were ordered below until wanted to board the supposed enemy. " After a chase of many hours," says Colonel Leach, " she turned out to be a neutral, and all our golden dreams of prize money vanished in an instant." Such was life at sea in the days of the long war with France.

On Christmas day the Seventieth arrived at Barbados and on the last day of the year at English Harbour, in the island of Antigua, the new station of the regiment.

During the first five months of 1804, says Colonel Leach, the health of the regiment was comparatively good, but then, just ten years after the epidemic of yellow fever at Martinique, a similar disaster fell upon the Seventieth.

" In the month of June we were suddenly visited with an attack of yellow fever, that eternal curse and scourge of Europeans, which in a few days filled the hospitals to such an extent as has perhaps never been exceeded in any regiment, and but rarely equalled. Between the months of June and October we buried two-thirds of the officers who came out with the regiment from England, six of whom were captains. The ravages occasioned by this infernal pestilence amongst the soldiers, their wives and children, bore a full proportion to that of the officers, and . . . by the end of 1804 the Regiment was a perfect skeleton, and could with great difficulty furnish men to perform the regimental duties."

The Seventieth landed in Antigua on January 1, 1804, with a strength of twenty-seven officers and 440 of other ranks fit for duty, with twenty-six sick, and although Colonel Leach's memory had deceived him as to the details when he wrote his book, the reality was bad enough. By the end of the year twelve officers and 152 of other ranks had died in the island, and doubtless other deaths had occurred among those who had been invalided.

The details of the casualties among the officers are given on the opposite page.

THE FRENCH REVOLUTIONARY WAR

OFFICERS OF THE SEVENTIETH (SURREY) REGIMENT
ANTIGUA, 1804

COLONEL
   John, Earl of Suffolk. General. (England).

LIEUTENANT-COLONELS
   Andrew Ross.
   Lewis Grant.

MAJORS
   Henry Elliot. Promoted Lieut.-Colonel 96th Regiment, 1808.
   James Williamson. Retired October 1, 1804.

CAPTAINS
   John Crawford. Died July 23, 1804.
   William Chambers. Died August 24, 1804.
   J. B. Ormsby. Died March 24, 1805.
   John Williams. Died June 15, 1804.
   Wm. B. Johnston. Retired 1809.
   Benjamin Lawrence.
   John Cameron. Retired January 1804.
   Thomas Winstanley. Died August 23, 1804.
   Usher Boate. Died October 12, 1804.
   Thomas Congreve. A prisoner-of-war in France.[2]
   William Spaight. Died October 25, 1804.

LIEUTENANTS
   Michael Joseph Cox. Exchanged to Royal Scots.
   Jonathan Leach. Promoted vice Cameron.
   James Cox. Retired 1805.
   John P. Hawkins. Promoted vice Winstanley.
   Charles D. Allen. Exchanged to 23rd Light Dragoons.
   Robert Lyons. Promoted vice Spaight.
   J. W. Chase. Retired 1804.
   C. L. Carruthers. Died July 24, 1804.
   George Johnston. Died September 24, 1804.
   Andrew Elliott.
   Charles Martin (Adjutant).
   William Keon. Died May 21, 1804.

ENSIGNS
   Henry Nichols. Promoted Lieutenant, May 5, 1804.
   William Owen. Promoted Lieutenant, May 6, 1804.
   Henry McDermott. Promoted in 88th Regiment.
   George Mellis. Retired 1804.

PAYMASTER
   William Hutchinson.

ADJUTANT
   Charles Martin.

QUARTERMASTER
   Smith.

SURGEON
   Robert Evans. Died August 3, 1804.

ASSISTANT SURGEONS
      Ratcliffe.
   Henry Hough.

NOTES

1. Of the officers of 1804, the following were survivors of the epidemic of yellow fever at Martinique in 1794 : Major Henry Elliot, Captains John Crawford, William B. Johnston and Usher Boate, of whom the second and last died. Major Elliot and Captain Johnston alone survived both epidemics.

2. Captain Thomas Congreve was a prisoner-of-war in France throughout the West Indian tour of 1803–10.

Colonel Leach mentions the curious circumstance that, owing to the great number of deaths in the garrison, General Dunlop, the Governor, ordered that all funeral ceremonies should be discontinued, and that the coffins of officers should be carried to the grave without band or drums and without a firing party. The General ordered that these instructions should apply, if necessary, to his own funeral. "The order," writes Colonel Leach, " was obeyed to the letter ; and both he and his brigade-major who died within a few days of each other, were taken to their graves in a light wagon, attended by the few of our our officers and soldiers who were able to do duty, and by a small party of artillerymen."

After this terrible epidemic the Seventieth apparently became case-hardened, or possibly the survivors adapted themselves to a mode of life that gave them a better chance, for the mortality in subsequent years was not abnormal. Colonel Leach, from whose diary we have quoted so freely, survived a severe attack of yellow fever, his remedy being, as he tells us, the heroic one of a jug of boiling Madeira. Thanks to the deaths of seven captains, Leach, who purchased his company, found himself moved up in a few months from second senior subaltern to second senior captain, but notwithstanding this good fortune he had had enough of Antigua. He exchanged into the 95th Regiment (now the Rifle Brigade), in which gallant corps he saw much service and rose to considerable distinction. He, however, never forgot his old friends in the Seventieth, and ends his " Rough Sketches " with the following words : " In the 70th Regiment there is not now an officer who was with us at the period of our embarkation for the West Indies, and in all human probability not one individual. My best wishes, nevertheless, attend the Regiment to whatever part of the globe the Fates may call it."

Colonel Wolfe, it may be mentioned, did not accompany the regiment to Antigua. He retired from the army in February 1804 and died in the following year.[1] He was succeeded in the command by Brevet-Colonel Andrew Ross, A.D.C. to the King, an officer whose name is frequently mentioned in the history of the Thirty-First. Colonel Ross commanded the Seventieth throughout its tour in the West Indies, from 1803 to 1810.

Of these long years there is but little to record beyond an occasional move of the regiment from island to island. In June 1806 the Headquarters of the Seventieth were moved to St. Christopher (or St. Kitt's, as it is more usually called), leaving two companies, under Lieutenant-Colonel Lewis Grant, at Antigua. A month later this detachment went also to St. Kitt's. During the year, in which the garrison of St. Kitt's suffered much from sickness, an attack on the island was threatened by a French squadron under Admiral Guillaume, with troops commanded by Jerome Bonaparte, afterwards King of Westphalia. Much alarm was caused in the island, but the French force, after reconnaissance, considered the garrison, which consisted of the 11th and Seventieth Regiments, with some artillery, too strong to be attacked, and went elsewhere. At this period (June 1806), it may be noted, all the men of the regiment, except four, were enlisted for life.

In 1807 Denmark was drawn into the international quarrels caused by the European league against Napoleon, and a state of war arose between that country and Great Britain. An expedition numbering about 2500 men was therefore prepared, under General Henry Bowyer against the Danish West Indian islands of St. Thomas and St. John; and a portion of the Seventieth, under Colonel Ross, accompanied the expeditionary force. The islands were, however, surrendered without any fighting, and the remainder of the Seventieth was sent to St. Thomas and its dependent islands and was there stationed during 1808 and 1809.

In 1810 an expedition on a larger scale was despatched under Lieutenant-General Sir George Beckwith, K.B., against the island of Guadeloupe, which had been restored to France at the short-lived peace of Amiens in 1802. The expeditionary force numbered rather

---

[1] Colonel the Hon. Arthur Wolfe, who died June 29, 1805, was the second son of Viscount Kilwarden, who was murdered in the streets of Dublin in 1803 during Emmet's rising.

over 7000 men, and was divided into two divisions and a reserve. The flank companies of the Seventieth were included in the expedition, which arrived off Guadeloupe on January 26, and by the 29th had landed almost unopposed at Port Sainte Marie on the east and Vieux Habitants on the west of the island. The two columns marched down the coast towards Trois Rivières, where the enemy had prepared fortified positions; but these, together with the guns in them, were abandoned on the approach of the British light troops of the eastern column. The light company of the Seventieth received special mention on this occasion.

The principal point of attack by the expedition was the town of Basseterre, and to guard it, General Ernouf, the French Commander-in-Chief, took up two strong positions in the mountains to the north-east and north-west of the town. Sir George Beckwith's object was to drive the two French bodies of troops, which were of inferior quality, into such a position that they must either submit to an attack or surrender. With this object it was that part of his expedition had landed on the west of the island.

General Beckwith advanced from Trois Rivières on January 30, and after a well conducted advance over difficult ground, made a successful attack on General Ernouf's force on February 4. The French force had taken up a strong position covered by the Rivière Noire, but General Beckwith had a sufficient superiority of strength to detach a strong turning force, while threatening the French front. The turning force, however, was conducted by its guide to a point much nearer than that prescribed, where a practicable ford was found, and its commander, Colonel Wale, chose this route in preference to the long turning movement on which he had set out. The result of the unexpected attack by the flanking force was decisive. The French, particularly a weak regular battalion, fought well, but were completely outmanœuvred and outnumbered, and consequently surrendered.

Sir George Beckwith's force, which was boldly and skilfully handled, lost fifty-two killed and 250 wounded, chiefly in the last day's fighting. The following officers of the Seventieth served at Guadeloupe with the flank companies: Captains Benjamin Lawrence, commanding the Grenadier Company, and Andrew Elliot, commanding the Light Company (both of whom died soon after the end of the campaign);

Lieutenants Tredennick, Edward Saunderson, M. W. Forde,[1] Samuel Harney, Donald McKay, and G. H. Hazen.

In consequence of the distinguished services of the flank companies of the Seventieth in this short campaign, the honour "Guadeloupe" was granted to the regiment in the year 1867.

After the capture of Guadeloupe the flank battalions were broken up, and the Seventieth companies rejoined the regiment at St. Thomas, where Captain Benjamin Lawrence died in January 1811 and Captains Andrew Elliot, Charles Martin and T. B. Edwards, and Lieutenants M. Maxwell, E Yates, F. Smyth, and A. Grant died later in the year.

In consequence of the heavy loss of life and sickness in the regiment the officers, non-commissioned officers, and drummers of four companies had been sent home in June 1810 to form a recruiting depôt at Ayr, the command of which was bestowed on Colonel Andrew Ross. A.D.C. The losses in the garrison of the West Indies by death and invaliding at this time amounted to 2000 yearly; but owing to the great demands on the army consequent on the Peninsular War, it was impossible to replace these losses, and regiments in the West Indies dwindled to mere skeletons. Those officers and men of the Seventieth who survived the campaign of 1810 did not attain old age, for on the issue of the war medal in 1848 there was not a single survivor of the combatant officers, and only eight rank-and-file of the regiment to claim it.

In 1811 the depôt was removed from Ayr to Stirling Castle and early in 1812 the remainder of the regiment was removed from St Thomas and joined the depôt at Stirling Castle, arriving in two detachments in April and June.

In 1812 the regiment lost its veteran Lieutenant-Colonel, who became a Major-General on January 1. Major-General Ross died a few months later in the year in Spain, where he held a command.

In January 1813 the Seventieth marched to Montrose to assist the civil power in suppressing riots there, and in February it was hurriedly

[1] Lieutenant Matthew William Forde survived the West Indian Campaign for many years, and becoming captain in the Seventieth in 1812 served subsequently in several regiments. In 1837 he left the British service and became a Colonel in the Sikh army under Maharaja Ranjit Singh. Colonel Forde, who was described as "an estimable and very amiable man," died at Peshawar of injuries received at the hands of his own men in the mutiny of the Sikh army in 1843.

despatched to Dundee on a similar duty, proceeding at the end of the month to Perth to guard a large number of French prisoners of war confined there.

In July of the same year the regiment proceeded to Ireland, and its destination having been rapidly changed from Belfast to Dublin, and from Dublin to Cork, it was finally ordered to embark for Canada, sailing from the Cove of Cork on September 1 and not arriving at Quebec until November 4. The delay was caused by the *Hastings* transport, in which a wing of the regiment was being conveyed, running ashore in the St. Lawrence on October 25. Part of the men and all the women and children were landed, 250 of the men remaining on board to lighten the ship by throwing heavy portions of the cargo overboard. By great exertions on the part of the soldiers and seamen, the ship was floated in twelve hours, but owing to rough weather the detachment and families ashore could not be got on board in less than two days and nights. In spite of considerable hardships there was no loss of life, and the regiment arrived at Quebec without a man, woman or child sick, an exceptional occurrence at the time.

It should be noted that the regiment at this time, like the rest of the infantry, had a boy company. This was rendered necessary by the extreme difficulty of obtaining sufficient recruits at the latter part of the great war with France.

Lieut.-General the Honble. Sir G. Lowry Cole, G.C.B., Colonel of the 70th (Surrey) Regiment.

70th (Surrey) Regiment.
Officers' uniform in bygone days.

CHAPTER XV

YEARS OF PEACE

After the great war—Service in Canada—Ireland in 1831—Gibraltar and Malta—The West Indies again—First tour of Indian service—Cholera at Cawnpore.

IN 1814 the Seventieth was stationed successively at Quebec, Montreal and Cornwall, and in the latter half of the year occupied posts on the line of communication from Cornwall to Cook's Point. In the month of January the Earl of Suffolk, who had been Colonel of the regiment for thirty-one years, was transferred to the 44th, and was succeeded in the Seventieth by Lieut-General the Honble. Sir Galbraith Lowry Cole, K.B., whose services in the West Indian campaign have been mentioned. In 1816 Sir G. Lowry Cole was transferred to the 34th Regt., and was succeeded in the Seventieth by General Forbes Champagné, who died on October 22 of the same year. Major-General Lord Howard, afterwards created Earl of Effingham, was then appointed Colonel, and retained the appointment until January 1832, when he was transferred to the "Buffs." In March 1815, on peace being concluded with the United States, the regiment was assembled at Cornwall, marching thence at the end of May to Kingston, where it remained stationed until April 1817, when it took up duty along the Niagara frontier, Headquarters being at Fort George. At this period the Seventieth was commanded by Colonel Lewis Grant, and at the very frequent inspections then usual was invariably reported to be in the highest state of discipline. The attention of the officers to the comfort of the men, and the good conduct of the latter, received much commendation.

In June 1819 the regiment returned to Kingston, remaining there until May 1821, when it was removed to Quebec, in which town it remained two years, moving in May 1823 to Montreal.

During this year Lieut.-Colonel Lewis Grant retired by sale and was succeeded in the command by Brevet-Lieut.-Colonel Charles McGrigor, an officer who had seen much service in India and had been present at the capture of Seringapatam in 1799. Colonel McGrigor held the command until 1829, when he retired through ill-health, being appointed a Knight of Hanover on retirement.

The Seventieth was allowed a longer stay than usual at Montreal, in which town it became highly popular. On its departure at the end of May 1826 the regiment received most gratifying assurances of the esteem with which it was regarded. The magistrates of the city, at a general meeting, unanimously passed a resolution in the following terms :

" Resolved—That the uniformly correct and praiseworthy conduct of the Seventieth Regiment while in garrison at Montreal under the respective command of Lieutenant-Colonel Evans and Lieutenant-Colonel McGrigor, and the services the regiment has always zealously rendered to the citizens whenever their services could be useful, have entitled the Officers, N.C.O.'s, and Privates of the regiment to the regard and gratitude of the Magistrates and inhabitants of Montreal."

At the same time the fire assurance companies and citizens of Montreal presented to the Sergeants' Mess a handsome silver cup, with an inscription couched in similar terms. This cup is still a treasured possession of the sergeants of the 2nd Battalion East Surrey Regiment.

On leaving Montreal in May 1826, the Seventieth was again stationed at and near Kingston until, in August 1827, after fourteen years' service in Canada, the regiment embarked at Quebec for transfer to Ireland, taking up quarters at Fermoy. At the end of the year the Reserve (or Depôt) companies joined Headquarters.

The Seventieth remained in Ireland till March 1834, making very frequent changes of station and being at times broken up in a large number of detachments. In spite of these drawbacks the regiment was invariably well reported on for its discipline and conduct.

One incident of the tour of duty in Ireland deserves record. In November 1831 a party of twenty men of the Light Company, under Captain G. B. Mathew, while employed with the same number of police in marching a party of arrested rioters from Doonane to Castlecomer, were followed by a dense mob of rioters, who demanded the release of the prisoners. On reaching a turnpike Captain Mathew found the road blocked and the hedges and house occupied by the mob. The escort was surrounded, and on Captain Mathew refusing to release the prisoners, was furiously assailed with stones and was fired on.

Several of the soldiers and police were knocked down and much injured, and the whole party was in imminent danger. Captain Mathew at length ordered the leading section to fire and then with another party drove the mob from the buildings and hedges. Five of the rioters were killed on the spot. After full inquiry, Lord Hill, the Commander-in-Chief, delivered his opinion in the following terms : " Horse Guards, 9th December, 1831. Lord Hill is gratified to learn that under circumstances of no ordinary difficulty the conduct of Captain Mathew of the Seventieth Regiment was conspicuous for judgment and decision."

No more difficult or responsible duty can fall upon an officer than to deal with an emergency such as Captain Mathew encountered, and his conduct may serve as a model on future occasions.

In January 1832 General Gage John Hall became Colonel of the regiment in succession to General the Earl of Effingham, G.C.B., transferred to " the Buffs." General Hall retained the Colonelcy until his death in 1854, when he was succeeded by Lieut.-General G. W. Paty, C.B.

The Seventieth again embarked for foreign service in March 1834, after a home tour of less than seven years, none of which had been spent in England. Its first station was Gibraltar, where the regiment lay for rather more than two years. While at Gibraltar the regiment lost three sergeants and thirty private soldiers from an epidemic of cholera which broke out soon after its arrival. In June 1836 the Seventieth was transferred to Malta, and in January 1838 the six service companies sailed once more for the West Indies, arriving at St. Vincent on April 26. Three companies were detached to Grenada. The four depôt companies at this period were stationed at Guernsey.

West Indian service was again unfortunate to the regiment, yellow fever breaking out both in Grenada and St. Vincent a few months after its arrival. At Grenada the three companies there stationed lost Captain H. G. Jarvis, Lieutenant J. G. Correy and thirty-two of other ranks, while at St. Vincent the three Headquarter companies lost Captain J. Morphy (a Waterloo officer), Lieutenant and Adjutant Moody, Ensign W. S. May, the Sergeant-Major, and seventy-six of other ranks. The casualties in the band were so heavy that it was found necessary to break it up.

Early in the year 1840 the Seventieth was moved to British Guiana, three companies being stationed at Demerara and three at Berbice.

In March 1841 this distribution was changed, the Berbice detachment being withdrawn, Headquarters and four companies remaining at Demerara, while two companies were sent on detachment to Barbados. In April the Headquarters and four companies from Demerara also proceeded to Barbados, and in May the six service companies were all conveyed to Canada, taking up quarters at and about Montreal. Sixteen months later the regiment was transferred to Quebec, arriving there on October 1, 1842, and taking up quarters in the Citadel Barracks. In May 1843 the Headquarters and service companies returned home, and were stationed at Portsmouth. The regiment had not previously been in England for forty years. The commanding officer at this time was Lieutenant-Colonel Joseph Kelsall, a veteran soldier of forty years' service, whose picture still adorns the officers' mess of the 2nd Battalion. In February 1844 Lieutenant-Colonel Kelsall retired on full pay, and was succeeded in the command by Major Edward James White.

The Seventieth did not remain quite two years in England, moving to Ireland in April and May 1845. While in Ireland the regiment, as was usual in past times, was broken up in small detachments, which were incessantly moved from one station to another. Nothing worse for a regiment than service in such conditions can well be imagined, the only experience gained by the officers being the handling of men on the march and in billets. In December 1845 Lieutenant-Colonel E. J. White retired on full pay, and was succeeded by Major Thomas Reed, who in turn retired in April 1847 and was succeeded in the Lieutenant-Colonelcy by Major M. W. Bigge.

In December 1848 the Seventieth received orders to embark for its first tour of duty in India, and on the consequent augmentation of establishment Major T. J. Galloway of the 33rd Regiment was brought in as 2nd Lieutenant-Colonel.

The regiment embarked at Cork in January 1849 in six ships belonging to the Honourable East India Company, and arrived at Calcutta on various dates in May and June, proceeding to take up temporary quarters at Dum-Dum. Five men, one woman, and six children died on the voyage. The regiment only remained three months at Dum-Dum, but in that short period lost seventy-nine men by disease, thirty-one of whom died of cholera. In October 1849 the Seventieth moved to Calcutta, and suffered from sickness in the following hot weather. In the month of May 1850 the deaths of three officers occurred. That of Major Edwards from fever, while Captain Hennis and Lieutenant Wilson died of cholera.

In December 1850 the regiment, under Lieutenant-Colonel Chute, moved by river from Calcutta to Allahabad, whence it marched to Cawnpore, arriving there in Ferbruary 1851. While at Calcutta the regiment lost seventy-nine men by disease, the same number that were lost at Dum-Dum. In a farewell Order, dated December 19, 1850, the orderly and soldier-like conduct of the regiment while at Fort William was recorded in terms of the highest praise. The Seventieth was stationed at Cawnpore for three years, during which time it suffered very heavily from cholera. One of the worst recorded epidemics of this terrible disease broke out in the regiment in May 1853, lasting until the beginning of September. In the month of August, when the whole regiment was in cholera camp, ten miles from Cawnpore, the deaths numbered 104, and in the course of the epidemic the regiment buried at and about Cawnpore two officers, Captain G. A. Schreiber and Ensign J. B. Watson, 344 men, thirty-seven women, and ninety-nine children. When the epidemic was at its worst many thought that the entire regiment was doomed to death, yet " nothing," it is recorded, " could exceed the soldier-like bearing of the soldiers of the regiment and the devotion shown by them to their stricken comrades."

Such an epidemic, it may be added, strains courage and discipline fully as severely as the most arduous campaign.

The Seventieth left Cawnpore on January 1, 1854, and marched to Ferozepore, where it was stationed till November 1856. The health of the regiment at Ferozepore was excellent until the months of August and September 1856 when cholera again carried off many victims. The deaths included one officer (Assistant-Surgeon Grant) and ninety men. The conduct of the regiment in this epidemic is again recorded as having been most admirable.

The next station of the Seventieth was Peshawar, where it arrived by route march from Ferozepore on December 8, 1856. The strength of the regiment on January 1, 1857, was twenty-five officers, forty-eight sergeants, 760 rank-and-file. The general health is noted as " very good." The strength of the depôt at Chatham on the same date was 194 men.

CHAPTER XVI

The Indian Mutiny

The importance of Peshawar—Colonel Chute's "Flying Column"—Military executions—The regiment supplies artillery and cavalry—An abortive rising.

Four months after the arrival of the Seventieth at Peshawar the rebellion in northern India, generally spoken of as the Indian Mutiny, burst like a thunder-storm on the weak and scattered English garrison and civil population. There had been premonitory symptoms in several quarters, and the more intelligent observers were aware of the danger of the situation, but generally speaking the civil and military authorities were taken by surprise. The first serious outbreak occurred at Meerut on May 10, 1857, and was immediately followed by a terrible massacre of Europeans at Delhi, few escaping with their lives. The ancient capital of the Moghul Empire thus fell into the hands of the mutineers, who declared the old king of Delhi their leader. The rebellion then became general in Oudh and all the regions of Hindustan; the recently-conquered Punjab, though strongly garrisoned and not disposed to sympathise with a Mahomedan insurrection, showing a grave tendency to take advantage of the difficulties of the British Government.

Fortunately the civil authorities of the Punjab were all men of exceptional talent and strength of character. Headed by Sir John Lawrence, the Chief Commissioner, they rose nobly to the emergency, and after some discussion it was rightly decided that any retreat would be suicidal, and that the entire Punjab should be held. By this decision Peshawar became one of the most important posts in India, and being, from its distance, very inaccessible, the regiments

THE INDIAN MUTINY

stationed there on the outbreak of the Mutiny could never be relieved, but retained their honourable and important but uneventful duties until the suppression of the rebellion. The great importance of Peshawar was derived from its position at the mouth of the Khaibar Pass, the main road from Afghanistan to India. In addition then to its first duty of suppressing the threatened mutiny of the Bengal regiments stationed in and near Peshawar, the weak British garrison had for two long years to stand on guard, almost unsupported, against the highly probable invasion of India by the Afghans and all the freebooters of Central Asia.

The European garrison of Peshawar consisted of two batteries of artillery and two infantry regiments, the Seventieth and 87th. Brigadier-General Sydney Cotton, commanding the Peshawar Brigade, having been placed in military command of the frontier district, Colonel Galloway of the Seventieth was appointed Brigadier of the station, and the command of the regiment devolved on Brevet-Colonel Chute.

Events moved rapidly, and within ten days of the receipt of news of the outbreaks at Meerut and Delhi it was decided to disarm four of the five native infantry regiments at Peshawar. The cause of this decision was the arrival on the night of May 21 of the news that the 55th Native Infantry had mutinied at Nowshera, a station twenty-four miles from Peshawar, and that the native cavalry regiment at the same station had shown itself untrustworthy. On receipt of this news at midnight, Colonel Herbert Edwardes, the Commissioner, and Lieutenant-Colonel John Nicholson, the famous soldier who was Deputy Commissioner of Peshawar, went to Brigadier-General Cotton and urged on him the necessity of acting immediately. Cotton, a veteran of forty-seven years' service, but active and decided as in his youth, accepted the risk and responsibility without hesitation, and ordered that the four native regiments in the cantonment should be disarmed at daybreak. No instructions were necessary, all had been thought out beforehand, and every officer knew what was to be done and what his duties would be. General Cotton therefore at once summoned to his house the commanding officers of the native regiments and ordered them to parade their regiments as quickly as possible for disarmament. The officers protested against the decision, and declared their belief in the loyalty of their men, but the order given was final, and the remonstrances, though listened to with sympathy, were of no avail.

SEVENTIETH (THE SURREY) REGIMENT
1857–59

COLONEL
    George William Paty, Major-General, C.B., K.H. In England.

LIEUTENANT-COLONELS
    Thomas James Galloway. Brevet-Colonel November 28, 1854.
    Trevor Chute. Brevet-Colonel November 28, 1854.

MAJORS
    Thomas Charles Timins. Brevet-Lieut.-Colonel February 6, 1855. Died February 6, 1855.
    George Durnford. Brevet-Lieut.-Colonel. Retired on full pay and promoted Hon. Colonel in the army, October 1859.

CAPTAINS
    Thomas Mulock. Promoted Major vice Timins.
    Edward L'Estrange. A Waterloo officer. Brevet-Lieut.-Colonel June 20, 1854.
    John William Hay. Died September 14, 1857.
    George Evatt. Died July 17, 1857.
    George A. Ryan.
    Sydney Cosby Jackson.
    Oswald Pilling. Served with Artillery—Peshawar.
    A. J. O. Rutherford. Commanding Depôt—Chatham.
    Henry Fred Saunders. Promoted Brevet-Major March 24, 1858.
    William Cooper.
    R. F. W. Cumberland.
    John Mackay McKenzie. Served with Artillery—Peshawar.

LIEUTENANTS
    Charles A. P. James. Promoted Captain September 15, 1857, vice Hay.
    Paul Fred de Quincey. Promoted Captain January 9.
    Attilio Scheberras. Adjutant. Promoted Captain 15th Regiment.
    George Augustus McNair. Promoted Captain 17th Regiment.
    Oates Joseph Travers. Served with Peshawar Light Horse. Promoted Captain July 18, 1858, vice Evatt.
    Charles Crawley. Promoted Captain in 15th Regiment.
    John T. N. O'Brien.
    William Crozier. Promoted Captain in 18th Regiment.
    Arthur Saltmarshe. Promoted Captain vice Mulock.
    Robert Whigham. Served with Peshawar Light Horse.
    W. F. T. Marshall.
    George Richards Greaves. Appointed Adjutant vice Scheberras.
    George Fred. Coryton. Promoted Captain in 10th Regiment.
    Matthew Bell. Died at Peshawar Fort, January 11, 1859.
    William Wiltshire Lynch. Severely wounded January 5, 1858. Promoted Captain in 2nd (Queen's) Regiment.
    John William Madden. Promoted Captain in 4th (K.O.R.) Regiment.

Alex. C. H. Tovey.
James Green. ⎱ Served with Artillery—Peshawar.
Charles William Quinn. ⎰
Henry Berkeley Good.
Henry Leake. Transferred from 44th Regiment.

ENSIGNS
Thomas Deering Backhouse. Promoted Lieutenant vice James.
Tho. R. Devereux Bingham. Exchanged to 98th Regiment.
Charles G. Stuart Menteath.
George Aislabie Hilton.
William Henry Ralston.
John Beldham. Promoted from Sergeant-Major.
Eustace Cay.
A. W. Crozier.
Alex. B. Wright.

PAYMASTER
Michael Thompson.

ADJUTANT
Attilio Scheberras.

QUARTERMASTER
William Nevell.

SURGEON
Samuel Currie.

ASSISTANT SURGEONS
Henry James Rogers.
James F. Deakin.
Joseph Watts.

The Native Infantry was soon formed up on parade, and the work of disarmament began. As a precaution the Peshawar force had been divided into two weak brigades, the British regiments being allotted to them according to circumstances. On May 22 General Cotton, accompanied by Colonel Edwardes, took charge of the right wing, to which the 87th Regiment was attached; while Brigadier Galloway, accompanied by Colonel Nicholson, supervised the disarmament of the left wing, supported by the Seventieth. The artillery (twelve guns) was divided between the two wings and was guarded by the British regiments.

In his book " Nine Years on the North-west Frontier of India " General Sir Sydney Cotton thus describes the incident:

" The disarming on that morning of nearly four thousand men took place as ordered, and happily without struggle or bloodshed. The affair was everywhere executed in the most dexterous manner. The infantry were marched away from their firelocks which had been piled as if for some drill purpose, and when clear of them, the European troops with loaded arms (who were concealed behind barracks and ready for action) rushed forth, seized the arms, and conveyed them under a sufficient escort to the arsenal. At all points was this carried out simultaneously and in like manner. The Sepoys, motionless with surprise, were utterly powerless."

General Cotton adds the interesting detail that it afterwards came to his knowledge that this very 22nd of May was the date fixed for a mutiny of the Peshawar troops. The step of disarmament was therefore taken in the nick of time, and probably saved India from a terrible disaster, for the whole of the wild borderland was waiting to decide what action it should take. The slightest hesitation or delay at Peshawar, and "the whole Punjab would have rolled up like a towel" to use the expressive phrase of a loyal native; and without the aid of the Punjab Delhi would not have been retaken in 1857.

On the day following the disarmament at Peshawar, a small column was despatched under Colonel Chute of the Seventieth to deal with the mutinous 55th Native Infantry at Hoti-Mardan, that regiment having been sent to that isolated station in consequence of its mutinous conduct at Nowshera. The column consisted of eight officers,[1] nine sergeants and 153 rank-and-file of the Seventieth, some irregular cavalry under Colonel Nicholson, and two guns. The men of the Seventieth were mounted on elephants, in consequence of the great heat. At Nowshera the column was joined by part of a newly raised 5th Punjab Infantry under Major Vaughan.

At daybreak on May 25, Chute's force came in sight of the fort of Hoti-Mardan, and as soon as it was seen from the walls the disloyal portion of the 55th lost heart, poured tumultuously out of the fort; and fled towards the hills of Swat. Colonel Chute directed an immediate pursuit, but the guns and infantry were unable to do any execution, and it was left to the cavalry under Nicholson to inflict the punishment. The flying 55th turned and fought desperately, but 120 of them were killed, and 150 captured, together with the regimental colours.

Immediately after the destruction of the 55th, the detachment of

---

[1] Colonel Chute, commanding the column, Captain Evatt, commanding detachment Seventieth, Captain Cooper, Lieutenants Travers, Saltmarshe, Tovey, and Menteath, and Assistant-Surgeon Rogers.

the Seventieth returned to Peshawar, taking with them 120 of the mutineers who had been sentenced to death. The sentences of two-thirds of these men were subsequently reduced to various terms of imprisonment, and on June 10 the remaining forty mutineers were blown away from guns in the presence of the entire garrison and of a great crowd of native spectators. The scene was horrible to those who witnessed it, and the writer well remembers the description of it given to him by a veteran officer of the regiment. The exact method of carrying out the execution is thus described by another officer who was present:

"The forty men condemned to death were brought out in batches of ten, and were placed with their backs against the muzzle of a field-gun. Their elbows were then lightly tied to the wheels of the gun, no word of command was given by the officer to the artillery detachment, but the gunners knew that when he raised his sword arm, they were to fire. This was done to save the men who were to be shot from hearing the word of command. I think this form of death was much more merciful than the alternative of either hanging or shooting, the charge of blank powder in the gun instantaneously breaking the body into some four pieces. This process was repeated until the whole body had been executed."[1]

During the absence at Hoti-Mardan of Colonel Chute's column, and twelve days prior to the blowing from guns of the mutineers of the 55th Native Infantry, an individual execution at Peshawar had caused a great sensation. This was the public hanging before all the troops in garrison, and the same great crowd of spectators from outside, of the Subadar-Major (senior native officer) of the 51st Native Infantry. This native officer had deserted with about 250 men of his regiment, but being promptly pursued had, with about half his men, been captured and brought back to Peshawar. The spectacle of these stern, but just and necessary, acts of justice, sparing neither high rank nor numbers, had an immense effect, and the news of them was bruited far and wide. The inhabitants of the Peshawar valley, "that nest of scorpions," as its neighbours called it, saw that the English, were they few or many, were determined still to be masters of India, and a like impression was made on the Afghan people and on the wild tribes of

[1] *Through Persia in Disguise.* By Colonel Charles E. Stewart, C.B., C.M.G., C.I.E.

the border. The consequence was that throughout the mutiny no serious attack was made on the Peshawar garrison, though the guards and pickets which protected the wide-spread barracks and other buildings at night were constantly fired on by small parties of marauders.

On June 3 Colonel Chute's column, in increased strength, marched to Abazai, one of the frontier posts close under the hills, and disarmed the detachment of the 64th Native Infantry stationed there. This regiment was ripe for mutiny, but being broken up among three forts the men were afraid to act, and each detachment was disarmed without offering any resistance. They were then marched in to Peshawar.

The teeth of the Bengal regiments being drawn, General Cotton at once set about increasing his active strength. With this object he called for volunteers from the Seventieth and 87th to perform mounted duties. Men came forward willingly, and with them General Cotton formed an efficient corps of irregular horse of a novel type, two-thirds of its strength being European and one-third native. This corps was named the Peshawar Light Horse. He found the plan answered well, the native troopers being proud of their association with the English soldiers and the latter getting on very well with their native comrades. In like manner General Cotton manned a battery of nine-pounders which was in the magazine at Peshawar, finding efficient drivers as well as gunners among the infantry soldiers. In consequence of the success of this measure a battery of native horse-artillery was also re-manned by British infantry volunteers. The number of officers and men contributed by the Seventieth was as follows :

Peshawar Light Horse .	. 2 officers, 3 sergeants, 1 drummer, 57 rank-and-file.
Horse Artillery .	. 2 officers and 23 of other ranks.
Artillery (dismounted) .	. 4 officers and 106 of other ranks.
Total .	. 8 officers and 190 other ranks.

The duty of training men for these novel duties at high pressure in the great heat of the Peshawar valley fell heavily on the officers, and the loss of so many men from the duty roster caused the necessary guard duties to press on the weakened ranks of the 27th, Seventieth [1]

---

[1] Deducting the Peshawar Light Horse and Artillery the effective strength of the regiment in August was reduced to seventeen officers and 376 other ranks. Night duty at the time was very heavy.

THE INDIAN MUTINY

and 87th, but all faced the hard work and bore the increasing strain with the most loyal and courageous endurance.

In the second week of June all danger of an invasion by the hill tribes of Swat was seen to be at an end, and Colonel Chute's column returned to Peshawar from its camp on the border.

Towards the end of August the disarmed regiments in Peshawar cantonments became very restless, and on the 27th of the month a rising appeared imminent, and all the European troops were kept constantly under arms, eating and sleeping rifle in hand. On the morning of the 28th General Cotton ordered a thorough search for arms in the native lines, the disarmed Sepoys being ordered to quit their huts for the purpose. Swords, hatchets, pistols, bayonets, powder, ball and caps were found stowed away in roofs and floors and bedding, and even drains; and exasperated by the discovery of their plans and by the taunts of the men of the newly-raised Afridi regiment who were carrying out the search, the 51st Native Infantry rushed upon the piled arms of the 18th Punjab Infantry and sent messengers to all the Hindustani regiments to tell them of the rising. For a few minutes a desperate struggle ensued. The 51st had been one of the finest Sepoy corps in the service and they took the new irregulars altogether by surprise.

But soon the Afridi soldiers seized their arms, " and then " (it is written in the life of Sir Herbert Edwardes) " began that memorable fusilade which commenced on the parade-ground at Peshawar and ended at Jamrud." The pursuit and slaughter of the flying mutineers was started by the Punjabis, and was taken up by the wing of the 27th Inniskillings (which had recently been transferred to Peshawar) and by the Seventieth, who shared barracks with them.

It is stated in Sir Herbert Edwardes' life that 700 men were killed in the pursuit, and Colonel Stewart adds the detail that sixty-three men who were captured were sentenced to death by a court-martial, and shot by firing parties of the 27th and Seventieth. One man of the Seventieth, Private Samuel Collins, was killed in the lines of the 51st Native Infantry on August 28, and one man whose name has not been recorded was wounded. One man of the regiment also died of exhaustion during the pursuit of the mutineers. The total number of Sepoy mutineers executed at Peshawar in 1857 was 523.[1]

These details of the suppression of the mutiny at Peshawar are given with no sense of satisfaction, but from a conviction that it is necessary that English soldiers should know what duties may devolve on them in times of emergency.

In consequence of heavy duty and the unhealthy climate of the Peshawar valley, there was a considerable amount of sickness in the regiment during the mutiny. In October 1857, when the strength of the regiment was very low, the average daily number of sick was 130, the cause being principally fever of a bad type. In the following month the fever became even more virulent, and twenty-seven deaths occurred, all caused by it. The regiment lost three officers at Peshawar, Captain Evatt dying in July and Captain Hay in September 1857. Lieutenant Bell, who was attached to the artillery, died in Peshawar Fort on January 1859, after the regiment had left the station. Major and Brevet-Lieutenant-Colonel Thomas Charles Timins died on his way up country, having come out from England in bad health in order to share in the campaign. Captain Evatt was a nephew of Captain and Brevet-Major John Evatt, who distinguished himself in the campaign in the West Indies.

Two officers of the Seventieth who had been absent on leave at the outbreak of the mutiny and were unable to rejoin, volunteered for duty on the way up country and had the good fortune to distinguish themselves. (1) Captain Henry Frederick Saunders, who served in Major-General Windham's operations round Cawnpore in November 1857, being at the time attached for duty to the 64th Regiment. In the action of November 28, 1857, all the officers of the 64th senior to Captain Saunders were killed, and he consequently assumed command of the regiment and brought it out of action—a very unusual occurrence. Captain Saunders was given a Brevet-Majority for his services. He subsequently exchanged to the 3rd West India Regiment. (2) Lieutenant William Wiltshire Lynch, who volunteered for duty with the small body of cavalry with General Havelock's force in the first advance on Cawnpore. This little corps, chiefly composed of officers

[1] *Life of Major General Sir H. B. Edwards*, vol. ii, p. 165.

THE INDIAN MUTINY

of disbanded regiments of the Bengal Army, did heroic service, and among its members Lieutenant Lynch was conspicuous for gallantry. He was severely wounded near Lucknow in the first relief of that garrison, and was promoted Captain in the 2nd (Queen's) Regiment for his services. Barrow's volunteer cavalry, though so weak in numbers, did fine service. They left Allahabad for Cawnpore twenty strong, and had lost three killed and eleven wounded when they reached Lucknow. Lieutenant Lynch rose to the rank of Major-General and died of cholera at Allahabad in 1888, when in command of that district.

By the month of February 1858 the strength of the regiment at Peshawar had considerably increased. A large draft of 287 men had been sent out from Chatham, and part of them had arrived at Headquarters. The health of the regiment, also, was completely restored. In July great satisfaction was caused by an order to proceed down country to Rawal Pindi, and late in the month the regiment marched to Nowshera, but was compelled to halt there by abnormally heavy rain. On August 10, owing to an extraordinary rise of the Kabul river, a great flood occurred at Nowshera; every private bungalow in the station was swept away and the officers and their mess suffered heavy losses. The barracks occupied by the men, being on slightly higher ground, escaped the general destruction. The Grand Trunk road was much damaged and the ferry boats on the river Indus at Attock were carried away by the flood.

It was consequently found necessary to postpone the move of the regiment to Rawal Pindi until September 27, Headquarters arriving at that station on October 5, 1858. The services of the Seventieth in the suppression of the Mutiny, in common with those of the rest of the Peshawar garrison, received but scanty recognition, the medal being at first granted only to the officers and men of Colonel Chute's flying column. It was eventually issued to the officers mentioned in the following roll and to 714 non-commissioned officers and men. It will be observed that the names of Major Saunders and Captain Lynch are not included in the roll, their claims having no doubt been submitted by the regiments into which they had been transferred.

OFFICERS' MEDAL ROLL SEVENTIETH REGIMENT INDIAN MUTINY CAMPAIGN

Lieut.-Colonel Thos. James Galloway.
,, T. Chute.
Major George Durnford.
Captain Oswald Pilling.
,, George Evatt.
,, R. F. Cumberland.[1]
,, W. S. Cooper.
Lieutenant Paul F. de Quincey.
,, G. A. McNair.
,, Charles Crawley.
,, William Crozier.
,, Robert Whigham.
,, G. F. Croyton.
Lieutenant Matthew Bell.
,, James Green.
,, O. J. Travers.
,, A. C. H. Tovey.
,, A. Saltmarshe.
,, C. G. S. Menteath.
Ensign Thomas D. Backhouse.
,, G. A. Hilton.
Lieut. and Adjt. Attilio Scheberras.
Quarter-master William Nevell.
Paymaster Michael Thompson.
Assistant-Surgeon H. J. Rogers.
,, Joseph Watts.[2]

After a stay of fifteen months at Rawal Pindi the Seventieth marched in January 1860 to Cawnpore, proceeding thence by rail to Allahabad, under orders for China, arriving at Allahabad on March 25. The move to China did not take place, and a year later, in January 1861, the regiment again moved, to Benares and Barrackpore. On the 24th of the month orders were received to embark for service in New Zealand, where a rebellion of the natives had been for some time in progress. The regiment consequently embarked in three divisions and arrived at Auckland, New Zealand, on May 11, 13, and 25, 1861. Cholera had unfortunately broken out in the early part of the voyage and thirty-one deaths had occurred (twenty-six men, four women, and one child) chiefly from that disease.

---

[1] Awarded clasp "Relief of Lucknow." Commanded reinforcements in Brigadier Greathed's column from Delhi to Agra. Served with General Sir H. Grant's, K.C.B., force from Agra to Lucknow, also at the relief of Lucknow, at the defeat of the Gwalior contingent, with the Commander-in-Chief's force present at the action of the Kalanuddee and occupation of Futtyghur.

[2] Awarded clasp "Relief of Lucknow." Served with the Alum Bagh garrison, also at the relief of Lucknow, and at the defeat of the Gwalior contingent, &c., with the Commander-in-Chief's force.

CHAPTER XVII

THE NEW ZEALAND WAR

Engagements on the Katikira and on the Waikato rivers—Relief of Pukekohe—Action of Rangiawhia—Action of Orakau—The " Gate Pah "—Action of Okea.

NEW ZEALAND is, of all British possessions, the country with the shortest history. The group of islands now known by this name, so full of natural beauty and so fortunate in climate, was unknown to Europeans until the reign of Charles I of England. The first discoverer was a Dutch explorer of that period, who found the islands peopled by a fine, warlike, and intelligent race called *Maoris*, who, according to their own traditions, had emigrated from Eastern Polynesia early in the fifteenth century. The New Zealand islands had apparently been uninhabited prior to this immigration.

Missionary enterprise brought England into contact with New Zealand in the year 1814, and soon afterwards individual settlers began to acquire tracts of land by purchase from the Maoris. As these settlers became more numerous, quarrels, and eventually small wars, arose between the settlers and the Maoris, and with a view to securing proper treatment of the latter, a British Commissioner was appointed, but with insufficient authority, in the year 1832. Eight years later, partly to secure a proper administration of the island, and partly to anticipate an expected annexation by King Louis Philippe of France, New Zealand was declared a part of the British Empire. The annexation took place on the almost unanimous vote of the ruling chiefs of the three islands, and by its conditions

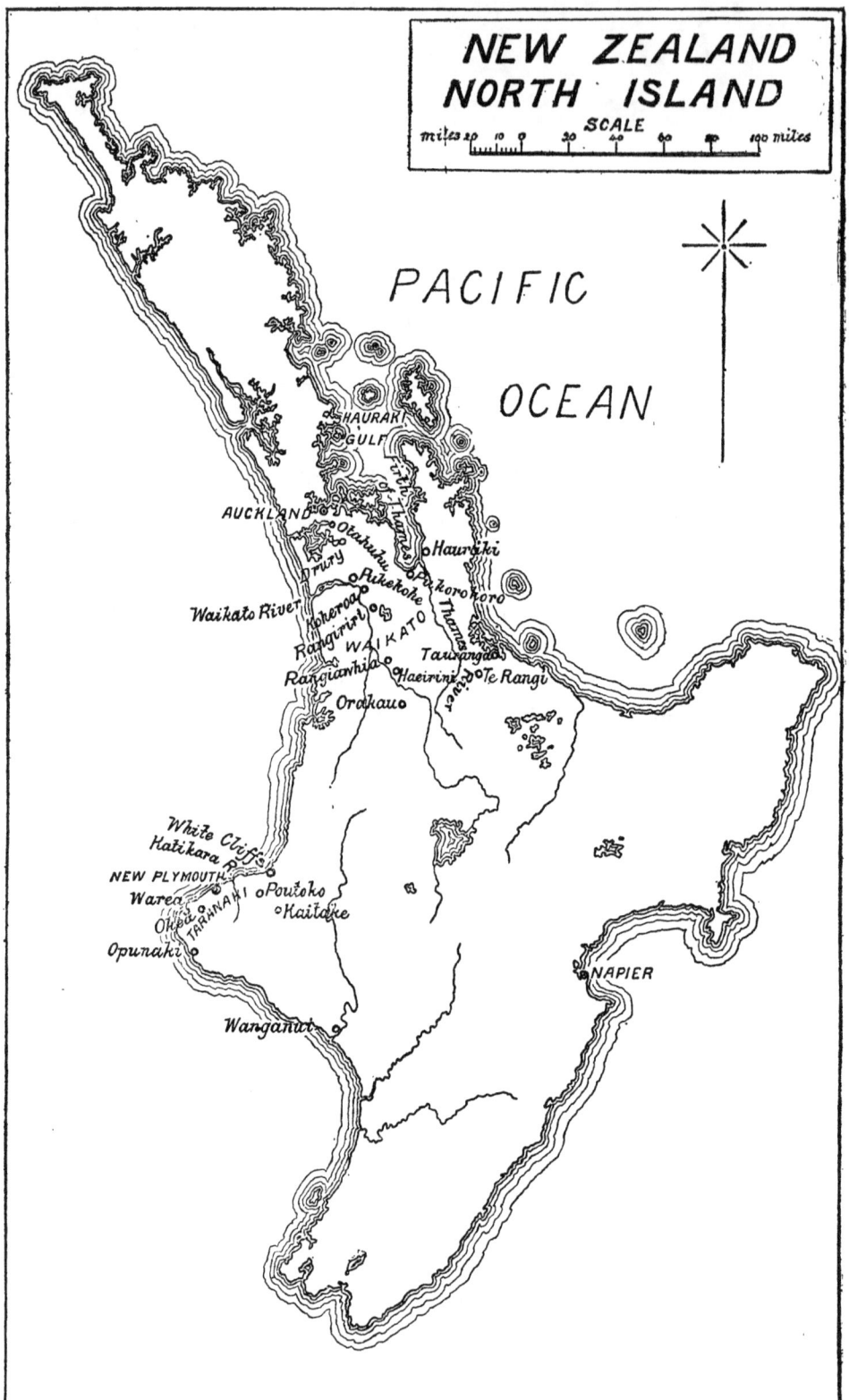

the Maoris received all the rights and privileges of British subjects.

Unfortunately the rapid increase of white settlers led to frequent small insurrections, and between the years 1860 and 1871 these became so serious that, after the suppression of the Indian Mutiny, when troops were available, the Home Government decided to send an adequate force to dispose of the now organised rebellion against British authority.

The seat of this rebellion was in the inland portion of the north island, which is about 500 miles long and of varying breadth, running to 200 miles in parts. This large area was most difficult for military operations, being in many regions densely wooded, and entirely without roads. The English operations were therefore at first confined to the neighbourhood of the coast, though as time went on means were found to use some of the rivers as communications. The Maoris were brave fighters, though without much military knowledge, and at the date of the arrival of the Seventieth Regiment at Auckland they were fairly well armed. They were skilled in forming stockaded entrenchments with deep ditches and flanking rifle pits, often placed in well-chosen positions. Had the Maoris been as united as they were brave, the task of overcoming them would have been so formidable, and the cost so great, that its performance would have taken a great many years. The tribes were however jealous and disunited, and it is generally estimated that at no time were there more than 2000 fighting men in the field. Even this small number offered, as will appear, a stout resistance to the much larger number of English soldiers who fought them with varying success.

When the Seventieth arrived at Auckland in June 1861, three tribes were united in active rebellion—the Taranaki, the Ngatiruanui, and the Waikato, of whom the last named was the most formidable. The Waikato frontier was distant only forty miles south of Auckland, and it was chiefly for the protection of this town that an encampment had been formed at Otahuhu, nine miles on the way to Waikato. The regiments at Otahuhu were the 1st Battalion 12th, 2nd Battalion 14th, 40th and Seventieth Regiments. Colonel Galloway fell into command of the camp, and the command of the regiment consequently devolved on Major Mulock, the next senior officer.

SEVENTIETH (THE SURREY) REGIMENT
1863–5

Colonel
    General Sir George William Paty, K.C.B., K.H. In England.

Lieutenant-Colonels
    Thomas James Galloway. Promoted Major-General March 27, 1863.
    Trevor Chute. Retired on half-pay and appointed Brigadier-General in Australia, March 6, 1863.

Majors
    Thomas Edmund Mulock. Promoted Lieut.-Colonel March 27, 1863, vice Galloway. Appointed C.B.
    George A. Ryan. Promoted Brevet-Lieut.-Colonel March 21, 1865.

Captains
    Arch. J. Oliver Rutherford. Promoted Major vice Mulock.
    William Cooper.
    Oates Joseph Travers.
    Arthur Saltmarshe. Severely wounded. Promoted Brevet-Major March 1, 1864.
    James Green. Retired February 2, 1864.
    George Richards Greaves. Promoted Brevet-Major March 1, 1864, and Brevet-Lieut.-Colonel March 21, 1865.
    Alex. C. H. Tovey.
    William Henry Ralston.
    Donald M. Fraser.
    Eustace Cay. Promoted Brevet-Major February 6, 1866.
    John Aug. Tighe.
    Alex. Boydell Wright.

Lieutenants
    Henry Berkeley Good. Promoted Captain vice Rutherford.
    Thomas D. Backhouse. Promoted Captain vice Green.
    Charles G. S. Menteath. Retired 1863.
    Henry Leake.
    Arthur Stronge Gilbert.
    Herbert John Hill.
    Charles Roger.
    Charles Clark Richardson.
    John F. A. Grierson.
    Norman Huskisson.
    Rodney Stuart Riddell.
    John Robert Collins.
    W. S. Feneran.
    Henry Bally. Killed in action August 2, 1865.
    Henry Fred. Greatwood.

Ensigns
    James McPherson. Promoted Lieutenant March 27, 1863.
    Henry E. Whidborne. Promoted Lieutenant February 2, 1864.
    George G. Cuppage.
    Charles R. Tylden. Severely wounded August 2, 1865.
    Robert Addison Clarke.
    Charles W. Howard.

George Young.
Edward Pearson.
Charles Townley Martin.
Thomas George Barrett Lennard.
Leyland Hornby.

PAYMASTER
Michael Thompson.   Hon. Major November 10, 1864.

INST. OF MUSKETRY
Henry Leake.

ADJUTANT
Herbert J. Hill.

QUARTERMASTER
William Nevell.

SURGEON
G. C. Meikleham.

ASSISTANT-SURGEON.
Thomas Hession.

In November 1861 disturbances broke out among the white mining population of Dunedin in the south (then called Middle) Island, and a detachment of 100 men of the Seventieth, under Major Ryan, was sent to Otago to keep order and protect the town of Dunedin. The detachment remained in Otago till June 1863.

No active operations against the insurgent tribes were undertaken prior to this date, but in December 1861, Lieutenant-General Duncan Cameron, the general officer commanding in New Zealand, began the construction by military labour of a road from Auckland to the Waikato frontier. The troops from Otahuhu were all employed in making this road, each regiment being allotted a certain number of miles which it had to guard while making the road, the last twenty miles of which ran through dense bush. The Seventieth was encamped along the road near Drury from December 1861 till June 1862, when Headquarters and seven companies returned to Otahuhu for the winter, the road having been constructed. The three remaining companies, under Major Rutherford, remained encamped near the Waikato river for the purpose of building a redoubt, to be called " the Queen's " Redoubt.

In March and April 1863, in consequence of an expected outbreak in Taranaki, the regiment was sent by detachments in H.M.S. *Harriet* and H.M.S. *Eclipse* to New Plymouth, being concentrated there by May 10, and on June 3 a detachment numbering eleven officers and 224 of other ranks took part in the first engagement of the war of 1863-65 at the mouth of the Katikara river. The force, which numbered only about 700 men, under the personal command of Lieutenant-General Cameron himself, had to cross the river, which had been fortified, before attacking the Maori position. General Cameron threw his strongest unit, the 57th Regiment, numbering about 400 of all ranks, across the river; the crossing being covered by shell fire from H.M.S. *Eclipse* at the mouth of the river, and supported by the fire of a skirmishing line of the Seventieth placed by Major Mulock along a high bank of the river. The 57th advanced and successfully charged the Maori position, the detachments of the 65th and Seventieth under Major Mulock following in support. The advance of the 57th Regiment over very broken ground was led by three detachments of picked men, to one of which was attached a party of nine men of the Seventieth, under Sergeant Cleary. This party was mentioned by Colonel Warre, 57th Regiment, in his report as having rendered good service, and one of the nine, No. 3517, Private William Wallace, was severely wounded. The Maoris fought gallantly, though surprised, and twenty-eight bodies were found in the position. The British loss was only one killed and nine wounded. The first operation of the war was therefore a distinct success.

On June 16 the detachment under Major Ryan rejoined the regiment from Otago, and on June 27 two companies under that officer returned to Camp Otahuhu, marching thence to Queen's Redoubt on the Waikato river. This move was in consequence of a threatened advance by the Waikato tribes against Auckland, which General Cameron decided to check by a counter advance. Owing to the necessity of finding garrisons at various threatened points and of protecting many outlying farms, only some 1800 men were found available for the advance, and in the first action, which took place on July 17, only 500 of all ranks were engaged. In this action a large force of Maoris which had entrenched themselves on the heights of Koheroa, opposite the camp of the 2nd Battalion 14th Regiment, were attacked by the troops immediately available, composed of the 1st Battalion 12th Regiment (about 150), 2nd Battalion 14th (about 300), and two officers and 102 other ranks of the Seventieth.

The action began about ten A.M., Lieutenant-Colonel Austen of the 14th Regiment advancing to the attack with his own battalion, the detachments of the 12th and Seventieth following in support under their own officers, as they came upon the scene of action. General Cameron himself hurried up also on hearing of the impending fight and took charge of the operations. The Maoris, who numbered between 300 and 400, made a gallant fight, but were driven from their entrenchments at the point of the bayonet. General Cameron in his report to the War office, dated July 20, 1863, wrote as follows: " I cannot speak too highly of the conduct of all the officers and men engaged, or of the able manner in which the troops were led by their commanding officers (among whom was) Major Ryan of the Seventieth."

The Maoris had from thirty to forty killed and many wounded. The British loss was three killed and nine wounded, all of the 14th Regiment. On August 9 Headquarters and the remainder of the regiment (except Captain Wright's company) returned from New Plymouth to Camp Otahuhu. On September 14 two small detachments of the advanced companies under Major Ryan and Captain Saltmarshe behaved with distinguished gallantry in the relief of a detached post of militia at Pukekohe. The detachments of the Seventieth numbered three officers and forty-three of other ranks, and the casualties in them were as follows :

Killed . . . . No. 712 Private R. Burdett.
                  No. 407   ,,   J. Turley.
Wounded . . . Captain A. Saltmarshe (severely).
                  No. 3108 Private J. Eley   do.
                       508   ,,   T. Dannehy do.
                        54   ,,   W. Patterson do.
                       134   ,,   J. Baxter   do.
                      3557   ,,   J. Slater (slightly).

Captain Saltmarshe and Lieutenant Grierson were " particularly mentioned " for gallant conduct on this occasion, and the former received a Brevet-Majority for his services. The killed and wounded were all carried from the field by Major Ryan's detachment. The action of Pukekohe, though on a small scale, was of a severe nature, the enemy being in considerable strength and well armed. All the wounds were gun-shot wounds.

On October 2 Captain A. B. Wright's company was engaged at Poutoko, near New Plymouth, but suffered no loss. Favourable mention of Captain Wright and his men was made by Colonel Warre, C.B., commanding in Taranaki.

In November 1863 the regiment was employed in an expedition under Colonel Carey, Royal Irish Regiment, which was conveyed by steamer to Hauraki on the Firth of the Thames, destroyed a Maori base of operations at Pukorokoro, and established a line of posts between the Firth of the Thames and the Waikato river. The expedition did some hard and useful work, but saw no fighting.

In the same month a force under the personal command of Lieutenant-General Cameron advanced into the Waikato country and fought a severe action at Rangariri on November 20 and 21. The British casualties amounted to thirty-nine killed and ninety-three wounded, and the Maoris lost heavily. General Cameron received the honour of K.C.B. on this occason.[1]

In February 1864 Sir Duncan Cameron concentrated a force for an advance against the Maori positions at and near Rangiawhia. The British force totalled about 1050 of all ranks, and the strength of the Seventieth included in it was eighteen officers and 380 other ranks. The regiment was now commanded by Lieutenant-Colonel Mulock, recently promoted to that rank vice Colonel Galloway, promoted Major-General. Major-General Galloway had on promotion been appointed to organise and command the militia and volunteers in the province of Auckland. Colonel Chute had retired on half-pay in 1863, and was now in command of the troops stationed in Australia.

After some delay, caused by transport difficulties, the force under Sir Duncan Cameron marched from camp Te Rore to Rangiawhia on the night of February 20, 1864, and captured the settlement with slight loss early on the 21st. On the morning of the 22nd it was discovered that the enemy had advanced to Haeirini, close to the British camp, and General Cameron at once marched out to attack him. The enemy's skirmishers were found a mile in advance of his position, lining a hedge,

---

[1] Among rewards granted to the troops in New Zealand at this stage of the war, Captain A. Saltmarshe and Captain G. R. Greaves of the Seventieth received the brevet rank of Major.

Sergeant A. E. Curtis, V.C., 2nd Bn., The East Surrey Regiment.

and were driven out " in the most spirited manner " by two companies of the Seventieth. The skirmishers were driven by the Seventieth companies into the road, down which they were pursued by the mounted men of the column. Meanwhile the 50th Regiment, supported by the 65th and the remainder of the Seventieth, assaulted the main position, which extended about 400 yards. The position was brilliantly carried by the 50th, and the success had an important effect, the Maoris abandoning a series of fortified positions in Waikato which could not have been captured without heavy loss. In his despatch General Cameron expressed his satisfaction with the troops, and thanked Lieutenant-Colonel Mulock, commanding the Seventieth, Captain and Brevet-Major Greaves, D.A.Q.M.G. and Captain Travers, who " ably conducted the transport duties with the field force." The casualties of the regiment at Rangiawhia were slight ; No. 197 Private J. Morris being severely wounded, and No. 1789 Sergeant J. Dunn and No. 3260 Private I. Muggeridge slightly wounded.

While the regiment was engaged in Waikato, Captain A. B. Wright's company was also actively employed in Taranaki. On March 25 Colonel Warre, C.B., commanding in that district, successfully attacked a strong Maori position at Kaitake. Colonel Warre's dispositions were bold and able, and an important success was achieved by him with very slight loss. Captain Wright's company had no casualties. It may be noted that a detachment of Otago volunteers took part in the capture of Kaitake.[1]

On March 30, 1864, 300 Maori insurgents of Waikato made a bold attempt to recapture the village of Orakau. They were, however, promptly attacked by Brigadier-General Carey, commanding the nearest station, who with a small force completely surrounded the Maori position, but failed on April 1 in an attempt to assault it. General Carey was re-inforced on the same day by the dispatch of 200 officers and men from Headquarters, the detachment including three officers and ninety-four of other ranks of the Seventieth, under Captain Cay. An April 2 the Maori position was no longer tenable, and as

---

[1] The 4th (Otago) Regiment of New Zealand is to-day allied to the East Surrey Regiment, a happy reminder of the Maori War.

women and children were known to be present, permission was offered to the Maoris to send them out into safety. The Maoris, however, refused the offer and declared that they would all fight to the death. Shortly afterwards the Pah was attacked and carried, but the surviving Maoris forced their way through the weak cordon of troops and escaped capture in the work. They were, however, pursued, and lost heavily while retiring, about 120 being killed and thirty-three taken prisoners. The British casualties were sixteen killed and fifty-two wounded; the detachment of the Seventieth losing No. 306 Private Thomas Maskell, killed, and No. 985 Private G. Courtney and No. 932 Private P. Pettit wounded. Captain Cay was favourably mentioned in Brevet-General Carey's report, and No. 854 Private George Dowling subsequently received a silver medal for distinguished conduct in the field, being the first soldier so decorated in the Seventieth. Private Dowling showed exceptional courage and determination in carrying a wounded comrade to safety under a heavy fire.

At the beginning of May 1864 the Seventieth was stationed in the posts on the Waikato river, but on the 28th of that month was transferred by sea to Taranaki, where reinforcements were required. A detachment of the regiment, under Major Ryan, remained however with the force under General Cameron, and did good service at the unfortunate action at the Gate Pah, near Tauranga, on the east coast. In the attack on the Gate Pah Major Ryan's detachment, which numbered 170 men of various regiments, was extended close up to the Maori position, with orders to keep down the fire of the rifle pits and to follow the assaulting column into the Pah. In Sir Duncan Cameron's report to the War Office, Major Ryan's services are thus detailed : " I must also specially mention the name of Major Ryan, 70th Regiment, who after covering the advance of the assaulting column with his detachment, followed into the work, and with Captain Jenkins, H.M.S. *Miranda*, was one of the last to leave it."

On June 21 a severe defeat was inflicted at Te Rangi, near the Gate Pah, on the Maoris by a force of about 800 men, chiefly of the 43rd and 68th Regiments, under Colonel Greer. The Maoris lost very heavily, and the winter rains setting in soon afterwards, active operations practically ceased.

THE NEW ZEALAND WAR

In October 1864 two detachments of the Seventieth (226 of all ranks, under Major Rutherford, and 151 under Brevet-Major Saltmarshe) took part in a successful expedition under Colonel Warre, C.B., against Te Arei Pah in Taranaki. The troops performed good service, making long marches over very heavy ground, but there was little fighting and the Seventieth sustained no casualties. In his report Colonel Warre spoke in high terms of Majors Ryan, Rutherford, and Saltmarshe, and of the willingness and steadiness of the men of the regiment.

The war still continuing, though in a somewhat desultory manner, the Seventieth found itself broken up early in 1865. On February 1 four companies under Major Rutherford were despatched by sea to Wanganui, a port to the south of New Plymouth, where they joined a column under Colonel Warre, C.B. In April two more companies, with a strength of 154 of all ranks, proceeded as part of a small column under Lieutenant-Colonel Mulock to establish a post at White Cliffs, some thirty miles north of New Plymouth. Eventually one of these companies, under Captain Ralston, was established at White Cliffs, and the other, under Captain Cay, formed a post at Opunaki, some forty miles to the south of New Plymouth. Captain Ralston's services in the White Cliffs expedition were favourably mentioned by Colonel Warre. On May 28 Major Rutherford's wing rejoined Headquarters at New Plymouth, whence three companies of the wing were immediately sent to Opunaki, where a force under Colonel Warre, C.B., was concentrated. On June 8, the two remaining companies of Major Rutherford's wing also joined Colonel Warre's column. After various operations of no great importance, a movable column under Lieutenant-Colonel Colvile, 43rd Light Infantry, was despatched on July 29 from New Plymouth to punish the rebel natives for repeated attacks made by them on the troops stationed at Warea, twenty-six miles to the south. On August 2 part of this column fought a sharp action at a village named Okea, in which a detachment of the Seventieth did good service.

Although his column only numbered some 220 of all ranks, Lieutenant-Colonel Colvile divided it into two detachments, despatching one entirely composed of officers and men of the Seventieth under

Brevet-Major Russell, 57th Regiment, to make a frontal attack on the Maori position, while the other under his own command attempted to take the position in rear. Owing to a miscalculation of the time required by the two detachments for their march, Major Russell's small column came in touch with the enemy single-handed. On approaching Okea, Major Russell posted picquets on four small hills which commanded the surrounding country, and sent Captain Cay forward with sixty rank-and-file of the Seventieth to reconnoitre the village. On reaching the village Captain Cay found it strongly occupied, but he at once charged with the bayonet and took the Maoris so much by surprise that they fled, leaving thirteen dead on the ground. Captain Cay then fell back on the main body, and as soon as he had joined Major Russell the Maoris closed in on the little column on all sides, firing with unusual precision and steadiness. Major Russell's detachment then fell back slowly to meet Lieutenant-Colonel Colvile's column, and being hotly followed up by the Maoris was compelled to make several stands, in one of which Lieutenant Bally was killed. In his report to Lieutenant-Colonel Colvile on the proceedings Major Russell expressed his satisfaction at the judgment shown by Captain Cay, and Lieutenant-Colonel Colvile, in his despatch to General Sir Duncan Cameron, also thanked Captain Cay, "for the very gallant manner in which he rushed the enemy's position, which he held with an inferior force and inflicted severe loss on the enemy." Lieutenant-Colonel Colvile adds: "I deeply regret the death of Lieutenant Bally, 70th Regiment, who was shot whilst performing his duty most nobly."

Major Russell also made special mention of Lieutenant Tylden, and of Sergeants Howe and Clority, all of the Seventieth Regiment.

In Captain Cay's own report of his capture of Okea he brought to notice "the conspicuous gallantry of Lieutenant Tylden, who was the first to enter the enemy's position, and was severely wounded in two places while leading on his company."

The following casualties occurred in this sharp action:

Killed—4.
    Lieutenant Henry Bally.
    No. 376 Private George Smith.
    ,, 350 ,, Charles Ralph.
    ,, 819 ,, John Brown.

THE NEW ZEALAND WAR

Wounded—6.

Lieutenant Charles R. Tylden (severely).
No. 371 Private John Lawton do.
„ 368 „ Samuel Royal do.
„ 316 „ John Ward do.
„ 2767 „ Patrick Maley do.
„ 350 „ John Saville do.

All the wounds were caused by musket shots.

Captain Eustace Cay was promoted Brevet-Major for his services at Okea.

Soon after the action of Okea a total change of policy was adopted regarding the Maori War. The Home Government, with the concurrence of that of New Zealand, decided on the withdrawal of the first five regiments on the roster for home, the second of these being the Seventieth. In August 1865, therefore, the regiment was withdrawn from Taranaki and concentrated at Napier, and in December it marched to Camp Otahuhu.

Early in January 1866 the Seventieth left New Zealand in two divisions, and arrived at Dover on March 28 and April 7, each division then marching to Shorncliffe, where the regiment was to be stationed.

The Maori campaigns in New Zealand, though of considerable duration, had not been as arduous as those of the British army frequently are. The enemy, though exceptionally brave, was not numerous nor very skilful, and the climate was very good. As an instance, the strength of the regiment on December 1, 1863, was 726 of all ranks, of whom all but seventeen men, several of whom were wounded, were fit for duty.

In addition to the rewards already mentioned, a medal was granted to the regiment for the Maori War, and Lieutenant-Colonel Mulock received the honour of a Companionship of the Bath. Brevet-Major Greaves, who had served on the staff throughout the war and had been repeatedly mentioned in despatches for forward gallantry and conspicuous ability, received further promotion to the rank of Lieutenant-Colonel. In addition to Lieut.-Colonel Greaves, the officers in the following roll received the New Zealand medal, as did 795 non-commissioned officers and men.

ROLL OF OFFICERS OF THE SEVENTIETH REGIMENT WHO RECEIVED THE MEDAL FOR NEW ZEALAND.

Lieut.-Colonel T. E. Mulock, C.B.
Major G. A. Ryan.
,, A. J. O. Rutherford.
Captain and Bt. Major A. Saltmarshe.
Captain W. H. Ralston.
,, A. B. Wright.
,, T. D. Backhouse.
,, H. Leake.
,, C. Roger.
,, A. C. H. Tovey.
,, E. Cay (Brevet-Major).
,, H. Hill.
,, J. A. Tighe.
Lieutenant A. S. Gilbert.
,, G. C. Cuppage.
,, H. E. Whidborne.
,, C. R. Tylden.
,, R. A. Clarke.
Lieutenant J. R. Collins
,, W. S. F. Feneran.
,, H. F. Greatwood.
,, R. S. Riddell.
,, C. W. Howard.
,, G. Young.
,, C. F. Green.
,, and Adjt. N. Huskisson.
,, E. Pearson.
Ensign T. G. B. Lennard.
,, L. Hornby.
,, H. B. Travers.
Paymaster M. Thompson.
Qr.-Master W. Nevell.
Surgeon G. C. Meikleham.
,, D. C. Wodsworth.
Assistant Surgeon T. O. Hession.

CHAPTER XVIII

INDIAN SERVICE—THE SECOND AFGHAN WAR

Home Service—India again—Peshawar and Cherat in 1875—Nowshera and Multan—The second Afghan war—The Dera Bugti desert—The advance on Kandahar—The march to the Helmand—The return to Kandahar and return march to India through Tal and Chotiali—The Seventieth becomes the Second Battalion East Surrey Regiment.

THE stay of the Seventieth at Shorncliffe was very short, the right wing of the regiment marching to Dover in July, followed by the left wing and Headquarters in August; and in April 1867 another change of station took place, the regiment being moved to North Camp, Aldershot.

On August of this year new colours were presented to the regiment by Lady Scarlett, wife of General the Hon. Sir J. Yorke Scarlett, commanding at Aldershot. These colours are still in use. The presentation was the occasion of a great gathering of old members of the regiment, several old officers and pensioners coming from far distant places in order to be present. The old colours were deposited in All Saints Church, Aldershot. In November 1766 Colonel Mulock, C.B., retired on full pay and was succeeded in the command by Brevet Lieut.-Colonel Ryan, who himself retired a few months later.

In October 1867 the honour " Guadeloupe " was granted to the regiment " in commemoration of the distinguished part which the flank companies took in the recapture of the Island of Guadeloupe under Sir George Beckwith in 1810."[1] On October 8, 1867, the Seventieth, under Lieut.-Colonel W. S. Cooper (who had succeeded to the com-

---

[1] Extract from Horse Guards' letter dated October 31, 1867, from the Adjutant-General to Lieut.-Colonel W. Cooper, commanding Seventieth Regiment.

mand on April 17 of that year on the retirement of Lieut.-Colonel Ryan), left Aldershot for the Northern District, Headquarters being stationed at Ashton-under-Lyne, with detachments at Carlisle and Bury.

On May 8, 1868, General Sir G. W. Paty, Colonel of the regiment, died. He was succeeded in the Colonelcy by Major-General Charles Hastings Doyle. General Paty had held the Colonelcy fourteen years.

The regiment, under Lieut.-Colonel Cooper, embarked at Liverpool on October 4, 1868, for service in Ireland and landed at Cork on October 8. Headquarters were stationed at Kinsale, and five companies furnished garrisons at various out-stations.

On October 10, 1870, Major-General Sir Henry Knight Storks was appointed Colonel of the regiment, vice Lieut.-General Sir Charles Hastings Doyle, K.C.M.G., transferred to the 87th Royal Irish Fusiliers.

The Seventieth remained in Ireland until October 1871, earning while in that country the good opinion of the military authorities and much popularity in its various stations. In consequence a large number of Irish recruits joined the regiment, which contained many Irishmen until the establishment of its depôt at Kingston-on-Thames in 1875 and the gradual development of the territorial system filled the ranks with men of Surrey.

On September 1, 1871, the regiment, being under orders for India, had its establishment raised to 1032 of all ranks, and at the end of the month the two depôt companies proceeded to Aldershot to be attached to the 100th Regiment. On October 5 the regiment itself left Dublin for Cork and on the following day embarked under Colonel Cooper in Her Majesty's Troopship *Crocodile*. After a prosperous voyage in which no casualty occurred, the regiment arrived at Bombay on November 9, whence it proceeded by rail to Deolali to be supplied with Indian equipment. After two days at Deolali the regiment went by rail to Lahore, whence it started on December 2 by march route to Rawal Pindi. During the hot weather of 1872 the regiment had two companies stationed at Bara Gali, and a detachment of seventy-seven of all ranks at Marri.

On August 14, 1872, a change of commanding officer occurred, Brevet-Colonel W. Cooper exchanging with Lieut.-Colonel H. de R. Pigott of the 19th Regiment. Lieut.-Colonel Pigott, the last officer who obtained command of the Seventieth under the purchase system, remained its commander for many years, being one of the twelve purchase Lieut.-Colonels who were removed from their regiments by a Royal Warrant in 1880. Lieut.-Colonel Pigott assumed command of the regiment in November 1872, and in the following month took it to the camp of exercise at Hassan Abdal, where it remained until February 13, 1873, on which day it returned to Rawal Pindi. The Seventieth remained at this station until January 1875, during which time hardly any changes took place in its ranks. The health of the regiment was good, and very few non-commissioned officers and men completed their term of service. The only additions to the strength of the regiment were caused by the arrival of two sergeants and twenty-five men from the depôt at Aldershot, and by volunteering from regiments leaving India. When, therefore, the Seventieth left Rawal Pindi for Peshawar on January 11, 1875, it was a seasoned regiment fit for any duty ; and in the able hands of Lieut.-Colonel Pigott it had attained a high state of discipline and efficiency. General the Right Honble. Sir Henry Knight Storks, Colonel of the Regiment, died on September 6, 1874, and was succeeded in the Colonelcy by General Thomas James Galloway, an old officer of the Seventieth.

In February 1875 a draft of sixty young soldiers arrived from the depôt. These were principally men enlisted for six years' colour service and six years in the Army reserve. The draft was in point of fact composed of men of good physique who turned out good soldiers, but they were received with much disfavour by the long-service men of the regiment, who, like all soldiers, disliked innovations.

During its first hot weather at Peshawar the Seventieth had no detachment in barracks in the hills. A detachment, varying in strength from 100 to 200 men, was placed under canvas at Cherat, but owing to the great heat of this year it was found necessary to exchange parties of men from time to time between Cherat and Peshawar, and the health of the regiment was a good deal tried. In the latter months of the year malarial fever of a very bad type laid hold of the regiment. Few died, but sickness was very great. The regimental records state that only five men escaped the epidemic, and large numbers undoubtedly had their constitutions permanently injured.

In December 1875 Captain de Coetlogon's company marched to Nowshera to take over charge of the infantry barracks, and in

February 1876 Headquarters and the remaining seven companies also marched to that station. At the end of the month Captain H. C. Darley's company marched to Fort Attock, there to be stationed.

On April 13, 1876, Headquarters, with eight [1] officers and 250 of other ranks, left Nowshera under sudden orders for Cherat, which little station was threatened by the Afridi tribes. They marched unopposed, but on the second day's march a few shots were fired at the rear-guard under Sub-Lieutenant H. W. Pearse, while in a narrow valley. In accordance with orders no notice was taken of the shots fired, and no further attack was made by the Afridis. The detachment at Cherat was for a time in a dangerous position, but in May detachments from the regiments at Peshawar were sent up and precautions could be relaxed. The Afridis were, however, in a disturbed state, two soldiers at Cherat were murdered during the hot weather, and a column was sent out from Peshawar to threaten punishment. In the following year the Jowaki expedition settled this part of the frontier for a time. A few days after Headquarters marched to Cherat, two companies under Captain de Coetlogon and Lieutenant Boothby were sent to Marri for the hot weather. A virulent outbreak of cholera occurred at Marri in July, and the detachment of the Seventieth lost Lieutenant Boothby and eleven men. About the same time seven men died of heat apoplexy at Nowshera.

In October 1876 Major Miller's company marched to Dera Ismail Khan, and Captain de Coetlogon's company to Multan, to relieve companies of the 92nd Highlanders; and on December 13 Headquarters and five companies marched from Nowshera to Multan, picking up at Rawal Pindi the remaining company from Marri. The length of the march was 454 miles, and it was completed on February 1, 1877.

The Seventieth remained at Multan until September 30, 1878, on which date Headquarters and seven companies, under Lieut.-Colonel H. de R. Pigott, marched with other troops for Quetta, orders having been received one week earlier to strengthen the garrison of that place and to be in readiness for a further move. The remaining company,

---

[1] Lieut.-Colonel H. de R. Pigott, Captain R. S. Riddell, Lieutenants F. H. Maturin, A. W. Munsey (Adjutant), H. M. P. Hawkes, Sub-Lieutenant H. W. Pearse, Major and Paymaster G. E. Huddleston, Quartermaster A. Jones.

INDIAN SERVICE—THE SECOND AFGHAN WAR

which was stationed at Dera Ismail Khan, was ordered to rejoin Headquarters during the march.

THE SECOND AFGHAN WAR

The causes that led to the second Afghan War are too involved for explanation in a regimental history. It must be sufficient to say that for two years before war actually broke out relations between Afghanistan and India had been strained nearly to the breaking-point, and that matters reached a climax in 1878 on the reception of a Russian Mission at Kabul. At this moment affairs in Europe were so disturbed that a war between Great Britain and Russia seemed almost inevitable, and it was therefore considered impossible to permit the Amir of Afghanistan to concede to Russia a sign of intimate friendship which he had consistently denied to the British.[1]

A Mission to the Amir with a strong escort was therefore despatched from Peshawar under Sir Neville Chamberlain in September 1878, but on the advance party reaching Fort Ali Masjid, on the Afghan frontier, passage to Kabul was formally refused. An ultimatum was then sent to Amir Sher Ali, and no reply having been received by the prescribed day, November 20, 1878, war was declared against the Amir on the following day. Hostilities having been for some time expected, no time was lost, and on November 21 three strong columns of British troops crossed the Afghan frontier at widely-separated points and began a rapid advance on Kabul and Kandahar, the two principal cities of Eastern Afghanistan. The three lines of advance were as follows—(1) From Peshawar, through the Khaibar Pass and Jalalabad on Kabul. (2) From Kohat, through the Kurram Valley, also on Kabul. (3) From Quetta, through the Khojak and Gwajha Passes on Kandahar.

The Seventieth Regiment having been allotted to the 3rd or southern column, we are only concerned with its movements, which began with the despatch of reinforcements, under Major-General M. A. S. Biddulph, C.B., to Quetta at the end of September 1878. The Seventieth, as has been stated, marched from Multan on September 30, two companies acting throughout the march as escort to E 4, the battery of Field Artillery stationed at Multan. On arrival at

[1] "Official Account of the Second Afghan War, 1878-80."

Dera Ghazi Khan the regiment was joined by the company from Dera Ismail Khan, under Lieutenant Ringwood, the numbers present with the regiment being then twelve officers, thirty-five sergeants, and 583 drummers, rank-and-file. The weakness of the regiment in officers and men was attributable to the epidemic of malarial fever at Peshawar in 1875, and to the fact that on leaving that station the regiment, instead of being sent for a time to a hill station, had been stationed successively at Nowshera and Multan, two of the hottest places in India. When therefore the Seventieth set off for Quetta, more than 200 men and several officers were stationed in various convalescent depôts, and other officers were on sick leave in England.

The officers present with Headquarters on leaving Dera Ghazi Khan were Colonel Pigott, Captains Hornby and Riddell (Acting Paymaster), Lieutenants Burnaby (acting Adjutant), Grey-Smith, Ringwood, Couper, Lumsden, Delamain, Sub-Lieutenant Carruthers, Surgeon-Major Whylock and Surgeon Maurice Knox. Surgeon Knox, a most popular officer, was, it may be mentioned, the last remaining medical officer who had been an officer of the Seventieth regiment.

The march from Multan to Quetta proved a very trying experience for the regiment, starting as it did in impaired health. The weather was extremely hot, and the crossing of the rivers Chenab and Indus was a severe trial, followed by a long and most arduous march across the Dera Bugti desert and up the Bolan Pass. The single-fly tents into which the men were crowded, in order to economise carriage, gave no adequate protection from the sun, and an even greater trial was the extreme scarcity and bad quality of the drinking water in the Dera Bugti desert.

Passing over the details of the march, it may suffice to say that the Headquarters of the regiment arrived at Quetta on November 16, and remained there till November 22, on which day the two companies escorting E 4 marched into Quetta in good health. These companies had been caught up a fortnight earlier by Major (Brevet-Lieut.-Colonel) Ralston, Lieutenant Pearse, and Sub-Lieutenant Hunter, who had found their way from Multan in pursuit of the regiment. The two first-named officers had resigned appointments in order to rejoin for active service.

On November 27 the Seventieth, forming part of a small column,

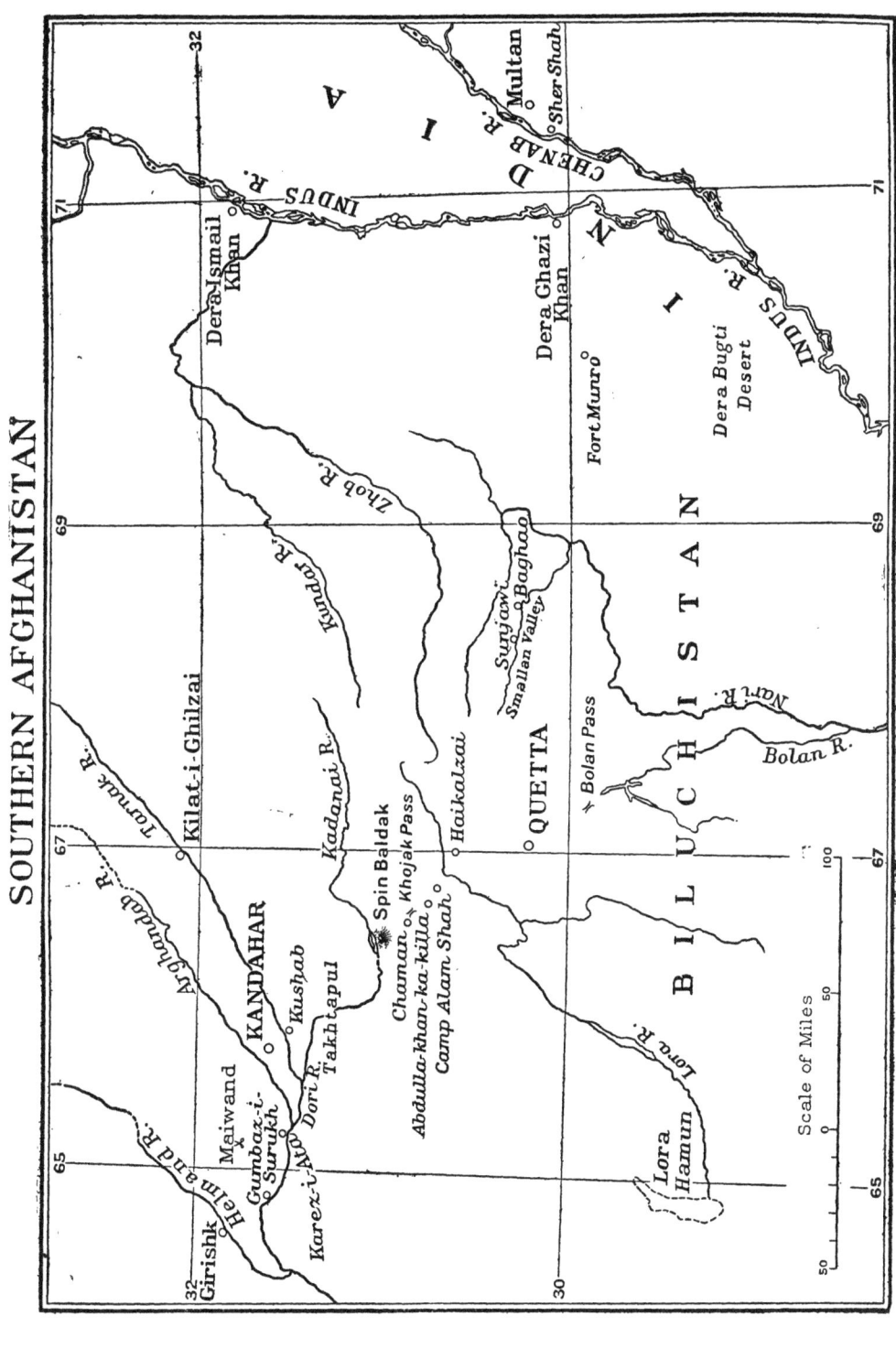

arrived at Haikalzai, at which place a British force suffered a reverse in the first Afghan War, but no enemy now appeared to bar the road. General Biddulph, however, had as yet no sufficient force available for an attack on the Khojak range, which lay close before him. The little column had no artillery with it, and the 32nd Pioneers, which had been stationed for some time at Quetta, was in a sickly state.

During the halt at Haikalzai (November 27 to December 6) Colonel Pigott gave the regiment running drill every morning early, and a longer parade later in the day. The rest from marching, combined with hard exercise in a cool climate, resulted in a great improvement in the health of the regiment. The only disadvantage of the running drill was that most of the men's boots were worn out, and could not be replaced. On December 6 the two companies escorting E 4 Battery marched into Haikalzai and rejoined the regiment, which marched on December 10 to Camp Alam Shah. Here Private Toogood was severely wounded by a Ghazi, but recovered from his wounds. The Ghazi was tried by a drum-head court-martial, and having been sentenced to death, was shot by a firing party of the Seventieth on December 11.

On December 12 the regiment made a short forward march and encamped in the mouth of the Khojak Pass, and such were the difficulties of the ground and the shortness of transport that it was not until December 24 that the right wing reached the head of the pass. During the interval a good deal of work had been done by the regiment in improving the roadway through the pass, but the chief cause of delay was the insufficiency of transport. Camels had died in immense numbers, chiefly from want of proper care, food and clothing. The transport problem had not at this time been much studied, and the lessons of the war of 1839 had apparently all been forgotten. Later on, after terrible suffering endured by the unhappy camels, and considerable hardships inflicted on the troops, the transport became efficiently organised and well managed. The faults mentioned were not attributable to the transport officers with the army, who all did their best in most difficult circumstances.

While Major-General Biddulph's force was in the neighbourhood of the Khojak range, a signalling party furnished by the Seventieth was stationed under Lieutenant Grey-Smith on one of the highest peaks of the range. The signallers, being insufficiently clad, suffered severely from the cold, and Lieutenant Grey-Smith's health was permanently injured. He and his party did excellent service.

On Christmas Day 1878, the Seventieth marched over the Khojak Pass. An extract from the diary of the officer on baggage guard that day may be of interest ; " I was on baggage guard and had desperate work to get everything over : camels falling down at every yard : many of them we actually held up and pushed along. There was not a single spare one, and I ended by putting two loads into *dhoolis*, one of which was carried by the bearers and the other by our own men." On the following day a large fatigue party of the regiment, under Lieutenant Pearse, was employed for twelve hours in lowering the artillery down a slide, the road being unfit for guns. A few gunners went down the slide with each gun and limber, to steer and steady them, the weight being taken by the infantry fatigue party by means of long drag ropes. Three complete batteries of artillery with all their stores and ammunition were lowered this day without an accident. The men of the Seventieth worked splendidly, without any food, the *bhistis* having thrown away the water with which the dinners should have been cooked, although warned that no water was obtainable at the summit. Lieutenant Pearse ordered the *bhistis* to be flogged, but the men with great good nature begged them off in consideration of their usual good service. It must be remembered that this incident occurred to ill-clad men working in bitterly cold weather at a height of 7000 feet.

The Seventieth remained at Chaman, at the northern exit of the Khojak Pass until January 4, 1879, when it marched thirteen miles to Spin Baldak. The Quetta Division had now been brigaded, and the Seventieth, with the 19th Punjab Infantry and the 30th Bombay Infantry (Jacob's Rifles) formed the 1st Infantry Brigade, under Brigadier-General R. Lacy. The Brigade-Major was Captain M. H. Nicholson, who afterwards rose to distinction.

On January 5 the cavalry covering the advance came in contact in the Takhtapul Valley with a large but inefficient body of Afghan horse, who were easily dispersed with considerable loss. The British cavalry, which was well handled, had two officers and nine men wounded. On January 6 General Stewart's two divisions, which had hitherto moved on separate roads, united at Abdur Rahman. In this march the Seventieth passed the scene of the cavalry action of the previous day, and the writer noted in his diary that he saw the bodies of nine or ten Afghans and one dead horse lying near the road.

On January 7 a further advance was made to Kushab, about seven miles south of Kandahar. The troops, to this moment, had hoped for a fight at that city, and were greatly disappointed to learn that it had surrendered. The governor with the small regular garrison had fled to Herat, no adequate preparations having been made to defend Kandahar against the overwhelming British force. Kandahar was a large and densely populated city, surrounded by a wall thirty feet high, with strong gateways. It would certainly have been able to make but a poor defence against General Stewart's force, but if the inhabitants had meant fighting the town could have been held house by house, and to reduce it would have entailed heavy loss of life. On January 8 General Stewart marched through Kandahar at the head of the 1st Brigade of each of his divisions. In consideration of the Seventieth having been the first British regiment to take the field, the lead was given to the 1st Brigade, 2nd Division, and the Seventieth was therefore the first British regiment to enter Kandahar since its evacuation in 1841.

The two brigades, after marching through the city, encamped about one and a half miles east of it, where they remained halted until January 15. It was now evident that there would be no fighting in southern Afghanistan, and there seemed no probability of need to assist the Khaibar and Kurram columns in their advance towards Kabul. Both columns had had a fair amount of fighting, but were effecting a gradual advance which evidently would in time break down the Afghan resistance. (Amir Sher Ali Khan, it may here be mentioned, died on February 21, and was succeeded by his son, Amir Muhammad Yakub Khan).

There being no necessity at Kandahar for the large force under General Stewart, and the country being unable to furnish supplies for it, it was decided that it should be dispersed. An adequate garrison was therefore detailed for the city of Kandahar, and on January 15 General Stewart, with the greater part of the 1st Division, set out eastward for Kilat-i-Ghilzai, a fortress on the Kabul Road. On the following day Major-General Biddulph, with part of the 2nd Division, marched westward to explore the whole country up to Girishk on the river Helmand, an important strategical position on the road to Herat. General Biddulph only took one infantry brigade with him, the 1st, which was increased in strength and efficiency by the addition to it of the 32nd Bengal Pioneers. The 29th Bombay Infantry took the place of the 30th, which remained at Kandahar.

The Seventieth, with the 1st Brigade, marched westward, keeping to the Herat road, close to the river Aghandab. On arriving at Karez-i-Ata (thirty-one miles from Kandahar) the force divided, a small column being despatched on the northern road to Girishk. The infantry brigade continued its march on the southern road to Gumbaz-i-Surukh, the most westerly point reached by the Seventieth in Afghanistan. This place was reached on January 27, and owing to the impossibility of obtaining supplies and to the weakness of the half-starved transport animals, the brigade halted, being then only some eighteen miles from the river Helmand. The 32nd Pioneers and a wing of the 19th Native Infantry were then sent to strengthen the northern column, which arrived at Girishk on February 2, and remained there till February 13. The remainder of Brigadier-General Lacy's Brigade marched on January 31 back towards Karez-i-Ata, where they could be conveniently supplied from Kandahar. The Seventieth had been on half rations of bread and groceries for several days, but a full meat ration was always obtainable in Afghanistan. On January 30 Major J. R. Collins and Lieutenant R. L. C. Birch joined the regiment from Multan, after a long and adventurous journey, and on arrival at Karez-i-Ata on February 1 a much-needed supply of uniform, boots, and other stores reached the Seventieth, whose only clothing since leaving Multan had been two suits of white drills, dyed khaki-colour.

The regiment remained west of Kandahar until February 26, having heard on the 14th that it was shortly to return to India on the reduction of the force in Southern Afghanistan.

The rumour of this reduction caused much unrest among the Afghans, and the rear-guard of General Biddulph's Division was attacked by irregulars of the Zamindawar district at Khusk-i-Nahkud, close to the ground on which the battle of Maiwand was afterwards fought. The rear-guard defeated their assailants, but Major Reynolds of the Sind Horse and four men of the cavalry were killed, and Colonel Malcolmson and twenty-three men were wounded. This was the only action of any serious nature shared in by General Biddulph's Division, and it will be observed that the attack was made directly the force was known to be retiring on Kandahar. The people round this city were also highly excited, and on February 7 a Ghazi attack was made on the camp there, in which Private Turner of the Seventieth was very severely wounded.[1]

On February 26 the regiment marched to Kandahar, and two days later left that city on its return march to India. On arriving in camp the regiment was joined by a draft from the depôt at Kingston-on-Thames of three officers and 162 non-commissioned officers and men. The officers with the draft were Captain (Local Major) Miller, Captain Brander, and 2nd Lieutenant Davies. The Seventieth arrived at Chaman on March 7 and was delayed there by heavy rain until March 11, when it began to cross the Khojak Pass by detachments. On the following day two companies, to which all the young soldiers and sickly men in the regiment had been temporarily posted, set out for India *via* the Bolan Pass, under Lieut.-Colonel Ralston, who had been ordered to resume his command of a hill depôt. With the Bolan party also went the following officers—Lieutenants Burnaby, Couper, Birch, Delamain, 2nd Lieutenants Smith and Waldron.

The Headquarters of the regiment, numbering eighteen officers and 512 sergeants, rank-and-file, having arrived at Abdulla Khan Ka Killa, the camp at the southern mouth of Khojah Pass, on March 16, set off on March 18 on its eastward march to India through unexplored country. On March 20 Lieutenant Harris, from Multan, and 2nd Lieutenant Wynyard, from England, joined Headquarters. The names of the officers with the Headquarters and six companies of the Seventieth while serving in the Chotiali Field Force were as follows:

FIELD OFFICERS. Colonel Pigott and Major J. R. Collins.
CAPTAINS. Local Major Miller and Captain Maturin.
LIEUTENANTS. Harris, Pearse, Ringwood, and Lumsden.
2ND LIEUTENANTS. Rodwell, Carruthers, Hunter, Davies, Bolton, Wynyard and Nagle (Adjutant).
QUARTERMASTER. A. Jones.
SURGEON-MAJORS. O'Brien and McCarthy; and SURGEON. M. Knox.[2]

[1] Private Turner had been left in hospital at Kandahar when the regiment marched towards the Helmand.
[2] In addition to the officers mentioned as having served in Afghanistan with the regiment, Captain F. F. F. Roupell served in Northern Afghanistan and received the medal.

Lieutenant Grey-Smith, who had served on Major-General Biddulph's Staff as signalling officer since the arrival of the regiment at Quetta in November 1878, also served in the Chotiali Field Force in charge of signallers.

The force under Major-General Biddulph, which was now about to open up the mountain region lying between Quetta and Multan, much of which was quite unknown to Europeans, was divided into three columns. The Seventieth was posted to the 3rd Column, commanded by Brigadier-General T. Nuthall, the other units of the column being two squadrons of the 8th Bengal Cavalry, four companies of the 12th Bengal Infantry and a company of Bengal Sappers and Miners. Great hope was felt in the regiment that if the warlike Maris and other tribes whose territory was about to be penetrated showed any fight, they would attack the rear column. In the event, however, only one attempt to check the Chotiali force was made, at Baghao in the Smallan valley, where on April 6, 1879, a vigorous attack was made on the leading column, commanded by Major Keen, 1st Punjab Infantry. The attack was beaten off with considerable loss to the enemy, Major Keen's column sustaining a few casualties.

The only warlike incident with which the rear column was concerned occurred on April 1, when the column was encamped in low-lying ground at Sunjawi. A body of Ghazis, said to have numbered 300, planned a rush into the camp, but at the appointed moment only one man devoted himself to death. This Ghazi, a mere youth armed only with a sword bayonet, sharpened however like a razor, rushed on alone, killed one native follower and wounded a sapper and miner. He then headed for the camp of the Seventieth, but came across a double sentry in front of the quarter guard. The nearest man of the pair, Private Cook of F Company, was severely wounded, but the other sentry ran up and bayoneted the Ghazi.

After a march in rapidly increasing heat through country, some of which was beautiful and finely wooded, and some in fertile but sultry plains, the regiment on April 23 arrived at Dera Gazi Khan, one of the frontier stations of the Punjab. The heat during the six previous marches had been great, and on April 18 two band boys, who had gone through the whole campaign in good health, died of exhaustion. The men of the band, it may be noted, were all serving in the ranks, while those of the boys who had been allowed to go on active service did duty as acting drummers.

The regiment crossed the river Indus on April 24 and the Chenab on the 27th. The heat was very great, but no harm was done by it. On the 27th the regiment received a farewell visit from Major-General Biddulph, who complimented Colonel Pigott and the officers on the healthy and hard appearance of all ranks. In his narrative of the march, published in the Journal of the Royal United Service Institution, Major-General Biddulph writes: " I found here the 70th, about to take the train, and I took the opportunity of inspecting the hospital. It was satisfactory to find that, notwithstanding the low condition of the men at starting, now at the close of a march of about 1200 miles, there were few sick and no serious cases of illness."

The Seventieth arrived at Multan on April 29, having entrained in great heat at Sher Shah on the previous evening; and reached Ambala on the morning of April 30. Here ended the hottest train journey that the Seventieth is ever likely to face, and it was followed by a very trying though short march, which began at midnight on May 1. The destination of the regiment was Sabathu, with a wing detached to Dagshai, but this short distance was not to be passed with impunity. On the second march from Ambala a fatal case of cholera occurred, followed by a death on the next day caused by an accidental over-dose of medicine, administered by the soldier himself. On the fourth march a second death from cholera occurred, and when on the following day, May 6, the regiment caught up the Bolan party at Dharampur, it was found that they had lost a sergeant and three privates, all from cholera. The regiment therefore when actually in sight of the comfortable barracks at Sabathu was compelled to pitch a cholera camp, in which it remained until May 23, when all danger had ceased. There were three more cases of cholera while the regiment lay at Dharampur, but happily none were fatal. The deaths between Multan and Sabathu, consequently, numbered seven, and of the cholera cases six out of nine were fatal. During the Afghan campaign the regiment had buried one sergeant, one corporal and sixteen privates, between the dates of its start from and return to Multan.

Colonel H. de R. Pigott was mentioned in despatches for his services during the campaign, as were Lieut.-Colonel Ralston, Lieutenant Grey

INDIAN SERVICE—THE SECOND AFGHAN WAR

Smith, and 2nd Lieutenant Nagle. In recognition of its services the Seventieth Regiment was permitted to bear on its colours the words, "Afghanistan 1878-1879"; and a medal was issued to 846 non-commissioned officers and men, and to the officers mentioned in the following roll:—

SEVENTIETH (SURREY) REGIMENT, AFGHAN MEDAL ROLL

Lieut-Colonel and Brevet-Colonel H. de R. Pigott.	Lieutenant W. A. G. Smith.
Lieut.-Colonel W. H. Ralston.	Sub-Lieutenant A. E. Couper.
Major J. R. Collins.	2nd Lieutenant M. G. Bolton.
Captain E. R. S. Brander.	,, G. A. Carruthers.
,, L. Hornby.	,, R. D. C. Davies.
,, F. H. Maturin.	,, J. G. Hunter.
,, J. J. C. Miller.	,, E. H. Rodwell.
,, R. S. Riddell.	,, H. L. Smith.
,, F. E. F. Roupell.	,, H. F. K. Waldron.
Lieutenant R. L. C. Birch.	,, R. D. Wynyard.
,, R. B. Burnaby.	2nd Lieutenant and Adjutant J. Nagle.
,, F. G. Delamain.	Qr.-Master A. Jones.
,, R. H. W. H. Harris.	Surgeon-Major J. McCarthy.
,, H. R. W. Lumsden.	,, J. O'Brien.
,, H. W. Pearse.	,, W. S. Whylock.
,, H. Ringwood.	Surgeon J. Hayes.
	,, M. Knox.

The regiment remained at Sabathu and Dagshai until near the end of the year 1879, when marching orders were received for Ferozepore. On arrival at Ambala, however, on January 2, 1880, the march was cancelled, and the regiment remained at Ambala until October of the same year, when it was moved by train to Dinapore.

On July 20, 1880, Colonel H. de R. Pigott retired from the command, being succeeded by Major and Brevet-Lieut.-Colonel W. H. Ralston. Colonel Pigott subsequently commanded the Liverpool Regimental District, and on retiring from the army in 1882, with the honorary rank of Major-General, emigrated to Canada, where he died in the year 1889. Colonel Pigott was a commanding officer of the old school. An accomplished soldier and a fine horseman, his stern system of discipline kept his regiment in a high state of efficiency and made a permanent impression on the characters of those who served under him.

While stationed at Dinapore, on July 1, 1881, under the re-organisation of the infantry which took effect from that date, the Seventieth Regiment lost its separate existence, and as the 2nd Battalion of the

East Surrey Regiment, returned once more to its old position of 2nd Battalion of the Thirty-First, which regiment now became the 1st Battalion East Surrey Regiment. Like the Thirty-First, the Seventieth also lost its old title of "Surrey" and the black facings which, being rare, the regiment valued highly.

For a few months after the amalgamation, the East Surrey Regiment possessed two Colonels, but General Thomas James Galloway dying during 1881, General the Right Honble. Sir Edward Lugard, G.C.B., Colonel of the 1st Battalion, became Colonel of the Regiment.

Sir Edward Lugard, whose distinguished services have already been recorded, retained the Colonelcy until his death on October 31, 1898, when General Sir George Richards Greaves, G.C.B., K.C.M.G., succeeded him. Sir George Greaves, an officer who in many campaigns had been distinguished by his energy and daring, had served for twenty-two years in the Seventieth Regiment.

PART III

HISTORY OF THE FIRST AND SECOND BATTALIONS THE EAST SURREY REGIMENT

JULY 1881 TO AUGUST 1914

*General the Right Honble. Sir Edward Lugard, G.C.B.,
Colonel of the East Surrey Regiment.*

CHAPTER XIX

Recent History of the 1st Battalion

Home service—A trip to Gibraltar—Nine months at Aldershot—Gibraltar again—A modern voyage to India—Peaceful service—Presentation of colours by Lord Roberts—Two years at Jersey—Ireland before the war.

In October 1881 the 1st Battalion left Dover for Ireland, and on arrival was stationed at Buttevant. The establishment at the time was very low, and the strength of the battalion was seventeen officers and 533 of other ranks. In the following month, however, the establishment was raised to twenty-four officers and 1016 of other ranks, and the battalion was quickly raised above this strength by the despatch of recruits from the depôt and by volunteering from other regimental districts. This rapid increase was in preparation of foreign service, and on August 2, 1882, the battalion embarked at Queenstown for Gibraltar, arriving there, after a fine passage, on the morning of August 6. This passage may well be compared with some recorded in the early history of the regiment.

In September 1882 the honour "Dettingen" was granted to the East Surrey Regiment in commemoration of the share in that battle borne by the Thirty-First Regiment in 1743. Change of air being apparently thought good for the 1st Battalion, it was sent home from Gibraltar in May 1883, eight months after its arrival there. The battalion was then stationed at Aldershot for nine months, returning to Gibraltar in February 1884. The reason for these movements cannot now be guessed.

After a somewhat similar period of service at Gibraltar the 1st Battalion, under Lieut.-Colonel George Bayley, embarked from Gibraltar for service in India in December 1884, in relief of the

2nd Battalion, which had been ordered on active service to Egypt.

In accordance with the arrangements newly introduced under the double battalion system, the 1st Battalion, on arrival at Suez, handed over 257 N.C.O.'s and men to the 2nd Battalion, receiving in exchange a draft of almost identical strength, of men liable for further Indian service. The 1st Battalion, after a good passage, landed in India on January 14, 1885, without sustaining any casualties on the voyage, a circumstance which shows the great improvement in the condition of the soldier brought about by modern conditions of military transport. The battalion proceeded by rail to Bareilly and thence marched to Ranikhet by wings, arriving there early in March. Eight months later (in November) the battalion marched *via* Moradabad and Delhi to take part in a camp of exercise between Delhi and Ambala. After the termination of the manœuvres, in January 1886, the battalion marched to Moradabad, where it remained encamped for three weeks, after which it again marched to Ranikhet, arriving there on March 5.

In December 1886 the battalion marched to Allahabad, a distance of 445 miles, and remained at that station for three years, marching in November 1889 to Calcutta. In January 1891 the battalion moved to Dum-Dum, finding a detachment of one company at Barrackpore. At the end of 1892 the battalion proceeded by route march to Agra, the distance of 667 miles being covered in fifty-seven marches. The strength of the battalion on arrival at Agra, February 14, 1893, was eighteen officers and 978 of other ranks. In the following month the battalion was armed with the Lee-Metford rifle, in place of the Martini-Henry rifle, which had been in use since April 1875.

Soon after the arrival of the battalion at Agra it was visited by enteric fever, which caused sixteen deaths, including those of Lieutenant Galloway and 2nd Lieutenant Van Someren; and in the hot weather of 1894 further deaths occurred from the same cause, including those of Lieutenant Rose and 2nd Lieutenants Walker and Lindsay. The 1st Battalion during its stay at Agra was commanded by Lieut.-Colonel and Brevet-Colonel Fitzroy Hart, C.B., under whom it earned a high reputation for efficiency. Colonel Hart completed[1] his period of command in June 1895 and was succeeded by Lieut.-Colonel F. F. F. Roupell, promoted from the 2nd Battalion.

In October 1896 the 1st Battalion moved to Jhansi and Nowgong, and almost immediately after arrival two more young officers, Lieutenant Goodridge and 2nd Lieutenant Fisher, died of enteric fever. Thus in less than four years the battalion had lost seven officers from this disease. In 1897 the battalion was again reported to be "in many respects exceptionally efficient and fit for field service," the individual intelligence and initiative shown by all ranks being especially observed.

In June 1899 Lieut.-Colonel Roupell was placed on half-pay on completion of his period of command, and was succeeded by Lieut.-Colonel W. J. H. Frodsham. In November of the same year the battalion moved to Lucknow, where it was stationed until, in January 1903, it was relieved by the 2nd Battalion from South Africa, and returned to England.

The Indian tour of the 1st Battalion had lasted more than nineteen years, and although the battalion had not had the good fortune to share in any campaign, it had maintained itself in a high state of efficiency for active service and had made consistent progress in war-training. A considerable number of officers and men had served as volunteers in minor campaigns on the Indian frontier, and towards the end of the South African War the 1st Battalion despatched a draft of four sergeants, six corporals and 140 privates, under Captain W. H. Paterson, to join the 2nd Battalion on active service.

On arrival in England in February 1903 the 1st Battalion was stationed in the Salamanca Barracks, Aldershot, where on May 26 of the same year, the battalion was presented with new colours by Field-Marshal Earl Roberts, K.G., the Commander-in-Chief of the Forces. The ceremony was of a most impressive nature, and in addressing the battalion Lord Roberts, in an inspiring speech,

---

[1] Colonel Arthur FitzRoy Hart, who subsequently became a Major-General and assumed the additional surname of Synnot, was a soldier of marked individuality and talent. To the end of his life he maintained the spirit of enterprise which had earned him distinction in many campaigns. In the South African War of 1899–1902 few general officers saw harder fighting or served in more widely scattered parts of the extensive theatre of war than did Fitzroy Hart, and his name will long be remembered by the East Surrey Regiment as that of one of its most distinguished officers.

reminded his hearers of the long and distinguished record of the East Surrey Regiment. While alluding to the glories of Albuera, Lord Roberts did not overlook the heavy loss of life endured in the wars in the West Indies, and he ended by a kindly reference to the services of the 2nd Battalion of the regiment in Natal, and particularly at Pieter's Hill, where it had lost heavily. A large number of men and several officers who had served in South Africa were at this time serving in the 1st Battalion. In concluding his remarks, the Commander-in-Chief said : " You may indeed be proud of belonging to a regiment which during an existence of two hundred years has served with distinction in so many climes and in every quarter of the globe."

On June 21, 1903, Lieut.-Colonel Frodsham completed his period of command, and was succeeded by Lieut.-Colonel Herbert Ringwood, an officer who served with the 2nd Battalion in the Afghan War.

On July 13, 1904, the old colours of the Thirty-First (1st Battalion East Surrey) Regiment were laid up with every honour in the Parish Church of Kingston-on-Thames, in the presence of Viscount Midleton, the Lord-Lieutenant of Surrey, who personally handed the colours to the Vicar of Kingston for safe keeping in his church.

Lord Midleton, in his address, referred to the recent speech by Lord Roberts on the glorious record of duty of the East Surrey Regiment, and pointed out how closely the history of the regiment was identified with the growth of the British Empire. "Many a gallant lad," said Lord Midleton, " who had attended service in that church, had laid down his life for his country on the field without thought of self and far from home and relatives. Such as had died for their country fully deserved the glorious sentence, ' Well done, thou good and faithful servant.' " On its departure from Kingston after the ceremony at the Parish Church, the detachment of the East Surrey Regiment from Aldershot was greeted by the townsmen of Kingston-on-Thames with very great cordiality and enthusiasm.

In September 1905 the Sikh colours (four in number) which had been deposited at Huntingdon in 1867, were restored to the 1st Battalion and are now among the treasured possessions of the officers' mess.

In October 1905 the battalion left Aldershot for Jersey. During its stay in the camp it had borne a high character, particularly in regard to its marching and shooting. In the same month died, at the age of eighty-two, Mr. James Biffen, late a private of the Light Company of the Thirty-First, who had highly distinguished himself in the Sutlej campaign, and had captured a colour at the battle of Sobraon, killing the Sikh officer who bore it. A party from the regimental depôt at Kingston-on-Thames attended Mr. Biffen's funeral.

On June 21, 1907, Lieut.-Colonel Ringwood[1] retired from the army on completion of his period of command, and was succeeded by Lieutenant-Colonel H. L. Smith, D.S.O., who had seen much active service with the 2nd Battalion and had been severely wounded in South Africa.

In November 1908 the battalion left Jersey for Plymouth, where it was stationed for nearly two years, proceeding to Kinsale in September 1910 on the termination of the manœuvres at Salisbury Plain.

On June 21, 1911, Lieut.-Colonel H. L. Smith, D.S.O., completed his period of command and retired from the army, his successor being Lieut.-Colonel J. R. Longley, who had served in the South African War with the Mounted Infantry. Under Lieut.-Colonel Longley, as will some day be related, the 1st Battalion East Surrey Regiment fully maintained its long-established reputation in peace and war.

The battalion moved to Dublin in September 1912, and was still serving in that command on the outbreak of the war with Germany in August 1914.

---

[1] Lieut.-Colonel Ringwood, who died in March 1910, was the first secretary of the Surrey Territorial Association and did excellent service in that capacity. He also was the originator of the National Reserve.

CHAPTER XX

The Second Battalion at Suakin

The Second Battalion in Egypt 1884-5—At Suakin—Reconnaissance of Hashin—Engagement at Hashin and occupation of the post—Advance to Tamai.

WE left the 2nd Battalion at Dinapore (see page 350), at which station it remained until January 1884, marching on the 13th of that month for Bareilly, a distance of 495 miles. One death occurred during the march.

The stay of the battalion at Bareilly was destined to be a short one, for on August 13 orders were received to move to Egypt. On the following day Captain C. A. G. Cumine, a popular officer, was killed by a landslip while riding to visit the guards by night at the Hill Depôt at Naini Tal.

The battalion moved by wings to Deolali on August 29 and 30, 1884, and embarked at Bombay on H.M. Troopship *Himalaya* on September 10. Colonel Ralston being on leave, the battalion embarked under the command of Lieut.-Colonel J. R. Collins, the strength present on leaving India being twenty officers and 838 non-commissioned officers and men. A list of the officers who served in Egypt with the battalion is given on the opposite page.

The battalion disembarked at Suez on September 26 and on arrival at Cairo was quartered at Abbasiyeh, the women and children going on to England in the *Himalaya*.

On January 1, 1885, a draft of 259 men, under Lieutenant Thomas, left for Suez, there to join the 1st Battalion, which was on passage to India. A corresponding draft of 263 men was sent to Cairo by the 1st Battalion to join the 2nd Battalion.

Suakin, 1885

On February 7 the 2nd Battalion was ordered to hold itself in readiness to proceed to Suakin, a port in the Red Sea nearly due east of Berber, where a field-force of about 13,000 men was about to be formed under Lieutenant-General Sir Gerald Graham, V.C., for service in the Eastern Soudan. General Graham received orders direct from the Secretary of State for War, but he was instructed to consider himself under the command of General Lord Wolseley, then in command of the Nile expedition for the relief of General Charles Gordon and the Egyptian garrison at Khartum.

Sir Gerald Graham's field-force was charged with two special duties: (1) the defeat and dispersal of the Hadendowa Arabs under Osman Digna, who represented the Mahdi in the country between Suakin and Berber, and was at the head of a formidable and fanatical army; and (2) the protection of the construction of a railway from Suakin towards Berber. Lord Wolseley's intention was to use, at a subsequent date, the Suakin-Berber railway as a line of supply after Berber itself had been captured; but at the time that the Suakin force was being formed it was not intended that the railway should be pushed more than about half-way to Berber.

ROLL OF OFFICERS WHO SERVED AT SUAKIN, 1885

LIEUTENANT-COLONELS
    Ralston, W. H. (Brevet-Colonel). Appointed C.B.
    Collins, J. R.

MAJORS
    Hornby, L. Promoted Brevet Lieut.-Colonel.
    Maturin, F. H.   ditto.
    Freeman, T. A.
    Burnaby, R. B.

CAPTAINS
    Frodsham, W. J. H. (Adjutant.)
    Couper, A. E.
    Smith, H. L.

LIEUTENANTS
    Dunsterville, A. B.
    White, F.
    Bayliss, E. G.
    Birch, J. R. K. Severely wounded. (Promoted in Cheshire Regiment.)
    Sloman, H. S.

Whiffin, H. E.
Ellis, W. H.
Bell, C. P. L.
Grant, K. M. P.

MAJOR AND PAYMASTER
Riddell, Sir R. S., Bart.

In addition to the above, Lieutenant M. G. Bolton served in the Nile Expedition, receiving the medal.

To carry out his orders General Graham was provided with the following force:

Four squadrons of British Cavalry.
One battalion of Mounted Infantry.
One regiment of Bengal Cavalry.
Three batteries of Artillery.
Three brigades of Infantry.
(1) The Guards Brigade (3 battalions)
(2) The 2nd Brigade   (4   ,,   )
(3) The Indian Brigade (3   ,,   )

The force was also liberally supplied with Royal Engineers, commissariat and transport, hospitals, etc., and especially elaborate arrangements were made for the supply of the water that would be required for all movements in the arid scene of operations. General Graham was provided with a large staff, at the head of which was Major-General Sir George Greaves, whose long and distinguished service in the regiment has already been mentioned.

The 2nd Battalion East Surrey Regiment, with the 1st Battalion Shropshire Light Infantry, the 1st Battalion Berkshire Regiment, and the Battalion Royal Marine Light Infantry formed the 2nd Brigade, their commander being Major-General Sir J. C. McNeill, V.C., K.C.B.

On arrival at Suakin on February 27, 1885, the battalion was encamped about a mile north of the town. Colonel Ralston had now resumed command of the battalion, which numbered nineteen officers and 792 of other ranks. Prior to the arrival of the remainder of the force, the troops at Suakin were considerably troubled at night by "snipers," and on March 7 Private Green was wounded. On the following day, the main body having arrived, the battalion joined the 2nd Brigade. On March 9 the rear-guard of the battalion was suddenly attacked by a small party of Arabs at about 3 A.M., and Lance-Corporal

J. Daniels, Private W. Roebuck, and Private J. Arbon received spear wounds. In view of the short period of comparatively cool weather available, Lieut.-General Graham had been ordered by Lord Wolseley to hasten the commencement of operations as much as possible. Consequently every shoulder was put to the wheel, and early on March 19 General Graham's Cavalry, Mounted Infantry, and Native Infantry advanced on its first enterprise against Osman Digna. The enemy, said to be about 7000 strong, held the line Tamai, Hashin, Handub, the main position being at Tamai. It was necessary to clear this position before any work on the railway could be undertaken. The task undertaken on March 19 was the reconnaissance of the position at Hashin, distant about ten miles from Suakin, and the operations of the day disclosed the difficult nature of the ground. A few casualties were sustained, which included Lieutenant J. R. K. Birch, East Surrey Regiment Mounted Infantry, who was severely wounded. Lieutenant Birch's conduct on this occasion was highly commended, and he was subsequently promoted captain in the Cheshire Regiment. Private R. Birfoot and Private H. Stanley, of the East Surrey Mounted Infantry, also were wounded.

On March 20, the day after the reconnaissance, the field-force, with a strength of 8200 men and ten guns, advanced on Hashin, the infantry forming three sides of a large square within which marched the guns, engineers, and transport. On arriving near Hashin the Royal Engineers and Madras Sappers, guarded by the 2nd East Surrey Regiment, proceeded to mark out and construct redoubts on four low hills, where it was intended to establish a post. Meanwhile the remainder of the force attacked the Arab position on two other hills, and after a short action drove the enemy from the hills towards Tamai. When, however, the British force was withdrawn from the captured position, they were briskly followed up by the Arabs and sustained some casualties. The force then withdrew to Suakin, leaving the 2nd East Surrey Regiment in the post which, together with the engineers, they had constructed during the day. The British losses in the action of Hashin were nine killed and thirty-nine wounded.

Hashin having been occupied, the next step decided on by General Graham was an attack on Tamai, Osman Digna's headquarters; and as the distance was too great for the operation to be performed in one march, it was necessary to form an intermediate camp about eight miles from Suakin. A force under Sir J. McNeill was despatched on March 22 on this duty, but the march proving a difficult one, General McNeill selected a halting place at a place about six miles out, called Tofrik. While the British force was engaged in making two zaribas, at about 3 P.M., they were suddenly attacked and sustained over 300 casualties. The attack was, however, repulsed, and the Arab losses were very heavy, over 1500 being killed on the spot in twenty minutes' fighting. No further serious attempt on the zaribas was made and they were held, as proposed, by three battalions, daily convoys with strong escorts being sent out from Suakin to keep up the necessary water-supply.

On March 25 the zariba at Hashin, being no longer required, was demolished, and the 2nd East Surrey Regiment and other troops stationed there were withdrawn. On the following day the battalion formed part of the escort of a convoy to Tofrik. The infantry, as usual, marched in a large square enclosing the convoy, the East Surreys being on the right. An attack on the convoy was repulsed with some loss, Private H. Phillips of the battalion being wounded. The battalion subsequently took part in several similar marches to and from Tofrik. By March 31 the Tofrik zaribas had been adequately stocked with water, and further operations could be undertaken. Tamai was reconnoitred on April 1, and an advance against that place was made on April 2 by a force of slightly over 8000 men. The force marched to Tesela Hill, three miles from Tamai, where a large zariba was formed for the main body under protection of the hill, which was held during the night by the 2nd East Surrey Regiment. Some sniping took place during the night, and Private H. Bradley of the battalion was killed. Tamai was entered on April 3 with slight opposition, but the enemy then retired to the hills, into which it was impossible to follow him. The force was then withdrawn by Sir Gerald Graham to the Tofrik zariba. Private J. Munn of the battalion was wounded this day.

On April 4 the field-force returned to Suakin, and the strength and enterprise of the enemy were so much reduced that the garrison of Tofrik could be reduced to one battalion of Indian Infantry, with two Gardner guns and a small naval detachment.

The Arab tribes near Suakin were now ready to make peace, only desiring assurance that Suakin would not be abandoned by the British, and the operations resolved themselves into minor movements against small local gatherings. Mobile troops being required, a camel corps was formed on April 15, to which the battalion contributed thirty-one non-commissioned officers and men.

The capture of Khartum and the death of General Gordon at the end of January 1885 rendered the future conduct of affairs in Egypt very uncertain. The British Government for a time adhered to its intention of advancing in the coming cold weather to recapture Khartum and destroy the power of the Mahdi, but meanwhile it was decided to hold no territory south of the province of Dongola and to reduce the troops in the eastern Soudan to an adequate garrison of Suakin. Lord Wolseley, having returned from the front to Cairo, proceeded to Suakin, where he arrived on May 2, to inspect the place and decide on the necessary strength of the garrison. In view of the condition of Imperial affairs, it had, however, already been decided to abandon the advances intended in the autumn, and on May 11 Lord Wolseley issued orders for the evacuation of the Soudan. These orders were executed with all possible speed, the large body of troops on the Nile being withdrawn under the supervision of Sir Redvers Buller. The Suakin field-force was broken up, the 2nd East Surrey Regiment leaving that place on May 23, and arriving at Alexandria six days later.

Before taking his departure from Suakin Lieut.-General Sir Gerard Graham had addressed the battalion on parade, speaking in the highest terms of its conduct and services; and in his despatches, or those of Lord Wolseley, the following officers and non-commissioned officers of the battalion received mention: Colonel W. H. Ralston, Lieut.-Colonel J. R. Collins, Major L. Hornby, Major F. H. Maturin, Lieutenant J. R. K. Birch; Orderly Room Quartermaster-Sergeant S. R. Curson, Quartermaster-Sergeant J. Cranwitch. Colonel Ralston received a Companionship of the Bath, and Majors Hornby and Maturin Brevet-Lieut.-Colonelcies.

In commemoration of the campaign the East Surrey Regiment was permitted to bear the words " Suakin 1885 " on its colours. The Egyptian Medal with clasp " Suakin 1885 " was conferred on the officers, non-commissioned officers and men who had taken part in the operations. A nominal roll of the officers appears on page 359.

In June 1885 Colonel Ralston, C.B.,[1] completed his term of command, and was succeeded by Lieut.-Colonel J. R. Collins. Two months later the 2nd Battalion left Alexandria for England, and landed at Portsmouth on September 7, proceeding on the same day to Dover, where it was quartered in the South-Front Barracks. The strength of the battalion on arrival was thirteen officers and 686 of other ranks, the casualties at Suakin having been slight. One officer and nine men had been killed and wounded, six men had died, and seventy-one had been invalided home.

On June 30, 1887, Colonel J. R. Collins was placed on half-pay, on completing six years' service as Lieut.-Colonel. He was succeeded in the command by Lieut.-Colonel L. Hornby. In April 1888 the battalion proceeded to Guernsey, and in February 1891 to Ireland, with Headquarters at Tipperary. On June 21 of this year Colonel Hornby retired from the command. He was succeeded by Colonel D. D. Chadwick, from the 1st Battalion, who retired on December 14, and was succeeded by Lieut.-Colonel R. W. F. Phillips.

In February 1893 the Battalion was ordered to Malta for a short tour of duty while on the home establishment. It arrived at Malta on March 4 and was stationed in that island until October 1895, when it returned to England and was again stationed at Dover.

In December 1896 Lieut.-Colonel R. H. W. H. Harris succeeded Colonel Phillips in command of the battalion, which in June 1898 proceeded under him to Inkerman Barracks, Woking. Here the battalion remained, forming part of Major-General Hildyard's Brigade at Aldershot, until in October 1899 it received orders to mobilize for the South African War.

---

[1] Colonel Ralston was in due course promoted to the rank of Major-General and was appointed Colonel of the Cheshire Regiment. He died in April 1914. General Ralston was a most genial and kind-hearted man and a good soldier. He was universally beloved in the East Surrey Regiment.

CHAPTER XXI

THE 2ND BATTALION IN THE SOUTH AFRICAN WAR

The Second Battalion on home service—The South African war—The 2nd Brigade sent to Natal—The action of Willow Grange or Brynbella Hill—The action of Colenso—The Spion Kop operations—The action of Vaal Krantz—The relief of Ladysmith—Cingolo and Monte Cristo—The fight on Wynne's Hills—Battle of Pieter's Hill—Skirmish at Elandslaagte—The Volunteer Service Company—The clearing of northern Natal—Operations in the Biggarsberg—Action of Alleman's Nek—Occupation of Standerton—On the lines of communication—Minor enterprises—With Colonel Colville's column—With Colonel Rimington's column—On the line again—Record of the Mounted Infantry company—End of the war—The battalion goes to India.

THE 2nd Battalion East Surrey Regiment received orders to mobilize for active service on October 7, 1899, and on October 11 was officially informed that it was to proceed to South Africa with the remainder of Major-General Hildyard's Brigade. The three other battalions of the Brigade were the 2nd battalion The Queen's, and 2nd Battalion Devon, and the 2nd Battalion the West Yorkshire Regiment. The four battalions had served together under General Hildyard for a considerable time, and had been associated in brigade training and in the summer manœuvres, which had been on a large scale They were therefore well acquainted with one another and with their brigadier and his methods, an advantage shared by no other infantry brigade that went in 1899 to South Africa. Major-General Hildyard's Brigade was numbered the 2nd, and with the 1st (Guards) Brigade was intended to join the 1st Division, under Lieut.-General Lord Methuen, but owing to the course of events this disposition was changed, the 2nd Brigade proceeding, as will be seen, to Natal, where it joined Leiut.-General Clery's 2nd Division.

On mobilization the 2nd East Surrey were in excellent health and hard training, the distance of their barracks from those of the remaining battalions of the Brigade having thrown on them the necessity of much extra marching. The serving soldiers, though young, were of good physique, and were of a decidedly high standard of education and general intelligence. 378 young soldiers, who were under twenty years of age, were left in England to mature for active service, and the battalion was brought up above war strength by the mobilization of 683 1st class army reservists belonging to the regiment, the greater part of whom had served as young soldiers in the 2nd Battalion, and had completed their colour service with the 1st Battalion in India. The reservists were permitted as far as possible, to choose the company in which they would serve, and as they all found friends and acquaintances in the ranks they settled down in their places as easily and readily as if they had never left the colours. The reservists, it may be added, were a very fine set of soldiers, steady and well conducted almost to a man. Their average age was twenty-eight years.

The battalion embarked at Southampton on October 20, 1899, under the command of Lieut.-Colonel R. H. W. H. Harris, the battalion staff consisting of Major H. W. Pearse, 2nd in command,[1] Lieutenant F. W King-Church, Adjutant; Lieutenant C. W. Fletcher, Quartermaster; and Lieutenant L. W. Johnson, Transport Officer. The strength on embarkation was twenty-six officers, one warrant officer, fifty-eight sergeants, fifty-three corporals, sixteen drummers and 1038 privates. The Headquarters of the battalion and seven companies were conveyed on the hired transport *Lismore Castle*, while the eighth company, under Major H. L. Smith, which could not be accommodated in the *Lismore Castle*, was conveyed in the *Harlech Castle*, which sailed the same day. The three other battalions and the Staff of the 2nd Brigade also sailed on October 20, as did the Guards' Brigade. The voyage to Cape Town was a favourable one as regards weather, and though the heat in the tropics was somewhat severely felt in the crowded transport, health continued good throughout the voyage. Every effort was made to keep officers and men in training by a constant succession of physical drills and other exercises, and also to impart instruction in fire control and to give practice in shooting for the benefit

---

[1] The appointment of 2nd in command of a regiment of cavalry or battalion of infantry existed at this period. It was subsequently abandoned.

Gallant Conduct of four soldiers of the 31st Regiment in Afghanistan.

of the reserve non-commissioned officers and men, some of whom had left the colours nearly four years before the mobilization. Just as the *Lismore Castle* was clearing the wharf at Southampton to the strains of the National Anthem, newspapers were thrown on board, with a brief account of the action of Talana, fought that morning in northern Natal. The news caused great excitement and was discussed throughout the voyage, most fearing that the war would be over before the battalion could reach South Africa. The only port of call was Las Palmas, reached on October 26, where no trustworthy news could be obtained, and it was not until November 5 that a homeward bound liner was met, which signalled : " Several battles in Natal, Symons successful." The *Lismore Castle* anchored off Cape Town at 8 P.M. on November 10, but no one came on board and no one was permitted to land.

Early next morning the transport was boarded by various staff officers, from whom details were obtained as to the actions at Talana and Elandslaagte, of the capture of Colonel Carleton's column at Nicholson's Nek, and of the commencement of the siege of Ladysmith. Lieut.-Colonel Harris was also informed that the battalion, with the rest of the brigade, was to sail as soon as possible for Natal, where invasion by the Boers was in full progress, and reinforcements were urgently needed. The *Lismore Castle* lost no time and sailed at 10 A.M., within an hour of the receipt of her orders, and in spite of rough and unpleasant weather crossed the bar of Durban Harbour soon after daybreak on November 14. No time was lost in disembarkation and the battalion left Durban for Pietermaritzburg in three trains as soon as the very limited baggage and stores could be landed. The journey to Maritzburg, as the town is usually called, was very interesting, for the battalion was loudly cheered at every railway station, and at several the inhabitants had kindly collected refreshments and fruit which they freely gave to their deliverers, who had arrived only just in time to anticipate the intended Boer raiding of southern Natal. The battalion arrived at Maritzburg in the evening, and received rough accommodation in the empty barracks ; on November 15, field equipment and transport were drawn from the ordnance stores, and at daybreak on November 16, the battalion again entrained for the north, its precise destination being for the moment uncertain.

A few words of explanation must now be given of the situation in Natal. President Kruger's ultimatum, couched in terms which made war inevitable, was sent to the British Government on October 9, 1899, and the Boers being fully prepared, the first shot in the South African War was fired on October 12 at Kraaipan, forty miles south of Mafeking, when the Boers captured an armoured train taking guns and ammunition to Colonel Baden-Powell. This was in the far western portion of the seat of the coming war, and on the same day, in the eastern portion, the Boers, about 23,000 strong, invaded Natal, threatening the advanced British force of 4000 men with eighteen guns at Dundee under Major-General Sir W. Penn Symons. Early on October 20 (the day on which the East Surrey sailed from Southampton), General Symons attacked a Boer force of 3500 men under Commandant Lukas Meyer in a strong position on Talana Hill. After heavy fighting the Boer position was captured, Major-General Symons, a gallant soldier, being mortally wounded. The command devolved on Brigadier-General Yule, who at first intended to hold his ground, but eventually decided to retire on Ladysmith, where Sir George White, the Commander-in-Chief in Natal, was at the head of some 8000 men. Sir George had only arrived at Ladysmith from Gibraltar on October 11.

Ladysmith was now strongly threatened with attack, both from the west, where a force of Free State Boers had entered Natal through the neighbouring passes in the Drakensberg, and from the east, where a force from the Transvaal had seized Elandslaagte, where it threatened the line of retirement of Yule's column. Hastily fortifying the hills round Ladysmith, General White was able to send out a column under Major-General French and Colonel Ian Hamilton, which on October 21 completely defeated the Elandslaagte Boers, capturing many prisoners and two guns, and clearing the road for Yule, whose troops after a fine march entered Ladysmith on October 26.

On October 30, Sir George White fought the unsuccessful action of Lombard's Kop, outside Ladysmith, an unfortunate episode of which was the capture of a column about 1000 strong, under Colonel Carleton, at Nicholson's Nek. It was now evident that the garrison of Ladysmith, if not withdrawn, would probably be besieged. Sir George White decided to hold Ladysmith, and with the object of keeping open his communications with Maritzburg, sent a small column

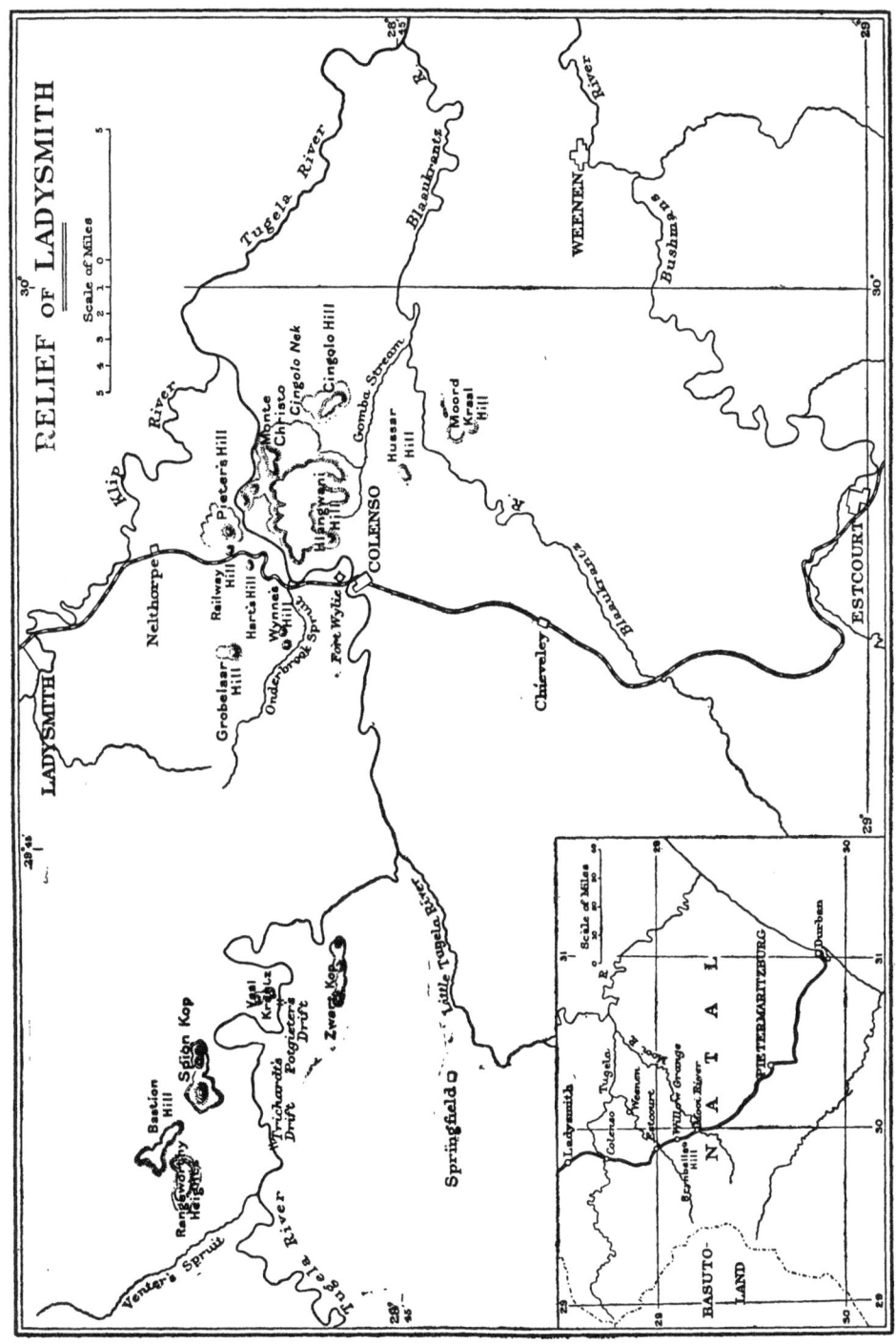

to Colenso to secure the crossing over the river Tugela. This was done on the evening of October 30, after Sir George White's reverse at Lombard's Kop. Colenso was held until the night of November 2, when the garrison of 1200 men, being seriously threatened by a superior force, was compelled to retire southward on Estcourt.

On November 9 the Boers made their first attack on Ladysmith, which was easily repulsed, and four days later, on hearing a false report that British reinforcements had arrived at Frere, a force of 4200 Boers, the flower of the invading army, assembled at Colenso with orders to push southward and examine the situation. At their head were Commandant-General Joubert, the Transvaal Commander-in-Chief, and "Fighting-General" Louis Botha, the young Commandant who was destined to make so great a reputation during the war.

On November 15 Commandant-General Joubert's expeditionary force achieved its first success by the capture of an armoured train from Frere, which was taken near Chieveley station, and later in the same day Major-General Hildyard arrived at Estcourt and assumed the command. With him came the 2nd West Yorkshire, the first regiment of his brigade to land, and on the following day the 2nd East Surrey also reached Estcourt.

Owing to the want of mounted men, it was found very difficult to locate and watch the Boer forces, and in consequence a large proportion of the infantry at Estcourt had to be held under arms at night, and work fell heavily on the newly-landed troops. On the night of November 17 an attack was expected, and the battalion furnished four and a half companies (out of seven) for out-post duty. The out-posts were relieved at 9 A.M. on the 18th, but no sooner had they marched back to camp than the Boers were seen all round Estcourt, riding about in a threatening manner. The out-post companies had therefore to hurry back, breakfastless, to their posts, which they did with the utmost cheerfulness. A section of D Company, under Lieutenant North, fired during the morning at a party of Boers who were examining a bridge on the railway about 1200 yards from them. These were the first shots fired by the Battalion in South Africa. Later in the day, the Boers, who numbered about 3000 men and were the main body under General Joubert, and were in full view of our picquets, were fired on by a naval 12-pounder gun, the presence of which was a surprise to them. They showed no inclination to fight, but sheered off to the westward, with the evident intention of getting on our lines of communication further south. Another body numbering 1200 men, under Commandant David Joubert, son of the General, was away to the east, moving southward on the Weenen Road, and later, as will be seen, these two bodies joined hands and placed themselves boldly between Major-General Hildyard's 5000 men at Estcourt and Major-General Barton's force of nearly equal strength, which was at Mooi River, twenty-three miles south. By 2 P.M. it was evident that no attack would be made on Estcourt, and the out-posts were reduced to their usual day strength.

On November 18 the 2nd West Yorkshire, under Colonel Walter Kitchener, were sent to guard Willow-Grange Station, seven and a half miles distant, but on the 19th orders were received from General Clery at Maritzburg to withdraw them, and, in the afternoon of that day, four companies of the East Surrey under Lieut.-Colonel Harris marched to Willow-Grange to assist, if necessary, in the withdrawal of the West Yorkshire. Warning was received in the evening that a night attack would be made on Estcourt during the absence of so considerable a part of the garrison, and Lieutenant L. W. Johnson rode out, by order of Major-General Hildyard, to recall Lieut.-Colonel Harris' wing. Lieutenant Johnson performed this duty, but he and his guide narrowly escaped being shot.

On November 20 the laager of the 1200 Boers under David Joubert was located, and a night attack on it was planned. The force detailed for this attack was commanded by Colonel Hinde of the Border Regiment, and consisted of 430 mounted men under Lieut.-Colonel Martyr; five companies Border Regiment, under Major Pelly, and three companies 2nd East Surrey, under Major Pearse. The infantry marched off at 9.45 P.M. and arrived at Willow-Grange railway station a little before 3 A.M. on November 21, but on further investigation the Boer position was considered too strong to be attacked. Colonel Hinde's column advanced, however, to examine the ground towards Mooi River, the East Surrey companies leading. The ground proved very hilly and the heat was great. The men, who had only landed after a long voyage a week previously, were much exhausted, but marched pluckily. At about 9 A.M. General Hildyard ordered the column to return to Willow-Grange, where it arrived at 11. Soon afterwards Boer scouts appeared in all directions, but no attack was made. At 4 P.M. the column set out for Estcourt, where it arrived about 8.30 P.M., meeting on the road some troops who had been sent out to cover the march. This was a hard day's work, particularly for the three East Surrey companies, who had marched to within a short distance of Mooi River, but a much harder one was to come next day. Major-General Hildyard was now fully informed of the position of the Boer laager, which was on Brynbella Hill, west of Willow-Grange station, and determined to attack it by night on November 22. For this purpose he entrusted Colonel Walter Kitchener with a column composed as under :

No. 7 Battery R.F.A., four companies 2nd Queens, 2nd West Yorkshire, seven companies 2nd East Surrey, and the Durban Light Infantry—a battalion of Natal Volunteers. In the afternoon of November 22 this force advanced to Beacon Hill, a high hill about half-way between Estcourt and the Boer position. A naval 12-pounder gun was placed in position on the summit of Beacon Hill. Colonel Kitchener decided to attack the Boer position with his own regiment and the seven East Surrey companies, and that the remainder of the force under Colonel Hinde should support the attack and press it home as soon as it was daylight.

"Action of Willow-Grange" or "Brynbella Hill"

During the afternoon an unusually heavy shower of hail fell, and blotted the British troops from the sight of the Boers, and when the storm cleared, Colonel Hinde's troops were seen retiring, very widely extended, while the West Yorkshire and East Surrey lay hidden behind Beacon Hill. Most of the Boers believed that the whole British column was returning to Estcourt, but others thought differently. Just as the East Surrey companies were taking up their position in rear of Beacon Hill, the Boers fired two shells at a venture, which narrowly missed them, but did no harm. This was merely by way of clearing the hill or drawing fire in case a picquet might have been left behind, for, as has been said, most of the Boers refused to believe for a moment that English troops would remain in the open in such weather. Unfortunately this opinion was not shared by a

German officer who was in charge of the Boer guns. He was not satisfied that all the English troops had retired, and after long argument induced the Boers to remove their guns from the front to the rear of the position on Brynbella Hill.

Early in the night a thunderstorm of great severity delayed the advance, and when at 9 P.M. the leading East Surrey company (Captain White's) moved off along a narrow and slippery hill path, heavy rain was falling and the weather was bitterly cold. The night was then pitch dark, except for the frequent flashes of lightning, and the storm was said to be the worst experienced in Natal for many years. Two Boers were reported to have been killed by lightning on Brynbella Hill. The advance in these trying circumstances was very slow; heavy falls among the rocks were frequent, and great difficulty was experienced in keeping touch. Thanks largely to the assistance of Mr. Chapman, a Natal farmer who knew every inch of the ground and had patriotically offered his services as guide, the East Surrey eventually arrived at the rendezvous and met the West Yorkshire near the foot of Brynbella. Here a halt was made to enable both regiments to get into their assigned positions for the attack, and by Colonel Kitchener's orders mess-tins were left on the ground, so that the coming advance should be noiseless. The plan of attack was that of an advance of double companies, one company of each regiment moving on the right and left respectively of a wall which ran up to the nearest point of the Boer position, where a strong picquet was posted. This plan ensured the two battalions keeping touch in the darkness, and would also prevent their becoming intermingled should it be necessary to reinforce the leading lines from the rear. At the foot of the last ascent but one, an unfortunate incident occurred, which threatened to warn the Boers of the coming attack. A section of D Company East Surrey had been detached some little distance to the right to act as a flank-guard. The sky clearing and the moon coming out brilliantly, suddenly disclosed this party to an officer, who thought them to be a party of Boers and ordered them to be charged with the bayonet. Unfortunately a number of shots were fired, Privates Reeves and Hunter, East Surrey, and a man of the West Yorkshire being killed, and five other men wounded. The firing was quickly stopped and order restored, and Colonel Kitchener decided to press on the attack as if no misadventure had happened. The first line was already climbing the steep ascent of Brynbella, and, strange to say, did not hear the sound of firing so close in their rear, nor did the sound of it reach the Boer sentry at the top of the hill close by, though he was alert and on his post.

The front line, composed of a company of the West Yorkshire and G Company (Major Treeby's) of the East Surrey, was well led by Major Hobbs, the second in command of the West Yorkshire. It reached the top of the hill at about 3 A.M., and succeeded in surprising the Boer picquet. Their sentry shot the man on Major Hobbs' left hand, but was himself immediately killed. The picquet fell back rapidly across the plateau firing vigorously in order to check the pursuit and to alarm their main body, which, with the recently-removed guns, was laagered on the further portion of the hill, some 1300 yards to a mile distant. The second British line, also composed of one West Yorkshire and one East Surrey company, under Lieut.-Colonel Harris, closely supported the first, and in its turn was followed by the third line, similarly constituted, under Major Pearse. The capture of Brynbella Hill, a position of great strength, in such severe weather and after the unfortunate episode immediately before the assault, reflected equal credit on Colonel Kitchener, who persisted in his plan when many men would have abandoned the attempt, and on the troops under his command. The outbreak of firing was an incident such as has often marred night attacks, and that in fact always makes them hazardous operations. When it is remembered that the battalions engaged were largely composed of reservists, and that they had only been eight days on active service, their conduct in so quickly regaining their order and steadiness will be appreciated by all soldiers.

As soon as the captured plateau was completely cleared and examined, the troops were disposed round it for defence, pending the expected advance of the remainder of the force to attack the Boer main body. Three cheers were given, by arrangement, to warn the naval gun on Beacon Hill of the position of our troops. The sun soon came out and revived the shivering troops, who in their thin clothing had suffered much from cold during the night. Soon after daylight the Boers seemed to realise that they had no further advance to fear, and they soon opened a rifle and pom-pom fire, which became rapidly heavier as the burghers found suitable points from which to fire. The troops on Brynbella were out-numbered, and but for the protection of the wall which had directed their advance up the hill, their losses must have been very heavy, for the enemy round them were the flower of the Boer army. Colonel Kitchener, on learning that no further attack on the Boers was contemplated, at once made arrangements to retire from his dangerous position. Reserving the post of honour to his own battalion, he directed Lieut.-Colonel Harris to retire the East Surrey companies as quickly as possible, and to take up any suitable position near the foot of Brynbella to assist the West Yorkshire in their retirement. Part of the East Surrey, under Major Pearse, were ordered to retire in like manner by the same slope by which they had ascended, this proving to be very exposed ground. While the East Surrey were leaving the hill the West Yorkshire kept up a hot fire, during which they sustained considerable casualties, and when their turn for retirement came the task proved to be a most difficult one. On retiring they were followed up by the Boers, now in an advantageous position, and many must have been killed or captured but for the gallant support afforded by about 150 of the Imperial Light Horse and King's Royal Rifles Mounted Infantry, who rode nearly to the summit of the hill by way of a shoulder with a practicable slope. At the last hollow before the summit these fine troops dismounted, and going forward at a run covered the retirement of the exhausted infantry, who still clung to the wall that has so often been mentioned. There were few finer things done during the war than that ride of the Mounted Infantry and Imperial Light Horse up precipitous Brynbella to face the deadly fire of Joubert's 1200 picked men.

When once clear of Brynbella, the West Yorkshire and East Surrey soon passed through the extended lines of the Queen's and Border Regiments, which had advanced close up to the foot of the hill, and the whole force then returned to Estcourt, pursued by a well-aimed but ineffective shell fire from the Boer guns.

Although the attack on Brynbella failed to achieve its main object—the capture of Joubert's guns—it accomplished highly favourable results. The invading Boers were much shaken by the unexpected night attack, and almost immediately returned to Colenso, retiring, as stated in Sir Redvers Buller's despatch, " in a manner that was more of a rout than a retreat." " General Hildyard," continues the despatch, " Colonel Kitchener, and all concerned deserve the greatest credit for the manner in which this operation was planned and executed."

The casualties in the 2nd Battalion East Surrey at Brynbella were as follows :

Killed—2.
No. 2903, Private H. G. Hunter.
,, 2984, ,, T. E. Reeves.
Wounded—12.
Sergeant-Major J. Anderton.
No. 1788, Colour-Sergeant S. Briffitt.
,, 3547, Sergeant T. Hayes.
,, 5651, Private W. Brewer.
No. 3419, Private E. Finch.
,, 5377, ,, G. Mallon.
,, 2670, ,, F. Smith.
,, 2414, ,, C. Casey.
,, 5414, ,, F. Lacey.
,, 2505, ,, A. Otway.
,, 3549, ,, W. Ruttley.
,, 3473, ,, J. Whalebone.

On November 24 Privates Hunter and Reeves were buried at Estcourt, and early on Sunday, November 26, the Estcourt force made the first move towards clearing Natal of its invaders by advancing to Frere. The day was very hot and the advance was made with caution, as Commandant-General Joubert's force were still close at hand and the British were weak in mounted men. The march consequently took nine hours (8 A.M. to 5 P.M.), and the baggage did not arrive till 10 P.M. As the troops at Estcourt left that place, those from Mooi River marched in and took their place, and on November 28 the 2nd Devon marched to Frere and completed the 2nd Brigade. On the same day E Company 2nd East Surrey, under Major H. L. Smith, caught up the battalion, and on December 1, 2nd Lieutenant Alexander, joined from the 1st Battalion in India, and 2nd Lieutenants Stafford and Le Fleming from England, completing the establishment of officers. The halt at Frere lasted for some days, though the troops daily expected to advance, and it was not until December 13 that the bulk of the force moved on to Chieveley, leaving the 2nd Brigade at Frere till the 14th, when it marched along the railway line to a point two miles beyond Chieveley, where it joined the remainder of the infantry.

ACTION OF COLENSO. DECEMBER 15, 1899

Having struck its tents, and packed them and its light baggage on the ox-wagons, the 2nd Brigade marched off at 4 A.M. towards the village of Colenso, following the line of railway, but keeping on the left of it for a considerable distance. The 2nd Queen's and 2nd Devon formed the first line; the 2nd East Surrey, the second line; and the 2nd West Yorkshire, the third line. The task committed to the 2nd Brigade was to cross the river Tugela by the iron foot-bridge, or, if this were blown up by the Boers, by drifts (or fords) stated to exist close to the bridge. Having crossed the river, the brigade was to capture the enemy's position at Fort Wylie and on the neighbouring kopjes, all of which were known to be strongly entrenched. This was to be the main attack, and it was to be supported as follows: On the left, the 5th Brigade (under Major-General Fitz-Roy Hart)[1] was to cross the Tugela at the Bridle drift, and then to move along the left bank of the river on the kopjes that were the objective of the 2nd Brigade. On the right, the mounted Brigade (Earl of Dundonald) was to advance on Hlangwane Hill, supported by the 6th Brigade (Major-General Barton). Both these brigades were ordered to guard the right flank of the 2nd Brigade. The 4th Brigade (Major-General Hon. N. Lyttelton) was to support either the 5th or 2nd Brigade as might be required. The Royal Artillery and naval guns were divided among the three attacks, and the flanks of the army and the baggage were guarded by small bodies of cavalry.

As will be seen from the above summary of orders, it was clearly intended that the passage of the Tugela was to be forced, but unfortunately the plan failed at a very early stage in its proceedings, the 2nd Brigade alone carrying out the programme allotted to it until ordered to cease its advance. As this narrative is mainly concerned with the doings of the 2nd East Surrey it must suffice to say that disaster befell the troops on both flanks. On the left Major-General Hart's Brigade, wrongly led (probably through a misunderstanding) by a Kaffir guide, advanced into an exposed position close to the Tugela, and at a portion

---

[1] Major-General A. Fitz-Roy Hart, C.B., had passed his regimental service in the Thirty-First, and had commanded it in India. He had seen much active service on the staff, and was an officer of conspicuous daring and energy.

of the river where there was no drift. As soon as General Buller saw the mistake, he sent orders to Major-General Hart to retreat, and his brigade was eventually withdrawn after suffering considerable loss. On the right things went even worse. No. 1 Brigade Division of the Royal Field Artillery, with six naval 12-pounders, had been ordered to take up position at a point where they could prepare a crossing for the 2nd Brigade. Under the direction of Colonel Long, commanding the artillery in Natal, the two field batteries advanced to within 1250 yards of Fort Wylie and not much more than 1000 yards from the long Boer trenches along the bank of the Tugela. In consequence the batteries, though most gallantly fought, suffered heavily, the detachments after an hour's firing being reduced on an average to four men per gun. The naval guns were fought equally pluckily, but with much less loss. At about 8 A.M. Sir Redvers Buller decided to abandon the attempt to cross the Tugela, but, in order to enable Colonel Long's guns to be withdrawn, he ordered Major-General Hildyard to advance his two leading battalions, taking care not to become seriously engaged, and thus to facilitate the retirement of the guns.

Major-General Hildyard then ordered the 2nd Queen's, his leading battalion, to advance on Colenso, and the 2nd Devon to cross the line and move up to Colonel Long's guns. By 9.30 A.M. Colenso had been occupied by the Queen's, and the leading half-company of the Devon had reached the guns. Both battalions had advanced with the greatest gallantry under the fire of the whole Boer army defending the river line.

The 2nd East Surrey, forming the second line of the brigade, was ordered by Major-General Hildyard to adopt the following formation during its long advance over the base and open plain that lay before it: "Column of half-companies, extended to 6 paces, with an interval of 80 paces between half-companies." In this formation the battalion advanced for a considerable distance with slight loss, though under a heavy fire and without any cover while moving. When lying down, the innumerable ant-hills with which the ground was covered afforded much protection. Extensions and intervals were kept with the greatest accuracy, and perfect steadiness was shown during the advance and the subsequent retirement.

At about 9.30 A.M., the advance of the Devon towards Colonel

Long's guns carried them to the right of the railway, and soon afterwards Lieut.-Colonel Harris ordered the right half-companies of the East Surrey, under Major Pearse, to cross the line also in order to support the Devon. In order to gain some sheltered ground Major Pearse closed the right half-battalion somewhat on its leading half-company, thus conforming to the action of the left half-battalion, which then was occupying a long trench on the ridge overlooking Colenso. This trench had been dug about two months previously by the Durban Light Infantry, when it was intended to hold the crossing of the Tugela. At 10 A.M. Major-General Hildyard sent orders to the Queen's and Devon that they they were to retire through the 2nd East Surrey, but owing to the difficulty of carrying orders to infantry closely engaged, the retirement did not begin for a considerable time and took long in execution. The " Official History of the War in South Africa " thus describes it :—

" The retirement was carried out with coolness and precision under cover of the 2nd East Surrey, who were holding a shelter trench on the west and a donga on the East of the railway. The officers and men of the Queen's and Devon doubled back in small groups through their files. By 2.30 P.M. the 2nd Brigade, except a half-battalion of the East Surrey, was beyond the range of the enemy's guns and by 3.30 P.M. had reached camp. This half-battalion of the East Surrey, under command of Major H. W. Pearse, remained for more than an hour in position near the plate-layer's hut, hoping to cover the withdrawal of the detachments near the guns. Finally, finding that no more men fell back, and that his command was becoming isolated, Major Pearse also marched back to camp."

One incident of the retirement deserves record. The companies of the Queen's in Colenso retired from the village under a very heavy fire. When nearly all had passed through the East Surrey, Lieutenant Wade (Royal Lancaster Regiment, attached) was told by a staff officer that some wounded men were in want of help, and that he would do well to move a section forward to cover their retirement. He at once advanced with the left section of B Company East Surrey, and moved beyond the wounded men. Lieutenant Wade and his party, after holding a house in Colenso village until the last men of the Queen's that could be moved had effected their retirement, returned to the battalion under a concentrated fire from all the Boer trenches, having an extraordinary escape. Lieutenant Wade, a brave and zealous officer, shortly afterwards rejoined his own regiment, and met a soldier's death at Spion Kop. He was liked and respected by all the East Surrey Regiment.

The heat of the weather was very great during the action of Colenso, and the sufferings of all ranks from want of water were considerable. So many hours of exposure to a severe fire without being able to fire a shot in return was no small trial of steadiness, but nothing could have been better than the conduct of the battalion. Among those who distinguished themselves, in addition to Lieutenant Wade and his men, was Sergeant Sexton, who was reported by Captain Gorman to have bandaged a wounded man in the open, under heavy fire; and Colour-Sergeant Clay, who refused to leave his company after being wounded in the arm.

The casualties in the battalion at Colenso were as follows:

Killed—1.
No. 2354, Private W. Taylor.

Wounded—31.
No. 2685, Colour-Sergeant H. Clay.
„ 2862, Sergeant A. Tinkler.
„ 4400, „ C. Dick.
„ 2283, „ S. Conen.
„ 2853, „ A. Cavell.
„ 3185, Corporal J. Stroud.
„ 5029, Lance-Corporal W. Lucy.
„ 5431, „ J. Pizzey.
„ 3190, „ W. Warner.
„ 4975, Drummer H. Hart.
„ 4622, Private C. Hollis.
„ 3017, „ J. Goddard.
„ 3076, „ J. Dachelor.
„ 3444, „ J. Peacock.

No. 3215, Private J. Summerton.
„ 4594, „ W. Snow.
„ 3476, „ J. Hilton.
„ 5063, „ A. Rogers.
„ 2532, „ A. Stratford.
„ 3262, „ T. Sergeant.
„ 5422, „ H. Markham.
„ 3165, „ J. Powis.
„ 3134, „ A. Harley.
„ 2387, „ G. Moss.
„ 2402, „ J. Tayton.
„ 3180, „ F. Reynolds.
„ 2753, „ J. Haynes.
„ 2418, „ F. Rutledge.
„ 3373, „ H. Hamlin.
„ 3353, „ S. Iggledon.
„ 3428, „ F. Brown.

Private G. Moss eventually died of his wounds in Netley Hospital.

After the repulse at Colenso it was necessary to remove the camp, it being on ground commanded by the Boer guns. No move was, however, made until the night of December 16, nor did the Boer artillery take advantage of the fine target offered to them. Presumably they had no ammunition to spare. The camp was struck after dark on December 16, the 2nd and 6th Brigades of infantry, with other details, taking up a defensive position two miles north of Chieveley station, while the rest of the army marched back to Frere. The weather continued very hot until the evening of December 26, when heavy rain set in.

On January 6, 1900, the Boer army round Ladysmith made their only serious attempt on the town, the principal attack falling upon Caesar's Camp, and Wagon Hill, a great plateau which was the key of the defensive position. The attack began very early in the morning, and about mid-day General Buller received a signal message from Sir George White that he was hard pressed. The troops at Chieveley were immediately ordered to threaten Colenso, in order to hold the Boers there from joining in the attack on Ladysmith. The 2nd Brigade consequently advanced straight on Colenso, while the 6th Brigade advanced along the line of the railway. The advance compelled the Boers to man their trenches, which were then heavily shelled by the British artillery. Towards evening firing was no longer heard from Ladysmith, and the Chieveley troops were drawn off under cover of a heavy thunderstorm. They were not fired on.

The Spion Kop Operations

The 2nd Brigade remained at Chieveley, maintaining great vigilance until January 10, 1900, on which day it marched westward to take part in Sir Redvers Buller's second attempt to relieve Ladysmith. The 6th Brigade remained at Chieveley to hold in check the Boer garrison of Colenso, and its place in the 2nd Division was taken by the 5th Brigade (Major-General Hart). The division concentrated at Pretorius's farm on January 10 and lay there till the 15th, forming a flank-guard to the main force which, together with a large convoy of supplies for the Ladysmith garrison, was collecting at Springfield. On January 15 the 2nd Division marched to Springfield, and on the following night marched off, leaving its tents standing, to mislead the enemy, and arrived at dawn on the 17th on the hills covering Trichardt's drift on the Tugela. It was Sir Redvers Buller's intention that his main body, under Lieut.-General Sir Charles Warren, should cross the river at this point, and, working round the Boer right, should eventually attack them in rear, while the remainder of the army, under Major-General Lyttelton at Potgieter's drift, should co-operate in the Boer front.

The 2nd Brigade remained at Trickardt's drift until the evening of January 18, the 2nd East Surrey crossing the Tugela by a pontoon bridge at 5 P.M. and bivouacking near the river. The battalion was on the move all the next day, and at night received orders to take up out-post duty for the brigade along Venter's spruit. Owing to the difficulty of the ground and the vagueness of the instructions received, the companies were not all in position until midnight. On January 20 an attack was made by the 5th and 11th Brigades and other troops on the Boer position on the Rangeworthy heights. The 2nd Brigade was not employed except that in the afternoon Captain Packman's company of the East Surrey was ordered forward to support the mounted troops who had captured a commanding height called Bastion Hill. The Queen's and West Yorkshire were also sent forward about the same time, but were not engaged.

Early on January 21 the remainder of the battalion went to the front, four companies under Lieut.-Colonel Harris advancing soon after 4 A.M., and the remaining three companies, which had been detached to guard the left flank, following under Major Pearse at 8 A.M. to the foot of Bastion Hill. Here Major Pearse's wing was joined by Captain Gorman's company, which had been with Lieut.-Colonel Harris, and was ordered by Major-General Hildyard to move up the valley east of the hill and place himself at the disposal of Colonel Kitchener, West Yorkshire Regiment, who was about to attack the Boer position with his own battalion and two companies of the 2nd Queen's. On arriving at the head of the valley, Major Pearse was directed to place as many of his men as could fire effectively in the firing line, and to keep up a heavy fire on the Boer trenches, until the moment when Colonel Kitchener's troops advanced into the open. Meanwhile the crest line further to the right was captured by four battalions under Major-General Hart, and the attack seemed to be going well. The four companies of the East Surrey, under Lieut.-Colonel Harris, had, however, a very difficult, if not impossible task, assigned to them. They were ordered to work their way over the rolling western slopes of Bastion Hill, and so to make a flank attack in conjunction with Colonel Kitchener's frontal attack from the east of the hill. Lieut.-Colonel

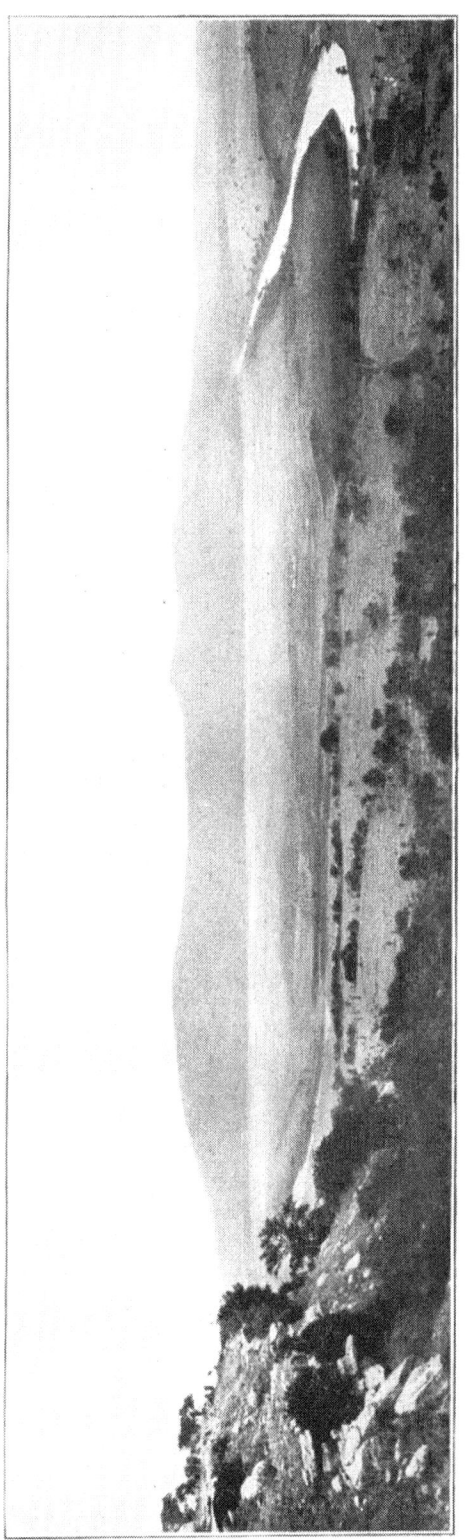

Spion Kop, Natal. General view of the Boer position.

Harris' dispositions and the movements of his four companies were as follows :

Major Smith's company (E) worked gradually up a very large donga some distance west of the hill, and, being sheltered by the ground, arrived at within 1400 yards of the Boer trenches, when it opened a steady fire. Captain Tew's company (B) advanced along the slopes of Bastion Hill itself, *i.e.* considerably to the right of E ; by careful and skilful use of folds in the ground Captain Tew arrived at a point about level with the position of E company. Captain Ellis' company (D) supported B company and gradually closed up to it, until early in the afternoon its front section was within 100 yards of the rear-section of B Company. F Company (Captain Packman) was placed by Lieut.-Colonel Harris on a spur running S.W. of Bastion Hill. Here the company had a clear view, and was in position to cover a possible retirement of the three companies in front, which had no artillery support and no other troops in reserve.[1] F company, though in reserve, was much exposed, and all the officers with it were hit. Lieut.-Colonel Harris and Captain Packman had bullets through their uniform, and Lieutenant C. P. Porch was very severely wounded in the leg while selecting a fire position for his half-company. Lieutenant Porch had received a severe injury to the head in the river Tugela three days earlier, but left the hospital to resume duty on hearing that the battalion was going into action. While Lieut.-Colonel Harris' companies were slowly advancing against the Boer right, Colonel Kitchener made his attack on the front. The attack was gallantly delivered, but the two movements were too widely separated to help one another, and the force allotted to the flank attack was too weak to hope for success. The frontal attack was consequently stopped at about 11 A.M., after over 100 casualties had been incurred. The half-battalion, under Lieut.-Colonel Harris, remained in the position described until evening, when they were withdrawn under a heavy but ineffective fire, and bivouacked at a farm near the foot of Bastion Hill where they were still within range, an ammunition mule being shot in the bivouac during the night. On January 22, the half-battalion again held the ridge on the S.W. of Bastion Hill. Major

---

[1] Late in the morning two batteries R.F.A. came into action on the left near Venter's spruit, which gave support to Lieut.-Colonel Harris' companies.

Pearse's half-battalion remained in action on Bastion Hill and on the crest line east of it, throughout January 21, and were, with the Lancashire Fusiliers, jointly responsible for the hill throughout the night. They remained in the same position all the following day (January 22), the Boer fire becoming heavier and more effective towards evening. At about 8 P.M. the half-battalion was withdrawn, after being in action for thirty-six hours, and the battalion was re-united at the bivouac occupied by the Headquarter wing on the previous night, Captain Gorman's company (C) only remaining on out-post duty at the extreme point of Bastion Hill.

On January 23 the battalion turned out at 2 A.M. and worked for some hours at defences which it had previously begun near the foot of Bastion Hill. On this night Spion Kop was captured by a force under Major-General Woodgate; and at 3 A.M. on January 24 the East Surrey, together with the 2nd Devon, marched across to Picquet Hill, a height to the west of Spion Kop and close to it with orders to be in readiness to support the troops on Spion Kop in any manner that might be ordered.

In this position the two battalions lay idle all January 24, 25 and 26, watching the severe fighting on Spion Kop on the first day and the removal of the wounded from that unfortunate spot on the 25th. During this day it became known that the attempt to capture the Boer position was abandoned, and orders to retire during the night were expected. The retirement of the battalion did not, however, take place until about midnight on the 26th, when the battalion left the position in perfect silence, being the last unit to move off. Just before the retirement, the Boers, who seemed to fear an attack, opened a very heavy rifle fire, by which two men of the battalion were wounded. No notice was taken of this fire. After marching a short distance, the battalion passed through the 2nd Devon, who formed the rear-guard to the whole force. It was broad daylight on January 27 when the East Surrey re-crossed the Tugela, a Boer shell at the moment falling into the river close to the pontoon bridge. The battalion then, under Sir Redvers Buller's personal orders, took up a position to cover the demolition of the bridges.

The casualties of the 2nd East Surrey during the Spion Kop operations were as follows:

Killed—5.

No. 2324, Private J. Smith.
„ 2886, „ H. Keep.
„ 5381, „ C. George.
„ 5506, „ H. Austin.
„ 5556 „ J. Porter.

Wounded—1 officer and 20 other ranks.

Lieutenant C. P. Porch.
No. 3164, Corporal J. Wilkinson.
„ 2432, Private A. Seward.
„ 3023, „ F. Bruce.
„ 3935, „ C. Clarke.
„ 2431, „ C. Copsey.
„ 2942, „ J. Martin.

No. 5303, Private W. Brunning.
„ 3067, „ S. Eade.
„ 2526, „ H. Smith.
„ 3571, „ C. Carvey.
„ 2603, „ T. Patterson.
„ 3284, „ S. Topping.
„ 2724, „ J. Corbett.
„ 3796, „ J. Soper.
„ 3749, „ W. Ford.
„ 3663, „ J. Arnold.
„ 5224, „ C. Gilbert.
„ 2366, „ H. Sharp.
„ 3357, „ W. Taylor.
„ 3519, „ H. Wiles.

These and previous losses were more than made good on January 30, when the battalion was joined by a draft of 130 men under Lieutenant de la Fontaine, bringing the strength of the battalion up to 1013, exclusive of officers.

Action of Vaal Krantz

While arrangements for the retirement from the Spion Kop region were in progress, Sir Redvers Buller and his staff were eagerly searching for a new point of attack. Presently they selected a portion of the Boer position east of Spion Kop, where a ridge called Vaal Krantz appeared to offer a favourable pivot for a piercing movement. This ridge was near the left of the Boer position facing Springfield, and the British having abandoned all designs against Spion Kop and the ground to the Boers' right of it, Spion Kop now formed the extreme Boer right. The British infantry lay in camp near Springfield from January 27 until February 4, by which time twenty guns had, with great labour, been placed in position on the summit of a wooded hill called Zwart Kop, to cover the intended crossing of the Tugela. On February 3 Sir Redvers Buller issued his orders for the capture of Vaal Krantz, which was entrusted to the 4th Brigade (Lyttelton), supported by the 2nd (Hildyard) and the 5th (Hart). The 11th Brigade (commanded, since Sir E. Woodgate had been mortally wounded, by Brigadier-General A. S. Wynne) was to assist by making a feint attack on the Boer right. This attack was to be supported by six batteries R. F. A., and a howitzer battery, which, at the appointed moment, were to change position and shell Vaal Krantz immediately before the real attack. The three brigades of infantry having marched from Springfield to their appointed bivouacs on February 4, moved at 7 A.M. on February 5 to a position close in rear of the intended crossing, about a mile from Vaal Krantz, and waited while the Royal Engineers, under Major J. L. Irving, with their accustomed gallantry threw a pontoon bridge over the Tugela. Almost at the same moment Brigadier-General Wynne advanced to make his feint attack, which was finely carried out. Vaal Krantz ridge was heavily shelled from Zwart Kop from early in the morning, and though thinly held by about 100 Boers, so heavy was the artillery fire that half of them were killed or wounded before Major-General Lyttelton delivered his attack. Lyttelton's troops advanced under a heavy fire from the Boer trenches on all the surrounding heights, and from a large number of sharpshooters, but pushing steadily on they captured Vaal Krantz, which was fully occupied by 4 P.M. The 2nd Devon, the leading battalion of the 2nd Brigade, followed close after Lyttelton's troops, with orders to capture a green hill to the eastward of Vaal Krantz; but as they were advancing, this order was cancelled, and the Devon were divided between a farm and a donga close up to the right rear of Vaal Krantz, while two companies held the extreme right of that hill. The 2nd East Surrey were following the Devon, but when two companies had crossed the pontoon bridge, the advance of the battalion was stopped and the companies recalled. One man only in them had been wounded. At dusk the battalion bivouacked on the eastern slope of Zwart Kop, Captain White's company (H) crossing the pontoon bridge and taking up a covering position on the north bank.

On February 6 all the infantry lay idle, except Lyttelton's brigade, on Vaal Krantz, which had thrown up defences during the previous night. The Boers attempted to re-capture the hill in the afternoon, but were repulsed. At dusk the three battalions of the 2nd Brigade advanced across the open to relieve the 4th Brigade on Vaal Krantz, crossing the Tugela by a pontoon bridge which had been thrown across immediately in rear of the hill. The East Surrey had one man wounded during the advance. Major-General Hildyard disposed his brigade as follows: The 2nd Queen's were posted on the left front and left flank, a very exposed position, which they held with great tenacity. The West Yorkshire, on the right, held a smaller kopje united to the main ridge by a nek. The 2nd East Surrey held the centre of the hill and the nek just mentioned, E, C and D companies being placed in the first line in the order named from right to left. B company remained at the bottom of the hill in order to carry up rations for itself and the five other companies on the summit. After completing this severe task at 5 A.M. on February 7, B company joined A and H companies, which formed a general support, under Major Pearse. They were posted immediately under the rear crest of the hill. F and G companies were detailed to guard the pontoon bridge, and entrenched themselves on the north bank of the river.

The 2nd Devon, having been already in action two days, were placed in reserve at the foot of Vaal Krantz.

The night of February 6 was one of very hard work for the three East Surrey companies in front, who made every exertion to improve the defences which had been built under great difficulties by the 4th Brigade. The left company, having good materials, made excellent cover, but the right and centre companies had to search in the darkness for stones to raise their walls. Major Smith, on the right, worked in his shirt sleeves with his men, in most exposed ground. A subsequent examination of Vaal Krantz showed that the centre company (Captain Gorman's) had dug every available stone out of the ground, going far to the front in the search, with the result that, although in the centre of the bombardment next day, only one man of the company was killed by shell fire. The three supporting companies scraped together what shelter they could, but their best protection lay in the steepness of the ground, which was very precipitous at their position.

The Boer artillery opened a bombardment of Vaal Krantz at dawn on February 7, and continued it till dark. Their guns had closed in on the hill, and the British artillery, in spite of its superior numbers and unceasing efforts, was able to do very little towards checking the Boer fire. As the 2nd East Surrey were in the centre of the hill, and so perhaps received the lion's share of the shelling, though the Queen's had more rifle fire to endure, we may quote a description of this day's fighting written by an officer of the 2nd Brigade, well known in literature under the name of " Linesman " :

"It was a terrible day for the 2nd Brigade," he writes, "a day of dull silent waiting in the blazing heat, listening to the interminable whistle and roar of shells falling among them lying flat in the stony sangars wondering where the next would burst, and who would be the next to be lifted, bloody and maimed, by the stretcher-bearers for that journey down the steep hill-side."

"Linesman" states that on this day Vaal Krantz was shelled incessantly by a 40-pounder and a 3-inch high velocity gun from Spion Kop, that is, from the left rear; by a big gun (94-pounder) from Doorn Kop on the right rear; by two high velocity French guns from the front; by pom-poms from both flanks; and by a battery of 7-pounder field-guns on Brakfontein, a high hill on the left. In three-quarters of an hour, he adds, 253 projectiles fell upon Vaal Krantz. They were counted by an officer, who then gave up the task. The steadiness of the three battalions was quite unshaken by this fire, and thanks to the effective cover made by the 4th Brigade and improved by themselves, their losses were surprisingly light. It was, however, hardly possible to move on the hill during daylight without being hit.[1]

A careful inspection of Vaal Krantz convinced General Buller that it was impossible to mount guns on it, and that without such a forward artillery position any further advance was impossible. General Buller therefore decided to retire once again, and the 2nd Brigade was ordered to vacate Vaal Krantz during the night, a delicate operation skilfully planned by Major-General Hildyard and steadily carried out by his brigade.

Shortly before nine o'clock the three battalions on the summit assembled quietly on the slope of the hill in rear of their positions, each company in the front line leaving one section widely extended to hold the firing line until 9.15. Just as the battalions began to descend the hill, the Boers opened a heavy fire at close quarters on the firing line, who responded with such vigour as to discourage any attempt on the part of the enemy to close with them. The firing line then with-

---

[1] The multiplication of artillery and particularly the immense volume of heavy shell fire to which troops have been subjected in the great war that began in August 1914 dwarfs all previous experiences. The writer, however, leaves the description of Vaal Krantz as it was originally written, for even judged by the standard of to-day the position of Hildyard's brigade on that rocky hill was no pleasant one.

drew silently, and followed the three supporting companies down the hill. The West Yorkshire, who had easier ground to traverse, arrived at the pontoon bridge before the Queen's and East Surrey, and the bridge being thus in use the two latter battalions had to wait in a crowded formation for some time. Had the Boers followed up the retirement, the brigade must have suffered heavy loss. The East Surrey sections left in the firing line were commanded by Lieutenants North and Anson, and 2nd Lieutenant Stafford. The last-named young officer, after reaching the place of assembly at the foot of the hill, returned to the summit in search of two of the men of his section who had lost their way in the darkness.

By 10 P.M. all the 2nd Brigade had crossed the pontoon bridge, and the Connaught Rangers had also retired from their position in the right rear of Vaal Krantz, crossing the Tugela by another bridge.

After having re-crossed the Tugela, happily for the last time, the 2nd Brigade formed up near the river in line of battalion columns, and lay down to pass the remainder of the night within easy reach of the Boer guns. At 4 A.M. on February 8, the brigade marched off, apparently unseen by the Boers on account of the morning haze. Just as the retiring army reached Zwart Kop, the Boer guns opened fire and continued to shell it for a considerable time, with little or no effect.

The casualties of the 2nd East Surrey at Vaal Krantz were as follows:

Killed—2.
No. 3303, Private A. Bartelloni.
" 5515, " J. Juniper.

Wounded—1 *officer and* 11 *other ranks.*
Captain F. White.
No. 2685, Colour-Sergeant H. Clay.
" 2553, Sergeant A. Cavell.
" 3190, Lance-Corpl. J. Warner.

No. 3471, Private H. Hogan.
" 3029, " E. Lyons.
" 2306, " W. Green.
" 3255, " E. Chamberlain.
" 3019, " W. Jackson.
" 4176, " J. Tripp.
" 3664, " E. Boyes.
" 3403, " C. Dell.

Captain White was severely injured by a shell from the 94-pounder on Doorn Kop, and Colour-Sergeant Clay, who had been previously wounded at Colenso, was very severely wounded by a shell in the feet. Sergeant Cavell had also been wounded at Colenso.

The 2nd Brigade encamped at Springfield after a long and hot march, followed by a similar march on February 10 to Pretorius's farm, and by a yet longer and more trying one on February 11. Moving off at 3 A.M. this day, it retraced its march to Chieveley, crossing the railway at that station and encamping some two miles beyond it on the left bank of the Blaaukrantz river, opposite the Weenen monument. As the East Surrey passed Chieveley station the naval signallers there received a message from the Boer heliograph on Monte Cristo to the effect that they knew where we were going and what we were going to do, and that they were quite ready for us. This showed a sportive spirit, but proved to be mistaken.

The Pieter's Hill Operations

The 2nd Brigade lay in its pleasant, well-wooded and well-watered camp on the Blaaukrantz river for two days of rest after the long strain of the Spion Kop operations, and on February 14 started on the new movement which, after fourteen days' fighting, was at last to clear the road to Ladysmith.

Sir Redvers Buller's orders for the advance were that the 5th Division (under Sir Charles Warren) was to capture an unnamed hill east of Hussar Hill, and that the 2nd Division (now commanded by Major-General the Hon. N. Lyttelton [1]) was to advance beyond it, where General Lyttelton would receive orders as to further operations towards Cingolo Hill. The movement was to be covered by the mounted troops under Lord Dundonald, and the artillery was to accompany the 5th Division, as the advance of the 2nd Division would be mainly over ground inaccessible to wheeled traffic.

Hussar Hill was occupied, almost without loss, early on February 14, and the 2nd Division advanced, in great heat over rough and thickly-wooded ground, to its allotted positions. On the following day the advance on the right was continued over very rough and precipitous ground, the 2nd Division occupying Moord Kraal Hill and some rising ground to its north-west. The 6th Brigade (Major-General Barton) also advanced to a position to the left rear of the 2nd Division, linking it up with the 5th Division. The artillery meanwhile continued to engage the Boer guns, and thus aided the movement against the Boer left. On February 16, Major-General Lyttelton sent the 2nd Queen's,

[1] Vice Lieut.-General Clery, who had been admitted to hospital after Vaal Krantz.

Boer Position—Pieter's Hill, Natal. (From the foot of Hlangwane Hill.)

widely extended, to examine the ground towards the Gomba river and to ascertain the Boer positions. The 2nd East Surrey advanced in support of the Queen's, and at night furnished seven companies for out-post duty. The Scottish Rifles, from the 4th Brigade, moved this day over ground on the left of the Queen's, and Lord Dundonald's composite regiment of Mounted Infantry, moving wide on the right flank, searched the lower slopes of Cingolo. The slow advance of the infantry against this height was caused by the scarcity of water and the uncertainty as to the Boer positions, but the reconnaissances of February 16 cleared up the situation, and the subsequent advance was more rapid. In the evening General Buller issued his orders for the following day, to the effect that the left of the Boer position, north of the Gomba spruit, was to be turned by the infantry, the 2nd Division aiming at the centre of the Cingolo Nek and, on reaching that point, swinging to its left. One brigade of the 5th Division was to move on Major-General Lyttelton's left, supported by the other brigade. The field batteries and howitzer battery, under Colonel L. W. Parsons, were to support the attack, and the mounted troops, divided between the two flanks, were to aid it; which, it may be added, they did most effectually. These orders were carried out on February 17, Cingolo Hill being captured by the 2nd Brigade in conjunction with the South African Light Horse and the composite regiment of Mounted Infantry. The 2nd Brigade advanced in the following order: 2nd West Yorkshire, 2nd Devon, 2nd Queen's, and 2nd East Surrey, the last-named coming off out-post duty as the brigade advanced. The ground proved extraordinarily difficult as soon as the Gomba was crossed (7.30 A.M.), for the hillside beyond was steep and rough with boulders of ironstone, and the bush so thick that men had to be dropped every ten paces to maintain connection between the companies. At nine o'clock the Boers on the northern slopes of Cingolo opened fire, and to manœuvre them out of position Major-General Hildyard ordered the 2nd Queen's to move out to the right and execute a circling movement. This task was very well carried out, and by 1 P.M. the leading companies of the Queen's reached the top of the spur, where they found some of Lord Dundonald's troops, who, by an even wider turning movement, had outflanked the Boer trenches and compelled the detachment of 300 men holding them to evacuate them.

By four o'clock the Queen's had advanced along the summit of Cingolo, and the Devon were about to advance on the nek and on Monte Cristo. The West Yorkshire and East Surrey were in support and close up. The work performed by the 2nd Queen's this day was so heavy that the 2nd East Surrey volunteered to carry rations and ammunition for them to the top of Mount Cingolo, while the 2nd Devon and West Yorkshire furnished parties to drag four guns of the 64th battery up the western slopes of Cingolo, so that they might aid in the attack on Monte Cristo next day.

At dawn on February 18, the guns on Hussar Hill opened fire on Monte Cristo, and at 6.40 the 2nd Brigade began its advance in two lines, the Queen's and West Yorkshire leading, followed by the Devon and East Surrey. In the left rear of the 2nd Brigade, the 4th Brigade moved along the lower slopes, and yet further to the left was the 6th Brigade.

Covered by long range volleys from the Devon and East Surrey, the Queen's and West Yorkshire advanced rapidly across the nek with slight loss, and then climbing quickly up the precipitous slope, in parts almost a cliff, had by 10.30 seized the southern knoll of Monte Cristo. There they were quickly reinforced by the Devon and half the East Surrey, the remainder of the battalion being for a time retained by Major-General Hildyard in the nek, as his sole reserve. The three and a half battalions of the 2nd Brigade then continued their advance with Lord Dundonald's troops on their right, and during the afternoon cleared all the main plateau of Monte Cristo, which they then prepared for defence, the West Yorkshire halting eventually at the southern, and the half-battalion East Surrey at the northern, end of the plateau. The rear half-battalion East Surrey joined the remainder of the brigade after a difficult climb in the dark, and spent most of the night in building defences against the Boer bombardment expected next day. The 4th Brigade, moving up on the left rear of the 2nd Brigade, had captured the Boer laager at the western foot of the hill.

At dawn of February 19, it became evident that the Boers had abandoned Hlangwane and the Colenso position, and large numbers of them could be seen in full retreat in the open plain towards Ladysmith, which town also lay at last in distant view of the 2nd Brigade. At 7 A.M. the 2nd East Surrey was ordered by Major-General Hildyard to push forward and reconnoitre the wooded ridges and valleys running to the north and north-east. This task was performed by four companies under Major Pearse, supported by the remainder of the battalion under Lieut.-Colonel Harris. Later in the day, a fifth company was sent to Major Pearse, with orders to take up defensive positions along the whole northern ridge of Monte Cristo, some two and a-half miles in extent, which commanded the river Tugela nearly up to the Klip River falls. The most advanced post, held by Captain Tew's company, was established on a conical hill overlooking a drift which, it was thought, the Boers might use for a counter attack. This drift might apparently have been used by our troops in order to turn the Pieter's position, but it was considered unsuitable for this purpose. Lieut.-Colonel Harris, with the three remaining companies, took up a position to guard two naval 12-pounders, which were mounted on the northern point of Monte Cristo. The East Surrey remained thus posted on February 19, 20 and 21, being supplied with rations with difficulty owing to the rugged ground on which they were posted and suffering considerably from want of water, which had to be brought by a long and steep climb from the Tugela. One man was wounded by a Boer sniper on February 20 when carrying water.

After the capture of Monte Cristo the only important Boer position on the south side of the Tugela was the great hill Hlangwane. This was attacked on February 19 by the 5th Division and part of the 4th Brigade, and the greater part of the hill was easily captured. By 7 A.M. on February 20, no Boers remained south of the river. This success had been achieved at the cost of 300 British casualties. Sir Redvers Buller having decided that he could not cross the Tugela at any point under the long ridge held by the East Surrey Regiment, decided to throw a pontoon bridge over the river near Hlangwane and then advance through Colenso ; and in preparation for this measure the 2nd Division (less the 2nd East Surrey) was moved on February 20 to the eastern slopes of Hlangwane. On February 21 the bridge was quickly constructed without loss by Major Irving's skilled Engineers, and the 5th Division was now ordered to take the lead. Accordingly the 10th Brigade (Major-General Talbot Coke) crossed the river early in the afternoon and advanced towards the Onderbrook spruit, where the first Boer position was believed to be. Here the brigade was checked, and as Sir Charles Warren held back the 11th Brigade (Major-General Wynne), no further progress could be made that day. The losses in the 10th Brigade were, however, not heavy, and at night Major-General Coke drew back his battalions to the Colenso kopjes, posting them on the left of the 11th Brigade. General Buller's intention for February 22 was to repeat the attack of the previous day in much greater strength, and with this object the 11th Brigade was directed to advance against the hills, afterwards called the " Wynne Hills " after its commander, the 2nd Division being ordered to cross the Tugela and follow in support. Accordingly Major-General Wynne advanced at about 2 P.M. on February 22, but at that time no troops were available to support him, as only two battalions of the 4th Brigade had crossed the Tugela and were required to guard the left flank. Soon after his advance began, Major-General Wynne was wounded, and on reaching the hills which they were attacking, his battalions, now commanded by Colonel Crofton, came under a severe cross-fire from several directions and got into difficulties. By three o'clock the Boer fire had strengthened so much that orders were sent to the 2nd Brigade to advance from the Colenso kopjes. The order took some time to reach Major-General Hildyard and the operation of advancing over bad ground exposed to fire also took time, so that until dark the only reinforcement that reached the 11th Brigade, was the 3rd Battalion King's Royal Rifles (of the 4th Brigade) which came up to Wynne's Hill East about sunset. At sunset the fire of the British artillery ceased, and the Boer attack on the troops on Wynne's Hill became so vigorous that immediate reinforcement was called for.

The 2nd Brigade at this moment was lying in mass, at quarter-column distance, close under a steep hill at the south end of the railway cutting, and about half a mile south of the Onderbrook spruit. The 2nd East Surrey, which was the leading battalion of the brigade, had reached this point with little loss, though Sergeant Chamberlain, a good non-commissioned officer, had been killed by a shell at about five o'clock. On receipt of the demand for immediate help, Major-General Hildyard ordered the 2nd East Surrey to advance as quickly as possible to reinforce the right of the advance line, followed by the 2nd Devon, who were to reinforce the left.

Lieut.-Colonel Harris' task was a most difficult one. The ground over which the battalion had to advance was quite unknown and very rough ; and in the increasing darkness each half-company in succession had to climb over a wall, change front to the right, and extend to six paces as they moved off. No information as to the position of troops in front could be given except by the sound of firing, and in such hilly ground this sound was often misleading. A staff officer, who came by from the front just as the advance began, advised Colonel Harris to keep his right on the path, but as it became impossible to see the path after a few minutes this gave little assistance. Guided however by the fire, which became louder and louder as the battalion advanced, and particularly by the sound of a machine gun, the leading half-company soon found and crossed the Onderbrook spruit, and presently arrived at the foot of the slopes leading up to the Wynne Hills. Just in front could be seen the nek between the hills. Lieut.-Colonel Harris, who, with his 2nd in Command and Adjutant, was a little in advance of the battalion, was here met by one or more officers and several men, who all eagerly asked for help and ammunition. Lieut.-Colonel Harris, after brief enquiries, decided to reinforce the troops on the plateau to his right front with four companies under his own command, and he ordered Major Pearse, with three companies, to act similarly on the left, the eighth company being detailed to hold the nek between the two hills. As the right was said to be severely pressed and the left to be weakly held, Lieut.-Colonel Harris decided to send companies alternately to the two flanks ; and leaving Major Pearse to carry out these orders, he himself ascended the right hill. The companies which followed Lieut.-Colonel Harris were those of Major Smith (E), Major Treeby (G), Captain Ellis (D), and A company, commanded since Vaal Krantz by Lieutenant C. H. Hinton.

In order to relate the experiences of these four companies during the night, it will be well to deal with them in pairs, A and G companies, with which were Lieut.-Colonel Harris and his Adjutant, remaining together, while D and E in the darkness became separated from them, though only by a short distance, and took their orders from Major Smith. The machine-gun under Lieutenant May was with these two companies during the night. To take Major Smith's companies first ; on beginning to ascend the hill they bore slightly to their right, and on reaching the crest Major Smith was told that there was no room for his men, and was directed to withdraw them to some kraals close by at the foot of the hill, which at that point was very steep. At 9.30 P.M. Major Smith was directed by the officer commanding 11th Brigade (Colonel Crofton) to send a company along the railway to the right to ascertain if the enemy was preparing an attack on that flank. This duty was performed by D company, its leading patrol under Sergeant H. J. Percy, a very daring non-commissioned officer, going a long distance along the railway and finding it quite clear of the Boers. D company eventually returned and formed up on the left of E. Soon after midnight Major Smith was again summoned by Colonel Crofton, whom he found with Lieutenant H. Wake of the King's Royal Rifles. Colonel Crofton said that some of the King's Royal Rifles were in a very dangerous position at the far end of the plateau above them, that they had suffered heavily, and were so near the enemy that they were unable to retire. Colonel Crofton then asked Major Smith to take his two companies forward at dawn with the bayonet, and get the riflemen out of their difficulty. He added that Lieutenant Wake would act as guide.

Major Smith at once moved his companies round the slope of the hill a short distance to the right, and when on clear ground advanced up the hill until he reached a large hollow near the crest, where he ordered both companies to extend and fix bayonets. He posted D company 200 yards to the left of E, with orders to advance as soon as they saw E move off in the early morning. Major Smith in his narrative of these events adds: "We then lay down and tried to sleep, but the hollow being full of wounded men and the fire passing over us being very heavy, we got little rest." Shortly before daybreak Major Smith ordered his companies to advance, and soon after topping the near crest of the plateau found himself passing through the right of A and C companies, which were then lying behind a line of sangars constructed by them during the night from the scanty material on the spot. Major Smith did not then see Lieut.-Colonel Harris, who was with A company on the left, but he told Major Treeby, commanding G company, what he was about to do and what orders he had received. Major Smith's narrative continues thus:

"I moved on some distance and saw a Kraal where a lot of the K.R.R. were sheltering, and on getting in line with them ordered my men to lie down and keep very quiet while the K.R. Rifles were retiring through them. This retirement made some noise, and the Boers who were very close, at once opened a heavy fire. I walked back to Lieutenant-Colonel Harris (whose position had been pointed out to me by Major Treeby) and asked him if he wished me to remain where I was or to retire. He told me I had better retire, and when I got back to my company I gave them the order to do so. As soon as they rose the fire became very heavy indeed and a large number of men were hit."

Major Smith, who by his gallant advance, had enabled all the unwounded King's Royal Rifles to retire from their position, was severely wounded during his own retirement, and his company had eight men killed and sixteen wounded. Privates Humphrey and Thurston carried Major Smith out of fire, and owing to the severity of his wound were compelled to move slowly. They were fired at all the time, but refused to leave Major Smith, and eventually carried him to the hollow whence the company advanced. Major Treeby, on hearing that Major Smith was wounded, at once went to his assistance, and was himself wounded in the shoulder while endeavouring to bandage Major Smith's wound.

To return to the movements of A and G companies, which had been the last to reach the foot of the plateau on the previous evening. Major Treeby was sent up the hill, which was very steep, in advance of the companies to find the firing line. On reaching the summit he found a scene of great confusion and a number of men of various battalions who in the darkness had lost their officers. With much exertion, Major Treeby rallied some of these men, and when the two companies arrived on the plateau soon afterwards, Lieut.-Colonel Harris formed them into line in single rank just under the crest, and posted one company to the right and the other to the left of these rallied men. As Lieut.-Colonel Harris could not ascertain in the darkness and confusion whether his companies were the first line or had other troops in front of them, he ordered them not to fire, to fix bayonets and lie down where they were, and to make the best cover that they could for themselves. This they did in the course of the night, and though loose stones were hard to find, the two companies made a fairly good line of sangars before dawn.

As already described, Major Smith's retirement by Lieut -Colonel

Harris' order brought the four East Surrey companies into a general line on the southern crest of the plateau shortly after daybreak on February 23; Colonel Harris then found that the ground occupied by A company, on the left of the line, which had been taken up in the dark, gave the company no field of fire, and he therefore ordered it to advance a short distance to better ground. The company, under Lieutenant Hinton, and accompanied by the Colonel, advanced without hesitation, but came presently under so heavy a fire that, after moving about 200 yards, Colonel Harris ordered them to halt and lie down. Several casualties were sustained, and Lieut.-Colonel Harris and Lieutenant Hinton were both wounded. Shortly afterwards Lieutenant Hinton was hit again and killed, and Colonel Harris received another dangerous wound. A company remained the whole day in this exposed position, without food or water, and within about 200 yards of three Boer trenches, which poured a deadly fire on them from the front and right flank whenever the slightest movement took place. The casualties were numerous, Colonel Harris receiving no less than nine wounds, and some of the non-commissioned officers and men being also wounded several times. The company suffered terribly from thirst, in the great heat, but nevertheless they gallantly held their ground and kept up a steady fire from their exposed position. Little piles of stones showed afterwards where these brave soldiers lay through these long twelve hours of peril, and behind every little shelter lay a heap of empty cartridge cases. Some men showed great courage and determination in crawling to the dead and severely wounded, taking their ammunition from their pouches and giving such water as could be found in the water-bottles of the dead to the wounded survivors. Among those specially brought to notice for devotion to the wounded was Private Lovegrove, who was granted the Distinguished Conduct Medal, but unfortunately died before receiving it.

After the death of Lieutenant Hinton, the command of A company devolved on Sergeant F. C. Leavens, a reservist, who behaved in an exemplary manner. At about five in the afternoon Lieut.-Colonel Harris was found by Private A. E. Curtis, who on discovering that the Colonel was still living, went to his assistance, and after being twice driven back by the Boer fire, succeeded in reaching him and in binding up some of his wounds. Private Curtis then tried to carry Colonel Harris off the field, but finding that he could not do so single-handed, called Private T. Morton, who at once went to his assistance. The two soldiers then carried Colonel Harris out of fire, thus saving his life. The place where Colonel Harris lay was so near the Boer trenches that no other disabled men were carried off, and nearly all the wounded who could not walk without assistance died where they lay. At dusk Sergeant Leavens brought A company back from their position, taking with him those of the less-severely wounded, who could be helped away to safety. The casualties of the company during the day were twelve killed and twenty-five wounded, nearly all the wounds being very severe. Sergeant Leavens and Private Morton were awarded the Distinguished Conduct Medal for their services on this occasion, and the Victoria Cross was conferred on Private Curtis, the grant being notified as follows in the *London Gazette* of 15th January, 1901.

"The Queen has been graciously pleased to signify her intention to confer the decoration of the Victoria Cross on Pte. (now Corpl.) A. E. Curtis, 2nd Battn. East Surrey Regiment.

"On the 23rd February, 1900, Colonel Harris lay all day long in a perfectly open space under close fire of a Boer breastwork. The Boers fired all day at any man who moved, and Colonel Harris was wounded eight or nine times. Pte. Curtis, after several attempts, succeeded in reaching the Colonel, bound his wounded arm, and gave him his flask, all under fire. He then tried to carry him away, but was unable, on which he called for assistance, and Pte. Morton came out at once. Fearing that the men would be killed, Colonel Harris told them to leave him, but they declined, and after trying to carry the Colonel on their rifles, they made a chair with their hands, and so carried him out of fire."

We must now return to the companies under Major Pearse which were posted during the evening of February 22 along the ridge to the left of the nek between the Wynne Hills. This ridge was found on the arrival of the companies to be held by a thin firing line of the Rifle Reserve Battalion under Major E. Stuart-Wortley. (This battalion was formed of reservists belonging to the battalions of the King's Royal Rifles and the Rifle Brigade in the Ladysmith garrison, and was entirely composed of veteran soldiers.) Major Pearse found that the officers of the Rifle Reserve battalion were satisfied with their position, now that support had arrived, and preferred that their men should remain as they were until the battalion should be ordered to retire. Major Pearse consequently posted his three companies in suitable positions along the slope of the ridge, which was very steep, and ordered them to build shelters. In consequence of information given by an unknown officer to the Major on arrival at the nek, he gave special warning to the company commanders to build sangars with flanking protection towards the left. These orders were so well carried out that although at dawn a galling flank fire swept the ridge, casualties were remarkably light. Soon after the companies had settled down, Captain Gorman, who had been posted at the nek, reported that there was not room there for more than half a company, and consequently joined the three companies with half his men. At dawn another section was withdrawn from the nek, which was left in charge of 2nd Lieutenant Stafford with one section.

At about 3 A.M. on February 23, the Rifle Reserve Battalion was ordered to leave the firing line, and its place along the ridge was taken by as many men of the East Surrey as the company officers thought it desirable to put in action. At dawn the advance of Major Smith's two companies on the right, followed by the advance of A company, under Lieut.-Colonel Harris, caused a heavy outburst of fire from the Boers in front, and this presently was aided by a flank fire from Grobelaar mountain; but the companies, thanks to their half-moon shaped defences, held their ground fairly easily.

Soon afterwards, in response to a message sent during the night to Major-General Hildyard, some companies of the 2nd Queen's, under Major Burrell, came up and were posted on the left flank, thus somewhat relieving the pressure from that direction. By this time Major Pearse had been informed that Colonel Kitchener had been appointed Brigadier-General to command the 11th Brigade, and on Major Burrell's suggestion he requested the Brigadier to send a machine-gun, or two if possible, to be placed at the extremity of the ridge. Brigadier-General Kitchener at once complied, sending the East Surrey gun, under Lieutenant J. C. May, and also the gun of the Royal Lancaster Regiment. Lieutenant May and his gun-team fought the gun from dawn to dusk under a well-aimed fire, which covered the gun and its shields with lead. Lieutenant May (who had a bullet through the helmet) and Lance-Corporal Fisher, who was severely wounded, were rewarded respectively with the

Distinguished Service Order and the Distinguished Conduct Medal.[1]

In accordance with orders, Major Pearse withdrew his companies from the ridge at about noon. The retirement under enfilade fire was a difficult one, but being well managed by the company officers did not cost many casualties. The left companies had Captain Packman and 2nd Lieutenant Benson wounded, and about twenty of other ranks killed and wounded. The remainder of the battalion, except A company, which owing to its exposed position could not be withdrawn until dusk, was also brought down from Wynne Hill East, and the seven companies were collected in the bed of the Onderbrook spruit by 2 P.M., where the men obtained some much needed food and rest.

The following officers, non-commissioned officers and men were brought to notice for distinguished conduct on February 22 and 23 by Lieutenant-Colonel Harris or Major Pearse :

Majors H. L. Smith and H. P. Treeby ; Lieutenant J. C. May, all three of whom received the Distinguished Service Order. Acting Pay-Sergeant F. C. Leavens, who commanded his company most bravely and efficiently after Lieutenant Hinton was killed. Lance-Corporals : A. E. Curtis, who was awarded the Victoria Cross for determined gallantry in saving the life of Lieut.-Colonel Harris ; J. Fisher, who distinguished himself with the machine gun ; and R. Parris, who was dangerously wounded while bravely attempting to carry a message to Lieut.-Colonel Harris. Privates T. Morton (who assisted Lance-Corporal Curtis to carry Lieut.-Colonel Harris away under close fire), J. Diamond, G. Ashcroft, D. Connor, W. Boxer, W. Lovegrove, W. Humphrey and A. Thurston. The two last carried Major Smith out of action after he had been wounded.

Of the above non-commissioners officers and privates, the following were awarded the medal for distinguished conduct in the field : Lance-Corporals J. Fisher and R. Parris, and Private T. Morton.

The 2nd East Surrey had sustained heavy casualties on February 23, losing six officers and about eighty of other ranks killed and wounded. These sacrifices, however, were willingly made, and the good work of the

---

[1] The remaining men of the maxim-gun party, who all behaved most bravely, were mentioned in Battalion Orders as having rendered exceptionally good service. They were Privates Gard, Pets, Thomas, Wood, and Leedham.

battalion was fully recognised by its superiors. Major Pearse, who had succeeded Lieut.-Colonel Harris in the command, and was now the only field officer with the battalion, received on February 25 the following memorandum, conveying the thanks of Lieut.-General the Hon. N. Lyttelton commanding 2nd Division, and of Major-General Hildyard, commanding 2nd Brigade :

> The Major General desires me to inform you how highly he appreciates the conduct of all ranks of the 2nd East Surrey Regiment in the operations of the 22nd and 23rd instant, when the battalion was employed in most trying conditions. The Lieut.-General Commanding the Division has asked him to intimate the high appreciation of the 3rd Battalion K. R. Rifles of the service rendered them on the morning of the 23rd, and to add his own cordial thanks.
>
> By Order.
> (Signed) CHRISTIAN VICTOR.
> Bt. Major

Major Pearse,
  2nd East Surrey Regiment.

This letter gave great pleasure to the 2nd East Surrey. It will be noticed that it was signed by Brevet-Major H.H. Prince Christian Victor, a grandson of Queen Victoria, who was attached to Major-General Hildyard's staff after the action of Colenso. The Prince unfortunately died during the campaign, to the great regret of all who knew him.

After dark on February 23 the 2nd East Surrey was ordered to bivouac in and round the kraals occupied on the previous night by D and E companies. The kraals were now Major-General Hildyard's headquarters. It was the intention of the General to keep the battalion in reserve for a day, but at an early hour on the 24th he was ordered to send reinforcements to Major-General Hart, whose brigade had suffered heavy losses in an unsuccessful attack on the previous evening. The East Surrey being immediately available, were sent on this duty. The movement along the bank of the Tugela was in parts exposed to fire, and the battalion had nine men wounded during its short march. On reaching General Hart's headquarters the 2nd East Surrey was immediately detailed to head an intended attack on the Boer position on Railway Hill, but this movement was postponed, and the battalion held in reserve during the remainder of February 24. On the two following days the 2nd East Surrey was posted on the right of General Hart's position, which had previously been much exposed. During the night of the 25th, at about nine o'clock, a party of Boers crept close up to the bivouac of General Hart's troops and opened a sudden and very heavy fire. The battalion was perfectly steady, and in accordance with orders already issued closed up to quarter-column, fixed bayonets, and waited for orders. Two companies were presently sent out on the right flank to clear the ground, and the Boers retired.

On the 25th (Sunday) an armistice was arranged with the Boer commanders, the flag of truce accompanying the message being carried by Lieutenant Barchard, who was fired at several times before the flag was understood. Under the armistice the surviving wounded of February 23 were carried in from Wynne's Hill and Hart's Hill. Their sufferings from thirst and their wounds had been terrible.

Battle of Pieter's Hill

Very early on February 27 Major Pearse was informed that the battalion was to take part in the general attack on the Boer position and would be attached for the fight to the 4th Brigade, commanded by Colonel Norcott. Being summoned to the brigade headquarters, Major Pearse was told that the battalion would be on the right of the first line of the brigade, the 1st Rifle Brigade being on the left. The second line was to be formed by the Scottish Rifles (half-battalion) and the third line by the Durham Light Infantry. At about nine o'clock Major Pearse and Lieutenant-Colonel Colville, commanding the 1st Rifle Brigade, accompanied Sir Charles Warren to a hill with a clear view of the whole Boer position, and had the plan of attack fully explained to them and were shown several of the Boer trenches. The orders for the attack were admirably drawn up, and as the attack could not begin until the Fusilier Brigade, on the extreme right, had arrived at its position, Major Pearse had time to explain not only to the officers, but to the men of each company, the part that each of the three brigades was to play in the coming attack, and particularly the duty assigned to the 2nd East Surrey. All ranks received their orders with coolness and cheerfulness, and showed a clear understanding of the task before them.

The attack was to be begun on the right, and the 4th Brigade was ordered not to advance beyond the railway until the Lancashire Brigade (in the centre) had reached a point which would compel the Boer commanders to evacuate the trenches in the low ground, the fire from which had caused heavy loss in General Hart's attack on February 23.

Owing to the heavy casualties among officers, six of the eight companies went into action with one officer, while two had two officers. The battalion staff was reduced to the Commanding Officer and Adjutant, and there was no officer with the machine-gun or signallers. The distribution of companies was as follows:

Firing line B company (Captain Tew) and H company (Lieutenant Barchard).
Supports   C   ,,   (Captain Gorman) and E company (Lieutenant Anson).
Reserve   A   ,,   Lieutenant North.
              D   ,,   Captain Ellis.
              F   ,,   Lieutenant de la Fontaine.
              G   ,,   ,,   May.

Captain Tew commanded the firing line, and Captain Gorman the supports.

The Battle of Pieter's Hill began by the successful advance of the Fusilier Brigade (Major-General Barton) against the Boer left, on Pieter's Hill, by which the Boers were completely surprised. The Lancashire Brigade, reinforced by the 2nd West Yorkshire from the 2nd Brigade and commanded by Brigadier-General Walter Kitchener were the next to attack, and advanced in fine style. They captured the lower slopes of Railway Hill with complete success, and, turning the advanced Boer trenches, took about sixty prisoners without themselves suffering serious loss.

Finally the 4th Brigade crossed the railway, which it had reached without many casualties, and began its attack on Hart's Hill, the right of the Boer main position. In accordance with brigade orders, the 2nd East Surrey and the 1st Rifle Brigade each had two complete companies in their firing line; and these four companies, extended to six paces from man to man, and closely supported by four more

Capture of Hart's Hill, Natal, February 27th, 1900.
(From a drawing by an Officer of the Devonshire Regiment.)

companies (two of each battalion), began the assault of Hart's Hill with a spirited rush up the lower slopes. The advance to the railway and the early stages of the assault were carried out under cover of a very heavy artillery fire, admirably managed, which enabled the infantry to advance with comparatively slight loss. As the leading half-battalion of the 2nd East Surrey began its advance up Hart's Hill, Major Pearse, who to that point had accompanied the supports, received a sudden order, sent by General Sir Redvers Buller himself, to move the rear half-battalion with all speed to the right, in order to reinforce the Lancashire Brigade, whose Commander was said to have demanded assistance. Lieutenant-Colonel Cooke, commanding the Scottish Rifles, received orders at the same time to follow the 2nd East Surrey.

On reaching the Lancashire Brigade Major Pearse was informed by Brigadier-General Kitchener that he was in no want of reinforcements and had asked for none. Lieutenant-Colonel Cooke, who arrived soon after with his four companies, received a similar reply to his offer of help. The Boer artillery at this time was shelling the 11th Brigade heavily, and the four East Surrey companies sustained several casualties. Under Brigadier-General Kitchener's orders they remained with the 11th Brigade until dusk, when Major Pearse was permitted to move them across to Hart's Hill and rejoin the four companies there, who meanwhile had well played their part in the capture of the position.

The firing line, ably handled by Captain Tew, had worked its way to the summit, closely supported by Captain Gorman's companies, which closed up to them with great eagerness during the attack, so that in the final rush for the Boer trenches the two lines were in part inter-mixed. The left company of the firing line being rather crowded out of place by the Rifle Brigade, was eventually somewhat in rear of B company, but all ranks and all the companies showed an excellent spirit. Private Brady of H company was brought to notice by Lieutenant Barchard, and was awarded a Distinguished Conduct Medal. He was promoted Corporal, and was killed in action later in the war, when a sergeant.

The hill having been captured, the four companies proceeded under Captain Gorman's orders to reverse the Boer sangars and to make the defences good against any attempt to recapture the hill. They were just completing this task, which had been carried out under fire, when they were joined by the four companies from Railway Hill. The casualties of the battalion during the battle of Pieter's Hill were four killed and one officer (2nd Lieutenant Brancker) and thirty-four non-commissioned officers and men wounded—one mortally.

The following passage in Lord Roberts' despatch, dated Bloemfontein, March 15, 1900, gives a brief summary of the battle:

> "On the 27th February Major General Barton with two battalions of the 6th brigade and the 2nd battalion Royal Dublin Fusiliers, crept one and a half miles down the river bank and, ascending an almost precipitous cliff 500 feet high assaulted and occupied the top of Pieter's Hill. This to some extent turned the enemy's left, and enabled Lieutenant General Sir Charles Warren, with the 4th Brigade under Colonel Norcott and the 11th Brigade under Colonel Kitchener, to assault the main position, which was carried by the 1st Battalion South Lancashire Regiment, 2nd Battalion East Surrey Regiment, and 1st Battalion Rifle Brigade, about sunset; sixty prisoners were captured and the enemy scattered in all directions."

This summary report was telegraphed to Lord Roberts by Sir Redvers Buller on February 28, the day after the battle.

At dawn on the 28th, the 2nd East Surrey and half-battalion Scottish Rifles, the troops holding the summit of Hart's Hill, were ready for a renewal of the action of the previous day, but soon discovered that the Boers had at last given up the position that they had held so tenaciously and were in full retreat towards Ladysmith. During the morning the East Surrey buried their dead under the large tree which had been the directing point of their attack, and there the men, or most of them, rested after their labours, which had been incessant since dawn on the 22nd. Some enterprising spirits explored the neighbouring Boer laager and returned laden with blankets and clothing from the store, most of which had presently to be thrown away. Trousers were in great demand, for many were completely worn out, as were most of the boots, but few of the latter could be replaced.

The battalion was visited on Hart's Hill by Major-General Lyttelton commanding the 2nd Division, and in the course of the morning Major Pearse was desired by the Colonel commanding the 4th Brigade to submit through him the names of officers and men who had distinguished themselves on the 27th. The officers recommended for reward were Captain Tew and Lieutenants Barchard and de la Fontaine. The non-commissioned officers and men were Colour-Sergeants W. Ladd, F. Robinson, and C. Dennis, Sergeants W. G. Lyne, F. Hillyard, and G. Joiner,[1] Privates E. Brady (specially recommended for gallant conduct), J. Hinton, T. Crawley, A. Long, and A. Sharp. The colour-sergeants and sergeants had all commanded half-companies in the action, owing to the death of officers, and had been reported as showing both dash and coolness. The four private soldiers last mentioned had volunteered to act as orderlies to the commanding officer. This was looked upon as a most dangerous duty, as a large proportion of the men who had previously acted as orderlies to Lieutenant-Colonel Harris or Major Pearse had been killed or wounded.

Having handed in his report and recommendations, Major Pearse received the following order :

> " The O. C. East Surrey.
>
> " When General Hildyard reaches this camp you are to rejoin him. The Brigadier wishes me to thank you for all your behaviour and support yesterday. Your men did most excellently and we are sorry to lose you.
>
> (Signed) HARRY WILSON,
> Bde. Major 4th Brigade."

11.20 A.M.
28.2.00.

Accordingly the battalion moved down presently from Hart's Hill and rejoined the 2nd Brigade on the level ground between Hart's Hill and Railway Hill, near the long trench captured on the 27th by the 11th Brigade. This trench had been used as a grave for some of the Boer dead, many of whom had also been buried in their trenches on Hart's Hill. It was subsequently admitted by the Boers that their losses on February 27 had been heavy.

The casualties of the 2nd East Surrey Regiment from February 18 to 27 inclusive were as follows :

---

[1] Sergeant Joiner later in the war was granted a commission as 2nd Lieutenant in the Northamptonshire Regiment.

THE EAST SURREY REGIMENT

Killed, 1 Officer and 26 of other ranks.
Wounded, 6 Officers and 133 „   „   „
Total, 7   „   „ 159 „   „   „

Killed.

Lieutenant C. H. Hinton.
Sergeant J. D. Chamberlain.
Corporal H. E. Warwicker.
    „   J. Wilkinson.
Lance-Corporal G. Synnott.
Drummer W. Blackmore.
No. 5467, Private C. Hibbert.
 „ 4806, „   W. Downing.
 „ 5531, „   J. Hunt.
 „ 3475, „   F. Long.
 „ 3231, „   H. Callan.
 „ 3653, „   H. Bond.
 „ 3438, „   J. Hill.
 „ 5365, „   T. Wild.

No. 3142, Private E. Blackburn.
 „ 5033, „   F. Llewellyn.
 „ 4385, „   H. Beach.
 „ 5428, „   H. Baldock.
 „ 2749, „   H. Bell.
 „ 5509, „   H. Sterling.
 „ 2693, „   H. Brown.
 „ 5607, „   W. Prior.
 „ 2462, „   G. Yeatman.
 „ 5273, „   J. Wilcox.
 „ 4377, „   J. Bond.
 „ 5505, „   C. Adams.
 „ 5499, „   J. Clayton.

Wounded.

Lieut.-Colonel R. H. W. H. Harris.
Major H. L. Smith.
    „   H. P. Treeby.
Captain F. L. A. Packman.
Lieutenant J. P. Benson.
2nd Lieutenant S. D. Brancker.
Colour-Sergeant F. Robinson.
Sergeant H. Jones.
    „   J. Cooper.
    „   H. Thomson.
    „   J. Godding.
Lance-Sergeant T. Fisher.
Corporal G. Stanley.
    „   J. Grist.
    „   H. Goddard.
    „   J. Self.
    „   H. Brown.
Lance-Corporal H. Curtler.
    „   A. Blatch.
    „   E. Blake.
    „   J. Fisher.
    „   W. Davies.
    „   R. Parris.
Drummer C. Southey.
No. 5476, Private W. Baker.
 „ 5451, „   J. Bartlett.
 „ 5691, „   H. Chance.
 „ 3548, „   F. Collett.
 „ 5482, „   G. Ashton.
 „ 3401, „   W. Jackson.

No. 2275, Private G. Lowe.
 „ 5462, „   J. Locke.
 „ 4660, „   F. Wallis.
 „ 3354, „   E. Tadgell.
 „ 3621, „   H. Park.
 „ 4260, „   J. Gatcombe.
 „ 5697, „   W. Cannell.
 „ 5700, „   J. Mulligan.
 „ 4820, „   F. Barrett.
 „ 3435, „   C. R. Brown.
 „ 4330, „   J. Whitton.
 „ 3509, „   R. Newman.
 „ 3504, „   H. James.
 „ 5721, „   G. Dover.
 „ 5430, „   C. Lowe.
 „ 5014, „   H. Lowe.
 „ 3256, „   J. Taylor.
 „ 5692, „   E. Webb.
 „ 4260, „   F. Cotton.
 „ 2332, „   A. Blake.
 „ 4627, „   H. Maynard.
 „ 3641, „   S. Garrod.
 „ 2451, „   C. Hall.
 „ 3299, „   G. Latuga.
 „ 2397, „   D. Butler.
 „ 3996, „   H. Tobutt.
 „ 3269, „   A. Glenister.
 „ 3090, „   J. Wanless.
 „ 1365, „   G. Wilton.
 „ 5530, „   F. Beale.

SECOND BATTALION IN THE SOUTH AFRICAN WAR 409

No. 5447,	Private	J. Franks.	No. 3708,	Private	W. Collins.
,, 3669,	,,	J. Lambert.	,, 3279,	,,	J. Bennett.
,, 2888,	,,	H. Spacey.	,, 3413,	,,	J. Edmonds.
,, 2843,	,,	G. Adamson.	,, 3150,	,,	W. Morris.
,, 5523,	,,	J. French.	,, 3223,	,,	H. Baker.
,, 4214,	,,	W. Upfold.	,, 2775,	,,	W. Simmonds.
,, 3308,	,,	H. Hepburn.	,, 3666,	,,	W. Lock.
,, 3526,	,,	R. Poynter.	,, 2537,	,,	W. Molly.
,, 4864,	,,	G. Brooks.	,, 5652,	,,	A. Ball.
,, 4939,	,,	H. Smith.	,, 5246,	,,	R. Bateman.
,, 4296,	,,	W. Maskell.	,, 3287,	,,	J. Horstead.
,, 2954,	,,	S. Dicks.	,, 2580,	,,	T. Brown.
,, 3497,	,,	R. Taylor.	,, 3599,	,,	A. Spittle.
,, 2274,	,,	A. Wood.	,, 2844,	,,	J. Herring.
,, 3277,	,,	P. Evans.	,, 3645,	,,	W. Stowel.
,, 2865,	,,	F. Taylor.	,, 3367,	,,	G. Manning.
,, 5703,	,,	J. Churchill.	,, 2626,	,,	A. Green.
,, 2783,	,,	C. Watkins.	,, 5489,	,,	W. Haynes.
,, 2458,	,,	P. Berry.	,, 4310,	,,	H. Raby.
,, 3685,	,,	W. Loader.	,, 5496,	,,	G. Sealey.
,, 5326,	,,	T. Murden.	,, 4930,	,,	W. Sheffield.
,, 5556,	,,	J. Porter.	,, 4867,	,,	G. Whitby.
,, 5403	,,	D. FitzGibbon.	,, 3169,	,,	W. Allen.
,, 2583,	,,	J. Sheay.	,, 2233,	,,	D. Pryor.
,, 2111,	,,	G. Williams.	,, 3658,	,,	J. Knight.
,, 2106,	,,	A. Bailey.	,, 4360,	,,	A. Attwood.
,, 2285,	,,	W. Bowles.	,, 2986,	,,	A. Wood.
,, 2365,	,,	T. Brooks.	,, 3113,	,,	G. Witsey.
,, 4246,	,,	R. Chatwin.	,, 2260,	,,	W. Coltman.
,, 4969,	,,	E. Coleman.	,, 3134,	,,	J. Harley.
,, 2808,	,,	E. Curtain.	,, 5548,	,,	F. Birch.
,, 4154,	,,	A. Ellis.	,, 5351,	,,	W. McFarlane.
,, 2260,	,,	A. Thurston.	,, 3014,	,,	W. Matthews.
,, 5342,	,,	T. Brown.	,, 5655,	,,	W. Roche.
,, 5793,	,,	J. McMahon.	,, 5453,	,,	J. Blundell.
,, 5501,	,,	A. Alexander.	,, 3091,	,,	W. Boxer.
,, 2745,	,,	B. Barrett.	,, 3027,	,,	H. Long.
,, 3487,	,,	F. Hopkins.	,, 5053,	,,	J. Willmott.
,, 5497,	,,	R. Skelley.	,, 3654,	,,	E. Boyes.
,, 5487,	,,	T. Hayward.			

Of the above the following died of their wounds:

Lance-Corporal Curtler.			No. 2233,	Private	D. Pryor.
No. 5556,	Private	J. Porter.	,, 3666,	,,	W. Lock.
,, 5497,	,,	R. Skelley.	,, 3658,	,,	J. Knight.

On discovering that the Boer army was in full retreat, Sir Redvers Buller decided to make the duty of passing supplies into Ladysmith his first care. He knew the skill of the Boers in fighting rear-guard actions, his mounted arm was not strong, and any further delay in supplying the starving garrison of Ladysmith might have serious results. Accordingly the infantry and artillery of the Natal army advanced a short distance, when the divisions, whose units had been much inter-changed, were re-organised; the bulk of the mounted troops halted at Nelthorpe, and only a small force under Lord Dundonald rode into Ladysmith on February 28. On March 1 Sir Redvers Buller himself entered Ladysmith, and a large convoy of food and medical appliances were driven into the town. The Natal army, except the 5th and 10th Brigades, moved up to Nelthorpe and bivouacked in heavy rain on the banks of the Klip river. The troops necessarily drank the water of this stream, polluted by the filthy Boer camps, in which sanitary precautions were unknown. To this circumstance, the outbreak of enteric fever which soon after attacked the troops may partly be attributed. The army halted on March 2, and on the 3rd marched through the streets of Ladysmith, which were lined by the garrison, a moving experience which will never be forgotten by those present.

The total casualties incurred by Sir Redvers Buller's army in the relief of Ladysmith numbered 5405, out of which over 1000 fell upon the 2nd Brigade. The 2nd East Surrey's casualties in the relief numbered 253 killed and wounded, thus composed:

Killed: One officer and thirty-six of other ranks.

Wounded: Eight officers and 208 of other ranks.

The battalion lost no prisoners.

In addition to the honours mentioned in the narrative, Lieutenant-Colonel R. H. W. H. Harris was appointed a Companion of the Bath, and Major H. W. Pearse was promoted Brevet-Lieut.-Colonel for services in the relief of Ladysmith. Both these officers received special mention in despatches as having shown themselves good commanding officers.

The 2nd East Surrey, with the other battalions of the 2nd Brigade, was encamped near Surprise Hill, on the outskirts of Ladysmith, from March 4 to 8. On the former day the tents and light baggage came up, and all ranks had an opportunity of changing the clothes which they had been wearing night and day since February 14. On March 8 the 2nd Division, with other troops, marched to Modder spruit, and on the 9th to a long ridge between Elandslaagte railway station and Sunday's river. Major-General Lyttelton disposed the camp on a wide front, so that the troops might have as much air as possible, in the interests of health, as the reaction after the exertions of the relief operations were now much felt by officers and men. Dysentery and enteric fever were rife, and a large number of deaths occurred, though the Natal army did not suffer nearly as severely from this disease as did Lord Roberts' troops at Bloemfontein.

On March 15 Captain Ionides joined the battalion, having volunteered from the 1st Battalion in India, and on March 20 Lieutenant-General Clery rejoined the 2nd Division from hospital. The following order was published on the occasion by Major-General Lyttleton:

> "In relinquishing command of the 2nd division, Major General Hon. N. G. Lyttelton, C.B., desires to express his appreciation of the manner in which the 2nd Brigade has performed its part in the difficult operations during which he was associated with it, and to express his regret that the exigencies of the service have so soon severed his connection with it."

The departure of Major-General Lyttelton was universally regretted, he having inspired all who came in contact with him with the highest respect, confidence and liking. General Lyttelton received the command of the 4th Division, composed of the Ladysmith Infantry, which was for a time sent to clean and healthy camps to recover its health. The 5th and 6th Brigades (now the 10th Division, under Major-General Sir A. Hunter) were sent early in March to Cape Colony. Finally, the Ladysmith sick, numbering over 2000, were sent down country to various hospitals or to England.

All these changes and movements threw so much stress on the broken railway that no immediate advance of Sir Redvers Buller's army was possible. The Boer army from Ladysmith had completely vanished from view until the middle of March, when it was ascertained that about 16,000 men with thirty guns were entrenched in the Biggarsberg. This being known, the position of the 2nd Division before Elandslaagte was obviously unsafe, being within easy range of the lower spurs of the Biggarsberg. The Boers, however, were uncertain as to what course of action they would pursue, and it was not until April 10 that they made any attempt to attack Elandslaagte. By that date Lord Roberts' advance through the Free State had drawn off a large portion of the Boer Natal army, and no more than 6000 or 7000 men remained on the Biggarsberg, with strong supports at Dundee.

On April 10, the Boers, led by General Louis Botha, made a sudden advance, and at 8 A.M. opened fire with three guns on the camp of the 2nd Division at a range of about 5000 yards. The camp of the 2nd East Surrey, which was about the centre of the division, received the first fire. The first shell just missed the commanding officer's tent, and passed over the ridge pole of a shelter under which the officers were eating breakfast. A couple of feet lower and the battalion would have been left almost without officers. The second shell struck a tent of C company and seriously wounded Private Daman, the tent-orderly. C and D companies had left camp before dawn, and had taken up a position on a kopje near the Sunday's river bridge, in support of the cavalry out-posts, and the 2nd Queen's were also in the plain before the camp, engaged at drill, when fire was opened. Consequently there was no risk of a sudden attack on the camp. The battalions in camp turned out quickly and without the slightest confusion from their tents, and moved clear of the camp under regimental orders. The camp was then struck, and the 2nd West Yorkshire were ordered up on the right of the 2nd Queen's, which battalion had reinforced the two East Surrey companies and was posted near the bank of the Sunday's river. Firing at long ranges continued about four hours, the Boers showing no inclination to press their attack. At dusk the whole British force was withdrawn from its exposed ground near the Sunday's river and took up a very strong position on the Elandslaagte ridge; that very position in fact that had been so gallantly captured by the force under Sir John French in the previous October.

The retirement from Sunday's river camp was covered by the 2nd East Surrey, which lay out all night along the railway line in case the Boers might attempt a night attack.

On April 12 the battalion, which had been largely reduced in strength by war casualties and sickness, received welcome reinforcements in the shape of 100 men from Maritzburg, under Lieutenant Smalley, and a volunteer service company, 105 strong, under Captain Collyer, with Lieutenants Brooks and Longstaff. This help came when it was much wanted, for all ranks, particularly the officers, were being seriously over-worked. On April 17, the 10th Division having left Natal, it was considered advisable to withdraw the troops from Elandslaagte, and the 2nd Division marched back to Ladysmith, arriving there on April 18 and encamping by Bell's spruit, on the east side of Surprise Hill, and about two miles from Nicholson's Nek. Enteric fever continued to prevail, and during April Captains Gorman, Ellis, Packman and Gilbert Cooper were admitted to hospital and subsequently invalided to England. Major Pearse and Captain Tew were therefore the only officers above subaltern rank remaining at duty who had embarked with the battalion on October 20. Reinforcements of officers and men were, however, well maintained, as on April 25 Major H. W. Benson and Lieutenant Colquhoun arrived from England with a draft of 100 men, and on the previous day Lieutenant Benson rejoined for duty, having quickly recovered from his wound. At the same time the 2nd Brigade lost its trusted commander, Major-General Hildyard, C.B., who was promoted to the command of the 5th Division, vice Sir Charles Warren, who took up a command in Cape Colony. Major-General Hildyard's departure was much regretted by all ranks in the 2nd East Surrey Regiment, who placed implicit confidence in his skill and judgment.

Major-General Hildyard issued the following farewell order to the brigade :

> " On relinquishing command of the 2nd Brigade, Major-General Hildyard, C.B., desires to convey to all ranks his keen appreciation of the good services rendered by them during the campaign in Natal. His experience of the several Battalions composing the Brigade when under his command at Aldershot during two training seasons made him confident they would prove efficient in the field. At Willow Grange, at Colenso, at Vaal Krantz, and at Pieter's they fully justified this expectation and he will always recall with pride their conduct on those occasions. The Major-General takes this opportunity of thanking Commanding Officers for the support they have uniformly given him, and all Officers, N.C.O's and men for their excellent behaviour on all occasions. He sincerely regrets that his connection with the Brigade has now been severed, but confidently looks forward to hearing of fresh honours being earned by it."

Major-General Hildyard was succeeded in the command of the 2nd Brigade by Lieutenant-Colonel E. O. F. Hamilton of the 2nd Queen's, the only Lieutenant-Colonel remaining in the brigade. Of the three others, Colonel Kitchener had been promoted Major-General from February 23, 1900, Lieutenant-Colonel Harris had been invalided to England on account of his many dangerous wounds received on that same day, and Lieutenant-Colonel Bullock was a prisoner-of-war. After Colonel Hamilton's appointment to Brigadier-General, therefore, all four battalions of the 2nd Brigade were commanded by Majors.

On May 1 Major Pearse was compelled by illness to hand over command of the 2nd East Surrey to Major H. W. Benson, and was sent to hospital at Durban. A few days later the long period of compulsory inaction which had followed the relief of Ladysmith came to an end, and on May 7, Sir Redvers Buller's Natal army began its advance through northern Natal, with the object of clearing the railway line in order that it might eventually become the main source of supply for the whole army in the Transvaal. Sir Redvers' first object was to drive the Boers out of the Biggarsberg, and to do this he decided to turn their left flank by an advance of the 2nd Division and other troops by Helpmakaar and Beith, while the 5th Division advanced up the railway, repairing it as it went.

The 2nd Division marched without tents from Surprise Hill on May 7 and reached Sunday's river camp on the 10th, where it was joined by Lord Dundonald's mounted Brigade and a strong force of artillery. On May 12 the whole turning force under Sir Redvers Buller himself advanced to Vermaak's Kraal, the 2nd East Surrey Regiment, with one squadron 19th Hussars, and two guns, forming the advanced guard, under Major Benson. On arriving at Vermaak's Kraal, Boers could be seen preparing a gun position about 8000 yards away, on the summit of the Biggarsberg. Two 4.7 guns were placed in position and laid on the Boer guns.

On May 13, Sir Redvers directed a movement against a very high and precipitous hill called Uithoek, which had been neglected by the Boers, being probably considered inaccessible to our troops. While the cavalry made a circling movement to the east of this hill, led by Thorneycroft's Mounted Infantry, the 2nd Brigade was ordered to advance against it, the Queen's, Devon, and West Yorkshire attacking, while the East Surrey remained in reserve and as escort to the guns. Thorneycroft's advance was but little opposed, and by 11.30 A.M.

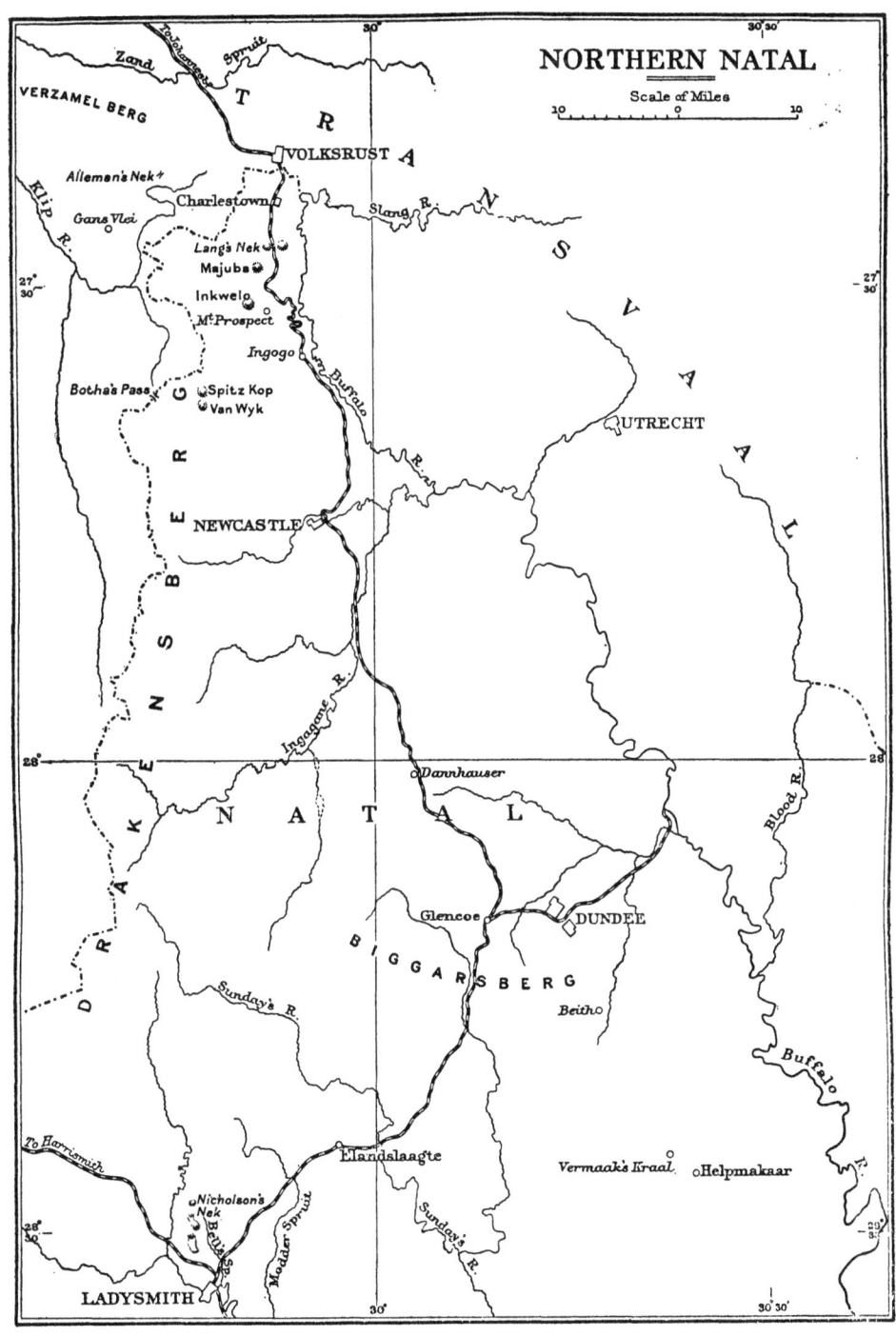

Uithoek had been occupied by the 2nd Brigade, the leading battalion, the Queen's, coming under a good deal of fire. The Boers were completely outmanœuvred and soon fell back on Helpmakaar, before which place the British force bivouacked for the night. During the night the enemy evacuated Helpmakaar and fell back on Beith, so that Sir Redvers Buller's bold and rapid manœuvring had turned the Biggarsberg with unexpected ease.

On May 14 the Boers attempted to make a stand about three miles north of Helpmakaar, but the mounted troops soon got them on the run and kept them going. Later the Irish commando, under one Lynch, attempted also to check the advance, but were driven back so easily that very few in the force knew of the existence of these renegades. A final stand was made by the Boers about fourteen miles from Helpmakaar, in a very strong position at Blesboklaagte. Here Lord Dundonald was ordered to halt by Sir Redvers Buller, the mounted troops having covered twenty-five miles during the day's pursuit, and having passed far beyond the infantry, which had halted at Beith. Lord Dundonald left a strong picquet to watch the enemy, his main body bivouacking at Meyer's Farm; and a patrol from the picquet entering Dundee during the night, found that the Boers had retired from that place. The entire Biggarsberg was therefore evacuated. The infantry entered Dundee by 1 P.M. on the 15th, the 2nd Brigade having covered the sixteen miles from Beith since 6 A.M., marching mainly through burning grass and finding no water on the road. After a day's halt, the force advanced on May 17 to Dannhauser (fourteen miles), the cavalry advanced guard pushing on to Newcastle, where they arrived at 10 P.M. to find that the enemy had passed through in the morning in full retreat. On May 18 the infantry marched twenty-four miles to Newcastle, and the 2nd East Surrey, forming the advanced guard, was the first infantry regiment to enter that place. At the mid-day halt rifles were piled and accoutrements taken off, to rest the men. The long grass was accidentally fired and the ammunition was endangered, many rounds exploding. Major Benson and three men were injured, but by great exertions all the rifles except four were saved. A number of water-bottles and haversacks were destroyed, a serious loss. The battalion was quartered in a farm outside the town. The 2nd Brigade was halted on May 19, while the 4th Brigade advanced

SECOND BATTALION IN THE SOUTH AFRICAN WAR 417

to support a reconnaissance of Lang's Nek by the cavalry. Lord Dundonald soon found that this vast position was held by the enemy in strength, and General Buller consequently decided to halt awhile and concentrate his strength before his next attack.

On May 25, the 5th Division marched into Newcastle, accompanied by more heavy guns, and the 4th Division from Ladysmith arrived two days later. Enteric fever was now prevalent in the force, and Lieutenant Le Fleming and Lieutenant Brooks of the volunteer service company were attacked by the disease, the latter dying at Newcastle, to the great regret of his own company and of the battalion.

On May 28 the 2nd Brigade advanced to Ingogo, the 4th Brigade being about four miles in advance at Mount Prospect and Inkwelo.

Sir Redvers Buller now had before him the arduous task of capturing or turning the Lang's Nek position. Strongly held as it obviously was, a frontal attack was not to be thought of. To Lord Roberts and Sir Redvers himself a turning movement round the Boers' right seemed to offer the best hope of success, but this entailed forcing a passage over the formidable Drakensberg, and as many of the Boer leaders were known now to despair of success, and were believed to be ready to come to terms, it was decided to approach them with a view to peace. Sir Redvers Buller was personally well known to the Boers, and much liked and respected by them, and this rendered him more likely to succeed with them than any other British Commander. Accordingly on May 30 Sir Redvers despatched a message to the Boer Commander on Lang's Nek, informing him that Lord Roberts had crossed the Vaal and pointing out the desirability of making peace; but on June 5 the Boer leaders declined further negotiations.

General Buller, whose plans were all formed and knew the ground well from experience gained in earlier campaigns, immediately put into execution his intended operations for the forcing of the Drakensberg, a barren and lofty range which forms the western boundary of Natal. Leaving a force under Sir Francis Clery facing Lang's Nek, Sir Redvers on June 6 ordered the South African Light Horse to seize Van Wyk's Hill, a height which commanded the south side of Botha's pass. This done, Major-General Talbot Coke, with three battalions and a battery, established himself on Van Wyk's Hill, on

2 E

which four heavy guns were then placed. The Boers attempted to re-capture the hill, but were easily repulsed.

On June 5, Lieutenant-General Hildyard attacked Botha's pass with his own (the 5th) Division and the 2nd Brigade, the 11th Brigade attacking the pass itself, while the 2nd Brigade moved against the heights east of Spitz-Kop, a very high point, which was attacked by the South African Light Horse. Spitz-Kop was seized without fighting, and the 2nd Brigade advanced, placing the 2nd Devon and 2nd West Yorkshire in the first line, 2nd East Surrey second line, and 2nd Queen's third line. As the advance proceeded, the first line covered so much ground that Major Benson sent Captain Ionides with four companies to support the Devon, while he with four companies supported the West Yorkshire; the ninth company,[1] under Lieutenant May, escorting the maxim guns, which with the pom-poms had been ordered to get to the summit of Spitz-Kop if possible. The ground was very rough, and the brigade had a precipitous climb of over 1000 feet up a very steep spur of Mount Inkweloane. The firing on reaching the top was heavy though ineffective. It was found that the Boer trenches were drawn back nearly 3000 yards from the crest, with perfectly level ground in front of them. Major Benson's companies, on reaching the summit, were ordered to take up the ground held by the West Yorkshire, who then moved further to their left. Fire ceased at dusk, and the force bivouacked where it was in a dense mist. No great-coats or food could be got up, and the cold was very severe. The 11th Brigade (Major-General Wynne) had in like manner captured the crest of the berg west of Spitz-Kop, and had passed the night there. The 10th Brigade had remained on Van Wyk. On the morning of June 9, Sir Redvers Buller rode round the out-posts of the 2nd Brigade and expressed himself delighted with the way the troops had gone up the cliffs. The Boers had evacuated their position before daylight, and the 2nd Brigade moved about a mile to its front and bivouacked on a ridge which gave some shelter, the baggage (except tents) coming up during the morning through Botha's pass. The 11th Brigade advanced this day about five miles in a north-westerly direction, following up the defeated Boers.

[1] The battalion was now formed of nine companies, the volunteer service company retaining its separate organisation.

On June 10 the 2nd Brigade, still accompanying the 5th Division and the remainder of General Hildyard's force, made a long and fatiguing march into the Free State, bivouacking at last at the junction of the Gansvlei and the Klip river. The early part of the march was made in a thick fog, during which the baggage was found making off straight for the Boers, outside the right flank-guard. The Boer rear-guard made one stand, but were speedily driven off by the South African Light Horse and the artillery. Beyond this rear-guard a force of the enemy, estimated at over 3000 horsemen, was seen establishing itself on high ground to the northward and directly between the British force and its objective, the villages of Charlestown and Volksrust in rear of Lang's Nek. Sir Redvers, therefore, had his troops warned to prepare for a fight.

Action of Alleman's Nek

The position held by the Boers before the British force was a well-defined spur which ran north-westward from the Drakensberg range across the wide valley between it and the Verzamel Berg in the Transvaal. The road to Volksrust, by which Sir Redvers Buller intended to advance, ran over this spur through a deep cleft called Alleman's Nek. The ridge on each side of the nek was very steep. Between the bivouac at Gansvlei and the point of attack lay more than seven miles of undulating country. The advance was led by the 11th Brigade, covered by the heavy artillery, and guarded on either flank by a mounted brigade. No opposition was offered, and Major-General Wynne soon established his brigade within five miles of Alleman's Nek, in a suitable position for it to act as pivot for the remainder of the force. The 2nd and 10th Brigades then advanced, and by one o'clock were concentrated under cover of the last roll in the ground before the nek. The cavalry at this time became engaged on both flanks, and an artillery duel opened. The Boer fire was at first heavy and rapid, but on our heavy guns coming up it was temporarily silenced about 2.30 P.M. The infantry was then ordered to advance to the attack, the 10th Brigade being directed at the high ridge to the right of the nek, and the 2nd Brigade at the nek itself and the hill to the left of it. Brigadier-General Hamilton placed the 2nd Queen's and 2nd East Surrey in first

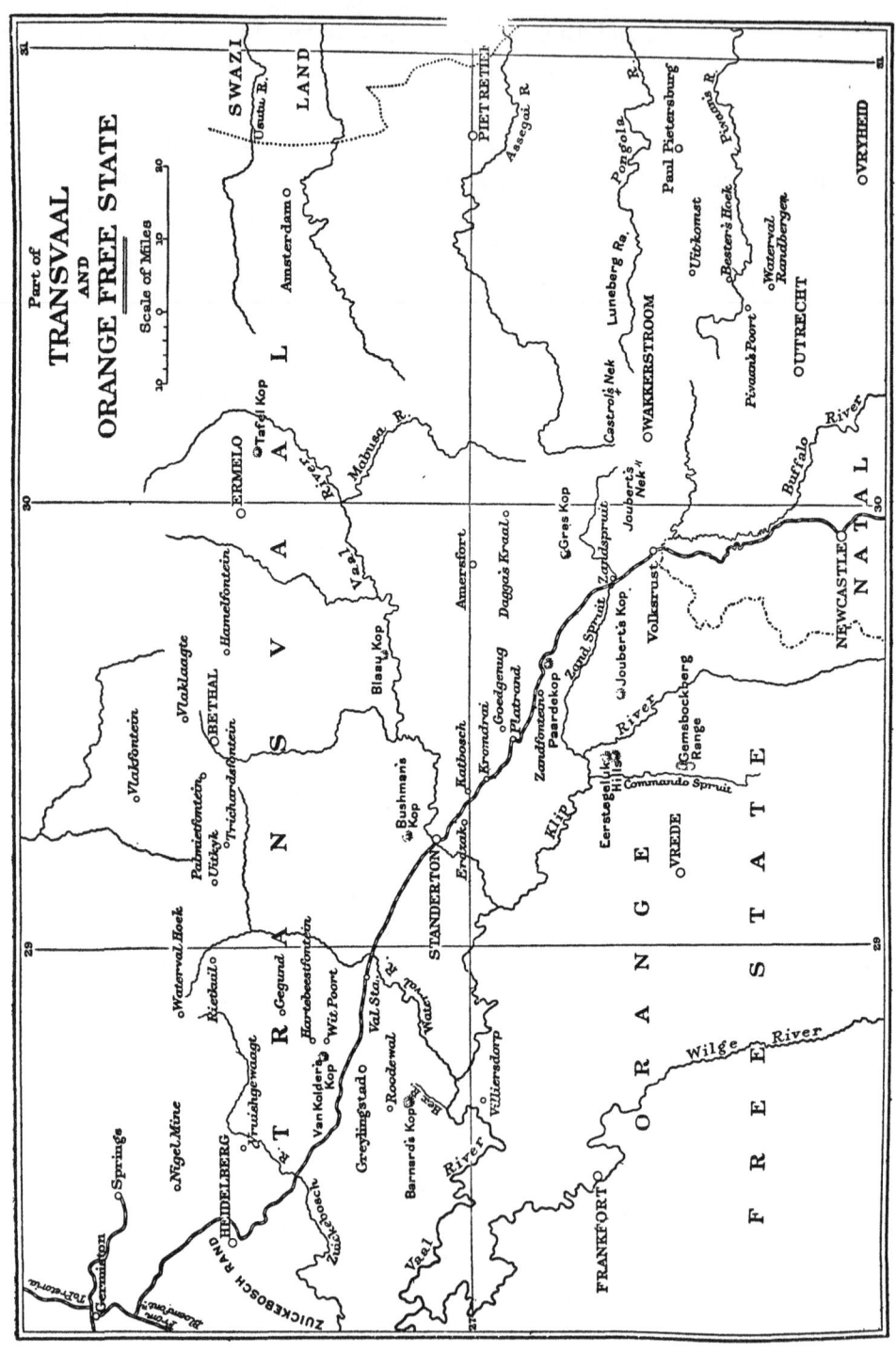

line, each with two companies in the firing line, two in support, and five in reserve. The 2nd West Yorkshire were in second line, in rear of the Queen's. The 2nd East Surrey, which were on the right of the first line, were ordered to attack the nek itself and the hill to the left of it, the Queen's attacking the ridge further still to the left.

Captain White, who had recovered from his wound received at Vaal Krantz, joined the battalion shortly before it went into action. The Boer position proved to be strong and difficult to approach, but the two brigades, very well handled and showing the best possible spirit, were not to be denied, and by 5 P.M. the whole position was in the hands of General Hildyard's force. The experiences of the 2nd East Surrey are clearly detailed in Major Benson's official report to Brigadier-General Hamilton, which follows:

The Brigade-Major,
    2nd Brigade.

    In accordance with Memo received I have the honour to report that on the 11th instant on the arrival of the Battalion under my command at the 2nd position taken up by the heavy guns, I was ordered to attack Almond's[1] Nek and the hill on the left of it, on the right of the position to be attacked by the 2nd Queen's.

    At 3 P.M. the Battalion advanced with two Companies extended in the firing line under Captain Ionides and two in support under Captain Tew, and five companies in reserve, under Captain White. On arrival of the firing line at about 800 yards from the Nek a heavy rifle and Pom-pom fire was opened on it from the hills on both sides of the Nek. The first casualty occurred here. The firing line advanced steadily until close in front of the Nek where there was a dip affording some cover. The fire on the Nek itself was so heavy that Captain Ionides halted his left company and advanced with his right company to drive the enemy off the hills on that side. This was carried out successfully by him with his company, supported by Captain Tew.

    Seeing that if I advanced directly on the Nek many casualties were likely to occur I moved the rest of the Battalion to the right, where they were sheltered by the hill, and when the fire in the Nek had been subdued, I directed them across the Nek to seize the hill which was our original objective. This was done without further loss. The Boers retired from the hills on the right and

---

[1] The official spelling of Alleman's Nek was not adopted until after the date of this letter.

were followed by Captain Ionides and his support, who advanced to the Kraal beyond and did some execution amongst them as they fled.

(Signed) H. W. BENSON, Major.
Com^{ing} 2nd East Surrey Regiment.

Charlestown,
15.6.00.

The capture of Alleman's Nek, and the clear evidence that Sir Redvers Buller's advance could not be stopped, decided the Boers to retire from the whole position, although in fact they had been able to hold their own in the high ground on their own left. A position here was, however, useless to them, as their main body at Lang's Nek was already in full retreat, and the Alleman's Nek commandos would consequently be cut off unless they quickly made their way to the north. On June 12 not a Boer remained in Natal, Sir Francis Clery had advanced and occupied the Lang's Nek position, and on June 13 the force under General Hildyard marched into Charlestown and Volksrust, the latter being the border town of the Transvaal.

The casualties of the 2nd East Surrey at Alleman's Nek were two private soldiers killed, and one officer and thirteen of other ranks wounded. Two of the wounded died almost at once. The names were as follows :

Killed and mortally wounded—4.

| No. 1103, Private H. Lofthouse. | No. 3399, Private H. Smith. |
| ,, 2227, ,, E. Burke. | ,, 5573, ,, A. Hicks. |

Wounded—1 officer and 11 other ranks.

2nd Lieutenant P. B. Stafford.	No. 4392, Private W. Davis.
No. 6369, Private J. Welman.	,, 4685, ,, W. Locke.
,, 1372, ,, J. Burke.	,, 3386, ,, H. Lewenden.
,, 2757, ,, J. Stead.	,, 2390, ,, H. Rose.
,, 3320, ,, A. Acourt.	,, 2869, ,, V. Storey.
,, 5423, ,, G. Fawdry.	

2nd Lieutenant Stafford, commanding the left company of the firing line, who was shot through the head from side to side, had a remarkable escape. The command of the company devolved on Colour-Sergeant Holmes, a cool and efficient non-commissioned officer.

The good judgment and initiative shown by Major H. W. Benson, in command of the battalion, and by Captain Ionides in command of the firing line, met with favourable notice. Major Benson was mentioned in despatches by Sir Redvers Buller and was awarded the Distinguished Service Order. The volunteer service company, under Captain Collyer, behaved perfectly steadily, but sustained no casualties. Captain Collyer was shortly afterwards invalided on account of enteric fever, and was succeeded in the command of the company by Lieutenant Longstaff, who was promoted to the rank of Captain.

On June 16, the 2nd East Surrey was ordered to march out to De Jaeger's Nek, on high ground to the north-east of Volksrust, in order to keep open the communications of a force under General Hildyard which had occupied Wakkerstroom. The battalion remained at De Jaeger's Nek until June 19, when it marched to Zandspruit to join its brigade in the advance to Standerton. The force arrived at Paardekop on June 21, the Boers retiring thence just before its arrival. Continuing its advance unopposed, Sir Redvers Buller's cavalry entered Standerton on June 22, and the 2nd Brigade arrived there on the 24th and encamped under the eastern end of the kop, or precipitous hill, north of the town. On June 30 Major Pearse returned from hospital and resumed command of the battalion from Major Benson, whose services during the advance from Ladysmith to Standerton had been conspicuous.

During July 1900 the battalion remained at Standerton, the garrison of which place gradually diminished as the railway line towards Pretoria was opened. On July 15, a draft of ninety-two men arrived from England. Early in August it was found necessary to establish additional posts to guard the railway south of Standerton, and the battalion furnished detachments of one company at Katbosch, where there was an important bridge, and at Erdzak, where a high road crossed the line. These posts were almost immediately increased to two companies each. At the end of the month, on the removal eastward of the 5th Division, the battalion was ordered to take over the important stations of Platrand, where three companies were stationed, and Volksrust, where Headquarters and four companies were to be posted. The Volksrust position had hitherto been very strongly held, and the half-battalion was dangerously weak to hold it. No other troops could, however, be spared, nor could the position be contracted, as it was necessary to keep strong posts on the surrounding high hills, on which guns were in position.

A and G companies, under Major Benson, were stationed on Hout Nek, a commanding height to the north of Volksrust, on which was a naval 12-pounder; and H company, under Captain White, held a similar post to the east, called Black Ridge, on which was a 4.7 gun. Volksrust itself, with all the rolling stock and other important stores, was almost without a garrison, and the Boers could have captured it any day, but at this stage of the war they showed little enterprise, and peace seemed to be near at hand.

Headquarters of the battalion remained at Volksrust until November 4, and the strength of the garrison frequently varied, but was always inadequate. For a time two companies of the 5th Division Mounted Infantry were stationed at Volksrust, under Major Chapman, Royal Dublin Fusiliers. (These companies and their commander subsequently highly distinguished themselves at the gallant defence of Itala.) On the removal of the Mounted Infantry to join General Hildyard's force operating about Wakkerstroom, the garrison became so inadequate that a company of the Dublin Fusiliers was lent to Major Pearse for the defence of the railway station. This company, however, was only thirty strong. On October 9, the volunteer service company left Headquarters for England, but on reaching Maritzburg was detained in South Africa for a further period of several months' duration, during which it was unfortunately detached from the battalion.

On the company leaving Volksrust, Major Pearse issued the following battalion order:

"October 9, 1900.

"The Volunteer Service Company joined Head-Quarters soon after the relief of Ladysmith, and has since done good work with the Battalion, sharing in the operations in Northern Natal, including the action of Alleman's Nek. The conduct of the company has been excellent and all ranks have shown a soldier-like spirit and a desire to take a full share in the hard work and dangers of the campaign. The Officer Commanding is sure that all the Battalion will join him in wishing the Volunteer company a pleasant journey home."

It may be added that the company continued to be well reported on as long as it remained in South Africa, and that it was very efficiently commanded by Captain Longstaff.

In consequence of a re-distribution of troops, Volksrust became, from November 4, a portion of the Natal command, and the headquarters of Major-General Talbot Coke. The 2nd East Surrey was consequently ordered to march to Platrand, its new headquarters, Major Pearse being appointed commander of the Platrand sub-section of the Standerton command. Under orders from Brigadier-General Hamilton, who met the battalion at Zandfontein, about four miles south of Platrand C company, under Lieutenant Benson, remained at Zandfontein, and formed a post there. This was an awkward place to defend, as it was commanded by high ground which could not be occupied. The next post northward was Platrand, where there was at first a considerable garrison, consisting of:

One troop Bethune's Mounted Infantry.
Two guns 64th Battery Royal Field Artillery.
Four companies 2nd East Surrey Regiment.

The remaining three companies of the East Surrey were stationed at important points on the railway, Leeuw Spruit, Kromdrai, and Katbosch.

On November 10 the garrison of Platrand was reduced by one company (E), which under 2nd Lieutenant Appleyard, formed a post on the Goedgenug ridge, about four miles north of Platrand. A party of Boers opened fire on the company from a neighbouring ridge while the trace of the work was being laid out, but no damage was done, and the post (which the regiment called " Good enough ") was quickly made extremely strong, and though quite isolated was never attacked. It proved very useful and enabled a large tract of country north of the railway to be kept clear of Boers.

On November 14 a small expedition (one troop B.M.I., two guns 64th Battery, and two companies 2nd East Surrey), under Major Pearse, cleared a large quantity of mealies from Boshoff's farm, north-east of Platrand. (Boshoff was a surrendered burgher living under the protection of the post at Kromdrai.) The mealies, stored in unoccupied farms, were of great importance to the Boer commandos. Wessel's farm, about two miles further on in the direction of Blaaukop, a Boer centre afterwards visited by the battalion, was found to contain a coil of dynamite. This could apparently only be intended for the purpose of destroying a railway bridge, so in accordance with orders, the farm was burnt and a notice placed on the premises stating by whose order it had been fired, and the reason. This farm and one other (for a similar reason) were the only ones burnt in the Platrand sub-district during the war. The expedition was "sniped" during its return march, but there were no casualties. The mounted men claimed to have wounded two Boers.

Many similar expeditions, under command of Major Pearse or Major Benson, took place during the stay of the battalion at Platrand, the strength being usually as above, though when a greater distance was to be traversed, an additional troop of cavalry was lent from Standerton for the occasion, and the strength of the infantry raised from two to four or even five companies when necessary. This entailed leaving the posts with skeleton garrisons, and also meant hard marching for the infantry, who had to rejoin their posts before nightfall, but all such work was most cheerfully performed. These expeditions resulted in the complete clearing of food stores for man and beast from all farms in the neighbourhood of Platrand, and Major-General Wynne, who had succeeded Sir Francis Clery in the Standerton command, expressed his approval of the measures taken. Much hard work also was done by the regiment in re-constructing and improving the defences of Platrand and the other posts. Engineering skill of no mean order was shown by many officers, non-commissioned officers, and men, and by no one more than Major Benson. Great attention was paid to sanitation, with good results to health.

On November 29 the Platrand column was strengthened by a squadron of the 13th Hussars from Standerton, and was sent out under Major Pearse in the Blaaukop direction, presumably with the intention of keeping the commandos there occupied, while Lord Roberts passed down the railway on his homeward journey. A brisk action took place, and the retirement of the little column was a somewhat hazardous operation, but the Boers were held off by the guns of the 64th Battery. The infantry rear-guard, under Lieutenants North and May, was well handled and retired steadily. One man of the 13th Hussars was dangerously wounded, and that no more casualties occurred was a piece of surprisingly good fortune.

In December the Boer commandos on the sides of the Platrand section of the railway began to show activity, and on the 19th of the month a demonstration towards Zandfontein was made by about thirty of the Verzamelberg Boers under Commandant Cornelius Erasmus, supported by a party of similar strength. A party of seven men of the battalion under Lance-Sergeant Jones, who had recently been mounted on captured or surrendered Boer ponies, were escorting a wagon into Volksrust, and being near Zandfontein were ordered to follow the Boers and observe their intentions. Sergeant Jones and his party, partly from inexperience and partly through the difficulties of the ground, were eventually entrapped in an ambush. Privates Cobb and Alington, who were surrounded at close quarters, were called upon to surrender, but both men made a gallant attempt to escape. Private Cobb, a young soldier, was killed, and Private Alington was dangerously wounded. Three days later Kromdrai, garrisoned by B (Captain Tew's) company, was fired into at night, and similar incidents were of frequent occurrence. They were intended to harass the men of the regiment, but had very little effect.

On December 19, Major Smith and Captain Porch rejoined from England, having recovered from their wounds. Lieutenant Hart also returned to duty, after a very severe attack of enteric fever.

On January 7, 1901, a second attack was made by the Verzamelberg commando, which numbered about eighty men. A strong party attempted to rush a mounted observation post between Platrand and Zandfontein. The four soldiers on the post held their ground pluckily for a time, but fell back on seeing that they were in danger of being surrounded.

On January 13, Lieutenant-Colonel R. H. W. H. Harris, who from the severity of his wounds had been unable to return to duty since he was carried off the field on Wynne's hill nearly a year previously, was placed on half-pay on completion of his period of command. Brevet-Lieutenant-Colonel H. W. Pearse was promoted to the Lieutenant-Colonelcy of the battalion, and Captain Finch White to the Majority, from January 14, 1901. On finally severing his connection with the battalion which he had commanded with so much gallantry and devotion, Lieutenant-Colonel Harris directed the publication of the following order:

"Colonel Harris in relinquishing command of the Battalion wishes to sincerely thank the Officers, Warrant Officers, Non-Commissioned Officers and men who so ably supported him in keeping up the high reputation which the Battalion has always held. Colonel Harris was exceedingly proud of the Battalion in South Africa: their excellent behaviour in camp, cheerfulness and endurance during most trying marches, and coolness, steadiness and courage under very heavy fire from an unseen foe, will ever be remembered by him with entire satisfaction. Colonel Harris deeply regrets having had to leave the Battalion while still at the front, but he has much pleasure in the knowledge that the command devolves on Major Pearse, who has the interests of the Battalion thoroughly at heart, and who at all times gave him the most loyal and entire support as second in command."

Early in February 1901 the "block-house system" was adopted in the Heidelberg-Standerton command, the post at Zandfontein being replaced by three block-houses. This not only made a dangerous post secure, but effected an economy in men.

On April 2, 1901, the names of the following officers, non-commissioned officers, and men mentioned in Sir Redvers Buller's despatches, published in the *London Gazette*, February 8, 1901, appeared in Battalion Orders:

Lieut.-Colonel R. H. W. H. Harris.
,, H. W. Pearse.
Major H. W. Benson.
,, H. L. Smith.
Captain H. S. Tew.
,, A. C. S. Barchard.
Lieutenant R. A. B. Chute (Promoted in the Manchester Regiment).
Lieutenant C. P. Porch.
,, V. H. M. de la Fontaine.
,, F. W. King-Church.
,, J. C. May.
,, R. V. O. Hart (A.D.C. to Major-General Hart).

Quarter-Master-Sergeant H. G. Clay; Colour-Sergeants H. J. Percy, W. Ladd, F. Robinson, F. Hillyard, and W. G. Lyne; Sergeant A. G. Joiner (promoted 2nd Lieutenant the Northamptonshire Regiment); and Privates W. Boxer, E. Robbens, H. Kemp, D. Conner, J. Diamond, G. Ashcroft, A. Thurston and H. Humphrey.

On the same date (April 2, 1901) on which the above Battalion Order appeared, part of the 2nd East Surrey Regiment was relieved from duty on the lines of communication, Headquarters and four companies, under Lieutenant-Colonel Pearse, joining the mobile column commanded by Colonel Colville of the Rifle Brigade; and the remaining four companies, under Major Benson, joined Colonel Rimington's column three weeks later. As the two half-battalions were widely separated while serving in these columns, it will be best to trace their experiences successively, by extracts from the diaries of two officers.

The Battalion Headquarters, with B company (Captain Tew), C company (Lieutenant May), F company (Captain Porch), and H company (Major White), with twelve mounted scouts and the machine-gun, left Platrand by train on April 7, 1901, and on arrival at Standerton at mid-day, marched out about four miles to Rademeyer's farm and joined Colonel Colville's column,[1] which remained at that place till April 10, when the column marched to Waterval river.

April 11. Marched to Wit Poort, harassed by 100 Boers, on our right and rear. The squadron of Johannesberg Mounted Rifles, who were newly raised and very raw, had a party of eight men ambushed and taken prisoners, six of them being wounded. This occurred while the column was crossing a river, and was a foretaste of many subsequent experiences.

April 12. A long march, about seventeen miles, to Hartebeestfontein. Sniped during most of the march.

April 14. Marched about seven miles to Vruischgewaagt, where we encamped in a strong position at the eastern extremity of the Zuikerbosch Rand, about fifteen east of Heidelberg and four miles south of the Nigel Mine. On the northern sky-line was the Rand, about thirty miles distant, but clearly visible.

The column remained at Vruischgewaagt camp till May 2, the chief incident during its stay being a surprise attack on Hans Botha's laager (April 29). Botha's Headquarters were near Bushman's Kop, and were completely surprised, but owing to a thick fog all the burghers except three managed to escape. There were a few casualties among the mounted men in the action which followed. B company accompanied Colonel Colville, but had no casualties. Captain Tew's horse was wounded.

May 2. Having been ordered at very short notice to take part in a projected "drive" about Blaaukop, the column made a long march to Van Kolder's Kop, a hill east of Greylingstadt, and on May 3 marched to Waterval river, molested by Commandant Albert's

---

[1] Also with the column were the 26th Mounted Infantry, one squadron Johannesberg M.I., four guns R.F.A., and one pom-pom.

commando as on the march up. May 4. Marched all day in great heat and bivouacked on the Ermelo Road at night-fall at a point about ten miles short of Uitkyk, our rendezvous for the "drive." May 5th (Sunday). The mounted troops, guns, and C company East Surrey (on mule wagons), marched at 4 A.M. and surprised three small laagers, capturing a Maxim-Nordenfeld gun. Remainder of the column marched south-east to Tweedronk, a hill near Blaaukop. There was a certain amount of fighting during the day, and Lieutenant Hemmingway, Mennés Scouts, was killed. He had served with the battalion at Platrand.[1] The drive was badly managed, and the Boers escaped, but an immense number of cattle and sheep were captured.

May 6 and 7. Clearing farms. Long march in the afternoon to Rademeyer's farm, where Lieutenant and Quartermaster Fletcher, who had long been in bad health, left the battalion for England, to the regret of all ranks who owed much to Lieutenant Fletcher's unwearied zeal and efficiency.

While at Rademeyer's farm, the first list of rewards for the South African War appeared in the *London Gazette*, and were published for the information of the battalion in orders of May 8, 1901.

The following rewards were allotted to the battalion :

To be a Companion of the Bath :

Brevet-Colonel R. H. W. H. Harris.

To be Brevet-Lieutenant-Colonel, dated 30th November 1900 :

Major H. W. Pearse (since promoted substantive Lieut.-Colonel.)

To be Companions of the Distinguished Service Order :

Brevet-Lieut.-Colonel B. R. Mitford (Staff).
Major H. W. Benson.
  ,,   H. L. Smith.
Captain H. S. Sloman (Staff).
  ,,   A. H. S. Hart (Staff).

Medals for Distinguished Conduct in the Field :

No. 3046, Colour-Sergeant H. J. Percy.
,, 2425, Lance-Corporal G. Fisher.
,, 5676, ,, R. Parris.
,, 5228, Corporal E. Brady.

[1] The squadron of Bethune's Mounted Infantry, stationed at Platrand, had been formed into a separate corps, called "Menné's Scouts."

May 9. Colville's column having been ordered to escort a large convoy of supplies for Major-General Locke-Elliot's columns, was strengthened by two squadrons of the 5th Dragoon Guards and two squadrons of the 13th Hussars, and marched through Standerton to De Lange's drift on the Klip river; distance about eighteen miles. Arrived late at the drift and C company East Surrey (rear-guard) was out all night. Remained in the Free State till we had handed over our convoy, and, on May 12, shifted camp to the north bank of the Klip.

May 15, 1901. Marched through the hills to the high ground south of Stoffel Lombard's farm, which we had often visited in the expeditions from Platrand. Crossed the Zandspruit drift before reaching our camp.

May 16. Marched about ten miles over very bad ground to Honingvlei. Saw no Boers, but captured much stock and cleared a number of farms.

May 17. Marched through the Verzamelberg, clearing farms. Found the country rich and full of stock. Camped on high ground about four miles from Klip river.

Halted on May 18, and on the 19th moved about two miles nearer the river. Cleared Joubert's farm, and one of the East Surrey companies was for a time in danger of being cut off. The 13th Hussars had a man wounded.

May 20. Marched towards Alleman's Nek for several miles and then, on receipt of fresh orders, turned and marched to Roodedrai.

May 21. Marched towards Vrede, crossing the Klip river at Roodedrai. From the drift we marched about six miles into the Orange Free State, over difficult ground, and encamped on the western slopes of Eerstegeluk Hills. There was a good deal of firing at long ranges, and one man of the 5th Dragoon Guards was wounded.

May 22. The mounted troops cleared farms in the Gemsbockberg, having three men wounded.

May 23. Marched six or seven miles, crossing Commando spruit. Delayed by an attack on our rear guard, but the Boers showed little spirit, owing no doubt to the fact that our column was strong in mounted troops during this trek.

May 24. Marched to our old camp on the south side of the Klip, delayed as yesterday by attacks on our rear.

May 25. Crossed as before to north side of the Klip; went to the same camping-ground, and found (apparently) the same gale of wind blowing. Halted here in bad weather, high gales and bitter cold, till May 31, when the column made a long march along the Klip river to Joubert's Kop. The 5th Dragoon Guards and 13th Hussars (two squadrons of each) left the column. During this march the 26th Mounted Infantry, under Major Wiggin, 13th Hussars, searched the ground along the south bank of the river, and had some fighting and a few casualties.

June 1. Had a halt, as only part of the convoy got across the drift last night.

June 2. Marched about fourteen miles towards Hex river.

June 3. Made a short march to high ground south of Hex River Mines. Hunted for buried stores and stock, with fairly good results on this day and on the 4th.

June 5. Marched to Villiersdorp and had a stiff skirmish.

June 6 and 7. Marched westward along the north bank of the Vaal, clearing farms. On the latter day reached Grobler's drift.

June 8. Marched back towards Barnard's Kop. Had a stiff skirmish, and the Mounted Infantry had Sir Rose Price, King's Royal Rifles, and one man killed, and five wounded.

June 9. Made a short march to Roodewal.

June 10. Moved quite a short distance towards Greylingstad, while the mounted troops cleared farms and collected stock.

June 11. Marched early to a Camp about three and a half miles south of Greylingstad, and halted two days.

June 13. Marched eight miles to Vogelstruisfontein.

June 14. Marched seven miles to camp near Waterval. The Queen's Mounted Infantry had a man killed during the march. Halted for orders.

June 20. Moved a short distance to Val station.

June 22. Made a rather long march up the Waterval (general direction E). A good deal of firing. One Boer at any rate was killed, as we found his body. On the following day (June 23), the column made a short march to Leeupan and took up a strong position, there being signs of an impending attack, which was delivered at about 8 A.M. on June 24 in a thick fog. The Boers (Ben Viljoen's commando) came on in considerable strength, and rode through some mealies right into the outpost line, between the left group of C company East Surrey and the right group of the 26th Mounted Infantry. No. 2604, Private J. Emmerton of C company 2nd East Surrey, was killed, and No. 6452, Private W. Edwards, of the same company dangerously wounded, losing his arm. A private of the Devon Mounted Infantry was also killed. One Boer was killed on the spot, and one other at least was known to be killed. Our out-posts were perfectly steady, and the attack was quickly repulsed. As soon as the fog cleared we buried Private Emmerton, the private of the Devon, and the Boer who fell in our out-post line side by side; and the column made a short march to Rietkuil. Ben Viljoen opened fire on us with a pom-pom as we were taking up our camping ground. Our guns promptly replied, and after about six shots silenced the pom-pom. We heard that the seven artillerymen with the Boer gun were killed on this occasion.

June 25. We spent much of this day trying to communicate with Colonel Grey's column, who should have been in touch with us.

June 26. Marched about sixteen miles through Waterval Hoek to a very high point called Nooitgedacht, which had been held by the Boers when we were at Vruischgewaagt. Colonel Grey's column marched about four miles north of us.

June 27. Marched about ten miles towards Vlakfontein, camping on good ground at Palmietfontein. Colonel Grey's column crossed our track and marched towards Greylingstad.

We halted at Palmietfontein, sending in a convoy to the line with captured stock and prisoners, and drawing fresh supplies.

On July 2 we marched back to Waterval Hoek, the mounted troops firing a good deal. On the road we met Colonel Grey's column, now commanded by Colonel Garrett.

On July 4 we made a very long march, continued till 2 P.M. July 5, in combination with General Walter Kitchener's column. We marched to Trichardsfontein, hoping to surprise Louis Botha with two commandos. We narrowly missed him.

July 10. Marched to Gegund. Four Boers surrendered to the East Surrey out-posts.

July 11. Marched to Greylingstad, and on the following day left Colonel Colville's column. The Head-quarter wing entrained at

Greylingstad at 4 p.m. and arrived at Zandspruit, its new station, at noon on the following day. The left wing, under Major Benson, had arrived there from Colonel Rimington's column two days previously. Colonel Rimington addressed the following telegram to Lieutenant-Colonel Pearse (published in Battalion Orders of July 10, 1901): " The wing of your Regiment now leaving my Column has rendered most excellent service."

At the request of Colonel Colville, the following Battalion Order was published on the July 14, 1901:

> " The Commanding Officer has much pleasure in informing all ranks of the Head-Quarters Half Battalion, that Lieutenant Colonel Colville, Commanding Mobile Column, has expressed to him his high opinion of the good conduct, willingness, and good marching of the 2nd East Surrey Regiment. Colonel Colville has expressed his intention of reporting most favourably on the conduct of all ranks during the last three months."

The following is a record of the experiences of the left wing while attached to Colonel Rimington's column.

On April 24, 1901, the several companies—A under the command of 2nd Lieutenant Appleyard, D under Captain Ellis, E under Major Smith, and G under Captain Barchard—concentrated at Standerton from their respective posts along the railway. Major Benson took over command of the detachment on April 26, 2nd Lieutenant Appleyard being appointed Acting-Adjutant and Quartermaster. 2nd Lieutenant Elphinston was appointed Orderly Officer to Colonel Rimington. On May 2, a detachment of volunteers, consisting of Lieutenant Prescott-Hallett, one sergeant and twenty-three men, joined and were attached to D company.[1]

The column consisting of four companies, 2nd East Surrey Regiment, 21st Imperial Yeomanry, 3rd New South Wales Mounted Rifles, section of Royal Artillery with pom-pom, and four guns of the Australian Artillery, under the command of Colonel Rimington, moved out of

---

[1] It had been intended that a second volunteer service company should join each battalion in South Africa when the first contingents were released from service. This plan, however, fell through owing to the high rate of pay offered to men joining the Imperial Yeomanry, and, as in the case of the East Surrey, many regiments only received a section instead of the second company.

Standerton at 2 P.M. on May 5, 1901, and marched to Vaalbank. The march was resumed on the 6th to Vellingkraal, from whence the mounted troops made a reconnaissance in force in the direction of the Watervaal river. On May 8, the column moved to Brakspruit, and the mounted troops, together with 100 men of the 2nd East Surrey Regiment in wagons, crossed the river and scoured the adjacent hills and the Hex River Mines, without however coming into close contact with the enemy. Major Benson accompanied this party, and on the return journey, in re-crossing the river, had the misfortune to wrench his knee, necessitating his reporting sick. Major Smith then assumed command of the detachment on the 11th, Lieutenant Anson taking command of E company. On the 10th a move was made to Platkop, and on the 11th the railway line was crossed at Vlaklaagte.

The column remained at Vlaklaagte on the 11th and 12th, and moved to Rademeyer's farm near Standerton on the 13th. The march was resumed on the 14th to Leeuwspruit, where the Vaal was crossed, and to Blesbock Spruit on the 15th, to Uitzicht on the 16th, and to Kaffir Spruit on the 17th. On the 18th the column marched to Tafel Kop, and on the 19th to Hamelfontein. On the 20th, in moving to Naudesfontein, the rear-guard was actively engaged, especially the New South Wales Mounted Rifles, and the section of the Australian Artillery.

The column halted at Naudesfontein on the 20th and 21st, and the country round about was scoured by the mounted troops, who were subjected to the annoyance of snipers, several casualties occurring. The column moved to Uitzicht on the 22nd, and here the practice of shelling the late camping ground directly the troops were clear commenced, as it was found that the enemy frequently came in small numbers to search for articles that might have been left by the columns. The column marched to Tafel Kop on the 23rd on its return journey to the line, to Uitgezacht on the 24th, to Drinkwater, Zevenfontein and Kaffir Kraal on the 25th, 26th and 27th, and Platrand was reached on May 29. A number of Boer prisoners were brought in, together with their families.

The column remained at Platrand until June 2, during which time opportunity was taken of re-clothing the troops, which they were much in need of, especially boots. Major Benson rejoined and resumed command of the detachment on May 31, Major Smith resuming command of E company.

On June 2, the column moved to Hankey's farm and marched to Amersfort on the 3rd, the detachment 2nd East Surrey being billeted in the church there.

On the 4th the march was resumed and the column halted for the night at Robertson's farm. On the 5th, the column moved and crossed the Mabusa river, encamping on the east side. The advanced guard got in touch with the retreating enemy, and the guns and pom-pom came into action, killing and wounding several of the Boers. The column moved on the 6th, descending on to the lower lands by a most precipitous path, alongside which deserted wagons, etc., gave evidence of the hasty flight of the enemy. Geelhoutboom was reached on the 7th and Driefontein on the 8th. From here the mounted troops went out and captured about sixty Boers, and an attempt was also made on Paul-Pietersburg, but the enemy was found to have fled. The march was resumed on the 9th and the column passed through Piet Retief, which was left burning; the weather at this time was very bad. The Assegai river was crossed after much difficulty, the drift being very bad, and the crossing taking place at night. Marionthal was reached on the 12th, and the prisoners and their families moved off the same day, Captain Barchard, who was sick, returning with them, transferring the command of G company to Lieutenant Anson. A halt of two days was made at Marionthal, after which the column moved down to the foot of Baken-Kap in the Luneberg on the 14th, camping in a grove of gum-trees for five days. A number of band instruments (said to have been captured by the Boers at Dundee) were found at Marionthal, and during the stay at Baken-Kap several performers amalgamated and presented most enlivening and enjoyable concerts during the early hours of the evening.

The mounted troops operated from here in conjunction with General Plumer's and other columns in the vicinity. Baken-Kap was left on the 19th and Uitkomst was reached on the 20th. The infantry marched from here on the morning of the 21st at 4 A.M., ascending a steep pass to the top of the mountains, which was found fortified but not occupied by the enemy. Besters Hoek was reached the same day and Pivaans Poort on the 22nd. A telegram was received from Lord Kitchener on the 24th, congratulating the column on its excellent work. Pivaans Poort was left on the evening on the 27th and the column marched until late at night, starting again very early on the 28th. Wakkerstroom was reached on the 29th, and the column halted until 30th. Castrols' Nek was reached on July 1 and Waterval Randbergen on the 3rd. Here the operations of the mounted troops resulted in the capture of large herds of cattle and sheep, and a few prisoners. Vryheid was reached on July 5 and Dagga's Kraal on the 6th. The column halted at the foot of Gras Kop on the 7th, and here Colonel Rimington made a farewell speech to the detachment 2nd East Surrey. He said that he was sorry to part from them, and that during the time they were with him they had performed their arduous work most cheerfully and without grumbling. Their duties had consisted of all the hard fatigues that go with column work without the excitement of a little fighting, which, he was sorry to say, he had not been able to give them, but he knew, had they had any, they would have acquitted themselves in a distinguished manner.

The detachment 2nd East Surrey left Colonel Rimington's column on July 8, marching to Paardekop, and entraining from there to Zandspruit on the 9th.

On returning to duty on the lines of communication the Headquarters of the battalion were stationed at Zandspruit, which had been the original place of assembly of the Boer army under General Joubert prior to the invasion of Natal in 1899 ; the ground occupied by them was still in a most dirty state, and the water supply appeared to be permanently unfit for human consumption. After much hard work, the defences were strengthened and drained, and the removal of several hundred wagon loads of refuse greatly improved the health of the garrison. Drinking water was brought from Charlestown or Standerton by rail, and eventually Zandspruit was rendered as healthy as other posts on the railway line. The Zandspruit section at this period extended from Paardekop to No. 4 Bridge, about midway between Zandspruit and Volksrust.

Owing to the battalion being at this time somewhat weak, the large post of Graskop (eight miles north of Zandspruit), was held by a detachment of "The Queen's" Regiment until September 7, when it was taken over by E company, under Major Smith. At the same time F company, under Captain Packman (who had returned from England), took over Dublin Hill from E company. Paardekop and the neighbouring posts of Kopje Alleen and Paardekop Hill formed a sub-section under Major Benson, under whom were Captains Tew and Barchard. This sub-section took charge, in addition, at the end of August, of the block-houses at Greno and Roodewal, which had been constructed to guard dangerous points on the line.

On September 3, 4 and 5 the section was inspected by Major-General Clements, who had recently succeeded Major-General Wynne in the Standerton command. General Clements was pleased to approve of the newly-constructed posts, which effected an economy of strength and also increased the safety of the railway.

It may here be explained that the Zandspruit-Paardekop section of the railway was peculiarly liable to attack, as the country both to the north and south was very mountainous, and many ridges and deep valleys rendered it easy for the enemy to approach it unseen. Owing to this circumstance, it was the natural crossing-place for messengers between the Boer forces in the Orange Free State and Eastern Transvaal, and such attempted crossings being usually covered by an attack on neighbouring posts, there were few nights on which firing was not heard in some portion of the section. Every effort was made to prevent crossings, and with very few exceptions, they were prevented. Patrols and night ambushes frequently watched the ground likely to be used, and it may fairly be said that the battalion earned the respect of the neighbouring Boer commandos while guarding the line. The section contained two 4.7 and three naval 12-pounder guns, which were placed in commanding positions at Graskop, Opperman's Kraal, Dublin Hill, Paardekop Hill, and Kopje Alleen respectively. In mounted troops it was weak, small detachments of Menné's Scouts in addition to the East Surrey Mounted Infantry being all that could be spared until quite near the end of the war, when a company of mounted infantry was added to the garrison. The East Surrey Mounted Infantry, however, rapidly grew in strength, and in time became a well-mounted body, some sixty strong. About half of them were stationed at Paardekop, under Lieutenant J. P. Benson, and the remainder were divided between Graskop and Zandspruit. The whole country round was denuded of horses by the combined work of the East Surrey Mounted Infantry and of the Intelligence Scouts, and the country was as effectively patrolled and watched as their numbers permitted.

On July 16, 1901, a very plucky reconnaissance into the Verzamelberg through Joubert's Nek was made by the party of Menné's Scouts from Zandspruit under Lieutenant Basil Lubbock. The patrol went several miles into the hills, and had finally to retire under a very heavy fire. One of the native scouts, whose horse was shot, was gallantly rescued by Lieutenant Lubbock and Sergeant Cima, who on Lieutenant-Colonel Pearse's recommendation were mentioned in Lord Kitchener's despatches for Distinguished Conduct in the Field.

On October 5, 1901, Lance-Corporal Long distinguished himself in action with the Mounted Infantry, and the good service performed by him on this occasion was recorded in Battalion Orders. This non-commissioned officer, who was an exceptionally good scout, had previously been mentioned in despatches for gallant conduct at Pieter's Hill.

On October 6, 1901, an all-night patrol from Fort Opperman, commanded by Captain Lambarde, Royal Artillery, surprised a Boer out-post in the Verzamelberg, killing one Boer and severely wounding another.

On October 9, 1901, the second list of South African honours and rewards, conferred on the army on the completion of Lord Roberts' command in Africa, appeared in the *London Gazette*. Those awarded to the 2nd Battalion East Surrey Regiment were as follows:

To be Companions of the Distinguished Service Order:

Lieutenant-Colonel H. W. Pearse.
Major H. P. Treeby.
Lieutenant J. C. May.

To be Brevet-Majors:

Captain H. S. Tew.
 ,, A. C. Barchard.

Awarded the Medal for Distinguished Conduct in the Field:

Sergeant-Major J. Anderton.
No. 3551, Colour-Sergeant W. G. Lyne.
 ,, 3606, ,,   F. Hillyard.
 ,, 3254, Sergeant F. Leavens.
 ,, 3091, Private W. Boxer.
 ,, 3015, ,,   W. Lovegrove.

Private Lovegrove unfortunately did not live to hear that his gallant conduct on February 23, 1900, had been rewarded.

On November 23, 1901, the 2nd Brigade was finally broken up by the removal of Brigadier-General E. O. F. Hamilton and his staff from Platrand to the Orange Free State. The 2nd Brigade had existed unchanged, save for the detachment of the 2nd Battalion West Yorkshire Regiment, since June 30, 1898. The Brigadier-General directed the publication of the following Order on his departure :

> " Before quitting the command Brigadier-General Hamilton wishes to express to all ranks his thanks, to the Officers for their support, and to the rank and file for the cheerful and efficient manner they have undertaken the trying duties connected with the safe-guarding of the line. The night work has been extremely arduous and has been most effectively performed. The Brigadier-General bids farewell to his comrades of the old 2nd Brigade with much regret, and had not his move been so sudden he would personally have expressed his thanks to them for the good work they have done for him."

On November 29, 1901, owing to the removal of a battalion from the Standerton-Heidelberg command, more ground was allotted to the custody of the battalion. Headquarters were moved to Paardekop (where they remained until the end of the war), and all posts up to and including the platelayer's cottage north of Warkenspruit were taken over from the Essex Regiment. Three days later it was decided that so much of the railway could not be adequately guarded without reinforcement, and a company of the Scottish Rifles under Lieutenant Chisholm was sent for duty in the section, and was stationed at Elandspoort and the neighbouring posts. This company remained attached to the battalion until April 21, 1902.

On December 17, 1901, a number of additional posts were made in the section, and to enable the East Surrey Regiment to find garrisons for them, the Scottish Rifles took over all the posts north of Kopje Alleen. No other change took place until the end of the year, the battalion being busily engaged in building posts and making wire entanglements and similar obstacles at likely crossing places. A draft of sixty-two non-commissioned officers and men joined from England on January 15, 1902.

On February 3, General Plumer's column made a drive from the east, through Blaaukop, with the intention of driving the Boers into the angle between the railway and River Vaal near Standerton. It was anticipated that the enemy would escape round General Plumer's left as he approached the line, and to prevent this, strong points were occupied by parties of the East Surrey Regiment, who went out on mule wagons to the most distant points, and by every available mounted man, including officers' servants on spare ponies. This drive, however, failed in some unexplained manner, the Boers getting away by way of the big dongas north-east of Blaaukop.

On February 5, in consequence of the movements of General Plumer's and other columns, a party of about 200 Boers made a determined attempt to force their way across the line, trying to find a weak spot in the defences. They made nine separate attempts in the course of about four hours, and fired heavily at several of the posts. The closest attack was made on a post close to No. 4 Bridge. This post was under repairs and the traverse to the doorway was unfinished. The garrison consisted of No. 5228, Sergeant Brady and six men of G company, who all behaved admirably. Sergeant Brady, who had received the Distinguished Conduct Medal for gallantry at Pieter's Hill, was killed, and No. 1441, Private Morris, and No. 5664, Private Callan, were severely wounded and No 4313, Private J. Russell, was slightly wounded. Private Russell and the remaining four men kept up a heavy fire, and the armoured train, which at this period frequently patrolled the Paardekop section coming up in the nick of time, the Boers were driven off. On the following morning a telegram was received from Major-General Clements expressing his satisfaction at the successful defence of the line, and his regret for the death of Sergeant Brady. Attacks of a similar nature, but on a smaller scale, were made on the nights of February 7 and 8, probably with the object of enabling Britz's commando to escape into the Verzamelberg from an impending drive by General Plumer. No crossing was effected and the drive took place on February 11. A party of forty-seven mounted men, under Lieutenant J. P. Benson held the Mooimesjesfontein ridges, and the intervening ground was held by detached infantry groups, every available officer and man in the section being employed. The drive was fairly successful.

Another drive took place on February 19, when a reinforcement of 105 men of the Royal Inniskilling Fusiliers were lent to the section. Two small parties of Boers endeavoured to cross the line near No. 4 Bridge Guard, but failed. The Inniskilling Company returned to Pretoria on February 22.

On February 23, a patrol of Mounted Infantry, under Lieutenant Benson, went to the top of Joubert's Nek and found that portion of the Verzamelberg deserted by Erasmus' commando, who had been swept up in the southward drive. Lieutenant Benson re-visited the Nek on February 26, and found that twenty-six Boers had returned. Gradually the commando slipped back, having escaped from the drive, thanks to their intimate knowledge of the ground. They were all local farmers, their sons and dependents.

On February 28, General Plumer made another drive on the north of the line, and on this occasion the Paardekop section turned out sixty mounted men of its own and forty men left at Paardekop by General Nixon's columns. The latter were mounted on sick or lame horses, but could hold detached posts well enough. The Boers again broke back and did not come south. The result of the manner in which our railway line and other lines were held during February 1902 was the complete success of the Harrismith drive, in which 819 Boers were captured.

On March 7, 1902, a draft of 150 men from the 1st Battalion, under Captain Paterson, arrived from India. This was a very fine draft of old soldiers. On March 11 Captain Paterson left for India, taking with him 150 men, mostly young soldiers.

On March 21, a party of thirty Boers attempted to cross the line from the north, but were driven back. It was stated that Britz's whole commando intended crossing, and this party was perhaps an advanced guard. On March 27, an expedition sent out from Graskop by Major White (who had relieved Major Smith at that post) captured two Boers after a long march, but were ambushed on their return journey, and had a Kaffir scout and five horses shot. Two Boers were killed in this engagement. On the same day Sergeant Perkins was slightly wounded by a ricochet bullet fired at one of the Mooimesjesfontein block-houses by a Boer sniper.

On April 2 the last draft from England arrived, mostly composed of young soldiers, with a few men who had been sent home on account of wounds or sickness.

On April 7, 1902, a party of about thirty Boers attempted a crossing, but were driven back.

On April 21, Lieutenant Chisholm's company of the Scottish Rifles were ordered to rejoin their battalion, and the posts occupied by them were taken over by the 2nd East Surrey Regiment, every large post being reduced to find the necessary men. A yet further spreading out of the battalion took place on May 1, when the railway up to and including Platrand was taken over. Captain Porch took charge of the Platrand sub-section.

On May 3, 1902, a party of Free State Boers under Field-Cornet Van Helsinger, supported by part of Cornelius Erasmus' commando from the Verzamelberg, attempted to raid cattle from Platrand under cover of a dense fog. The alarm was quickly given, and the Mounted Intelligence Scouts turned out, without warning the East Surrey Mounted Infantry that anything was going on. The Scouts were briskly engaged with the Free Staters, and one of them was killed. The Mounted Infantry then heard the firing and turned out, under Lieutenant Benson, without the loss of a moment. The Boers were speedily driven off, Field-Cornet Van Helsinger being severely wounded. The shots fired in this affair proved to be last heard by the battalion in the South African War.

On May 14, the volunteer service section, under Lieutenant P. Hallett, left for home, the following Battalion Order being published on this occasion. Private Lee, one of the section, died suddenly during the previous night from heart failure.

Battalion Order :

"The Commanding Officer wishes to place on record the excellent conduct and good services of the Volunteer Service section under Lieutenant P. Hallett, which is about to return to England on the expiration of its engagement. All the officers under whom the section has served speak most highly of the soldierlike conduct and willingness shown by all ranks in the section, which have been most creditable both to their own battalions and to the battalion with which it has served in the Field."

No further incident worthy of note occurred until Sunday, June 1, 1902. During church service on this day the Commanding Officer received a telegram saying that peace had been signed on the previous evening. So ended the South African War, in which the 2nd Battalion East Surrey Regiment had been engaged from first to last.

On June 2 the following telegram was received :—

"Lord Kitchener to Officer Commanding Paardekop 2nd June. Please communicate to your troops the following message which I have received from his Majesty the King and for which I have thanked him in the name of all concerned. Begins : 'Heartiest congratulations on the termination of Hostilities. I also congratulate my brave troops under your command for having brought this long and difficult Campaign to so glorious and successful a conclusion.'"

On the declaration of peace the strength of the 2nd Battalion in South Africa was as follows :

Officers	31
Warrant officer	1
Sergeants	54
Corporals	48
Drummers	8
Privates	925
Total	1067

The battalion itself occupied fourteen important posts, each of which was sub-divided ; the total number of posts occupied being seventy-one. The battalion, in addition to its own strong party of Mounted Infantry under Lieutenant J. P. Benson, furnished at the time a company of Mounted Infantry which, under Captain de la Fontaine and 2nd Lieutenants Appleyard and Storey, was serving in the 26th Mounted Infantry. A short record of the services of this company will be found on page 446.

In addition to the thirty-one officers mentioned above, the following officers of the Regiment were serving on the Staff in South Africa :

Brevet Lieut.-Colonel B. R. Mitford. Mentioned in Despatches. D.S.O.
Major H. S. Sloman. Mentioned in Despatches. D.S.O.
Major A. B. Dunsterville. (Brevet of Lieut.-Colonel.)
Major H. D. Lawrence. Mentioned in Despatches.
Captain J. R. Longley. (Adjutant Canadian Scouts.)
Captain A. H. S. Hart (afterwards Hart-Synnot). Wounded. Mentioned in Despatches. D.S.O.
Captain L. G. Ionides. (Brevet of Major).
Lieutenant R. V. O. Hart (afterwards Hart-Synnot). Twice mentioned in Despatches. D.S.O.
Lieutenant E. M. Woulfe-Flanagan. (Wounded.)
Lieutenant F. S. Montague-Bates.

SECOND BATTALION IN THE SOUTH AFRICAN WAR

A certain number of non-commissioned officers and men were also detached from the 2nd Battalion during the war, many of whom did conspicuously good service. Among these special mention may be made of No. 5582 Private J. Devitt, who showed the highest gallantry and devotion while attached to the Royal Artillery. Private Devitt and a gunner saved a pom-pom gun from capture by a large number of Boers, fighting at close quarters. For this gallant act Private Devitt was promoted to the rank of Corporal and mentioned in Despatches by Lord Kitchener.

The battalion at the end of the war was in excellent health, the average daily number of sick during the last month being six.

The casualties of the battalion throughout the war were as follows:

	Killed.	Wounded.
Up to the Relief of Ladysmith	1 officer and 36 other ranks.	8 officers and 208 other ranks.
Subsequent to the Relief	— ,, ,, 9 ,, ,,	2 ,, ,, 26 ,, ,,
Total killed	1 ,, ,, 45 ,, ,,	Total 10 ,, ,, 234 ,, ,,

A total of 290 killed and wounded

In addition, one officer and sixty-six non-commissioned officers and men died in South Africa of disease during the war, almost all of enteric fever. Their names were as follows:

Lieutenant S. F. Brooks.
No. 1433, Q. M. S. McKenzie, J. A.
,, 2691, Sergeant Angell, G.
,, 3135, Corporal Breadon, G.
,, 3657, ,, Lillis, J.
,, 5612, ,, Swift, C.
,, 5038, Lance-Corpl. Butler, C.
,, 2350, ,, Barker, F.
,, 1413, ,, Handley, T.
,, 5801, ,, Rose, C.
,, 5811, Private Alexander, A.
,, 5882, ,, Andrews, J.
,, 6493, ,, Bennett, W.
,, 3037, ,, Berryman, W.
,, 2296, ,, Blizzard, J.
,, 5850, ,, Bond, J.
,, 5140, ,, Broawn, S.
,, 5910, ,, Bryant, W.
,, 964, ,, Charman, W.
,, 4247, ,, Clifford, C.

No. 4397, Private Collins, H.
,, 3409, ,, Cork, W.
,, 5319, ,, Cox, W.
,, 3435, ,, Croft, A.
,, 6195, ,, Cropper, C.
,, 3454, ,, Davis, C.
,, 6343, ,, Dawkins, W.
,, 3415, ,, Durant, J.
,, 5454, ,, Foreman, C.
,, 3472, ,, Freakly, H.
,, 3601, ,, Furneaux, F.
,, 2518, ,, Hall, D.
,, 2673, ,, Harris, E.
,, 3052, ,, Healing, A.
,, 5760, ,, Heath, T.
,, 4656, ,, Hope, W.
,, 6495, ,, Hopkins, J.
,, 2729, ,, Horlock, J.
,, 6373, ,, Horseman, J.
,, 4592, ,, Howlett, S.

No. 5483,	Private	Hull, G.	No. 3498,	Private	Shade, J.
,, 5744,	,,	Huntingford, G.	,, 5394,	,,	Smith, W.
,, 2473,	,,	Jenkins, F.	,, 4923,	,,	Smythe, S.
,, 6039,	,,	Lane, R. H.	,, 5837,	,,	Sullivan, C.
,, 6152,	,,	Leavens, F. G.	,, 2244,	,,	Sygraves, H.
,, 6963,	,,	Lee, C.	,, 5659,	,,	Travers, J.
,, 4304,	,,	New, E.	,, 1608,	,,	Weir, S.
,, 5540,	,,	Parker, E.	,, 3473,	,,	Whalebone, J.
,, 5634,	,,	Peters, P.	,, 5054,	,,	Wheatley, J.
,, 6494,	,,	Rance, W. R.	,, 4785,	,,	Winson, W.
,, 6485,	,,	Roberts, H.	,, 2756,	,,	Wiseman, A.
,, 3335,	,,	Ruffell, C.	,, 6160,	,,	Wood, C.
,, 5678,	,,	Sayers, P.	,, 6201,	,,	Wooden, F. B.

Record of the Mounted Infantry Company

In November 1900, a number of new Mounted Infantry battalions were formed, and amongst others the 2nd Divisional Mounted Infantry Battalion from regiments who were originally in the 2nd Division.

Each infantry battalion had to furnish half a company. Fifty of the 2nd East Surrey, added to the same number from the 1st Battalion Durham Light Infantry, were henceforth to be known as No. 2 Company 2nd Division Mounted Infantry. The command of the company was given to Captain Ionides, 2nd East Surrey Regiment, whilst the four section commanders were Lieutenants Montague-Bates and de la Fontaine of the East Surrey Regiment; Lieutenants Soltau-Symons and Matthews of the Durham Light Infantry. The battalion commander was Major W. S. Kays of the King's Royal Rifles.

The training of the battalion took place at Standerton, where the Mounted Infantry was usefully employed in clearing neighbouring farms of all supplies. We rarely met with any Boers on these occasions, but on December 26, 1900, whilst removing some forage from a farm called Kareebosch on the Vaal, we were suddenly attacked by some 300 Boers, who by chance happened to be returning from a peace meeting at Blaaukop. They galloped to within 200 yards of us, and attempted to cut off our line of retreat. No. 5794, Private H. Goodey, 2nd East Surrey Regiment, was wounded in the foot, and also a man in another company; whilst three Boers were killed and one badly wounded. For a first fight as mounted troops this was most encouraging.

On January 26, 1901, our company was ordered to join Colonel

Colville's mobile column, which consisted at that time of one battalion of infantry, four field guns, and now also of our Mounted Infantry company.

The column proceeded to Greylingstadt and joined in General French's first great drive towards the Swaziland border. We kept in the general line with the other columns and marched due east, almost parallel to the railway. When we reached a place called Uitkek on the Standerton-Ermolo road, a large convoy was sent out to us from Standerton, which we had orders to escort on to Ermelo on account of the number of Boers about. We handed the convoy over to General French on February 10, and took over from him over a hundred waggons of Boer women and children and wounded soldiers, about 6000 head of cattle and 30,000 sheep. The chance of capturing a small column hampered by wagons and cattle was not lost sight of by Commandant Britz and his Blaaukop commando, and we had great difficulty in crossing some of the spruits ; but a wholesome respect for our four 15-pounders prevented them from coming into too close contact with us. As it was, they succeeded in re-capturing some of the cattle and most of the sheep. No. 5588, Private F. Reid, 2nd East Surrey Regiment, was slightly wounded in the neck. It was one of the hardest treks our company ever did. Being the only mounted force, our patrols were always out before dawn, we had to furnish the advance guard and flankers on the exposed flanks ; most of the day was spent in skirmishes with the enemy and we had to find out-posts at night. We were not sorry to return to Standerton, to give both men and horses a rest and to rejoin the remainder of the Battalion of Mounted Infantry.

From Standerton we took part in various expeditions, sometimes alone, sometimes attached to columns. In May 1901, an attempt was made to surround Commandant Britz's commando on Blaaukop by means of converging columns. The Standerton column, consisting of our Mounted Infantry and several companies of the Devon, marched along the left bank of the Vaal in the direction of Blaaukop. The attempt was a failure, the Boers breaking through the cordon drawn round them. On our way back to Standerton Captain Ionides, riding alone through a farm, spied a Boer crouching behind a tree. Without dismounting, he fired at him with his Mauser pistol, and wounded him in the back. A search was at once made for any other hidden burghers and two more were discovered, amongst whom was Adrian de Lange, a commandant who had given General Buller much trouble.

On May 12, 1901, the 2nd Division Mounted Infantry received orders to join Colonel Colville's Column (with which was the Headquarter wing of the East Surrey Regiment) at De Lange's Drift on the Klip river. The column was to act in conjunction with several columns under General Locke-Elliot, who had organized a drive through the Northern Free State towards Natal. We kept along the northern bank of the Klip, crossed the Verzamelbergen, where we gathered together 2500 head of cattle and 25,000 sheep, which we sent into Volksrust. We then crossed into the Orange River Colony and returned to De Lange's Drift. On the way back to the drift, we ran into Commandant Malan's commando and had a few casualties.

The column's next trek was in a westerly direction along the right bank of the Vaal. No. 3583, Lance-Corpl. E. Thorne, 2nd East Surrey Regiment, was shot through the foot by a Boer sniper.

On approaching Villiersdorp, Major E. A. Wiggin, 13th Hussars, who had succeeded Major Kays in command of the Mounted Infantry, gave Captain Ionides the order to charge a small kopje on the bank of the Vaal. To our surprise, as we charged the hill, the Boers, instead of bolting, held on to their position. The reason was soon apparent. A barbed-wire fence, with but one small opening through it, ran round the foot of the kopje. We all made for this opening, and the Boers concentrating their fire on it, made it seem improbable that any would get through. But the Boer loses his nerve at close quarters. Captain Ionides and Lieutenant de la Fontaine, on reaching the summit of the kopje, had just time to shoot the last Boer as he was mounting his pony. Major Wiggin and Lieutenant Matthews, galloping after the next burgher, took him prisoner after shooting him in the back.

Our casualties were nil, though five dead horses near that wire fence told the tale of some narrow escapes. Captain Ionides' horse was slightly wounded.

Buys was the commandant of that district, and a very bitter foe, having lost his son at Ladysmith. We searched his farm and unearthed three brand-new Stehr rifles and several thousand rounds of ammunition. Buys' mode of action was to harass our rear-guard and endeavour to cut it off from the main body. In one of these rear-guard actions Lieutenant Sir Rose Price, King's Royal Rifles, of the Mounted Infantry, was killed.

Our column then moved in a northerly direction, and crossing the railway line at Vaal Station kept along the banks of the Waterval river. On June 24, 1901, a dense fog prevented us from leaving camp at the usual time. While we were waiting for it to clear, the Boers tried to rush the column. Our out-posts, who had fortunately not been withdrawn, gave us timely warning, and we drove the enemy back without difficulty. One of our sentries was killed and two wounded, while two dead Boers left behind paid the penalty of their rashness. That same evening a pom-pom, turned on to our baggage, nearly put it to flight, but the pom-pom was soon silenced by our guns, which found the range almost at once. Our company was advance guard as we approached Waterval Hoek, the headquarters of Pretorius' laager, and the Boers holding a kopje which we charged, stayed there rather too long, and we shot one of them through the leg, who turned out to be Commandant Klasse. He escaped capture, but was lame during the remainder of the war.

Our column then joined hands with General Walter Kitchener's, but a combined night march on Trichardsfontein led to no results, and we returned to the line, reaching Greylingstadt on July 11, 1901. There Kaffirs brought us news of a large number of cattle on the banks of the Vaal near the Hex River Mine, so we started at 11 P.M. one night to capture them. A dense fog next morning interfered with our plans, and the Boers got wind of our coming. When the fog lifted, we could see wagons and cattle making off on the far side of the Vaal. We immediately gave chase and a two-mile gallop resulted in the capture of two Boers, five wagons, four cape carts and 800 head of cattle, but a good many must have escaped. From Greylingstadt the column took a circular tour north of the line to Standerton. The second day out No. 2 section holding a kopje were pom-pomed. Though the enemy had the exact range, and the shells fell between the men, no one was hit. While retiring before some Boers, a corporal of the Durham's lost his horse. Lieutenant Matthews, with great gallantry, took the corporal up behind him, but he fell off and was unfortunately killed. On reaching Standerton we were informed that our official title had been altered from the 2nd Division Mounted Infantry to the 26th Battalion Mounted Infantry, and that we were to be known as such in future.

Colonel Colville left Standerton again on August 3, 1901, and two days later pitched his camp near Trichardsfontein. Our scouts reported the presence of Pretorius' laager somewhere near the Waterval. Colonel Colville's plan was to leave his infantry in camp and pursue the enemy with a really mobile column. Besides the Mounted Infantry, he took two field-guns, a pom-pom and a few infantry (Queen's Regiment) in wagons.

A start was made at 2.30 A.M. on August 6, 1901, along the main Pretoria Road, but we soon branched off to the left. At day-break we made out a couple of white covered wagons in the far distance, and as the sun rose we were able to distinguish in the plain beyond dozens of wagons, cape carts, horsemen, etc. They were all on the move. The alarm had evidently been given. Major Wiggin immediately gave the order to gallop after them. Captain Ionides started off at once and we went as hard as we could go for about ten miles, gradually overtaking most of the wagons, till our tired horses could go no further.

Our total bag amounted to twenty-one prisoners, twenty-one wagons, 2000 rounds of ammunition, 1500 head of cattle and 2500 sheep, in addition to which two Boers were killed and eight wagons which could not be removed were burnt. As we retired, our company was rear-guard, and under cover of a grass fire, several Boers succeeded in getting fairly close to us and sniping us. No. 5539, Private W. Connor, 2nd East Surrey Regiment, was dangerously wounded in the head, Private Rugman had his horse shot, and Captain Ionides, Lieutenants Matthews and de la Fontaine all had their horses wounded.

The column then returned to Standerton.

Our next trek was on August 20, 1901, along the southern bank of the Klip river, through the range of hills known as the Gemsbockhoekberg. The infantry were left encamped at the foot of this berg, while the mounted troops made a night march towards Natal. No Boers were captured, but a certain number of cattle were driven in.

Colonel Colville decided on taking these, together with some Boer families, into Newcastle. We crossed the Drakensberg over Muller's Pass, which is so narrow in parts that a few Boers could have defied a whole army. We went through the pass at night without any opposition. It was the first time since the declaration of war that a column had been through that pass. On the way to the pass, No. 3946, Private C. Sadgrove, 2nd East Surrey Regiment, was wounded in the arm. We returned to our infantry camp by Botha's Pass and then moved on towards De Lange's Drift. While charging a kopje, No. 3457, Private T. Tierney, 2nd East Surrey Regiment, was very severely wounded in the leg. The column halted a few days at De Lange's Drift and then moved westward in the Orange River Colony. On September 5, 1901, a man in the bodyguard (a company of Commander-in-Chief's bodyguard had been added to the column) was dangerously wounded. Major Wiggin called for a volunteer to assist in bringing him in. No. 4289, Sergeant J. Lane, immediately offered to do so. It was a plucky thing to do, as the Boers were firing at him the whole time. The following day the column crossed the Vaal at Robert's Drift. Our company was rear-guard, and a section of the Durhams sent to drive in some cattle had two men wounded by Boers concealed in a mealie field. An ambulance had to be sent for, and, being a long way ahead, it took a long time coming. In the meanwhile other casualties occurred. Lieutenant Matthews was dangerously wounded. Sergeant Sykes, Durham Light Infantry, was killed, while Lieutenant de la Fontaine, No. 4289, Sergeant J. Lane, and No. 4609, Private F. Howard, all of the 2nd East Surrey Regiment, were slightly wounded. A day's rest at Standerton and the column was on the move again, this time in a north-easterly direction along the left bank of the Vaal. Crossing the Vaal at Roodeval, we called in at Ermelo for supplies. There we heard of General Louis Botha's intended invasion of Natal, and received orders to proceed at once to Volksrust, which we reached on September 25, 1901.

It was now decided to build a block-house line to Piet Retief and the Swaziland border. During its construction the column served as a covering party. When close to Piet Retief, we heard that Louis Botha's commando was retiring north, through Swaziland. We made an attempt to intercept them, but only succeeded in capturing sixteen wagons. After the completion of the block-house line, we remained on the Swazi border to prevent Boers gathering there in any large numbers. A night march on November 6, 1901, to Mahamba's Drift on the Assegai river, led to the capture of fifteen Boers, and another night march on the 14th of the same month to a place called Kwakeni, south of Mahamba's Drift, added twelve more prisoners, six wagons, 5000 rounds ammunition, 400 head of cattle to our previous captures. In December 1901 and the beginning of January 1902, we made thirty more captures by means of these night raids on farms. At the end of January we took part in a combined operation with General Plumer's columns. The block-house line formed a right angle near Castrols' Nek, and it was General Plumer's intention to drive the Boers into this angle. Our column was to take up a certain position by dawn on the morning of January 25, 1902. The whole column was to have gone, but heavy rain had made the roads impassable for wagons and guns, so the Mounted Infantry only were sent. Starting at 10 P.M. on the 24th, we rode twenty miles over frightful country, every small ditch and stream, swollen by rain, forming a most serious obstacle in the dark. We only just reached our destination on the Assegai river before daylight, and could see General Plumer's columns each in its appointed place. The bursting of a shell showed us the enemy on a flat-topped hill in front of us. It was a pleasure to watch them galloping backwards and forwards pursued by pom-pom shells, looking for some means of escape. We received the order to close in on them, when the Boers, seeing that they must be captured, surrendered.

Our bag was two killed and forty prisoners. We then joined General Plumer, and by means of several very long night marches, tried to capture Louis Botha, who was in the Elandsberg mountains with 200 men. But he succeeded in crossing the block-house line.

Colonel Colville was then ordered to Volksrust and told to hold a range of hills extending from Zandspruit and Alleman's Nek to the Drakensberg, as a big drive was to take place in the Northern Orange River Colony. We were there three days, but no Boers attempted to break through our line. We then were sent down to Newcastle, and on to De Jager's Drift on the Buffalo river, where we remained till about March 10, 1902, when we pushed on to Vryheid. From

Vryheid we trekked on to Paul Pietersberg and Piet Retief, and up to the block-house line once more. Near the Assegai river we ran across Chris Botha with a commando of 300 men. We captured one of his men and wounded another. From the block-house line we made a night march to the Tafel Berg to try and catch Chris Botha, but without success. We only stumbled across two Boers of the Utrecht commando.

On April 11, 1902, the column was ordered down to Wakkerstroom. There Colonel Colville left us and handed over the column to Colonel Mills, of the Dublin Fusiliers.

On April 16 we started off for Utrecht and camped above the town at Knight's farm. A night march from there resulted in our surrounding six Boers in a farm near the Blood River Poort. On May 5 our column left Utrecht for Vryheid, where the Boer commandos had been less worried than in most places. The Zulus, however, driven to desperation by rough treatment on the part of the Boers, saved us the trouble of attacking the latter, as the night before we arrived they had risen and killed about sixty Boers at a farm called Holkranz near the Pivaan river.

We were still at Vryheid when the glad tidings of peace were wired out to us.

On June 16 General Bruce Hamilton came down to Vryheid, where 650 Boers surrendered to him. From June to September 1902, we trekked about the hilly country between Vryheid and the Zulu border, to keep the peace between the Boers and Zulus, who had always been on the verge of rising since the fight at Holkranz.

At the end of August 1902, we were ordered back to Natal, and disbanded at Mooi river on September 6, 1902; the horses being handed in, and the officers and men returning to the battalion. It should be mentioned that early in March 1902 the 2nd East Surrey half-company was reinforced to a strength of about seventy, and formed into a Mounted Infantry company under the command of Captain de la Fontaine; Captain Ionides being employed on detached duty until his transfer to the 28th Battalion Mounted Infantry.

During the existence of the East Surrey Mounted Infantry half-company and company, the following officers did duty with it, in addition to those mentioned:

Lieutenant J. K. T. Whish.
,, W. Appleyard.
,, F. B. Storey.

The company always bore a high character for efficiency and good conduct in action.

It sustained the following casualties:

Killed or died of wounds.
No. 5539, Private W. Connor.
,, 2739, ,, E. Morris.

Wounded.
Lieutenant de la Fontaine.
No. 4289, Sergeant J. Lane.

No. 3583, Lance-Corpl. E. Thorn.
,, 4609, Private H. Howard.
,, 5794, ,, H. Goodey.
,, 5588, ,, J. Reid.
,, 3946, ,, C. Sadgrove.
,, 3457, ,, W. Tierney.

On July 2, 1902, Major-General Clements was transferred to the command of the Pretoria district, and published the following farewell order:

"On leaving the Standerton-Heidelberg District, Major-General Clements wishes to place on record his appreciation of the assistance he has received from all ranks during the time he has commanded the District.

To the troops who have, for such a long period, guarded the lines of communication and block house lines, a monotonous and most trying duty, he gives his thanks, it being due to their exertions and watchfulness that so few crossings have been effected and that the traffic has not been interrupted."

The demobilization of the battalion began on July 5, when Major F. White with the first party of 100 reservists started for England. The remainder of the reservists were sent home as rapidly as possible, and on September 18, 1902, the battalion, reduced to a strength of about 320, proceeded by march route to Volksrust, where it remained under canvas until its departure for India.

On September 26, 1902, the battalion was inspected by Lieutenant-General the Hon. Sir Neville Lyttelton, K.C.B., Commanding in the Transvaal and Orange River Colonies. The Lieutenant-General was pleased to express his pleasure at the smart appearance of the battalion and camp, and also his high appreciation of the services of the battalion during the campaign.

In Lord Kitchener's final dispatch, Lieutenant-Colonel H. W. Pearse, D.S.O., Major H. W. Benson, D.S.O., and Captain and Adjutant

F. W. King-Church received favourable mention for their services. Captains L. G. Ionides and F. W. King-Church were promoted to Brevet-Majorities, and Major A. B. Dunsterville received a Brevet-Lieutenant-Colonelcy for service on the staff.

A Medal for Distinguished Conduct in the Field was also awarded to Sergeant-Major H. G. Clay.

Two medals were granted for the South African War and one or both of them was received by all ranks of the 2nd Battalion who served during the war. The roll of officers who were thus rewarded is as follows:

ROLL OF OFFICERS WHO RECEIVED THE QUEEN'S SOUTH AFRICA MEDAL AND CLASPS

Lieut.-Colonel R. H. W. H. Harris, C.B.
,, H. W. Pearse, D.S.O.
Major A. B. Dunsterville (Brevet Lieut.-Colonel).
,, H. W. Benson, D.S.O.
,, H. L. Smith, D.S.O.
,, H. P. Treeby, D.S.O.
,, F. White.
,, H. S. Sloman, D.S.O.
,, B. R. Mitford, D.S.O. (Brevet Lieut.-Col.).
Captain W. H. Ellis.
,, W. H. Gorman.
,, F. L. A. Packman.
,, H. D. Lawrence.
,, J. R. Longley.
,, W. N. R. Gilbert Cooper.
,, H. S. Tew (Brevet Major).
,, A. H. S. Hart, D.S.O.
,, A C. S. Barchard (Brevet Major).
,, W. H. Paterson (1st East Surrey, attached).
,, L. G. Ionides (1st East Surrey, attached) (Brevet Major).
,, H. D. Smalley (1st East Surrey, attached).
,, R. A. B. Chute (4th Manchester, attached).
,, L. W. Johnson (3rd Royal Warwicks, attached).
Lieutenant C. P. Porch.
,, C. H. Hinton.
,, H. V. M. de la Fontaine.
Lieutenant R. E. N. North.
,, J. C. May, D.S.O.
,, E. St. G. Anson.
,, J. P. Benson.
,, R. V. O. Hart, D.S.O.
,, C. E. A. S. Currie.
,, J. K. T. Whish.
,, T. M. Hutchinson.
,, L. J. Le Fleming.
,, C. F. Colquhoun (1st Battalion).
,, R. G. Alexander.
,, H. A. Neild (4th East Surrey).
,, N. G. P. de. C. Tronson (1st Leicesters).
,, P. B. Stafford.
,, S. D. Brancker.
,, H. T. K. Messenger.
,, C. T. Simcox.
,, W. Appleyard.
,, F. S. Montague Bates.
,, R. Campbell Ross.
,, A. Elphinston.
,, F. B. Storey.
,, L. M. Miller.
,, I. O'G. Maunsell.
,, A. de V. Maclean.
,, P. M. Whale.
,, G. Gould.
,, T. E. Stafford.
Lieut. and Adjt. F. W. King-Church.
Lieut. and Qr.-Master C. W. Fletcher.

On January 5, 1903, the battalion, under the command of Major H. L. Smith, D.S.O., left Volksrust for Durban, embarking on January 9 in the Transport *Syria*. Strength: nine officers and 306 non-commissioned officers and men. Lieutenant-Colonel Pearse, D.S.O., who had gone to England on leave on the demobilization of the battalion shortly after the end of the war, rejoined at Durban and resumed command. A draft under Brevet-Major Barchard of 103 men (including the band), nine women and seventeen children, also joined Headquarters at Durban.

The battalion arrived at Bombay on January 23, 1903, and reached Lucknow on February 1, relieving the 1st Battalion, which had proceeded to England.

CHAPTER XXII

Recent History of the 2nd Battalion

Two years at Lucknow—Sitapur and Ranikhet—Mhow—Athletic successes—Efficiency and good health—The battalion visits Burma for the first time—A country of many detachments—Back to India—Manœuvres in Eastern Bengal—Chaubattia—The coming of war.

From its arrival at Bombay in January 1903 until its embarkation at that port for the seat of war in Europe in November 1914, the history of the 2nd East Surrey was uneventful.

Lucknow, the first Indian station at which the battalion was stationed, was in many respects a good one for the purpose of breaking the officers and men into Indian methods of soldiering, as the large garrison ensured comparison and competition with other units. A large number of non-commissioned officers and men, with a few officers, had been left at Lucknow by the 1st Battalion, and these seasoned and steady soldiers, well accustomed to the country, proved very valuable.

Coming as it did from a long campaign, the battalion had much leeway in technical education to make up. The South African non-commissioned officers and soldiers were thoroughly efficient for war, but their training in the military arts of peace was necessarily scanty. Very few of the non-commissioned officers had passed a school of instruction, and many of them who had been promoted for good conduct in the field and for soldierly quality were at a disadvantage educationally.

In like manner nearly all the subaltern officers, though well acquainted with field duties, had yet much to learn of the book-science of their profession, and it was necessary for them to attend schools of musketry and other classes of instruction in order to qualify themselves for promotion. The officers of the battalion also had, for the most part, been granted no leave for a long period, and for the first two years of the Indian tour of duty the battalion was consequently very short-handed in officers.

To meet this difficulty the commanding officer found it necessary to work the companies in pairs, so that each two companies should have one officer at least capable of imparting instruction in practical training. This arrangement was approved by Major-General Walter Kitchener, C.B., who commanded the Lucknow Division in the early days of the service of the 2nd Battalion in that station. Major-General Kitchener had served in close connection with the battalion during the relief of Ladysmith and took great interest in its welfare.

A few days after the arrival of the 2nd East Surrey at Lucknow the battalion paraded under Lieutenant-Colonel Pearse for the presentation of the Queen's South African medals.

Major-General Kitchener, before handing the medals to the recipients, made a stirring address to the battalion, making special mention of the night advance of the battalion on February 22, 1900. The General stated that in his opinion this episode was the turning point in the Relief of Ladysmith, and that the staunchness of the battalion under Colonel Harris and their present commanding officer in a most critical moment, rendered invaluable service.

At a later date (October 22, 1903) the King's South African medals were presented to the battalion by Major-General Black, then commanding the District. The General, after referring to the services of the battalion in the early stages of the war, observed that the King's medal specially marked the long period when the infantry was broken up into a great number of small posts. This dispersal was calculated to try the discipline and *moral* of a battalion to the utmost, and it was, in the General's opinion, the highest praise that could be given to the 2nd East Surrey to say that they had emerged with unimpaired discipline from this long trial.

The battalion remained stationed at Lucknow for two years only, being moved to Sitapur in January 1905 in consequence of a regrouping of the British infantry in India carried out by Lord Kitchener, the Commander-in-Chief.

The battalion arrived at Sitapur on January 12, and two days later Brevet-Colonel H. W. Pearse, D.S.O., completed his period of command and went on half-pay. Colonel Pearse had served in the East Surrey Regiment for thirty years, less one month, and all his regimental service had been passed in the 2nd Battalion.[1] He was succeeded in the command by Brevet - Lieutenant - Colonel A. B. Dunsterville.

The health of the battalion during its two years at Lucknow was very good, and in both years the battalion was reported to be thoroughly efficient and fit for active service. Work was carried on throughout the hot weather, proper precautions being adopted in periods of exceptional heat, and this measure resulted in far better health than prevailed in former times when work during the hot season ceased as soon as the sun was high above the horizon.

Lieutenant-Colonel Dunsterville joined at Sitapur from England in February 1905, and a month later the Headquarters and four companies marched to the hill station Ranikhet, where they passed the hot weather.

In October these companies returned to Sitapur, and the winter months were occupied in a very thorough course of field training. The year 1906 much resembled its predecessor, half the battalion again proceeding to Ranikhet in March and returning to Sitapur in October. In November the battalion moved to Mhow, being then in the highest state of efficiency and in fine health. The representatives of the battalion, it may be recorded, carried all before them this year at the Lucknow Assault-at-Arms, and the battalion won the Southern-Indian Command Musketry Challenge Shield.

The record of the 2nd Battalion at Mhow during the remainder of Lieutenant-Colonel Dunsterville's period of command was similar to that of the two years at Sitapur. It was a time of hard and honest work, resulting in a high state of efficiency. In 1907 Major-General Stratford Collins, C.B., Inspector of Infantry in India, a very severe critic, reported in the most favourable terms on the admirable condition of the battalion. Health was extraordinarily good at the time of

---

[1] Colonel Pearse was subsequently appointed an Assistant Director on the Headquarter Staff of the Army and retired on pension in January 1911, after 36 years' service.

the inspection, there being only one case of enteric fever, and practically no other illness of any kind. Those who know India will realise the meaning of these facts.

On the termination of his period of command Lieutenant-Colonel Dunsterville was promoted to the rank of Colonel, and shortly afterwards retired on pension. His successor in the command of the battalion was Lieutenant-Colonel H. S. Sloman, D.S.O., whose promotion was dated January 15, 1909. At the same time Major H. D. Lawrence rejoined the battalion from the Staff on appointment as second-in-command. From February 3rd to 18th the battalion took part in the Fifth Divisional Manœuvres to the south of Mhow, and on the 25th of the same month it was inspected by General Sir Edmund Barrow, commanding the Southern Army.

The remainder of the year was uneventful, nor does the early portion of 1910 call for special remark. On September 13, 1910, the battalion entrained for Bombay, and two days later embarked in the R.I.M.S. *Dufferin* for conveyance to Burma.

On September 22 the battalion disembarked at Rangoon, and proceeded up country by river, Headquarters and four companies being stationed at Thyetmyo, two companies at Mandalay under Major Gilbert-Cooper, and two at Meiktila under Major Paterson. The discomfort of this river-move was very great, as it was carried out before the rainy season was over.

During November the battalion was inspected at these stations by Brigadier-General Hastings, commanding the Mandalay Brigade.

In December 1910 the Headquarter wing was inspected at Thyetmyo by General Sir Edmund Barrow.

In February 1911, owing to a reduction in the garrison of Upper Burma, a change of stations took place, Headquarters and three companies proceeding to Shwebo, and leaving one company under Captain R. E. N. North at Thyetmyo. The two companies stationed at Mandalay under Major Gilbert-Cooper moved at the same time to Bhamo, the battalion being thus split up into four widely separated detachments. This distribution continued throughout the remainder of Lieutenant-Colonel Sloman's period of command, and indeed during the remaining two and three-quarter years in which the battalion remained in Burma, but so loyally and efficiently did everyone work that nothing but good reports were earned by the various detachments.

Lieutenant-Colonel H. S. Sloman, D.S.O., vacated the command of the battalion on May 2, 1911, on appointment to the Headquarter Staff of the Army, and was succeeded on the following day by Lieutenant-Colonel H. D. Lawrence. Lieutenant-Colonel Sloman's connection with the battalion was a long one, during which he rendered valuable service in the maintenance of discipline and efficiency.

In 1912 and 1913 it was found necessary to withdraw the Bhamo detachment to Shwebo during the hot weather and rains. There were thus five companies at Headquarters, but unfortunately at a time when battalion training was impossible. In February 1913, however, the detachments were temporarily reduced, and 600 of the battalion, formed in six companies, were moved up for manœuvres at Myothit on the Yunnanese frontier. The battalion on this occasion earned the highest commendation, the smartness and efficiency of all ranks being conspicuous. The report of the Divisional commander ran as follows: "A very fine battalion, steady and smart at drill. The men are well trained and work with dash and enthusiasm. It is a pleasure to see them at work. The officers are a fine body, full of zeal and energy, in every respect fit for service."

At length the period of service in Burma came to a close and at Christmas 1913 the battalion began to concentrate from its distant stations for passage to Chaubattia and Bareilly. By January 2, 1914, all the detachments were united at Rangoon, and two days later the battalion, with a strength of 922, embarked once again in the R.I.M.S. *Dufferin*. The relief of the battalion was not however carried out in the usual manner, as it had been considered to assemble a body of troops in Eastern Bengal, a secluded and (to soldiers) almost unknown portion of the Empire. On January 8, the battalion disembarked at Chittagong, a prosperous port in which no white troops had been seen for over a century. The arrival of the battalion had unfortunately been awaited by the inhabitants of Eastern Bengal with much alarm, the disloyal element having spread dire reports of atrocities to be expected on the part of the white soldiers. The excellent conduct and strict discipline of the battalion was, however, immediately appreciated. From Chittagong the battalion marched to Dacca, where it again earned very high praise at the manœuvres about that ancient city. Concerning these operations General Sir James Willcocks, commanding the Northern Army, wrote: " I saw the battalion this winter at drills and also at Divisional manœuvres at Dacca. It is a good corps and very well commanded by Lieutenant-Colonel Lawrence. The drill is good and the work in the field is lively and intelligently carried out."

At the end of the manœuvres the battalion left Dacca by river steamer for Digha Ghat, near Bankipore, the capital of the newly formed province of Bihar and Orissa, whence it took train for Bareilly and Katgodam. From the latter station the battalion made a double march in very bad weather to its wintry quarters at Chaubattia, where it was serving on August 4, 1914, when Great Britian declared war against Germany in consequence of her violation of the neutrality of Belgium.

The journey of the battalion to England, and thence to France, and its services in the great European war will be related hereafter in the second volume of this history.

INDEX

Abercromby, General Sir Ralph, 65, 70, 74.
Afghan War, the first, 161–73.
    ,,   ,,   the second, 335–50.
Aire, Action of, 145.
Albaro, Action of, 94–95.
Albuera, Battle of, 120–6.
Alington, Private, Brave conduct of, 427.
Aliwal, Battle of, 197–9.
Alleman's Nek, Action of, 419–23.
Anderson, Captain C. (killed at Sebastopol), 223, 224.
Anson, Lieutenant E. St. G., 389, 404.
Antigua, Seventieth Regiment at, 298–300.
Appleyard, 2nd Lieutenant W., 425, 434, 444.
Arbuthnot, Lieut.-Colonel Robert (mortally wounded at La Vigie), 68, 70.
Ardesoife, Lieutenant A., 17.
Ashcroft, Private G., 401.
Attree, Captain F. S. (killed at Sebastopol), 223, 224.

B

Badowal, Action of, 194–7.
Baird, Captain James, 20, 21, 35.
Baldwin, Major George (mortally wounded at Ferozeshah), 177, 193.
Bally, Lieutenant Henry (killed in action), 324, 332.
Barcelona, Attack on, 11, 12.
Barchard, Lieutenant A. C. S., 403, 404, 407, 428, 439.
Barnes, General Sir Edward, 159.

Beauclerk, Colonel Lord Henry, 35, 40.
Beckwith, 2nd Lieutenant John, 5, 16, 19, 20, 21.
Bell, Lieutenant Matthew, Death of, 318, 320.
Benson, Major H. W., 413, 414, 416, 421, 428, 434.
Benson, 2nd Lieutenant J. P., 401, 438, 442, 443.
Bernard, Lieutenant and Adjutant W. (killed at Ferozeshah), 193.
Berville Camp, Brave defence of, 63–5.
Biffen, Private James, Captures a Colour at Sobraon, 208.
Biffen, Private James, His funeral, 357.
Biggarsberg operations, 414–6.
Birch, Lieutenant J. R. K., 359, 361.
Birch, Lieutenant R. L. C., 345, 349.
Blakeney, Lieut.-Colonel George, 4, 16, 17.
Blakeney, William, Lord, 16 (*note*).
Bolton, Lieut.-Colonel (afterwards Colonel) (mortally wounded at Moodkee), 159, 162, 168, 171, 178, 183.
Bolton, Lieutenant M. G., 349, 360.
Bolton, Lieutenant and Adjt. William, 177, 200, 204.
Boxer, Private W., 401.
Boy company, 304.
Brady, Private (afterwards Sergeant), 405, 441.
Brenchley, Lieutenant John (mortally wounded at Moodkee), 177, 179.
Brooks, Lieutenant S. F., 417, 445.
Brynbella Hill (*see* Willow Grange).
Burgoyne, His campaign, 47–53.
Burgoyne, Lieut.-General, 47.
Byng, Major-General John (afterwards F.M. Earl of Strafford), 127, 141.

C

Cabul, Thirty-First at, 170.
Cagliari, Surrender of, 14.
Cambridge, H.R.H. Prince George (afterwards Duke of), 216.
Campbell, Lieut.-Colonel Wm. Howe, 98, 102.
Canada, Service in, 46, 304.
Carew, Major Thomas, 3, 4.
Carib War (*see* St. Vincent).
Cathcart, Colonel Honble. Charles, 17.
Cawnpore, Cholera epidemic at, 309.
Cay, Captain Eustace, 324, 331, 332, 333.
Chatham, Major-General the Earl of, 76, 79.
Christian Victor, H.H. Prince, 402.
Churchill, Colonel C. H. (killed in action), 162.
Churchill, Colonel Joshua, 12, 14.
Chute, Colonel (afterwards General Sir) Trevor, 308, 312, 314, 316, 320, 324.
Clarke, Major-General Thomas, 54, 55.
Clay, Colour-Sergeant (afterwards Sergeant-Major) H., 380, 389.
Cobb, Private, Brave death of, 427.
Cole, Captain Honble. G. Lowry (afterwards General), 277, 278.
Colenso, Action of, 377–80.
Collins, Major (afterwards Colonel) J. R., 333, 345, 349, 358, 363, 364.
Coote, Lieut.-Colonel (afterwards Lieut.-General Sir) Eyre, 271, 273, 274, 277, 287.
Corfu, Thirty-First at, 218.
Corsica, Occupation of, 96.
Courtney, Captain William, 4, 8.
Craigie, Major-General P. E., 225, 233.
Cranwitch, Quartermaster-Sergeant J., 363.
Crimean War, 218–26.
Cumberland, H.R.H. William, Duke of, 30, 31, 34, 40.
Cumine, Captain C. A. G. (accidentally killed), 358.
Curson, O.R. Quartermaster-Sergeant S. R., 363.
Curtis, Private A. E. (awarded Victoria Cross), 399, 401.

D

Dacre, Lieut.-General Lord, 216, 218.
Dalway, Lieutenant Alexander, killed at Fontenoy, 35
Darrah, Lieutenant Nicholas, Death of, 247.

Dettingen, Battle of, 23–8.
Devitt, Private J., Gallant act of, 445.
Douglas, Captain Honble. R., 20, 21, 21 *note*.
Doyle, Lieut.-General Sir C. Hastings, 336.
Drakensberg, Operations in the, 417, 418.
Drummond, Captain William, 19.
Dunsterville, Major A. B., 359, 455.

E

Eagar, Captain Francis, 98.
Eagar, Captain (afterwards Colonel) R. J., 225, 226, 227, 230, 231, 232, 235
Egmont-op-Zee, Action of, 78–80.
Elandslaagte, Action at, 412.
Ellis, Captain W. H., 360, 395, 404, 413.
Elwyn, Lieutenant James, 99.
Estcourt, 370.
Evatt, Captain George, 312, 314, 318.
Evatt, Brevet-Major John, 277, 278, 294.

F

Fearon, Lieut.-Colonel R. B., 75, 89, 98, 152, 153.
Ferguson, Captain (afterwards Major) Patrick, 259, 260, 268, 269.
Ferozeshah, Battle of, 184–194.
Ferrol, Skirmish at, 87.
Fisher, Lance-Corporal S., 400, 401.
Fletcher, Lieutenant and Quartermaster (afterwards Major) C. W., 430.
Florida, 43.
Fontaine, Lieutenant H. V. M. de la, 385, 404, 407, 428, 446, 448, 450, 451.
Fontenoy, Battle of, 30–36.
Forster, Lieutenant Francis (killed at Alkmaar), 75, 81.
Frodsham, Captain (afterwards Colonel) W. J. H., 355, 356, 359.

G

Gahan, Assist.-Surgeon R. B. (killed at Moodkee), 177, 180.
Garris, Action of, 143, 144.
Garvock, Captain (afterwards General Sir) John, 177, 199, 208, 209, 210.
Genoa, Thirty-First at, 94–6.
George I, King, 16.

INDEX

George II, King, 18, 23, 26, 27, 28.
Gibraltar, Capture of, 9.
Gibraltar, Defence of, 9–11.
Girdlestone, Captain J., 99, 111, 135, 136, 138, 149.
Glasgow, Seventieth Regiment raised at, 42.
"Glasgow Greys," old nick-name of Seventieth Regiment, 239.
Goodliff, Lieutenant James M., 129.
Goring, Colonel Sir Harry, Bart., 14, 16, 17.
Gorman, Captain W. H., 382, 384, 404, 405, 413.
Gough, General Sir Hugh (afterwards F.M. Viscount), 172, 182, 184, 185, 189, 190, 191, 208, 215.
Greaves, Lieutenant (afterwards General Sir) George R., 312, 324, 329, 334, 360.
Green, Captain Charles, 47, 51.
Green, Corporal Joseph, 22, 22 *note*.
Greenwood, Lieutenant Joseph, 163, 168.
Grenada, Island of, Seventieth at, 247, 245.
Grey-Smith, Lieutenant W. A., 340, 342, 343, 347, 349.
Grierson, Lieutenant J. F. A., 324.
Guadeloupe, Capture of, 59, 64, 287–292.

H

Halkett, Lieut.-General Sir Colin, 159, 216.
Hallett, Lieutenant P., 443.
Handasyd, Colonel William, 18, 19, 20, 21, 35.
Harding, Sir H. (afterwards F.M. Viscount), 192.
Hargrave, Colonel William, 18.
Harris, Lieutenant (afterwards Brigadier-General) R. H. W. H., 346, 349, 364, 366–99, 408, 410, 427, 428.
Hart (afterwards Hart-Synnot), Major-General Arthur FitzRoy, 377.
Hart (afterwards Hart-Synnot), Captain A. H. S., 444.
Hart (afterwards Hart-Synnot), 2nd Lieutenant R. V. O., 444.
Hart, Lieutenant Henry William (killed at Moodkee), 177, 180, 182.
Hawkshaw, Ensign (afterwards Lieut.-Colonel) Edward, Letter of, 82, 85.
Hawkshaw, Lieutenant J. S., 69, 70, 75, 82 *note*.

Hay, Lieut.-Colonel Adam (mortally wounded at La Vigie), 67, 70.
Hay, Captain J. W., Death of, 312, 318.
Helder, Expedition to the, 74–86.
Hesse Darmstadt, Prince George of, 9, 12.
Hewett, Ensign (afterwards General Sir George Hewett, Bart.), 245, 246, 248.
Hildyard, Major-General H. J. T., 365, 378, 379, 388, 402, 413.
Hill, Lieut.-General Rowland (afterwards F.M. Lord), 98, 149.
Hilliard, Colour-Sergeant F., 407, 428.
Hinton, Lieutenant C. H. (killed in action), 398.
Holmes, Lieut-General Henry, 40.
Hornby, Ensign (afterwards Colonel) Leyland, 333, 340, 349, 363.
Huberton, Action of, 48.
Huntingdonshire Regiment, The, 54.

I

Ionides, Captain Luke G., 411, 418 421, 422, 447, 455.
Irving, Captain (afterwards Lieut.-Colonel) Robert (killed in action), 248–67, 274–7, 284–7.

J

Jack, Sergeant and Mrs., Death of, 154.
Johnson, Lieutenant L. W., 366, 371.
Johnston, Captain Richard (killed at La Vigie), 68, 70.
Johnstone, "Governor" George, 44.
Jones, Quartermaster-Sergeant, afterwards Ensign William (killed at Sobraon), 179, 205.

K

Kandahar, Seventieth Regiment at, 344, 346.
Kent, Burning of the, 152–6.
Kerr, Colonel Lord John, 17.
King-Church, Lieutenant (afterwards Brevet-Major) F. W., 395, 455.
Kitchener, F.M. Lord, 444.
Kitchener, Colonel (afterwards Lieut.-General) F. W., 372, 374, 375, 400, 405, 458.
Knox, Surgeon (afterwards Brigade Surgeon) Maurice, 340, 349.
Kojak Pass, 342, 343.

L

Lackey, Private, 223.
Ladevèze, Lieutenant A. R. de, 17, 17 *note*.
Ladysmith, Relief of, 409–10.
Lane, Sergeant J., Brave conduct of, 451.
Lawrence, Captain (afterwards Colonel) H. D., 444, 460, 461, 462.
La Vigie, Attack on, 67–71.
Leach, Ensign (afterwards Colonel) Jonathan, 296, 297, 298, 300.
Leavens, Sergeant F. C., 398, 399, 401, 439.
Leeson, Lieutenant R. E., 222, 223.
Le Fleming, 2nd Lieutenant L. J., 376.
Leith, Lieut.-Colonel Sir Alexander, 75, 81, 138, 142, 148.
L'Estrange, Ensign George (afterwards Sir George), 132, 133, 140, 142, 144.
L'Estrange, Major Guy (afterwards Lieut.-General Sir G.), 98, 102, 122, 125, 127, 150, 151.
Lisbon, 2nd Bn. Thirty-First at, 102.
Lodge, Captain William (killed in action), 98.
Long, Lance-Corporal, 439.
Longley, Captain (afterwards Lieut.-Colonel) J. R., 357, 444.
Longworth, Captain D. F., 177, 200, 205, 207, 210.
Lovegrove, Private W., 439, 440.
Lowe, Private John, Letter of, 85.
Lugard, Lieutenant (afterwards General Sir Edward), 163, 177, 199, 209, 210, 350.
Luttrell, Lieut.-Colonel Alexander, 3, 4, 12.
Lynch, Lieutenant (afterwards Major-General) W. W., 318, 319.
Lyne, Colour-Sergeant W. G., 428, 439.
Lyttelton, Major-General Honble. N., 390, 402, 406, 411.

M

Mackenzie, Major-General J. R., 104, 105, 106, 112.
Manchester, Thirty-First at, 58.
Marine Regiments, Rules and Instructions of, 4.
Marine Regiments, Uniform of, 6.
Marshall, Captain G. C. (died in Afghanistan), 168.
Martinique, Capture of, 279–86.
Mathew, Captain G. B., 306, 307.
Maturin, Lieutenant (afterwards Lieut.-Colonel) F. H., 338, 346, 349, 359, 363.
May, Lieutenant J. C., 400, 428, 439.
McCabe, Sergeant (afterwards Captain) Bernard, 205, 208, 216.
McIlveen, Lieutenant Dalway (killed in action), 167.
Meade, Brigadier-General the Honble. Robert, 89, 92, 93.
Melle, Action of, 36–9.
Messina, Thirty-First at, 91.
Minorca, Thirty-First at, 41.
Mitford, Major (afterwards Brigadier-General) B. R., 444.
Montagu, Lieut.-Colonel Edward, 21, 25.
Montagu, Lieut.-Col., Killed at Fontenoy, 35.
Montague-Bates, 2nd Lieutenant F. S., 444, 446.
Monte Cristo, Capture of, 392.
Montjuich, Capture of Fort, 11, 12.
Montreal, Seventieth Regiment at, 305, 306.
Moodkee (or Mudki), Battle of, 176–183.
Moore, Brigadier-General John (afterwards General Sir John), 70, 72.
Morne Pied, Seventieth Regiment at, 281, 282.
Morton, Private F., 399, 401.
Mulgrave, Colonel Lord (afterwards F.M. Earl of), 55, 125, 157.
Mulock, Major (afterwards Colonel) T. E., 324, 326, 328, 329, 334.
Munro, Lieutenant (afterwards Lieut.-General Sir) Hector, 240, 241.
Murray, Captain Richard (mortally wounded at La Vigie), 68, 70.

N

Napier, Captain (afterwards F.M. Lord), 182.
Nares, Captain G. S., 282.
Nelson, Admiral Lord, His funeral, 91.
Nicholson, Brigadier-General John, 311, 314.
Noel, Lieutenant (afterwards Colonel) E. A., 177, 188, 190, 205.
North, Lieutenant R. N., 370, 389, 404.

O

Ogle, Captain Newton, Death of, 287.
Orakau, Action of, 329, 330.
Orthes, Battle of, 144–6.
Otago (4th) Regiment, 329 *note*.
Oughton, Lieut.-General Sir Adolphus, 43, 54.

INDEX

P

Packman, Captain F. L. A., 383, 401, 413, 438.
Parris, Lance-Corporal R., 401.
Parslow, Colonel John, 241, 243.
Paterson, Captain W. H., 442.
Paty, General Sir G. W., 336.
Pearse, Sub-Lieutenant (afterwards Colonel) H. W., 338, 340, 346, 374, 410, 428, 430, 439.
Pender, Lieutenant T. (mortally wounded), 171.
Peninsular War, 98–149.
Pentenny, Private William, His gallant conduct, 88.
Percy, Sergeant H. J., 396, 428.
Peshawar during the Mutiny, 310–9.
Peshawar in peace, 337.
Peterborough, Earl of, 11, 12.
Phillips, Lieut.-Colonel R. W. F., 364.
Pieter's Hill, Battle of, 403–7.
Pieter's Hill operations, 390–403.
Pigott, Lieut.-Colonel H. de R., 336, 337, 338, 340, 346, 349.
Pollard, Lieutenant J. L. R. (killed at Ferozeshah), 163, 169, 177, 180, 186.
Pollock, Captain John, killed at Fontenoy, 21, 35.
Porch, Lieutenant C. P., 383, 428, 429.

R

Ralston, Ensign (afterwards Major-General) W. H., 313, 324, 331, 333, 340, 348, 349, 359, 363, 364
Recco, attempted landing at, 94.
Riddell, Captain (afterwards Lieut.-Colonel Sir) R. S., 324, 340, 349, 360.
Ringwood, Lieutenant (afterwards Colonel) H., 340, 346, 349, 356, 357.
Roberts, Field-Marshal Earl, 355, 356.
Robertson, Lieutenant (afterwards Colonel) James P., 177, 180, 181, 187, 190, 192, 226.
Robertson, Captain John (killed in action), 89.
Rosetta, Disaster at, 92, 93.
Ross, Captain (afterwards Major-General) Andrew, 53, 59, 63.
Roupell, Captain (afterwards Colonel) F. F. F., 346 note, 349, 355.
Ruth, Private, 223.
Rutherford, Captain A. J. O., 324, 330, 333.
Ryan, Major George A., 324, 327, 330, 333.
Ryan, Private, 223.

S

Saltmarshe, Captain (afterwards Colonel) Arthur, 324, 327, 331, 333.
Saratoga, Capitulation of, 52, 53.
Saunders, Captain H. F., 312, 318.
Sayers, Lieutenant H. K., 171.
Scarlett, Honble. Lady, presents Colours, 335.
Sexton, Sergeant, 380.
Shanghai, Thirty-First at, 233.
Shaw, Captain Charles (died in Afghanistan), 167.
Shovell, Sir Cloudisley, 13, 14.
Shovell, Loss of his Fleet, 14.
Simpson, Captain Noah, 47, 52.
Sind-ho, Action of, 229.
Skinner, Major (afterwards Lieut.-Colonel) Thomas, 162, 168, 169, 171.
Sloman, Lieutenant (afterwards Colonel) H. S., 359, 444, 460, 461.
Smith, General Sir Harry, 176, 183, 186, 195, 197, 198, 199, 206, 213, 216.
Smith, 2nd Lieutenant (afterwards Lieut.-Colonel) H. L., 346, 349, 357, 359, 366, 383, 387, 396, 397, 401, 428, 430.
Spence, Major (afterwards Colonel) Frederick, 173, 177, 179, 186, 190, 194, 200, 204, 208, 210.
Spion Kop operations, 381–5.
Stafford, 2nd Lieutenant P. B., 376, 389, 400, 422.
Stafford, Lieutenant Egerton, 22, 35.
Stafford, Captain Edward, 89.
Staunton, Lieut.-Colonel, 221, 225.
Stewart, Captain Honble. T. H., 99, 117.
Stewart, Major-General Honble. William, 119, 121, 122, 123, 138, 141.
St. Lucia, Capture of, 58, 59.
St. Pierre, Action of, 140–3.
Storey, Lieutenant F. B., 444, 454, 455.
Storks, Major-General Sir Henry Knight, 336, 337.
Stuart, Major-General James, 55.
St. Vincent, Island of, 44, 45, 246, 247.
Suakin, 2nd Bn. The East Surrey Regiment at, 359–63.
Suffolk, Colonel the Earl of, 270

T

Talavera, Battle of, 106–12.
Tang-koo, Action of, 230.
Taranaki, 325, 330.
Taylor, Captain, killed in action, 5, 15.
Tew, Captain H. S., 383, 404, 405, 407, 421, 428, 439.

Tezin Pass, Action at, 169.
Tientsin, Thirty-First at, 230–3.
Timins, Brevet Lieut.-Colonel T. C., Death of, 318.
Toulon, Attack on, 13.
Trapaud, Ensign Cyrus, 27, 243.
Tritton, Ensign C. H. G. (mortally wounded at Sobraon), 205.
Tritton, Ensign R. B. (died in Afghanistan), 171.
Treeby, Major H. P., 374, 395, 397, 401, 408, 439.
Trevor, Lieut.-General Honble. H. O. (*see* Lord Dacre).
Tryon, Major-General William, 247, 254, 270.

V

Vaal Krantz operations, 385–90.
Vigo, Attack on, 7, 8.
Villiers, Colonel George, 3, 4.
Vittoria, Battle of, 133–5.
Volunteer Service company, the, 412, 423, 424.

W

Wade, Field-Marshal, 29.
Wade, Lieutenant, Royal Lancaster Regiment, 379, 380.
Waikato, 326, 328.

Walker, Captain William (killed at La Vigie), 68, 70.
Walsh, Lieut.-Colonel Ralph, 43, 44, 45.
Warde, General Sir Henry, 157, 159.
Warren, Lieut.-General Sir Charles, 381, 390, 403.
Watson, Major John Williams, 98, 112.
West Indies, Losses of the Army in the, 72.
Whish, 2nd Lieutenant J. K. T., 454.
White, Captain (afterwards Major) Finch, 389, 421, 424, 427.
William III, King, 1.
Williams, Private, Captures a Colour at Sobraon, 208.
Willow Grange (or Brynbella), Action of, 372–6.
Wolfe, Colonel Honble. Arthur, 296, 300, 301.
Woodward, Sergeant Christopher, 22, 22 *note*.
Wright, Captain (afterwards Major) A. B., 324, 329.
Wynyard, 2nd Lieutenant R. D., 346, 349.

Y.

York, H.R.H. the Duke of, 76–81.
"Young Buffs," Old nickname of Thirty-First Regiment, 28.

www.ingramcontent.com/pod-product-compliance
Lightning Source LLC
Chambersburg PA
CBHW060416300426
44111CB00018B/2867